A NONPROFIT ORGANIZATION OPERATING MANUAL
Planning for Survival and Growth

ARNOLD J. OLENICK and PHILIP R. OLENICK

The Foundation Center
New York • 1991

Library of Congress Cataloging-in-Publication Data
Olenick, Arnold J., 1918–
  A nonprofit organization operating manual / by Arnold J. Olenick and Philip R. Olenick.
    p.   cm.
  Includes bibliographical references and index.
  ISBN 0-87954-293-4 (paperback) : $29.95
  1. Corporations, Nonprofit—Management. 2. Corporations, Nonprofit—Finance.
3. Corporations, Nonprofit—Accounting.
I. Olenick, Philip R.   II. Title.
HD62.6.044 1991
658′.048—dc20   91-12292
                                                                      CIP

To our selfless colleagues in the conspiracy of goodness—a million points of light who struggle on undimmed, unsung, underpaid and underfunded, to make the world a better place than you received it; and to our little Jeannie: may she know the better world you are making—this book is dedicated with love and respect. It is your caring, your serving others—your constant reminder that "Every man for himself" could be freedom's epitaph—that makes democracy work—often in spite of itself.

Arnold J. Olenick and Philip R. Olenick

ACKNOWLEDGMENTS

This is a book given a second life. Its predecessor, by the same team of authors, was published by Prentice-Hall, Inc., in 1983 as *Making the Nonprofit Organization Work: A Legal, Tax and Financial Guide*—a title which accurately defined its scope. This new work is an outgrowth that has been greatly expanded in scope. It now includes chapters and materials covering strategic and program planning, organizational development and personnel administration, fundraising, and the business and tax planning issues involved in creating income-producing ventures.

Because of the wide scope of subjects covered in this work, we were fortunate in being able to get valuable input from three management consultants in the areas of strategic planning and organizational development: Richard H. Dougherty and Jacqueline Michelove of the Boston area and Mark Michaels of Urbana, Illinois, whose inputs to Chapters 3 and 4 were invaluable. By no means of lesser importance was the assistance of Melinda Marble, a Boston-area fundraising consultant, who reviewed Chapter 8.

These four professionals added considerable strengths; any shortcomings are the responsibility of the authors.

Contents

PART THREE. OPERATIONAL MANAGEMENT

List of Figures and Tables

Preface

Even in the best of times it has not been smooth sailing for nonprofit organizations, and the political weather of the 1980s churned up stormy seas that threaten organizations not fitted to ride them out.

This book is for those who lead and staff nonprofits. Competing for a slice of a shrinking pie and asked by society to do more with less, you confront the difficulty of maintaining financial health. This book is designed to guide you in acquiring and managing the resources so crucial to the life of your organization.

Paying for accounting, legal, and tax know-how can be expensive for underfunded nonprofits, which often have trouble affording bookkeeping, let alone professional services. Yet recognition is dawning that to struggle along without such services can be far *more* expensive, maybe even ruinous. Professional services are, in fact, commonly the price of admission to the world of foundation and corporate support, not to mention government grants and tax exemption (the ticket to get in).

Accountability for Success

Accountability—as well as accounting—is stressed as the key to management success, for "whoever pays the piper calls the tune." When other people's money makes your organization possible, they earn a stake in how you use it. Budgets and accounting create the structure for accountability: moreover they help you to plan, to track your progress, and to see whether you're getting where you intend to go.

Shaping up Legally

The first two chapters take you step by step through the major tasks involved in establishing a nonprofit entity, starting with whether you should incorporate, what formal documents you need as your "birth certificate," the ins and outs of tax exemption, plus the kinds of registration required by government agencies—federal and state—to make you "legal."

Staying Legal

As important as *admission* to tax-exempt status is staying in good standing. The ground rules are spelled out in later chapters, including which activities and procedures are required, permitted, and prohibited. Annual reports required by federal and state agencies for keeping your tax exemption are explained, with notes on their preparation. Potential obligations to file various tax returns, such as payroll and sales taxes—even though you're otherwise tax-exempt—are fully explained, with step-by-step illustrations provided as appropriate, and explanations of any specialized record keeping that may be necessary.

Strategic Planning

The chapters on Organizational Planning and Organizational Building can make a major contribution to the success of any nonprofit organization. They explore the concepts that are the territory of management consultants.

Organizational Development

The chapter on Organizational Building covers the major issues of board development, board-staff relations, and human resource management.

Fundraising

A life-and-death function, one that needs no selling to the nonprofit manager. The major aspects of winning foundation, corporate, and government grants and contracts are explored in depth, as is how to write a successful funding proposal. The basics of fundraising from individual donors are outlined as well.

Income-Producing Ventures

For many readers, this chapter may be the most interesting in the book. It explains not only how to go about creating and operating such a venture, but also the legal and tax problems that must be considered.

The Budget: Your Navigational Radar

In-depth treatment is given this subject, not only in developing effective budgetary control, but also in how to proceed with the budget-building process itself, in human as well as technical terms. A step-by-step approach is used to show you how practical worksheets are prepared. The Center for Community Service, an imaginary nonprofit, is used as case material. (Financial statements and tax returns will make use of the same case materials, so that you get an integrated picture.) The operating budget is presented as a central policy and planning document, created, as already suggested, as a road map of where you want to go, and a radar to keep you on course. It is viewed as a living document for motivating and measuring effectiveness and efficiency, not as an irksome straitjacket.

In addition, cash budgeting and management are explored, as well as capital budgeting and managing financial crises—all in light of the legal responsibilities involved.

Accounting for Non-Accountants

A well-kept secret is that accounting is not for accountants: it is *their* product, but *you* are its intended consumer. You are able to drive a car without understanding thermodynamics or internal combustion, yet you need to know the names of its principal parts to use the car correctly and take care of what goes wrong. The same realities apply to accounting, so we have included explanations of its language, concepts, and systems, as well as a thorough example of double-entry bookkeeping, a useful guide for those willing to tackle it for their organization, or those who want to sharpen tools acquired in on-the-job training. This chapter, written for non-accountants, spans the subject from the simplest debit-credit entries through the more advanced areas of accrual and adjusting entries and full-fledged systems, including short-cut methods and low-cost computer use.

The preparation, use, and significance of financial reports are also explained and illustrated. Operating performance reports comparing actual vs. budgeted figures are illustrated and analyzed and the differences made clear between budgeting for internal purposes and for grant proposals, including the controversial area of overhead cost.

Handling Audits and Auditors

A comprehensive discussion of how to handle audits and auditors completes the coverage of accounting and tax problems. It includes audits by tax, regulatory, and funding agencies, as well as those done at your request by public accountants. How to handle potential problems in the first type of audit is spelled out, as are the positive benefits to be sought from the second.

Other Features

The appendices offer a full range of supplemental resources, including a fully worked out illustration of the accounting cycle, from transactions through financial statements, plus a list of useful directories and periodicals, and a bibliography.

We firmly believe that nonfinancial administrators, board members, and staff of nonprofit organizations, large and small, need to understand the nontechnical material in these pages, which is too important to be left entirely to technicians.

The smaller the organization and the less it can afford a technical/professional staff, the more important it becomes for its leaders to grasp financial matters. Awareness of financial management tools and resources will help you to make sure you are getting reliable, timely information your organization needs to be successful. People who are willing to undertake financial responsibilities for nonprofit operations can get maximum use out of this book as a guide to the essentials of the job. Finally, although this book is not written primarily for accountants or attorneys, we believe that they will find it of great value, especially if their experience in the nonprofit field is limited, or for their nonprofit clients' use. Its greatest value may well prove to be in promoting a greater understanding and appreciation of accounting and accountants, the law and lawyers, and by them of the nonprofit world, that often has struggled along without their know-how.

Part One

Long-Range Considerations

Chapter 1

Becoming—and Staying—Tax-Exempt

For purposes of paragraph (3), an organization described in paragraph (2), shall be deemed to include an organization described in section 501(c)(4), (5), or (6) which would be described in paragraph (2) if it were an organization described in section 501(c)(3).

EXCERPT FROM SECTION 509 OF THE INTERNAL REVENUE CODE

It ocasionally has been observed that the words of the Internal Revenue Code, do, in fact, make sense—it's the sentences that sometimes don't. In fairness to the Code, it should be pointed out that the quote above is the most compact and efficient way of saying what it says—to those who can understand it. The problem is that the Code tries to deal with every possible way of evading its provisions and has thus become incredibly detailed. Worse, it becomes incomprehensible (except to specialists) whenever the answer given by each incredibly detailed rule is that you should go look at another.

In recognition of this problem, the Internal Revenue Service publishes many pamphlets that try to paraphrase the Code's rules in normal sentences and paragraphs. Unfortunately, this does not work either. While the Code deals in abstract categories that at least shorten the verbal equations, the IRS's pamphlets spell it all out in detailed descriptions that can make a simple rule incomprehensible because the "if" and the "then" are so far apart.

The problem with both approaches is that they basically do the same thing: describe the rules. What these approaches omit are the reasons for the rules, which would enable you to figure out what the rules mean for yourself. In addition, once the purposes behind a rule are understood, it becomes easier to read, even if it *is* long and densely worded. We only get stuck when we hit a passage that "makes no sense," which really means a passage we don't understand the reason for.

This book is designed to show the reasons behind the rules, both the legal rules and the accounting rules your group has to deal with to get and handle money. The intent is not only to give you the answers, but, just as importantly, to make you familiar with the concepts that frame the questions. This chapter in particular deals with an area where the rules are modified from time to time. By dealing with the root concepts, which change less often, it becomes possible to understand the periodic loosening and tightening of rules as representing temporary gains by one philosophical camp or another. (The best example of this is the tension between "freedom of speech" and "fair play" that is expressed in restrictions on political activity by groups subsidized by the tax system.) Once you understand the debates you can update the rules in this chapter, and learn which direction the trenches have moved, by looking at the most recent edition of Publication 557, *Tax Exempt Status for Your Organization,* available free of charge from the IRS.

ADVANTAGES OF TAX-EXEMPT STATUS

The two main reasons you will want tax exemption are:

1. Your group can accomplish more with the money it gets if it is exempt from having to pay income taxes, and

2. Your group can raise money more easily if it also qualifies as a tax-deductible organization.

Besides these self-evident advantages, there are less obvious advantages to exempt status. For example, exemption from paying federal unemployment taxes is available to 501(c)(3) organizations, and section 501 organizations can often get reduced-rate bulk mailing privileges. (See the IRS "Organization Reference Chart" in Chapter 2 for a list of the kinds of exempt groups, by section number.)

Most states also exempt some charitable, religious or educational organizations from income, property, or sales taxes, and federal exemption can help to show that you qualify.

Thus, there are advantages to be gained in the ease of raising funds, in improved purchasing power with those funds, and in the ability to hold onto (for next year's activities) any surplus funds that you may have generated by activities in pursuit of your tax-exempt function. What it all boils down to is that you can get more done.

Are There Disadvantages to Exemption?

That depends on what you are trying to accomplish. There are definite limitations upon the political and lobbying activities of all categories of exempt organizations, although the limitations vary from category to category. (See "Political and Legislative Activity," later in this chapter.) This may pose a real problem if your goals require such activities, and may require separately funded companion groups, or it may pose no problem at all if such activities are not needed to advance or defend the goals of the group.

There is paperwork associated with getting and keeping tax-exempt status, but it is not much, and the ongoing annual tax and corporate information filings involved usually require about the same amount of effort as in a small business. Increased record-keeping and reporting does become necessary when a tax-deductible section 501(c)(3) organization engages in legislative lobbying, in order to show that it has not done too much of it. In addition, unless they want to be treated as foundations, most 501(c)(3) groups must prove to the IRS that they're "publicly supported."

Considering the advantages of tax exemption and deductibility, the small amount of paperwork involved is worth it—if you qualify.

SIGNING UP WITH THE SERVICE

How should *your* group go about becoming tax-exempt and even tax-deductible? First of all, you have to pick a section of the law that your proposed activities fit into and set up along the lines explained in this chapter and Chapter 2, *Creating the Right Legal Structure*. Whether you use corporation or association form (discussed in Chapter 2), you'll need to put together a written governing document that establishes and governs the organization, and which sets out the organization's purposes and powers.

In addition to this chapter and Chapter 2, you should also have at hand a copy of IRS Publication 557, *Tax Exempt Status for Your Organization*, which can help update you on any changes since this book was written, and fill you in on special requirements for particular types of organizations. (For example, a school must have a formal policy against racial discrimination, which is outlined in IRS Publication 557.)

Secondly, you should apply to the IRS for recognition of your exempt status on Form 1023 (section 501(c)(3) groups only) or on Form 1024 (most other groups), preferably within 15 months of the effective date of your governing document. (If you apply within 15 months, your exemption and deductibility will be granted retroactive to your governing document's effective date. Otherwise, your exemption, if granted, would start as of the postmark on your application, or, if none, the date your completed application was received by the IRS—unless you've got a good excuse for filing late.

However, the IRS ruled in 1985 that retroactivity to the date of organization will be allowed if you had no gross receipts for your first two years and no more than $15,000 in contributions in the third year, if you file Form 1023 within three months of the end of the third year.

Form 1023 Filing Exemptions

Not all 501(c)(3) organizations are required to file Form 1023. If your group is a chapter or unit of a larger organization that has previously been issued a "group exemption letter," you may either file your own independent Form 1023, or you may simply rely on the existing group exemption letter. If your organization is a church, or church-affiliated auxiliary or an association of churches, you need not file Form 1023. Of potentially widest applicability is the rule that 501(c)(3) organizations (other than private foundations) with "normal" annual gross receipts of $5,000 or less need not file Form 1023. Organizations in existence for less than three years qualify if their gross revenues for the first year are $7,500 or less, or $12,000 or less for the first two years combined. After that, your last three years' combined gross revenues (up through and including the current year's) must stay at or below $15,000 or you'll have to file Form 1023.

Why You Should File Form 1023 Even When It's Not Required

Even though your group may not *have* to file a Form 1023 because your normal annual gross revenues stay within the limits described above, you'll probably choose to file one anyway. Why? Because few things are as reassuring to potential contributors (and to foundation grant officers) as a copy of a letter from the IRS to you, informing you that your application for recognition of your group's tax-exempt status under section 501(c)(3) has been granted, and that contributors to your group may deduct their contributions on their tax returns. (Not only does the IRS send you such a letter, it also regularly publishes a list of tax-deductible organizations, so a potential contributor can double-check your letter in the library.) Without such a determination letter from the IRS, *each* potential contributor would have to evaluate (on its own) the organization's likelihood of being found to qualify under section 501(c)(3) in the course of an audit of the *contributor's* tax return. This is really living dangerously, as auditors are not the people at the IRS who normally handle 501(c)(3) questions.

There is a second reason for filing even if you are not required to. If, someday, the IRS does not agree that your group qualifies for tax-exempt status under 501(c)(3), your group might end up having to pay income taxes on the contributions it got. You should nail this question down *before* you raise (and spend) the contributions rather than take the chance of being hit with a tax bill that you may not be able to pay.

Therefore, if you're a 501(c)(3), you should file Form 1023, even if you're not required to. There is a filing fee, which you compute using Form 8718 *User Fee for Exempt Organization Determination Letter Request*, and submit along with the 1023.

Why Groups Other Than 501(c)(3)s Should Apply for Recognition

If your group is designed to qualify under one of the sections of 501(c) other than 501(c)(3), you should file Form 1024. (For some sections, there is no form to be filed. See the IRS Organization Reference Chart in Chapter 2). You should file to nail down, in advance, the fact that the group will not be subject to federal income taxes other than the tax on unrelated business income. Otherwise, you run the risk of your group's ultimately having to pay income taxes on all the contributions it has received (and probably already spent). (If no form is specified for your kind of group, use Form 1024.) There is a filing fee, which you compute using Form 8718 *User Fee for Exempt Organization Determination Letter Request*, and submit along with your application.

Successful Applications Are Public Documents

There is one trade-off in filing for exemption: if the IRS grants your application, the Code makes all of your filings public documents, available for inspection and copying by anyone. That's the way accountability works. There is an exception for trade secrets, patents, processes, styles of work, or apparatus, that allows you to mark on your Form 1023 or 1024 particular materials as *Not Subject to Public Inspection*, and to include, in writing filed with the Form, the reason you say the materials are secret and how their release would harm you. This does not guarantee that the materials will not be released, but it puts you in the best position to convince the IRS not to release them. (Lists of contributors filed with the IRS are automatically confidential.) Starting in 1988, the Code requires all 501(c) or (d) organizations to maintain a file with exact copies of the application for recognition of exemption and all annual returns, with all attachments (except list of contributors), which may be inspected during regular business hours by anyone, with a $10 per day penalty for violations.

What to Tell the IRS on These Forms

Forms 1023 and 1024 are designed to elicit from you the information needed to show that you qualify for the tax status you are claiming. They ask about your structure, purpose, officers, activities and plans, and, of course, about your finances. Don't be put off by all the schedules that don't apply to your kind of organization. Just be grateful you can skip them. They make up about two thirds of each form.

Don't just answer the exact question they ask and then stop. *Bring up* things that might help them understand your position, in the course of answering their questions.

You should also seek legal advice in completing the Forms, particularly Form 1023, where you have to deal with the tricky issue of private foundation status, or, under any section, if there could be any disagreement over whether you really fit.

Determination Letters and Advance Ruling Periods

Once you've sent the IRS your Form 1023 or 1024, along with copies of your governing document, bylaws, and financial data (along with any other materials the IRS asks for in the instructions for the Form), the IRS is in a position to evaluate whether you qualify for exemption from income taxes. However, if you are applying for exemption under section 501(c)(3), and the IRS decides that you *do* qualify for exemption, the IRS must also decide whether to treat you as a private foundation or not. (Private foundations must comply with many more restrictions than other 501(c)(3) groups, as descibed later in this chapter, under "Avoiding Private Foundation Status.")

Some kinds of 501(c)(3) groups are automatically excluded from private foundation status, such as churches, hospitals, and schools, and groups operated in conjunction with or for the benefit of recognized public charities. These groups can get a definitive ruling from the IRS that they are not private foundations at the same time as their eligibility for exemption under section 501(c)(3) is evaluated.

In contrast, groups that say that they are not private foundations because they are "publicly supported" need a track record of actual (not projected) support to prove their case. (The various "Public Support" tests under sections 509(a)(1) and (2) are explained later in this chapter, under "Avoiding Private Foundation Status.") If a newly created organization has a first tax year of at least eight months, an "advance ruling" must be requested, in which case the group may be treated as not being a private foundation for its first three tax years. At the end of the three years, the IRS will evaluate the actual financial information for all three years and issue a definitive ruling based on the cumulative totals. Even if your first tax year is eight months long or longer, it may be a good idea to request an advance ruling period rather than an immediate determination, unless it is clear that you can meet the public support tests based on your first year's numbers. (If your first tax year is eight months long or longer, your advance ruling period would be two years long, instead of three.)

How to Get an "Extended" Advance Ruling Period.   If you feel that your group will eventually be able to be publicly supported, but that it may take longer than two or three years before your numbers will meet the public support tests, you may choose the "extended" advance ruling period: the group's first six tax years (five years, if the group's first tax year is eight months or more). In this case, all five (or all six) years are added together in making the support tests.

Note: If you want an extended ruling period you must ask for it at the outset—you can't switch back and forth.

Advance Ruling Periods Are Not Always Permitted by the IRS.   Getting an advance ruling period is not automatic. Your answers to the questions about your acitivities and operational information (Part III of Form 1023) are looked at not only to determine if you qualify for exemption, but also to see if it looks like you'll have a reasonable chance of raising sufficient "public support" to meet the support tests by the time they are made. Therefore, it is a good idea to *tell* the IRS about the ways your group can show some of the "public support factors" covered later in this chapter under the 10% "facts and circumstances" test. (Even if you are relying on 509(a)(2), where the "facts and circumstances" test does not apply, the presence of these "public support factors" will help persuade the IRS that you've got a reasonable chance of eventually meeting the applicable tests.)

What If They Rule Against Us at the End?   If, at the end of your advance ruling period, you don't meet the support tests, your group would have to pay the normal foundation excise tax of 2% of all net investment income you received (if any) during the course of the advance ruling period.

In addition, it *is* possible for failure to meet the support tests to result in loss of a group's exemption. This is because if a group fails the support test it is considered to be a "private foundation." In order to qualify under 501(c)(3), foundations must have more required clauses in their governing documents than a nonfoundation 501(c)(3). For this reason it is a good idea to include a section with the language required of foundations, so that if the IRS rules that your group *is* a foundation, your documents have the language needed to maintain your exemption and deductibility under section 501(c)(3). This section could begin by saying that you don't intend to be a foundation, but if you turn out to be, the following provisions will apply. Have a lawyer write this for you if you are in a borderline situation.

Appeals and Declaratory Judgments

Your application will normally be granted or denied by the IRS District Director for the key District in which your group's principal office is located. However, the key District Director also has the choice to seek technical advice from the IRS's National Office.

How to File a Protest with the Appeals Office.   If the key District Director rules against you, you have 30 days to protest the ruling to the Appeals Office. To do so, you should file with the key District Office a protest that includes the following:

1. Your group's name, address, and employer identification number.
2. The statement that you want to protest the determination.
3. The date and identifying symbols on the determination letter.
4. The facts that show that your group is entitled to a different determination.
5. The laws or rules you are relying on (as you may have guessed, it's a good idea to get legal advice, and if at all possible, representation, if you have to appeal).
6. Indicate whether you want a chance to present your case directly in a conference with someone from the appeals office.

You should also include at the end of the protest the following declaration, signed by a principal officer or trustee of your group:

> Under penalties of perjury, I declare that I have examined the statement of facts presented in this protest and in any accompanying schedules and statements, and to the best of my knowledge and belief, it is true, correct and complete.

If the protest is prepared and submitted by a lawyer, a certified public accountant, or other individual enrolled to practice before the IRS, that preparer will include his or her own substitute declaration. (See IRS Publications 556 and 557.)

The National Office Has the Final Say (Within the IRS).   If the key District Director ruled without seeking technical advice from the National Office, the Appeals Office can review and reverse the determination. Or, it may seek technical advice from the National Office itself. The Appeals Office cannot reverse the National Office on any issue on which the Natonal Office has already advised the key District Director. The key District Director or the Appeals Office may seek the National Office's technical advice. Also, the organization itself may request that the National Office be asked for its advice on the application form or in the protest.

If the National Office has ruled against you, you can protest that (also within 30 days) to the Conference and Review Staff of the Exempt Organization Technical Branch in the National Office. If the National Office's advice has not been requested, the Appeals Office is the last stop within the IRS.

If 30 days go by after you've been issued a proposed adverse determination letter, and you don't protest, the adverse determination becomes final. (In addition, if you have not protested, you can't go to court for a declaratory judgment, described below.)

Declaratory Judgments—Taking the IRS to Court.   If you've taken all the steps to protest and are still sent a notice of final determination that is adverse to your group, or have not gotten a final determination out of the IRS after 270 days from when you mailed in your completed application, you can go to court under certain circumstances. You can appeal to the courts if the issues involved grow out of exemption under section 501(c)(3), deductibility under section 170(c)(2), private foundation status under section 509, or private operating foundation status under section 4942.

For this you'll need a lawyer. You'll have 90 days from the issuance of a notice of final determination (or from the end of the 270-day period) to file a petition for declaratory judgment with the U.S. Tax Court, the U.S. Court of Claims, or the U.S. District Court for the District of Columbia.

If you lose at the IRS on issues of exemption under sections other than 501(c)(3), there is no direct appeal to the courts. Instead, the group would be treated by the IRS as an ordinary taxpayer, and would raise the issues in court in the context of an IRS claim that it owes taxes and should have filed a business tax return, not a Form 990 information return.

State Tax Breaks

In addition to federal tax exemption, many states offer tax exemptions to nonprofit organizations from income taxes, sales taxes, property taxes, and other taxes. These exemptions sometimes track federal exemptions and sometimes don't, so legal advice may be needed. These exemptions generally are available to charitable, religious, or educational organizations. You should check with your state's Corporations Division, Secretary of State's Office, and any taxing authorities in your state and city to find out what tax breaks are available to your organization, and how to sign up. (And be careful: if you're exempt from state sales taxes on what you *buy*, that does not make you exempt from collecting sales tax on what you *sell*.)

State Charitable Registration

Most states now regulate fundraising by public charities, and require registration and annual reports (sometimes audited) from groups that solicit funds from the public. In addition, many such states set outside limits on how much of the funds raised may go for fundraising expenses as opposed to the purposes for which they were contributed. Inquire at the Attorney General's office about such requirements, and make sure you comply with them.

STAYING EXEMPT—A NEVER-ENDING PROCESS

You can't just get exemption once and then forget about it. You must make sure that you stay exempt, which means that you must make sure that you can prove that you've followed the rules of your exemption and not done things you're not allowed to do. This means that you'll need to develop systems to keep track of what you have done and to require prior approval, by leaders in the group aware of the rules, of any activities that could cause the IRS to challenge your exemption. You should find a lawyer willing to advise you on an ongoing basis, particularly if you're applying under section 501(c)(3).

You'll be filing Form 990 every year to show that you're following the rules, unless you meet one of the exemptions from such filing. Chapter 16 describes Form 990 and the rules about how to file and who must file. Much of this book is aimed toward showing you how to produce the kinds of records the IRS needs access to in support of your answers on Form 990 and the application form. The same (or similar) records will help you deal with foundations and with state agencies, so your record-keeping systems should be designed with enough detail to enable you to generate reports for each purpose, a design task you should enlist both legal and accounting aid in tackling (or at least reviewing).

Who Qualifies for Exemption?

In Chapter 2, we reproduce (with some additions of our own) an IRS table listing the major categories of tax-exempt organizations. In evaluating your organization's application for IRS "recognition" of its tax-exempt status, the IRS will ask itself two basic questions: (1) is your group *organized* exclusively for exempt purposes? and (2) is it *operated* exclusively for exempt purposes? The organizational test focuses on your governing documents—your articles and bylaws discussed in Chapter 2. The operational test looks at what you do, and how you raise and use funds.

The "Substantiality" Test for Nonexempt Activities

The key to the test is the fact that the term "exclusively" has been read by the courts to mean "primarily," in that a nonexempt purpose or activity will disqualify a group from exemption only if it becomes a "substantial" part of the group's purpose or activities. Thus a highly subjective judgment must be made by the IRS about what your group is "really" doing, and why it's really doing it. (At least for lobbying, the concept of "substantial" has fairly recently been defined by Congress on a percentage basis. See "Political and Legislative Activity" later in this chapter. This may, in time, become a source of analogies for measuring whether other nonexempt activities are "substantial.")

The best defense against the accusation that a substantial activity is "really" a business is to show that it is actually carried on to further an exempt purpose. Once again, however, this requires a subjective judgment by the IRS. Are you operating on a larger scale than is necessary to further your exempt purpose in order to make more money? If the IRS feels that you are "really" just a business, and you are "really" trying to get tax-exempt status in order to help you compete unfairly with other businesses, you will ultimately have to show convincingly (if not to the IRS, then to the courts) that all but an insubstantial part of your activities are either clearly exempt or contribute importantly to carrying out your exempt purpose. (For more discussion of the permissible amount of nonexempt activities, we refer you once again to "Political and Legislative Activity," later in this chapter.) Form 990 now asks some probing questions in this area. (It used to rely on you to recognize this issue. Not anymore.)

THE TAX ON UNRELATED BUSINESS INCOME

For a full discussion of this subject and the new IRS reporting requirements intended to smoke out such income, see "Possibly Taxable Types of Income" in Chapter 9.

The law does more than just limit the amount of effort you may devote to revenue-producing activities that don't advance your stated goals. It actually taxes you, at standard corporate income tax rates, on your net income (after the first $1,000) from such activities, if they are regularly carried on and resemble a trade or business. Again, the idea is to prevent you from competing unfairly with taxpaying businesses. As just noted, Form 990 has recently been rewritten to search out non-exempt and taxable activities.

It gets tricky, however, when the IRS decides to single out a revenue-producing part of an un-questionably exempt activity as an "unrelated trade or business."

Example: Let's say your group publishes a newsletter that furthers your goals by spreading the word and helping coordinate your activities. In addition, let's also say that you sell the newsletter to members and others, and that the newsletter carries paid advertisements. The sale of the newsletter would be "exempt function income," as selling the newsletter contributes importantly to your exempt purposes. However, the IRS could zero in on the sale of advertising, call it a separate unre-lated business, and would tax it on any excess of advertising revenue over advertising costs (including its share of overhead)—even if your group, as a whole, is losing money.

There are some exceptions to this, however. For example, as the advertising depends upon the newsletter's existence, if the newsletter is running at a loss because its subscriptions (exempt function income) don't cover its costs, *that* loss can be used to offset any profit made on advertising. (If it couldn't, the newsletter publishing activity could be losing money but still paying taxes—which would not happen to a newsletter published by a business. Fair's fair.) However, you cannot create a loss to offset unrelated business income from other activities that do not directly depend upon the newsletter's existence. (How these things are calculated is discussed in Chapter 16.)

Another group of exceptions relates to activities that are saved from being classified as unrelated trades or businesses. They are excluded because substantially all of the merchandise is donated to the organization for it to sell. There are other exclusions as well, for trades or businesses operated by charitable organizations, state colleges, local employees' associations, unions, farmers' associa-tions, or business leagues primarily for the convenience of their members and of others involved in their exempt activities.

This last exclusion leads to some fine distinctions. For example, at a convention or trade show held by a union or a business league, if booths are rented to exhibitors, the rental income is unre-lated business income if exhibitors are allowed to make sales. Purely informational booths are presumed to be for the convenience of the conventioneer, but sales booths are clearly for the benefit of the exhibitors—or so says the law, which must often rely on such approximate tests.

There are still other exclusions, for certain hospital services—even for the proceeds of bingo games—but these are the major ones. For more information on the unrelated business tax, see Chapter 16, which explains how it is computed, and also get the most recent revision of IRS Publication 598, *Tax on Unrelated Business Income of Exempt Organizations.*

POLITICAL AND LEGISLATIVE ACTIVITY

What? Me Lobby?

A major area that tax-exempt organizations have to limit carefully is political and legislative activity—trying to influence elections or legislation—even if it directly and substantially contributes to accomplishment of a group's tax-exempt purposes. You may not think that *your* group will have any reason to lobby, but that's not a safe assumption. A health center or school might need to support or oppose changes in the laws regarding the licensing of itself, or of its professional staff, or regarding "third party" payments in the form of insurance, loans, or grants. An arts or cultural group might want to voice support for continued or increased public appropriations for the arts. A library might have to oppose proposed laws to ban certain kinds of books. And even if your group does not support or oppose changes in the laws, it will have a great interest in the status of laws regarding its rights and duties as an employer.

It is almost impossible to completely avoid any need to deal with legislation, as the legislatures are where all the elements of society collide in the process of deciding what the society needs. The legislative bodies pass laws to bring about desired goals by providing funding or regulating conduct. Someday you may need to do something the law forbids, or keep on doing something the law presently allows; or you'll need to stop someone else from doing something wrong that the law presently allows; or you'll need to oppose a cutback in appropriations in some area.

If your efforts serve to support or oppose legislation or a referendum, you're lobbying—even if you never contact a legislator and merely urge your members (through your newsletter) to get involved, or to tell their friends. Even giving a telephone interview to a radio reporter who asks you to discuss a legislative controversy could constitute lobbying. If your interviews might affect how listeners regard a particular candidate for public office, you may even be electioneering.

Why the Law Limits Political and Legislative Activities

Since furtherance of your exempt purposes would seem to require many kinds of involvement with the political process, whether extensive or fleeting, even if only to maintain the status quo in some area, you might think that such activity would be unrestricted. However, even though they would advance the group's exempt purposes, political and legislative activities by exempt organizations are subject to limitations on their extent, sometimes give rise to a tax, and (depending on the particular part of the Code you are exempted under) may even be prohibited entirely. The reason for this is that the economic leverage the tax system gives to exempt organizations (particularly those that are tax-deductible for contributions) makes it unfair to allow them to apply that leverage to influencing the government. That is an extreme statement, and goes well beyond the actual rules in its restrictive intent, but it is the animating spirit behind these restrictions.

The same contribution costs the wealthiest contributors less, after taxes, than it costs others. It would be very dangerous to our society's democratic system to have political contests fought out between tax-deductible groups. On the one hand, you might have a group backed by 33% (top bracket) taxpayers, whose $100 contributions actually cost $67 (the other 33% being reimbursed by a tax reduction equal to 33% of the tax deductible $100 contribution). And on the other, you might have an opposing group backed by 15% taxpayers, whose $100 contributions actually cost $85. Then again, you could have a group backed by those who take the standard deduction[1] or are too poor to pay any taxes, whose $100 contributions actually do cost $100. Of course, such an obvious stratification might not occur very often, but the point it makes is clear. Those with the most to spend should not be given a discount on democracy. (Looked at another way, the nondeducting taxpayer can give $100, the 15% taxpayer can give $117.65, and the 33% taxpayer can give $149.25—all for the same after-tax cost of $100. That's what's referred to as tax "leverage.")

Political Activity

The passion and force behind the argument just discussed is at its greatest where the debate concerns political activity by tax-deductible organizations.

Therefore, it should not come as a surprise that tax-deductible charitable organizations are entirely prohibited from attempting to influence elections for public office, and that even non-partisan distribution of the various candidates' answers to questions, or of analysis of their voting records, may be closely scrutinized by the IRS for bias in the framing of questions or in the selection of topics.

This prohibition is not limited to attempts to influence election campaigns. The Code's definition of "political activity" includes any attempts to influence "the selection, nomination, election, or appointment of any individual to any Federal, State, or local public office or office in a political organization, or the election of Presidential or Vice-Presidential electors, whether or not such individual or electors are selected, nominated, elected, or appointed."

In fact, intervention in politics is not allowed to business corporations either, and is limited in amount (as "nonexempt activity") in most other categories of nonprofits and taxed at corporate rates in nonprofits that have significant investment income. Congress has tried to channel most such activity into organizations exempt from tax under section 527 of the Code (which can be a separate bank account opened by a 501(c)(3) organization). The purpose is to keep the funding for political intervention separated from (and thus less able to be subsidized by) the funds that support other kinds of tax-exempt or business activities.

A tax-exempt section 501(c)(4) lobbying organization can thus either spend money on a campaign itself and be both taxed at the highest corporate tax rate (assuming the presence of investment income) and limited in the total amount it may spend, or it may open a separate segregated bank account and solicit separate contributions to that fund, which could qualify as a separate section 527 political organization, and which would be neither taxed on, nor limited in the total amount of, such activity. However, the funds must be separate and clearly earmarked for this use by the contributors, or else they'll represent expenditures by the 501(c)(4) and may be taxed.[2] Section 501(c)(3) charitable organizations cannot take advantage of these provisions, as they may

---

[1] The Economic Recovery Tax Act of 1981 allowed a limited percentage of a limited amount of charitable contributions to be taken on the returns of taxpayers who take the standard deduction and don't itemize, for tax years beginning in 1982 through 1986. The limit came off in 1985, and the percentage hit 100% in 1986, but this whole provision expired at the end of 1986. Thus, for one year (1986) those who didn't itemize were able to take the same deduction as those who did, temporarily cutting one of the basic problems with the charitable deduction. Now, however, we're back where we started, with no deduction allowed unless one itemizes.

[2] It might not be a bad idea to ask contributors to note such earmarking on the face of the check, and for the group to save photocopies of all such checks, to show as proof. In addition, all amounts advanced to pay for initial fundraising appeals should be paid back by the 527.

not intervene in elections at all.[3]

The amount of political activity 501(c) organizations (other than 501(c)(3)) may engage in is determined in a negative way: (1) The group must be operated exclusively for exempt purposes; (2) Political activity fits into no group's exempt purpose except section 527 political organizations; (3) "Exclusively" means that no nonexempt activity (unrelated business, electioneering, social activities for members) may become a "substantial" part of an organization's activities.

The test is not strictly quantitative in terms of expenditures or revenues, but involves a subjective evaluation of the way the group operates.

As with unrelated business activity, the test is largely subjective and asks basically the same question: what are you "really" up to? In fact this same test applies to all "nonexempt" activities. It includes those which either don't contribute importantly to furthering your exempt purposes, and even some that do, but are specifically excluded from your exempt activities by law.

The exception to all of this is the tax-exempt section 527 political organization for which political activity *is* its exempt purpose. If you want to set up a 527, you should refer to the Federal Election Campaign Act (which begins at section 431 of Title 2 of the United States Code) regarding organizational and reporting rules.

Influencing Legislation

As we leave the field of combat over who *should* govern, and move to attempts to convince those who *do* govern of the justice of one's cause, the balance shifts. The First Amendment right to petition the government for redress of grievances begins to overshadow objections to the unfair economics of tax deductibility—at least in the eyes of Congress. (A less kind view might be that the members of Congress are less afraid of lobbyists than of well-financed political opposition. "You may try to persuade us, but you may not try to replace us.") Since Congress feels legislative activity by tax-exempt groups is less dangerous to democracy than political activity, the Internal Revenue Code does not undertake to limit legislative activity by all tax-exempt organizations. Tax exemption, by itself, is not that much of an advantage. Thus, lobbying groups often choose to be exempt under section 501(c)(4).

However, tax deductibility of contributions is a significant advantage that makes the after-tax cost of contributing lower, the richer the taxpayer is. Because of that, Congress limited the amount of lobbying activity tax-deductible (Section 501(c)(3)) organizations could engage in. (Contributions to some other categories of 501(c) organizations, 501(c)(5) labor groups and particularly 501(c)(6) business leagues, are also tax-deductible, not as charitable contributions, but as ordinary business expenses. While these groups are not directly limited in the amount of lobbying activities they may engage in to further their members' common business interests, a member may not deduct any portion of its contribution that pays for lobbying activities in which the member does not have a business interest, nor may any member deduct the cost of an appeal to the general public, regardless of whether it has a business interest in the subject of the appeal.)

Before we get to the rules about how much lobbying is too much (and what happens if the limits are exceeded), we should know what kinds of activity the limits apply to in the first place.

IRS Regulations under Section 501(c)(3) will deny you exemption if your primary purpose can

---

[3]The 1987 tax law amendments added a set of penalty taxes on (c)(3)s that make political expenditures: 10% on the group and 2½% on its manager plus, if the expenditure was not attempted to be corrected, 100% on the group and 50% on the manager. The IRS may make immediate assessment of the penalties in cases of "flagrant violation" and may seek an injunction against further violations.

only be attained through the passage or defeat of legislation and you actively lobby. They'll call you an "action" organization and send you away. Thus, the following applies only if your "primary" purpose is not the passage or defeat of legislation.

"Influencing Legislation" Defined. The definition and exceptions that we're about to describe, together with the percentage limits we'll talk about later, were adopted by Congress in 1976 as Code sections 501(h) and 4911, a set of rules many 501(c)(3) organizations can voluntarily "elect" to have apply to any current or future tax year, instead of the vaguer "substantiality" test. (Private foundations, churches and church-affiliated groups, and 501(c)(3) organizations controlled by groups exempt under other parts of section 501(c) are all precluded from making such an election.) Theoretically, not even the definition of "influencing legislation" may apply to a group that has not filed a 501(h) election. However, the definition and exceptions of "influencing legislation" are very similar to the definition and exceptions of "influencing legislation" in the previous case law under 501(c)(3). Congress should make the definition and exceptions of "influencing legislation" explicitly applicable to nonelecting organizations as well. This would bring greater clarity to the law without affecting the underlying policy.)

The Congressional Balancing Act

A good deal of the complexity in this area arises from Congress' extending its balancing of free speech and fair play to the level of evaluating particular types of activities that can influence legislation. Thus, in defining the term "influencing legislation" in Section 4911 of the Code, Congress adopted a broad definition but tacked on a number of exceptions for activities it considered either (a) innocuous or (b) vital to preserve the right of petition.

The broad definition is that "influencing legislation" means "any attempt to influence any legislation through an attempt to affect the opinions of the general public or any segment thereof,"[4] (known as "grass roots" lobbying) or "any attempt to influence any legislation through communication with any member or employee of a legislative body, or with any government official or employee who may participate in the formulation of the legislation."

"Legislation" is defined in the same section as including "action with respect to Acts, bills, resolutions, or similar items by the Congress, any State legislature, any local council, or similar governing body, or by the public in a referendum, initiative, constitutional amendment, or similar procedure." "Action" is defined as "the introduction, amendment, enactment, defeat, or repeal" of legislation.

The exceptions are for kinds of activities that, although they come within the broad definition just quoted, are specifically excluded from it because of congressional recognition of their relative harmlessness or their importance to allowing freedom of speech and the right of petition.

One approach that was *not* adopted was to create an exception for any legislative activity in pursuit of a group's exempt purposes. Such an exception would quickly swallow up the rule. Groups whose primary objectives can *only* be attained by legislative action and which lobby to that end are considered "action" organizations ineligible for 501(c)(3) status.

---

[4]Regulations that were being adopted at this writing narrowed the definition of grass-roots lobbying to require reference to specific legislation, a point of view, and encouragement to take action. However, mass media communications less than two weeks before a vote would be considered to be grass-roots lobbying even without reference to specific legislation, unless it is shown that the timing was a coincidence.

1. Exception Number One is for *"making available the results of nonpartisan analysis, study or research."* The key word here is *"nonpartisan."* The presentation must be fair and balanced, presenting alternative viewpoints, and must stop short of advocating legislative action or inaction. This exception flows both from the relative harmlessness of such activity and from its essentially "educational" nature—i.e., it is not only *in pursuit of* a 501(c)(3)-type purpose, but *it is itself* a type of activity exempt under section 501(c)(3).

2. Exception Number Two excludes from the category of lobbying the *"providing of technical advice or assistance . . . to a governmental body or to a committee or other subdivision thereof in response to a written request by such body or subdivision . . . "* Thus the same technical advice may or may not be considered to be lobbying, depending on how it came to be given. The sentiment behind this exception is the feeling that a group should not be trapped into using up its quota of lobbying in responding to requests for assistance in its area of expertise. The exception is worded as narrowly as it is to avoid abuse by a group that asks a friendly committee member to ask for its views.

3. Exception Number Three relates directly to the right of petition. This exception covers *"appearances before, or communications to, any legislative body with respect to a possible decision of such body which might affect the existence the organization, its powers and duties, tax-exempt status, or the deduction of contributions to the organization."* If this reminds you of the right to defend yourself, you're right. When you're fighting for your organizational survival, the meter isn't running. It does not affect how much lobbying you may do on other issues.

4. Exception Number Four covers *"communications between the organization and its bona fide members with respect to legislation or proposed legislation of direct interest to the organization and such members . . . "* However, there are exclusions from this exception. If the organization encourages its members to:

    a. lobby the government themselves, or
    b. urge nonmembers to either
       i. lobby the government, or
       ii. spread the word

this exception does not apply, and the organization's message to its members is considered to be "influencing legislation." If it falls under b(i) or (ii) it is counted as "grass-roots lobbying"—the importance of which will become clear shortly. Once that tangle has been straightened out, what it comes down to is that you can tell your members that legislative action is needed, and it won't be considered lobbying unless you also encourage them to *do* something. Clearly this exception is based both on the First Amendment right of association and the argument that since it doesn't urge action it represents relatively harmless free speech (although we shudder at the expression).

5. Exception Number Five from the definition of "influencing legislation" is for *"any communication with a government official or employee other than:*

    i. a communication with a member or employee of a legislative body (where such communication would otherwise constitute the influencing of legislation), or
    ii. a communication the principal purpose of which is to influence legislation.

This one boils down to saying that if you communicate with someone in government *outside* the legislative branch, it will only be considered to be lobbying if trying to influence legislation is the *main reason* you are communicating with them. But if you communicate with someone *in* the legislative branch, it is lobbying unless you *avoid* influencing legislation. (Why didn't Congress say so more clearly? Maybe because nobody expects anyone to read the Internal Revenue Code unless they're paid to—usually by the hour!)

How Much Lobbying Is Allowed?

Now that you know what is (and what isn't) considered to be "influencing legislation," how much of it may you engage in? If you are tax-deductible as a 501(c)(3) charitable organization, this is an issue of no small importance, for if you get called out for doing too much, you may have to pay a tax on the excess, and (depending on how extreme and/or persistent an offender you are) you may even lose your tax-deductible 501(c)(3) status. In addition, section 504 of the Code denies recognition as a tax-exempt 501(c)(4) social welfare organization to any group that had been recognized by the IRS as a 501(c)(3) but that has lost its exemption for excessive lobbying.

You see, 501(c)(3) charitable organizations and 501(c)(4) social welfare organizations have essentially overlapping kinds of purposes, which are general enough that many kinds of organizations could seek exemption under either section. The difference is more one of powers and activities than one of purposes. The tax-deductible 501(c)(3) may not intervene in elections at all, and may only influence legislation a little, while a tax-exempt (but not deductible) 501(c)(4) social welfare organization may intervene in elections a little and may lobby extensively. But you have to decide in advance that you are a 501(c)(4) and forego the deductibility of charitable contributions that 501(c)(3) organizations benefit from. If you choose and obtain recognition under 501(c)(3) and then go over the lobbying limits to the extent that you lose your 501(c)(3) status, you may not convert to a 501(c)(4) status, nor may you set up and operate a new group as a 501(c)(4) and transfer to it the old 501(c)(3) group's assets (which it may have been able to amass because of its tax-deductible status).

So with all these red danger flags waving we come to the ultimate question: *How much is too much?* Before the elective rules were adopted (and today for any group that does not file a 501(h) election with the IRS) the rule was the vague "substantiality" test (as with unrelated activities). The rulings and cases make it clear that a high dollar expense can kill you, but a low dollar expense might not save you, since it is an *activity* test.

The worst thing about the "substantiality" test in a First Amendment context is the test's subjectivity, which renders it useful for harassment of groups that is really motivated by disagreement with their views. The effect is to lead many groups to exercise self-censorship, out of fear.

The elective rules were enacted by Congress to help solve this problem. Under the elective rules, the "substantiality" test is replaced by a "percentage of exempt purpose expenditures" test, on a sliding scale. If you file a 501(h) election, your group's "lobbying nontaxable amount" would be 20% of the first $500,000 of exempt purpose expenditures, plus 15% of the second $500,000, 10% of the third, and 5% of anything over that. The lobbying nontaxable amount may not exceed one million dollars. Your "grass roots nontaxable amount" would be 25% of your "lobbying nontaxable amount." (See the definition of grass-roots lobbying under the heading "The Congressional Balancing Act.") Congress will let you lobby it, but legislators are still not crazy about letting you start a campaign to affect the public's opinion on a legislative matter. After all, the line between issue propaganda and electioneering can get very hazy if there is a strong association in the public mind between a particular issue and a particular legislator or candidate. In addition, each dollar spent stirring up a "write your Congressman" campaign may have more impact than the same dollar spent on direct lobbying. They'll let you go over their heads to the public a *little* on legislative issues (25% of your lobbying nontaxable amount), but they'd rather you came to them directly (the other 75%).

In calculating your exempt purpose expenditures and lobbying expenditures, items of capital equipment are included only on a straight-line depreciation basis.[5] (You can't boost your lobbying quota by 20% of the value of the word processor you just bought, but only by 20% of this year's straight-line depreciation of the word processor.) In addition, in making this calculation, you must exclude from your exempt purpose expenditures any amounts spent on a "separate fundraising unit" of your group, or paid to an outside organization for fundraising.

Most importantly, you must allocate your rent, utilities, and other fixed overhead, along with staff salaries, on the basis of how much time is spent on lobbying and grass-roots lobbying, and you must include these amounts as expenditures toward the quotas.[6]

If you exceed either nontaxable amount (lobbying nontaxable or grass-roots nontaxable), you will become liable for a 25% tax on the greater of the two discrepancies (not on their sum). Thus, if you had a lobbying nontaxable amount of $20,000 (and therefore a grass-roots nontaxable amount of $5,000), but spent $22,000, of which $7,500 was for grass-roots lobbying, the tax would be 25% of $2,500 ($625) because the $2,500 difference between $7,500 and $5,000 is larger than the $2,000 difference between $22,000 and $20,000.

Even if you're willing to pay the tax, you can't just spend as much as you want. There is still an outside limit. The Code expresses it as a pair of ceilings. The lobbying ceiling amount is 150% of the lobbying nontaxable amount; the grass-roots ceiling amount is, similarly, 150% of the grass-roots nontaxable amount. Section 501(h) expressly denies exemption under section 501(c)(3) to any electing organization that "normally" makes expenditures in excess of either ceiling. According to the IRS, "normally" means on the average over a four-year period, and is determined by doing the calculations above based on the group's combined total expenses for the past four years. If the result is over 150%, you'll lose your exemption.

If you're doing so much lobbying that you're regularly exceeding your nontaxable amounts and are bumping up against the ceilings, you should consider setting up a companion 501(c)(4) social welfare organization and channeling your permissible expenditures through it.

Such an arrangement greatly simplifies the record-keeping needed to show that the 501(c)(3) group has complied with its limits. If the two groups are physically separate and share neither office facilities nor staff, all that need be kept track of is how much money the 501(c)(3) contributed to the 501(c)(4). If the 501(c)(4) operates out of the office of the 501(c)(3), an allocation of floor space (and thus of rent and utilities), must be made, so that the value of the rent that is being (in effect) donated to the 501(c)(4) can be included in the calculation. If the two groups share staff, salaries and over-head will have to be allocated on the basis of the percentage of their time spent on lobbying. In this case you're back where you started with just the 501(c)(3) in terms of record-keeping. (The mechanics of such allocations, which are the same whether expenses are allocated between programs, functions, or organizations, are explained in Chapter 6.)

However, there are other advantages, besides convenience in record-keeping, that recommend the use of a 501(c)(4) group for lobbying. Beyond whatever can be contributed by the 501(c)(3), the 501(c)(4) is free to solicit additional funds on its own. Contributions to the 501(c)(4) will not be

---

[5]Depreciation is explained in Chapter 10.
[6]Allocation of overhead is explained in Chapter 6.

deductible as charitable contributions, but this need not be an insuperable obstacle. It should be remembered that some people actually do give money to groups in order to support their activities, even when there is no tax saving involved. The great majority of individuals don't itemize their deductions, but take the standard deduction instead. To them, tax deductibility is largely irrelevant,[7] but they still make contributions. The 501(c)(4) is therefore not really disadvantaged when it comes to soliciting funds from them. The main disadvantage comes in trying to get large contributions or foundation grants which *are* usually governed by whether the recipient group has 501(c)(3) status.

In addition, like any other tax-exempt organization, the 501(c)(4) may operate revenue-generating activities to support its lobbying efforts. (See the discussion under "The Tax on Unrelated Business Income" earlier in this chapter.)

To Elect the Lobbying Provision or Not?

As indicated above, the elective provisions (501)(h) were designed to replace the uncertainty produced by the "substantiality" test with an expenditure test. Remember that, until Congress clarifies the law, nonelecting groups are taking a gamble in relying on the precise wording of any of the exceptions above. If your group foresees the need to engage in any activity that could be called "influencing legislation" by the IRS, by not electing you increase the risk of having to defend your activities against challenge by an unfriendly IRS agent. Even if you win such a battle, it'll cost you—in terms of money, time, and even potential harm to your reputation.

As an additional reason to elect, the 1987 tax law amendments added a 5% penalty tax on groups that lose their exemptions for excess lobbying—if they have not filed 501(h) elections—and a 5% penalty on the organization's manager, if the manager knew the exemption was in danger.

The lobbying election is not irrevocable. It can be used one year at a time, and can be made or revoked using IRS Form 5768. You may make the election at any time during the tax year to which it applies (which may be a fiscal year). It will then continue in effect for future years unless you revoke it. A revocation must be filed prior to the beginning of the tax year to which it applies. (You can change your mind and reinstate the election at any point during the year.)

Why Not Elect 501(h) Status?

The main argument against electing is that it makes you analyze the time spent by each paid staff member of the 501(c)(3) who devotes part of his or her time to lobbying (either direct or grassroots), breaking that staffer's time down by activity, in order to make an allocation between lobbying and nonlobbying and also between direct and grass-roots lobbying. If a companion 501(c)(4) with a separate staff is used, this objection disappears. The same is true if, within the 501(c)(3), all lobbying activity is carried out by staffers who do nothing else during particular days or weeks, avoiding the need for daily time breakdowns.

Even if you can't avoid this kind of time analysis by one of the expedients just mentioned, the IRS only requires that the allocation be made on a "reasonable" basis, and if you are not already making a detailed time breakdown for some other purpose (such as for budgetary planning or to comply with the terms of a grant) the IRS will probably be satisfied with good-faith estimates. An

[7]But see footnote 1 under *Political and Legislative Activity* above, for recent temporary changes in the law.

estimate that is an average of (and is documented by) daily, weekly, or monthly estimates made by the staffers themselves is obviously more credible than an estimate that is basically a "guesstimate" made by a group's leaders based on the whole previous year's activity.

However, the IRS does not say how the allocation is to be arrived at, so it becomes a matter of the IRS having to say that the approach you took was unreasonable. And that's difficult for them to say in the absence of independent evidence (which could include your own newsletter and public statements), that your staff spent significantly more time lobbying than you estimated. Of course, if your time allocations look fishy, such as by allocating no part of the time of a top staffer who has responsibility for the issue about which you're lobbying (like your chief executive), this may be challenged as contrary to common sense and you may be asked for more convincing proof.

In any event, since all you'd normally report to the IRS each year are lump-sum total expenses for direct lobbying and grass-roots lobbying, the basis for these figures is needed mainly for backup documentation in case of an audit. Even if you don't make the lobbying election, you'd still be well advised to have a similar kind of factual backup to show that you have not engaged in a "substantial" amount of lobbying—and activities would have to be monitored and controlled, not just expenditures.

Affiliated Groups

If your 501(c)(3) organization controls or is controlled by another 501(c)(3) organization, and either of them makes the lobbying election under section 501(h), then, under 4911(f) all computations of lobbying activity must be made as if the controlled and controlling groups are one organization, basing the lobbying nontaxable and ceiling amounts on the groups' combined exempt purpose expenditures. Thus, a nonelecting member of a group of affiliated organizations (which could have more than two members) still has to generate the same factual record as the electing members.

If there is any tax due on excess lobbying, each electing member of the group must pay a 25% tax based on its proportionate share of the excess. If the 150% ceiling is "normally" exceeded by the group, each electing organization loses its tax exemption. (The nonelecting members are not taxed, but are treated under prior law and could lose their exemptions for having engaged in "substantial" lobbying activity.)

In an ironic way, the affiliated organization rules, while they look like additional regulation, are actually the opposite. Anyone who has had to deal with budgets knows that his or her flexibility is greatly increased by the ability to transfer funds from one account to another. What aggregation does is allow you to (in effect) transfer quotas from group to group, and concentrate your lobbying activity where you need it the most, instead of having to spread it around among all the groups on a basis proportional to their size. Therefore, aggregation represents more of a boon than a burden. But you can't aggregate with just anyone (the bigger and more legislatively inactive the better): the price is that one group's independence on legislative issues must be sacrificed.

What are "Affiliated Organizations"?

The degree of control that one 501(c)(3) organization must have over another before the two are considered to be "affiliated" is specified in section 4911(f)(2)(A) and (B) as only if:

(A) the governing instrument of one such organization requires it to be bound by decisions of the other organization on legislative issues, or

(B) the governing board of one such organization includes persons who—

    (i) are specifically designated representatives of another such organization or are members of the governing board, officers, or paid executive staff members of such other organization, and

    (ii) by aggregating their votes, have sufficient voting power to cause or prevent action on legislative issues by the first such organization.

"Limited Control"

Section 4911(f)(4), one of the most impenetrably worded provisions of the Code, deals with the situation where the local chapters of a national organization are bound by their charters to the national organization's strategy on national legislation only, and there are no voting interlocks between the groups that could control their actions with regard to state or local legislation. In such a situation of "limited control," the usual aggregation rules do not apply. Instead, in evaluating the *controlling group's* compliance and tax liability, all expenditures by the controlled groups with regard to national legislation are treated "as though" the controlling group "has paid or incurred those amounts." But no aggregation of exempt purpose expenditures is made, so all lobbying activity with regard to national legislation must be measured against the controlling group's own individual lobbying quota.

With regard to the *controlled group* or groups, each one is evaluated on its own, "as though such organization is not a member of such affiliated group." The IRS's instructions for Schedule A for Form 990 direct the controlled groups to omit from their own returns expenditures with regard to national legislation that are treated "as though" they were made by the controlling group. (See Chapter 16).

AVOIDING PRIVATE FOUNDATION STATUS

Any 501(c)(3) organization that is required to apply for recognition of its tax-exempt status is also required to give notice to the IRS that it is not a "private foundation," to avoid being treated as one. (For exceptions to both requirements, see "Signing Up With the Service," earlier in this chapter.)

Two questions immediately occur to most people when they receive the above (rather cryptic) advice from the IRS:

1. What is a "private foundation" anyway?

2. Why should we avoid being treated as one?

Once these questions have been answered, a third, more urgent one appears:

3. How can we avoid "private foundation" status?

Taking it from the top:

What are "Private Foundations"?

Private foundations are, in the classical, stereotyped sense, endowments created and controlled by a single individual or family or firm, or by a small group of them. (There is no affirmative definition of the term "private foundation" in the Code that could help sharpen the above description, only a list of types of organizations that are *not* private foundations.)

Private foundations are the "banks" of the nonprofit world. They are where you'll probably go looking (in addition to government agencies and, sometimes, businesses) for grants to help support your group's activities. They get their money as charitable contributions, same as you, and apply it for 501(c)(3) purposes, same as you. However, because of the concentration of economic power represented by a 501(c)(3) entity in a small number of people's hands, and because of the danger of tax fraud (at the expense of charitable applications of the funds), private foundations are held much more closely to traditional fiduciary obligations of care than other 501(c)(3) organizations. They are not even allowed to make the section 501(h) lobbying election just discussed, and are subject to other restrictions and taxes that do not apply to 501(c)(3)s in general.

In case you're thinking, "Well, we don't make grants, so we're not a foundation," you should know that there's a special group of private foundations that look a lot like ordinary 501(c)(3) groups. They don't make grants to other 501(c)(3)s but instead directly carry on exempt activities themselves. They're called "private operating foundations," but they're still subject to almost all of the same rules as other private foundations. You may have to be one if you get your funding from only a few sources, as you'll see. They are discussed below, under "'The Private Operating Foundation' Option."

Why Avoid Being Treated as a Private Foundation?

The short answer to this question is that private foundations are subject to many more rules than other 501(c)(3) organizations: rules about how they may operate, who they may make deals with, how much of their money they must spend, what they may spend it on, and what they may not. As noted above, they may not make the lobbying election, among others. In addition, private foundations are subjected to taxes on their assets, as well as numerous penalty taxes to enforce the other rules, including taxes on the individuals involved (whether as officials or employees) in violation of some of the rules. (The penalty taxes range from 2½% to 200% of the amounts involved. You wouldn't want to read the full answer, as it would be almost as long as this chapter. If you're really interested, get hold of IRS Publication 578, *Tax Information for Private Foundations and Foundation Managers.*

How To Avoid Private Foundation Status

Certain kinds of 501(c)(3) organizations are automatically excluded from the private foundation category, other 501(c)(3)s must show that they are "publicly supported organizations" or that they are operated for the benefit of one.

The kinds of 501(c)(3) organizations that are automatically excluded are:

- Churches and conventions or associations of churches.

- Educational organizations that normally maintain a regular faculty and curriculum and that normally have a regularly enrolled body of students in attendance.

- Hospitals and hospital-affiliated organizations that principally provide medical or hospital care or medical education or research.
- State colleges.
- Governmental units.
- Organizations that are organized and operated exclusively to test for public safety.[8]

There are two tests to qualify as a "publicly supported" organization (also called "public charities"). Either one can get you out from under the private foundation rules. One is under sections 509(c)(1) and 170(b)(1)(A)(vi), the other is under section 509(a)(2).

The Section 509(a)(1) and 170(b)(1)(A)(vi) Test. Your group can qualify as being publicly supported if it normally gets a "substantial" amount of its support from government or foundation grants or from contributions from the general public. In this context, "substantial" means one third, and "normally" means a four-year average up to and including last year, unless your funding has changed substantially this year (in which case this year gets averaged in as well), or unless you are a new organization, in which you average in all the years you've got.

Under both this test and the test under section 509(a)(2) described below, the "public support fraction" that is used looks like this:

$$\frac{\text{"Public Support"}}{\text{"Total Support"}} \times 100 = \text{"Public Support Percentage"}$$

This looks simple enough, but there are lots of rules about what kinds of money count toward "Public Support" and "Total Support."

Factors to Consider When Computing the Numbers. 1. Grants and contributions do not include *moneys the organization earned in the course of its exempt operations,* whether in the form of the sale of literature, or as a payment from a government agency to carry out a particular task for the benefit of the agency (rather than of the public). These are considered "related gross receipts," and *are not included in "public support" nor in "total support."* While excluded from the fraction, these amounts may still disqualify a group if it gets almost all of its funding from related gross receipts and only an insignificant amount from "public support." However, such groups may still qualify as "publicly supported" under the section 509(a)(2) test, described later. In-kind contributions of services (which are not tax-deductible by the contributor), are also excluded from both "public support" and "total support."

2. *Net income from unrelated business activities,* even if not carried on regularly enough to subject the group to taxes, still *counts toward "total support," but not towards "public support."*

3. *If any contributor* (other than a governmental unit or another 170(b)(1)(A)(vi) organization[9]) *contributes more than 2% of a year's total support, that contribution is included in full in "total support," but nothing beyond that 2% counts towards "public support."* (Even a grant from a governmental unit or another 170(b)(1)(A)(vi) organization can run afoul of this rule, if the original source of the funds was a contribution from an individual that was earmarked for the recipient group.) Husbands and wives share a 2% limit, as do all members of a "disqualified" entity.

---

[8]This category is an anomaly. Omitted from section 170(c)(2)(B), which defines "charitable contributions," it is the only group of nondeductible 501(c)(3) organizations.

[9]That is, an organization that is excluded from private foundation status under the test we are describing.

A "disqualified person" is a person or entity that is close to the organization. How close is too close? For starters, officers, directors, responsible employees, "substantial contributors," or anyone who owns 20% of a substantial contributor, and members of the families of any of the above are all "disqualified persons" under section 4946, along with entities that are 35% owned by any of them. Under section 507(d)(2), a "substantial contributor" is anyone who has contributed or bequeathed more than $5,000 to the organization, if they gave more than 2% of the total contributions or bequests received by the organization by the close of the tax year in which their contribution or bequest was received. Once someone becomes a "substantial contributor" they are treated as one from then on, even if they stop giving. Such status will change only after 10 years of no further giving.

If the organization is a trust, the creator of the trust is considered to be a "substantial contributor."

4. Finally, the IRS recognizes that a group that normally meets the test may receive an unusual grant in a particular year that would cause the group to fail the test, through no fault of the group's own. To deal with this, *the IRS will allow the exclusion of some unusual grants from both "total" and "public" support* in making these calculations. Many factors are considered by the IRS in evaluating whether a grant may be excluded, including the group's past history of meeting the one-third of support test, and its activities designed to make the group publicly supported in the past. Another consideration is whether the grant came from a "disqualified person" or from a disinterested person attracted by the group's tax-exempt purpose and public outreach activities. Another factor could be whether the grant was in the form of a bequest in a will (which is hard to time for the best IRS impact) or was an ordinary gift. Also, whether the grant was of cash or of assets of particular value to the group's exempt purpose; and other factors listed under IRS regulations section 1.509(a)-3(c)(5)(ii). The IRS has recently decided to stop giving what it terms "comfort rulings," however, in situations where it feels there is no need to go beyond the published materials.

To help digest and assimilate all that, let's look at an example. Listed in the left-hand column is a breakdown of different kinds of funding a particular group might have. The second column shows the amount that counts toward "public support" for the purposes of this test, and the third shows how much counts toward "total support."

	Amount Received	Public Support	Total Support
Govt. Bureau A (grant for public's benefit)	$ 10,000	$ 10,000	$ 10,000
Govt. Bureau B (grant for agency's benefit—related services)	6,000	—	—
General Public (contributions of less than 2%)	100,000	100,000	100,000
(gross receipts for related services)	10,000	—	—
(net income from unrelated business, after taxes)	5,000	—	5,000
Gross Investment Income	100,000	—	100,000
Contributions in excess of 2% limit	100,000	—	100,000
Totals	$331,000	$110,000	$315,000

Since $110,000 is more than one-third of $315,000, the organization would qualify as "publicly supported" under this test.

The Facts and Circumstances Test under Sections 509(a)(1) and 170(b)(1)(A)(vi).   If your organization cannot qualify automatically because its "public support" is less than $33^1/3\%$ of its "total support," but its "public support" is at least 10% of its "total support," and the group is set up and operated in such a way as to attract new public or governmental support on an ongoing basis, then the IRS will look at the way the group is set up and operated to determine whether the group meets the IRS's "facts and circumstances" test.

Under the "facts and circumstances" test, the IRS looks at such "public support factors" as the sources of the group's funding (the more public and governmental the identity of its funders the better), the extent to which it is open to public participation in its programs or policy formation, the extent to which the membership of its governing body (its Board of Directors or Trustees) represents the interests of the public through inclusion of public officials (or their appointees), or of experts in the organization's subject area, or of community leaders, and not merely the interests of a limited number of donors.

In the case of membership organizations, the inclusion, on the Board of Directors, of Directors elected by the membership helps, and membership solicitations and dues should be designed to encourage membership by a broad cross section of people interested in the group's activities.

The closer to 10% your group's support fraction, the more closely these factors will be scrutinized. The closer to $33^1/_3\%$ you are, the less they'll matter. No one factor is determinative—it's a subjective test.

The Section 509(a)(2) Test.   If your group cannot qualify under the tests just described, there is still hope. The tests we've been looking at exclude support from "related gross revenues," and focus on gifts. If your group operates a business that furthers your exempt purposes, those revenues would be excluded from the tests we've just described, but they can be taken into account under the section 509(a)(2) test, and would count toward both "public support" and "total support." Once again the goal is to show at least $33^1/_3\%$ of your "total support" as being "public support." However, under this test, you must *also* show that no more than $33^1/_3\%$ of your "total support" comes from the combination of gross investment income and unrelated business income (less any tax on the unrelated business income). Thus, if you count related revenues towards public support, you have to meet a *double* "thirds" test: no less than one-third public, no more than one-third unrelated business or investment.

Another difference from the first set of tests is that contributions from "disqualified persons" are excluded *entirely* from "public support"—not just to the extent they exceed 2%. But they do count in full towards "total support." In fact, there is no 2% limit on contributions under this test, only a limitation on whom contributions may come from to qualify as "public support." "Public support," under this test, can come *only* from the general public, from governments, or from groups excluded from private foundation status either automatically (described earlier) or under the first set of "public support" tests—but not from those excluded under *this* test.

Another detail is that "related business income" from any one individual or from any government agency will count toward "public support" under this test only to the extent that it does not exceed the greater of $5,000 or 1% of the group's "total support," although it will count in full towards "total support."

Finally, while the IRS will allow the exclusion of unusual grants on the same basis as described above, there is no 10% "facts and circumstances" fallback test under section 509(a)(2). The $33^1/_3\%$ automatic and 10% "facts and circumstances" tests under 509(a)(1) stem from the IRS's having to flesh out the meaning of section 170(b)(1)(a)(vi)'s vague phrase "a substantial part of its support." Under section 509(a)(2), a one-third level is specifically mandated; thus the IRS cannot interpolate a 10% fallback rule here.

Table 1–2 is another example to help you work through the above rules.

TABLE 1-2.

	Amount Received	Public Support	Total Support	Investment Income
Govt. Bureau A (grant for public's benefit)	$ 10,000	$ 10,000	$ 10,000	—
Govt. Bureau B (grant for agency's benefit— related services)	6,000	5,000[a]	6,000	—
General Public (contributions)	100,000	100,000	100,000	—
(gross receipts for related services)	10,000	10,000	10,000	—
(net income from unrelated business)	5,000	—	5,000	5,000
Gross Investment Income	100,000	—	100,000	100,000
Contribution from disqualified persons	100,000	—	100,000	—
Totals	$331,000	$125,000	$331,000	$105,000

[a]Includable in "public support" up to the greater of $5,000 or 1% of "total support" (see text).

As $125,000 (Public Support) is more than one-third of $331,000 (Total Support), and as $105,000 (Investment Income) is less than one-third of $331,000, this organization qualifies under this test. Different organizations will find it better to come under one or the other test. The main advantage of this test is that it lets you count related income towards public support. The main advantage of the other test is that if you can't make the one-third test there is still the 10% fallback rule. (Both tests are illustrated and worked through in Chapter 6 under Schedule A, Part IV.)

If your group's funding involves any of the kinds of income that is limited by the various "thirds" tests, or that is classifiable under different categories, you should be sure to get professional advice.

The "Private Operating Foundation" Option

Some groups get their funding from just a few grants. They may not be able to meet either of the public support tests outlined above, and will have to accept being treated as a private foundation, because each of their funding sources may become a "substantial contributor" and thus a "disqualified person" whose contributions don't count towards public support.

However, they do have the option to be treated as an "operating foundation" rather than the usual grantmaking foundation. To the naked eye, an operating foundation looks like any other 501(c)(3) group. It does not have to give away its funds to other groups but can engage in its own program activities. The difference is that it is subject to the limitations imposed on foundations, including not being allowed to make a 501(h) lobbying election, and having to file a Form 990-PF rather than an ordinary Form 990. (This form, while similar in many ways to a Form 990 plus its Schedule A, is required of all foundations, regardless of how much money they handle, with daily penalties for failure to file.)

Qualification as an operating foundation requires that you directly spent in pursuit of your exempt purposes at least 85% of the lesser of your adjusted net income (from Part I of your Form 990-PF) or your minimum investment return (from Part IX of the Form 990-PF), and also meet one of the following: an "assets test," an "endowment test," or a "support test." (Elderly care facilities covered by 4942(j)(3) have to use the endowment test.) These are computed, based on the previous four years, in one of two ways. You may choose whether to simply add up the last four years, or whether to meet the test for each of three of the four years (you'd only do this if the figure for one of the years would kill a four-year total. You have to be consistent; whichever method you use for the

85% expenditure test, you have to use the same method for the other test you select (assets, endowment, or support).

If you don't have investments, your bank account will be the basis for the minimum investment return, which is a hair under 5% of your assets. This figure will proably be smaller than your adjusted net income. Showing that you've spent 85% of the lesser of these directly on your exempt purposes will probably not be difficult.

Similarly, the assets test requires that 65% of your assets be devoted directly to your exempt activities or related businesses.

The endowment test requires that you directly spent or made grants in pursuit of your exempt purposes amounting to two-thirds of your minimum investment return. Unless you have many investments, and relied on adjusted net income for the 85% test because it was less than 5% of your investments, you'll have little problem with this test.

If, for some reason, you can't meet either of these tests, you'll meet a new version of the public support test, one very different from the public charities test. Instead of one-third, you're looking to show: (a) that 85% of your noninvestment support comes from the general public and at least five exempt organizations that are not private foundations controlled by the same people that control your group or are funded by the same "disqualified persons" that fund you (and who keep you from qualifying as a public charity); (b) that not more than 25% of your noninvestment support comes from any one of the exempt organizations; *and* (c) that not more than one-half of your total support comes from investment income.

If you are going to use this option, be sure to get hold of a current copy of Publication 578, *Tax Information for Private Foundations and Foundation Managers*, and Form 990-PF and its instructions.

WHY YOU MAY WANT A LAWYER'S HELP

This book can help you answer many of the questions that may come up and can provide generalized guidance in many areas. It is wise to seek a lawyer's advice. The attorney you consult should preferably be someone who is willing to work with you on an ongoing basis.

In particular, you may want to have a lawyer review your organizing documents (your Articles, Bylaws, Constitution, etc.), your application for IRS recognition of your exemption, and your annual reports. In addition, you may want to have a lawyer review the terms of any major grants or contracts and any reports to funding agencies.

How to Work with a Lawyer

Unless you have a lot of money and can afford to pay your lawyer to do all of the work for you, the best way for you to work with a lawyer is as an advisor, with the understanding that you will do much of the fact-gathering and writing of "first drafts." Obviously, you'll want to seek the lawyer's advice before you get into any of the "iffy" areas.

Sometimes you can find a lawyer (perhaps one of your members) who is concerned enough about your goals to make a substantial commitment of time on a voluntary or reduced-fee basis. It is particularly useful if the lawyer is willing to attend board meetings regularly and help guide the group in tracking required filings. If this happens to you, congratulations. However, if you are paying for legal services, don't jump too fast to put your lawyer on your board as a voting member. While such arrangements were once common, they are now seen as ethically questionable, as the lawyer could end up voting to give himself or herself work.

What to Look for in a Lawyer

Nonprofit organizations have areas of legal concern ranging from tax exemption to compliance with state corporation laws, employment laws, and other laws ranging from sales taxes to the licensing of some kinds of activity. Many of these areas overlap with the concerns of small businesses, but some do not, particularly those relating to tax exemption.

While this book can help you get a feel for the issues involved with federal tax exemption, it does not really try to cover all of the legal concerns listed above, other than flagging some of them as issues for you to look into, as the law on many of them varies from state to state.

Some attorneys have practices that span the whole range of what you need, and if you can find one who is sympathetic to your group's goals and whose assistance you can afford, you are all set. More likely, however, you'll be able to find lawyers who service small businesses but don't know much about tax exemption, or who are familiar with business, individual, and estate and gift taxes but who have little contact with nonprofit groups other than the well-established charities to which their clients make contributions.

There's not a lot of money to be made in representing small (or even medium-sized) nonprofit groups, although the larger charities can often get assistance from lawyers who represent a board member or major contributor in other matters. Because tax exemption is not a lucrative specialty, it is not easy to find someone who has a feel for the issues involved. It is a cliche that some lawyers will tell you what you can't do while others will tell you how you can. Clearly, a lawyer who knows the ins and outs of tax exemption can help you accomplish more than one who is intimidated by the subject and interprets prohibitions on your activities more broadly than necessary "just to be safe."

If you can't find a specialist in tax exemption, you're probably better off with a small-business lawyer who is willing to learn about tax exemption than with a pure tax lawyer. Small-business lawyers will be able to help you in other areas, as well as with tax exemptions. In addition to this book, other sources of initial orientation for a lawyer who wants to learn about tax exemption include Bruce R. Hopkins' *The Law of Tax-Exempt Organizations* (Ronald Press, John Wiley & Sons, NY), which can provide leads for further research; and Howard L. Oleck *Nonprofit Corporations, Organizations, and Associations* (Prentice-Hall, Englewood Cliffs, NJ), which is a good introduction to nonprofit corporation law in general, and particularly with regard to bylaws and matters of internal procedure. It includes samples of bylaws and other documents for various kinds of groups. An excellent three-volume service keyed to the Code and Regulations is Marilyn E. Phelan's *Nonprofit Enterprises: Law and Taxation* (1985, with annual updates in May. Callaghan & Co., Wilmette, IL).

How to Get Names of Lawyers

- Ask your members. One of them may know someone who can help. (One of them may *be* someone who can help!)
- Ask your accountant. Your accountant's familiarity with your particular situation may lead to an appropriate referral.

- Ask people in other groups similar to yours.
- Ask a local foundation for names of lawyers who represent groups they've funded.
- Call a local bar association's referral service. (They usually advertise in the consumer *Yellow Pages* under "Lawyer Referral Services.") These services usually ask participating lawyers to list areas in which they would like to receive referrals. Look for someone who lists one or more of the following: "Charitable Organizations," "Nonprofit Organizations," "Exempt Organizations," "Tax Exemption" (obviously, the above are all roughly equivalent, but the person at the referral service may not be familiar with all of those terms). If these fail, ask for "Small Businesses," "Corporation Law," or "Tax Law." Bar association referral services will often only give out one name at a time, but in large cities there are frequently competing referral services run by city, county, and state bar associations..
- Look in the consumer edition of the *Yellow Pages* under "Lawyers Grouped by Types of Practice." ("Business to Business" editions of the *Yellow Pages* may contain only the straight alphabetical listing of "Lawyers.") Amazing as it may seem, as incomplete as this listing is (it costs money to be listed in each category), it is the only generally available listing of lawyers grouped by specialty.

Chapter 2

Creating the Right Legal Structure

PROPER ORGANIZATION: THE ROAD TO SUCCESS

If your group wants to be able to handle significant amounts of money, the single most important factor is how it is organized. While this book is about coping with the accountability expected of nonprofits, this chapter focuses on your group's organizing documents, which are the sources of some of the most basic promises to be accountable.

Your group's articles of incorporation, charter, or constitution, together with its bylaws (rules of internal operation) are as important as its activities in defining it to the outside world. Not all groups need to assume the same degree of accountability: each one is assumed in return for some form of special treatment that you may or may not need (or want). Thus, these documents must be designed (and, when necessary, revised) with care.

It should also be pointed out that in addition to defining what *kinds* of accountablility can be expected of your group, its organizing documents can help you control *who* is to be accountable— and for what. (See "Why Incorporate?" later in this chapter.)

Organizational Design

The process of organizational design is neither easy nor immediately productive of obvious direct progress toward a group's programmatic goals. As a result, it can get ignored or postponed while more exciting activities are pursued. Ultimately, however, many groups find it necessary to rent an office, or hire staff, or buy or rent equipment, or even award scholarships or other direct financial assistance in order to reach their goals. At that point, it does become necessary to set up a structure that can get and handle funds.

Note: This chapter is premised on the assumption that your group needs to be a separate organization. Some activities do not need a whole organization to support them, and do not justify the time, money, and effort needed to create and sustain tax-exempt status on their own. If this is the case with your activity, it may be wisest to approach an existing group to become one of its projects. The basic compromise is in the loss of independence that this may mean, but it also means your activities can begin sooner.

Getting Started

The best way to begin the design process is to back up and define your group's goals. What are you trying to accomplish? This should be followed by a sketch of what you might want to do in order to reach your goals. These goals should not be carved in stone at this point by formal adoption by the group, as it will most likely be necessary to fine-tune them to fit the requirements of the Internal Revenue Code and your state's nonprofit incorporation law. But without an initial idea to work from, it is very difficult to know what kinds of organizational structure will best serve your needs. (Chapter 3 discusses formulating your goals.)

Choosing an Organizational Structure

Once the "what" and the "why" are sketched out and in front of you, it then becomes possible to start thinking about the "how" in terms of available resources. Can free office space, labor, or supplies be relied on? If not, what sources of funding are available? Will it be necessary to rely on large foundation or government grants, or is it reasonable to expect that the group could be supported by large numbers of small individual contributions? How much of the group's support might come from fees charged by the group for goods or services related to the group's ultimate purposes? How much of its funding could it raise from some "unrelated" business? (See chapters 1 and 16 about the tax on unrelated business income.)

None of these questions can be answered with certainty unless the group is already operating, but all of them affect and are affected by the choice of its organizational structure. Some activities your group might want to engage in may be forbidden to groups eligible for the funding you see as easiest to obtain. It may be necessary to divide the activities between two or more separate groups and fund them separately. With all this in mind, let's look at the various kinds of accountability. This includes the promises that must be made and kept, the benefits obtained based on them, and the price in increased paperwork or reduced freedom of action.

THE NONPROFIT ORGANIZATION

There are two ways to get money, short of coercion or theft: you can simply ask for it, or you can give something in exchange for it. In turn, there are two kinds of things an organization can give in exchange for money: (1) goods and services (including, in the case of a business, a cash return in the form of dividends), or (2) tax benefits. If your group's goals can be reached through activities that bring in revenues that are more than sufficient to cover expenses, it could raise its initial bankroll by promising to share the surplus revenues among those who provided the funds. This is, of course, how ordinary commercial organizations work. There are good reasons not to use this approach, however, reasons that involve credibility, economic efficiency, and control over the future direction of the organization. These can be best understood by looking at what it means to be a nonprofit organization.

Focus on Programs Not Revenues

The essence of nonprofit operation is to carry on an activity because it is important, not as a way to generate profits for investors. No one gets a cut of a profit, if there is one, and the focus is not on making sure there is a surplus, but on making sure that the group's goals are met. This does not mean that a nonprofit organization must operate at a loss (a popular misconception), nor that it cannot hire people and pay them for their work (another, less common error). However, it should not be generating profits at the expense of its goals by charging too high a fee for benefits it provides and, as a result, excluding people who should be helped. If it is simply doing and spending less than it ought, it has broken faith with its supporters, even if it is not acting illegally. On the other hand, if a nonprofit is paying its officers or directors too much for their work, it may justly be accused of secretly paying them profits, and not really being a nonprofit organization at all.

Nonprofit operation is important in establishing in everyone's minds, both in the group and in the community, that the group's focus is on its program, not on its revenues. Beyond any question of image, this focus will also be a "litmus test" of the motivation of those who provide the organization's funding. Even if they retain a say in how the group operates, and in what it does, they can be expected to try to further the group's shared goals. They will not try to hijack it into some other direction in order to earn a higher rate of return, which is always a risk in any organization that tries to achieve noneconomic goals in a profitable way.

Benefits of Tax-Exempt Status.   These are benefits that are inherent in nonprofit operation. They may or may not be enough to balance the greater difficulty of raising funds than through standard investment, but many groups cannot generate a profit in any event. Aside from its own inherent benefits, nonprofit status is a prerequisite to tax-exemption and tax-deductible status. If the group's purpose is sufficiently in the public interest, it makes no sense to tax it. Since its activities lessen the load on the government, it should be allowed to apply any surplus it generates to more good works, not taxes. Thus, if your group can fit its purposes into one of the categories recognized in the Internal Revenue Code, it may be able to accomplish more with *tax-exempt* status, as income taxes would not take revenues away from activity in pursuit of exempt purposes. (A list of these purposes is included later in this chapter.)

Why You May Wish To Obtain Tax-Deductible Status

Some nonprofits also qualify for tax-deductible status, as "charitable organizations," which encourages contributions by allowing their supporters to reduce their own taxable incomes by their contributions (to the extent the contributions exceed the value of any goods or service obtained), and thus reduce their taxes.

Here, of course, is where the action is. If you want to be able to attract large grants and contributions from foundations and individuals, you will probably feel that it is worth the trouble to obtain tax-exempt status under Section 501(c)(3) and tax-deductible status under Section 170(c) of the Code.

It is not legally necessary to get such status yourself to get foundation money. A foundation (they are, themselves, 501(c)(3) organizations) does have the option to pursue its charitable purpose by means of grants to individuals or other nonprofit organizations that are not themselves 501(c)(3) organizations, but only if the foundation maintains "expenditure responsibility." However, since expenditure responsibility means justifying the activities of the groups that get the money in terms of 501(c)(3)-type purposes, and requires a high degree of oversight and reporting, it is understandable that foundations would rather deal with organizations that have already proved all that to the IRS's satisfaction. They might make an exception occasionally, but only if they are really committed to a project that can't be done any other way. Generally, however, the lack of previously established deductibility will greatly diminish your chances.

Individuals don't even have the option to maintain expenditure responsiblity. They *have* to make their contributions to tax-deductible organizations—although some of them could be foundations.

Disadvantages of Tax-Deductible Status

However, tax deductibility carries with it significant limitations on political activity, and the need to show that you're not a foundation. Depending on the nature of your organization and its supporters, tax deductibility may be an unnecessary hindrance, if most of its contributions are small amounts given by people who do not itemize their deductions on their tax returns, and thus can't claim the deduction for charitable contributions.

The reason for the prohibition on electoral activity, and the limitation on lobbying to influence legislation, is that, unlike tax exemption, which is simply the public agreeing not to tax an activity's revenues, tax deductibility means that the public chips in (through the tax system) and gives a discount. In effect, the contributor is deciding how the public should spend part of its money. To make it worse, since the value of the deduction is tied to the contributor's tax bracket, richer contributors get a larger discount on their contributions, or can (for the same after-tax cost) leverage more public money. A fairer alternative would be the use of a tax credit, but as the laws presently stand it makes perfect sense to limit the use of the tax-deductible form in conducting publicly subsidized political campaigns. (The why's and wherefore's of tax exemption and tax-deductible status are discussed in greater detail later in this chapter and also in Chapter 1.)

WHY INCORPORATE?

The Internal Revenue Code allows unincorporated groups as well as corporations to become tax-exempt and tax-deductible. So why bother incorporating?

Limited Liability of Individuals

Corporations are an odd mix of both heightened accountability and lessened personal risk. They were invented as a way for investors to put money into a venture but limit their potential personal liability to the venture's creditors solely to the money invested. Their own personal assets are not, in general, put at risk. How is this done? Why should not all of a person's funds be available to that person's creditors? The trick is the creation of an "artificial person" to carry on the business. The individual investors never have to enter into the corporations's contracts, so they don't have the creditors in the first place: the corporation has the creditors. Similarly, officers of the corporation who make it clear that they are acting on behalf of the corporation don't put their own credit on the line.

It should be pointed out that incorporation is a privilege extended by the state because the legal fiction of a separate artificial person is helpful to others, not just to the members of the corporation. It makes clear to all just who has control of any assets. Because it is so helpful, the courts will very seldom allow creditors to go after individual members' personal assets. However, if a corporation is treated by an individual as his or her own personal property, with no regard for the need to keep adequate records and to keep its funds separate, a court may decide that its separate identity is really a sham. In such a case, the court might be willing to allow a creditor to collect from the individual.

Some tax and criminal laws, and some consumer protection laws, do, in fact, make individuals personally liable for corporate acts for which they are responsible. Since fines against corporations do not hurt any "natural" person (human being!) directly, and are simply passed along to consumers as part of the cost of doing business, these laws, which are designed as much to deter bad acts as to compensate the victims, try to make human beings accountable for the corporate activities they control.

Limited Immunity of Responsible Individuals

While the reason corporations were invented is to allow the normal debts of an enterprise to be confined to that enterprise, this does not mean that you can be careless just because the corporate form is being used.

In fact, the area of liability on the part of board members and officers for negligence on their part in supervising their organizations' activities—as separate from simple liability for debts—is one where caution must be exercised. If someone is seriously harmed, and the members of the board or officers had reason to know that such sort of danger existed but did not investigate and prevent it, they could be sued personally. This can even go so far as to result in liability to an individual patient because of insufficient care in hiring the head of a medical service. Similarly, if the board has, through inattention or otherwise, allowed business practice that results in the organization being short-changed, they may find themselves being asked to make the organization, or its creditors, whole.

While the most catastrophic lawsuits generally arise out of personal injuries, with personal liability focused on negligence in supervision or hiring of staff, there are exceptions. If the board does not maintain adequate budgetary control (which is far easier than evaluating the competence of professional staff, and thus less easily excused), they could be held liable for a trusted staffer's having robbed the organization blind.

Chapters 5 and 6 deal with the budgetary process, but it should be noted here that it is a simple precaution to adopt a resolution or bylaw that to make any expenditure over a specified amount requires authority from either a line item in a budget adopted by the board, or, in the absence of such a line item, directly from the board itself. While such a provision may seem clumsy, inflexible, and bureaucratic, it is the only reliable way for a board to maintain control over the organization's expenses that its fiduciary responsibility requires.

The moral, for the officer and directors, is to pay attention. Don't take a title for the prestige it conveys if you are not able to actually keep track of what is going on. In fact, while the "reasonable business judgement" rule used to insulate directors and officers of commercial corporations from liability for simple errors of judgment is applicable to nonprofits as well, the fact is that the level of supervision required of directors of nonprofit organizations may well be higher under your state's law than that required of directors of commercial corporations. Given the activity's tax-exempt status, this is a public trust, not just a business. Investors in a business can be expected to protect their interests by riding herd on the directors—they get to elect them, and large investors will often sit on the board themselves. The public's ability to watch out for its interests in a nonprofit organization is much less, justifying a greater duty of care by the directors of a nonprofit group.

A more subtle moral, for the nonprofit group itself, is to consider carefully the issue of indemnification of board members and officers. Many corporate bylaws provide that if the board members or officers are sued, the corporation will reimburse them for legal fees and damages. Such provisions are often necessary to get anyone to take on the legal risks of becoming a director or officer. It is worth paying careful consideration to limiting the corporation's liability in such situations by either limiting the reimbursement in amount, or totally excluding it for wrongful acts. Otherwise the organization may be put out of business by its promise to reimburse. (This can be a ticklish clause to word. If the level of wrongfulness or negligence that serves as the threshold for exclusion of reimbursement is set so low that it matches the threshold for personal liability, the promise to reimburse becomes a mirage—if it's needed, it's not available.)

Insurance is, of course, the most attractive way to deal with this, but may be very difficult and expensive to obtain. Less obvious, but equally important, is choosing people who will pay attention is the best way to limit this risk—and it may be healthy that there may be some situations where reimbursement is not available. It will help keep board members attentive.

Continuity of Relationships

Beyond offering personal protection to members of the board and officers, the corporate form is something familiar to foundations and the IRS even if they don't quite understand what it is that your group does. The corporate form provides for continuity in terms of who it is they are dealing with: an independent legal entity with its own assets and liabilities and a public list of people who control its actions, so they know who has the right to make promises, and who doesn't.

Control of Assets

An unincorporated association is, by contrast, a very clumsy form in which to own property, particularly if it must be sold. It may require a vote of the whole group to do anything. Or it may not—and the outsider may have a hard time figuring out who has the right to act for the group, or to whom to look for payment of a debt. For directors, officers, or members, the other side of this coin is heightened potential risk of personal liability for the group's debts or for each other's acts. In addition, while the IRS requires written organizing documents before they will grant special tax treatment, you give up the benefits of incorporation just described by not calling those documents Articles of Incorporation and filing them with the state.

Incorporation Is Worth the Effort

Incorporation involves filing a certain amount of paperwork with the state on a regular basis, and it requires you to go through state-specified minimum internal procedures to make changes in your organizing documents. These must be written with both the IRS and the state requirements in mind, particularly the "purposes" and "powers" clauses, which must satisfy both. This may take some thought, not because the requirements are inconsistent, but because they may use slightly different words to say the same thing. It is therefore a very important step, and one that should be taken carefully; but if your group needs to handle significant amounts of other people's money, the benefits of incorporation far outweigh its burdens.

COMPANION ORGANIZATIONS

Because of the limitations the Code places on how much legislative activity "charitable" 501(c)(3) organizations may carry on, and because it precludes totally all but the most nonpartisan electoral involvement by charitable organizations, it is common to see clusters of companion "charitable," "civic," and "political" organizations. Civic 501(c)(4) organizations *may* have legislative lobbying as a primary purpose, and may engage in a limited amount of electoral intervention on behalf of, or against, candidates, as long as it is not a primary purpose of the organization. (For a definition of what activities are included, see "Political Activity" in Chapter 1.)

Note: "Political organizations" are a new category of exempt organizations that don't come under Section 501 but under Section 527. A political organization's exempt function is precisely what is forbidden to 501(c)(3) organizations and is taxable (and limited) in other "501(c)'s," namely influencing federal, state, or local elections.

Three Ways the IRS Allows You to Set Up Companion Organizations

1. Any 501(c) organization can establish a separate fund to finance political activities that can be treated as a separate section 527 political organization.

2. A 501(c) organization can establish a separate 501(c)(3) organization to carry out those parts of its activities that qualify under 501(c)(3).

3. A "501(c)(3)" (other than the kind just described, churches, or governments) can elect to be allowed to engage in a limited amount of lobbying activity as is described more fully in Chapter 1.

One way it can simplify the procedure is to contribute its allowable quota to a companion lobbying group, such as a 501(c)(4).

Warning: If two or more 501(c)(3) organizations have a close enough relationship to allow one to control another, they are considered "affiliated" and if any of them elects to be allowed to lobby, they are all treated as one organization for the purposes of the lobbying calculation. They could conceivably all lose their exemptions together if the limits are exceeded. Two groups are affiliated (a) if the documents of one group require it to obey decisions of the other with regard to legislative issues, or (b) if the board of directors of one group has members who are representatives, directors, officers, or paid executive staff members of the other, and who together have enough voting power to cause or prevent action on legislative issues. (See "Affiliated Groups," in Chapter 1.)

DRAWING UP THE ARTICLES AND BYLAWS

The Articles—Windows to the World

To qualify as an organization eligible for tax exemption, a group has to make some promises. The IRS requires that these promises be made not just anywhere, but in the document that governs the group. Most groups are *not* governed by a document. But to get tax-exempt status from the IRS, yours must be. A governing (or organizing) document is a signed statement that sets out the group's name, purposes, powers, classes of membership, initial officers and directors, and its principal office. This document could be called a Constitution, Charter, or Articles of Association; if the group is a corporation, it may be called Articles of Incorporation or Articles of Organization.

Since the term "Articles" bridges both corporations and unincorporated associations, and since the IRS expects the same promises from both, we'll use the shorthand term "Articles" throughout and we'll note where the requirements for corporations and associations differ.

All states require that corporations file articles (usually with the Secretary of State) in order to become incorporated.

Information contained in the Articles.   Articles filed with the state are public records, available to anyone. They make possible the most basic forms of accountability. Think about how you, as a member of the general public, would deal with a corporation about which you knew nothing but its name and address. Part of the basic accountability required to create an independent legal "person" is that, as a member of the public:

a. If you are harmed by someone using only a corporate name, you can find out the names of the people who control the corporation and how to find them. This information must be reported periodically (at least annually) even if it does not change, so the state knows the corporation still exists.

b. If you are approached to contribute money, you can find out what the corporation's purposes are.

c. If you are approached to join, you can find out if there are different classes of membership, and if so, what voting power each has.

The "purposes" and "powers" clauses.   From the point of view of the IRS, the most important parts of the articles are the "purposes" and "powers" clauses. The "purposes" clause must limit your group's activities to those in pursuit of the purposes you specify—which must be strictly limited to the exempt purposes listed under the Internal Revenue Code provision you choose to come under. The "powers" clause is where the IRS expects you to promise not to pay a profit to the members, directors, officers, or other individuals, and that if the group is dissolved its assets will be disposed of only for exempt purposes or to another tax-exempt organization. If you seek tax-deductible status, the IRS will also expect the group to promise not to devote any substantial part of its activities to attempts to affect legislation, and not to take part in campaigns on behalf of any candidate for public office.

The Bylaws—Protecting Yourself

While the articles represent promises to the outside world, a group's bylaws are tools of *internal* accountability. By specifying how the directors and officers are to be selected and removed, what sorts of decisions must be referred to the membership, and other procedural rules, the bylaws represent the contract among the members of the group about how the group will be run. The state doesn't care whether your bylaws provide for a self-regulating board, representative democracy, or direct democracy, but it may well require that there be a written set of rules. It is a good idea to have bylaws to minimize internal disputes about who has the power to make particular decisions or take particular actions.

As the basic gound rules for internal operations, the bylaws should be made available to all members, at least upon request. If your group applies for tax exemption, the IRS *will* want to see its bylaws as well as its articles. The main interest of the IRS in the bylaws is to see that they don't contradict the articles and that they provide sufficient internal controls, in the form of pinpointing responsibility, to enable the group to keep the promises in its articles.

If your group is applying for tax-deductible status and is not a private foundation, the IRS may have to look at the bylaws in deciding whether your group qualifies as a "publicly supported" organization. If your group is a membership organization, the IRS may prefer that it have some members of its board of directors (or other governing body), who are elected by the membership. (See "Avoiding Private Foundation Status," in Chapter 1.)

In general, the IRS will look at bylaws to determine whether a group is what it claims to be.

Adoption and Modification of Articles and Bylaws

Articles can be adopted by being signed by a group of incorporators or associators, although some states now provide for single-incorporator nonprofit organizations. All corporations must file their articles with the state. The articles become effective upon the state's "acceptance for filing" of the articles after an examination to make sure that the state's rules for forming corporations have been followed, and (in some states) a character check on the incorporators to see if they have criminal records that might disqualify them as public trustees.

Articles can be amended by a vote of the members. State law will usually specify a minimum percentage vote needed to amend corporate articles—often set at two-thirds. A corporation (and, in some states, an association) would then file "Amended or Restated Articles" with the state.

Bylaws are adopted either by the incorporators or associators (prior to the filing of articles with the state) or by the members (afterwards), depending on state laws. Bylaws usually specify how they may be amended, but state corporation law may set outside limits on these rules, and often specifies what the bylaws may or must cover, such as the selection of directors and officers, how meetings are called, and how voting is conducted.

It is usual to hold a meeting to adopt or amend articles or bylaws. Minutes should be taken at such meetings, and someone (usually the clerk) should make sure not only that the requirements of state law, the articles, and the bylaws are complied with, but also that an adequate record is made to show that all the rules were followed, noting such facts as the names of people present, the number needed for a quorum, the number voting for or against, and anything else that shows that the requirements were met. There is nothing unusual about adopting or amending articles or bylaws. The only way it differs is that state law or the bylaws may require a higher quorum and/or a higher percentage of the vote than usual.

Resolutions

Just as the corporation may adopt Bylaws, it may also adopt Resolutions. The basic difference is that a resolution is a single act, rather than an ongoing rule. Resolutions can be used to approve a contract, adopt a program, set dues, or even to adopt or amend a set of bylaws. Many things, like dues levels, could either be written into the bylaws, where they may be difficult to change, or they could be established by resolution, which can usually be approved or repealed by a simple majority. It thus makes sense to pay attention to individual rules, to see which really need to be hard to change, and which should be flexible.

Researching Your State's Law

Before you sit down to prepare a draft of your bylaws and articles, read copies of all the forms and literature provided by the Secretary of State's "Corporations Not for Profit" law, or the

"Charitable Corporations" law. If you can't find any of these try looking under "Eleemosynary Corporations." (Yes, it's really a word, and an awful one, but they use it.) Other possiblities include "Philanthropic" and "Corporations for Other Purposes" (other than making money, that is). A good librarian can help out.[1]

Find the section that lists the purposes for which a nonprofit (or whatever they call it) corporation can be formed. Most likely it will have a list of many specific kinds of purposes and a few general ones, like "civic," "educational," "benevolent," "religious," and "charitable." The Internal Revenue Code has lots of specific and general kinds of purposes too. Here's an abbreviated list (Fig. 2-1) in chart form, from IRS Publication 557, *Tax-Exempt Status for Your Organization* (available free from the IRS). Once you've found the section or sections that you're interested in, you can look up the exact wording of the purposes in the Internal Revenue Code. Before you make your final decision, you should read Chapter 1 to make sure you know what you're letting yourself in for.

WRITING THE FIRST DRAFT OF YOUR CORPORATE PAPERS

While you should not expect to write the final version of your corporate papers, it is useful to have at least an outline of a few points sketched out before you sit down with your attorney. Advance planning will help to focus the discussion, and your research will enable you to understand the alternatives laid out by the attorney. Points you should be ready to deal with include the following:

1. For what you want your group to do, is tax-exemption enough, or is deductible status necessary? You can approach this in two different ways. First, lay out what sort of activities you want the group to engage in, both immediate and long-range. This will help identify nonstandard "powers" that need to be specified in your articles if they are not granted as a matter of course.

Next, come up with a broad formulation of what sort of benefits you want your group to confer on the public, to help fit it under one or more of the categories that justify according a group tax-exempt status. (See Fig. 2-1.)

This will help specify the group's "purposes" in its articles. (You may also include some of the most important types of activities, with language indicating that your purposes will include them but are not limited to them.)

If you expect to be getting your money mainly through small contributions, or through fees that are clearly for activities in pursuit of your "exempt purpose," you may not need to leap the high hurdles the tax code places around tax-deductible status. (If you expect to be supported entirely by fees, you may consider simply incorporating as a business.) If you are looking for foundation grants or large contributions from individuals, you may have no choice other than tax-deductible status. You should review Chapter 1 to help decide this basic issue, and discuss the options with your attorney. The law is not stable, and changes may influence your decision.

The IRS has standard language that you should use in your purpose and powers clauses, which promises that the group will not break the rules. IRS Publication 557 and the instructions accompanying forms 1023 (tax-deductible tax-exempt organizations) and 1024 (nondeductible

---

[1] Get to know a local law school or courthouse law library. They usually contain not only statutes and cases but also encyclopedias and handbooks with sample forms, often keyed to your state's requirements. Many are open to the public.

Organization Reference Chart

Section of 1954 Code	Description of organization	General nature of activities	Form No.	Annual return required to be filed	Deductibility of* Charitable Contributions Allowed
501(c)(1)	Corporations Organized Under Act of Congress (Including Federal Credit Unions)	Instrumentalities of the United States	No Form	None	Yes, if made for exclusively public purposes
501(c)(2)	Title Holding Corporation For Exempt Organization	Holding title to property of an exempt organization	1024	990[1]	No[2]
501(c)(3)	Religious, Educational, Charitable, Scientific, Literary, Testing for Public Safety, to Foster Certain National or International Amateur Sports Competition, or Prevention of Cruelty to Children or Animals Organizations	Activities of nature implied by description of class of organization	1023	990 or 990-PF[1]	Generally, Yes
501(c)(4)	Civic Leagues, Social Welfare Organizations, and Local Associations of Employees	Promotion of community welfare; Charitable, educational or recreational	1024	990[1]	Generally, No[2,3]
501(c)(5)	Labor, Agricultural, and Horticultural Organizations	Educational or instructive, the purpose being to improve conditions of work, and to improve products and efficiency	1024	990[1]	No[2]
501(c)(6)	Business Leagues, Chambers of Commerce, Real Estate Boards, Etc.	Improvement of business conditions of one or more lines of business	1024	990[1]	No[2]
501(c)(7)	Social and Recreation Clubs	Pleasure, recreation, social activities	1024	990[1]	No[2]
501(c)(8)	Fraternal Beneficiary Societies and Associations	Lodge providing for payment of life, sickness, accident, or other benefits to members	1024	990[1]	Yes, if used for Sec. 501(c)(3) purposes
501(c)(9)	Voluntary Employees' Beneficiary Associations (Including Federal Employees' Voluntary Beneficiary Associations formerly covered by section 501(c)(10))	Providing for payment of life, sickness, accident or other benefits to members	1024	990[1]	No[2]
501(c)(10)	Domestic Fraternal Societies and Associations	Lodge devoting its net earnings to charitable, fraternal, and other specified purposes. No life, sickness, or accident benefits to members	1024	990[1]	Yes, if used for Sec. 501(c)(3) purposes
501(c)(11)	Teachers' Retirement Fund Associations	Teachers' association for payment of retirement benefits	No Form	990[1]	No[2]
501(c)(12)	Benevolent Life Insurance Associations, Mutual Ditch or Irrigation Companies, Mutual or Cooperative Telephone Companies, Etc.	Activities of a mutually beneficial nature similar to those implied by the description of class of organization	1024	990[1]	No[2]
501(c)(13)	Cemetery Companies	Burials and incidental activities	1024	990[1]	Generally, Yes
501(c)(14)	State Chartered Credit Unions, Mutual Reserve Funds	Loans to members. Exemption as to building and loan associations and cooperative banks repealed by Revenue Act of 1951, affecting all years after 1951	No Form	990[1]	No[2]
501(c)(15)	Mutual Insurance Companies or Associations	Providing insurance to members substantially at cost	1024	990[1]	No[2]
501(c)(16)	Cooperative Organizations to Finance Crop Operations	Financing crop operations in conjunction with activities of a marketing or purchasing association	No Form	990[1]	No[2]
501(c)(17)	Supplemental Unemployment Benefit Trusts	Provides for payment of supplemental unemployment compensation benefits	1024	990[1]	No[2]
501(c)(18)	Employee Funded Pension Trust (created before June 25, 1959)	Payment of benefits under a pension plan funded by employees	No Form	990[1]	No[2]
501(c)(19)	Post or Organization of War Veterans	Activities implied by nature of organization	1024	990[1]	Yes
501(c)(20)	Group Legal Services Plan Organizations	Legal services provided exclusively to employees	1024	990[1]	No[4]
501(c)(21)	Black Lung Benefit Trusts	Funded by coal mine operators to satisfy their liability for disability or death due to black lung diseases	No Form	990-BL	No[5]
501(d)	Religious and Apostolic Associations	Regular business activities. Communal religious community	No Form	1065	No[2]
501(e)	Cooperative Hospital Service Organizations	Performs cooperative services for hospitals	1023	990[1]	Yes
501(f)	Cooperative Service Organizations of Operating Educational Organizations	Performs collective investment services for educational organizations	1023	990[1]	Yes
521(a)	Farmers' Cooperative Associations	Cooperative marketing and purchasing for agricultural producers	1028	990-C	No
527	Political Action Committees	Influencing elections			No
528	Certain Home-Owners Associations				No

*Author's clarification.
[1]For exceptions to the filing requirement, see Part I, Chapter 2 and the instructions for Forms 990 and 990-AR.
[2]An organization exempt under a Subsection of Code Sec. 501 other than (c)(3), may establish a charitable fund, contributions to which are deductible. Such a fund must itself meet the requirements of section 501(c)(3) and the related notice requirements of section 508(a).
[3]Contributions to volunteer fire companies and similar organizations are deductible, but only if made for exclusively public purposes.
[4]See Part III, Chapter 8.
[5]Deductible as a business expense to the extent allowed by section 192 of the Code.

FIGURE 2–1. ORGANIZATION REFERENCE CHART

tax-exempt organizations) reflect the language the IRS expects to see. Your attorney can customize them for your state. For example, references to which court will decide who gets your assets, if the organization dissolves without taking care of it, may need to be written in conformity with your state's nonprofit corporation law. In addition, your purposes and powers clauses should pledge fealty to your state's statutes as well.

2. What sort of internal organization do you want? The state and the IRS do not say that you must be a membership-run group or must be a group whose board chooses its own successors. You must, however, select one form or another (or a hybrid). There have to be written bylaws, so a decision must be made about what they will say. Bylaws make it clear what the chain of command is and can help eliminate acrimony over who is to make a particular decision.

Do not expect your attorney to make this decision for you, but once you make the basic choice, the attorney can prepare, for your comments and revision, a draft of bylaws that reflect the chosen approach.

3. What will the name of the organization be? Secretary of State incorporation offices can look up whether the name you want to use is available, and yours will probably be able to let you reserve it for a short period of time for a nominal fee, while you prepare the articles and bylaws. Your attorney can do this for you, but you could also do it yourself, and save your attorney time.

You should be aware, however, that their check is limited to their own files, to see whether they have another corporation with the same name. However, an unincorporated group, or a corporation in another state, might be using a confusingly similar name, or someone may have a trademark on a name like the one you've chosen. In either case, they might try to make your change your name. If this is a real worry, you might consider having your attorney use a search firm that specializes in searching trademark registrations in Washington and all the states, and even phone books and trade directories, so that you can have some assurance before you invest a lot of time and money in publicizing the name you've chosen.

4. Who will be the officers and directors? This question might be deferred until the papers are almost done, but you will have to face up to it eventually, and you may find that the people you choose are not happy with the way the papers read. It's thus a good idea to choose them and bring them in on the process early, at least to make suggestions before the papers are formally adopted and filed. Choose people whom you can trust to devote a lot of time to the group. People with a lot of fame but little time can serve as advisors to the group—you might even put together an advisory board or council—but don't give them more responsibility than they have time to handle. It's in neither your nor their interest to have a problem develop because they were not around enough to prevent it.

Dates and Other Details

The answers to the four questions above will form the most important parts of the articles, but be sure to fill in *all* the blanks. List incorporators, officers, and directors and their addresses, specifying differing classes of membership, specifying the date of the annual meeting of the members, and specifying the corporation's fiscal year.

Which Fiscal Year?

The choice of fiscal year should be discussed with your accountant, if your group has one, and your treasurer and clerk. The annual meeting will probably have to be within a certain time period (such as six months) after the end of the fiscal year, under state law or the rules of the state secretary.

Every organization, whether nonprofit or business, incorporated or unincorporated, is required by law as well as accounting rules to "close its books" on the same date each year; however, the date need not be December 31, but may be the end of any month of the year. The choice of fiscal year is entirely up to the organization and must be made when it begins operations, so that it knows just how many months are left until the year ends. Even if you don't incorporate, the IRS requires that this information be supplied on the form applying for exempt status.

Therefore, the decision cannot be postponed, but what month should you choose? Suit the convenience of both the organization and those responsible for its accounting and reporting to interested parties (the IRS, foundations and government funding agencies, the board and officers, and to any other outside parties who may receive annual reports).

Since there may be a lot of work involved in closing the books, preparing reports, and perhaps being audited by a public accountant, the best time to close the books is when the activity of your organization normally slows down, and when peak activity of your public accountant is past. A fiscal year ending June 30 or September 30 works well in many cases. Unless you prepare monthly reports, it is usually convenient to end on a calendar quarter (March, June, September, or December).

Drafting the Bylaws

Drafting and adopting the bylaws can be the hardest and most acrimonious part of the organizing process. It is your internal contract, the club's rules. Unlike articles, which are short and simple and general, bylaws are usually long, and complicated, and sometimes too specific. We can't give a universal set of bylaws. We can give some advice, however. Bylaws are frequently regulated by state nonprofit corporation law, which may list required or prohibited types of provisons. The basic issues include the extent to which responsibility for essential functions is clearly assigned; the extent to which the decision-making process (including elections) is clearly defined at each organizational level; and the extent to which policy and operational decisions are delegated to the board or are retained by the membership.*

An excellent place to start is to approach a successful organization that has the kinds of activities and membership you'd like to have, and ask if you may have a copy of their bylaws to use as a starting point in drafting your own. They'll either be flattered or suspicious (maybe *both*) but they'll probably give you a copy, since it's a public record at the IRS.

Don't just copy your model, wherever you get it. (Other possible sources include legal practice sets at law libraries, bar associations, and legal stationery stores.) Tailor it to fit your organization. If it places responsibility for important decisions in the wrong place, change it! If the model makes itself too easy or too hard to amend, change it.

But be realistic. Don't lock yourself into a meeting schedule you can't keep to. Set a minimum of required meetings, and *allow* others more often. And don't load too much responsibility onto too few people (difficult advice to follow, to be sure).

*See "Your Governing Board" in Chapter 4.

Remember that if you are going for recognition by the IRS as a "publicly supported" 501(c)(3) organization, and if you are setting up as a membership organization, the membership should be able to elect some members of the organization's governing body (usually its board of directors). As noted earlier in this chapter, the IRS will look at bylaws in deciding whether your group is what it claims to be.

Chapter 3

Organizational Planning

If you are a new nonprofit, or an established one considering a new program, perfecting your organizational form, or just taking stock, this chapter is one to read. Perhaps you have been considering a major change in direction, or in your organizational structure. The ideas and approaches to planning detailed here can help you make sense of what can be a vague and confusing process.

PLANNING—THE KEY TO SUCCESS

The point that needs to be made from the outset is best made by a famous quotation that has been ascribed to many different people: "How do you know when you're there, if you don't know where 'There' is?" Too many organizations (including businesses) have the notion that you can play it by ear . . . stick to "doing what comes naturally," and it will all work out somehow. Typical comments: "Planning looks like textbook stuff: a bit abstract, just too much work, and boring at that." "Who has the time, when there's so much that needs to get done *now*?" "We're liable to get locked into a plan: we need to be flexible in meeting our constituents' needs."

Those are the alibis of the losers, of organizations that flounder along, like corks on the sea, the victims of wind and waves.

Winners understand the need to take a good hard look at themselves, at where they want to go, and how they plan to get there. A good plan can accomplish a lot for your organization:

• Impress funding sources and donors. (This is first because it's an overriding concern.) Nothing makes a better impression than showing that you know where you're headed and how you propose to get there. It sets a framework of accountability and for evaluating not only how you'll use funds, but also how well. It is also a public relations tool for getting all kinds of support, for the same reason, including volunteers and in-kind services and donations.

• Create a framework for organizational management. An organizational framework becomes a guideline for action. People know and can anticipate their roles, and coordination of activities is facilitated, which is not only good for morale, but helps you reach your goals and objectives. (The best way to avoid going from crisis to crisis is to plan ahead.)

● Help achieve the most with the resources available. Setting priorities and limits, which you do in planning, helps prevent wasting money, time, and effort.

● Help greatly in measuring results by providing a yardstick to measure them against. For example, serving 10% more people than last year may look good, but not if you planned (and were funded) to serve 25% more.

Elements of Planning

The Process.   The planning process is a complex one that involves not only setting goals but also determining that the human side of the process works productively. One of the reasons it is not more often undertaken—or done successfully—is that it requires an array of uncommon skills in the one who leads and shapes the process, often the board chairperson. To avoid frustration and wasted time when the leadership lacks those skills, many organizations engage a consultant to aid in planning the process and to be available as a resource to make it work.

The End-Products. What follows is an overview of what an effective overall planning process should have as its end-products:

● **A mission statement:**   who you are and why you exist

● **A vision statement:**   what "business" you are in, and in general terms, what you plan to do, and what kind of organization you will need to do it

● **Strategic plans:**   Primarily long-range in nature, they identify organizational goals and they target a client or patient base.

● **Annual plans:**   an outline to advance your goals and set short-term objectives to be achieved during the year

● **A human resources plan:**   who you need on staff—paid and volunteers—and how they will be organized

● **The logistics needed:**   what we need, where and when, in the way of property, facilities, and supplies, to carry out plans

● **Funds and other donated resources:**   what is needed to pay for the human resources and to meet other logistical requirements

● **Sources and types of funding:**   fees, grants, donations, endowments, in-kind contributions, borrowing, etc.

● **Work plans:**   the time frame for projects and other tasks to be performed during the year.

● **Policies re:**   dealing with the target population and with market prices vs. subsidized prices, quality controls, and performance evaluation methods, as measures of both program results and individual performance

● **Organizational issues:**   board, staff, and volunteer roles and relationships, beyond the provisions of bylaws

● **Marketing and public relations:**   getting your message across to potential clients or patients, funding sources, and the community at large; grantsmanship, fundraising, marketing, and public relations.

Some of these subjects are covered in this chapter; others in later ones. All are vitally important. Plans are not made for their own sake, nor should they be seen as set in concrete. The management cycle begins and ends with planning, as shown in Fig. 3-1.

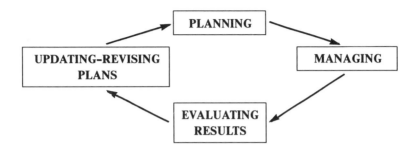

FIGURE 3-1. THE PLANNING CYCLE

Your Mission Statement

In Chapter 1, we looked at the statement of purposes required in an organizing document. A mission statement is related in content, but it serves a different purpose. It is something like a credo, in that it expresses your raison d'etre: *why you exist and what you hope to accomplish.* If it is to be of any value in keeping your organization true to its purpose, it must be brief—anything longer than one or two short sentences is bound to get either too fuzzy or too specific. It should not go into the what or the how of your plans, because the same goals can be achieved in more than one way, and methods of doing so can change with time. Nor should the where or who be stated because these too may change. However, if the clear intent is to serve only a specific locality or geographic area, that should be included.

Having eliminated how, when, and who, we are left with where, why, and what: why you exist and what you hope to accomplish *as an end result.* Example: "XYZ is organized to address the severe shortage of affordable housing for low-income families in the city of Gottbucks. Our goal is to create such housing in order to improve the well-being of disadvantaged residents, which will benefit the community as a whole." Notice the absence of how, when, and by whom. A mission statement can serve as a constant reminder and frame of reference for all organizational plans and activities. Such a guideline can help everyone involved avoid going off on tangents and losing sight of your true mission. Continuity is important to the community as a whole as well as to donors and other funding sources.

The value of the mission statement assumes that it is kept very much in evidence—not in the back of a file—and that your mission is not set in concrete. It may have to be reexamined and reevaluated if major developments should eventually make this desirable or necessary, and it should be reviewed every few years at least.

Another valuable purpose is served by the process of winnowing out your true mission. It forces you to focus on what you're all about, and in the process discover and resolve potential differences in philosophy, concept, and emphasis among your leadership. It may even unearth hidden agendas!

A Word about Terminology

The dictionary doesn't help much in sorting out words like *strategic, goals,* and *objectives.* Common organizational usage of the word *strategic* refers to long-range, key, or basic plans. The phrase business plan is sometimes used interchangeably with strategic plan. We've decided to limit its use later on to the planning of for-profit ventures undertaken by nonprofits.

Goals are usually seen as the end toward which planning is aimed, although they often imply a somewhat shorter timeframe, a year, rather than several years.

Objectives are commonly seen as intermediate targets that advance the organization toward its goals, stated in measurable terms. There is a well-known saying, "If I can't measure it, I can't manage it." These are the usages that will be assumed in this book.

Note that one thing that makes it harder to run a nonprofit than a business successfully is the absence of a "bottom line" in dollars. Since profit is the main goal and objective of a business, it is a primary measure of perfomance. It should not be the primary goal of a nonprofit. Finding more meaningful performance measures is far more difficult; they require much care in their selection.

Some other key words, phrases, and abbreviations are worth defining here. They will be used often, so let's get their meaning clear.

- **CEO (Chief Executive Officer):** A generic term for the top staff operating officer. Nonprofits may call theirs Executive Director, Director, Administrator, President, Dean, etc.

- **CFO (Chief Financial Officer):**   a generic name for the controller. Nonprofits may call their hands-on financial person the Financial Manager, Fiscal Director, Controller, Business Manager, Accountant, etc.

- **Program Director:**   sometimes called Program Administrator, Program Manager, Department (or Unit) Manager, Head, Administrator.

- **Revenue and Support:**   Although often lumped together, "revenue" refers to money that is earned, such as program service fees, admissions, etc., amounts earned under contracts with government agencies or under restricted grants from foundations or corporations (*as* it is earned), and investment income. "Support" usually refers to other funds received that are not earned, such as unrestricted grants for general support, cash or in-kind contributions, and membership dues. Where we refer to revenue and support without any need to differentiate, we'll use the word *income.*

- **Support Services:**   general adminstrative services common to the agency as a whole, rather than to a specific program or department. It will apply to the services (and costs) of the CEO, CFO, and their own staffs, if any, and will include fundraising (development), public relations, or similar agency-wide functions not limited to a specific program or department.

- **Segment:**   a generic word use to avoid having to spell out all the subdivisions of an agency and their alternate names (program/department/division/unit, or functions like program/administration/fundraising).

- **Performance Indicators (sometimes called criteria or standards):**   results that can be measured objectively—in quantitative terms that can be observed and verified. (See Chapter 15.)

STRATEGIC PLANNING

Before planning can begin, the core leadership must share or develop a clear common vision of the organization's future. Where do you want to be and what will you look like five or ten years from now? This is a key leadership role, whether in a nonprofit, a business, or in government. The dream starts here. The plan itself then becomes a fleshing out of that dream. The vision must deal with what we plan to do, not how we plan to do it.

The Vision Statement

A vision statement goes beyond the mission statement to set forth the programs proposed to accomplish the organization's perceived purpose. Like other aspects of planning, vision will change as client needs vary and as both context and leadership of the organization change. The vision statement guides strategic planning.

What "business" are we in? You'd better state that in *broad* terms so that the statement doesn't become obsolete too soon. It should reflect your statement of purpose. In fact, in the process of developing a vision statement you may find that you need to amend your statement of purpose to make it reflect current reality. (Don't forget to report any such changes to the IRS, as required, at least in your annual Form 990.)

> Just suppose IBM had answered it years ago with "Why, we make punched-card tabulating equipment," or Burroughs Corporation had answered, "Adding machines, of course." And suppose both had stuck to their answers. (Seen any of those gadgets around lately?) A top IBM exec cast light on IBM's success not too long ago by saying that they are not in the computer business but in the problem-solving business. So IBM survived and became a giant, as new problems suggested new products to solve them.[1]

What is our operating environment? In the broadest possible terms it includes everything external to the nonprofit organization that potentially affects its functioning. That may include the following factors:

1. The various potential sources of funds: individual, foundation, corporate, and governmental.

2. Other support sources: umbrella and parent organizations, volunteers and pro bono support groups, suppliers and lenders, the media, and the community itself. (Even the noncontributing general public helps support the nonprofit by paying income, real estate, and sales taxes that otherwise would have to be paid by the organization or its private donors, who get a tax deduction for their contributions.)

3. The "marketplace": those who are the direct beneficiaries of our services, whom we often call "customers," because they are identified as clients, patients, students, patrons, and members by different kinds of nonprofits.

4. Government regulatory agencies: IRS and state.

5. Employee or client organizations.

6. Competitors: nonprofit and sometimes business competitors.

[1]Arnold J. Olenick, *Managing to Have Profits,* McGraw-Hill, New York, 1989, p. 3.

7. Other environmental factors, including trends and changes in economic conditions and demographic factors that affect the context in which the organization operates.

The "goldfish bowl" syndrome.   With the exception of the last two of the items listed, it is useful to recognize that all are what are sometimes called "stakeholders" of the nonprofit: they have a stake in what it does and must be seen as expecting some level of accountability. A burden that the nonprofit must learn to bear is staying afloat in a goldfish bowl, surrounded by a world of "kibbitzers," all of whom may have a right to look over its shoulder, to some extent.

What kind of programs do we envision?   On what scale and in what location?

What facilities and skills will be needed?   In a general way, the kinds of facilities and specialized skills should be determined.

Organization.   What basic kind of structure and leadership will be required to run the organization? Nonprofits are unusual in most cases in having more diffusion of responsibility and authority than other organizational types. Except in large ones, such as hospitals, museums, and universities, limited resources compel the use of volunteers in many roles: board members, officers, as well as people rendering program and support services. Some are membership organizations, which draw on their members for such activities—in addition to dues. This is the subject of Chapter 4.

When your leadership achieves agreement on the organization's vision, the strategic plan starts to put flesh on its bare bones.

When Is Strategic Planning Done?

Your community may change demographically or be affected by national or local political or economic developments, such as changes in government policies, recession, or unemployment. The target population you serve may shift, broaden, or narrow, as may their needs or demands for services. That may compel a review of your strategic plans—and even of your mission statement at times. Wisdom counsels at least a preliminary review every three or four years to make sure that neither statement has become outdated. This kind of review is sometimes referred to as an environmental scan. Sticking with documents that clash with reality is a sure prescription for trouble, since they can be used by people in the organization to block new programs and activities they may dislike, yet that are responsive to current needs.

What Is In a Strategic Plan?

We have said that developing a mission statement makes you focus on *why* and *who* you are, and a vision statement on *what* you want to do and be. A strategic plan makes you look at *how* you plan to do it, at least in general terms. It should seek to answer the question "How do we get from where we are now to where we want to be?" In the process, it makes you define your goals and policies, which helps eliminate the fuzziness and superficial consensus under which many noprofits (and businesses) operate.

Here is where any hidden agendas must be ferreted out, whether philosophical or selfish ones. Properly done, strategic planning is a process that strengthens consensus and unity and gives any organization a more focused sense of purpose and direction.

Essentially, the plan spells out the vision in more concrete terms.

Elements of a Strategic Plan

Our "turf" (sometimes referred to as the nonprofit's "domain"). Who are the people we plan to serve, how many (which may differ from year to year), where are they—and where should we locate our facilities to serve them? Fuzziness is dangerous here; we must define our constituency (clients or patients) *in terms that are relevant to our vision*; for example, by their income level, specific problems or needs, where they live or work, ethnicity or gender, and relevant physical disabilities or psychological problems.

Take the catch-all slogan, "creating affordable housing." Notice what a cliche the word "affordable" has become. Affordable to whom? One family's affordable housing is another family's luxury apartment! This is where focus enters into planning.

Another question might be, Do we plan to do a little for a lot of people, or to make a big difference in a few people's lives? Once you get into discussing such issues as quantity vs. quality you'll often find that your leadership is not of one mind about them. It is essential to arrive at consensus early on; otherwise there will be trouble when the group starts to make its plans more concrete.

Remember that we are thinking in basic, long-range terms here, so program-planning methods such as needs assessment are not yet appropriate. Developing a business plan is another subject to be covered, but not yet. As already noted, we'll look at creating a business plan in Chapter 9 on (for-profit) income-producing ventures.

What makes our organization special? Why should anyone come to us or lend us support? What have we to offer—in terms of know-how, ideas, professional or language skills, policies, facilities, location, values, and other resources? Have we a good track record? How do our resources compare with those of others providing the same, similar, or substitute services? What weaknesses need to be corrected? In business this is known as our *competitive position*.

Programs. Taking our strengths, weaknesses, and competitive position into account, what programs will we develop and operate to bring to life our vision and serve the needs of constituents? What types and methods of delivering the needed services? There is usually more than one method of service delivery, so alternatives need to be studied in terms of relative cost effectiveness. If we plan more than one program, what is the order of priority for funding: if we can't do them all, should we limit the number of programs or the amount to be spent on each one?

Setting goals and objectives. What do we plan to accomplish over time—say three to five years—to solve the problems identified in our mission statement, fully or partially? What intermediate—annual—targets can we project? How will we measure whether we have achieved them? These are what professionals call *performance indicators* or *performance criteria*.

Support services. In planning activities, it is dangerous to overlook nonprogram services and facilities like administration, financial management, and fundraising, among others. These must be planned for and paid for. Potential funding sources will expect to see this as part of your planning.

Resources. What resources can we tap—in funds or in volunteer services and in-kind contributions—to pay for what we plan to do? It is in this area that a nonprofit organization differs most from a business, since its services are rarely paid for in full by the clients who use them. The "buyer" is often someone else, in whole or in part. To what extent do we plan to offer our services free; to what extent for a fee or charge?

What kinds of major funding sources will be available to pay for or subsidize our services, and in what proportions: government agencies, United Way or similar agencies, foundations, corporations, or major individual donors? It's not big news that this is a key question. What's important is doing all the thinking, research, and leg work involved. The general subject of funding the organization will be explored in Chapter 8.

Sources of funding.   "He who pays the piper. . . ." There is an element here that can easily be overlooked and that can have an impact on achieving your vision: what professionals call your *funding mix.* Every nonprofit organization needs to think through, as a long-range issue, the extent to which it wants to be self-supporting, as compared with being dependent on government or other funding sources. The answer depends in large part on the nature of the programs. Many nonprofits in the human services field are funded almost entirely by state agencies and function essentially as state contractors.

That is also true to a considerable extent in the community economic development field, where CDCs (Community Development Corporations) need governmental help in building or rehabilitating properties. It is less true in the fields of the arts, education, and health services, where admissions and fee-for-services are more common.

You may have little choice regarding the sources of your funding in the early stages of development, but it is something to think about in longer-range terms. There are practical as well as philosophical aspects of this question, since being dependent on anyone gives the funder a degree of control over what you can do and how you can do it.

A 1988 research report entitled *The State and the Voluntary Sector* (New York: Foundation Center) includes a survey of 300 New York nonprofits with state contracts.

> More than half the respondents said they believed that non-profit organizations had become too reliant on the state government for financial support.
>
> Approximately half . . . felt that the receipt of state funds had "significantly changed the program priorities" of non-profit agencies, and . . .
>
> More than a third felt that government financing had "actually changed their missions." The report said that non-profit groups had often shaped their programs to match requirements for state grants. . . .

Your board needs to think long and hard about this possibility before you "go for the easy buck." The choice is sometimes clear-cut: do it their way, and survive as a captive agency, or cling to your own vision and mission and struggle to make ends meet. That's being between a rock and a hard place, but life is never simple.

Start-up funding.   If you are a new or young organization, start-up funding may come before the other funding question. What are often called "seed money" grants are not always easy to get. You may need money for technical assistance such as legal and accounting services, organizational, program, fundraising or marketing (formerly called "development") consultants. In some nonprofit areas there may be government agencies that supply such grants or some of this assistance, which may also include workshops on these subjects. If you're not lucky there—or until you are—you may be able to borrow limited amounts from board members or loyal supporters. There may also be a revolving loan fund in your area, although these are sometimes earmarked for emergency needs rather than start-up activities. (Banks rarely lend money for such purposes.)

Donated services.   If you're diligent—or fortunate—you may be able to get some professional services as an in-kind contribution from professionals willing to provide services free or at cut rates. (Perhaps you can get one or more of them on your board or advisory committee.)* Sometimes it is possible to have state agencies, other nonprofits, or business firms lend, pay for, subsidize, or other-

---

*See "How to Work with a Lawyer" in Chapter 1.

wise provide professionals to perform services you otherwise could not afford. Look hard at anything you get for nothing, however; you may get just what you paid for!

Donated equipment and supplies. Business firms and individuals who might not give money may be willing to make an in-kind contribution of these, including used equipment or vehicles you need or clothing that you need or can sell. Watch out for donated computers, photocopiers, and other electronic equipment. Often they prove to be an "unkind contribution": more of a headache than a boon! The motive to give may be to get a tax deduction for equipment that is unusable or unsaleable by the giver, rather than putting it out with the trash.

THE ANNUAL PLAN

The strategic plan lays down the "yellow brick road," in long-range terms; usually of three to five years. It is a vision of the future as we would like it to unfold. To get from here to there, we must of course break the future into bite-size pieces. If we could really predict and plan the future accurately, what a different world it would be! To move along on the strategic path, we need mileposts, annual plans that are integrated with the strategic plan to keep it moving. Annual plans are not different, only more specific, as though we've switched the objective lenses on a microscope for greater magnification of the detail. Now we need to flesh out the vision still further, adding the specific logistics:

Programs. Assuming that we handle more than one program, which ones will we continue, which will start, which will end? When will we start or finish each program? What is the order of funding priority, or level of service activity, if we can't fund all of them fully? Each program needs a plan of its own, covering the details listed below. The relationship of funding sources and programs must be worked out, since there can be more than one source of funds for a program, and more than one program paid for by a single funding source.

The separate program plans must then be integrated with the overall plan of the agency. What performance indicators will we use to evaluate whether the plans are achieving their intended results?

People. Unless we aren't changing what we do, what people will we need, with what skills? Where will they be assigned in the organizational structure? How many of each, at what pay scales? Can we get volunteers or in-kind services contributed by another agency for some or all of what we need? Part-time? Full-time? Permanent? Temporary—for how long? It may need to include support services (administrative and fundraising) as well as program people. This is the key part of the plan, as far as funding goes.

Purchased services. What services can or should we obtain from outsiders: freelancers, consultants or other professionals, contractors, or the like? There are a number of such categories of service, ranging from janitorial to legal and accounting, including fundraisers and PR people. (There are pros and cons here: We have more control over what our own staff does and how they do it; it may, however, cost less in some cases to engage short-term services outside. We may not be able to afford all services on a salaried basis, and some skills are only available on a fee basis.) Transportation, delivery, and insurance are some other items that need to be considered in planning.

Facilities. Do we have enough (or too much) for what we plan to do? What facilities need to be added or eliminated? How much space, at what rents? What other equipment or vehicles? (Whether to rent or buy is a question to consider in the budgeting process.) Do we have adequate communications facilities?

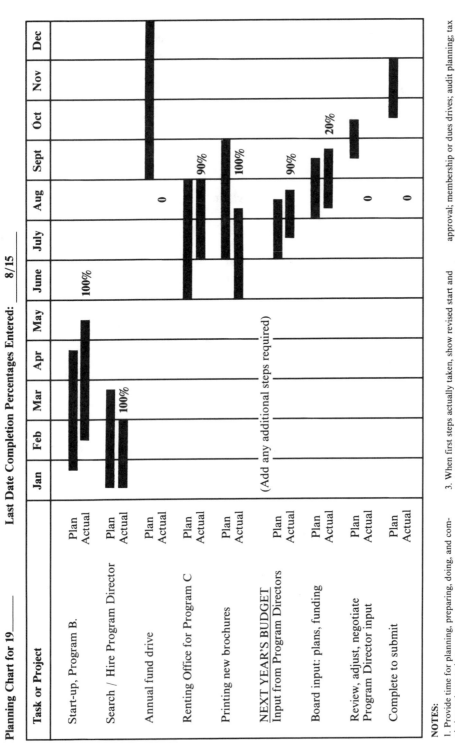

Planning Chart for 19____   **Last Date Completion Percentages Entered:** ___8/15___

Task or Project		Jan	Feb	Mar	Apr	May	June	July	Aug	Sept	Oct	Nov	Dec
Start-up, Program B.	Plan												
	Actual												
Search / Hire Program Director	Plan												
	Actual			100%									
Annual fund drive	Plan						100%		0				
	Actual												
Renting Office for Program C	Plan									90%			
	Actual												
Printing new brochures	Plan									100%			
	Actual												
NEXT YEAR'S BUDGET													
Input from Program Directors	Plan									90%			
	Actual												
Board input: plans, funding	Plan										20%		
	Actual												
Review, adjust, negotiate Program Director input	Plan								0				
	Actual												
Complete to submit	Plan								0				
	Actual												

(Add any additional steps required)

NOTES:

1. Provide time for planning, preparing, doing, and completing task or project.

2. Show planned start and end dates to nearest week on upper ("Plan") line.

3. When first steps actually taken, show revised start and end dates. Under current week, show estimated percent task or project is completed. (Revise end date if necessary.)

4. Other uses: grant or contract proposals, processing, approval; membership or dues drives; audit planning; tax return preparation/completion; ordering/receiving program supplies and equipment; periodic program evaluations, internal or by funding agency, etc.

FIGURE 3–2. GANTT PLANNING CHART

Supplies. What supplies will we need, when, and how much of each? What quality can we afford? What are the best sources of supply? If merchandise is involved, again, how much and what kind? Will we buy or make it? Where?

Now all of this may be obvious, as you read it. As a matter of fact, that may be true of many things in this book. On the other hand, you'd be surprised how often we have heard people confess to overlooking one or more of them in planning. So look on this as a convenient checklist.

The Role of Work Plans

Strategic and annual plans set the framework of what is to be done. The only way to ensure follow-through is to create, at least for new activities, a step-by-step guide to when each move will be made, and by whom. Such guides are usually called work plans or action plans.

Starting a new program? When do you hire—or reassign—the program director, other staff, and volunteers? When does any needed training begin, and for whom? When does the person responsible for it order supplies? Equipment? Facilities? Outside services? What administrative support or fundraising is needed and when? What publicity and when? If you have the dates or time frames spelled out for starting and completing each step, you can follow up on whether these things are happening. Otherwise your plans can easily become wishes instead of reality.

Experienced nonprofits and businesses use what is called a Gantt Chart for the purpose of detailed follow-up. The chart is often attached to an office wall, to keep it in plain sight at all times. For each important new or major planned activity, program, project, or event, the chart shows when it starts, how long it is expected to take, and when it is expected to end.

Because many activities start and end at different times throughout the year, it not only assures that none will be overlooked, it also provides lead time, assessment of the executive's workload, and necessary delegation or time shifts. Fully used, the charting system also tracks the *actual* starting and revised completion dates of each item listed. (See Fig. 3–2.)

How All These Pieces Fit Together

Thus far we've looked at ten parts of the organizational planning process. It may be useful at this point to summarize the order in which tasks are accomplished, the periods of time they cover, how long each takes, and how specific or general its content is. Fig. 3–3 is an attempt to line up the planning components in relation to these characteristics:

Planning Document or Statement	Sequence of Item	Period of Time Covered	Detailed or General	Length of Document
Mission statement	–First–	–Long–	–General–	–Short–
Statement of purposes				
Vision statement				
Strategic plan				
Goals				
Annual plan				
Objectives				
Performance indicators				
Logistics				
Human resources				
Work plan				
Gantt chart	-Last-	-Short-	-Detailed-	—Long—

FIGURE 3–3. CHARACTERISTICS OF PLANNING COMPONENTS

Marketing and Public Relations

In long-range, strategic terms, marketing and PR are subjects that relate to the basic positioning and image of the organization in the community or field of activity, rather than to the details of these activities on a day-to-day basis. The earlier discussion of strategic planning dealt with this aspect of marketing and PR. (These terms are used rather than the more ambiguous term "development," which can be mistaken for organizational development. They have come into increasing use in the nonprofit world, where they used to be looked on with some distaste. "Marketing" will be used to include fundraising and grantsmanship, the subject of Chapter 8.)

MANAGEMENT BY OBJECTIVES

Although the term "management by objectives" (MBO) may be losing favor, it will be used here to identify a set of valid concepts. Essentially, they are what this whole book is about. It consists of a set of methods and policies that all well-run organizations use. It is also more profound than it sounds, for it embodies a philosophy and style of management that is democratic and participatory.

• Specific and measurable objectives are established for the year. In looking at the important values of planning, we pointed out that an effective plan gives you something against which to measure your actual results, so you can tell how well you're really doing. We also spoke of setting objectives for the year. It is vital to understand that objectives are only meaningful if they are stated in measurable terms: not "improve (or increase) services to clients" but "hire one more counselor to give more time to each client," or "handle an increase in the caseload of 20 clients," or "increase the caseload by 15% this year." These are objectives that can be measured objectively; the others cannot, and can only give rise to arguments about whether or not objectives are being achieved. That is the general meaning of the term performance indicator.

• Involve the key players in setting objectives: program directors at the very least; also fundraisers and PR people when they can make a contribution to the discussion or when they need to understand the plans fully. (This is what Japan is teaching U.S. industry.) Imposed objectives create resentment if unrealistically high; underachievement, if too low. Either situation leads to poor general morale and an atmosphere that promotes high turnover or burnout.

• Set individual performance indicators, wherever possible, involving each person in helping to set the measures by which his or her work will be evaluated. It is both unfair and ineffective to hold people responsible for failure to carry out plans they were not involved in making.

• Provide frequent feedback for all levels of management, and for individual staff members when feasible, that permits everyone to see "how'm I doing?" In other words, compare actual results with those originally planned.

• Keep on top of outside developments, being always ready to improve, polish, expand, contract, revise—even abandon—a given plan. Such outside influences could include changes in the local or national economy, legislation or regulations affecting the program or its funding, demographic or economic changes in your target clientele, the appearance—or disappearance—of competition from other agencies or business firms. Plans should never be set in concrete. There's no way to evaluate results against a plan that has ceased to be meaningful.

We examine these problems in further detail in Chapter 5, in terms of budgeting, and in Chapter 15, in terms of nonmonetary performance evaluation.

Chapter 4

Organization Building

Organization building is not always considered in strategic planning of nonprofit groups, perhaps because it is an ongoing problem, not just a long-range planning issue. Yet it needs to be thought about carefully in long-range terms as well.

The complex of relationships in a typical nonprofit organization is looser and more vague than would be possible in most business firms, primarily because volunteers are used at all levels. Volunteers normally serve as board members and officers, and they frequently provide program or support services.

The organizational relationships in a typical nonprofit are shown in Fig. 4-1.

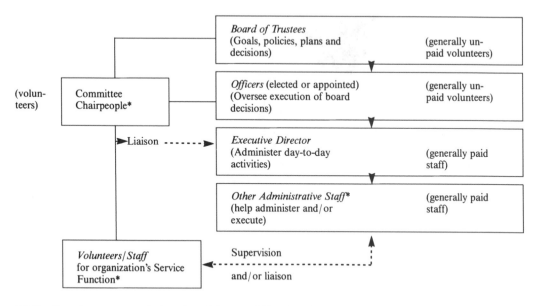

*Staff and/or volunteers carry out basic service and support activities, depending on the nature of the organization and the extent of its funding.

FIGURE 4-1. ORGANIZATIONAL RELATIONSHIPS IN A TYPICAL NONPROFIT

YOUR GOVERNING BOARD

It has been estimated that as many as 13 million people serve on nonprofit governing boards. This body—usually called the board of directors or trustees—will, in long-run terms, determine how successful your organization will be. Experienced nonprofit professionals know this well. Often, unfortunately, the nonprofit was started by one or two dedicated people who become its key paid staff members, and who see the board as an unavoidable legal and fundraising necessity. Human nature being what it is, we all want freedom from any limitations on what we do or how we do it.

Yet the most experienced professionals among nonprofit executives know that a strong, active, and committed board is essential to creating and building a strong organization. One fact that must be kept in mind: it is the board that has ultimate legal authority and responsibility for all activities and resources of the organization. That is true regardless of who founded the nonprofit or how the board was chosen. This fact is too often unknown to board members, yet it may have serious implications. They can, for example, be sued individually under certain circumstances for things done by the organization, a point that is discussed below.

Board Responsibilities

Although the nonprofit's key staff members do most of the day-to-day work, it is the board's responsibility to supervise and approve decisions affecting goals, policies, plans, and programs. The board also has basic responsibility for funding all programs and support services. There are two opposing attitudes on this point: (1) nonprofits that accept the three G's of board membership, attributed to the Junior Le   —"give it, get it, or get off"; or (2) those who may instruct a new executive director that "pai   raising the money to pay your salary," (which almost guarantees that this activity .   .y attention.)

Board Membership

The three G's are the better policy, if *"it"* refers not only to money, but to time, talent, and expertise, as well as to prestige or valuable contacts. Because the board is the key to all else, there is no room on it for people who join only for what they may get out of it: ego gratification, career advancement, or business contacts. There is also no room for people who are board members in name only, and rarely show up for meetings. Their lack of commitment can become contagious to hard-working board members who see them as taking a free ride. (The bylaws should prevent this by including a "deadwood" provision for dropping members who miss a certain number of meetings without explanation or good cause. Nor should there be room for board members who come but never do anything to help.)

One way to help prevent this problem is by having your bylaws provide for rotating board membership. Members should be elected (or appointed) annually, so that new blood can be added. If longer terms are desirable, the greatest of care must be taken in recruiting and orientation of new members, and strategies developed for dealing with the "deadwood" problem.

Who are good candidates for membership? People who can bring one or more of the following resources to your organization, especially if they become officers:

- Money or the ability to raise it through their own connections, talents, or energies.

- Experience and wisdom, preferably in your field of operations. However, solid business experience can also be of value, since you are running a "business," at least in a financial and managerial sense. But—DANGER, SHARP CURVE—the "bottom line" outlook of business people can divert a nonprofit from its mission. Safeguards must be found to prevent this, without losing the valuable skills and talents such board members can bring. Emphasis on organizational goals at board meetings might be one such safeguard (see Chapter 3).

- Professional skills. If you're lucky, you may be able to attract an attorney, a CPA, or professionals in the management, marketing, or fundraising fields as board members. Such professionals can be invaluable assets to the organization, if they are there to serve your mission, not primarily their own careers.* A former CEO of your own agency or one in the same nonprofit field would be a real asset.

- There is also a value in having one or two "names" on your letterhead: people who are well known, people who can lend prestige and open doors for you. But remember the "deadwood" problem pointed to above. If they are not expected to do much, their real function should be one accepted by other board members. On the other hand, you may be able to get some of the same benefit by asking them to serve on an advisory board (see below).

- If yours is a community-based organization, or one that represents the interests of different constituencies or member organizations, logic dictates that representative individuals from each key constituency be included. Your bylaws might well contain this provision.

  It is important to recognize the likelihood that in such a board, factions may develop among those with common interests and viewpoints. This can lead to conflict. When such conflict occurs beneath the surface, suspected but not given overt expression, it can endanger the health—even the existence—of your organization. Preparation or review of the mission and vision statements should resolve any such issues. Disagreements should surface in the process of the board's consideration of strategic or annual plans, when priorities in programming and resource allocation are being discussed.

- Should the CEO or other staff members serve on the board? This is not an easy question to answer. Because the board hires the CEO, there is a potential conflict of interest in working for yourself, in a sense. It is not unusual, however, especially in small organizations, particularly those whose CEO was a founder and has held the job a long time. The relationship of the board and CEO obviously is a critical one, and is explored later. The CEO's participation in board meetings is essential, yet should not necessarily be based on board membership.

Recruiting and Orientation

Identifying and recruiting is usually the responsibility of a nominating committee made up of existing board members. The potential values and difficulties just discussed should be kept in mind when recruiting board members. Fairness dictates that prospective board members understand what will be expected of them—the "three G's."

New members need to understand your organization's purposes, resources, organization, and history. They should be invited to an orientation session, where they receive copies of key docu-

---

*See prior comment re: conflicts of interest in Chapter 1 ("How to Work with a Lawyer").

ments: the constitution, bylaws, any organizational chart, a list of officers, key staff people, and functioning committees. Policy and procedure documents, work plans, recent financial reports, and current budget are also useful. Before their first meeting, new board members need to see minutes of board meetings and agendas.

Board Size

A question often asked is, "How big should a board be?" Too small a board risks having an inadequate range of knowledge and abilities, paralysis due to absences, a possible narrow outlook, and limited numbers to chair or people committees. The plus side is the tightness and unity that can develop in a small group. Too large a board can become unwieldy, and requires a tighter rein to engage members in activity. On the other hand, it can add more skills and serve the interests of more constituencies. There is really no magic number, since the size and complexity of the organization and its mission are factors. (Somewhere between nine and twelve seems to work for many small to medium-size groups.)

Term of Service

How long should members serve? There's no easy answer to this question. There is no substitute for experience and knowledge of the organization's affairs and people, yet there is always the potential for stagnation, weariness, and an inbred outlook.

The infusion of new blood and new energies is just as important. Many groups do this by providing in their bylaws for overlapping terms of membership; for example, one-third of the members may be newly elected each year for a three-year term. To accomplish this, the process is begun by having one-third elected to a one-year term, one-third for two years, and one-third for three. Thereafter, one-third of the membership is replaced annually.

Operating Budgets

The operating budget matches funding needs with projected expenses. Budget approval is a key board responsibility, although budgets are generally prepared by staff and submitted to the board for approval. Review for this purpose should be a key function of the finance committee. The same should apply to any necessary budget revisions.

Staffing and Personnel Policy

The board hires the Chief Executive Officer (CEO), whom we shall refer to as the "CEO" throughout, since the title varies in nonprofits: most common is Executive Director, or Director (vague, since it may refer to a board member unless they're called trustees), Administrator, Dean, or even President in some cases. After the determination of basic goals and policies, this hiring decision is the most important decision a board makes. The CEO is the one person whose abilities and talents will either make or break the organization. Care in the search for, compensation, and supervision of a CEO, including periodic evaluation of the CEO's job performance, are similarly major board responsibilities.

The following recommendations are made regarding the hiring process for a CEO.

● Adequate time must be provided for the process if you expect to get a winner. Use of the Gantt (planning) chart in this connection is highly recommended. (See Fig. 3-2) in Chapter 3.

● Criteria need first be established regarding the characteristics as well as the qualifications considered most desirable in a CEO. Education and related experience are important, but management ability and philosophy and management style—past or potential—can be of particular significance.

A seasoned professional in your area of operations does not necessarily make a good CEO. The candidate's value system, personality, and communications skills are also important. The successful candidate may well have to deal with antagonism from unsuccessful in-house applicants and an initial "show me" attitude on the part of the whole stff. The candidate's likely attitude towards and relationship with the board, and whether he or she would make a good "fit" with the organization are also crucial in the selection process.

● Serious consideration should be given to inviting key staff members to take part in the interviews, and to provide input to the personnel or hiring committee during the selection process. The perspective of paid staff may be useful in forming hiring criteria, as well as in revealing possible causes of any past problems.

If the CEO position is posted within the agency, any staff members applying for it should be given an explanation of the conflict of interest that would be represented by their participation in interviews. They should nonetheless be invited to offer suggestions regarding selection criteria or procedures. For these reasons, such a procedure should preferably become formalized as part of the agency's personnel policies, not left to the chance of being overlooked.

● Each candidate must understand the nature of the position being interviewed for, which should include a clear written job description, and of the mission, vision, and present situation of the organization. Any serious problems regarding such key matters as the agency's financial condition or prospective funding, or the adequacy of staffing levels, need to be disclosed to the leading candidates *before* a final hiring decision is made. A new CEO will discover them very quickly anyway, and may otherwise feel that he or she has been misled. You don't want to lose this key person as a result, something the authors have seen happen.

● Because the role of CEO is so central to the success of the nonprofit, those charged with the hiring process must be prepared to negotiate adequate compensation, benefits, and, frequently, incentives to hire a really desirable candidate. (While bonuses are uncommon in the nonprofit world, there is much to recommend the idea of an annual bonus to the CEO and key staff based on meeting or surpassing objectives.) In any event, the performance indicators that the board will use in evaluating the work of a CEO should be made explicit and an annual review should be provided for.

This is a major career decision—often a once-in-a-lifetime choice—for a well qualified professional, therefore obstacles need to be dealt with. Examples include other offers, temporary unavailability due to existing job or personal commitments, and relocation problems and costs, including housing problems. Such obstacles should be expected and overcome, not seen as deterrents.

The all-volunteer nonprofit organization is exceptional in its approach to staffing and operations. Many small or new groups operate without paid staff—by either necessity or preference. Local cause-oriented groups and local chapters of professional and trade associations are notable examples. The experience of most nonprofits of which we are aware is that without at least one paid staffer, even on a part-time basis, the organization is likely to labor under grave difficulties.

We know from long experience that many groups show incredible dedication and selflessness. Nonetheless, many such nonprofits have eventually fallen apart because other commitments or opportunities of its volunteer leadership sooner or later take priority: the need to make a living or raise a family, for example. Another possible outcome is burnout and loss of key leaders. For literature on coping with this serious problem, contact the Association for Volunteer Administration at P.O. Box 4584, Boulder, CO 80306. (See also the bibliography.)

Hiring Other Staff

Authority for staffing the organization is usually delegated to the CEO, although the board may have good advice to offer when it comes to key program directors or fundraising officials. Assignment of the responsibility and authority for hiring and firing must be made clear from the outset.

Personnel Policies

No matter how much delegation a board may prefer, in the final analysis the health of the organization is its own responsibility. Therefore the board should recommend, oversee, and approve compensation and fringe benefits, recruiting, job descriptions and titles, periodic review, performance evaluation, hours of work, overtime pay, incentives, and promotions.

Authority without accountability is an unhealthy situation for a CEO—or anyone else—to be in. More than one organization has been put in jeopardy by an unsupervised CEO who managed to turn off key program directors or support people by bureaucratic habits, or by arbitrary or unfair decisions. Unless there is some channel or vehicle for key staff people to communicate serious concerns to a board committee or officer, the organization may be headed for real trouble.

For example, a landmark lawsuit in Massachusetts held a hospital's trustees individually liable for the death of a patient in the operating room, based on their negligence in the hiring of the chief of surgery, to whom they had clearly delegated total authority, with no system of checks or balances.

> ACCOUNTABILITY is at the very heart of the world of the nonprofit. It includes accountability of the agency itself to society, funding agencies, government, and community; of its board, for its fiduciary responsibility; of staff to board and of board to staff.

Board Meetings

Board meetings should have as a goal the involvement of members in committee or support activities. Those who always have excuses should be replaced at the end of their term of board membership.

Nothing turns off and loses active member participation, or destroys a board's effectiveness, like poorly planned or badly run meetings. A carefully thought out and timed agenda is key. What you don't want is a grab bag or laundry list. It should be sent out with the meeting notice, well in advance of the meeting, with minutes of the previous meeting, to permit thought and preparation.

It should not attempt to bite off more than the board can chew in the time provided. Regular board meetings should focus on decisions to be made or approved, in a business-like way, and not used for brain-storming, spur-of-the-moment proposals, or unnecessary argument. These activities are for committee meetings.

The chair of the meeting should make sure the agenda is closely adhered to—that discussion is relevant and not extended unnecessarily. Someone, preferably the corporate secretary or clerk, should always be designated to take minutes, which should also be as concise as possible, recording primarily decisions made and actions taken. All these are of course obvious rules to experienced people: would that they were always followed!

Board Committees

An effective board does not do most of its work at board meetings, but rather through committees. Ideally, working committees should be created to deal with planning, finance, program oversight, personnel, and other activities, depending on the nature of your organization, such as membership, meetings, etc. The finance function is often divided between a development or fund-raising committee and one responsible for financial management and budgets. Some committees may include non-board members or volunteers, and commonly work closely with paid staff responsible for the same or related activities. There is usually an executive committee, commonly consisting of the officers plus key board members, such as former officers, to function between board meetings in place of the board, and a nominating committee to recommend officers and board members when appropriate.

Advisory Board

Some people may be willing to play a limited role of potential value to your group, if only to lend prestige. You may even prefer some people to serve in an advisory capacity because of political considerations, conflict of interest, or the like. An advisory board is a way of having your cake and eating it in that respect, since board membership confers control.

Roles of the Officers

The organization's bylaws are the authority for electing or appointing officers from among the membership of the board and defining their roles. Here it is worth considering the three key officers from a functional standpoint: the Chairperson or President, the Treasurer, and the Corporate Secretary or Clerk. These are the leaders with the heaviest legal responsibility for the ongoing activities of the nonprofit, since they commonly sign its correspondence, legal documents, and tax returns and, in the case of the Chairperson or President, is its most common public representative, although the CEO often assumes that role. Their potential importance to the success of the organization is second only to that of the CEO and CFO.

The chairperson. The board chairperson should be a real leader, and someone who has served on the board, preferably on its executive committee, for at least a year. It is his or her role to be the keeper of the vision of the organization, to inspire and motivate its board and staff, and to oversee their functioning in keeping with the principles spelled out in this chapter; to act as the chief liaison between the CEO and the board, to represent the community and to represent the nonprofit to the community. This is no mere honorary title, but a job requiring a far greater commitment of time and energy than other board members.

One or more vice-chairs (or vice-presidents) may be desirable to help share the load and chair meetings or otherwise act in the chair's absence or inability to act. Committee liaison is a useful role for a vice-chair.

The Treasurer.   The board treasurer should fulfill the same functions with respect to the CFO and the financial well-being of the organization, and not merely sign checks. Central to both their roles is a smooth and full flow of communication from the staff, reporting on what is going on. The key word is again accountability.

The Corporate Secretary/Clerk.   The board secretary/clerk is not a staff clerical position, though it may sound like one: it is a legal office provided by state charter, responsible for maintaining important corporate documents and records. These include not only the original and amended certificate of incorporation (called articles of organization in some states) and the original and amended bylaws, but also important decisions of the board and membership, if any, as reflected in the corporate minutes.

The Secretary/Clerk is usually charged with taking the minutes of membership, board, and executive board meetings. Good minutes are short on discussions and long on decisions and resolutions. They should also refer to any budgets, contracts, leases, deeds, mortgages, engagements of legal counsel, auditors and consultants, and other such important decisions and actions, including ratification of actions taken by the staff, officers, or Executive Committee on behalf of the organization. As noted in connection with the discussion of board meetings, copies of the minutes should be sent to each board member in advance of the next meeting, and errors corrected at that meeting.

Board Development

In addition to the orientation of new board members discussed earlier in this chapter, well-run nonprofits concern themselves with further development of board members. A serious nonprofit encourages its officers and key committee chairs to attend seminars and workshops intended to sharpen their skills and effectiveness. It also encourages things like annual or other periodic retreats, where the organization's leadership, including key staff members, can step back from things in a relaxed atmosphere that helps put things in perspective, free of time pressures and phone calls. On-site visits to see programs in action are excellent ways to promote understanding of real-world problems not always clear in a board meeting.

There should be a periodic—perhaps annual—evaluation of the work of the organization, and of the board, based on comparing objectives and budget against actual performance. Good work by the responsible members should always get due recognition, unsatisfactory performance approached in a constructive way intended to improve it, not to destroy egos. This applies both to officers and board members.

At long last there is a national nonprofit organization founded to help in the area of board development. It is the Center for Non-Profit Boards, located at 1225 19th St., N.W., Suite 340, Washington, DC 20036; phone (202) 452-6262. It is sponsored and funded by major foundations and umbrella groups, including W. K. Kellogg Foundation and Independent Sector. It offers publications plus advice on board development, responsibilities, and relationships.

Board development is an area in which a knowledgeable consultant can also be a valuable resource, as is the case with planning processes and organizational problems in general.

OPERATING MANAGEMENT AND STAFF

In the best-run nonprofits (and businesses), the CEO has the delegated authority to choose staff. Key board members should assist and have an input to the process with respect to important staff members such as program/department directors and financial managers (the CFO). Their reactions to candidates can be most important and helpful. The treasurer should certainly be involved in the hiring of the CFO, with whom an important relationship has to be established.

Staffing Needs

Staffing requirements are of course driven by plans for programs and support services and are closely geared to the budget. Typically, 70 percent to 80 percent or more of nonprofit budgets go to payroll and benefits, depending on the type of activity the organization pursues. The important consideration is the "fit" between newly hired people and the organization, in terms of aspirations and mission; in terms also of personality, ideology (in some cases), and life-style. Experience, demonstrated skills, and, where appropriate, credentials are important, but someone who has it all will not necessarily prove to be effective in the wrong organization or job.

Especially for key staff, thinking through the specific hiring criteria and qualifications, and reducing them to writing, are a great help. **And never forget:** an "equal opportunity" employment policy is an *essential* in the nonprofit field.

Hiring

The hiring process must be taken seriously. It is well recognized that it is not organizational structure but people who decide the success, stagnation, or failure of any organization, nonprofit or business. The saying "marry in haste, repent at leisure" applies here. It is recommended that the Gantt (planning) chart shown in Fig. 3-2 be used when filling a key position.

Resumes.   You can't really tell a lot from resumes, so don't rely on them too much as a screening device. You're often surprised by what you get in person.

References.   Don't neglect checking them, even though people rarely give the name of anyone they think won't praise their work. It's a good idea to call key people not named, who are with former employers, schools, or other places named in the resume. Not all references do what is expected and may provide important insights not obtainable in interviews. There is reportedly a growing tendency for people asked about former employees or colleagues to balk at saying anything negative in an evaluative sense, to avoid possible lawsuits. It is therefore advisable to ask only for factual information.

Length of service.   Patterns of employment in past jobs are important; people who change jobs often may be unreliable, either because of the quantity or quality of their work, personal traits, or because they get dissatisfied too easily.

Motivation.   Another fundamental point is motivation. Credentials, skills, and prior experience are no match for real motivation. With it, everything is possible; without it, very little. Some of the best people we have met in responsible positions learned everything they know on the job. They would never be where they are if they had been hired on the basis of what their resume showed. (A corollary is that the true function of a leader or manager is to motivate people to give their best.)

Compensation.   Staff members of nonprofits, however idealistic or highly motivated, need first of all to be paid decently, at the very least at a competitive market rate—not just that of other non-profits! They also need to be encouraged and motivated by officers and board members who are leaders, not bosses. No matter how dedicated they may be, it is not either fair or realistic to count on people working for substandard salaries. Those who are good at their jobs will eventually leave because of financial pressures, resentment, or career opportunities. A few statistics, based on a Massachusetts study, might be instructive.[1] Personnel costs for providers of human services, including non-payroll personnel (consultants, temporaries, etc.), have been estimated to represent as much as 75% of the overall budget: 62% for compensation, 13% for fringe costs (including payroll taxes.) Yet this huge dent in the budget is based on very low salaries.

The same study showed average full-time social service salaries in 1985 to be at the bottom of the heap: 15% below hospitals, 16% below health services, 19% below education, 26% below businesses, and 34% below other professions. Full-time human service employees with over 16 years' education (presumably college graduates) were paid 21.8% less than the average of people in other lines of employment with the same schooling.

Running an organization as a training school for employees who move on to jobs that pay better is expensive in the long run. All that staffers know about the organization will leave with them, and the agency will at best coast until a qualified replacement is found and learns the ropes. (And the cycle may then be repeated endlessly). We place this first, even before what staff is needed, for proper emphasis.

The study cited earlier indicated a turnover (separation) rate in Massachusetts human service agencies averaging 42.4% a year; but in smaller agencies, with one to twenty employees, the rate was a staggering 73.6%!

Board members, and especially officers, who commonly have full-time responsibilities elsewhere, should ask themselves whether it is fair to exploit the typically idealistic people who make the nonprofit world *their* full-time responsibility, or to ask them to raise the money for their own salaries. This is a threat to staff morale that can hurt the organization's mission. (And let it be said here that everything done or proposed in a nonprofit needs to be measured against its potential effect on mission.)

Government agencies that fund nonprofits are not notably generous about allowable staff salaries. A study published by the Commonwealth of Massachusetts in 1988 compared human services job titles of state employees with similar job titles in human service nonprofits funded by the state. As might be expected, there was a considerable gap, at the expense of the nonprofits, one that was expected to be narrowed in the future.

The Massachusetts study cited previously indicated that the percentage of average private non-profit salaries to equivalent state salaries in the same job titles was as great as 61%. (Since 1984, the state has been working gradually at increasing funding to shrink this gap.)

Benefits.   The make-up of the benefits package is, of course, a policy decision, driven by funding, but its importance should not be overlooked. Health insurance, paid sick leave, vacations, and overtime pay are key questions nowadays, especially to prospective staff members.

In the Massachusetts study cited above, "fringe costs," which also included payroll taxes, were 21% of "salaries," which as noted included non-payroll personnel.

The "1988 National Nonprofit Wage & Benefits Survey" by the Technical Assistance Center of Denver, CO, covered a cross section of various kinds and sizes of agencies. It reported the following

[1]Massachusetts Council of Human Service Providers, Inc., "Confronting Effectiveness: Social Investment in Massachusetts," Boston, Nov., 1988.

patterns nationwide:

- 75% of nonprofits pay some employee health insurance costs; 60% pay a major portion.
- 77% provide a two-week vacation after one year.
- 71% provide 9 to 11 paid holidays a year.
- 74% pay sick leave, commonly up to 10 or 12 days.
- 48% provide some personal leave (17% allow unpaid parental leave).
- 50% offer some form of retirement plan.

The reported trend was toward increased employee benefits, with child care and better insurance increasing in importance.

Pension plans are becoming more important in stable organizations. (The IRS accepts profit-sharing plans for nonprofits, believe it or not!) Employee benefits are incentives not only to attract new people, but sometimes to retain present staff members, especially when they take on new personal responsibilities such as marriage or children. You'll need professional tax advice to set up such a plan. Always remember, anything to do with taxes is always subject to changing rules.

Note: Starting in 1987, the federal income tax laws permitted employers to pay up to $5,000 *tax free* to employees for day care costs of children and other dependents. (This may be a way of increasing the take-home pay of some of your staff by shifting part of their salary to day-care payments.) There are specific rules on how to set up such a plan, which must not discriminate in favor of higher-paid staff, applies only to eligible dependents, is cut in half for married individuals filing a separate return, etc. (See your tax advisor on this.)

Incentives. Incentives for better work are not often thought about in nonprofits, except in larger ones. Bonuses are uncommon, probably unfairly so; raises are often hard to finance, and most are across-the-board, cost-of-living increases when given; in effect they are longevity/seniority raises. Promotional raises are more common, though promotions represented by higher job titles in lieu of raises are all too frequent in the nonprofit (and profit) world.

Nonmonetary rewards. Incentives are at least as important as economic benefits, especially in the nonprofit world, where the latter are so hard to come by.

There are many success stories about the use of nonmonetary rewards, such as praise or recognition, as ways to improve employee performance.[2] A congratulatory visit, memo or phone call from a top executive for outstanding or much improved performance can work wonders.[3]

Where a nonprofit has several programs, locations, or other separate units, posting or otherwise publicizing outstanding or even improved performance by a unit is another way to build its own morale, and that of other units, which may enter into the spirit of competition. There is usually something good to be said about almost anyone. A unit or individual may be working harder or getting more or better results, in terms of quantity or quality of service or product. They may have stayed within, or well below, a budget allowance; achieved or exceeded a quota. It is no secret that everyone basks in approval and praise: the more public the better.

Promotional opportunities. People expect increasing responsibility and authority as they gain experience. A new staff member can often look forward to becoming a program or segment mana-

[2]See B. M. Carlson and J. A. Collins, "Motivating Managers with Positive Reinforcement," *Management Accounting,* March 1986, p. 120.
[3]Arnold J. Olenick, *Managing to Have Profits,* McGraw-Hill, New York, 1989, p. 120.

ger. In a small nonprofit, the only step up for a program director (or other segment director) may be to the CEO job. This may be an unrealistic hope, or one far off in the future.

Where there are a number of programs or segments, there may be an existing or planned middle management slot for a supervisor to manage a group of related segments. There may be an opportunity for lateral mobility: managing a larger, more important program or segment. Otherwise, only the good luck of having someone who is both good at a particular job and content with it will hold a valued staffer in the long run.

An equal opportunity employment policy includes promotional opportunities, not just hiring.

Assignment of people. Not everyone does everything equally well, no matter how well motivated they are. Many organizational problems result from forcing a "square peg into a round hole," resulting in substandard performance or job dissatisfaction. A good fit between the needs of the position and the talents, interests, and skills of the employee or applicant is thus key to good work. As previously suggested, a resume is no basis for judging the person, without a personal interview.

Most creative or imaginative people, for example, lose interest in a job that lacks challenge, variety, or influence over the conditions and methods of work, as well as over its end-product. It resembles what's called pride in craft.

These are often your more secure risk-takers, for whom job security is not a paramount consideration. Others, less secure, may also have pride in craft, yet prefer a relatively simple, repetitive job they're comfortable with, where they have no fear of failure. But most people need a little of each. They also need to be able to keep (or gain) self-esteem and the esteem of co-workers, which comes from a sense of being valued.

Job titles and descriptions. Title and job description too are important questions for staff people. Titles are sometimes acceptable, for career reasons, as fringe benefits. Job descriptions must be clear, correct and up-to-date, if a potential source of conflict is to be avoided. It is not unusual for someone to be criticized for not doing something expected of them, and being able to say "Hey, that's not in my job description." Worst of all is operating with no written job descriptions at all. (All of this applies to the CEO's job description as well.)

Overlapping jobs and turf problems are best avoided by unambiguously describing duties in writing, and updating those descriptions periodically—especially when duties are changed. To be of maximum value, a job description should contain the following information in full detail:

1. An unambiguous job title.

2. Brief description summarizing the function (or functions) of this position within the organization.

3. To whom the person is responsible. A supervisory or administrative position should also indicate what job titles (or volunteers) are supervised by the individual, and the extent of the supervisor's authority with respect to such people.

4. Typical tasks required to be performed, in some detail, including the degree of autonomy in decision-making; reporting duties if any, liaison required with other employees, board members, or volunteers; methods of supervision and evaluation of or by others; budgetary responsibilities, if any; sources of needed information, oral or written, etc.

5. Required experience and education for the job.

Hours of work. This is of course another of the areas in which nonprofits are inclined to take advantage of their staff, and of interns and dedicated volunteers as well.

Staff Hours.   Attention must be paid to applicable provisions of the wage and labor laws, which may require overtime pay. This is sometimes handled by granting "comp time" (an equivalent amount of uncompensated time off). This may be illegal under the federal wage and labor law or under the comparable state law.[4] State labor laws vary widely. Unpaid overtime may be permissible for some administrative and supervisory employees, such as your CEO and program or department managers, and for certain other administrative employees, such as accountants, or professional employees, such as social workers, as well.

It is important to know whether a staff member is exempt for this purpose from state and federal coverage, as it applies to specific jobs. Otherwise a disgruntled present or former staffer may create problems for you, even if you are never otherwise audited. You can find general answers to this question by obtaining a copy of the U.S. Department of Labor Regulations, Part 541, which defines the terms "executive," "administrative," and "professional" for the purposes of obtaining exemption from the federal wage and hour law. For example, an executive is one who is paid a regular salary, generally must supervise at least two other full-time employees, and has the authority to hire or fire such employees—or has influence over such actions. But note that exemptions are usually reviewed on a case-by-case basis, and depend on specific facts.

You need also check the comparable rules published by your state's labor department. Some state laws are tougher than the federal law. You may also find that the terms of any federal or state grant or contract you have may deal with this issue.

Volunteers and unpaid interns.   Other than occasional "drop-in" types of volunteers, utilizing volunteer services should be treated as serious business. It can relate to board members and officers, but it needs also to apply to volunteers needed to do necessary work in programs and services such as bookkeeping, clerical support, and fundraising, among others. Only people who are willing to make a serious commitment can be depended on for such tasks if the organization is to be able to rely on them for its proper functioning. They should be considered essential resources, and their time commitment scheduled on a regular basis. This is part of the planning process, since they are, or should be, part of the human resources plan, which may well affect the personnel budget.

Performance Evaluation Criteria.   These are often called "Performance Indicators," and need to be made explicit. They are too rarely explained (or thought through) by the leadership. Staffers, including the CEO, need to know what they are measured by, how much is expected of them, and what they get "Brownie Points" for, both quantitatively (how much work) and qualitatively (what caliber of work). Morale may be improved even for people who are not new, when the rules of the game are clearly stated and fairly followed. Suspicion of favoritism or prejudice are best prevented that way.

Managing People

Once the staff is on board, how well they work together is, of course, a major determinant of how good a job they will do. The paragraphs that follow offer some of the considerations that are important to that end.

Training staff.   No matter what skills or experience new people bring to an agency, there is

---

[4]There are specific rules and exceptions, covered by The Fair Labor Standards Act of 1938 (Dept. of Labor, Employment Standards Div., Wage & Hour Div., WH Publication 1318). They cover minimum wages (Sec. 6), maximum hours (Sec. 7), child labor (Sec. 12), exemptions (which are few) (Sec. 13) and students, interns, etc. (Sec 14). The Salvation Army was held to be in violation of the minimum wage section in 1990, for example. (See *New York Times*, 9-16-90.)

always need for training in some respect. Skills need constant development and updating as methods and technology change. New hires need to be oriented to your policies, procedures, problems, and people, even more than do new board members. A staff manual can help a lot in this regard. It should include the mission statement, statement of purposes and vision statement; personnel policy and benefits; organizationl structure; titles and lines of authority and responsibility; and principal operating procedures and policies, including report forms. Each person's job description should also be presented, together with the evaluation procedures and the performance indicators that will be used in their evaluation.

People do not absorb, take seriously, or remember everything they read, unfortunately. Policies and priorities that exist *only* on paper are rarely heeded. Some policies need a more personal touch, such as a discussion of the organization's atmosphere and political climate.

For example, encourage staff input and stress an atmosphere in which the leaders do not "shoot the messenger" of bad tidings—if such an atmosphere exists. Another example is the importance of staff input toward planning and budgeting, including feedback about actual program or support service results and problems.

Staff Supervision

This is the CEO's job, not the board's. It is one that calls for leadership, a quality that may be in-born, but can be developed, if the will is there. A boss is not a leader, nor is a leader a boss. Modern management theory (which is taught more often than practiced!) counsels sensitivity to the needs of others, not demanding that they "shape up or ship out." That tough approach demotivates people and eventually hurts the organization, and should be taken only as a last resort.

People have their own personal goals and needs, which inevitably come ahead of those of the group. The key to good performance is finding ways to link the two: to create situations in which what's good for the organization is also good for the employee. Most people in nonprofits want to do a good job, because they believe in the organization's mission. (If it were just for the money, they could in most cases earn more in the business world!) What's needed is to create a work environment that encourages good performance. Aside from the elements already discussed, others can affect job performance.

Personal relationships.   It may be all too obvious to say that the way people act toward one another can make or break an organization. Board members and paid staff inevitably have different points of view, which can be a source of tension and conflict, if the right working relationships are not established. Relationship of staff and officers is particularly important.

Most nonprofits have board committees responsible for certain operating or support functions; the relationship of committee chairs and key staff members is another key area that can help or hurt the agency.

Staff members may supervise the work of volunteers, who may or may not also be board members. This is an area of potential problems. Staff are involved in the day-to-day functioning of the operation, whereas the board meets infrequently (monthly, or less often), and the officers and executive committee, if any, usually meet more frequently, regularly see staff, and exercise the authority and responsibilities of the board. They thus commonly see themselves as *de facto* as well as legal "bosses."

On the other hand, day-to-day reponsibility for running the show lies with the staff. Staff members are employees, often underpaid and overworked, who have a first-hand, day-to-day grasp of what is going on. Volunteers feel good about rendering their services without pay, may have more social status, and may feel they have an extra "moral" claim to be listened to respectfully by a paid member of the staff. They properly expect appreciation for their efforts, even deference, in the case of board members and officers. Herein lie the seeds of potential misunderstanding and tension.

Contrast this situation with that of a business firm, where the officers and managers are the same people. Even there, an officer may in substance tell a front-line manager "You're doing it wrong," with the (probably unspoken) reply "You don't know what you're talking about." The big difference is usually that the officer has often come up through the ranks, and may in fact know what he or she is talking about. This is less often the case in a nonprofit. The resulting tension can be quite destructive. Yet either or both individuals may be right—or wrong—depending on their respective knowledge, experience, and skill.

As in so many other situations, however, if differences of opinion are approached with good will, in a problem-solving mode, putting "turf" issues aside, only good can result. That way, each party begins to understand the other's problems and viewpoint, which makes it possible for a solution that integrates what they have to offer. In the final analysis, staffers are board employees. The delicate balance of contending views, arising from different roles and perspectives, is the nonprofit's equivalent of governmental checks and balances.

Creative tension is good for any organization. Democracy itself is recognized as being probably the most frustrating and inefficient of organizational structures; yet authoritarian societies like the U.S.S.R. and Japan have been forced to recognize its ability to unleash the greatest creative energies. The same considerations apply in all of the following relationships within a nonprofit: officers and board; managerial staff and the people they supervise; and officers or staff and volunteers performing program or support services. The creativity is fed by several elements.

Atmosphere. An atmosphere designed to free people's imaginative and creative energies, within the limits of established policy and with a basic regard for established procedures, can be extremely beneficial. Does that mean doing everything the way it has always been done? Of course not. Never taking risks or trying anything new, for fear of failure? Applying rules blindly, without considering the needs of the specific situation? By no means! A true leader discourages such attitudes, and gets across to colleagues the feeling that they are trusted; that the point is to get the job done, and done well, so long as you don't do anything in the process that hurts anyone—or the organization.

Responsibility and authority. You can't give someone a job without the authority (budgetary as well as organizational) needed to carry it out. Perhaps worse yet is giving someone authority without holding the person responsible for how it is used.

Accountability is a two-way street. You can't hold people accountable to you or the organization for their work or resources they control, unless they feel that those to whom they are accountable are in turn accountable to them for their own well-being and job satisfaction.

Communication. Effective communication is usually the key to solving organizational problems. Playing things close to the vest is a key to creating them. The more openness there is—about goals, plans, budgetary and other resource constraints, performance indicators, rewards, disciplinary policies, and the like—the better the atmosphere for good work. But equally important is learning to listen. (That's not the same as waiting politely for the other person to stop speaking!—A well-known song, "The Sounds of Silence" by Paul Simon, decried "people hearing without listening.")

People not only want to be heard, but to be listened to and taken seriously. A current popular response infuriates intelligent people: "I hear you," or "I hear what you're saying." This is a noncommittal answer that usually means "I disagree," without saying so.

People also want to be free to consult and interact with anyone in the organization who can be a source of information, or who needs to get information they possess—without fear of getting in trouble for "not going through channels." Such channels should exist only for the purpose of supervision and accountability, not to cut off necessary communications between parallel or supporting activities. Well-run organizations recognize the importance of liaison (the new pop term is "interfacing") between individuals whose work is related. That relationship among staff may be between steps in a process (teachers of consecutive grades), parallel activity affecting the same individuals (teachers and counselors), related activities (program directors and financial managers), or others.

If operations are to move smoothly, then information, ideas, questions, and help must be able to move in whatever direction best promotes its mission, goals, and objectives at that moment. If there is information that cannot properly be shared for some good reason, this should reflect considered policy, not someone's desire to monopolize it. The simple reason is that knowledge is power; the agency prospers when that power is shared. An individual may seek to increase personal power by becoming the sole possessor of certain information, which will often be at the expense of the agency's effectiveness in carrying out its mission.

> One of us once served as financial manager of a nonprofit, but was told by its CEO, in no uncertain terms, "Don't ever speak to the treasurer without my permission!" It only *seems* irrational: she wanted to be seen as the source of all knowledge by the officers and board. She may also have feared that her weak grasp of financial matters might be found out if the treasurer got his information directly, rather than through her. Yet what that could do to the agency's financial health should be obvious. This illustrates the kind of destructive bureaucratic behavior already described.

Another danger to the organization is a manager, at any level, who "shoots the messenger bearing bad news." One who can't abide an unpleasant truth or accept anyone else's disagreement, ideas, or constructive criticism is effectively cut off from much of the most valuable information a manager needs to be effective. Such isolation almost guarantees that subordinates will be or become "yes-men" or leave. If you want only good news, that's the only kind you'll get. Examples from history are legion.

In the absence of open communication, cynicism and suspicion grow like evil weeds, rumors proliferate, cliques form, and an atmosphere develops of everyone for himself (or herself.) That of course is the death of teamwork—and of a viable organization.

Fairness.   It would be hard to exaggerate the importance of fair play. People will only follow rules if they know they will be applied fairly, "without fear or favor," as the old cliche has it. It helps a lot if they perceive the rules themselves to be fair; no one can abide a double standard that says "Yes, well the rule applies to you, but not to me."

The sign of the destructive bureaucrat (the word itself is neutral) is the arbitrary misuse of power. This involves covertly trying to be free of any constraints, all the while being careful to cover their tracks and their rear, and in the process, fawning on the powerful above and, usually, bullying those below. This is an atmosphere destructive of the organization's mission, the kind that breeds "whistle-blowers." (The space shuttle tragedy is an example of what can result.)

Trust.   The binding force in any organization is mutual trust between leader and led, and among peers. Real teamwork involves trusting the other's judgment, ability, honesty, and sense of fair play. That other may be the CEO or program director, a board officer or member, a staff member, or a volunteer. Like motivation, with trust, everything is possible; without it, not much. In fact, motivation probably derives more from mutual trust than from almost anything else, including good pay.

But how to create that trust? Trust must be earned by showing that you know what you're doing and mean exactly what you say; you deliver on promises and can be relied on to come through when you're needed. It means accepting responsibility for errors, rather than using alibis, excuses, or buck-passing. It means showing fairness always. Above all, it means showing that you put the organization's mission first.

Does it mean trusting everyone blindly?—Obviously not. That's where accountability comes in, via performance measurement and reporting; where the use of internal controls over the custody and use of resources becomes essential; where effective procedures and meaningful rules are needed, based on well-thought-out policies, and are enforced and followed—with a decent respect for the specific needs of different situations. Clearly, the word "trust" should have a common-sense meaning, but an atmosphere where trust is lacking is one destructive of genuine accomplishment.

Finally, neither fairness nor trust can last in an atmosphere that permits any form of discrimination to be practiced, whether by race, religion, sex, disability, or age. Prejudice is not illegal—discrimination *is*.

Grievance procedures. There is no way to avoid all of the many possible mistakes in dealing with personnel. If morale and motivation are to be preserved, a written grievance procedure, faithfully and fairly executed, is an important safeguard. Everyone knows the rules of the game, and if something goes wrong, the organization can correct any arbitrariness or abuse of authority.

The board should be the court of last resort, through a personnel committee, even if it functions only for that purpose. This is the only way in which the board can exercise its overall supervision of the staff—and of the CEO's use of authority. It should not have to rely on "whistle-blowers" within the organization, who may not emerge, or may not otherwise have the right to communicate with the board.

No matter how obvious (or even unrealistic) the above set of recommendations may appear, they are included because of the sad fact that such ideas tend to be honored more in the breach than in the observance. They do not cover everything there is to know about organizational life, the subject of whole books on management and organizational behavior, but to ignore them or brush them aside is to guarantee a nonprofit that's eventually going nowhere.

Part Two

The Vital Role of
Financial Management

Introduction

A Cautionary Tale

The Center School was planning to hold a belated celebration last week: a U.S. Department of Education official was coming to present the school with its award as one of the 287 "schools of excellence."

The award was announced last spring, but school officials decided not to attend this fall's award ceremony because they were too busy trying to cope with a financial crisis that threatened to close the school, which serves children with learning disabilities.

The eight-year-old school is still open, thanks to an 11th-hour, emergency appeal to parents and friends that raised nearly $300,000 in 10 days.

Experts say the school's experience is a cautionary tale of what can happen when an institution focuses too much on its mission and not enough on its finances.[1]

Here is an analysis by expert observers of why it happened:

- The immediate crisis was the result of "an unexpected drop in student enrollment but also of the institute's spending money it expected to receive from two foundation grants that never came through." (The moral is, "you can't live on promises": the Center School had "hired several new staff members on the basis of oral assurances from two foundations that the institute was in line to receive grants worth hundreds of thousands of dollars." P. S. They didn't.)

- An established pattern of deficit spending: revenues grew 300% between 1983 and 1988, but expenditures grew 400%.

- Little fundraising effort other than two annual dinners that brought in under $60,000, representing about 2% of the budgeted expenses. Foundation grants brought in only $80,000, in the previous year. The budget was funded by tuition and fees; when these fell off, a crisis resulted. They were apparently too low to begin with, according to one parent, Leslie Lenkowsky, who is also Deputy Director of the National Center for Nonprofit Boards.

He also pointed to the important responsibility of an agency's board in raising funds; other informed observers "agree that the institute's board should have taken a more active role in overseeing the organization's finances and should have made sure that funds were raised."[2]

A more recent story reported that the school did eventually go under, in spite of all efforts to stay open.[3]

[1] *The Chronicle of Philanthropy,* December 20, 1988, p. 13.
[2] *Ibid.*
[3] *Chronicle of Philanthropy,* August 8, 1989.

This is a story that has happened over and over in the nonprofit world. It clearly dramatizes a basic theme of this book: you can't spend what you haven't got, and the greatest program in the world can fail if a board does not take to heart its responsibilities for fundraising and financial oversight.

OVERVIEW OF PART II: THE VITAL ROLE OF FINANCIAL MANAGEMENT

Accountability: Missing Piece of the Puzzle

The words we use not only reflect our attitudes and misconceptions, they often determine our behavior. Take the word "give," as it's used in the nonprofit world: if you really think anyone *gives* your organization money, but *buys* goods and services from a business firm, you're heading for trouble. Some of the trouble many nonprofits are in stems from that misunderstanding.

Whether your funding source is an individual donor, a foundation, a corporation, or a government agency, it is merely paying for specific socially desirable activities that might not otherwise happen. More bluntly, your sources are buying—or investing in—activities they believe in and want to support, even though they are usually buying them for someone else. That is what your exemption from income tax is based on in the first place.

In other words, the "gift" comes with strings attached, not ribbon. The strings: *accountability*, something we have said would come up frequently in this book, and for good reason. Accountability is a pervasive issue and a problem for nonprofits because reliable sources of funds are crucial to survival.

Most funding agency grants go to nonprofit organizations that can not only demonstrate sound program ideas and capability, but have the functional credibility that only sound financial management can supply. The leadership of such organizations has the know-how to use money wisely and to account for what it does with its funding. And the heart of effective financial management is a good system and process of budgetary controls.

The Payoff for Sound Budgetary Control

If long-run success of any nonprofit depends on an effective board, good budgetary control is the key to effectiveness in a more immediate sense. Nonprofit professionals know that sound budgetary control can yield the following results:

1. Force attention to the planning process, including programs and their support functions. This sort of focus makes planning it more thoughtful and concrete; it requires attention to priorities in the use of resources.

2. Insure that you provide enough resources to pay for all program and support service needs.

3. Prevent overspending during the present fiscal year. This guarantees that the organization will avoid "going in the red." The budget is a document embodying decisions of the board regarding how much is to be spent, and for what. (If it's not in the budget, it wasn't meant to be paid for—no matter what anyone said.) The CFO does not make such decisions, but must carry them out faithfully. That is why the budget is the key to internal accountability for the use of funds.

4. Monitoring expenses against budget allowances; control, maximize, and minimize waste of your limited resources.

5. Help in integrating all planned activities by providing an overview of the resources required by each and the impact of each on total resources.

6. Help to create genuine teamwork, mutual understanding, and trust. The budgeting process, ideally, is participatory, because competing needs have to be considered. Properly handled, a common understanding of financial constraints will lead to reasonable budgetary compromises, which can create a good atmosphere.

7. Provide an orderly way to cope with unplanned developments, by budget revision or adjustment in the area of income as well as outgo.

8. Provide one important performance measure of the agency and its managers at all levels: CEO, program and fundraising director. The ability to manage resources and to meet budgetary targets provides both an essential assessment tool and an excellent motivating device for good financial performance.

9. A sound budgetary control process is good evidence to funding agencies (and the best guarantee) of both credibility and accountability.

Four Kinds of Budgets

A budget is a projection of the sources and uses of resources. A budget is always a plan expressed in dollars (not a financial report of actual transactions). But there are four kinds of budgets. In discussing budgetary planning, don't have one type of budget in mind when you mean another.

1. Operating budget. This is your operating plan expressed in dollars: the kinds and amounts of planned income and planned expenses for a specific projected period (usually the fiscal year). The operating budget is the subject of Chapters 5 and 6. It will be your primary financial planning tool, one that includes all income and the expenses of all programs, funds, and support services.

2. Grant or contract proposal budgets. Unless your entire operation is funded by a single agency, *these* budgets normally cover a single program, fund, or project. They may also cover partial support of general operations. They are explored in Chapter 8, which deals with fundraising.

3. The cash budget (or "cash flow budget/projection"). As demonstrated in Chapter 7, it is not the same as your operating budget—even if you are using the cash basis or method of accounting. Budgeting for cash flow is primarily a short-range planning tool used to make sure you can meet your payroll and other regular bills on time by anticipating any shortfalls.

4. Capital budgets. Not used in a formal sense by every nonprofit, except the larger ones, the capital budget plans for major expenditures to add to or replace major equipment, like vehicles, furniture, and computers, or buildings (or substantial repairs to them). The amount, timing, and methods of financing such outlays are the principal elements of a capital budget, as described in Chapter 7.

Accountability and Accounting

Accountability means being answerable for one's actions, and for resources put into one's care—having to "give an account of them." *Accounting* means more than keeping accounts: it is a whole body of theoretical and practical knowledge about many aspects of a nonprofit's accountability, both internally and externally. Accounting relates to such activities as receiving resources, using them, and having custody or control over them by the organization and those who serve it.

Accounting for the use of resources is also one major way of accounting for what a nonprofit is doing, since one objective way its activities are measured is what it uses its money and other resources for.

Modern accounting evolved from a book on math written by an Italian monk over 500 years ago, which first set forth a double-entry bookkeeping system for keeping track of commercial transactions in Mediterranean trade. It has, in its modern form, been embraced by business, government, and nonprofit organizations as a systematic basis for recording and reporting the exchange and use of economic resources. Accounting means keeping track and keeping score through keeping books, though it is a lot more than that. It should be seen as a means to an end, not an end in itself. It will help your nonprofit achieve its goals by: 1) monitoring activities, 2) getting the most—and the best—for your money, and 3) promoting confidence in your organization and its credibility, by demonstrating full and reliable accountability.

Try not to look on it therefore as just a necessary evil, a headache, or bureaucratic red tape. It is not a mystery, nor does it involve higher mathematics. (After all, there aren't too many geniuses doing it.) A basic grasp of its concepts is too essential for your health as an organization—your fiscal fitness—to allow it to be the private domain of accountants, bookkeepers, or even treasurers. To be an effective nonprofit leader of any kind, you too must understand and be able to use basic accounting and financial management concepts and terms in planning, managing, and decision-making.

The chart below (Fig. 1) shows the relationship of financial management and accounting to the operating functions of a nonprofit organization.

MANAGEMENT FUNCTIONS	PLANNING	MANAGING	ANALYZING/ EVALUATING RESULTS	REVISING/ UPDATING PLANS

RELATED FINANCIAL MANAGEMENT FUNCTIONS	BUDGETING & SYSTEM DESIGN	MONITORING INCOME & EXPENSE; CASH MANAGEMENT	ACCOUNTING, FINANCIAL REPORTING & ANALYSIS	REVISING/ UPDATING BUDGETS

FIGURE 1. THE SUPPORTING ROLE OF FINANCIAL MANAGEMENT AND ACCOUNTING IN A NONPROFIT ORGANIZATION.

The fundraising (development) function is not included in Fig. 1. It is not usually thought of as part of financial management as such, but is explored in Chapter 8 because it is closely related.

The four chapters that follow deal with financial planning and management in what we hope is an unexpectedly "reader-friendly" way.

Chapter 5

The Operating Budget:
Key to Planning and Control

We are about to look at the basics of developing a reliable operating budget. The brief overview preceding this chapter, of what is involved in financial management, has important ideas needed to understand its important role in running your organization effectively.

This chapter and the one that follows focus on the operating budget, which is basic to the other three budgets defined in the preceding overview. We begin with basic budgeting: how it relates to planning and evaluating performance, the mechanics involved, whether your objective should be just to break even, and how to predict cost behavior, pricing issues, and the timing problem in budgeting. It will deal with your overall agency budget, while also considering problems involved in budgeting for different programs or contracts.

FIVE STEPS IN BUDGETING

Once the operating plan for the coming fiscal period is approved by your board (see Chapter 3), the budget can be worked out from the logistics involved:

1. Expenses are commonly estimated first. This is the simple process of multiplying the number of people, quantity of supplies, amount of space needed, etc., by the estimated cost per unit of each such item. Normally this process is handled by the staff, who are the most familiar with the details. A tentative expense budget should then be submitted to the board for review and approval. There are some instances, covered in the next section, in which the income side comes first. The expense budget is only tentative at this point.

2. Next comes an assessment of potential sources of income. This is best accomplished by the people involved in fundraising, including the board. It may well involve different kinds of funding: grants, fund drives, and fees for service, among others.

Some groups have relatively stable and predictable kinds of income, such as from government contracts, recurring annual grants from United Way or similar funds, or earned income from client fees, or they can relate the total of major expenses to ticket sales. When this is the case, the income side of the budget may be calculated first, and then expenses projected.

3. In either situation expenses must be brought into line with reality. Attention may have to be

shifted back and forth between projected income and outgo before a balanced budget can be written.

4. The final proposed budget must then be reviewed and approved by the board, after any fine-tuning required.

5. During the year the budget must be evaluated periodically to determine whether projected and actual income and expenses are in line. If not, and the variances (amounts over or under budget) are substantial, due to incorrect estimates or new developments, the budget must be updated and revised if it is to be of any use at all.

The heart of budgetary control is studying and investigating the cause of variances between budgeted figures and actual income and expenses. To use a budget known to be out-dated by events or known errors is to invite wrong conclusions and decisions.

THE BOARD'S ROLE IN BUDGETING

Here is where the board's ultimate responsibility for the well-being of the organization, discussed in Chapter 4, becomes essential and inescapable. The annual plan is assumed to embody the board's decisions and policies as to the kind, level, and priorities of program activities needed to advance the mission and objectives of the agency (see Chapter 3). The budget *is* the plan expressed (primarily) in dollars; it incorporates decisions regarding the allocation of what are always scarce resources. Thus the budget and the plan must be inseparable. To say, "We plan to increase the number of clients served by 20%," but not provide sufficient monies for the increased expenses that will result, is just talk. To say, "Okay, you'll have an assistant next year" is an empty promise unless the proposed staff member's salary and benefits are in the budget.

These are matters too important and complicated to be handled at a regular board meeting, unless it is dealing with a real financial crisis. The well-run organization has a budget or finance committee, whose job it is to work with the CEO and CFO in developing the budget, and during the year to monitor and help revise it, if necessary. The board itself must of course approve the initial budget and any such revisions. This approval should never be a mere rubber-stamp formality.

WHEN SHOULD BUDGETING BEGIN?

Perhaps a better question is when should planning begin, since the two are one. An obvious answer is "Not after the new fiscal year starts!" (We've seen that happen, believe it or not.) Not even the month before. Planning and budgeting are complex processes. If they are to be more than going through the motions, they demand adequate time—to think, research, discuss, solicit, and receive input from those who must live with (and within) the budget, do the calculations, and identify funding sources. Even in the simplest, single-program nonprofit, that process should take at least two months, unless the organization is stable with regard to both activity level and funding.

A budget timetable or calendar is a useful working tool, to make sure it all gets done in time. It should include the first four of the "Five Steps in Budgeting" presented earlier in this chapter. A date should be attached to each, allowing a realistic amount of time to accomplish it, preferably based on past experience. When there is more than one program or segment, and input is needed from segment managers (program directors, department or unit heads, the fundraising director, the business manager, etc.) more time will be needed to get this layer of input, to negotiate, revise, and resubmit requests. Where grant or contract proposals to funding agencies are basic to the budget, the planning schedule must include the necessary time to develop and submit them and obtain approval, which commonly takes many months. Other fundraising efforts, such as direct-mail or telephone campaigns, print advertisements, or personal solicitation, take time to plan, organize, and carry out. (See Fig. 6–1 in Chapter 6 for an example of a budgeting timetable.)

THREE BASIC APPROACHES TO BUDGETING

Using Last Year as a Base

Other than newly minted organizations, the most common way budget estimates are made is what professionals call "incremental budgeting": "How much was this item last year and what changes should we make?" This has only one thing to recommend it: it's easier than detailed planning, which requires converting plans to logistics, logistics to dollars. Incremental budgeting works fairly well only in stable situations, with the same levels of the same ongoing activities each year. Its flaw as the sole way to budget, in most situations, is that it is backward-looking.

1. It assumes that what we did last year was the best we can do. It is better to base our projections on the most up-to-date estimates of possibilities and opportunities—in terms of income as well as outgo. How much *could* we bring in, and what economies *could* we make without reducing program quality or level?

2. What if plans or costs have changed since last year? That could mean increased (or decreased) program levels, such as number of clients or patients, new programs or services, increased staff or facilities planned; increased prices, pay scales or fringe benefits. Such changes must be taken into account.

3. There is a problem of timing: since we have to do our budgeting before the year ends, we don't yet know what "last year's" figures are. A budget worksheet is a useful device for reviewing the year-to-date figures and projecting income and expenses for the rest of the year (see Fig. 5–1).

	Actual Amounts Year-to-Date	Estimated Amounts		Increase or Decrease	Tentative Final Budget
		Balance of Year	Current Year		
REVENUE AND SUPPORT (listed by type or source)	————	————	————	————	————
OPERATING EXPENSES (listed by types)	————	————	————	————	————
NET INCOME	————	————	————	————	————

FIGURE 5–1. INCREMENTAL BUDGET WORKSHEET

Note that this approach is not based squarely on converting the annual plan's logistics into what they will cost, except to the extent the proposed increases and decreases can do that. Because the estimates for the balance of the year may not be absolutely accurate, we still won't have this year's true amounts as a basis for next year's budget.

A tip: Don't project the balance of the year mechanically. For example, at the end of September, don't simply add one third to each of the year-to-date amounts; rather, use your most up-to-date budget projections for the fourth quarter, or better yet, try to predict what will actually happen through the end of the year. Be sure that your books are up to date, so that you will have the latest actual figures as your basis for any projections.

Logistics-Based Budgeting

A better way to budget is to "price out" the logistics for all activities planned for the next year. This approach is sometimes (incorrectly) called "zero-based budgeting" (ZBB), apparently because it starts from zero rather than building on the previous year's figures. (Actually ZBB is a much more complex and sophisticated method suited primarily to very large organizations such as governments.) It is a forward-looking method that first considers the plan and then determines how to finance it.

A Combined Approach

A practical compromise is used by many organizations. Stable costs like core staff payroll, rent, and other recurring expenditures can be estimated on an incremental basis and adjusted for known increases or decreases in rates and prices. Expenses that vary with the level of activity, such as additional payroll, space rental, program supplies, and increased utilities usage (telephone and electricity), are then projected on the basis of the annual plan. Worksheets are shown below using the logistics-based method for expenses as well as for revenue and support, using hypothetical figures.

Yet another approach, flexible budgeting, can also be used. It involves cost behavior analysis and is examined later in this chapter.

THE BUDGET: A DELICATE BALANCE

It's easier to figure out how much you need than how much you'll get. Though we've said most nonprofits budget expenses first, to get it out of the way, let's first look just at the mechanics of budgeting revenue and support, since Chapter 8 will deal with how you go about generating income. The rest of this chapter and the next one will deal with the more complicated problems of budgeting expenses.

To avoid going in the red, it's better to estimate income (our generic term for both revenue and support) on the conservative side, expenses on the high side. While income limits what you can afford, expenses determine what you need to bring in. Which comes first? The two sides of the dollar equation must be worked together for a balanced budget. Operating plans must be realistic, based on anticipated income; new or increased sources may have to be developed to make priority plans possible.

Is Breaking Even Good Enough?

Most small nonprofits would feel great just to be able to break even. But let's look a bit deeper and look ahead, past that happy day. Would that be good enough? One school of thought holds that breaking even is the only legitimate financial goal of a nonprofit: that whatever funds are received should be spent on delivering services, and therefore that any "profit" is somehow illegitimate.

It is to be hoped that this viewpoint is on its way out. Though it may seem a contradiction in terms for a nonprofit to "make a profit," that is more a semantic question than a matter of substance.

What distinguishes a nonprofit from a business is not whether it earns a profit, but what becomes of it. For a business, profit is the primary goal, the main incentive to invest, since all profits legally belong to the owners. Profits are paid to them either in dividends or high salaries.

No one owns a nonprofit in the legal sense. Unless profits are used to enrich its leaders—a violation of the law exempting it from taxes—they will be used to carry out its mission. Making a profit should be a performance indicator of your organization. It should never be the most important one.

Practically speaking, a nonprofit must earn profits to survive. Assuming that correct accounting methods are used (see Chapter 10), profits are the only way to generate funds for the following:

1. Repayment of loans or advances.

2. Investment in capital improvements like equipment and property

3. Working capital: i.e., funds needed to pay the rent and payroll until approved funding actually comes in.

4. Reserves to carry the organization through periods of underfunding.

5. Funds to invest in program expansion or in income-producing ventures or activities.

Woe betide the nonprofit therefore that just manages to break even each year: any of the above needs that are not provided for may well cripple the organization.

Pricing and Rate-Setting Issues

Someone must pay for whatever a nonprofit provides in the way of goods or services. Some agencies function like charities, in that they provide free services and look to funding agencies and donors for all their resources. Others charge for what they provide, in one or more of the following ways:

1. At full market value, like a business.

2. At cost plus some percentage to cover overhead (indirect or general expenses).

3. At cost. But how is that defined? Only the direct costs of the goods or services? What do these include? What about shared occupancy costs? Indirect, shared costs such as administrative expenses? (See Chapter 6.)

4. Below cost (however defined), at a price subsidized by grants or donations?

5. Some combination of all these, perhaps using "scholarships" or "sliding-scale" fee schedules, which are related to ability to pay.

The above methods are suggested as policy options. How to deal with them in a technical sense is examined in Chapter 6. Prices charged to clients, patients, or customers is a board decision that is part of its strategic and annual plans. It will often be based on objective factors such as how well you are funded, whether you need to meet competition, and client's ability to pay.

Price subsidies paid to the nonprofit by government or other funding agencies—often called rates—are decided by the funding agency or negotiated. Having a good handle on actual costs can be a major factor in getting an adequate return.

Pricing with Multiple Programs

Here is a dilemma that has faced many nonprofits, one with philosophical as well as practical aspects: What if you have two programs, one of which is operating "at a profit"; the other, "at a loss"? Should you raise prices in the "losing" program? Cut its expenses to where it breaks even? Find a way to shift some expenses to the other program?

The ultimate decision may result from philosophical rather than practical considerations, but first the practical aspect:

- How have you defined the expenses that are being charged to each program? (This is a complicated process that is explored in Chapter 6.)

- If you're considering raising prices in the "loser" program, what if clients can't afford to pay, or simply won't? They may either go somewhere else, or just do without.

Businesses recognize that they should not expect every product to make a profit, and they often set prices on one product or service deliberately low to help sales of a more profitable one. (Kodak got started by giving away box cameras so that people would buy film. Stores use advertised "loss leaders" to bring in customers.)

In a nonprofit setting, one program or department might subsidize another. If a program is important to your mission, it need not break even. Why risk losing your target market, either by raising prices or cutting the amount or quality of service? Would changing to a more popular service to increase the total revenue be consistent with your mission, or would it betray it?

The best answer may be one of the following:

1. Adopt the view that it doesn't really matter if one program subsidizes another.

2. Look for legitimate cost savings in the "losing" segment that do not hurt the program—for example, through economies, increased efficiency, use of volunteers, or in-kind contributions of services, facilities, or supplies.

3. Seek increased funding or donations for that program that will balance income and outgo.

Never forget that you're not running a business. Your primary goal is not profit for its own sake, but to succeed in your mission by meeting the needs of those it seeks to serve. It is here that what we call "the bottom line mentality" can endanger your whole cause. It could alienate your community, your clients, and your donors or funding agencies, who might begin to see you as a business and withdraw their support. (On the other hand, you can't go on operating at an overall loss either!)

Estimating Income Realistically

A successful business bases its sales forecasts, which represent its primary income, on a combination of such methods as market research; test marketing; sales estimates by its marketing and sales personnel; studies of demographics, economic conditions, and trends; competitors' efforts; prices and products affecting its market share. The result is at best an educated guess, unless the firm has a corner on the market.

It is the fortunate nonprofit that can use many of these techniques, although they should be used wherever appropriate, especially where the organization is engaged in a for-profit venture. This is an area in which nonprofits differ greatly, depending on the nature of their mission and organizational structure.

As discussed in Chapter 8, human service nonprofits are often captive agencies of a state, which has found it more cost-effective to contract out services than to provide them directly. In such cases, an agency's funding source is relatively stable and predictable. Human service agencies in some fields may therefore find it difficult to raise additional funds to use in strengthening programs or support services, supplementing inadequate salaries, or adding new, non-contract programs because they are perceived by donors and funders as being sufficiently "wealthy." Similar problems occur in other nonprofit fields, as in the case of community development corporations trying to develop affordable housing.

Other types of nonprofits may have more freedom of operation, but their funding is less reliable. Because this book seeks to be of value to the maximum number of nonprofit leaders, we now deal with a wide range of problems that affect funding.

To begin, what follows is a generic list of the common types of income and the factors involved in estimating each type for the budget:

1. Routine types of income (dues, individual contributions, investment income). Unless you are starting from scractch, use last year's figures, broken down by quarter (or monthly), as a base. Consider how economic conditions and planned activities, such as drives, can be expected to affect them. Changes in available funds will affect investment income.

2. Service income (fees and admissions charged to patrons or clients). Again, use last year's amounts and monthly patterns, if such income is stable, and the anticipated effects of the same factors as above. Take account of planned changes in prices and activity level. Revenues of short-run projects—such as those of performing arts groups—should be estimated conservatively.

3. Fundraising events and drives should be considered, and the funds expected to be raised should be estimated conservatively. Again, consider the economic conditions and the level of effort planned. Previous results can be used as a starting point.

4. Foundation, government, or corporate grants should be classified by type (unrestricted and restricted, or program grants) and each evaluated as to how definite it is. Installment payments due from prior grants must, of course, be taken into account. Grants to fund entire programs should be linked in the budget to related expenses, so that both aspects can be cancelled if the funds are not granted. This is one value of program budgeting, described in Chapter 6.

The need to raise revenues adequate to pay for budgeted costs must be constantly kept before the planners. The board must take all necessary steps to assure adequate funding. The *timing* of cash flow on a quarterly or monthly basis is also a matter of considerable concern: you cannot pay February's bills with a grant due next November.

To project the timing of regular monthly revenues, the new estimated total can be broken down according to percentages derived from the past. (Table 5–1). Assume that routine revenues such as membership dues or service fees totaled $100,000 last year, and were collected in the quarterly amounts shown below. If the estimate for these revenues for next year is $125,000, then quarterly revenues can be projected by applying the percentages derived from last year's quarterly collections to the new total.

TABLE 5–1. PROJECTED QUARTERLY REVENUES BASED ON PERCENTAGE DISTRIBUTION OF PREVIOUS YEAR'S INCOME

	Last year's actual revenue	% of last year's total received each quarter	Projected revenues
1st quarter	$ 20,000	20%	$ 25,000
2nd quarter	20,000	20	25,000
3rd quarter	20,000	20	25,000
4th quarter	40,000	40	50,000
	$100,000	100%	$125,000

A Working Example

To give you an idea of how budgeting techniques work in practice, let's look at a hypothetical example of a nonprofit organization. We'll call it . . .

CENTER FOR COMMUNITY SERVICE, INC.[1]

Revenues Anticipated: The Center has been in existence for several years, and until the current year ending December 31, it had a single program, Program A. A grant of $15,000 has again been approved for the coming year by ABC Foundation.

In addition, a state agency grant of $8,800 has been approved. This will cover the salary and fringe benefit costs of an administrative assistant needed to lighten the workload of the executive director. At this stage, all paid staff work on a part-time basis.

Other revenues have been from annual fundraising events held during the spring and winter months, annual dues from about 100 members, and a small amount of interest on the bank account. Program A is making a modest charge for its services. Program A revenues are expected to total $15,000 this year, and $17,000 next year. A neighborhood bank has also provided 2,000 square feet of space, rent-free, with an estimated value of $500 a month.

The XYZ Foundation is reported to be in the final stages of approving a $46,000 grant for Program B, a new type of service to be provided by the Center without charge.

Services and Facilities: Assuming that the XYZ grant comes through, the next year's paid staff will consist of an executive director (ED), an administrative assistant, program directors for Programs A and B, plus an administrative assistant/secretary for Program B. Fundraising is done by the ED, with the help of a paid outside consultant.

Program B will also have a paid outside program consultant. Other essential outside services will include an attorney and public accountant, each paid a regular fee for services

---

[1]Note that budgeted and actual amounts for this agency are integrated throughout this book, to permit tracing data.

during the year; the CPA is also paid extra for annual audit services, provided at a reduced fee. A maintenance company provides a weekly janitorial service for a regular monthly fee.

As for other facilities, Program A has a station wagon and some equipment, which originally cost about $8,000; another $4,800 of office furniture and equipment is used for administration and fundraising. Program B will rent all additional equipment necessary: an automobile, copying machine, and typewriter.

Expenses Projected: The Center carries basic insurance, including employee health, workmen's compensation, liability, and fire protection. All employees are covered by contributions made under the Social Security (FICA) and state unemployment laws, and deductions are made from weekly payroll checks for FICA and federal income taxes withheld. The board has also authorized $1,000 a year as a budget "cushion," or contingency reserve, to take care of unexpected items.

Other expenses are the ones common to nonprofits, such as travel and conferences, supplies, telephone, printing and stationery, postage, utilities, and miscellaneous office expenses.

Putting the Budget Together

Now that you have been formally introduced to the Center for Community Services, Inc., it is time to pull all the relevant information about the Center together in a systematic form, and use it to start our exploration of the budget process itself. First, we will need a projection of revenues for the coming year, as illustrated in Table 5–2.

TABLE 5–2. SCHEDULE OF ESTIMATED REVENUES

Source	Estimated amount for year	Estimated amount per quarter			
		1Q	2Q	3Q	4Q
Foundation grants					
ABC Foundation					
(Program A—approved)	$ 15,000	$ 5,000	$ 5,000	$ 5,000	
XYZ Foundation					
(Program B—pending)	46,000	15,000	11,000	10,000	$10,000
State government grant					
(approved)	8,800	2,200	2,200	2,200	2,200
Free rent (definite))	6,000	1,500	1,500	1,500	1,500
Fundraising events	11,000		5,000		6,000
Program "A" revenues	17,000	4,000	5,000	3,000	5,000
Membership dues (100 @ $27)	2,700	1,000	500	200	1,000
Interest income	500	125	125	125	125
Estimated total income	$107,000	$28,825	$30,325	$22,025	$25,825

Later in this chapter, when we get down to preparing the budget for the organization, we'll pick up these figures and incorporate them into the operating budget.

How to Estimate Expenses

Projected expenses for a coming year depend on the planned activities for that year, and on the specific goods and services required. Working out the necessary details is commonly the job of the staff, but is always subject to board approval.

It's clear that you will want to develop a logical and reliable way to estimate what your various expenses will be next year, and more than that, by quarterly or monthly periods.

In putting the annual plan to work, start with the detailed plans of program activities and support services worked out by the board. You'll need the following information to begin:

- How many people will you need to carry out these activities? With what skills, and for how long? When will any new people come on staff? What employee benefits and employer payroll taxes will be incurred?
- Where will they work and what facilities (space and equipment) will they need?
- Will they need transportation? How often, how far, and by what means?
- How often do you expect to advertise or do mailings, and how big is your mailing list?
- What part of these needed resources can you have donated as an "in-kind" contribution?

These are not all of your costs, but some of the larger ones that are most affected by plans and decisions of the board.

Notice that up to this point, money hasn't been mentioned—but only those things you automatically have to think about. *Next,* we'll talk about money.

LOGISTICS-BASED BUDGETING: SAYING IT ALL IN DOLLARS

Once the needed resources and their uses have been defined, each must be translated into dollars. Those closest to the process should be in the best position to calculate or estimate what each element in the plan (facilities, goods, and services) will cost. For example: payroll costs are the product and the sum of the number of people, the pay scales they will accept, the total hours per day and periods of time they'll be employed, plus "payroll fringe costs." These include payroll taxes and any benefits the nonprofit can offer (vacation pay, health insurance, pension costs, etc.).

Remember that only the mechanics of logistics-based budgeting will be covered here: should you project any expenses on an incremental basis, use the procedures explained previously.

Before attempting to write the new budget, it is useful to analyze budget variances (amounts over and under budgets). Analyzing such variations for the current budget period can be of help in budgeting for the next period, because they may reflect one or more of the weaknesses in the last budget, rather than poor performance or later events which required its revision.

The Five Most Common Errors in Budgets

1. Mistakes in arithmetic when pricing goods or services.

2. Known changes in prices or pay scales not taken into account. On the income side, this can also apply to changes in grants or contract rates.

3. Known changes in plans affecting quantities of goods and services, not taken into account.

4. Expense (or revenue) items overlooked in the budget.

5. Expense or revenue items included in error, that are no longer relevant.

Budgeting should be a collective effort; it will be harder for such errors to go unnoticed if enough people get in the act, or if someone has the job of checking prices, quantities, and arithmetic. Once a system is firmly in place, experience will guarantee that the leadership will get sharper in detecting errors. Budgeting is a skill you develop with experience.

Typical Examples of Budget Calculations

Salaries. Salaries are usually the largest and most important expense of a nonprofit, and they are often the easiest to project (Table 5–3).

Make a list of personnel you expect to have on the payroll (by job titles), and indicate their rate of pay for next year, and also by quarter and month. If you have hourly staff, you should calculate planned hours × hourly rate. Don't overlook overtime and provisions for covering vacation or other paid leave.

TABLE 5–3. SAMPLE ESTIMATE OF SALARIES

Position	Monthly salary[a]	Annual salary	Salary per quarter
Administration			
Executive Director	$1,667	$20,000	$ 5,000
Administrative assistant	667	8,000	2,000
Program A Director	1,333	16,000	4,000
Program B Director	1,500	18,000	4,500
Administrative assistant/secretary	750	9,000	2,250
Total salaries	$5,917	$71,000	$17,750

[a]Source: Board resolution, contract or current payroll records. These are all part-time scale.

"Pretty obvious and elementary," you might say. True, but not all expense items are that easy. Suppose that the staff were not all full-time, permanent employees, but one or more worked only part of the year. It would take a bit more figuring to get the total for the year, and for each quarter, or for each month, if you are preparing a month-to-month budget.

Note: Unless your revenue and expense levels are the same each month, budget items should be estimated—or at least broken down—by quarterly period, even month by month. The obvious way to derive monthly or quarterly estimates—dividing the year's totals by twelve (or four)—is more dangerous than helpful, because seasonal or periodic fluctuations cannot be taken into account.

Printing and stationery costs. Another example that's a bit more complex would be calculating printing and stationery costs. A problem might be deciding whether the expenses should be in the month the materials were bought, or if they should be spread over the periods in which they were used. As a practical matter, the latter procedure is usually not worth the time and effort involved. Table 5–4 offers a practical guide to making an annual estimate.

TABLE 5-4. SAMPLE ESTIMATE OF PRINTING AND STATIONERY COSTS

Item	Quantity per year	Price[a] amt./per	Annual cost	Bought per quarter
Letterheads	500	$30/1,000	$ 15	All in 1st Q
Envelopes	500	32/1,000	16	All in 1st Q
Brochures for Program B	1,000	30/100	300	$150 1st Q & 2nd Q
Fundraising letter (self-mailer)	500	50/100	250	$125 1st Q & 2nd Q
			$581	

[a]Estimating expenses frequently involves checking prices with suppliers of goods and services. The more carefully these are analyzed, the more accurate your estimates will be.

Making Means and Ends Meet

It is often desirable to consider both minimum and maximum (or optimum) amounts for many items. This is so because exact costs are hard to anticipate, and certain activities can sometimes be done either better *or* cheaper, which may mean using either more or less expensive resources. In such cases, budget strategies depend on how adequate and firm the funding prospects are. If financing looks promising, estimating expenses at generous levels will provide a cushion that may help prevent running short of funds later, as well as providing funds to do the best job possible. On the other hand, if there is a resistance to the proposed budget by the board, or if funding falls short, setting expenses at generous levels leaves room to cut back items, if necessary.

If preliminary totals of anticipated expenses are considerably *below* anticipated revenues—even using optimum expense levels—the board should consider whether to add or expand activities, or whether to replace or acquire additional capital equipment, or whether to accumulate funds for such acquisitions later on.

Should even minimal levels of expense exceed projected revenues, the board must develop ways to increase funding. Otherwise one or more activities or expense items must be scaled down or dropped. For example, substituting a temporary or part-time staff member for a full-time one, renting equipment rather than buying it, or using cheaper supplies. Perhaps certain required items of goods or services could be secured as an "in-kind" contributions, or some staff functions might be provided by volunteers.

The Qualitative Effect of Budgeting Changes

While efficiency and economy are important, the nonprofit is not a business, and cannot afford to lose its effectiveness to achieve them. That is why we put *first*, among the possible alternatives above, that of the board's shouldering its basic responsibility for providing essential funding.

A STEP-BY-STEP GUIDE TO PREPARING A BUDGET WORKSHEET

A budget worksheet offers an orderly and systematic way of doing well what is often done badly on the backs of old envelopes! The worksheet helps to organize the budgeting process in a way that helps to minimize errors and oversights.

Step 1—Expense Budget Worksheet

The expense budget worksheet (Table 5–5) is used to price out details and accumulate totals for each of the items in a budget. The detailed information itself is the key; a worksheet can only *organize* the process. The estimates of quantities and prices of goods and services are up to you. No worksheet can improve them.

TABLE 5–5. LOGISTICS-BASED EXPENSE BUDGET WORKSHEET

Item	Base Amount	Annual total[a]	Quarter Ending			
			Mar. 31	June 30	Sept. 30	Dec. 31
Salaries						
Exec. Dir.	$1667/mo	$20,000	$ 5,000	$ 5,000	$ 5,000	$ 5,000
Admin. assist.	667/mo	8,000	2,000	2,000	2,000	2,000
Prog. Dir A	1333/mo	16,000	4,000	4,000	4,000	4,000
Prog. Dir B	1500/mo	18,000	4,500	4,500	4,500	4,500
Admin. asst. B	750/mo	9,000	2,250	2,250	2,250	2,250
Total salaries		71,000	17,750	17,750	17,750	17,750
Payroll fringe costs[b]						
FICA		4,352	1,088	1,088	1,088	1,088
State unemp. ins. tax		810	479	236	95	—
Health ins.		2,500	625	625	625	625
Total fringe		7,662	2,192	1,949	1,808	1,713
Occupancy						
Rent (donated)	$500/mo	6,000	1,500	1,500	1,500	1,500
Utilities						
Elect. & heat	200/mo	2,400	600	600	600	600
Water	20/mo	240	60	60	60	60
Janitorial svce.	150/mo	1,800	450	450	450	450
Total occupancy		10,440	2,610	2,610	2,610	2,610
Telephone						
Administration	$50/mo	570	150	150	120	150
Program A	25/mo	275	75	75	50	75
Program B	25/mo	275	75	75	50	75
Total telephone		1,120	300	300	220	300
Printing & stationery[c]						
Letterhead—500 @ 30/M		15	15	(Based on acquisition,		
Envelopes—500 @ 32/M		16	16	not usage)		
Brochures, Prog. B, 1000 @ 30/C		300	150	150	(periods in	
Fundraising letter 500 @ 50/C		250	125	125	which used)	
Total printing & stationery		581	306	275		
Postage						
Administration—300 @ 25¢		75	20	20	15	20
Program B—600 @ 25¢		150	75	75		
Fundraising—200 @ 25¢		300	150	150		
Total postage[d]		525	245	245	15	20
Travel & conferences						
Administrative	$ 60/mo	650	180	180	120	180
Program A	50/mo	550	150	150	100	150
Program B	120/yr	110	30	30	20	30
Total travel & conferences		1,320	360	360	240	360
Subtotals (carried forward)		$92,648	$23,763	$23,489	$22,643	$22,753

TABLE 5–5. LOGISTICS-BASED EXPENSE BUDGET WORKSHEET (continued)

Item	Base Amount	Annual total[a]	Quarter Ending Mar. 31	June 30	Sept. 30	Dec. 31
Subtotals (brought forward)		$92,648	$23,763	$23,489	$22,643	$22,753
Supplies						
Program A: "x" - 60 @ $19		1,140	570	300	270	
Program B: (unknown)		—	—	—	—	—
Total supplies (timing based on acquisition, not usage)		1,140	570	300	270	—
Equipment rentals (Prog. B)						
Office typewriter	$300/yr	300	75	75	75	75
Copying machine	$960/yr	960	240	240	240	240
Automobile	$95/mo	1,045	285	285	190	285
Total equipment rental		2,305	600	600	505	600
Professional fees						
Consultants						
Fundraising	$2,400/yr	2,400	600	600	600	600
Program B	2,400/yr	2,400	600	600	600	600
Legal	500/yr	500	125	125	125	125
Accounting						
Quarterly fee	150/Q	600	150	150	150	150
Annual audit	500/yr	500	500			
Total professional fees		6,400	1,975	1,475	1,475	1,475
Miscellaneous expenses						
Office expense	$30/mo	330	90	90	60	90
Insurance						
Liability	200/yr	200	50	50	50	50
Workmen's comp.	300/yr	300	75	75	75	75
Fire	100/yr	100	25	25	25	25
Contingency reserve	1,000/yr	1,000	250	250	250	250
Total miscellaneous expense		1,930	490	490	460	490
Grand Totals		$104,423	$27,398	$26,354	$25,353	$25,318

[a]Lower amounts in certain categories in the 3rd Quarter are due to closing shop during July.

[b]Payroll fringe costs (taxes and benefits): FICA is the IRS abbreviation for Social Security Tax. Not many nonprofits calculate each of these items separately as shown above, preferring the shortcut of using a flat percentage of payroll for all periods. The average for the year shown above would have been 10.79%; it varies each quarter, as employees exceed the cut-off ceiling on unemployment insurance. (A flat amount using 11% could have been used for all quarters to simplify the job.)

[c]The cost of letterheads and envelopes is shown in the period to be bought, not in the period used. To show the alternative method, brochures and fundraising letters were treated as expense in period used.

[d]1990 first class rate. Lower nonprofit rate may be available.

You'll notice on the worksheet that the list of budgeted salaries shown earlier in Table 5–3 makes up the first group of words and figures. The only difference is that we've set up four quarterly columns so that we can derive quarterly totals later on.

You'll also see that the calculations for printing and stationery expenses from Table 5–4 make up another group. The other expense categories and amounts are intended to represent typical examples, and are by no means all the items that might be included. All items except the "Payroll Fringe Costs" group should be self-explanatory. Payroll fringe costs, which include payroll taxes and, in this case, health insurance, are explained in detail in Chapter 17. (See also footnote b, Table 5–5.)

Step 2—Preparing the Operating Budget

The first thing you will have to decide is which form of budget to use. There is no single standard or best form. Because it must reflect the activities of organizations that come in many sizes and shapes, and which conduct activities of innumerable types, a budget is more a concept than a standard format. Although general-purpose formats for budgets and budget worksheets are illustrated later in this chapter, they must be designed or adapted to meet the specific needs of the nonprofit using them.

How to "Invent" a Line-Item Budget

Once you have the raw data you need for budgeting (revenues and expenses), what should your budget look like? First of all, you're probably wondering if you need all those complicated calculations in the budget itself. Chances are you'll agree the answer is "no." Second, it is obviously necessary to compare expenses against revenues to see if they are "covered." Finally, since you'll need to use the budget more than just once a year, you'll want to divide it into a series of monthly or quarterly budgets.

Putting these ideas into operation, you'll end up with the simplest budget format—the one used most widely by small or new nonprofits, the "line-item" budget (Table 5–6). It consists of columns of figures for the year and by quarter, showing the total amount budgeted for each kind of expense (salaries, rent, etc.) without regard to program or activity. This form may be adequate for a small and non-complex nonprofit, one with only a single kind of activity.

There is one rule that applies to every form of budget: if the budget is to be of any value in evaluating actual results, it must be prepared using the same classifications, categories, and accounting methods as those used in the financial reports. For example, the budgeted cost of apples cannot be readily compared with the actual cost of the apples bought, if the latter are included in an expense item called "Fruit." (This will be spelled out more clearly in Chapter 12, under the explanation of Charts of Accounts.)

The data in Table 5–6 come from the Schedule of Estimated Revenues (Table 5–2) and the Expense Budget Worksheet (Table 5–5).

Now, trace the figures, item by item, from the Revenue Schedule and Expense Worksheets to the Operating Budget, and you will notice that the amounts have merely been transferred (or "posted," in accounting jargon) from the worksheets to the budget itself, using the quarterly columns provided to make it easy to obtain a total for each quarter.

TABLE 5–6. CENTER FOR COMMUNITY SERVICE, INC.
QUARTERLY OPERATING BUDGET (LINE-ITEM FORMAT)

		Quarter ending[a]			
	Annual total	**Mar. 31**	**June 30**	**Sept. 30**	**Dec. 31**
Estimated Revenues					
Foundation grants					
ABC (Program A—approved)	$ 15,000	$ 5,000	$ 5,000	$ 5,000	—
XYZ (Program B—pending)	46,000	15,000	11,000	10,000	$10,000
Government grants					
(Admin. assistant—approved)	8,800	2,200	2,200	2,200	2,200
In-kind contribution (free rent)	6,000	1,500	1,500	1,500	1,500
Fundraising events	11,000		5,000		6,000
Revenues from Program A					
Services (show by program)	17,000	4,000	5,000	3,000	5,000
Membership dues (100 @ $27)	2,700	1,000	500	200	1,000
Interest income	500	125	125	125	125
Total estimated revenues	107,000	28,825	30,325	22,025	25,825
Budgeted expenses					
Salaries	71,000	17,750	17,750	17,750	17,750
Payroll fringe costs	7,662	2,192	1,949	1,808	1,713
Occupancy	10,440	2,610	2,610	2,610	2,610
Telephone	1,120	300	300	220	300
Printing & stationery	581	306	275		
Postage	525	245	245	15	20
Travel & conferences	1,320	360	360	240	360
Supplies	1,140	570	300	270	
Equipment rentals	2,305	600	600	505	600
Professional fees	6,400	1,975	1,475	1,475	1,475
Office expenses	330	90	90	60	90
Insurance	600	150	150	150	150
Contingency reserve	1,000	250	250	250	250
Total expenses before depreciation[b]	104,423	27,398	26,354	25,353	25,318
Depreciation[c]	2,577	645	644	644	644
Total budgeted expenses	$107,000	$28,043	$26,998	$25,997	$25,962
Excess of revenue over expense	–0–	$ 782	$ 3,327		
Excess of expense over revenue[d]	–0–			$ 3,972	$ 137

[a]Quarterly, rather than monthly, columns have been used here, to save space. An operating budget finds maximum usefulness for control and evaluation purposes when it is set up and compared with actual revenues and expenses on a month-to-month basis.

[b]In preparing budgets from worksheets, make use of the grand total or any other group totals as a cross-check of accuracy in transferring figures. For example, the five column totals above marked "Total expenses before depreciation" should agree with the corresponding figures on the "Grand totals" line in the worksheet (Table 5–5).

[c]Depreciation is included for the sake of completeness and comparability with financial reports. For the reasons for using it and where the figures come from, see Chapter 10.

[d]Interim excesses of expenses over revenues, as shown in the third quarter, are not significant in an operating budget, which is usually prepared on an accrual basis (see Chapter 6); i.e., the timing of expenses is based on date incurred, not when paid. They are crucial, however, in a cash budget, or where the operating budget takes such timing into account.

USING COST BEHAVIOR PATTERNS IN BUDGETING

Just to get the feel of this subject, just suppose you had only one program, and your board planned to increase its activity level, in terms of the number of people served next year, by 25%. If this year's total expenses are $80,000, would you advise the board that you will need $20,000 more (25% more money) to cover increased costs? Most people, even if it's a new question, give the right answer to that question intuitively. They point out that not all expenses would increase in the same proportion as the number of clients.

While some costs are *variable* (change in proportion to activity level), others are *fixed* (do not change with the activity level). Thus your rent is usualy fixed, unless you add space; program supplies used generally vary with the number of clients.

Now suppose you've determined that a quarter of your current expense is variable, the rest fixed. You'd then be in a position to give your board a more reliable rough estimate of how much more funding you'd need, as follows:

	Present costs	Increase	Next year
Variable costs	$20,000 (25%)	$5,000	$25,000
Fixed costs	60,000	–0–	60,000
Total	$80,000	$5,000	$85,000

Without considering this distinction, you'd be exaggerating the size of the problem.

Keep somewhere in the back of your mind, nevertheless, that even fixed costs are only fixed within a certain range of activity, which accountants call the "relevant range." For example, with your present program space, you can often handle up to a certain number of clients. Above that number you might need more space; considerably below it, you may need less—meaning possibly less rent to pay.

Knowledge of how your agency's own costs behave can be an important budgeting tool. Note at this point that all expenses can be classified into one of the following behavior patterns:

1. Variable costs, which change in proportion to some activity level (not always number of clients).

2. Fixed costs, which are unaffected by changes in activity level.

3. Mixed costs, which are part variable, part fixed. Telephone expense, for example: a fixed minimum charge, plus variable charges depending on usage—which incidentally may vary with fundraising activity rather than number of clients. (Some people call these "semi-variable costs.")

4. Step-variable fixed costs are used to describe fixed costs that go up in jumps (steps) when activity increases by certain numbers. An example would be salaries of case workers, teachers, or nurses, who could each handle up to a certain number of people; above that number, you'd need to add salary for another person in that job category.

(These cost behavior patterns are illustrated graphically in Fig. 5–2.)

Using these cost behaviors makes possible still another budgeting approach, *flexible budgeting*.

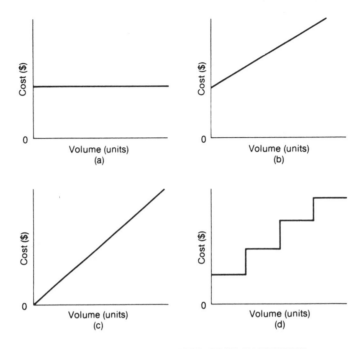

FIGURE 5-2. COST BEHAVIOR PATTERNS:
(a) fixed costs, (b) mixed costs, (c) variable costs, (d) step-variable costs.

FLEXIBLE BUDGETING AND COST BEHAVIOR

You now have a fourth approach to budgeting, which you can use in some cases instead of the other three or in combination with one of them. You might also use it to get a preliminary or tentative idea of your next year's budget, while awaiting the full process to take its course. You could use your new understanding of cost behavior as follows:

1. Variable costs: First find either the cost per unit of service (number of clients, hours, etc.) for each type of expense, or the percentage of the total revenue of the activity that type of expense represents. Next, project the planned number of service units, or the estimated revenue from that activity, and multiply it by either the cost per unit or the variable cost percentage already determined, whichever is appropriate.

2. Fixed costs: Unless there is a known increase in an item of expense, it can be the same as last year. Otherwise any necessary adjustment can readily be added, such as a rent increase, planned raise in salaries or employee benefits, increase in a payroll tax rate or taxable ceiling. Don't overlook any required increases for step-variable fixed costs resulting from planned increases in level of an activity. As we will discuss in Chapter 6, other true fixed costs do not increase based on increases in the number of service units, so don't make the mistake of trying to use a "fixed cost per unit," since the more units fixed costs are divided by, the lower the cost per unit!

3. Mixed costs: These require a two-step calculation as noted: the fixed portion is handled as a fixed cost, the same as above; the variable portion as a variable cost. Mixed costs can be tricky, because the variable portion does not necessarily change in proportion to changes in the number of service units. The variable may be other usage of the item, such as increased telephone expense for fundraising. This fact must be taken into account in budgeting or other uses of the data. Only when mixed costs are large in amount will this make much difference.

It's not always easy to know how much of a mixed cost is fixed. Telephone expense is clearly reported on the monthly statement. Other costs, like utilities, may have some normal minimum regardless of activity level; for example, you use a certain amount of electricity just to keep your office open. If mixed costs are big enough to warrant the effort, there are ways to separate their fixed and variable components, as shown below.

Separating Mixed Costs into Their Components

There are several methods for separating mixed costs into their components,[2] but only a simple one is given here. It is known as "HI–LO" analysis, and can be used to project the behavior of a single mixed cost, or even to obtain a rough projection of total operating costs, where there is a fairly stable level of fixed costs and a linear—i.e., proportional—relationship between the variable portion and the volume of activity. To analyze a single mixed cost, such as Supplies Used, you first list the cost of supplies used for a series of months in the recent past, and the volume of activity for the same periods, as follows (here, number of clients determined activity level):

Month	Activity level (No. of clients served)	Cost of supplies used
Jan.	100	$250
Feb.	200	450
Mar.	250	550
Apr.	300	650
May	220	490

Next, select the lowest month (in this case January) and subtract each of the two figures from the related ones from the highest month (April):

	Volume	Cost
High (April)	300	$650
Low (Jan.)	100	250
Increase	200	400

Then, since the cost of supplies increased $400 with an increase in volume of activity of 200, the variable portion of Supplies Expense is taken to be $\$400/200$, or $2 per client. The fixed portion of Supplies Expense can then be found by using either the high or low month and subtracting from its total Supplies Expense the variable portion associated with that volume level, as follows:

[2]The others are "scatter diagrams" and regression analysis, which are explained in texts on managerial accounting.

	High (Apr.)	Low (Jan.)	
Number of clients	300	100	(n)
Multiply by variable cost per client	× $2	× $2	(VC)
Total variable costs	600	200	
Balance of total cost of supplies (fixed)	50	50	(FC)
Total supplies expense	$650	$250	(TC)

In other words, Fixed Cost (FC) equals Total Cost (TC) minus total Variable Cost (VC). Note that it is $50 in both cases.

Now supplies Expense can be projected for any planned level of activity by the simple formula FC + n(VC); in this case the estimated expense, for say 280 clients expected in June, would be $610, calculated as follows:

$$\frac{FC + n(VC)}{\$50 + (280 \times \$2)} = \frac{TC}{\$610}$$

The same forumla can be developed for any mixed cost. The one other thing to watch out for is that fixed costs can change, if there is a change in level of activity that results in adding people to the payroll or requires additional rent for more space, for example. The formula works only within a particular range of activity (the "relevant range") in which fixed costs are stable.

Projecting Total Operating Expenses

Analysis of operating expenses in total can be used to yield a crude projection of what total expenses would be at varying levels of volume. Instead of a single kind of expense, total expense is used, along with activity level. This is more useful for brainstorming than for actual budgeting, where the question is, "What if?" To be specific, one can ask and answer the question: "What if our level of activity were to increase (or decrease) from its present level to a level of X clients (or other volume measure)? What would total expenses be, approximately, and therefore, how much more money would we need?"

The question of the relevant range would be of great importance in such a projection, and any increase in fixed costs that would be necessitated by the increase in volume (additional payroll, space, etc.) would have to be added to the fixed component of total costs in arriving at the estimate.

BUDGETING OF PROGRAMS AND FUNCTIONS

Annual IRS Form 990 and state information returns of nonprofits require that each item of expense be broken down to show the portions incurred for programs, management (administration), and fundraising. In addition, the total expense of each program is required for Form 990, and for each item of program expense, by certain state forms. This presents a problem, especially for smaller nonprofits, whose accounting systems rarely provide the program breakdowns, without reworking the figures or making "guesstimates."

In some cases, even though a nonprofit has more than one program or service, the activities overlap or are integrated under the direction of a single manager. In such cases, if segregating the costs of each is too difficult, or if evaluating them—or the manager—separately is genuinely not worthwhile, then it may not make sense to try budgeting and tracking them individually.

If that expedient is used, it is still very much worthwhile to budget and track the three broad categories—program, management, and fundraising expenses—separately. Such tracking provides control and evaluation, useful by-products of the IRS requirement.

Too few nonprofits are able to use their budgets effectively for control or evaluation. If costs are lumped together, even when programs are individually budgeted, the result is often to discourage program budgeting altogether, certainly to make such a budget something that is never used during the year. Yet without program budgeting, a budget cannot become the powerful instrument it can be, as explained in the Overview of Part Two under "The Payoff for Sound Budgetary Control."

Program budgeting—more properly termed *functional budgeting*—includes a breakdown of each line item into portions that apply to each major function of the agency: programs, administration (management), and fundraising. (Chapters 11 and 12 will show how to set up the books so that you can compare actual with budgeted figures, in order to monitor and control income and expense, and to evaluate how well you're doing during the year.)

"Inventing" the Program, or Functional, Budget

How do you accomplish budgeting by cost categories? One look at your expense worksheet (Table 5–5) will make it clear that

1. You can't use the group totals.

2. You can pick out the expense items specific to each program ("A" and "B") and to fundraising, plus a few that seem specific to general administration. One need not be a CPA to take the next step intuitively. Group them by program and by each of the "support services," as general administration and fundraising are usually called. What you're doing is reshuffling them. (See Table 5–5).

Looking back, we have achieved what we set out to do. Notice that the layered form of program budget shown in Table 5–7 can actually be used whether the nonprofit has only a single program, a group of activities and programs sharing the same staff and facilities, or separately administered program activities. These are shown here as line items grouped by program and by general administration and fundraising functions. (This is the format of a typical government budget, which is often referred to as a line-item budget, even though the items are grouped by program.)

TABLE 5–7. CENTER FOR COMMUNITY SERVICE, INC.
QUARTERLY OPERATING BUDGET[a] (PROGRAM OR "FUNCTIONAL" LAYERED FORMAT)

	Annual Total	Quarter Ending			
		Mar. 31	June 30	Sept. 30	Dec. 31
Estimated revenues					
Foundation grants					
ABC (Program "A"—approved)	$ 15,000	$ 5,000	$ 5,000	$ 5,000	—
XYZ (Program "B"—pending)	46,000	15,000	11,000	10,000	$10,000
Government grants					
State (Admin. assistant—approved)	8,800	2,200	2,200	2,200	2,200
In-kind contrib. (free rent)	6,000	1,500	1,500	1,500	1,500
Fundraising events	11,000		5,000		6,000
Revenues from Program "A"					
Services (show by program)	17,000	4,000	5,000	3,000	5,000
Membership dues (100 @ $27)	2,700	1,000	500	200	1,000
Interest income	500	125	125	125	125
Total estimated revenue	107,000	28,825	30,325	22,025	25,825
Budgeted expenses					
A. *Program services*					
Program A					
Salary—Program Director	16,000	4,000	4,000	4,000	4,000
Payroll fringe costs	1,642	478	424	370	370
Travel—P.D. & volunteers	550	150	150	100	150
Telephone	275	75	75	50	75
Supplies	1,140	570	300	270	
Total program A	19,607	5,273	4,949	4,790	4,595
Program B (tentative) (direct costs only)					
Salaries—Director & assistant	27,000	6,750	6,750	6,750	6,750
Payroll fringe costs	2,980	846	765	705	664
Consultant	2,400	600	600	600	600
Telephone	275	75	75	50	75
Travel expense	110	30	30	20	30
Equipment rental	2,305	600	600	505	600
Printing brochures	300	150	150		
Postage	150	75	75		
Total Program B	35,520	9,126	9,045	8,630	8,719
Total program costs	55,127	14,399	13,994	13,420	13,314
B. *Support services*[b]					
Administrative salaries	28,000	7,000	7,000	7,000	7,000
Payroll fringe costs	3,040	868	760	733	679
Travel & conferences	660	180	180	120	180
Legal & accounting	1,600	775	2675	275	275
Occupancy	10,440	2,610	2,610	2,610	2,610
Telephone	570	150	150	120	150
Stationery & postage	106	51	20	15	20
Miscellaneous expenses (combined)	1,930	490	490	460	490
Total administrative expenses (carried forward)	$ 46,346	$12,124	$11,485	$11,333	$11,404

TABLE 5–7. CENTER FOR COMMUNITY SERVICE, INC.
QUARTERLY OPERATING BUDGET[a] (PROGRAM OR " FUNCTIONAL" LAYERED FORMAT) (continued)

	Annual Total	Quarter Ending			
		Mar. 31	June 30	Sept. 30	Dec. 31
Total administrative expenses (brought forward)	$ 46,346	$12,124	$11,485	$11,333	$11,404
Fundraising					
Consultants	2,400	600	600	600	600
Printing	250	125	125		
Postage	300	150	150		
Total fundraising expenses	2,950	875	600	600	
Total support services	49,926	12,999	12,360	11,933	12,004
Total expenses before depreciation	104,423	27,398	26,354	25,353	25,318
C. *Depreciation*	2,577	645	644	644	644
Total budgeted expenses	$107,000	$28,043	$26,998	$25,997	$25,962
Excess of revenue over expenses	–0–	$ 782	$ 3,327		
Excess of expenses over revenue[c]	–0–			$ 3,972	$ 137

Note: Expense amounts are those developed in the Expense Budget Worksheet, Table 5–5.

[a]To have any value in controlling expenditures and evaluating performance, the account classifications in the budget must correspond to those in the financial statements.

[b]Note that no allocation has been made of the portion of certain fixed overhead costs applicable to program or fundraising services, such as Occupancy costs, although other joint costs such as telephone have been allocated on an estimated basis.

[c]Interim excesses of expenses over revenues, as shown in the third quarter, are not significant in an operating budget, which is usually prepared on an accrual basis (see Chapter 6); i.e., the timing of expenses is based on date incurred, not when paid. They are crucial, however, in a cash budget, or where the operating budget takes such timing into account.

Program, or "Functional," Budgets in Columnar (Matrix) Form

The budget format shown below in Table 5–8 is used generally in larger nonprofits, but is applicable to all, primarily for annual budgeting and external financial reporting. (The same format is also used by some states, such as New York and Massachusetts, in the annual report forms required of tax-exempt organizations.)

This format is a more compact and integrated presentation of expense data, which permits analysis by either line-item (natural expense) classification, or by program and support functions, and it cross-references both. Where programs are revenue-producing, as in the performing arts, revenues can be directly compared with related expenses, to determine their adequacy. The format can also be used where there are retricted funds: Program B is a case in point.

TABLE 5–8. CENTER FOR COMMUNITY SERVICE, INC.
ANNUAL OPERATING BUDGET (PROGRAM OR "FUNCTIONAL" COLUMNAR FORMAT)

	Total	Program services		Support services	
		A	**B**	**Administration**	**Fundraising**
Estimated revenues	$107,000	$32,000	$46,000	—	$29,000
Budgeted expenses					
Salaries	71,000	16,000	27,000	$28,000	
Payroll fringe costs	7,662	1,642	2,980	3,040	
Occupancy*	10,440			10,440	
Telephone	1,120	275	275	570	
Printing & stationery	581		300	31	250
Postage	525		150	75	300
Travel & conferences	1,320	550	110	660	
Supplies	1,140	1,140			
Equipment rentals	2,305		2,305		
Professional fees	6,400		2,400	1,600	2,400
Office expenses	330			330	
Insurance *	600			600	
Contingency reserve	1,000			1,000	
Total expenses before depreciation	104,423	19,607	35,520	46,346	2,950
Depreciation*	2,577			2,577	
Total budgeted expenses	$107,000	$19,607	$35,520	$48,923	$ 2,950

Note: Data compiled from Table 5–5. Revenues are combined. Revenues are shown only in total, to save space. All nonprogram revenues have been arbitrarily assigned to fundraising for convenience, although there is no clear relationship. (A fifth column could be added for unallocated items.

*This format also raises more clearly the question of whether certain joint costs should be allocated. Here, Occupancy costs and Insurance are shown under Administration, although they would probably cover all four functions, and would be allocated on an external financial report, as might depreciation.

The columnar format is useful primarily as a bird's-eye view or x-ray on an annual basis, since it cannot easily be used for control or evaluation on a monthly or quarterly basis. It is useful for comparison with annual operating statements prepared in the same format for external reporting. (See Chapter 15). Another version, in which all joint and other overhead costs are allocated to program services, is explained and illustrated in Chapter 6.

It is not essential to prepare special budget worksheets in order to divide the budget itself horizontally into separate programs, general administration, and fundraising functions. The figures for each can be derived from the worksheets shown, and then transferred into columnar form if desired. Table 5–8 shows a final budget in this form, which permits later comparison with Operating Statement data presented in the same form.

If, despite reservations noted in Chapter 6, the budget is designed to allocate all overhead expenses to program and support functions, a separate worksheet is needed to lay out such calculations. This would ordinarily apply only to a nonprofit with revenue-producing programs, such as a performing arts group, or to an organization with one or more restricted grant funds, which must be accounted for separately. This is discussed in detail in Chapter 6.

When a Contingency Format Is Needed

Where funding for a new program or expansion is based on a pending grant, the contingency form of budget, shown in Table 5–9 permits board approval regardless of the outcome. Here the revenues and expenses of new Program "B" are shown in a separate column. Either the left- or right-hand column then becomes the final budget, depending on whether the grant is approved. (If the grant is refused, the board would either have to find another $10,480, or find a way to reduce expenses by that amount. The illustration here assumes that the grant is all but definite.)

TABLE 5–9. CENTER FOR COMMUNITY SERVICE, INC.
CONTINGENCY OPERATING BUDGET FORMAT (Data condensed from Table 5–8)

	Existing or basic programs	New/expanded programs	
		Required increases	Expanded budget
Anticipated revenues[a]		**(Program B)**	
Foundation grants			
ABC Foundation (approved)	$15,000		$15,000
XYZ Foundation (pending)		$46,000[b]	46,000
Other Sources	46,000		46,000
Total anticipated revenues	$61,000	$46,000	$107,000
Budgeted expenses[a]			
A. Support services[c]	49,296		49,296
B. Program services			
Program A	19,607		19,607
Program B		35,520	35,520
C. Depreciation	2,577		2,577
Total budgeted expenses	71,480	35,520	107,000
Excess of revenue over expenses		$ 10,480	–0–
Excess of expenses over revenue	$10,480		–0–

[a]See details of revenues and expenses in the annual total column of Table 5–7. In practice, the budget would show the same detail as that shown in the annual total column of Table 5–7, but not quarterly or monthly amounts, until the budget is finalized.

[b]It is assumed that $10,480 or about 21% of Support Service expenses, has been included in the grant proposal budget for Program B. It has not been allocated here, but accounts for the excess revenues for Program B and would cover the shortage in the existing budget level. In other words, grant approval would balance the budget by picking up part of overhead.

[c]For the sake of simplicity, it has been assumed that no increase in Support Services would result from adding the new program, which may not be the case.

USE IT OR LOSE IT—LEARNING BY DOING

The best way to master budgeting basics is by putting what you've read in this chapter to work immediately, even if your next annual budgeting period is a long way off. A suggestion: use the budget worksheets and formats in this chapter as soon as possible, starting with Tables 5–2 and 5–5. You might want to start by using them to budget the next quarter.

Now that we've taken a good look at the basic ideas involved in budgeting, the next chapter considers some of the more subtle and tricky aspects of the subject, which you'll find has some sophisticated angles.

Chapter 6

Internal Program Budgeting: The More Subtle Issues

Now that we have explored the essence of operational budgeting, let's look at some important issues that enter the budgeting picture:

- Organizational aspects of the budget process: who should do it and why
- Games people play with budgets
- The budget in controlling
- Responsibility accounting and organizational control
- Allocating joint costs and overhead
- Other accounting problems in budgeting such as accrual vs. cash basis, and donated goods and services
- The power of break-even analysis

The material in this chapter will give you a good working knowledge of operating budgets. More advanced aspects will call for the services of a professional, or someone with firsthand experience.

BUDGETING: TOP-DOWN OR BOTTOM-UP?

In Chapter 4, some of the common roles and relationships in a typical nonprofit were described. The trouble with organizational charts is that they imply a bureaucratic process that matches their vertical structure. But this is not the case with a good many successful organizations. A nonprofit organization's main "invested capital" is the collective idealism of everyone involved—regardless of official title or job description. Teamwork is what matters. And the teamwork concept must start with the budget-making process itself. If the budget is to be fully accepted and carried out, every key member of the team has to support it enthusiastically. Each must feel a sense of ownership in the plan—never that it has been imposed from above or from the outside.

HOW TO MAKE SURE EVERYONE BUYS THE BUDGET

1. *The Board.* Unless they are involved in the budget-making process, board members may not become directly involved in fundraising, a key function. If they merely "rubber-stamp" someone else's budget, they will feel no sense of shared responsibility, either for obtaining projected amounts of funding, or for turning plans into realities. Worse, they may later assume the role of critics. Ultimate responsibility for planning lies with the board. And the budget, which expresses those plans, is their responsibility to adopt.

2. *The Officers.* The need for a sense of personal "ownership" applies with special force to the officers and committee chairpeople, for they are involved in overseeing or carrying out the activities planned in the budget. Naturally, if they participate in planning and budgeting activities, they will have an interest in seeing that these activities succeed. (A common alibi—in the absence of such participation and commitment—is "No one asked me about it, so why blame me if it doesn't work?")

3. *The Staff.* As the ones closest to the front line, with a close-up view of what works, the intimate familiarity of the staff with what needs to be done, and what it takes to do it, is absolutely essential to the budget process. Without major input from the staff, their answer to any criticism will be the one cited above. Any organization that ignores this reality, and hands them a budget as a finished product of the board or its officers and committees, courts disaster.

There is, however, the reverse of this issue. If the staff—or worse, the CEO alone—prepares the budget merely for unquestioning board approval, the board members will probably not have a psychological investment in its success. There is also a substantial risk that the plan will be unrealistic, overly ambitious (or overly modest), and that either adequate funding will be impossible (especially with reduced board commitment), or that the planned activity level will be too low to carry out the nonprofit's purposes. The first alternative will result from unrealistic optimism, the other from a play-it-safe attitude more typical of bureaucrats in business or government. They may be more concerned with covering their flanks than with effective achievement of the organization's stated goals.

An example of a budget calendar for a multi-layered organization is shown in Fig. 6–1. This is for a complex nonprofit which has departments, some of which supervise programs. Note that the role of Controller/Accountant is purely mechanical for expense budgets ("assembles"). The only time he or she should *prepare* the income budget is when it is quite stable, and based on predictable revenues. A staff or committee Budget Request Form is shown at Fig. 6–2.

GAMES PEOPLE PLAY WITH BUDGETS

In any size nonprofit, especially one with a number of programs or activities under different managers, the necessary budget requests often take on an element of gamesmanship. This behavioral aspect of the budget process has been fully described by Robert N. Anthony and Regina Herzlinger in *Management Control in Nonprofit Organizations,* Rev. Ed. (Homewood, Ill.: Richard D. Irwin, Inc., 1980),[1] a basic reference work of particular value for leaders of larger or complex nonprofit organizations.

[1] See "Budget Ploys," p. 344ff.

TASK	TARGET DATE	RESPONSIBILITY
I. PREPARE PRELIMINARY DESCRIPTION OF ALL PROGRAMS PLANNED FOR NEXT YEAR	AUG. 1	DEPARTMENT HEADS OR PROGRAM DIRECTORS
Objectives		
Advantages		
Personnel Requirements		
Estimated Cost		
II. PREPARE FIRST DRAFT OF DEPARTMENTAL BUDGET	SEPT. 1	DEPARTMENT HEADS
III. ASSEMBLE EXPENSE BUDGETS	SEPT. 15	CONTROLLER/ACCOUNTANT[a]
IV. PREPARE INCOME BUDGET	SEPT. 15	CONTROLLER/ACCOUNTANT
V. REVIEW FIRST DRAFT OF BUDGET	OCT. 10	BUDGET COMMITTEE
VI. FINAL DECISIONS ON NEXT YEAR PROGRAM	OCT. 30	BUDGET OR EXECUTIVE COMMITTEE
VII. REVISION AS REQUIRED	NOV. 15	DESIGNATED DEPARTMENT HEADS
VII. PRESENTATION TO BOARD OF DIRECTORS OR MEMBERS	DEC. 1	EXECUTIVE DIRECTOR

Source: Joseph K. Barry and Charles Mundt, *Financial Management Handbook for Associations.*, U.S. Chamber of Commerce, Washington, D.C., 1973, p. 28.

FIGURE 6-1. BUDGET PREPARATION TIMETABLE.

Budget request for fiscal year ending: _____ , 19 _____   Date submitted: _____

Activity (identify *one*): _____   Committee: _____
                                                                      (Name)

Program: _____   Administration: _____   Fundraising: _____
                  (Name)

Name of person making request (print): _____

Signature: _____   Title: _____

DETAILS OF PROPOSED BUDGET ALLOWANCES:

Item	July–Sept	Oct–Dec	Jan–Mar	Apr–June	Total
Program supplies	_____	_____	_____	_____	_____
Office supplies	_____	_____	_____	_____	_____
Equipment (list below)	_____	_____	_____	_____	_____
Local transportation (Via: _____)	_____	_____	_____	_____	_____
Travel allowance (for: _____)	_____	_____	_____	_____	_____
Copying & printing (explain below):	_____	_____	_____	_____	_____
Postage (explain):	_____	_____	_____	_____	_____
Telephone (estimate):	_____	_____	_____	_____	_____
Other (identify):					
_____	_____	_____	_____	_____	_____
				Total:	_____

Explain equipment or other major items below:

Quantity	Unit of Measure	Category and Description	Est. Unit Price	Estimated Total
_____	_____	_____	_____	_____
_____	_____	_____	_____	_____
_____	_____	_____	_____	_____
_____	_____	_____	_____	_____

FIGURE 6–2. BUDGET REQUEST FORM

The most obvious game in budget negotiations is the one played between the upper and lower layers of leadership. The upper level offers less than it is willing to allow; the lower one asks for more than is really needed, to be safe (called "padding.") Somewhere in between what is asked for and what is offered, a compromise both can live with is arrived at, and horse trading usually ends with both sides saving face. Other games, which may or may not be played consciously, sometimes affect the process:

Other Common Budget Ploys

Game or Ploy	Retort
"But that's not too much: it's only what we spent last year, plus an adjustment for inflation."	"So what? What do we really *need* to spend?"
"I have a better handle on these costs than you do. Why not just take my word for it?"	"OK, *show* me."
"Without the full amount, we just can't function effectively."	"Be specific as to why that is so."
Burying sticky items in broader categories; i.e., those most likely to be challenged or reduced.	"Please supply greater detail."
Maneuvering against a budget cut by singling out essential areas as those that will have to be cut back, gambling that the cuts will be restored to avoid hurting the organization, e.g., cutting program costs rather than administrative costs.	"Why were *these* areas selected, not others?"

THE BUDGET AND EXPENSE CONTROL

If the budget is to be an action plan, it exists to be followed. It is not, however, a straitjacket. The budget is a projection of expected events and activities, of what funds they will bring in, and of what costs they will incur. As long as these expectations prove valid, the budget is the board's authorization to incur the related costs. When anticipated funding falls through, or costs unexpectedly increase by means outside the organization's control—say, a big rent increase—the flight plan must be adjusted; the budget must be revised to reflect reduced or altered funding and areas in which expenses will have to be cut back.

If genuine control over expenditures is to be achieved, there must be a way of using the budget as a guide to decisions involving commitment of funds. Most commitments are more or less long-term, fixed amounts, such as overhead costs, administrative salaries, and rent. Costs of program activities are more controllable and variable, and involve either decisions about activity and expenditure levels, or about the timing of costs during the year. To "come out even" with budget authorizations, data must be made available monthly—or at least quarterly—regarding the following:

1. Budgeted expenditures for the year-to-date.

2. Expenses actually incurred—whether or not yet paid—up to the same date.

RESPONSIBILITY ACCOUNTING AND ORGANIZATIONAL CONTROL

A major concept in managerial accounting, of which budgetary control is a part, is that of "responsibility accounting." In a nonprofit, that means that managers are accountable for the program or function that is their responsibility. In using a format referred to earlier, one that breaks down the budget by programs and by support functions (each activity is a "cost center"), the manager accepts responsibility for the agreed budgeted amounts, and is then held accountable for implementing that budget.

Subsequent comparison—on operating statements using the same format— of actual expenditures with budgeted amounts, becomes an effective control device. The administrator of a particular activity has no alibi for deviations from budget—at best a persuasive explanation of circumstances that were beyond his or her control.

Strictly speaking, the program director or other functional administrator cannot be held responsible for costs over which he or she has no control. Thus, a viewpoint that argues against allocation of indirect costs applies with considerable force, where a budget or operating statement charges an administrator with expenses controlled by someone else. This viewpoint will be developed in the next section. Such decisions and how they affect performance evaluation are covered in Chapter 13.

Allocating Joint Costs to Programs and Functions

One of the most troublesome problems in budgeting and accounting is what to do about costs that cannot be solely attributed to a particular activity or function, but that would be incurred whether or not the activity existed. These are generally referred to as "overhead" or "indirect" costs, sometimes also as "joint costs." They do not vary directly with the level of activity, even where directly related to the activity itself. An example would be a single rent paid for a building or suite of offices used by various functions and programs of the nonprofit. Another would be the time an executive director spent in direct supervision of a program, or in direct fundraising activity, requiring an allocation of part of his or her salary to that program or activity.

One school of thought holds that all such joint costs must be fully charged to each program and function of the organization, because the segments could not operate effectively without those services. If there are program revenues, such as admissions or fees for services, the operating budget will then project an anticipated "profit" or "loss" from each program or service, after *all* costs— both direct and allocated—have been taken into account (Fig. 6–3). The basic philosophy underlying this "full cost" concept is that service revenues and support must cover all relevant costs and stand on their own. It is a "bottom-line" concept, and is prescribed by the rules of the American Institute of CPAs for financial reporting to external users. (Those rules do not cover internal reporting; see Chapter 10).

Why Internal Reporting Is Different

While these considerations apply for external reporting, we believe that there are good arguments for not getting involved with such allocations when it comes to internal budgeting or internal analysis and decision-making. Of course this does not mean that you keep two separate sets of books. It merely means that any expenses allocated to programs in your records may be combined and shown on internal reports in total.

The arguments against allocation derive from the underlying differences between nonprofit organizations and business enterprises:

1. It is useful to know whether or not a program's revenues will exceed its *direct* costs; yet it is neither necessary nor desirable that each program fully cover indirect costs allocated to it.

2. Selecting only programs that can pay for themselves, or charging prices to make sure they do, can be both self-defeating and destructive of the nonprofit's efforts to attain its goals. Unlike a business, effectiveness of a nonprofit's performance is measurable not in money or "profits," but in terms of how well it is achieving its basic goals: how well it meets the needs it set out to serve.

3. If a particular program is important in meeting those goals, must it "break even"? Increasing admissions or service fees may discourage attendance by the target group for which the organization exists; changing the program to one that is more "popular" may be inconsistent with the nonprofit's very purpose. It is the *goals* that must be kept uppermost in mind. If increased funds are necessary to maintain a program that cannot fully cover its indirect costs, it is the board's responsibility to raise the additional funds, or to reconsider the goals, if necessary.

4. Let us assume that these arguments apply to a program that is "breaking even" after allocation of all joint direct costs. Then is there justification, where internal analysis is concerned, for allocating indirect "overhead" costs, which exist independently of programs and are generally the minimum costs required just to keep the doors open? Certainly it seems that these costs must be funded by basic support, grants, contributions, or dues, rather than by program revenues. It is up to the board to make sure that "overhead" is adequately funded, or to reduce it where appropriate. The solution is not to be found in manipulating its allocation. Nevertheless, *total* income must cover *total* expenses, or you're in trouble. (Note again that our argument concerns only the internal use and interpretation of overhead cost data.)

This topic is explored in greater depth in Chapter 13, in the section headed "Using the Bottom Line in Performance Evaluation."

How to Allocate Indirect (Overhead) Costs to Programs

If the second argument has not been convincing and you still prefer to allocate indirect expenses to programs or other segments, three possible approaches are illustrated below:

1. *Pooling indirect costs.* The simplest way by far is to combine all such costs into a single total, usually called "Total Administrative and General Expense" (or "Overhead"), and to allocate shares of this figure to the segments involved on some "logical" basis. (An argument can be made for at least three logical methods, each of which usually yields a different result, as will be illustrated later.) Aside from the method used, the allocation involves deciding what proportion of certain shared costs should be borne by each segment, and transferring those costs out of the segment to which they were first charged. For example, some percentage of total administrative expenses might be allocated to each program and perhaps to fundraising, or total fundraising costs might first be added to overall administration and those combined costs allocated. The important thing is to consider the purpose of allocating certain expenses, bearing in mind the problems involved in the general approach, pointed out in method 3 below. This is much simpler than allocating expenses individually, nonetheless.

2. *Allocating only joint costs.*   Tables 6–1 and 6–2 show a way of allocating individually only expenses that clearly relate to all segments. They include the salary of the Executive Director, who spends time in all four service areas shown, as well as the portions of rent, insurance, and other expenses that bear some individual relationship to the four services. Some logical relationship has been chosen for each line item of joint expense: space used, for Occupancy Expense (which is mainly rent), Office Expense and fire insurance; estimated hours per month for Executive Director's salary; budgeted payroll dollars for workmen's compensation insurance, which is usually based on payroll—though different premium rates are used for different occupations, etc.

Once such a logical relationship has been established to describe a service area's share of an item, especially a minor one, that factor can be converted into a percentage of that item's total. Only the percentage need then be used thereafter.

An alternative method of allocating joint costs that is both more scientific and more time-consuming is to measure directly the *actual* past usage of certain items. Some examples follow:

a. *Payroll costs (and related fringe costs).*   This can be based on an analysis of a past period's time sheets for each staff member, which can be one or more test periods or—if you're a glutton for punishment—a whole year. (And who says next year will be the same?)

b. *Office expenses.*   Some organizations keep logs of how much postage, how many photocopies, how much stationery is used by each segment. Some keep telephone logs, at least for toll calls, or have their phone bills broken down by department, by the billing company (some can do this). This is a good practice for monitoring who's using how much of what, but the work involved in allocating each of these expenses for budgeting or bookkeeping purposes often outweighs its value.

3. *Allocating all support service expenses.*   This is a method that is generally used only in organizations whose income is virtually all earned, such as hospitals. It carries the first method one step further, by reallocating administration and fundraising expenses to operating departments or programs.

Carried out fully, *all* support service expenses can be considered indirect costs of each service area because they are necessary to the operation of each area. If they are fully allocated to the other segments, they disappear as separate totals, as is shown later in Table 6–4. That will make it hard to see how much was budgeted for management, how much for fundraising; and comparing actual vs. budgeted amounts becomes difficult. If such a form of budget and financial report is desired, it might be valuable to prepare a preliminary or supplementary budget (and financial report) that shows these amounts *before* allocation to programs.

How to Show Allocations on Budgets and Reports

Rather than have allocated expenses disappear into the direct expenses of programs, some agencies group all program expenses under one heading and show their total, then group support service expenses under a second heading, with a separate total. The combined total of program and support expenses is then shown and subtracted from revenue and support to arrive at net income. (See Fig. 15–1 in Chapter 15.)

**TABLE 6–1. OVERHEAD ALLOCATION WORKSHEET:
ALLOCATION OF JOINT COSTS ONLY, TO PROGRAM SERVICES**
(Applicable to columnar or matrix budget format)

Allocable expenses[a]	Basis of allocation	Totals of allocation base and expense	Program Services		Suport Services	
			Program A	Program B	General ad-ministration	Fund-raising
General administrative salaries (Time of Executive Director spent in direct supervision of the function:)						
	Est. Time: Hrs/mo.	150	30	60	15	45
	% of total	100%	20%	40%	10%	30%
Allocation	in dollars	$20,000	$ 4,000	$ 8,000	$ 2,000	$ 6,000
Occupancy	Sq. Ft. spaced used	2,000	800	1,000	120	80
	% total	100%	40%	50%	6%	4%
Allocation	in dollars	10,440	4,176	5,220	626	418
Office expense[b]	Same basis as Occup.	100%	40%	50%	6%	4%
Allocation	in dollars	$ 330	132	165	20	13
Insurance Liability	Est. Risk[b]	100%	20% (auto)	70%	10%	0
Allocation	in dollars	$ 200	40	140	20	0
Workmen's comp.	Payroll	$71,000	$16,000	$27,000	$28,000	0
	%/total	100%	22.5%	38%	39.5%	0
Allocation	in dollars	$ 300	$ 68	$ 114	$ 118	0
Fire	same as occupancy	100%	40%	50%	6%	4%
Allocation	in dollars	$ 100	$ 40	$ 50	$ 6	$ 4
Total all insurance—	Allocation	$ 600[c]	$ 148	$ 304	$ 144	$ 4
Depreciation (values of assets)[b]		$12,885	$ 8,085	Rented	$ 3,100	$1,700
Allocation: 20% of value = dollar amounts		$ 2,577	$ 1,617	0	$ 620	$ 340
Total joint fixed costs Allocated		$33,947	$10,073	$13,689	$ 3,410	$6,775

Note: Table 6–2 is a budget based on this worksheet.

[a]See Tables 5–5 and 5–7.

[b]Figures assumed for purposes of this illustration.

[c]Amount may not be material enough to warrant such a complex allocation. Based on experience, for example, the following year's budget might allocate the combined insurance expense on a 25%–50%–25%–0% basis, using the percentage of each column's total to total insurance.

TABLE 6-2. CENTER FOR COMMUNITY SERVICE, INC.
ANNUAL OPERATING BUDGET (with only joint costs allocated to function)

	Total	Program Services		Support Services	
		A	B	Administration	Fundraising
Estimated revenues[a]	$107,000	$32,000	$46,000		$29,000
Budgeted expenses					
Salaries[b]					
Program personnel	$43,000	$16,000	$27,000		
Support personnel	28,000	4,000	8,000	$10,000	$ 6,000
Payroll fringe costs[c]	7,662	1,642	2,980	3,040	—
Occupancy[b]	10,440	4,176	5,220	626	418
Telephone	1,120	275	275	570	
Printing & stationery	581		300	31	250
Postage	525		150	75	300
Travel & conferences	1,320	550	110	660	
Supplies	1,140	1,140			
Equipment rentals	2,305		2,305		
Professional & consulting	6,400		2,400	1,600	2,400
Office expense[b]	330	132	165	20	13
Insurance[b]	600	148	304	144	4
Contingency reserve	1,000			1,000	
Depreciation[b]	2,577	1,617		620	340
Total budgeted expenses	$107,000	$29,680	$49,209	$18,386	$ 9,725
Excess (deficiency) of					
revenues over expense	–0–	$ 2,320[d]	$(3,209)[d]	$(18,386)[e]	$19,275[e]

[a]Revenues shown only in total to save space. Revenues unrelated to programs arbitrarily allocated to fundraising.

[b]Items affected by allocation worksheet (Table 6–1).

[c]No reallocation made to match administrative salaries allocated to function (a practical compromise).

[d]Note that although this is a "break-even" budget in total, allocation of overhead on program budgets must conform with rules of granting agencies, and differences may result in excess or deficiency of program revenues as shown.

[e]Note that estimated nonprogram revenues (support) for the year exceeded the total cost of support services by $889, the difference between $29,000 and $28,111, i.e., $18,386 + $9,725.

Another worksheet is required where all nonprogram costs, meaning support services, are also allocated to programs.

Such a worksheet is used to allocate the costs of all support functions to programs (and to any separate funds), while adding any direct and/or joint costs to those program expenses that also have such costs. (See Table 6–3.) The resulting figures can then be transferred to the actual program budget. The budget will then show *all* costs under Program Services (Table 6–4). Support function costs (general administration and fundraising) are included in other line items, as in a line-item budget (see Table 5–6), and the total of each expense category (salaries, occupancy, etc.) then appears allocated across the program or fund columns (see Table 6–4).

TABLE 6–3. OVERHEAD AND SUPPORT SERVICES ALLOCATION WORKSHEET
(Applicable only to budgets allocating all costs to programs)

Allocable budgeted expenses	Joint costs	Support service costs[b]	Total estimated expenses (100%)	Program "A" (41%)	Program "B" (59%)
Salaries					
—Direct			$43,000[a]	$16,000	$27,000
—Joint	$12,000[b]		12,000	4,000	8,000
—Support (balance)[b]		$16,000[c]	16,000	6,560	9,440
Total salaries			71,000	26,560	44,440
Payroll fringe costs—Direct			4,662[a]	1,642	2,980
—Joint	0[d]		0	0	0
—Support (balance)		3,040[e]	3,040	1.246	1.749
Total payroll fringe costs			7,662	2,888	4,774
Occupancy					
—Direct			0	0	0
—Joint	9,396[b]		9,396	4,176	5,220
—Support (balance)		1,044[c]	1,044	428	616
Total occupancy			10,440	4,604	5,836
Office expense					
—Joint	297[b]		297	132	165
—Support (balance)		33[c]	33	14	19
Total office expense			330	146	184
Insurance					
—Joint	452[b]		452	148	304
—Support (balance)		148[c]	148	61	87
Total insurance (balance)			600	209	391
Depreciation					
—Joint	1,617[b]		1,617	1,617	0
—Support (balance)		960[c]	960	394	566
Total depreciation			2,577	2,011	566
All other support service expenses					
Travel & conferences		660			
Legal & accounting fees		1,600			
Telephone		570			
Stationery & postage		106			
Contingency reserve (bal. of misc.)		1,000			
Fundraising expense—Total		2,950			
Total all other support services		6,886[c]	6,886	2,823	4,063
Totals of allocated exp.	$23,762	$28,111	$51,873	$21,599	$30,274
Total of direct costs included above			$47,622	17,642	29,980
Total estimated expenses included in worksheet			$99,495	$39,241	$60,254

[a]See Table 5–7 and Table 6–2.
[b]See Table 6–1. Support salaries include Administrative Assistant—$8,000.
[c]Allocated arbitrarily on a basis of percentage of total revenues.
[d]Omitted as unwarranted complexity and not material.
[e]Used same percentages as for Support Salaries.

TABLE 6–4. CENTER FOR COMMUNITY SERVICE, INC.
ANNUAL OPERATING BUDGET—PROGRAM FORMAT (All revenues and costs allocated to programs)

	Combined totals	Program A	Program B
Estimated revenues			
Program services and grants	$ 78,000	$32,000	$46,000
Fundraising and other sources	29,000[a]	8,700	20,300
Total revenues	$107,000	$40,700	$66,300
Budgeted expenses			
Salaries	$ 71,000[b]	$26,560	$44,440
Payroll fringe costs	7,662[b]	2,888	4,774
Occupancy	10,440[b]	4,604	5,836
Telephone	550[c]	275	275
Printing & stationery	300[c]		300
Postage	150[c]		150
Travel & conferences	660[c]	550	110
Supplies	1,140	1,140	
Equipment rentals	2,305		2,305
Professional fees—consultants	2,400[c]		2,400
Office expense	330[d]	146	184
Insurance	600[d]	209	391
Depreciation	2,577[d]	2,011	566
Other support service expenses	6,886[e]	2,823	4,063
Total budgeted expenses	$107,000	$41,206	$65,794
Excess of revenue over expense	–0–		$ 506
Excess of expense over revenue		$ 506	

[a]Allocated based on an arbitrary estimate that fundraising efforts will relate to program services on a 30% to 70% basis.

[b]Item combines direct expenses plus allocated joint and support service costs (Table 6–3).

[c]Direct costs only: the portion included in support services is allocated as part of "other support service expense" (Table 6–3).

[d]Consists of allocated joint costs only. Any also included in Support Services are also allocated as part of the last expense item (Table 6–3).

[e]Total of $51,873 less portions already included in other items (Table 6–3).

[f]Support service costs, wherever allocated on worksheets, distributed to programs on the ratio of program revenues (services and grants) at 41% and 59% respectively (Table 6–3).

Note that the effect of such allocation is to distribute *all* overhead costs (general administration and fundraising) as well as joint costs from the "Total" column to the program columns. The result is to make each "bottom line" (excess of revenues or expenses) look worse, to little or no purpose.

This has virtually no effect on planning, control, and evaluation of program directors, except perhaps to make them appear responsible for things over which they have no control—hardly a morale builder. The worst situation is one in which program directors have little or no input to the budget process, and perhaps only a vague understanding of it. This may lead to a suspicion that overhead or joint costs are being excessively and unfairly allocated to their programs, either in error or from some suspected political or bureaucratic motive. Its only value would be in setting prices for program services, where no nonprogram revenues (support funds) are received.

A Case in Point

A specific illustration should serve to drive home the point we have made, that the allocation of indirect support services is inherently arbitrary and can be harmful. We refer here to such items as general administrative and fundraising expenses, not those directly attributable to a program. In our illustrated operating budget (Table 6–4), note that we chose to allocate general administrative and fundraising costs in a logical way: on the basis of percentage of program revenues, as well as nonprogram revenues (see worksheet, Table 6–3). The resulting "bottom line" shows Program A as operating at a "loss" of $506; Program B, at a "profit" of the same amount.

Let us suppose we had chosen another equally logical basis to allocate the $28,111 cost of indirect support services, such as the percentage of each program's direct *costs* to the total of direct costs. In our example, the calculation involved would be as follows:

	Direct Costs (Table 5–7)	% of combined total	Allocation of support service costs
Total Program A	$19,607	35.5	$ 9,979
Total Program B	35,520	64.5	18,132
Total program costs	$55,127	100.0	$28,111

Note that in our worksheet (Table 6–3), by using percentage of program revenues for our allocation (41% and 59% respectively) we got another program breakdown of the $28,111, with the differences below:

	Allocation method			Program expenses
	Table 6–3	New	Differences	will be
Program A	$11,526	$ 9,979	$1,547	Less
Program B	16,585	18,132	1,547	More
Combined totals	$28,111	$28,111	–0–	

If the new allocation were carried through, here is what would happen (see Table 6–5):

	Program services	
	A	B
Estimated revenues	$40,700	$66,300
Budgeted expenses	41,206	65,794
Adjust for new allocation of support service costs	- 1,547	+ 1,547
Budgeted expenses as adjusted	39,659	67,341
Excess of revenues (profit)	$ 1,041	
Excess of expenses (loss)		$ 1,041

Now program A appears to be making a $1,041 profit, instead of suffering a $506 loss; the reverse appears true for Program B. Yet all we have done is change the method of allocation, from one logical but arbitrary basis to another. We believe that the danger in evaluating program results or program directors, and of making program or personnel decisions on this basis is made clear by this example.

TABLE 6–5. SUMMARY OF SUPPORT COST ALLOCATION FROM TABLE 6-3

Categories of indirect Support services Budgeted expenses	Balances to be allocated	Allocated to program	
		A (41%)	B (59%)
Allocated to line items			
Salaries	$16,000	$ 6,560	$ 9,440
P/R fringe costs	3,040	1,246	1,794
Occupancy	1,044	428	616
Office expense	33	14	19
Insurance	148	61	87
Depreciation	960	394	566
Total allocated to line items	$21,225	$ 8,702	$12,523
All other support service expenses			
Travel & conferences	$ 660		
Legal & accounting	1,600		
Telephone	570		
Stationery & postage	106		
Contingency reserve (misc. exp.–bal.)	1,000		
Fundraising expense	2,950		
Total—other	$ 6,886	$ 2,823	$ 4,063
Totals—support service expense allocated	$28,111	$11,526	$16,585

THE CONNECTION BETWEEN ACCOUNTING AND BUDGETING

We have pointed out the need to use the same classification of items and accounting methods as those used in the financial reports to permit data comparisons that are valid. There are thus several accounting problems that must be considered in budgeting, just as in financial reporting, if performance reports are to be reliable.

Accrual Basis vs. Cash Basis Accounting

The distinction between the two basic methods of accounting, cash basis and accrual basis, is explained fully in Chapter 10. Operating budgets tend to project the timing of expenses instinctively on an accrual basis (meaning when costs will be incurred, not paid) even where the books and financial reports are on a cash basis. In planning ahead, it is more natural to think in terms of when an expense will be incurred than when it will be paid.

Since in accrual basis accounting, costs are recorded when incurred instead of when paid, and since operating budgets tend to imply this method, they must be adjusted for timing differences in preparing a cash budget. If, however, timing of payments is somehow taken into account in the operating budget, there is no difference between them in the way expenses are handled.

There are, however, certain expense items in an accrual basis budget that require special comment. For one, full accrual basis treatment, according to accounting theory, requires that costs be reflected when incurred rather than paid. But it also requires that the costs of items that apply to more than one period, or benefit more than one period, be spread across ("amortized over") such periods.

Examples from Sample Budgets

In our illustrative budgets in Chapter 5 we showed the cost of Printing & Stationery (Table 5-4) in the quarters during which the items were purchased, and not those in which the supplies were used up. This is convenient, and commonly done for budgeting purposes, but it is not, strictly speaking, true accrual basis accounting, not at least if the items are significant ("material") in amount. To illustrate the point still further: In Table 5-4, if the brochures for Program "B" and the bill for $300 are expected to come on December 31 of the final quarter of the year, instead of in the first quarter ending March 31, their cost would properly apply to the year following our budget year. If, however, all the brochures were distributed the day they arrived, they would not be included in the budget for the following year at all, and would rightly be included in the budget for the present year. Whether the nonprofit wants to get this sophisticated in its budgeting depends not only on how material an item is, but, more importantly, how it will be handled on the Operating Statement. The question of comparability for performance evaluation is basic to this decision.

Similar considerations arise with respect to revenues. Where the organization accrues revenues on its financial reports, comparable accruals will be required on operating budgets, if valid comparisons are to be made in performance reports. In projecting estimated revenues in our budget illustration, we did not say whether we did it on a cash or accrual basis. Since most of the amounts were substantial, we solved the problem by showing them in the columns for the quarters in which they would probably be received. We did this, rather than accruing any items that became definite commitments sooner.

A method that treats revenues on a cash basis by budgeting them for the quarter in which they are expected to be received is the preferred route to take, if the internal Operating Statements will be prepared the same way. It is doubtless the one used by most nonprofits.

The opposite may also apply: restricted grant funds received in one period, to be used in the next, are not considered income until the program begins, and then only to the extent of expenditures. Until then, they are considered *obligations*. (See Chapter 10, "Examples of Deferred Revenue Items.")

Donated Goods and Services

Some examples of in-kind donations are rent-free space, supplies and equipment, volunteer services, and expenses paid on behalf of the nonprofit by others.

This is a tricky area of budgeting, as well as accounting: in past years inexperienced nonprofits tended to ignore it. However, the U.S. Annual Report (Form 990) now provides for optional reporting of certain in-kind contributions (see Chapter 16). Consider also what can be accomplished by including the value of such "in-kind" contributions in budgets and financial reports:

1. Including the value of in-kind contributions projects a true picture of the full scope of the organization's activities. For example, volunteers may perform most of the organization's service functions. To omit these services unfairly diminishes the apparent size of the organization and the scale of its activities. This can hurt when seeking funding (see Chapter 8).

2. Organizational expenses paid for by others represent both revenue and expenses of the nonprofit for which it is accountable. It's as though they gave you the money and you then paid for the expense.

3. Where matching grants are involved, a foundation may accept such "soft match" items (not in cash, but in kind) in meeting part or all of the requirements.

4. Certain kinds of items that would have to be paid for, if they were not donated or paid for by others, should be accounted for. Otherwise, if ongoing commitments for them are not forthcoming, costs will have to be covered by cash outlays. To ignore them is to overlook this potential problem when planning. Free rent, supplies donated, or key volunteer services are examples.

5. If the budget is used for control and evaluation of activities, as it should be, it must be prepared on the same basis as actual operating statements. Since good accounting requires that the books and financial reports include certain kinds of donated goods and services (see Chapter 10), omitting them from operating budgets makes comparisons of some actual vs. budgeted figures clumsy if not impossible.

When such items are included they should be shown in the budget at their estimated value, in the same manner as they are valued for bookkeeping and reporting purposes (see Chapter 10). Any items not entered in the books may be shown as supplemental information on the budget and operating statement, in units at least (e.g., volunteer hours), if not in dollar value. This can take the form of footnotes or narrative comments.

THE POWER OF BREAK-EVEN ANALYSIS IN PLANNING/BUDGETING

Nonprofits that charge for services (or products), or are funded on a per-client basis, can make good use of a planning tool known as "break-even analysis." It can be used to determine in advance a number of different figures that are important to planning operations and fundraising events:

1. What price to charge for services or products to cover program costs. (See Chapter 3 re: the policy issues involved.)

2. Given a certain price, how many clients or patrons are required to break even—i.e., to cover program costs?

3. Where program revenues are insufficient to cover costs, how much must be raised by grants or donations to subsidize program prices?

Examples of nonprofits that can use this tool are those that sell tickets to performances or special events, or for use of their facilities, and those that are paid a fee or dues for services to patrons, clients, or members. In arriving at the amount of a grant or contract, this may take the form of a rate set and paid by a funding agency or insurance company for each client or case. A grant may also be based on an estimated or required minimum number of such service units. (If the actual number served is less than the estimate, the result to the nonprofit will be to increase its "profit" from the grant—if the actual number is acceptable to the funding agency.)

Problem Areas to Watch Out for

● Which costs should be included in the calculation? Only direct costs resulting from the activity itself, or also a share of "overhead" costs that would be incurred in any event? Should costs include depreciation of fixed assets used in the activity? (See Chapter 10.)

● Which costs vary in proportion to volume—i.e., to the number of patrons, clients, or members using the service? (called "Variable costs")

● Which costs remain the same regardless of volume? (called "Fixed costs")

● Which costs, if any, have a combination of these characteristics: what part is variable with volume, what part is fixed?

A more complete discussion of these issues can be found in Chapter 5, under "Using Cost Behavior Patterns in Budgeting."

Six Types of Cost Situations

1. *Variable costs only.*   If all of a nonprofit's personnel are volunteers and its facilities are donated, its remaining costs may all be variable with volume. Take the case of a cooperative day-care center operating out of members' homes, with no paid staff. The fee paid by co-op members would have to cover only the cost of food and supplies provided each child. Assuming that the total or average cost of food and supplies per child can be calculated or estimated with reasonable accuracy, the cost and charge per child for a month is easy to compute:

Cost per lunch	$1.50	
Cost per day for supplies (crayons, paper, etc.)	.50	
Cost per day	2.00	
Cost (and fee) per month (22 weekdays)		$44.00

2. *Fixed costs only.*   Where no costs vary with the number of people served, fees charged must be spread over fixed "overhead" costs. Take the case of a counseling center with paid staff and rent, which provides only advice. The fee to be charged clients would have to be the total costs per month divided by the number of client visits per month. Assuming the following costs (all fixed):

	Per month
Counselors' salaries	$1,800
Rent	300
Telephone, utilities, etc.	100
Total costs per month	2,200
Number of client visits/month	200
Fee per visit = $2,200/200	$ 11

In the above calculation, the number of client visits is known (or assumed). Suppose instead that the fee has been decided in advance, say at $10 a visit. How many client visits will be needed per month in order to cover costs—i.e., to break even? The calculation is simple enough:

$$\frac{\text{Total costs}}{\text{Fee}} \quad = \quad \text{Number of visits required}$$

or

$$\frac{\$2,200}{\$10} \quad = \quad \text{220 visits to break even}$$

But, you say, that is perfectly obvious! Be patient. It was just a warm-up, to get used to the basic mental approach. It gets a bit more complicated when there are both fixed and variable costs present.

3. *Both fixed and variable costs.*   Suppose the day care center already described grew to where it could boast paid staff and rented quarters. Like the counseling center, these are fixed "overhead" costs, while the food and supplies costs are variable, increasing with the number of children. The pricing calculation would be as follows (the fixed costs used are those shown for the counseling center):

Pricing calculation

Fixed costs per month		$2,200	(FC)
Cost of food and supplies per child, per month (i.e., variable cost)	$44 (VC)		
× number of children per month[1]	× 50 (n)	= 2,200	(Total VC)
Total costs per month		$4,400	
Divided by number of children		50	(n)
Monthly fee per child to break even		$ 88	(P)

It is convenient to express the above calculation as a simple algebraic equation, using the symbols shown next to the items:

$$P = \frac{FC + n(VC)}{n}$$

The calculation of the number of children needed per month to break even at a given price (of $88) is merely a restatement of the one above, with a different unknown:

Break-even calculation

Monthly fee (price) per child	$ 88	(P)
Minus variable cost (VC) per child	- 44	(VC)
"Contribution Margin" (net income) per child	$ 44	(CM)
Total fixed costs per month (FC)	$2,200	(FC)
Fixed costs divided by contribution margin		(FC/CM)
equals number of children to break even	= 50	(n)

[1]Assumed figure.

Again, expressing the above calcuation in equation form:

$$n = \frac{FC}{P - VC}$$

4. *Costs partly covered by grant.*   A variation on the situation described in example 3 would be a case in which the services are not to be fully paid for by program fees, but partly by a grant or other funds. If the monthly grant is \$2,000, then using the same data as in example 3:

Pricing calculation

Total costs (FC = \$2,200; Total VC = \$2,200)	\$4,400	
Less: covered by grant (per month)	2,000	(G)
Balance to be covered by fees	2,400	
Divided by number of children per month	50	(n)
Fee to be charged per child per month	\$ 48	(P)

Or in equation form:

$$P = \frac{FC + n(VC) - G}{n}$$

The new calculation of break-even volume would be:

Break-even calculation

Total fixed costs per month	\$2,200	(FC)
Less: covered by grant	2,000	(G)
Balance to be covered by Contribution Margin	200	
Contribution Margin (P - VC):		
Fee charged as above	\$ 48	(P)
Less: variable cost per child	44	(VC
Contribution margin per child	4	
Balance of fixed costs to be covered (above)	200	
Divided by contribution margin per child	4	
Equals number of children to break even	50	(n)

And in equation form:

$$n = \frac{FC - G}{P - VC}$$

(Note that the total grant would be the monthly grant times the number of months the program is to operate.)

5. *Funds required to subsidize some clients.*   Suppose the nonprofit day-care center wanted to charge a lower price (or nothing at all) to low-income famiies. How much would it need in

support funds (grant or contributions)? Let's assume that the regular fee per month is $50. The fee to be charged ten low-income families per child is $25. The total number of children is 50. The calculation would look like this:

Operating costs		
Fixed	$2,200	
Variable: 50 × $44	2,200	
Total costs per month		$4,400
Program revenues		
Regular fees: 40 × $50	2,000	
Reduced rate: 10 × $25	250	
Total program revenues		-2,250
Supplementary funds required per month		$2,150

6. *Planning special events.* Many nonprofits use special events as part of their fundraising efforts. If the price of the ticket to a dinner, for example, is to cover costs only, with funds to be raised by an appeal during the evening, the break-even calculation would be essentially the same as in example 3 above:

$$\text{No. of ticket sales to break even} = \frac{\text{Total fixed costs}^2}{\text{Price} - \text{Cost per meal}}$$

Or if the number of guests is known, the tickets can be priced to break even using the following calculation:

$$\text{Price} = \frac{\text{Total fixed costs}^2 + (\text{No. guests} \times \text{Cost per meal})}{\text{Number of guests}}$$

If, however, the ticket price is intended to yield a profit to the organization, and not merely to cover costs, the calculation may be modified to include the target amount to be raised that way. It is added to the fixed costs in each of the above calculations, as follows (assuming $1,000 is the target):

$$\text{No. of ticket sales needed} = \frac{\text{FC} + \$1,000}{\text{Price} - \text{Cost per meal}}$$

and

$$\text{Required price} = \frac{\text{FC} + \$1,000 + (\text{No. guests} \times \text{Cost per meal})}{\text{Number of guests}}$$

If the special event is a concert or other occasion in which there are no variable costs per patron, only fixed, the calculations are the same as those shown in example 2, in arriving at a break-even price or attendance figure. If the event is intended to raise money from the ticket price, not just to break even, then the target amount to be raised is added to fixed costs, as above. The calculation would be as follows, assuming $1,000 is the target amount:

---

[2]Fixed costs include advertising, printing, hall rental, waiters, and any other overall costs of the event except food and beverages, which will vary with the number of guests.

$$\text{Ticket price} = \frac{FC + \$1,000}{\text{No. of tickets}}$$

$$\text{No. of ticket sales needed} = \frac{FC + \$1,000}{\text{Ticket price}}$$

Of course, if there are to be various ticket prices, the calculations will have to be modified and an average price used or derived.

Caution: In all of the above kinds of calculations, three things can make or break them:

1. Including relevant costs that need to be considered, without overlooking any. An example of this is a catered dinner, where the caterer usually will hold you to a specified minimum number of servings whether you sell that many reservations (or collect for them) or not. You may have to figure in a certain percentage of income as a loss in such cases.

2. Correctly classifying relevant costs as fixed or variable, since incorrect classification will end up distorting your results.

3. Making certain that all factors are figured on the same basis (e.g., time period).

For example, in example 1, above, we figured cost of food and supplies on a daily basis, but then multiplied this figure by the number of days' service per month (22), because all other figures were on a monthly basis. Other calculations were on a basis of number of visits, number of guests, etc., and all figures used had to be expressed in a manner that was both comparable and aimed at producing the appropriate measurement needed.

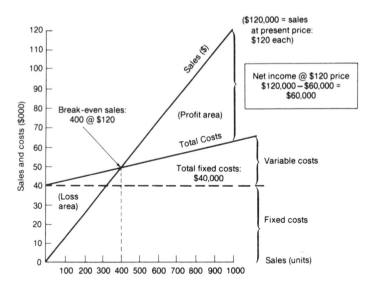

FIGURE 6–3. A TYPICAL BREAK-EVEN CHART

Source: From Arnold J. Olenick, *Managing to Have Profits,* McGraw-Hill, New York, 1989.

Using Break-Even Charts in Planning

In the business world particularly, the above equations are commonly used in preparing graphs of a company's sales and its fixed and variable costs at various levels of sales volume. Such costs can be shown in units of sales or service, dollars, or percentage of capacity. The beauty of such a graph is that it shows not only the volume needed to break even but also what the profit or loss would be at various volume levels. Fig. 6–3 is such a graph; it was constructed by the following steps:

1. Draw a horizontal line across the graph at the level of fixed costs, which in this case is $40,000.

2. Starting at this level, mark two or three points showing what total variable costs would be at each level of volume, by multiplying each of the selected levels by the variable cost per unit, if sales are in units, as shown, or by the variable cost percentage. Connect these points to make a line, which will represent total costs, since the amounts for variable costs are added to the total fixed costs. (That's where the variable cost line began.)

3. Starting at zero, mark two or three points representing sales or revenue at each level of volume: selling price times units sold, or an assumed dollar amount, the upper limit of which is sales at full capacity. (Note: Variable costs per unit are $20; selling price is $120.)

Where the total sales line crosses the total costs line ($48,000), the two are equal, so the organization will just break even. To the right of that point sales exceed costs, and the vertical distance between the lines measures the profit at any given level of volume. Below that level (to the left of the break-even point), the organization will show a loss, the amount of which is similarly measured by the vertical distance between the sales and cost line at any given volume level.

Graphs like this one must be used with care, since any change in the assumptions they are based on will change the break-even point and the amounts of profit or loss. For example, if the price per unit is changed, or the variable cost per unit, or the variable cost as a percentage of the price, or the planned fixed costs are changed, the graph must be redrawn, just as the equation would have to be recalculated. On the plus side, however, possible changes can be projected in this way, to predict their effect on net income.

Chapter 7
Cash and Capital Budgeting

If there is any subject seen as a life-and-death matter by nonprofits, cash flow is it! Staying afloat is the name of the game here, and our phrase for how you sometimes have to do it is "beg, borrow or stall!"—But that comes after you're in trouble. This chapter is about survival planning, by anticipating cash flow—to the extent you can do so in the nonprofit's uncertain world.

In case you think you've already taken care of that with your nifty operating budget, think again, or you may be in for a big (and unpleasant) surprise.

THE CONCEPT OF CASH FLOW

Cash flow is a much misused and misunderstood term, in the business world as well as that of the nonprofit. Correctly used, it means the excess of cash received over cash paid out during a given period. Organizations sometimes approximate it by adding to the net income ("profit") any expenses that did not require the current use of cash, such as depreciation expense. That has misled a lot of people, since it ignores cash received and paid that does not directly affect the bottom line.

What is important to understand about cash flow is its timing and its cyclical nature. Fig. 7–1 illustrates the flow of cash: where it comes from and where it goes. It is interesting that credit is a concept that has a place in the cash flow cycle. One way to view the purpose and effect of credit on the cycle is to see it as merely delaying the *timing* of cash payments from when they would be made if all transactions were strictly for cash. A way to view the role of your creditors in that respect is to imagine that they have loaned you the money to pay for current supplies and expenses, which you will pay back later. That puts the repayment in a different period than the expense itself.

A well-run organization can make good use of three different working tools in staying on top of cash flow:

1. An annual cash flow budget, for over-all financial planning, since the operating budget only deals with the income and expense part of your activities.

2. A month-by-month cash budget, to anticipate possible cash shortfalls during the year that won't show up in the annual cash flow budget.

3. A monthly worksheet, for scheduling payments, assigning priorities if necessary, and for making sure you'll have enough in the bank to cover the payments.

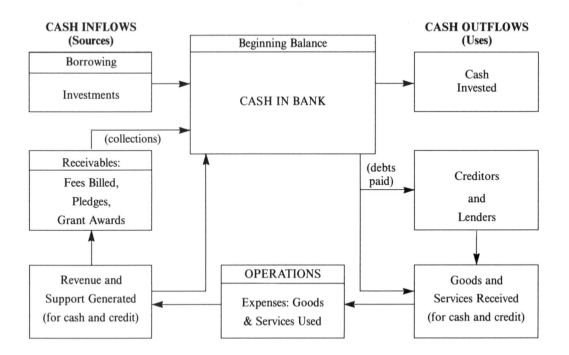

FIGURE 7-1. THE CASH FLOW CYCLE.
Note that the cash balance is decreased if total outflows exceed total inflows.

A CASH BUDGET ENHANCES AN OPERATING BUDGET

In our overview of the role of financial management that preceded Chapter 5, we briefly made the point that a cash budget is necessary. Now let's see why the two are different, and why both are needed:

1. To project your incoming and outgoing cash, you can't stop at income and expenses, as you do in an operating budget. There are deposits and payments that are neither income nor expenses. Take for example money borrowed. That's a debt, not income, since it must be repaid eventually.

Other examples are payments of amounts owed, loans or advances by the agency, and purchases of equipment or property. These are not expenses, yet they must be taken into account, therefore all such cash transactions must be covered in the cash budget.

2. Even the monthly amounts of income and expenses are not exactly the same in a cash budget as in an operating budget. For example, when you prepare your operating budget, your

mind is on what income you expect to earn or be granted, and what expenses you expect to incur—not *when* you expect the cash to be received or paid. Both income and expenses may fall in a later month—sometimes even in the next fiscal year. It is also possible that you will receive or pay for something in an earlier month, such as collecting a grant in the last month of one year that applies to a program beginning in the first month of the following year. (In Chapter 10 we will come back to this mind-set, a description of the accrual method of accounting.)

Note also that the operating budget deals, as its name indicates, only with income and expenses, regardless of when cash changes hands. To repeat, it is therefore not an overall financial budget, which would include other sources and uses of cash. It is prepared on a basis we will later refer to as the accrual basis.

Your cash budget differs from the operating budget both in what it contains and in the timing of when income and expense items are included (Fig. 7–2). In fact, timing is the crucial difference. There's no point in using an operating budget that might show a "profit" for a given month or quarter, when in fact there might be a cash shortage that will have to be covered.

A chart summarizing the differences between operating and cash budgets is shown below at Fig. 7–2.

Type of Item	Operating Budget		Cash Budget	
	Included?	When?	Included?	When?
Revenue & support:				
Services for cash	Yes	Date earned	Yes	Date of collection
Services on credit	Yes	Date earned	Yes	Date of collection
Grants awarded	Yes	Date earned	Yes	Date of collection
Pledges	Yes	Date earned	Yes	Date of collection
Cash donations	Yes	Date earned	Yes	Date of collection
Investment income	Yes	Date earned	Yes	Date of collection
Other sources of cash:				
Borrowed money	No	—	Yes	Date cash received
Investments sold	Gain only	At sale	Yes (all)	Date cash received
Other assets sold	Gain only	At sale	Yes (all)	Date cash received
Operating expenses:				
Paid in cash	Yes	At payment	Yes	Date paid
Incurred on credit	Yes	Incurred	Yes	Date paid
Paid in advance	Yes	As used	Yes	Date paid
Other uses of cash:				
Loans repaid	No	—	Yes	Date paid
Cash invested	No	—	Yes	Date paid
Equipment purchases	No	As used (via depreciation)	Yes	Date paid

FIGURE 7–2. COMPARISON OF ITEMS INCLUDED, OPERATING AND CASH BUDGETS.

A BUDGETED CASH FLOW STATEMENT: POWER TOOL
IN FINANCIAL PLANNING

Let's start with the big picture: your financial plan for the year as a whole. When your operating budget for the year is completed, to do a cash flow projection you still must add to it the nonincome and nonexpense items already mentioned, even before considering the more detailed question of timing.

You'll probably need to consult all of your annual planning documents. The operating budget tells you how much you plan to spend for expenses and where you plan to get it. (In this case, you can work on revenue and support first, expenses afterwards.) The organization's annual plan should reflect any planned purchases of equipment and increases or reductions of debts; if not, these are matters to be determined and provided for. Work plans should normally consider when new equipment is to be bought, which will help with the timing. Your capital budget, formal or informal, which we will cover later in this chapter, is the source of information about how much you plan to spend on new capital equipment, and how you plan to pay for it, which affects the timing.

When you've pulled together all of the above figures, there is one more step: the timing of income and expense payments. You need to consider whether there are any items omitted that may affect the first month or two of the fiscal year you are budgeting. These would include any expected inflows or outflows of cash that relate to the current year. (Let's number the years we are talking about for clarity: the current year, Year 1; next year, Year 2; the year after next, Year 3.) Here are examples: collections in Year 2 of grants, pledges or service fees set up as receivables in Year 1, or payment in Year 2 of expenses or other obligations of Year 1. These payments should be *added* to the income and expense figures derived from your operating budget for Year 2, which will not include payments of amounts that apply to Year 1.

The same process in reverse should be undertaken for the final months of Year 2 (the budgeted fiscal year): income and expenses included in the operating budget that will not be paid until Year 3. These items should be *subtracted* from the amounts of income and expense derived from the operating budget, which include Year 2 income and expense that will not become cash transactions until Year 3.

At best, this is a wide-angle view, since trying to anticipate how much cash will come in each month for a whole year is virtually impossible. And if the cash doesn't come in, you can't spend it; that means that your month-by-month cash budget for expenses is even less reliable than your budgeted cash inflow. A budgeted cash flow statement for a year, before developing monthly amounts, is shown in Table 7–1.

TABLE 7-1. CENTER FOR COMMUNITY SERVICE, INC.
BUDGETED STATEMENT OF CASH FLOWS

Cash flow from operations

Budgeted net income per operating budget[a]		–0–
Add back noncash expenses[b]		
Depreciation	$2,577	
Amortization of prepaid insurance	300	
Add/deduct changes in balances of receivables/payables[b]		
Net (increase)/decrease in receivables	–0–	
Net increase/(decrease) in accounts payable	–0–	
Increase/(decrease) in accrued expenses	200	
Increase/(decrease) in accrued taxes	–0–	
Increase/(decrease) in withholding taxes payable	$ 500	
Total adjustments		$3,577
Net cash from operations		3,577
("Net cash used for operations" if negative)		

Cash flow from planned investments

Proceeds of planned sale of fixed assets[c]	–0–	
Payments for planned purchase of fixed assets[c]	(2,000)	
Money market account investment/transfer	–0–	
Net cash from (used for) investments		$(2,000)
Balance		$1,577

Cash flow from planned financing

Planned borrowing	4,000	
Planned payments on loans, mortgages, etc.	$(2,000)	
Net cash from (used for) financing		$2,000
Budgeted net increase (decrease) in cash		3,577
Add: cash balance—beginning of year		$2,000
Budget cash balance—end of year		$5,577

[a]It is possible, but far more time-consuming, to work with the details of income and expenses instead; however, these amounts are shown on the Operating Budget. This short-cut is usually used.

[b]Changes in these balances adjust the Net Income from an accrual basis to a cash basis.

[c]Actual cash proceeds of sale are substituted for gains or losses on the sale of assets. Only down payments and cash purchases are shown here.

Using the Budgeted Cash Flow Statement

At this point you have a financial overview useful for answering some basic financial questions. For example, as a general proposition, will our projected cash inflows for the year cover our planned cash payments for expenses, plus other nonexpense outlays?

If the answer is no, as it may well be, how do we bring the two into agreement? Can we realistically plan for increased fundraising, and if so, what type? This will give us early warning to start the planning, which takes time (see Chapter 8). If we cannot raise funds, what outlays can be deferred or even reduced (an equipment purchase, for example)? If none of the above, we know that arranging for borrowing may be the only answer. Since that too takes time, we are in a position to start the process early.

If the answer is yes (inflows will cover outflows), it probably means the previous work that made the cash flow statement possible—our annual plan and operating budget—was done carefully and thoroughly. Before deciding to go on a spending binge, however, don't overlook the timing factor. Never forget that all accounting statements and budgets chop up the past and future into arbitrary windows of time: a year, a quarter, or a month. That fat cash balance projected for the year's end may be a beautiful illusion that will evaporate the following month when some big outlay is necessary!

If that is not a problem, meaning you'll have more cash than needed, you'll now have the pleasant problem of deciding what to do with the excess cash. Your options are fairly clear:

1. Increase the budgeted allowances, where appropriate, to put some or all of it to use—such as bringing staff and/or salaries into line.

2. Buy that equipment you need, but didn't think you'd have enough money for this time around.

3. Pay off back debt to improve your credit rating and reduce or eliminate interest charges.

4. Invest it (conservatively) to earn revenue. Use this investment as a cash reserve, to be drawn on when you have a future shortfall.

The thing to see here is that the cash flow budget is a power tool for overall financial planning. It should, to the extent possible, be worked on in parallel with the operating budget, since operations and finances need to go hand in hand. At the end of your fiscal year, an actual cash flow statement should be prepared, to see whether your overall financial plan was carried out as intended (see Chapter 15). If your actual ending cash balance is a lot different than was projected, a line-by-line comparison of the actual cash flow statement with the budgeted one will pinpoint why that happened. That will then serve as a review of your agency's overall financial performance, as distinguished from the results of its program and support activities. As the only financial report that makes this possible, the cash flow statement should be used far more often than it usually is.

YOUR MONTH-BY-MONTH CASH BUDGET

A month-by-month cash budget can serve to fine-tune the annual cash flow budget. There's no point going to sleep happy that your total cash inflows budgeted for the year will exceed your budgeted outflows. Money doesn't flow like a river, but often comes in spurts—or perhaps "dribs and drabs" would be more descriptive. When you look at it on a month-to-month basis, therefore, you may find one or more months in which your outflow exceeds your inflow. Unless you start out with enough in the bank to cover a shortfall, you'd be in trouble. That's why you need a month-by-month cash budget. You may be able to get by with an operating budget that shows quarterly amounts, but without a cash budget laid out by months, you are risking problems.

As with the operating budget, it's best to start preparing your cash budget with the money to be spent, then the funds you expect to receive, month by month. If any month shows a shortfall, that's something you'll have to plan how to cover. It may mean drawing on invested funds, if you have any, arranging for a short-term loan or a special fund drive, or perhaps changing the timing of one or more expenditures. We'll be looking at cash management as such in Chapter 14. Here it is a matter of anticipating such problems in the planning stage.

**TABLE 7–2. CENTER FOR COMMUNITY SERVICE, INC.
MONTHLY CASH BUDGET WORKSHEET**[a]

Cash Balance—beginning[a]	Operating budget 1st quarter	Date payment due[b]	Cash budget for month of:[c]		
			Jan. $ 2,000	Feb. $ 3,285	March $ 7,919
Estimated cash receipts					
Revenues (operating budget)					
ABC Foundation grant	$ 5,000	Feb.		$ 5,000	
XYZ Foundation grant	15,000	(monthly)	5,000	5,000	5,000
State grant	2,200	(monthly)	800	700	700
In-kind (rent)	1,500	(noncash)	—	—	—
Program "A" services	4,000	(as shown)	1,000	2,000	1,000
Dues	1,000	(as shown)	500	400	100
Interest	125	(monthly)	20	20	85
Total estimated revenues	28,825				
Estimated cash revenue			7,320	13,120	6,885
Nonrevenue receipts[d]					
Temporary loans borrowed Jan.		(repay in Apr.)	2,000		
Est. total cash received			9,320	13,120	6,885
Est. total cash available			11,320	16,405	14,804
Estimated cash disbursements					
Expenses (operating budget plus worksheet)					
Salaries (all)	$17,750	(monthly)	5,917	5,917	5,916
Less taxes withheld (30%)			1,775	1,775	1,775
Net salaries			4,142	4,142	4,141
Payroll fringe costs[e]					
Payroll taxes	1,567	(for previous Q.)	674	—	—
Health insurance	625	(for previous Q.)	375	—	—
Rent (donated)[e]	1,500	(noncash)	—	—	—
Electricity & heat[e]	600	(monthly)	200	200	200
Water[e]	60	(March)	—	—	60
Janitorial services[e]	450	(monthly)	150	150	150
Telephone (all)	300	(monthly)	100	100	100
Printing & stationery	306	(Feb.)	—	306	—
Postage	245	(Jan.)	245	—	—
Travel & conferences	360	(as shown)	60	180	120
Supplies	570	(Feb.)	—	570	—
Equipment rentals	60	(monthly)	200	200	200
Professional fees[e]					
Consultants	1,200	(monthly)	400	400	400
Legal	125	(March)	—	—	125
Accounting (Q/annual)	650	(Feb./Mar.)	—	150	500
Office expense	90	(monthly)	30	30	30
Insurance[e]					
Liability (prepaid 1 year)	50	(March)	—	—	200
Workmen's comp.	75	(prior quarter)	75	—	—
Fire (prepaid 1 year)	25	(Dec.)	—	—	—
Contingency reserve	250	("cushion")	84	83	83
Depreciation	645	(noncash)	—	—	—
Total estimated expenses (carried forward)	$28,043		$6,735	$6,511	$6,309

**TABLE 7-2. CENTER FOR COMMUNITY SERVICE, INC.
MONTHLY CASH BUDGET WORKSHEET[a] (continued)**

	Operating budget 1st quarter	Date payment due[b]	Cash budget for month of:		
			Jan. $ 2,000	Feb. $ 3,285	March $ 7,919
Cash Balance—beginning[a]					
Total estimated expenses (brought forward)	$28,043		$6,735	$6,511	$6,309
Add: nonexpense payments:		For Dec., Jan.			
Withholding taxes paid		& Feb.	1,100	1,775	1,775
Equip. installment payments		(monthly)	200	200	200
Est. total cash disbursements			8,035	8,486	8,284
Est. balance end of month			$ 3,285	$ 7,919	$ 6,520

[a]Cash balance at beginning of January comes from December 31 checkbook balance—actual or estimated. February 1 and March 1 balances are carried over from "Estimated Balance—End of Month" (January and February). "Estimated Total Cash Available" equals beginning balance plus cash receipts. "Estimated Balance—End of Month" is total cash available minus total cash disbursements.

[b]Information in "Date Payment Due" column is based on analysis of payment arrangements or possibilities affecting timing. Note items paid in advance, such as insurance for the whole year, and items due creditors willing to defer payment; e.g., audit fee.

[c]Note especially noncash items (in-kind contribution of free rent and rent expense, also depreciation) and handling of withholding taxes (deduct from current period salary, pay in following period. January payment for December W.T. and payroll taxes reflected lower payrolls last year, before Program B increase).

[d]Data for nonrevenue receipts and nonexpense payments: from the books, supplementary records (payroll, amounts receivable or payable, etc.). Budgeted equipment purchases would appear here. (It is assumed that there were no other unpaid expenses or revenues as of January 1.)

[e]Data derived from Tables 5-5 and 5-6, "Mar. 31" column.

Still, you must start somewhere, in order to anticipate the best you can any months in which you may run dry. You can't afford to let that happen unexpectedly, because unpaid bills can damage your credit, and unpaid salaries can ruin morale. An illustration of a monthly cash budget is given in Table 7-2. It is developed from the monthly or quarterly operating budget, taking into account the timing of items they contain (see "Mar. 31" column in Tables 5-5 and 5-6), the Budgeted Statement of Cash Flows (Table 7-1), and the text preceding it. The footnotes to Table 7-2 give detailed explanations.

Cash flow budgets can be prepared more easily with microcomputer spreadsheet programs (see Appendix 11C).

WHERE TO FIND THE DATA YOU NEED

Now that you've broken your operating budget down by month, you have a fair idea of how much expense you'll *incur* each month. But how much will you need to *pay out* in the same month? Is the budgeted amount of income each month the same as the amount of cash you expect to deposit? Probably not. Don't forget about the differences in timing, or about other obligations and plans.

Timing Differences

To calculate timing differences and their effects, use the same approach as described above for preparing the income and expense parts of the annual cash flow budget. Adjust the beginning and end of each month to a cash flow basis. Shift amounts from the month expenses are incurred to the month that cash will be paid for them. Use the same technique for shifting income. The footnotes below Table 7–2 give further information about some of the detailed procedures necessary.

If your annual statement is prepared on an accrual basis, your balance sheet may contain items such as Accounts, Pledges or Grants Receivable or Accounts Payable and Accrued Expenses. If your monthly or quarterly statements are prepared the same way during the year (regardless of how your books are kept), you should find the same balance sheet items. You can use them nicely to help your cash budgeting. All you need to know or anticipate is what your collection or payment patterns are.

For example, if you usually pay all your bills the following month, January's Accounts Payable and Accrued Expense should be February's Payments for Expense. The same approach may be used—probably somewhat less reliably—with your receivables, unless you have a good idea of how long they usually take to collect.

You can often come pretty close by examining past patterns: if grants are generally recorded as receivables when approved, and received, say, two months later, you can enter their budgeted collection two months after the actual or anticipated approval date. If 20% of the service fees billed are usually collected in the same month, 70% the following month and the balance two months later, you can apply these percentages to the fee income budgeted each month to find the months in which to include them in the cash budget.

Here's a worked out example for service fees, based on the above percentages:

	Total Amount	To be collected in		
		January	February	March
Accounts receivable Balance 12/31	$63,000	$56,000	$ 7,000	$ 0
Budgeted fees				
January	50,000 (100%)	10,000 (20%)	35,000 (70%)	5,000 (Bal.)
February	40,000 (100%)	0	8,000 (20%)	28,000 (70%)
March	60,000 (100%)	0		12,000 (20%)
Estimated Fees Collected		$66,000	$50,000	$45,000

This example assumes that December 31 Accounts Receivable consisted of the remaining balances of November and December fees earned. It also assumes that 20% of fees are collected in the month earned, 70% the following month, and the remaining 10% the month after that.

This type of calculation is used in automated cash flow budget spreadsheets used on microcomputers (sometimes via the use of a so-called "template"). Using the computer saves a lot of time. (See Appendix 11C.)

Don't overlook other sources of information about incoming cash. Items that may be contained in "off-the-books" records include pledges, unrecorded receivables for grants awarded or for reimbursements on contracts or grants, anticipated payments to your organization on the principal of notes or loans receivable, on installment sales you have made, on mortgages receivable you hold as investments, or on past sales of realty. (Any interest that will be earned should have been included in your operating budget.)

A similar approach can be used if you usually pay part of your bills in the month received, and for payments due on the principal of installment sales, loans, notes, and mortgages you owe to others. (Again, any interest expense should be in your operating budget.)

Cash Budgeting in the Real World

The work of the CFO (financial manager) should involve monitoring your cash needs on a weekly (or bi-weekly) basis, depending on how often you pay your staff. To do a good job of this, two working tools are needed:

1. The monthly cash budget, shown in Table 7–2, would usually show a whole year. Because of space limitations, we have shown only three months. The best way to use the budget is to keep adding a new month at the end, dropping the first month: that way you always have the long view ahead.

2. A worksheet covering only the current month, which gets down to the detailed planning within that month: whom do we pay when, based on how much we'll have in the bank each week, is a tool of cash management, rather than budgeting in the usual sense. It is explored further in Chapter 14.

Items Not from the Operating Budget

Notice in Table 7–2 that "cash receipts" includes monies borrowed as well as income: the temporary loan to be borrowed in April. Note also the nonexpense payments: payment of taxes withheld and of equipment installments. The loan repayment scheduled for April would also appear in this section, during the month of April.

HOW ACCRUAL BASIS ACCOUNTING AFFECTS THE BUDGET FIGURES

We gave a brief definition of accrual basis accounting in Chapter 6; however, if the subject is new to you, the following introduction may be useful. The cash budget illustrated in Table 7–2 made use of certain unstated assumptions about the operating budget on which it is based:

1. That expenses were projected basically (though not fully) on an accrual basis, and revenues essentially on a cash basis. (For example, the three grants, if approved by January 1, might be considered first quarter revenues, but the anticipated amounts due quarterly have been shown instead.) A few items in the operating budget were, for the sake of simplicity and realism, actually recorded on a cash basis: e.g., letterheads and envelopes (under Printing & Stationery) and Supplies, which were based on date purchased, not date consumed.

2. That there will be little quarterly or month-to-month variation in expense items and that most expenses will be paid in the same quarter as incurred. Any exceptions have been taken into account in the operating budget, or in the cash budget worksheet (Table 7–2). Note for example the effect of increased payroll for Program B on the amount of withholding and payroll taxes paid in January vs. February.

3. That no salary payments are due after the end of the month earned; otherwise the cash budget would have to take that into account, and January's salary payment would

be lower than February's due to accrued (unpaid) January salaries under the new program exceeding similar amounts carried over from December. The accrued payroll taxes for the previous quarter (ended December 31) are lower than those accrued for the current year's first quarter, which will be due in April. (It has been assumed that all payroll taxes and health insurance premiums are due quarterly; in practice, they may be due monthly.)

Caution: It is important to note that where any of these assumptions do not apply, the step-by-step process of adjusting from operating to cash budget would be affected accordingly. Thus, where any expenses do vary substantially in amount between periods, the time lag between incurring and paying them will show the amounts in the wrong period, unless this pattern is taken into account.

WHEN YOUR BOOKS ARE ON THE ACCRUAL BASIS

We haven't discussed the distinction between budgets or financial statements prepared on the accrual basis and keeping your books that way, which is not the same thing. That comes up in Chapter 10. Since we won't be talking about budgeting again after that, this is the only appropriate place to deal with that situation. This material will be clearer later, when you need to deal with it.

Where the books are kept on a full accrual basis, the unpaid expenses at the end of each month are shown as accrued expenses or accounts payable (see Chapter 11), which then do not show up as expenses in the month paid. The same applies to any revenues that have been accrued on the books but not collected.

A cash budget worksheet prepared from an operating budget prepared on a *full accrual* basis is illustrated in Table 7–3. Differences in amounts from Table 7–2 result from the timing differences noted in the worksheet itself. Its complexity suggests preparing the cash budget independently.

TABLE 7–3. CENTER FOR COMMUNITY SERVICE, INC.
CASH BUDGET WORKSHEET FROM FULL ACCRUAL BASIS OPERATING BUDGET

	Quarter ending March 31		Cash budget, month of		
	Operating budget	Cash budget	Jan.	Feb.	March
Cash balance—beginning of period[a]		$ 2,000	$ 2,000	$ 8,797	$13,431
Estimated cash receipts					
Total est. revenues:					
derived from operating budget (see Table 5–6)	$28,825	27,325	7,320[b]	13,120[b]	6,885[b]
Add: accounts receivable beginning balance (collected)		5,000[c]	5,000[c]		
		32,325	12,320	13,120	6,885
Less: acct. rec.—ending balance (uncollected)		5,000[d]			5,000[d]
Cash basis revenues		27,325	12,320	13,120	1,885
Nonrevenue receipts					
Temporary loans (due Apr.)		2,000	2,000		
Estimated cash received		29,325	14,320	13,120	1,885
Estimated cash available		31,325	16,320	21,917	15,316
Estimated cash disbursements					
Expenses (operating budget plus worksheet)					
Salaries (earned: all)	17,750	17,750	5,917	5,917	5,916
Less taxes withheld (30%)		5,325	1,775	1,775	1,775
Net salaries (take-home pay)		12,425	4,142	4,142	4,141
Payroll taxes (incurred)	1,567	1,567	522	522	523
Health insurance	625	625	208	209	208
Rent (donated)	1,500	(noncash)	—	—	—
Electricity & heat	600	600	200	200	200
Water (due Mar. for Jan./Feb.)	60	60	—	—	—
Janitorial service	450	450	150	150	150
Telephone	300	300	100	100	100
Printing & stationery (due Feb.)	306	306	—	306	—
Postage	245	245	245	—	—
Travel & conferences	360	360	60	180	120
Supplies (due Feb.)	570	570	—	570	—
Equipment rentals	600	600	200	200	200
Consultants	1,200	1,200	400	400	400
Legal (pay Mar.)	125	125	—	—	125
Acctg. (pay Feb./Mar.)	650	650	—	150	500
Office expenses	90	90	30	30	30
Insurance					
Liability (1 yr, prepay.)	50	200	—	—	200
Workmen's comp. (prior Q.)	75	(accrued)	—	—	—
Fire (1 yr, prepaid Dec.)	25	(noncash)	—	—	—
Contingency reserve	250	250	84	83	83
Depreciation	645	(noncash)	—	—	—
Total current expense (carried forward)	$28,043	$20,623	$ 6,341	$ 7,242	$ 7,040

**TABLE 7-3. CENTER FOR COMMUNITY SERVICE, INC.
CASH BUDGET WORKSHEET FROM FULL ACCRUAL BASIS OPERATING BUDGET (continued)**

	Quarter ending March 31		Cash budget, month of		
	Operating budget	Cash budget	Jan.	Feb.	March
Total current expense (brought forward)	$28,043	$20,623	$ 6,341	$ 7,242	$ 7,040
Add payment of accounts payable/accrued expenses (accrued at end of previous month)					
Salaries (4th week of previous month		917	917	1,479	1,479
Payroll taxes (prior Q.)		674	674		
Health insurance (prior Q.)		375	375		
Water (two previous months due)		50	50		
Insurance—Workmen's Comp.		75	75		
Total accruals paid currently		2,091	2,091	1,479	1,479
Subtotal		22,714	8,432	8,721	8,519
Less accrual of accounts payable/accrued expenses (accrued at end of current period)					
Salaries (last week of current period)		1,479	1,479	1,479	1,479
Payroll taxes (current Q.)		1,567	522	522	523
Health insurance (current Q.)		625	208	209	208
Total accruals eliminated		3,671	2,209	2,210	2,210
Cash basis expenses		19,043	6,223	6,511	6,309
Add nonexpense payments					
Withholding taxes paid for prior period		4,650	1,100	1,775	1,775
Installment payments—equipment		600	200	200	200
Estimated total cash disbursements		24,293	7,523	8,486	8,284
Estimated balance end of period		$ 7,032	$ 8,797	$13,431	$ 7,032

[a]Note that balance at beginning and end of the quarter (Jan. 1 and March 31) are the same as balances at the beginning of January column and end of March column.

[b]Only monthly totals shown here. Details would be derived as in Table 7-2.

[c]Represents ABC Foundation grant—balance due from prior year grant accrued at December 31.

[d]To eliminate accrual of uncollected ABC grant at March 31.

[e]The ending balances differ from those in Table 7-2 as a result of differences between amounts accrued at the beginning and end of each period. Also reflected are differences in the amounts of revenues and expenses that would be reported on an operating budget prepared on a full accrual basis.

BREAK-EVEN CASH FLOW

This is a suggested tool that can serve as a rule-of-thumb in day-by-day financial management. You probably won't find it in textbooks. The idea is to list your basic recurring monthly cash outlays for such items as payrolls, payroll taxes and employee benefits, rents for space and equipment, installment payments on loans, mortgages, and equipment purchases, plus an average figure for other recurring expenses paid monthly, such as supplies, office expense, travel, auto expense, and consultants, among others.

Business people call this the minimum "nut," the amount of cash you need each month to cover expenses. In the best of all possible worlds, that amount would always be available (in a checking account plus temporary investments like savings or money market accounts). You should plan to collect at least this amount each month to replenish bank accounts. If income does not at least match the monthly "nut," it's a signal to do something about it now, rather than wait for the inevitable crisis to develop.

Ideally, an organization should try to build up reserve funds of three (or at least two) month's "nut," to carry it over the bad times when a grant falls through or is delayed.

MINIMUM CASH BALANCE

Whether or not you have a reserve available, your budget should include a minimum balance (to be decided by the board or the treasurer), budgeted for as a matter of prudence. If the budgeted (or actual) ending balance falls below that minimum, you know steps need to be taken to bring it up to par. Your cash flow may be too tight at a given time for this minimum to be enough to cover your monthly "nut," but that is a goal you can work toward in your annual budgets. This can be thought of as a reserve or contingency fund, if you wish—a so-called "rainy day" fund—perhaps one based on the break-even cash flow figure discussed above.

If your projection shows one or more months in which the ending balance will fall below the established minimum (or is just plain negative), you can take steps to raise or borrow enough money to bring your balances up to where you want them to be.

CAN YOUR BALANCE BE TOO BIG?

Although having a cash balance that is too high may seem like dreaming, it is our hope that using what you learn in this book could bring it about. (Even if you usually have trouble just staying afloat, you may be notified of a big grant or pledge that temporarily will create a large cash balance when it comes in.) In such cases, the answer to the question whether it can be too large is yes, but only if it refers to your checking account balance, which is what your cash budget usually projects. To deal with such a happy event you should develop a policy for dealing with excess cash. What you should not do is leave it in an account that earns no interest; it belongs, at least temporarily, in a savings account (which is insured under F.D.I.C.) or a money market account (which may not be insured). Its use for other purposes should be planned in the budgeting process, or in a budget revision. Even a temporary cash excess should be reflected in your budget revision because you don't want to spend it on such things as equipment or debt repayment. It is pretty likely that you'll need those funds to pay regular expenses. For example, March may show an excess that will be eaten up by expenses in April and May. This is especially true with "up-front" grants (which are becoming very hard to get!)

The best planning is to invest funds temporarily in a safe, interest-bearing account, or in a certificate of deposit that will mature just before the time you'll need it. (It's best to invest in accounts insured by F.D.I.C.). Don't overlook planning to use as much of the temporary excess as you can to build up a "rainy day" reserve fund.

This approach to budgeting is more a form of cash management and is dealt with in depth in

Chapter 14. Nevertheless, you should anticipate any such "problems" in budgeting cash, and have a plan and policy for dealing with them when the time comes.

CAPITAL BUDGETING

Capital budgeting is a subject that can be approached on different levels, from simple to very complex. Sophisticated techniques are used primarily by large, complex organizations. We will within this chapter adopt a simple, common-sense approach that can be used for routine capital budgeting. The Appendix to this chapter offers an overview of some more sophisticated methods. Those who need them (or who don't suffer from math anxiety!) can pursue them in greater depth if necessary, in books aimed primarily at larger business firms and nonprofits.

A Simple Basic Approach to Capital Budgeting

Budgeting for the purchase of major items of real property or costly equipment may be looked upon as a special variant of cash flow budgeting in a nonprofit organizaton. What is different about it is essentially a longer time frame, and the linking of the uses of funds with their proposed sources.

Factors to consider in capital budgeting.
● How well the present equipment or property serves the needs of the organization, in terms of its condition or capacity. Whether repair and maintenance costs have reached the point where it would be economical to replace worn equipment with new, or even consider factory-reconditioned/used equipment.

● What alternative facilities would cost under alternate plans of financing: outright purchase, installment purchase, borrow-and-buy, long-term rental.

● What sources exist for financing each of these alternatives: special grants, installment purchases, long- or short-term loans. From which sources and on what terms, including collateral, could this money be raised? Is a special fund drive among supporters a possibility?

● The cash flow aspect presents itself with respect to the payment of installment loans or rentals, including any interest factors which may be present, explicitly or implicitly. For example, a piece of equipment may cost $1,000 if paid for in cash, or $1,100 if paid for in 24 monthly installments. The difference is what accountants refer to as implicit interest, which is an additional acquisition cost, in terms of cash outlay.

Examples of considerations that influence capital budgeting. Let us assume that our fictitious organization, the Center for Community Services, Inc., needs a new $12,000 van and has the alternative of acquiring one through any one of the following arrangements: (Note: all figures are rounded)

1. Pay $12,000 cash.

2. Borrow funds to purchase for cash. Repay loan in one year at 12% interest in 12 monthly payments of $1,066.

3. Pay for it in 24 monthly installments of $565, including finance charges (interest).

4. Rent on two-year lease at a monthly rental of $450.

5. Accumulate (save the funds) over the two-year period before purchasing for cash. This is called a "sinking fund."

Assume that the Center could invest spare funds at 5% per annum, compounded monthly, and that if purchased the vehicle could be sold at the end of two years for $5,000.

The approach to this somewhat complex decision might be as follows:

Alternatives		Total cost	Cash outlay per year
1.	*Purchase for cash* (if cash available)	$12,000	$12,000
	5% interest lost (two years) if taken from savings.	1,259	(first year only)
	(compounded monthly)	13,259	
2.	*Borrow funds to purchase with cash*		12,792
	Cost of 12 monthly loan payments of $1,066	12,792	(first year only)
3.	*Installment purchase*		6,780
	Cost of 24 monthly payments of $565.	13,560	(2 years)
4.	*Rent on two-year lease*		5,400
	Cost of $450 per month rental for 24 months.	10,800[1]	(2 years)
5	*Sinking fund*		
	Save up for the purchase over a two-year period: monthly amount needed to be deposited, at 5% interest, compounded monthly, to accumulate to $13,230 in two years is $525.[2]	$12,600	$6,300 (12 × $525)

This last alternative is not directly comparable to the first four, since it involves postponing acquisition of the vehicle for two years. It is useful as a long-range planning alternative, however.[3]

Intuition would tell you that anything costs less if you save for it than if you pay with borrowed funds (which includes installment purchases). On the other hand, during an era of high inflation, it was often argued that the erosion of the dollar at rates as high as 12% made it advantageous to pay with borrowed funds. The loan repayments or installments will be made with dollars worth less and less, and thus easier to come by, whereas the value of dollars accumulated by savings will shrink with time; it will therefore take more of them to buy the same item, as illustrated in alternative 5, above. (Inflation is moderate at this writing.)

Analyzing the results of calculations in the example.

1. Rental requires the lowest cash outlay per year, but it results in twice as much cost (or more), for it must be renewed annually, possibly at an increased rate. (And you never own the item.)

---

[1]Note that while rental appears to be cheaper, this rental continues each year you need a car, whereas with other options you have a fully paid car after 2 years.

[2]At an annual inflation rate of 5%, the vehicle would cost $13,230 in two years, not $12,000. Due to the interest earned, the vehicle would cost less than $13,230. The monthly deposit was derived from present value tables, discussed in the appendix to this chapter.

[3]In order to save, revenues must exceed expenses, excluding depreciation expense, which does not involve a cash outlay. Thus a break-even result *after* adequate depreciation means funds are being accumulated.

2. Installment purchase over two years takes a lower cash outlay per year than the one-year loan. Repaying the loan over two years at 13%, if possible, would reduce cash outlays per year to $6,846, which is still more than the installment payments ($6,780.)

3. Based on the above data, and assuming the vehicle is needed *now*, the best options would be:

    (a) pay in installments in two years;
    (b) borrow and repay over two years.

Note that this example is based on arbitrary data. Different terms could change the analysis—and your decision. There is no substitute for working out such an analysis yourself, using the actual terms of loans, installments, leases and interest rates, and after shopping for the best deal available.

In the first and last alternatives, an unpredictable factor is interest rates, which change over time. It is therefore best to use a conservative rate in such calculations.

In weighing the decision to buy, it is also wise to find out the trade-in and resale value of any vehicle or equipment being replaced by the new one. (The Center has one vehicle in use in Program A.) (And don't forget the new one's eventual value.)

Business enterprises use a more complex approach to capital budgeting involving, among other things, the time value of money.[4] This involves the use of compound interest, and "present value" tables. A large nonprofit considering purchase or lease of a building or major equipment might want to consider such an approach. Should such substantial acquisitions be planned, advice should be sought of a professional in the field of financial management. Your bank may be able to help with advice. (See the appendix to this chapter for an overview.)

Capital budgeting formats checklist. There is no typical form for the capital budget of a nonprofit organization, only the need for a clear and orderly presentation of the board's plans for major asset acquisitions, including its plans for funding them. A capital budget should cover at least the following points and future annual periods:

- Major asset acquisitions planned: descriptions, acquisition dates, suppliers, whether additions or replacements of existing assets, and estimated costs.

- Mode of acquisition: lease or purchase; trade-in or sale of present asset being replaced, and estimated value for that purpose.

- Source of funds to purchase: savings or investments, cash borrowings or installment payments, source of borrowings. If a special fund drive is possible, over what period? Indicate grant proposal (if possible) and list names of funding agencies. (The latter course is dangerous unless already explored with such agencies and encouragement has been received.)

- Sinking fund: schedule of deposits or payments on loans or installments, showing individual amounts and grand total for each month and year covered in the capital budget.

- Capital assets and related liabilities: show whether these are to be set up as restricted funds (e.g., plant fund; see Chapter 13).

The capital budget then becomes an adjunct and resource in preparing both the cash budget and the operating budget. It is both a long-range planning tool and an operating document to be used in executing the plan, for it sets forth schedules to be followed in acquiring capital assets and paying for them.

---

[4]Also income-tax considerations, which can affect a nonprofit subject to the tax on Unrelated Business Income (see Chapters 1 and 16).

Such acquisitions will affect accounting and budgeting in the following areas:

- Cash flow budgeting, for their financing and presumed reduction in repair and maintenance costs.
- Balance sheets, which should reflect both the cost of assets purchased and any related loan or installment obligations undertaken (and elimination of assets replaced).
- Operating budgets and operating statements, which should reflect the reduced repair and maintenance costs, and presumably increased depreciation expense covering the new assets over that of the assets replaced.

The role of depreciation.   Although nonprofit organizations have not used depreciation accounting, and many have even treated the cost of capital assets acquired as a current expense, the new rules prescribed for external financial reporting by nonprofits (see Chapter 15) will probably end those practices and bring nonprofit accounting into line with overall accounting theory in these respects.

A 1978 policy statement issued by the American Institute of CPAs made the observation that depreciation accounting is designed to charge each period for its share of the cost of using an asset, making depreciation expense analagous to rental expense.[5] At the same time, it points out that depreciation "is sometimes confused with funding replacements," which is a separate financial question.

While this is unquestionably true, some organizations properly relate the two by "funding depreciation"—i.e., setting up a sinking fund in which amounts equal to the periodic depreciation expense are deposited in a special "sinking fund savings account" or otherwise invested. The investment plus accumulated investment income is then tapped for asset replacement. (The board should designate this a "board restricted fund": see Chapter 13.)

The point made previously about the effect of inflation on the funding of replacements is relevant here, for the amount of depreciation is based on the cost of the present asset, not what it will cost to replace it at an inflated price in the future. The addition of interest or dividends to the amounts added to the sinking fund will help offset the effect of inflation, however.

Other Basic Issues

Not only comparative costs are involved in capital budgeting, but also other factors of a serious nature:

- A wrong decision can result in hiring—or not hiring—people who would be involved in operating or managing the property or equipment—or worse, in eventually laying people off, if the decision was a bad one.

- How efficient is the new equipment? How easy to learn, maintain, and repair? Will the seller or manufacturer provide support in these areas? Service contracts? On-site or nearby authorized service? What about ready availability of repair or replacement parts, components, or supplies? How big a job is installation? Will it require any additional costs for special wiring, plumbing, or work on the building? How flexible is it for different uses?

- Money may also be wasted on fundraising, advertising, training, or other related activities, if a bad decision is made.

---

[5]Statement of Position 78-10 (Dec. 1978), paragraphs 107 and 111.

- If assets are bought and are not usable, the money is tied up wastefully, and there may well be ongoing related costs that cannot be easily avoided, such as insurance, security, and maintenance. Space can be tied up that could be used more advantageously.

- Money invested unproductively is money not available for productive purposes. Opportunities for better use of the funds are thus lost.

- A mistaken decision not to invest the funds also represents a lost opportunity, which may have a material effect on the organization's future, especially if nothing as good turns up.

APPENDIX 7A

Capital Budgeting for Sophisticates

If basic math holds no terrors for you, you can use far more scientific approaches to capital budgeting than those offered in the body of this chapter. They will pay off in the long run, especially if large amounts of money are involved. The approaches used in the chapter are sufficient when you're thinking about a new car or computer, since the dollar differences between choices are not great. In dealing with big capital outlays, such as realty or heavy equipment like machinery or trucks, or investing in an income-producing venture, however, the dollar differences are too big to ignore.

The methods described here also provide added defenses against salespeople and realtors who might otherwise dazzle you with figures that look convincing, but that fall apart under scrutiny.

TYPES OF CAPITAL BUDGETING DECISIONS

1. *How to finance a capital acquisition.* This is the kind of decision looked at (using simple concepts) in the foregoing chapter. It seeks to answer the questions, "which method costs the least?" and "which one can we handle with our cash flow and available funds?" (The answers to these questions may be different, if cash is tight: you can always save money if you have money!) It may also involve the question of whether to buy or to lease.

2. *Would it be a good thing to invest in at all?* In a business, or an income-producing venture of a nonprofit, you are looking at return on investment, either in profits on goods or services sold, or in cost savings. This involves some complex considerations. In many nonprofits you are not paid, or not paid fully, for your services. A somewhat different approach is then necessary, sometimes one involving much imagination. This is the area of benefit–cost analysis.

3. *Should we replace an old asset? If so, when?* This, of course, involves a look not only at the cost and benefits of the new asset, but also at how these compare with the costs and benefits of continuing to use the old one.

THE TIME VALUE OF MONEY

One complicating factor mentioned but not illustrated in Chapter 7 is the recognition that a dollar received today is worth more than a dollar received a year from now. That is true quite aside from inflation, because if you put today's dollar in a savings account or some other stable investment, it should be worth more than a dollar in a year.

Thus if you could earn 6% on your money, today's dollar would be worth $1.06 a year from now.

(That's called the *future value* of the dollar.) Putting it another way, assuming a 6% interest rate, that year-off dollar is only worth a little over 94 cents today: you'd have to invest 94.34 cents today at 6% to add up to a dollar in a year. That's called the *present value* of $1.00, a year from now, using a 6% discount rate. If you took a promissory note from someone else to your bank, that's how they'd figure out how much to give you for it, depending on their rate of interest. Also, they would take into account whether interest was to be compounded, and if so, whether it would be on a monthly or daily basis, which would affect the amount of cash you'd receive.

It can get more complicated if you are talking not about a single amount, but about a series of payments, such as installments on a mortgage or equipment purchase, or rentals on a lease, whether you are paying or receiving them. There are three ways to do the arithmetic involved.

1. *Present value tables.* These are published separately or appear in textbooks on accounting and finance. Using such a table of present values, all you do is look up a factor based on the number of periods in which interest is to be compounded or payments made and the interest rate to be used. You then multiply that factor by the amount of principal involved.

For the future value of a present sum, you use a future value table, but for the present value of a future sum, you use a present value table. For the present value of a series of equal payments, or for the total future value of such payments, you use annuity tables. For the periodic payment needed to reach a certain amount in the future, you use a "sinking fund" table. (An annuity is a fixed amount to be paid or received per period. A sinking fund is a fixed amount deposited per period, to save up and pay a certain total.)

2. *Calculators and computers.* Some spreadsheet programs for microcomputers have some or all of the equations for present value tables pre-programmed. All you have to do is enter the variables: amount, interest rate, and number of periods. There are even sophisticated hand-held calculators that can do the same, usually business or finance models, which usually at least can calculate present and future values. With the equations that follow, you can do basic present and future value calculations without much trouble, even on most simple digital calculators.

a. *Present value:*

$$P_n = \frac{F_n}{(1 + r)^n}$$

Where: P_n is present value; F_n is the future value at the end of n periods; r is the interest rate per period; and n is the number of periods. (Where interest is compounded monthly, a monthly period is used for both r and n. Thus an annual interest rate of 6% compounded monthly for two years would be shown as .06/12 or .005 per period (½ of 1%) for 24 periods.)

b. *Future value:*

$$F_n = P (1 + r)^n$$

Where: F_n is the future value after n periods; P is present value; r is the rate per period, and n is the number of periods.

Calculator tip: to raise $(1 + r)$ to a power is easy: If the rate is 6%, $(1 + r)$ is 1.06; $(1 + r)^2$ is 1.06 × 1.06. Then you press the equals key for each higher power: one more time for $(1 + r)^3$, etc. (This may not work on all calculators.)

CAPITAL BUDGETING TECHNIQUES

Now that you have a handle on present value concepts, let's look at some alternative capital budgeting techniques (not all of which use them, incidentally).

The Cost of Financing a Capital Asset

Taking present value into account, what will it cost to add a capital asset? Things look a bit different when the time value of money is considered. Take, for example, the five alternative ways to acquire a vehicle, considered in Chapter 7. Three of them, #1 (purchase for cash), #2 (borrow the money), and #5 (saving up with a sinking fund) did take time value into account, since they considered interest on the money. Alternatives 3 and 4 did not.

Alternative #3 (installment purchase).   If you used an annuity table and assumed a rate of interest included in the installments of 12%, the present value of these installments would be $12,003, not the $13,560 shown.

Alternative #4 (rent on two-year lease).   Using the same approach, the present value of the rent payments would be $9,560, not the $10,800 shown.

Note: The present value of the loan payments is $12,000, since the bank would base the loan installments, including interest, on present value tables.

The outcome of the analysis is changed now. The present value of the payments on the installment purchase is about the same as that of the bank loan. (That would almost always be the case, since both would be based on present value tables: only the rate of interest used would differ, unless there are other hidden charges.) The reason the total and monthly cash flow are different is that the loan is being paid off in a shorter time, so each payment must be higher. The longer the loan, however, the more total interest you are paying, assuming the rate is the same.

Since the total of the payments is unequal, always find out what *effective* rate of interest is being charged. You have a right to know this under the Truth in Lending Laws.

The cost of the lease is less than that of the other alternatives, but you don't own a vehicle at the end of the two years, so it's not a valid comparison. If you want to take this factor into account as well, you need some estimate of the trade-in value of the vehicle at the end of the lease period and what the present value of that amount is, at the rate of interest you can earn on your money.

With all needed data in hand, you can rank the various alternatives in order of desirability, using all the criteria referred to above: total cash payout, monthly payout, cash cost net of trade-in value after the relevant number of years (when the vehicle has been fully paid for), net present value of payout before and after trade-in value. You can then make a scientifically valid decision, based on which method of paying ranks highest in the areas most important to you.

Let's work this out for the example above, assuming there is no tax aspect. We'll take an uneducated guess that at the end of two years, the trade-in value of the van will be $8,000. The present value of this amount, at a savings rate of 5% (as used for the sinking fund), is $7,240. We can now produce the comparative table shown in Fig. 7A–1, taking everything into account:

Alternative Methods of Measuring Cost	Buy for cash (#1)	Buy on bank loan (#2)	Installments (#3)	24-month lease (#4)
A. Total cash payout + int.	$13,259	$12,792	$13,560	$10,800
Total cash payout / month	–0–	1,066	565	450
B. Present value of payout	12,000	12,000	12,003	9,560
C. Total cash payout	12,000	12,792	13,560	10,800
Less 2-year cash trade-in	8,000	8,000	8,000	–0–
Net cash cost	4,000	4,792	5,560	10,800
D. Present value (P.V.)	12,000	12,000	12,003	9,560
Less P.V. of trade-in	7,240	7,240	7,240	–0–
Net present value	4,760	4,760	4,763	9,560

FIGURE 7A–1. COST COMPARISON OF VARIOUS ACQUISITION METHODS.

Tax Aspects

If you are subject to the federal tax on Unrelated Business Income, assets used in connection with earning this income cost less than may appear, because the depreciation on such assets reduces your income tax. You can even write off in full up to $10,000 of the cost of such assets (other than real property), in the year you put them into service. This is a consideration that must be factored into your decision.

Analysis of Alternative Cost Methods

The alternatives presented in Fig. 7A–1 are analyzed in the paragraphs that follow.

● Method A shows the same figures given in the sample calculations in Chapter 7 (A Basic Approach to Capital Budgeting), which ranks the lease as costing the least.

● Method B repeats what we looked at a few paragraphs ago: it still favors the lease. However, both ignore the trade-in value of the van.

● Method C, based on cash payout alone, but considering the cash value of the trade-in, makes buying for cash look best (and the lease looks awful!).

● Finally, using the most scientific approach, shown in Method D, any of the first three ways to acquire the van costs about the same—less than half the cost of a lease, with the figures given.

From a monthly cash flow viewpoint, buying on installments is the choice many nonprofits would make, because (1) they may not have the money to pay cash, (2) they now understand that the lower cash flow required by the lease is a snare in a delusion, and (3) the bank loan requires almost twice the monthly cash payout as the installments, even though its total payout is lower. On the other hand, if you can get a two-year bank loan with the same rate of interest, the monthly payments should be about the same as the installments. The importance of getting the lowest interest rate is clear.

CAPITAL BUDGETING WHERE BENEFITS AS WELL AS COSTS ARE INVOLVED

The decision to acquire property sometimes involves another consideration: its use to produce income or reduce present costs. This is a more complex capital budgeting decision not common to any but large nonprofits.

Payback Period

A typical situation you might face is one in which a salesperson says, "The amount you save (or earn) using this equipment will be enough to pay what it will cost you in (say) three years."—The length of time may vary, but the claim is a common one. Let's see how you verify this kind of claim, which may or may not be a valid one from your point of view. This is of course a simple calculation (payout period = total cost divided by annual savings or earnings). The thing to watch is how the amount saved or earned per year is calculated (and by whom!) and whether the truth of the claim can be demonstrated. You should check these out carefully, and not just accept the assertion, since you may not make the same assumptions in areas such as costs or income. It is a good idea to ask for recommendations from independent present users.

Most commonly, any potential savings are in payroll costs, yet these can differ substantially, depending on which staffer uses the equipment: salary rates vary, as do energy and ability. Savings in staff time may only save money if using the equipment enables you to hire fewer people, for example, although any time saved may result in its being used to earn money. Savings in fuel or electricity are more reliably predictable, if the basis can be shown.

Rate of Return

Another approach can be used in comparing the profitability of investments in income-producing ventures. Compare the projected rate of return of each on the average amount of the proposed investment. The calculation would look like this for each proposal:

$$\frac{\text{Net income (after taxes, if any)}}{\text{Average investment}} = \text{Rate of return}$$

The average investment is the original outlay divided by two, if the whole investment is made at the beginning, or in equal installments. You can now rank proposed projects by rate of return, and can reject any with a rate below some desired minimum.

Net Cash Benefit

Here's another way to approach the decision, using cash flow over the life of the asset—an aspect that the payback period ignores. To make it approximate a real-life situation, let's assume we are paying for an asset in monthly installments over two years—either on a bank loan or installment purchase. The asset will generate a monthly cash benefit (savings or earnings), to be called "cash inflow." We can compare that with the payout over its expected life, which we'll assume to be five years. (Let's ignore trade-in value here, to simplify things.)

	Cash inflows	Cash outflows
Monthly amounts × 12 =	$ 400	$ 500
Annual totals	$ 4,800	$ 6,000
Total no. of years	5	2
Total cash flows	$24,000	$12,000

In this case, although annual cash flow is a negative figure, $1,200 ($4,800 minus $6,000), during the first two years, it is all gravy thereafter: a $4,800 a year inflow. Over the expected life of the asset, inflows are twice outflows—if our assumption about inflow is correct. Any tax saved by depreciation, or any trade-in value after five years, will further improve the picture.

Net Present Value

How does the present value of the inflows compare with that of the outflows, a more scientific approach? We can use the tables for the present value of an annuity to find our answer. Let's assume an interest rate of 5% on the inflows, as we have in all our examples, and assume that 12% is being charged on the installments. We can find the present value of the outflows—the amount we'd have to pay in cash for the asset—as follows:

	Cash inflows	Cash outflows
Monthly amounts	$ 400	$ 500
Number of payments		
5 yrs × 12 mos	60	
2 yrs × 12 mos		24
Rate of interest	5%	12%
P.V. factor (table)	52.990706	21.243387
Monthly amount × P.V. factor =	$21,196	$10,622
Net present value = inflows minus outflows, or $10,574.		

The result using present values is similar to the previous result, because the present value of the inflows is twice that of the outflows. If we could stretch out the payments or pay a lower interest rate, the savings would be even greater. For example, if we paid the same loan (assumed to be $10,622) over three years instead of two, the monthly payout would approach $353, which is less than the monthly inflow for the first two years. The total cash outflow would be about $12,700 (only 700 more, in added interest), and the present value of the payments would be the same. Shopping around might also get you a better interest rate.

This kind of analysis can also be used in connection with buying a building, rather than continuing to pay rent, or buying it to rent out. The rent saved or earned would be the inflow, but monthly cash operating costs would have to be added to the outflow of mortgage payments. If the U.B.I. tax applies, you must also consider the annual income tax cost.

Interest Rate Used for Inflows.   In the above calculations, we've used a current savings bank rate of 5%. But if this were a capital asset to be used in an income-producing venture, you would want a higher rate of interest than you get on savings. There's no point investing in such a venture otherwise. In the calculation, you might use 8%–12%, depending on your desired return on investment. The resulting present value of inflows would then be quite different: At 10% it would be $18,826 instead of $21,196. In general, an investment is acceptable if the present value of inflows exceeds that of outflows.

The net present value approach can also be used in choosing between investments in equipment, property, or income-producing ventures. What would be compared would be the inflow side, if the required cash payments are the same.

Profitability Index Approach

The profitability index is a variant used where alternative income-producing ventures requiring different initial investments are being considered. The profitability index is calculated by dividing the present value of the net cash inflows or benefits by the initial outlays. Only proposals with an index (ratio) greater than 1.00 are acceptable. The proposal with the highest index above 1.00 will give the greatest return on investment. Note that this is better than merely subtracting the initial outlay from the present value of the inflows, since differences in the size of the investment or inflows may result in choosing the project with the higher net present value, rather than the one with the greatest percentage return on investment.

It is also far superior to using the rate of return approach shown above, unadjusted for present values.

Asset Replacement Decisions

A common decision that must be made is whether to replace an aging item of equipment. Common sense tells you that as things age, their repair and maintenance costs begin to get out of hand. Replacing them may often save money in the long run. But how do you determine whether this time has arrived? The calculation is similar to those already presented, but it is more complex, because the costs and benefits of both the old and new equipment are involved. An example follows.

Let's assume the following figures:

	Old equipment	New equipment
Original cost	$10,000	$12,500
Present trade-in	1,500	—
Cash operating costs per year	7,500	4,500
Cost to overhaul old equipment	2,000	—
Trade-in value, 6 years from now	6 years	2,500
Years of remaining life	6 years	6 years

Here is how you might calculate the relative costs of the two alternatives. Let's assume that you want a return of 10% on any invested funds.

	Year	10% cash inflows (outflows)	Present value factor	Present value of cash flows using 10% rate
Alternative A: Buy new equipment				
Cash outlay	1	$(12,500)	1.000	$(12,500)
Trade-in value of old equipment	1	1,500	1.000	1,500
Cash operating costs per year	1–6	$ (4,500)	4.3552607	(19,599)
Trade-in value of new equipment	6	2,500	0.5644739	1,411
Present value of net cash outflows				$(29,188)

Note: We used 1.000 for transactions for the first year, the Present Value of an Annuity table for six years' costs and the present value of the future trade-in after 6 years.

	Year	Cash inflows (outflows)	Present value factor	Present value of cash flows using 10% rate
Alternative B: Keep & overhaul old equipment				
Cost of overhaul	1	$ (2,000)	1.000	$ (2,000)
Annual cash operating costs	1–6	(7,500)	4.3552607	(32,664)
Present value of net cash outflows				$(34,664)
Net present value: favors new equipment (P.V. of outflows of new less than of old)				$ 5,476

Note: We used 1.000 for the overhaul at the start of the first year, the present value of an annuity of six payments at 10% for the annual cash operating costs.

Investment in Working Capital

Many investments in capital equipment result in the need for additional working capital to bring the equipment on line.* Equipment usually requires funds for maintenance and the wages of someone to operate it. This need for working capital must be planned for as well.

If There Are No Obvious Savings or Earnings

Many program or project proposals are made for an intended social benefit, and not necessarily for any clear savings or earnings that may result. This is generally the realm of politics or philosophy, and numerous arguments pro and con are advanced. The problem is inherently that of weighing the expected benefits against costs, since there are never enough resources to do everything that might be desirable. That translates into priorities in the use of resources.

*"Working capital" will be defined later, but can here be thought of as cash requirements.

While the outcome may turn on political pressures rather than anything else, it is nearly always necessary or desirable to do what is called a benefit–cost (or cost–benefit) analysis. While this is the subject we have been examining, the problem here is how to measure *in quantitative terms* what the benefit is, when the true benefit may be general social well-being or happiness. It is sometimes possible to find something to quantify. For example, the benefit of training welfare mothers to become employable, at a given cost, can be compared with the potential reduction of the welfare rolls plus the increased income tax revenues projected from such employment.

Unfortunately measuring such direct outcomes in dollars is not always very reliable, nor are many other approaches. Yet the attempt should be made, if possible. Imagination and creative thinking are the keys. This is the cutting edge of performance measurement, and choices of such measures tend to be controversial.

Where no clear quantifiable benefit can be recognized, two other approaches can be used:

1. Use a so-called surrogate measure, which seeks to quantify the result or benefit indirectly. An example is a written or verbal questionnaire asking clients, students, or patients to evaluate the value or benefit of the program or service to them. These are tabulated, averaged, and a measure of benefit arrived at. Peer reviews of program personnel are another surrogate measure.

In many cases measures like these are challenged as being too subjective; some professionals question the ability of a nonprofessional recipient of a service to evaluate it in a meaningful way. (Example: is a student competent to evaluate a teacher's effectiveness? Can or will a student do so objectively? What about the potential influence of grades received?)

2. In the alternative, benefit–cost analysis, as most often used, may well come down to a method of weighing alternative proposals only. Will proposal A yield a greater quantity (and/or quality) of service than proposal B, for the same amount of money? Or if they both produce the same results, which one costs less? This kind of benefit–cost analysis is undoubtedly the kind most commonly used. It is often simple common sense dressed up by the scientific-sounding term Benefit–Cost Analysis. As noted previously, the decision may ride more on political or social considerations than on economic ones, such as which proposal has the most public appeal or political clout.

Second-Guessing Your Decisions

A final step in the capital budgeting process should be to review the decision as it works out in practice. Most capital budgeting decisions involve estimates and projections regarding benefits, sometimes of costs as well. Clearly, each decision needs to be reviewed with the advantage of hindsight (which is always 20–20), in order to evaluate its results. Basically the question is, did it work out the way we thought it would? If it did, wonderful! If not, you can profit from such a review by discovering what you overlooked or miscalculated in making the projections and decision. Remember the saying that "anyone who does not study history is condemned to repeat the same mistakes."

Chapter 8

Fundraising

They tell the story of how, some years back, one of our top choreographers sent back an R.F.P. (request for proposal) with these words written across the top sheet: "I don't make proposals, I make dances!"

True or not, we can all relate to a good story. Whether it worked, we can't say. If it did, she either had a fairy godmother at the other end, or more likely, nothing succeeds like success.

Try to put yourself behind the desk of that grant officer you are asking for funding. She or he is literally swamped with competing grant requests. The result: what Tom Wolf called the "three-pile phenomenon. There is a 'yes' pile, a 'no' pile and a 'maybe' pile . . . by far the largest."[1] The well-known applicants usually have the inside track to the "yes" pile. Your first goal must be to make that big "maybe" pile. (Your longer range goal is of course to get on the "yes" pile in future years.)

If individuals are your fundraising target, they are swamped the same way in what is seen as "junk mail" (or "junk phone calls!"). They have their own three piles, and often the "no" pile is mail that gets tossed, unopened.

The Plan of this Chapter

1. *Generic fundraising methods.* No two nonprofits are the same, even if they are in the same field. But basic fundraising concepts and techniques can be used or adapted by most of them.

2. *Different types of fundraising sources and how your approach should differ.*

3. *Different nonprofits and different funding situations.*

4. *Charity begins at home.* Improving your cash flow and "bottom line" by how you mind the store: pricing, marketing, and getting the most for your money.

5. *Income-producing ventures.* Ways to earn money with no strings attached are covered in Chapter 9.

---

[1]Thomas Wolf, The Nonprofit Organization (Englewood Cliffs, N.J. 1984; Prentice-Hall) p. 160.

IT CAN'T WORK IN A VACUUM

In a business, marketing both drives and is determined by all other activities and plans. Fundraising, the nonprofit equivalent of marketing, must be an integral part of the organizational whole. It cannot be seen as the private specialty or mere bag of tricks owned by a hired gun. Professional fundraisers come and they go, whether they serve on staff or as consultants.

Nonprofits that survive and succeed therefore make fundraising a permanent and ongoing activity, one that continually involves the board as well as the CEO (chief staff officer). To quote an expert on the subject, Brian O'Connell, President of Independent Sector,

> One of the cruelest and most inappropriate things a board can do is to call for increased income
> and leave it to staff to produce or else![2] ... The good development directors are worth what they
> are being paid, but those very same specialists are good in large part because they know—and will
> tell you—that they can only succeed to the extent that the board and staff leadership are committed
> to and involved in the fund raising. It will not work for the board to assign the task to the executive
> director, and it will not work for him or her to pass the assignment on to the fund raising director.
> On the other hand, if the three work together as a team, the results can be absolutely terrific.[3]

Regardless of the kind of nonprofit you're in, or its situation, an isolated or over-specialized approach to fundraising is doomed to fail. Here's why:

1. Funders and donors don't "give money"—they invest in programs they want to see happening. According to Melinda Marble of Tufts University's Filene Center, when fundraising is a fully integrated activity,

> ... it can be an empowering experience for the organization. The best fund raisers think about
> what they do not as begging, but as developing resources and self-sufficiency for the organiza-
> tion. They see themselves, not as supplicants, but as offering opportunities to funders to spend
> their money wisely for community good.[4]

The one who has the most knowledge about a program which is needed to sell it is generally its manager or director. But having the knowledge is not enough. You also have to know the most effective way to present it, and how it fits into the agency as a whole. For information about hiring outside consultants to run a fundraising campaign, see "Fundraising Consultants," later in this chapter.

2. You may not be the only kid on the block. Other nonprofits may offer competing programs, maybe not better, maybe a bit different. More than programs, your funder is buying sound people, well-run organizations, that can deliver effectively. Fundraising succeeds when it is totally immersed in what's going on—or is in the works—in the whole agency, and therefore conveys this convincingly to a targeted funding source.

3. Fundraising is only one part of the over-all resource-generating activity of many nonprofits, sometimes called its "funding mix." Policy decisions regarding this mix should drive and direct fundraising, taking into account other sources of funds, such as membership dues, the sale of products or services (e.g. admissions), investment income, or endowment income.

---

[2]See *Fund Raising*, (Independent Sector, Washington, DC: 1987), p. 8
[3]*Op. cit.*, p. 10.
[4]Private correspondence with the authors.

4. Other policy decisions that may affect fundraising include program priorities and preferred funding source (government agencies, United Way, foundations, corporations, individuals), as well as such decisions as increases in support staff or facilities.

5. Strategic plans regarding such matters as growth, new programs, or income ventures, all affect fundraising needs and approaches. If plans aren't clear and understood by the fundraiser, chances are they won't be made clear to your funding source either.

FUNDRAISING IS INFORMATION PROCESSING

Getting the over-all task in focus breaks it down into information inputs, information processing, and information outputs.

1. Information inputs.

a. About the nonprofit itself: program plans, resources available and needed (staff and volunteers, facilities, equipment, supplies, funds), track record, financial strength and accountability, tax status, board oversight.

b. About the target population: a needs assessment, demographics, and any other information that relates to the giving patterns.

c. About competition (same as "a", above).

d. About potential funding sources: names and addresses, policies, interest areas and restrictions, size of grants or donations, application procedures and deadlines, key personnel.

e. Media costs: direct mail, telemarketing, print and broadcast media, production and delivery.

2. Information processing.

a. Analysis and evaluation of data presented in 1a–e, above.

b. Statistical analysis where appropriate (it is appropriate for the information given in paragraphs 1a and b, above).

c. Selection of most relevant and significant data from each area 1a–d, above.

d. Cost–benefit analysis of fundraising media or methods.

3. Information outputs.

a. Fully worked out fundraising and work plans.

b. Funding and grant proposals.

c. Media use proposals and budgets.

These are the work products of the fundraising function, and they reflect the effectiveness of your fundraising program.

As shown in Chapter 3, planning involves not only setting goals and objectives, but also planning how to get from here to there, and how to know when you've arrived. A goal or objective is not, "we need to write ten proposals," but "We need to raise $100,000 in grants by June 30." The plan might be, "We need to finish and mail ten proposals by March 31, averaging $30,000 each, to be followed up on April 30 and May 31." The work plan would assign the tasks, along with start and finish dates for each, and would allow time for data collection, research, and analysis, in addition to writing.

(Just in case you're wondering, "Why write $300,000 worth of proposals to raise $100,000?"—a .333 batting average is enough to make it into the big leagues.)

MAJOR FUNDING SOURCES

The first question a fundraiser asks is "who is giving how much to whom these days?" The Grantsmanship Center publishes an annual catalog, which offers a summary of the most recent statistics available. It is of interest that overall giving more than doubled between 1980 and 1989: from $48.7 billion to $114.7 billion, whereas federal grants decreased during the same period. The data published by *Giving USA*, shown in Figs. 8–1.A and 8–1.B, can yield some highly significant information.

Although nearly all sources and recipients of nongovernmental funding indicate increases over 1988, when these figures are adjusted for inflation, corporate giving actually declined for the third year, as did funds received for education. Health care held about even; arts and culture rose only 5.4%, public/society benefit (including the environment) 8%, and religion 7.4%.[5]

If you assume that in 1989 virtually all contributions to religious groups came from individuals and their estates, little or none from foundations or corporations, then of the $66.6 billion in nongovernmental funds received by nonprofits other than religious groups ($114.7 minus $48.1), only $11.7 billion ($6.7 + $5.0) came from foundations and corporations (about 18%), whereas about $54.9 billion (82%) came from individuals and their estates ($96.4 + $6.6 - 48.1).

This calls into question the tremendous emphasis most nonprofits give to the pursuit of foundation and corporate grants, which represented only 10.2% of nongovernment funding in 1989, whereas individuals and estates represented 47.9%. While proposal writing takes less time, work, and money than organizing fund drives and other approaches to individual donors, the mounting competition for such grants calls this excessive emphasis into question.

We will nonetheless deal next with the ever-popular subject of proposal writing, and save individual fundraising methods for later.

FACTS ABOUT FOUNDATION GRANTS

Foundations are the major targets of the proposal writing process. In 1987 there were over 27,000 U.S. foundations, many of them small or local ones. However, 93% of foundaton grant funds came from only 6,615 foundations in 1989, according to the Foundation Center, New York. Foundations represented only 6.7% of nongovernmental funds received by nonprofits in 1989. The size of their grants, interest areas, and criteria for funding vary widely:

- Some make only very large grants to universities, hospitals, or major cultural institutions; others make very small ones; most are somewhere in between.

- Some make grants only within their own region—state or city—others, nationwide or even internationally.

- Some have diverse interest areas; some are narrowly focused on one or two.

- Most will make grants only to exempt organizations; some will make grants to individuals as well.

---

[5]As reported in *The Nonprofit Times*, June, 1990.

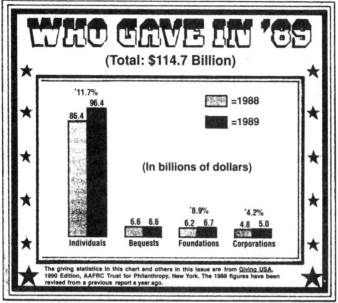

©THE NONPROFIT TIMES. Design/Illustration by Jim Feld

FIGURE 8–1. A. 1988 and 1989 SOURCES OF NON-GOVERNMENTAL FUNDS.*

Where the money goes

SECTOR	1989	1988*	Change
Religion	$54.32	$48.09	13.0%
Education	$10.69	$10.23	4.5%
Health	$10.04	$9.58	4.8%
Human Services	$11.39	$10.49	8.6%
Arts, Culture	$7.49	$6.79	10.3%
Public Benefit	$3.62	$3.21	12.8%
Other	$17.15	$15.48	10.8%
*Revised			
Source: Giving USA, 1990			

FIGURE 8–1. B. 1988 and 1989 RECIPIENTS OF NON-GOVERNMENTAL FUNDING.*

*From *Giving USA, 1990*, AAFRC Trust for Philanthropy, 1990.

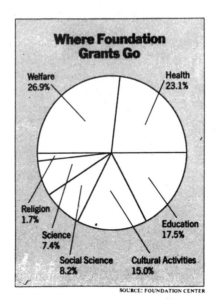

FIGURE 8-2. WHERE FOUNDATION GRANTS WENT IN 1988
(*The Chronicle of Philanthropy,* July 11, 1989.)

CHURCHES AS A SOURCE OF GRANTS

Often overlooked by community groups, churches act not only as charities for individuals, they also give grants and donations to non-church–related nonprofits. In 1986 these totalled $1.9 billion, no small amount.

CORPORATE AND BUSINESS FUNDING SOURCES

There are about 14,000 corporate foundations and giving programs in the Foundation Center's database. They commonly make grants primarily in the localities in which their major operations are located, to promote their community status. Although corporations are permitted to deduct 10% of profits from taxes for contributions, corporate funding has averaged only between 1% and 2% of profits annually. They gave 5% of nongovernmental funding received by nonprofits in 1989. Direct corporate grants are generally aimed at promoting the welfare, interests, and image of the corporation, its employees, and officers. For example, companies in the pharmaceutical and high technology industries tend to make many grants that foster research related to their own fields, but some are more broadly and socially responsive with their largesse.

A major portion of corporate giving is funnelled through the United Way and similar community chest types of organizations, much of it via employee payroll deductions. Some corporations also have giving programs that match employee donations.

Corporate grants tend to be more informal, less restrictive, and less tightly monitored than those of foundations. Corporations tend to be more generous with in-kind gifts than with cash contributions or grants. In-kind contributions may include the following:

● Free or sharply discounted merchandise (e.g., computers and software,[6] food or clothing from wholesalers or retailers.)

● Loaned executives and professional or other employees, on a released-time basis.

● Free use of facilities: space, use of computers, copying or printing equipment, and the like.

● Use of mailing facilities and postage meters.

● Services of advertising agencies in the design and production of brochures, media selection, or production of public service announcements (PSAs) for radio or television broadcast. (Stations usually donate free time for PSAs).

● Professional firms may provide pro bono legal, accounting, or consulting services free or at reduced rates.

● Local merchants may donate merchandise.

ZEROING IN ON GRANTS

How do you find the best targets for your grant proposals? You can't afford to sit around waiting for requests for proposals (RFPs) to come in the mail, unsolicited: not too many funding agencies offer them. Here is where knowledge, information, and being "plugged in" to what's going on is of crucial importance. There are numerous research and information resources available, which are important tools in the fundraiser's trade. We list below only some of the best known. A reference librarian, especially one working with a collection of nonprofit books and publications, is your best resource for further information.[7]

● *The Foundation Directory*, published annually by the Foundation Center, lists all private and corporate U.S. foundations with at least $1 million in assets or which made $100,000 in grants. There were 6,615 in 1989, and they gave over 93% of all foundation grant money. You can research foundations by geographic area, key personnel, and fields of interest.

● The *Foundation Grants Index Annual*, also published by the Foundation Center, lists 43,000 grants of $5,000 or more. *Source Book Profiles*, and *COMSEARCH*, a computerized database on foundation giving, and the *National Data Book* which lists foundations giving the overwhelming bulk of grant money, are also published by the Foundation Center in New York.

● In addition to these directories, announcements of foundation grants and RFPs can be found in periodicals like *The Chronicle of Philanthropy, Nonprofit Times,* and *Tax Exempt News.*

---

[6]Apple Computer and Lotus Development Corp. are two of the leading donors in this respect.

[7]The Foundation Center, 79 Fifth Ave., New York, N.Y. 10003 has a network of 170 cooperating library collections, in all 50 states, a leading resource. Their WATS line is 800-424-9836.

- *The National Directory of Corporate Giving* (Foundation Center).
- *Corporate Foundation Profiles* (Foundation Center).
- *Corporate 500–Directory of Corporate Philanthropy* (Public Management Institute, San Francisco).
- *Corporate Fundraising Directory* (Public Service Materials Center, New York).
- *Taft Corporate Directory* (Taft Corp., Washington, DC).

Note: It may be better to start with any large companies located in your immediate area of operations. They are usually your best bet.

GOVERNMENT GRANTS AND CONTRACTS

The federal government has long been a major funding source for nonprofits, either with direct grants and contracts, or as the source of funds for many state and local funding programs. During the Reagan era, federal funding programs were severely cut back and some dropped entirely. In view of the huge federal deficit, it seems doubtful that many cuts will be restored in the near future. The following table shows a comparison of where federal funds went in support of nonprofit organizations in 1980 and 1986, the latest figures available at this writing, and the changes between the two years. Amounts (expressed in billions of dollars) are adjusted for inflation and are stated in Constant Fiscal Year 1980 dollars.[8]

Type of nonprofit organization	Estimated		
	FY 1980	**FY 1986**	**Change**
Health care (excludes Medicare)	$ 1.5	$ 1.0	-$0.5
Social service	6.5	3.9	-2.6
Community development	2.6	1.5	-1.1
Education/research	5.6	5.2	-0.4
Arts/culture	0.4	0.2	-0.2
Foreign aid	0.8	0.7	-0.1
Totals	$17.3	$12.5	-$4.8

Figures available for federal support in 1988, in constant dollars, indicated the following increases and decreases from 1980:[9] The data indicate a continued reduction since 1980, in constant dollars, meaning purchasing power of grant funds received.

	1980	**1988**	**Change**
Educational and social services	$ 12.1	$ 8.6	-29%
Community development	2.6	1.3	-50%
Health (includes Medicare)	25.0	32.0	+28%
Foreign aid	0.8	0.7	-13%

[8]A. J. Abramson & L. M. Salamon, *The Nonprofit Sector and the New Federal Budget*, (The Urban Institute Press, Washington, DC: 1986), p. 69

[9]Same authors, as quoted in *The Chronicle of Philanthropy*, Oct. 25, 1988, p. 19.

Note: No 1988 data were available for Arts and Culture, nor separately for Education and Social Services.

The primary current sources of information on federal grants are as follows:

● Catalogue of Federal Domestic Assistance, which lists most funding programs of all federal agencies.

● FAPRS, the Federal Assistance Programs Retrieval System, a computerized database of these programs, which can be researched on request.

● The *Federal Register,* a daily U.S. government publication (Monday to Friday).

● *Commerce Business Daily*, also a federal publication, lists all U.S. RFPs of over $5,000.

● Guidelines for use in the budgeting and accounting for federal grants are contained in OMB (Office of Management and Budget) Circular A-110, available from the Superintendent of Documents, Washington, DC.

● Some federal agencies publish current information on grants, procedures, or policies. These include *American Education* (Department of Education), *Humanities* (National Endowment for the Humanities), and *NSF Grant Policy Manual* (National Science Foundation). Others respond primarily to grant proposals initiated by nonprofits.

● Your local congressional representatives' offices can often provide helpful information about potential grant opportunities.

Facts about Government Grants and Contracts

Government grants and contracts generally require particular know-how. They also often involve compliance with more restrictive demands than those of foundations, in the area of accountability and documentation, and are more subject to audits or audit requirements. In government, you are commonly dealing with layers of the bureaucracy, and your proposals may be submitted to outside professionals for review, which can add four to six months to the process. Government funding is often granted on a reimbursement basis, which means that you must spend money from your own resources before you can collect.

With federal RFPs you are often in a bidding situation; there are eligibility rules to meet, and sometimes a matching funds requirement, which can be as much as a three-to-one match on your part. Policies and procedures vary between federal agencies.

Some agencies may require an environmental impact statement, an affirmative action plan, or other special attachments to your proposal. It is essential to get a copy of the guidelines of the agency you are wooing before you invest time on proposal development. State funding is generally a bit less complicated to obtain than federal funding, though this varies between states.

The cutbacks and shifts in federal funding have transferred much of the funding and administration of nonprofit programs to state and local governments, some of which originates at the federal level. Since the dissemination of information about grants and contracts is hit-or-miss in most states, your research burden is greater. The suggestion about using knowledgeable people to minimize research time applies here with equal force. Networking with other nonprofit leaders in your field is one good way to find out which agency is funding what. Canvassing appropriate agencies directly may be desirable or necessary. This can be done through telephone or other directories. Your legislators may also be helpful. If there is a state or local association of nonprofits in your field, joining it can be of great value.

You may be able to get a technical assistance or R & D (research and development) grant from a government agency to pay for a consultant to do the research and coordinate the proposal writing.

Local government may be a funding source as well. The Community Development Block Grant program (CDBG) of the Department of Housing and Urban Development (HUD) is a prime example for nonprofits in the fields of local economic development, such as affordable housing. CDBG funds have also been used to fund activity in areas such as job development, training and counseling, social services, and land and building conservation, among others.

School systems, county court systems, and police departments may be willing to help fund such programs as day-care, or classes, workshops, and counseling in the areas of substance abuse, employment, pregnancy, or adult education.

Some local government agencies have been excellent sources of such in-kind contributions as the free use of space or facilities, and the part-time services of professional staff members. These are easier to get than cash from any organization in the public or private sector, since it usually involves no line-item they need to justify in their own budget and no out-of-pocket cost.

A PRIMER ON PROPOSAL WRITING

Whether your target funding agency is a foundation, United Way affiliate, a corporation, or a government agency, institutional grants normally require a formal written grant (or contract) proposal. Whether it is self-initiated, or submitted in response to an RFP (request for proposal), this is the way many nonprofits garner much of their support. How well you do it can be a life-or-death issue.

While the actual writing of a proposal takes some skill and talent, these abilities can only add style, polish, and good packaging: they are no substitute for content. As already pointed out, it is the person in charge of the program or developing it who knows what it's all about, and must therefore have a hand in the content area. The basic information needed is:

Key Program Information

- Who needs the program and why, and how was this ascertained? The "who" should be specified in terms of numbers, location, income and/or educational level, gender, age, and ethnicity, as appropriate.

- What alternative methods could be used to address the need, and why were the one(s) chosen considered best or most cost effective?

- What are the program's objectives and how results are to be measured?

- If an ongoing program, what kind of measurable, objective evidence is there that it is accomplishing its objectives? Making a difference?

- If a new program, how long will it take to become operational, and how long will it continue?

- What are the credentials of the staff and consultants who will manage and guide the program?

- What provision is there for evaluating the program's effectiveness?

- How much will the program cost, or how much per year? What other sources of funds will be tapped to help pay for it, including your own? What are the specific amounts of the different costs involved? (A realistic budget must be included.)

Note that this is part of the Information Input stage, its crucial element, of course.

Key Information About Your Agency

• When the organization was founded, and when it was granted tax-exempt status by the IRS. Your mission statement or statement of purpose.

• What other programs it provides and how they are funded.

• Who your key staff and board personnel are, their backgrounds and credentials. Copies of their resumes, an organizational chart, and names of key members of your advisory committee, if any, especially those in the field of the proposed program, are essential.

• Financial statements, independent audit reports, if any, for the past few years; any pertinent statistical data about program results; evidence of accomplishments; and public recognition, including awards, press clippings, and other records of significant accomplishments.

WRITING A FORMAL PROPOSAL

Before writing a proposal, it is important to obtain a copy of the RFP and grant or contract guidelines of each agency to which it will be addressed, and to tailor the proposals or transmittal letters carefully to meet those requirements.

Now that you have tracked down and pulled together the necessary information, the rest is a straight writing job. The outline of a formal proposal should look something like this:

1. Letter of transmittal

2. Cover or title page

3. Table of contents

4. Brief description of the program

5. Needs assessment statement

6. Statement of program objectives

7. How the program will work. Why this method was chosen to address the need.

8. The organization's capabilities and track record

9. How the program will be evaluated

10. Proposal budget (including other sources of funding the program)

11. Program work plan, time line, and future

12. Appendix: Resumes of key staff and board members, evidence of the organization's accomplishments and recognition, brochure, financial statements, IRS determination letter, organization chart.

If a different outline is prescribed by your target source, follow theirs, of course, but include all of this material.

The Letter of Transmittal

The letter of transmittal is your "grabber" and needs your best effort. Whether the proposal gets read at all may well depend on it. In many cases it will contain the brief description of your program proposal, which is what you have to sell to the funding source, so here is where writing talent can pay off.

There are two basic guidelines: the letter must be long enough to tell the essence of your story effectively, yet short and punchy enough to be read and digested quickly. That calls for a good precis writer, someone who can boil complex ideas and facts down into the minimum of words needed to convey them clearly and convincingly. This is not a job to stint on or rush.

The letter should distill the key highlights of outline items 4 through 8, and should state "up front" how much money is being requested, as well as other sources of funds available or being requested.

The name, address, and telephone number of the contact person in your organization should be supplied.

Many agencies and foundations supply application forms and may not require a letter of transmittal at all. Unless instructed *not* to write one, do so anyway.

Dressing up Your Prosposal

A report cover, title page, and table of contents help make an attractive and convenient package.

Brief Description of Program

Some funding agencies request a description of the program as a part of the proposal; if not, the summary included in your letter of transmittal may be sufficient. Nevertheless, repeating it in the body of the proposal itself may be wise, since it is possible that the proposal may be passed on to another reader without the letter of transmittal.

The description of your program may well be the first thing read. In a large funding organization that receives hundreds or even thousands of proposals, your proposal may first go through someone whose job it is to screen out the clearly unacceptable. The brief description or summary may be all this person reads, so it had better be on target and have economy of language.

Here is where the advice given by Strunk and White in their book *The Elements of Style* can pay off handsomely.

The Needs Assessment

A statement of the societal need or cause your program is meant to address is an essential part of any proposal. New organizations in search of programs, and new programs within established nonprofits, need to do a lot of homework. A proposal not grounded in key facts will often lack the real-world framework necessary to its credibility.

That may mean research, if you are addressing a need that is not well recognized either in general or within your locale. The needed research can be done in several ways. Here are some tips that may save you some false starts and dry holes:

- Don't reinvent the wheel. You may find that the facts you need have already been collected by someone else—a government agency, university, or another nonprofit—and may at most need some updating. The U.S. Census publications are a goldmine of local information on demographics. State, county, and local agencies conduct and publish studies: contact such departments as health, police, courts, labor, planning, housing, community development, social services, envrionmental affairs. Reference librarians can also be great sources of information and leads. Computerized inter-library loan consortiums can expand your reach tremendously, as can the use of on-line databases.

● Other published data. Don't overlook the major indexes which are keys to articles and books that may contain data and ideas:

- *Reader's Guide to Periodical Literature*—covers an index of U.S. periodicals
- *Social Sciences Index*—English language journals
- *New York Times Index*—the journal of record
- *The Public Affairs Information Service*—the international index to books and periodicals
- Many others, some more specialized and therefore better focused. Ask your reference librarian.

● Saving time with experts. Interviewing people who are either primary souces of the information you seek, or who know where to find it, can save you days—even weeks—of chasing down blind alleys. Most research time is spent locating and getting access to material and winnowing the wheat from the chaff. Key professionals who are knowledgeable about pertinent literature can be found in the agencies referred to above.

A tip: where your program addresses a social ill or problem, be aware of possible political and ideological blind spots or biases, which may affect the validity of published or oral information obtained. It is well to cross-check sources, to maximize reliability. Local government officials are especially reluctant to disclose bad news about community problems. A well-designed interview questionnaire will help focus your questions, and save time.

● Vox populi—Some programs to alleviate community ills can also benefit from widely publicized and well organized hearings or forums conducted in the affected community. The people who live with the problems are best qualified to say what they are and how they might be solved. If English is not their primary language, interpreters—better yet, anyone familiar with that you're trying to do and who speaks their language—are an ingredient essential to the success of such a meeting.

● Conducting a needs survey—If you have the time, resources, and talent, a well-designed community survey can be the most valid and effective way of assessing needs. It is recommended primarily as a last resort, because a survey of opinions or attitudes—even of facts—requires using a high-level professional to yield valid results. A valid needs survey requires valid questionnaire design, statistical sampling methodology, and methods to collect, tabulate, evaluate, and interpret the data in the survey report. *Note:* A non-professional job may be worse than none at all, leaving your results open to challenge or skepticism.

The Needs Statement

The needs statement should succinctly summarize the methodology of the needs assessment, identifying (1) who did it and when; (2) information sources and evidence, their currency and reliability; (3) the method(s) used and why chosen; and (4) samples of any questionnaire used.

The findings should be stated briefly and in quantitative terms, wherever possible. The statement should close with a summary interpreting the data, including expert outside support wherever possible.

Statement of Program Objectives

It is obvious that program objectives must be presented that meet the needs already identified in your needs assessment, and by the most effective means identified. Consistency here is clearly a must. Your objectives are basically the *outcomes* you plan to achieve in a given time period.

Objectives are mere hopes if not stated in measurable terms. (See the discussion of objectives in Chapter 3.)

Be careful not to promise more than can be realistically delivered within the proposed funding and time frame of the grant. Never forget that a grant proposal, once accepted and funded, is not a gift, but in effect a contract, one in which you promise certain results for a specified amount of money. What recourse your funding source has, if any, in the event you don't fulfill *your* end depends on the wording of the grant and guidelines.

You may be asked to return any unspent grant funds, or funds used for non-grant purposes. In any event, failure to deliver may not only prevent future funding from that source, it might well damage your chances with other funding agencies: the grapevine works all too well!

Another reason not to promise too much is that it may damage your credibility to the extent that you will not receive the funding. Grant officers commonly have a fairly good idea of how much can be done with a given amount of money. If you are exceptionally efficient and productive, and can make a good case of it, that's a different story.

Grant officers are commonly realistic about the extent to which a given need can be met—or social problem solved—with a typical grant. They are quick to pull back the curtain on the Wizard of Oz, looking for the smoke and mirrors. So don't try to palm off aspirin as the Cure for Cancer.

How the Program Will Work

This is the place to sell your product. If your needs assessment was done effectively, it should have pointed to the kind of program most likely to meet the identified need, within the constraints of time and resources. That's the one you're proposing, of course. If, on the other hand, the program design was specified in the RFP by your funding source, it usually means that it was sent to other nonprofits as well. Your job, then, is to show why your program design, your methodology, resources, and skills are the best ones for the job they want done. Subtle differences can become important here, such as cost-effective methods and economies, quality control, performance indicators, and accountability. Experience in the same or similar programs means a shorter learning curve and the promise of results sooner. Therefore, a relevant track record is your best asset.

Finding out the background, preferences, and predilections of the funder can help you couch your program description in the most attractive way. (If you know they buy a particular school of thought, it hardly pays to play up your disagreement with it.)

Important: How specific you are in your program description will be the best evidence, other than a directly relevant track record, that you know what you are doing, understand what such a program requires, have done your homework, and have planned the program carefully, covering all the factors that make for success. A comprehensive program description should include the following aspects of your program design:

- Where: locations to be used and their facilities.

- Who will do the work: numbers and job descriptions of staff (plus any interns or volunteers). Names, titles, and background of key professionals already on board—staff and consultants. Staff organization.

- Criteria, selection, and training process if any new staff is required.

- Description of program methods and procedures. These will depend on what type of work you do. They'll be specific to the nature of your organization (human services, health, education, arts, etc.) and the type of program. Staff manuals and written program materials may cover this.

Except for arts and cultural programs, most nonprofits deal with their target populations as individuals (clients, patients, students) rather than as audiences. Their modes of operation, therefore, have generic similiarities, which can be listed here. Their program descriptions should cover the following:

- How clients (patients, students) are found and recruited or otherwise attracted.

- Registration, individual needs assessment, and counseling procedures, as appropriate.

- Record-keeping systems used or planned, with key sample forms, if appropriate or novel.

- Adequate descriptions of specific program services covered in the proposal and procedures; program supervision and oversight. If there are alternative and better-established methodologies or agencies that could be used, a rationale for using yours may well be appropriate, especially if it has not achieved as much recognition or acceptance as the others. Its novelty or innovative aspects must be demonstrated to be a program strength, not a risk. Grant and contract officers need a good reason to stick their necks out.

- Duration of service to clients.

- Exit interviews, counseling, or follow-up services, such as referral, placement, and continued services.

- Provisions for evaluation of outcomes or results, at the client (patient, student) level. Performance indicators to be used. Specifics of reporting procedures for rendering accountability (unless prescribed by funding agency).

Capabilities and Track Record

Funding agencies look for more than a good program concept: they want to be certain that you have the ability and resources to carry it out successfully. For that, a comprehensive yet concise statement of your agency's purposes, resources, accomplishments, and capability to execute this program is a vital part of your proposal. It should contain the information listed above under key information about your agency. Helpful supporting documents such as resumes and other attachments are also useful addenda. Audited financial statements help, if favorable.

Program Evaluation

One thing that can convincingly show your seriousness and professionalism is a strong section on how, when, and by whom your program will be evaluated. There are always at least two dimensions in any program evaluation:

1. Inputs of resources and efforts that were committed to it in terms of staff time, full-time equivalent (FTE) staff assigned for supervision, facilities, and supplies, among others. These are input or process measures, which should have been set forth in your statement of objectives and your program description.

2. Outcomes. The results of your program in terms of service to clients, and the like. This can be measured in terms of number of clients, visits, counseling hours, patient/days, FTE students, or the like, depending on the nature of your program. Program impact is another outcome measure of great importance and is the hardest to measure. It looks at the effects of your program efforts in terms of what it did for clients, rather than how many were served, or how much time or attention they received. Here the question would be, for example, not how many job counseling hours or clients were served, but how many actually got jobs? Not patient/days worked, but number or percent who were cured. The problem is how to demonstrate that these results were a direct consequence of your program (See Chapter 15).

For proposal purposes, it may be sufficient to include a short statement of what performance indicators will be used to measure input effort and service outputs in quantities and results or effects. Data forms to be used to track individual clients should be attached, plus statistical formats to be used in summarizing and analyzing overall program performance. The evaluation section should also indicate who will be responsible for recording client data and for compiling, analyzing, and evaluating it for the program as a whole.

The timing of any interim reports used to monitor the program and of final reports should also be indicated. Also, whether and how results will be reported to the funding agency and other interested parties, including publication, if planned, should be made clear.

If a control group is to be used to validate results as being attributable to your program, that should be stated, and the means of accomplishing the controlled study indicated.

THE PROPOSAL BUDGET

The art of budgeting for planning and managing the agency's operations was given intensive analysis in Chapters 5 and 6. Why bring up budgeting again?

There are several excellent reasons, as follows:

1. A proposal budget usually covers only one program, or at most a few related programs, not the agency as a whole.

2. Even if there are no programs outside those covered by the proposal, there may be other funding sources. Funding for one program can be shared between two or more funding agencies; part may be paid for by earned revenues—fees or other charges for program services, investment income, individual donors, special events, and the like.

3. One major funding source may pay for two or more programs, covered either by a single grant or separate ones.

4. The budget and accounting guidelines of a funding agency are not often the same as those most appropriate for the agency's own internal management use—the ones dealt with in Chapters 5 and 6.

This section will deal with these differences and the best way to approach setting up a winning proposal budget, suggesting some vital principles along the way. Bear in mind that the proposal budget is not just an attachment, but a part of the proposal that can help make or break it.

How Much to Request

● Not too little, or you lose credibility. There is a real danger in promising to do too much with funds that clearly would be inadequate.

● Not too much either, or you may lose your audience. Almost as bad as promising too much is asking for too much money. Grant officers want their money's worth; they will not consider a proposal that suggests either great inefficiency and lack of productivity or an unstated desire to make a profit from the grant.

Since a line-item budget is usually requested, that means first a careful inventory of the necessary resources (staff time, space, facilities, supplies, utilities, etc.) based on the previous description of "How the Program Will Work," and "The Program's Work Plan and Future" (discussed below in another section), which look at stages and timing issues. The approach to this was explained in Chapter 5, which should be used as a starting point when approaching any budget. The emphasis here is on program budgeting.

Why Grant Proposal Budgets Are Crucial

There are two general types of grants. The first is a restricted grant to fund a particular program or activity. The second is an unrestricted grant, which generally can be used as the organization sees fit. Needless to say, the latter are as hard to come by as they are desirable. They may often omit any requirement for reporting to the grantor. Such grants are generally fairly small ones, sometimes intended as "seed money" to help a new nonprofit get off the ground.

Program grants are, on the other hand, most commonly restricted grants, either explicitly or implicitly, made to further a particular kind of activity or service the grantor desires to promote. A natural corollary is the notion that such a grant is not intended to fund the grantee's "overhead," those minimum operating costs for core personnel and facilities without which the nonprofit organization's doors would close. Most funding agencies are realistic enough to recognize, however, that some portion of such costs may be properly allocated and charged to the program grant, especially where part of the adminstrator's time and part of the organization's premises are devoted to the needs of the program. The same applies to other joint costs, such as telephone, utilities, supplies, and secretarial and office expenses.

Why grant budgets need a different approach.   This realization gives rise to an important distinction between the philosophical approach to an internal budget, discussed at length in Chapters 5 and 6, and that involving a grant budget. Entirely different considerations most commonly apply. Thus, where it may be impracticable, or even undesirable to allocate overhead to programs in an internal budget, the reverse is true with grant budgets. Here the purpose of the document is different, and as in all accounting applications, it is the purpose of an item that governs its treatment. Since the purpose of the budget is to obtain the fullest possible funding, overhead should be allocated to the grant budgets up to the full permissible limits indicated in the guidelines or instructions. (That is why they generally are quite clear in this regard.)

Major agencies publish standard guidelines regarding expense items that are allowable or unallowable, and acceptable formulae for charging or allocating indirect costs. A good example of such a document is Circular A-122, published by the U.S. Office of Management and Budget in 1980.[10]

Agencies that resist funding overhead.   There is room for argument in the area of overhead, when the funding agency objects to allowing any overhead costs to be charged to the grant. The fallacy here is that without the goods or services represented by so-called overhead, the organization itself could not exist, and neither would the program being funded. If it were unable to pay for an executive director, general secretarial services, office rental, accounting, or bookkeeping, how well could a given program function? One program director we know underlined this to an unsympathetic grant officer by pointing out that, "On the budget of your own foundation, you are classified as overhead!" While this may not actually have been the case, the barb struck home.

In most cases, this is not the policy. For example, in the Office of Management and Budget (OMB) guidelines cited above, provision is made for allowing a reasonable portion of indirect overhead costs to be allocated to the program grant. This is also the case with large foundations, generally speaking. The problem is, of course, that the rules are specific to the organization making the grant, and there is usually an uphill battle if they take a narrow approach to overhead allocation. You might ask whether it makes sense to require responsible grant supervision and accountability if no funds are provided to help pay for the costs of CEO, office rent, bookkeeping, and auditing (which may even be an imposed requirement).

Special Problems of Proposal Budgets

Not all nonprofit administrators keep in mind the fact that proposal budgets serve a different purpose than internal budgets, and that they must be approached with a different mindset.

Funding agency guidelines.   The only rules that apply here are the funding agency's rules—not which accounting or budgeting principles are best for other purposes. Since the foundation, corporation, or government agency is paying the piper, it has the right—and the power—to call the tune. The best to hope for is some flexibility and sensitivity on the part of the grant or contract officer applying the rules.

One practical problem that results is that different agencies often have different budgeting formats, rules, and procedures—even different within the same state government.

"Overhead" costs.   What is called "overhead" by many also travels under the aliases of "indirect expenses," "administrative expenses," "general expense," "joint expense," "allocated expense," and even "support costs." Worse yet, some of them may mean the same thing to some people, but different things to other people. There is no uniformity in their usage, even among accountants. So play it safe by observing which term your funding agency uses and what it covers.

Some funding agencies say up front, "we don't pay for overhead." But you may think of certain

---

[10]Its full title is "Cost principles for nonprofit organizations." OMB Circular A-110, "Grants & Agreements With Institutions of Higher Education, Hospitals & Other Non-Profit Organizations," sets forth other guidelines for applying for, managing, and reporting on grants.

things as overhead, indirect expense, for example, which to them may be legitimate line items.

Example: Rent, office supplies, utilities, which to you may be part of overhead, or indirect expenses; yet your program will use some percentage of the space you rent and the supplies and utilities consumed, and so should logically bear that percentage of the total costs.

The best way to finesse these issues is by showing a defensible amount for each item (including occupancy costs) as a line-item rather than part of "indirect expense."

One big area that is a no-man's land is that of administrative salaries. Funding agencies are likely to pay the salary (plus payroll taxes and benefits package) of a program director plus a secretary or administrative assistant of a particular program or department. When it comes to the portion of the CEO's time spent on program oversight, however, they may balk.

Percentage allowances.   The trend of funders in minimizing arguments over administrative, overhead or indirect costs is to allow nonprofits to add a certain percentage of the total budget or of certain line-items to their direct program costs to cover these expenses. Each funding agency picks its own percentages and how to apply them. Thus one agency allows 20% of program payroll to cover payroll taxes and employee benefits; it then allows another 15% of total direct program costs (including total payroll costs) for administration. Some funders use a percentage of total payroll costs to cover indirect or overhead costs.

In these cases, it is sometimes possible to get approval both for these percentage allowances and for line-items of shared administrative expenses, which you might otherwise assume are already included in that allowance.

Shared program personnel.   In a nonprofit with two or more programs, it is often economical or necessary to have one staff person divide time between them, rather than to hire two part-time employees. Funders will generally approve the appropriate percentage of such a person's payroll costs.

Direct program costs.   These are generally the easiest to budget and have approved, as long as they are appropriate and reasonable. It is here that you need to sharpen your pencil (or focus your computer screen), and be as specific as possible, so that your grant or contract officer understands your intent. If you are budgeting a staffer for six months of the program, show the annual salary cost, divided by two, or the monthly rate times six, not just the net amount. A half-time counsellor employed in the program for nine months, whose full-time monthly salary is $2,500 should be shown as: "Part-time counsellor: $2,500/month × 50% × 9 months = $11,250." Program supplies like food should be shown in terms of the monthly (or weekly) allowance per client, times the number of months (weeks) of the program, times the estimated (or contracted) number of clients.

Consultants or other contracted services should be clearly identified as to their nature and their hourly or daily rate multiplied by the budgeted hours or days contracted for or anticipated.

Travel and local transportation by staff that relates to the program should be specified and justified to convince your funder that it is necessary and useful to the program itself. The amount and kinds of travel and travel costs should be detailed.

Equipment costs.   Equipment can be a fuzzy area, since accounting principles treat the cost of an equipment purchase of more than a nominal amount—anything having an ongoing useful life of over a year—as an asset not an expense. (See the discussion of depreciation expense in Chapter 10.) If the funding agency allows an equipment purchase as a line-item, the result is a difference in the expenses according to the program budget (in reports to the funder), and your overall budget and financial statements, which will translate into a different "bottom line" and balance sheet (where the item will be included in assets and fund balances).

(Some government agency contracts, such as in Massachusetts, provide that any such equipment is legally the property of the state at the end of the contract period. Whether this is a serious practical issue or not is between you and any such agency. It does not seem useful to speculate about it here.)

Line-item control.   A recurring issue between nonprofits and their funding agency often arises near the end of a grant or contract period, when the nonprofit has used up the allowance for one expense but finds itself below budget on another line. Some funders have no objection to your shifting the unused allowance, at least with their permission; others will not approve this practice, or may allow you to go over budget on a given item by a specified percentage. Ten percent is common. It is wise to find out their policy at the proposal-writing stage, for planning purposes.

Unallowable expenses.   These are expenses that usually will not be funded, particularly by governmental agencies. They include fundraising costs and promotional costs not clearly related to program needs. Some foundations and corporations are willing to cover part or all of such expenses.

Matching funds.   The matching requirement is common with government grants and contracts, but it can apply to nongovernmental grants as well. The important thing to learn is whether the term means matching in cash, or whether a "soft match" (in-kind) is acceptable; and if so, what restrictions, if any, govern the types of in-kind items that are eligible.

This can be a make or break matter. Public television producers may earn matching funds for a federal grant by offering coproduction credit to another television station in exchange for free use of a studio, cameras and editing equipment, and certain technical staff.

Where only a cash match is permitted, there would seem to be nothing improper about converting a soft match of, say, free rent into a cash match by an arrangement to pay the rent and have it refunded as a contribution. This could apply to many types of in-kind contributions.

A cash match can be made out of your other sources of unrestricted funds, such as program fees, dues, investment income, or cash reserves. It can also come from other partial grants for the same program. It is not unusual for a nonprofit to approach two or more foundations with budgets showing the proposed grants of each as a matching grant on another proposal. In some cases, each might pick up certain costs only, rather than share in all of them.

Some funders may require that cash matches come from new donors, or they may restrict their match in other ways.

Funding "leverage."   Foundations like to see matching grants from any source and substantial in-kind grants, because these provide a multiplier effect on their own funds, often referred to as "leverage." When a $20,000 grant is instrumental in generating $50,000 worth of services by such means, the foundation can pride itself on having obtained a lot for its money. This, incidentally, is an excellent reason to show substantial in-kind services in a proposal budget. A small volunteer organization with only one or two paid staffers looks like small potatoes in a budget or financial statement, unless a valuation is placed on the services of its volunteers. One we knew had a cash budget of $30,000 (for executive secretary and rent), but $150,000 worth of professional services by its CPA volunteers.

"Miscellaneous" is a dirty word.   A large unexplained amount shown as Miscellaneous, Sundry, or Other will undoubtedly be viewed skeptically. Show its composition instead. Some funding agencies may approve a modest amount for contingencies, to cover unanticipated expenses or cost increases, but this is a negotiated item. (The best plan is to anticipate, and provide for everything.)

Unanticipated yet unavoidable costs.   There are a few necessary costs, which can be substantial, yet are often overlooked. One is insurance. Some human service programs must have liability insurance for injuries to clients in the course of the program. Unemployment and Workmen's Compensation and, in some states, disability income insurance are mandatory for employees.

Another is the cost of an audit, which may be thought of as an overhead or administrative cost, yet may be mandatory in connection with a government contract. This is an area of growing contention, since mandating an expensive activity should carry accompanying funds to pay for it. (An audit by an independent public accountant of even a small nonprofit can cost upwards of $2,000–$3,000). Some state agencies will pay a share of general audit fees based on their share of total funding.

Proposal budget formats. There is no standard form for a proposal budget. Your funding agency may specify or provide one for you, which you should then use, or modify only as necessary to present your budget effectively.

The budget formats shown in Chapters 5 and 6 can be used or readily adapted to serve as proposal budgets. To save repetition and space, however, a proposal budget is usually a combination budget worksheet and budget, since it shows calculations that would normally be shown only in a budget worksheet. Another difference is that it will not normally be an overall budget for the nonprofit, but will only cover specific programs. Finally, a proposal budget will often omit a revenue and support section and show only expenses, or it may show other revenues or support contributing to a program as a subtraction from the total of budgeted expenses.

Expense categories. The names or groups of expenses provided in budget forms provided by funding agencies will often differ to some extent from the names you are accustomed to using in your own budgets and accounting records (the Chart of Accounts). Always use theirs, not yours, and determine significant differences, as, for example, what is or is not included in a line-item: Do "fringe costs" include payroll taxes plus employee benefits? Do occupancy costs include utilities and janitorial service? If you own instead of renting your location, should you include depreciation on your building or payments of mortgage principal? (The latter is not proper accounting, since it is not an expense.)

If you are proposing a single program to be fully funded by the one agency, the format is quite simple. The illustration shown in Table 8–1 would need to be modified by eliminating the last two lines with dollar amounts: what is labeled "Total expense budget" would be renamed "Grant funds request."

If you are required to match grant funds, whether with program revenues or other funds, Table 8–1 can be used as shown. Of course you'd change "program revenues" to whatever other source is appropriate, such as "General funds." If funding is to come from more than one agency, the budget formats shown may be useful.

Note: If in-kind contributions are part of the budget, they should be shown twice, once as revenue (if shown), again as an expense. Thus pro bono legal services would appear as follows:

Revenue	
In-kind contribution—legal services	$2,000
Expense	
Legal fee—in kind	$2,000

That way, the contribution does not affect your "bottom line."

**TABLE 8-1. CENTER FOR COMMUNITY SERVICE, INC.
GRANT PROPOSAL BUDGET—PROGRAM A[a]**

Expenses[a]	
Salaries (All staff is part-time)	
Program director (50% of FTE: $32,000)[b]	$16,000
Executive director (10% of FTE: $40,000)	4,000
Total payroll	20,000
Payroll fringe costs (12%)[c]	2,400
Occupancy (40% of total)	4,176
Telephone	275
Travel and conferences	550
Program supplies	1,140
Office expense	132
Insurance	148
Depreciation—program equipment	1,617
Contingency reserve[d]	1,562[d]
Total expense budget	32,000
Less: estimated program revenues	17,000
Grant funds request	$15,000
Estimated value of volunteer services	$ 7,500
(750 hours @ $10/hr)	

[a]These are the same figures as shown in the Annual Operating Budget, Program "A" column, in Table 6–2 (Chapter 6), with the exception of amounts for payroll fringe costs and contingency reserve (see notes c and d).

[b]"FTE" means "full-time equivalent" salaries, a phrase widely used.

[c]ABC Foundation, the proposed grantor, allows 12% of payroll for fringe costs. This figure has been substituted for the $1,642 budget in Table 6–2 and would be also if that amount exceeded $2,400.

[d]A contingency reserve of up to 5% of total budget is commonly acceptable. The amount shown was chosen to round off the total to $32,000.

Specialized grants.   Grants for technical assistance, research and development, or "seed money" for start-up costs, can be fairly simple in format, following the single program grant format. The elements of expense involved are usually self-evident, although a seed money grant budget would commonly cover overhead costs for a period, rather than program costs, and would list major general expenses for core staff, occupancy, and utilities, plus possible consulting fees, employment ads, and other related costs.

Budget narrative.   Whether or not one is requested, the budget narrative is the place to explain or amplify aspects of your budget, in order to head off reader misunderstanding: why certain rent or salaries may seem out of line; why you need certain positions; or details of employee benefits. This can be not only a defense of your figures but also a demonstration that you have budgeted knowledgeably, not by "guesstimates."

The format illustrated in Table 8–2 makes full disclosure of all line-items and who is to pay for them, in what shares. It is cumbersome and time-consuming to prepare and may create more problems than it solves. However, it has the virtue of giving the funding agency a total picture of where the money for each item will come from, and it makes a good impression by showing the depth of planning that went into the proposal.

TABLE 8–2. PARTIAL FUNDING PROPOSAL BUDGET SHOWING LINE-ITEM DETAIL.

Expense category	Calculation	Total expense	Sources of funds			
			Funding request	Other agency	In-kind contrib.	Own funds
Personnel costs	Percent and					
(List by job title)	amount of FTE	XXXX	XXXX	XXXX	XXXX	XXXX
Payroll taxes	% of payroll	XXXX	XXXX	XXXX	XXXX	XXXX
Employee benefits	(same)	XXXX	XXXX	XXXX	XXXX	XXXX
Total personnel costs		XXXX	XXXX	XXXX	XXXX	XXXX
Consultants and/or contract services (describe)	Hours or days & rates	XXXX	XXXX	XXXX	XXXX	XXXX
Non-personnel costs (examples)						
Occupancy	(% of rent)	XXXX	XXXX	XXXX	XXXX	XXXX
Program supplies		XXXX	XXXX	XXXX	XXXX	XXXX
Administration or indirect expenses	(% allowance)	XXXX	XXXX	XXXX	XXXX	XXXX
Total budget		XXXX	XXXX	XXXX	XXXX	XXXX

A compromise format that takes less time and study to work up is similar to Table 8–2, but shows each additional source of funds, in total only (Table 8–3).

TABLE 8–3. PARTIAL FUNDING PROPOSAL: LINE-ITEM DETAILS OMITTED.

Expense Category	Calculation	Total Expense
(From Table 8–2)	(From Table 8–2)	(From total expense column only)
Total funds requested		XXXX
Other funding sources		
Other agency (or agencies)	XXXX	
In-kind contributions	XXXX	
Own funds (specify type)	XXXX	
Less Total of other funding sources		XXXX
Funds requested (balance)		XXXX

There are other advantages of using the format shown in Table 8–3: (1) it avoids any commitment or constraints regarding who will pay for what, and as a result (2) it makes it possible to submit proposals before that question can be nailed down; it also (3) provides a certain amount of flexibility in negotiating allowances for particular line-items that might otherwise be prematurely locked in.

In fact, Table 8–2, showing full details, is probably best used as an internal planning document, to help you answer that tough question, "so where's the money coming from?"

The Program's Work Plan and Future

If you have a good planning process in place, like the one described in Chapter 3, you will have no problem at all defining your program's work plan. In fact, you may already have dealt with the work plan of the program for which funding is being requested. If you've been waiting to be sure you get funding before doing the detailed planning, you'd be better off doing it at this point, at least in broad outline: it impresses a potential funding source.

You probably won't be able to attach dates to each step, since you won't yet know when—or even whether—the program will start. But you can give approximations of how long each step or phase will take, to show you've done your planning homework. A work plan can be a major asset to a proposal.

Finally, a word about the program's future, assuming you intend that it have one. At least a general statement is desirable of how you see the program developing and perhaps expanding—or phasing out, if the need being addressed decreases or ends. Of equal importance, describe other sources of funds that you envision as being available to keep the program going.

Foundations and corporations are not enthusiastic about open-end funding commitments: they usually prefer to see themselves as helping desirable new programs get off the ground. Think about possibilities of generating program revenues or support from your community, other foundations, or your profession. That sort of information shows an enterprising spirit that implies you aren't asking the funding source to support you forever.

Sources of internal data for your proposal.   Here is where good files pay off. You need to mine them for the data you need. Places to look include your strategic plan; annual plan; publicity you've received or sought by press releases, newsletters, and brochures; minutes of meetings; important correspondence; studies or reports you've made or that have been made about your agency; past reports or proposals to funders; financial reports and budgets. Last but not least, input should also be sought from present and past officers, board members, key staffers, clients, and key volunteers (e.g., committee chairs), who may be sources of valuable information or ideas.

Appendix of Supporting Materials

The proposal appendix will include the supplementary attachments that may be required by your proposed funding source. The following documents should be supplied, even if they aren't requested.

- Resumes of your CEO and proposed program staffers.

- Resumes of your officers, and important board members who might lend prestige. A list of key board members, with their telephone numbers, may be welcomed. (Those who are knowledgeable, of course!)

- A good, professional brochure if available, showing your program offerings, facilities, and accomplishments. If you have none, produce one or write these things up as a statement.

- Recent and past financial statements, especially if audited, unless they do you more harm than good. Graphs or pie charts showing your sources and uses of funds, unless they show too high a percentage spent on administration and fundraising.

- A copy of the IRS Determination Letter granting you tax exemption, always required.

- Any other valued evidence of recognition of your programs and accomplishments, such as awards or laudatory letters.

- A copy of your organization chart may be helpful, especially if yours is a complex, multi-service organization.

The Personal Touch

Funders fund people, not proposals. We learned this the hard way when we discovered that a grant that was just about to be approved was put on hold when the executive director mentioned to the grant officer that he was leaving the organization.

Personal contacts are important. A visit, or at least a phone call or two, before submitting the proposal is worthwhile, so you are seen as a person, not a faceless piece of paper, when your proposal arrives. (This is unfortunately not always possible, until you have already submitted a proposal.) A follow-up call reestablishes the personal aspect. If you're in the running, you may be invited to visit the funding agency. Send only the most knowledgeable and articulate representatives, and make sure they go prepared for all possible questions about the proposal, especially about the budget and any other funding sources in prospect. This is your big selling opportunity: you can't afford to blow it by looking like amateurs.

The other aspect of how important people are should have been dealt with by the resumes of key people submitted with your proposal and any important and relevant personal publicity you can include, or otherwise bring to the funder's attention.

What if the Answer Is No?

The odds against getting a first grant from a funding agency are high. That means you'll get many more turn-downs than grants. Instead of crying over spilt milk, try to use refusals as a foot in the door for next year. The sophisticated grantwriter sends a "thank you" letter to the funding agency for considering the proposal. If the rejection was more than a mere form letter, the foundation or corporation should be seen as a potential future funding source.

It is worthwhile then to phone your thanks and ask how your proposal could have been improved on, to make it more acceptable. Take notes and file them in a future proposal file, including the name and title of the person who was helpful with such information. You'll have a better chance next time.

FUNDRAISING FROM INDIVIDUAL DONORS

As pointed out earlier, since individuals and their estates represent nearly 82% of all non-governmental funds received by nonprofits, whole books are devoted to this subject (see the bibliography). All we have space for is a series of checklists of the various methods, with some suggestions about their relative requirements of money, time, and people, plus the type of nonprofits for which each is usually most appropriate.

Things to Consider in Fundraising from Individuals

Here is a short checklist of general considerations in selecting fundraising methods:

- Timing issues: planning, organizing, lead time, and execution time: how long before the money starts coming in?

- Relative effectiveness and fundraising potential: not in general, but in your particular situation.

- Costs involved: start-up and ongoing expenses.

- Amount of staff time required: how many additional staff, volunteers, and/or temporary employees are required?

- Volunteer time required and number of volunteers.

- Special skills or consultants required?

- Additional equipment or supplies needed?

- Possible negative (or positive) impacts on your image and on important funding sources?

- Potential tax effects: taxability and deductible costs.

Direct One-to-One Methods

Generally speaking, these labor-intensive methods are most commonly used by community organizations or those large enough to pay large numbers of solicitors or to attract numerous volunteers. They take considerable time and effort to plan and organize properly and often no little money for printing and/or phone expense. They also involve record-keeping and security problems, if cash is being handled, since "money has no memory." (See Chapter 11 on this.) Here is a list of possible methods and techniques:

- Door-to-door solicitation of residents or businesses.

- Personal fund drives involving members or volunteers. The yield from these can be greatly increased by the use of challenge grants from funding organizations and sustainers (pledges to give a certain amount per month or year).

- Major donors can be approached for tax-deductible gifts of securities or other property, and to consider deferred-giving plans such as bequests, charitable trusts (annuity trusts, "unitrusts" or net income trusts), and insurance contracts, among others. You'll need expert legal advice on these.[11]

- Raffle book sales.

- Telemarketing media, using paid or volunteer personnel (becoming a touchy subject).

- Street or shopping mall tables and booths.

- Coin boxes or cans in stores.

- Paid professional fundraisers (not consultants), who frequently work on a commission basis. (The latter arrangement is becoming controversial.)

---

[11]See Stanley S. Weithorn in *New York University 14th Biennial Conference on Tax Planning for the Charitable Sector* (Matthew Bender, New York: 1985), Chapter 9.

Special Events

These require even more time, effort, and organization. In addition to the one-to-one aspect in selling tickets or the like, they take longer to plan and organize, may involve outlays of funds, and sometimes involve the risk of loss, if a minimum number of takers is guaranteed to the theater, restaurant, or other organization. In such cases, it is important to use the break-even analysis planning technique explained in Chapter 6, since your aim is to make money, not lose it.

Important: Some of those listed may be subject to the federal tax on Unrelated Business Income. (See Chapters 1 and 16.) Another thing to handle carefully is stating clearly on tickets and publicity which part of the price is tax-deductible: only the excess of the amount paid over the fair value of whatever is received (a meal, entertainment, etc.). This is a growing area of IRS enforcement, and is covered by IRS rulings.[12] Here are some examples that may surprise you:

—"The IRS position is that no part of any payment for raffle, lottery, bingo game admission ..." or similar items is deductible.

—A ticket purchased to a benefit performance is deductible if it is refused or returned, but not if it merely goes unused.[13]

Special Events Checklist

- Dinners (or other meals): annual, testimonial, award, or anniversary.
- Dances and parties, including costume types
- Theater parties and concerts, including benefit performances
- Picnics and barbecues
- Sports events and exhibition games
- Fashion, art, and flower shows
- Excursions and tours: sight-seeing, homes, museums, and boating
- Group travel and package tours
- Children's holiday or summer entertainments (puppet shows, etc.)
- Auctions of art, antiques, donated merchandise, etc.
- Rummage or tag sales, flea markets, bazaars, and fairs
- Sales of volunteer services: car wash, sitting, speakers bureau, etc.
- Contests, games of chance: Bingo, roulette, lotteries
- Closed-circuit or satellite television meetings. (Used by national or regional organizations to reach local chapters or audiences, or by any organization to make possible a live broadcast of an important personage or event from another location.)

---

[12]See the message from the Commissioner of Internal Revenue that appeared in *The CPA Journal*, November 1988, p. 6, citing Revenue Ruling 67–246, 1967–2 C.B. 104, which describes the rules in detail. This ruling is reproduced in full in IRS Publication 1391, available from IRS Forms Supply (WATS line: 800-424-3676).

[13]From, "How Much Really *Is* Tax Deductible?" pp. 8–12. (Independent Sector, Washington, DC: March, 1989.)

Media Appeals

You'll need expert help with many of these from media pros. Try to get such assistance donated in whole or in part from those sympathetic to your cause.

- Television and radio "PSAs" (free public service announcements), perhaps using your own audio tape

- Telethons, interviews, news coverage, and call-in shows

- Cable access channels and VCR cassettes

- Print media: press releases, interviews, features

- Direct-mail appeals to members, mailing lists, or "occupant"

- Sale of ads in newsletter, special event, or annual programs or other publications (may be subject to tax on Unrelated Business Income. IRS rules use the length of time spent on selling the ads as a determining factor: spending more than a few months generally makes the income subject to U.B.I. tax.)

- Outdoor advertising signs

- Posters in store windows, on walls, and light poles

- Sound trucks

- Leaflets (flyers) distributed under doors, to cars (under windshield wipers), or to occupants

- Stunts: cross-country walkathons, marches, bicycle rides, etc.

If you want more detailed explanations of how to conduct individual fundraising campaigns, these methods are covered in depth in other books.[14]

CHARITY BEGINS AT HOME

While this may come as unexpected in a chapter on fundraising, our experience has taught us that many a tough financial situation that may seem to have only fundraising as a solution can be solved by looking inward rather than outward. There are many ways of improving your cash flow.

Near the beginning of this chapter, we spoke of the importance of marketing your programs to funding agencies. Still another important way to generate income is by doing a more effective job of marketing your present programs *to your target population.* More "paying customers"—regardless of who pays for them—means more income. There may be competitive factors to consider as well (See Chapter 9.)

Improving the prices or rates you get for your services from clients, patients, patrons, third-party reimbursement or funding sources, to the extent you can control them, is another way to boost your income. Sadly, too many nonprofits set (or agree to) these prices without realizing that they actually lose money on each person served. The reason is that they fail to take all costs into account. The costs not counted are usually the indirect costs that need to be included, if activities are to make

---

[14]See Michael Seltzer, *Securing Your Organization's Future* (Foundation Center, New York: 1987) and Joan Flanagan, *The Grass Roots Fundraising Book* (Contemporary Books, Chicago: 1982).

money—or at least cover all operating costs. Otherwise, the more people you serve, the more money you lose! How to solve this problem is dealt with in the section on break-even analysis near the end of Chapter 6.

Distasteful as it may sound, you can improve your cash flow and "bottom line" by sharply reducing or even eliminating any waste of your resources. This involves improving efficiency, productivity, or economy, wherever you can without hurting program quality or effectiveness. In other words, professionalize your operations in the areas of budgeting and cost controls.

You can also stretch your resources and get more for your limited funds by seeking possible in-kind contributions. Use volunteers, work-study students, or interns where they can be effective; get free or discounted rent, supplies, equipment, use of facilities or professional services. Business donors and government agencies are often more willing to help that way than with cash, which they control more tightly, a point made previously.

A nonprofit should not be run like a business: its purposes are quite different. Nevertheless, you owe it to your target population and those who fund you to run it in a businesslike way. This is really part of accountability, which is at the core of this operating manual.

OTHER CONSIDERATIONS IN FUNDRAISING

Excessive Expenditure of Funds

No one just "gives you money." They invest in activities they want to promote. If you spend too much on fundraising—or on management, for that matter, rather than on programs—a question may be raised regarding your real purposes. Not only may funders or donors ask about your purposes, state authorities regulating charities can, in extreme cases, revoke your tax exemption, and so can the IRS, if program purposes appear not to have been met.

A recent case in point involved PTL; Boys' Town was an older example. The *New York Times* (11/26/88) cited some other recent horror stories: two medical research funds, which raised $3.6 and $5.7 million respectively, but used only 2 and 6 percent of the funds raised on projects related to their stated purpose! Several states even passed laws, later declared unconstitutional, setting a fixed percentage of income that could be spent on fundraising! They still can regulate it, where it gets excessive.

How much is too much is a debatable question. The point is to keep fundraising within reasonable limits. In a fairly recent case, the Federal Tax Court upheld the IRS in denying tax-exempt status under Section 501(c)(3) to a senior citizen group because of excessive fundraising costs. It held that the organization was not being operated exclusively for a charitable purpose, and that money was spent to benefit certain individuals rather than program beneficiaries.

All of its funds were raised by telephone solicitation, and it paid a 25% commission to its solicitors. Almost a third of its remaining funds were paid them on advances against future commissions—some of which were never earned. Under 9 percent of the remaining income was actually spent on program services. While this was an extreme case, it does make the point.

Registration of Fundraising Activities

This is another problem to be aware of: many states require nonprofits to register and/or render supplementary information regarding their fundraising activities. A Model Act was adopted in 1986 by the National Association of Attorneys General and the National Association of State Charity Officials, in the hope that it would be enacted into law by individual states.[15] In addition, many states, including New York and Massachusetts, require that professional fundraisers—in some cases also fundraising counsel or others—register with the state as well.

Fundraising Consultants

While larger nonprofits usually have staff development or fundraising directors, many small and medium-sized organizations find it more cost-effective to engage a consultant. As a consequence, fundraising consulting has become a large profession. Even some agencies that have a staff director may retain an outside consulting firm to handle specialized types of fundraising, such as direct-mail solicitation, special events, capital campaigns, and cultivating deferred giving, such as bequests and charitable trusts. Professional firms are better equipped to handle these types of fundraising than they are ongoing community fundraising activity, for which activity they are also very expensive.

When engaging any professional—whether it be a public accountant or an attorney, an organizational development, management, computer or fundraising consultant—the rule of *caveat emptor* (let the buyer beware) applies. Attorneys and public accountants are at least bound by well-established professional rules of conduct, though not all are equally expert in the problems of nonprofits. The other professions mentioned are only beginning to develop rules and standards of ethics and competence, and are rarely licensed by any government agency.

Anyone can therefore call himself or herself a consultant in these fields (just as anyone can claim to be a professional tax preparer). Before contracting with anyone, therefore, it is wise to request references to present or past clients—and to follow them up. Another growing practice is to issue an RFP (request for proposal), with a set of specific points to be covered, in addition to the way fees will be determined.

These points could be drawn from some of the considerations and ideas covered in this chapter or in Chapter 9. A professional should be familiar with these concepts and should have no trouble dealing with them in a proposal. If a consultant can show membership in the appropriate professional society—one that has a clear set of rules of conduct and standards of competence—this is a big plus.

Practices by fundraising consultants that need particularly to be guarded against follow:

1. Offering "canned" solutions to problems, or proposing solutions before becoming adequately familiar with your problems. While this may work in certain specialized types of fundraising, you may do better by studying this chapter and the next, and other books cited, and then doing the job yourself, because you know your own situation, at the very least!

2. Plunging into action on fundraising activities without any effort to find out whether that is your only or most pressing need. We pointed out in other chapters that unless the nonprofit has proper organization, planning, and financial management, more funds may only mean more problems, rather than solutions to existing ones.

---

[15]Copies are available from the National Health Council, 622 Third Avenue, New York, NY 10017-6765.

Before deciding that what is needed is a fundraising consultant or director, the sophisticated administrator or officer will seek diagnostic advice: your problem may be organizational or financial management, neither of which will be cured by an infusion of funds alone. Not so many years ago, National Public Radio nearly went "belly-up," not because it couldn't raise enough money, but because, as its auditors noted, there was a nearly total lack of financial control. Its deficit far exceeded its total budget.

Chapter 9

Income-Producing Ventures

Although this is not a new subject for large nonprofits, the funding crunch and tax law changes in recent years have forced many smaller ones to seek new, independent ways of earning money. Others have developed an urge to find unrestricted sources of funds to provide for any of a number of things: better staff salaries and benefits, cash reserves, equipment purchases, major repairs, expansion or renovation of their premises to pay off debt, subsidize prices of other programs, or test new programs.

THE DANGERS INVOLVED

Before deciding on any new venture, go back to Square One and study your mission statement (see Chapter 3). You cannot afford to undertake any project that is not consistent with your mission. (If you want to change the mission, of course your board and membership have the power—though you may have to amend your bylaws and/or articles of incorporation to make it legal.)

If a new venture diverts you from your mission or goals, you may lose credibility and support from your community, donors, or funding sources. If the "bottom line" becomes so central to your thinking that you begin to look more like a business than a tax-exempt organization, people won't want to give you money. It is also possible that you will lose your tax exemption if the venture is part of your own organization's activities. Finally, you may develop organizational schizophrenia, with a Jeckyll-and-Hyde complex—or worse yet, Mr. Hyde may win out.

Perhaps the worst outcome, however, is that you may lose money, not make it. This is a real possibility that must be carefully guarded against. This chapter should help you avoid that possibility.

THE APPROACH OF THIS CHAPTER

1. We will look at the pros and cons, as well as the considerations involved in setting up new income-producing ventures in each of the following ways:

- A new tax-exempt program within your present organization.

- A venture within your agency that may be subject to the federal tax on Unrelated Business Income (UBI).

- A venture set up as a new organization, either tax-exempt or taxable.

- A joint venture or limited partnership between your present agency, or a new one, and a business firm or private investors.

2. While tax issues may be key, we will also consider other important considerations that cannot be overlooked.

3. A feasibility study is important in making you look before you leap.

4. The key importance of developing a business plan, including all financing and marketing aspects, as a vehicle for attracting capital and taking stock of all the ingredients, problems and opportunities that must be considered.

ADVANTAGES OF TAX-EXEMPT INCOME

Aside from the chief and obvious advantage of tax-exempt income, that all net income generated adds directly to your bottom line, there are others to think about. We listed many ways to raise funds that would probably be held tax-exempt in Chapter 8 (see Direct One-to-One Methods, Special Events, and Media Appeals). In addition to those listed, it is useful to note that any activity run entirely by volunteers, or selling donated merchandise, is presently nontaxable. That can expand the lists of fundraising methods to include gift shops and other stores, and cake or cookie sales. (Note, however, the famous Girl Scout Cookies program, which has always used volunteer members, has been called into question recently, and Congress is examining this whole area of taxation.)

Section 501(c)(3) (tax-deductible) organizations are generally exempt from paying property and sales taxes as well as income taxes (although they must collect and pay over taxes on their own sales). There are some cases in which nonprofits may be willing to waive the exemption from real estate taxes for political, public relations, or even ethical reasons; alternatively, some voluntarily pay the equivalent amount in service fees.

For example, community development corporations will sometimes do so because they need the goodwill of the municipality to operate successfully—sometimes even to obtain financing—and they find it prudent not to remove properties from the existing tax base.

Other Advantages of Tax-Exempt Activities

Quite aside from the obvious benefit in paying no corporate income tax, there are other advantages to be considered:

- Reduced postage rates.

- Savings of time and money for U.B.I. tax planning and compliance (aside from the tax itself).

- Avoiding the risk of losing tax exemption by undertaking too much taxable activity. Setting up a tax-exempt affiliate to conduct taxable activities is no guarantee against this, since some income received from such an affiliate, if "controlled," (see below) can become taxable income to the controlling nonprofit. Exempt income is better for your public image, although it might invite complaints from local small businesses if it "muscles in on their territory."

- Last but not least, exempt income is likely to fit in with your existing mind set and helps you avoid straying from your mission and the resulting organizational schizophrenia.

POSSIBLY TAXABLE TYPES OF INCOME

It is not always certain whether a specific activity is subject to the tax on Unrelated Business Income (See Chapters 1 and 16). The tests governing this question are complex, and relate not only to the nature of the activity, but also to who carries it on, where, how, and whether *it is related to your exempt purposes*, as stated in your articles of incorporation, as the very name of the tax indicates.

Sales of donated merchandise, or merchandise sold by volunteers are exempt. Facilities such as lunch rooms and parking lots operated at the organization's location for the convenience of its patients, clients, staff, members, visitors, etc., are exempt; but not if located elsewhere.

Note: It is important to understand that income generated to fund mission-related exempt programs of the nonprofit are not tax-exempt for that reason alone.

This part of the tax law has been under intense review by Congress and may be changed. As of this writing, here are some examples of taxable (or borderline) income-producing activities that might be considered. These do not exhaust the possibilities, of course, but can act as a provocative checklist (see Fig. 9–1). Your imagination is the only limit, as long as you remember the guidelines regarding taxability. The following *may* be taxable:

Merchandise Sales

- Sale of calendars containing program-related information, dates of activities and events. (Borderline.)
- Sales of merchandise and premiums given for contributions: T-shirts, umbrellas, and hats with the organization's logo. (Probably taxable.)
- Sales of buttons, bumper stickers, and window decals with program-related messages or logo. (Borderline.)
- Sale of refreshments at meetings, events, performances, including by vending machines on premises. (Probably tax-exempt.)
- Sales of program-related educational or informational materials: books, pamphlets, magazines, newsletter, video or audio tapes, films, and phonograph records. (Possibly exempt.)
- Sale of program-related merchandise: e.g., visiting nurse associations selling medical supplies, etc. (May be exempt if sold to patients.)
- Manufacture or purchase and sale of merchandise unrelated to exempt purposes, including franchised operations. (Taxable.)

Sales of Services

- Sale of advertising space in publications or programs sold at events. (Taxability depends on how frequently, and what period of time is covered by sales efforts, and whether the publication itself is profitable.)

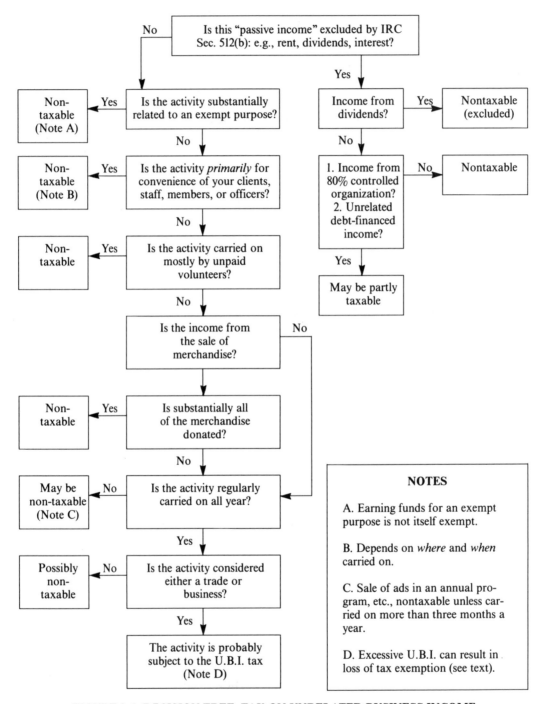

FIGURE 9-1. DECISION TREE: TAX ON UNRELATED BUSINESS INCOME
This is a general guide only; get professional advice.

- Sale or rental of mailing lists. (Exempt only if to an exempt organization.)
- Classes in arts, crafts, English, hobbies, sports, etc. (Exempt if part of exempt purposes.)
- Operating a group health insurance plan covering a group of related or affiliated nonprofits for an administration fee. (Probably taxable.)
- Administering a cooperative buying service for nonprofits to obtain quantity discounts on office or program supplies, equipment, or services. (Status unclear.)
- Sale of staff services: counseling, consulting, training, copying, typing, word-processing, addressing. (Similar to classes above; the first three are likely to be exempt.)
- Renting unused time on your computer or copying equipment, or doing desk-top publishing or data processing. (Probably taxable.)
- Catering or delivery service. (Probably taxable, unless performed by volunteers.)

How Much Taxable Income Is Too Much?

We pointed out that a nonprofit can jeopardize its exempt status by earning so much taxable income that it begins to look like a profit-making enterprise. Just how much is too much is not stated in the tax laws, however. Our advice is that when your gross income from taxable ventures passes 15% of your total revenue and support, it's time to start watching it, although some professionals recommend staying below that level to be safe. Certainly at 30% of the total, you're heading for trouble.

Legislative and Enforcement Activities

There has been developing agitation by small business within the federal government for tougher rules making it hard for nonprofits to operate for-profit activities at all. The Small Business Administration issued a paper and helped introduce a bill on the subject in Congress. The House Ways and Means Committee has indicated its interest in such legislation, and its Subcommittee on Oversight (J. J. Pickle, Chairperson) has been holding hearings and exploring proposals to toughen U.B.I. tax, or even to deny tax exemption to nonprofits conducting businesslike activities. A decision has not yet been made, as of this writing.

Defensive lobbying by the nonprofit community has thus far succeeded in blocking major changes in the law, except with regard to disclosure requirements. As a compromise, IRS expanded the reporting requirements by adding a whole new page to Form 990 which seeks to enforce the tax on Unrelated Business Income by requiring nonprofits to classify all income other than grants and donations into three categories:

- Income subject to the U.B.I.T.
- Income excluded from the tax by the Internal Revenue Code, with a code supporting this exclusion
- Income considered to be related to the organization's exempt function. Each such item must be explained in a new schedule provided for the purpose.

Another new requirement was added requiring disclosure of information about any taxable business in which the nonprofit owns a 50% or greater share.

Mr. Pickle reportedly has proposed extending coverage of the U.B.I tax to cover the following activities of nonprofits, which usually are exempt:[1]

● Gift shop sales of souvenir items costing over $15 and other noneducational items, other than art reproductions.

● Bookstore sales of the same kinds.

● Nonprofit hospital sales to nonpatients of drugs, and sale or rental of health-related equipment, such as hearing aids.

● Exercise and health centers, unless they admit disadvantaged community residents free or at low cost.

● College travel agencies sales, unless required of students or faculty in a degree program.

Scouting organizations fear that their sales of uniforms, publications, and cookies might also be affected, though the law exempts sales by volunteers.

CREATING A SEPARATE AFFILIATE

Working through an affiliate is sometimes recommended. This could take one of several forms. It might be another tax-exempt organization intended to conduct a level of taxable activities which, if done by the organization itself, might jeopardize its own exempt status. Loss of an affiliate's exemption would not be disastrous. Note also that if 80% of the members of the board of directors of a nonprofit represent or are controlled by another nonprofit, income which might otherwise be nontaxable might be subject to U.B.I. tax imposed on the controlling corporation.

The more common situation is to set up a fully taxable venture, in the form of a subsidiary corporation owned or controlled by the nonprofit, a sister corporation not so controlled, or a partnership or joint venture with another nonprofit or a business firm. The latter approach is common in the field of community economic development, since it opens up major sources of venture capital and borrowing power.

Minimizing the Tax on Unrelated Business Income

If a business venture is profitable, the probable income tax involved should not be a major consideration in planning. The tax rate is 15% on the first $50,000 of net taxable income, 25% on the next $25,000, and 34% on the top bracket, which starts at $75,000. The first $1,000 is exempt. If you can raise $51,000 that is fully taxable, the tax cost would be $7,500 (15% of $50,000, after the $1,000 exemption). A net income after taxes of $43,500 is not bad.

This is one area in which you need a *business* tax expert's advice: the methods to minimize the tax bite are the same as for any business income tax. Some of the common methods follow:

● Allocating a portion of indirect and administrative expenses, including payroll costs—even if you don't do so now. Here it saves money. Be sure to do so on a defensible basis: IRS watches for manipulation, and can change your allocations.

● Using tax-saving methods of depreciation and inventory valuation, where applicable.

---

[1] *The Chronicle of Philanthropy*, February 7, 1989, p. 18.

● If you sell merchandise, you'll have to use the accrual method of accounting when selling merchandise on credit (it is required by IRS rules); it's therefore to your advantage to do so when buying on credit, even if you don't use the accrual method now.

● Review your accounting system, to make sure it clearly separates taxable income and expenses from those that are tax-exempt, and facilitates tax reporting. (Professional help is also needed here.)

● Be aware that the IRS is alert to all the gimmicks and is skilled at upsetting schemes to conceal taxable income or to inflate deductions.

SETTING UP A SUBSIDIARY BUSINESS CORPORATION

The general advantages and disadvantages of setting up a subsidiary are shown in Fig. 9-2. A more comprehensive chart is shown in Fig. 9-3.

General Considerations

Legal issues.   Liability for the subsidiary's debts, including lawsuits and tax obligations, is limited to its invested capital. The nonprofit owning the controlling interest could also be held liable for its subsidiary's debts if the boards of directors of the two overlap too much, especially if the nonprofit's operations are closely intertwined with the day-to-day management of the subsidiary. Insurance may cover this in some cases, but legal advice and assistance is necessary. The state of incorporation has some regulatory authority over the company and generally imposes corporate taxes as well.

Capital needs and funding methods: debt vs. equity, pro and con.   How much capital will be needed? Can the parent NPO afford to invest or lend the required funds? There are risk factors here: you don't want business losses of the subsidiary to drag the nonprofit parent corporation down with it. The use of outside investors and lenders is a possible means of expanding the potential base of funds, but it also brings with it questions of control, interest rates, and dividend policy.

The IRS.   The IRS is involved with control issues, since they also can make income received from the subsidiary subject to U.B.I. tax on the nonprofit parent if the parent owns over 80% of its stock. It's better to control a bit under that level therefore, so that interest, rent, royalties, and other income received from the subsidiary are not taxable. (Dividends are not taxable in any event, but remember that they are paid out of the profits left after federal and state income taxes have been paid.)

Payroll tax problems.   Where some members of the staff are employed by both entities, they must be paid separately, or one entity must bill the other for part of their services.

Accounting.   When the activity is operated outside the nonprofit, the two accounting systems must be entirely separate. There may be problems in allocating joint costs, e.g., rent on shared space. We therefore recommend that allocations be handled via cash transactions between entities, not as mere bookkeeping entries. Loans or advances between the two organizations should be evidenced by a promissory note, with due date and market rate of interest.

Note: Relationships between the nonprofit and its subsidiary should be conducted on a well-documented, arm's-length basis, to avoid the potential for loss of exemption by the nonprofit organization. That means charging or paying the market value of anything significant transferred from

FIGURE 9-2. SHOULD A NONPROFIT SET UP A FOR-PROFIT SUBSIDIARY?

ARGUMENTS PRO

LEGAL REASONS

1. Isolates the assets of the NPO from claims of creditors and lawsuits: the NPO is the "Parent Company" of the subsidiary.

2. May facilitate borrowing from banks. (May also make possible outside investors.)

TAX REASONS

1. If substantial income (over say 15%) of the NPO is derived from activities not related to its exempt purposes, NPO could lose its tax exemption. (Does not apply to dividends received from subsidiary, or interest.)

2. Setting up a separate corporation will prevent this, at the cost of paying a corporate tax to IRS and state.

3. Losses can be carried forward & back.

ACCOUNTING REASONS

1. It is somewhat easier to defend the deductions against for-profit revenues in a separate corporation than if allocated within the NPO itself. The record-keeping is probably simpler where the entire entity is separate.

2. It makes possible using different accounting methods—e.g., accrual instead of cash basis—in the for-profit activity only.

MANAGERIAL REASONS

1. If a different management and/or Board is used, with business skills, the chances of a for-profit enterprise succeeding is greater than if run by the same leadership as the NPO.

ARGUMENTS CON

1. May be able to protect assets by carrying insurance against lawsuits—not other debts. If subsidiary not treated at arm's length, the parent could be held liable for debts.

2. Could borrow only if adequately financed. Outside investors may affect policy.

1. If for-profit activities *are* reasonably related to the exempt purposes, this isn't a problem. The expenses and technical problems aren't worth incorporating a subsidiary.

2. If not an excessive (say 5% or less) part of gross income, NPO files a 990-T and pays the same corporate tax (to IRS only?) without the complications of a separate corporation.

(NOTE: In either case, business accounting concepts will have to be mastered.)*

1. With proper accounting records and procedures, allocation of indirect expenses to for-profit activities can be justified.

2. Use of different accounting methods might be somewhat confusing, except to a sophisticated management.

1. If the for-profit activity is managed by a different manager with business skills, the difference in "mind set" would not be a problem, though the board itself would need to have a mix of skills, and perhaps a committee to supervise the for-profit activity.

*Special business accounting issues: inventory valuation, accelerated depreciation, etc.

FIGURE 9–3. ORGANIZATIONAL OPTIONS FOR NONPROFIT ENTERPRISE[2]

Retain as a Program Division	Create a For-Profit Subsidiary (Wholly or Partially Owned)	Create a Separate NPO
A. Legal and Tax Considerations		
1. If the activity of the division is substantially related to the exempt mission it will not pay unrelated business income tax (UBIT). If there is unrelated income, tax must be paid. If unrelated income is substantial, exemption may be questioned.	1. The business will pay taxes, like any commercial endeavor, at commercial rates. It can take business deductions, e.g., depreciation.	1. Same as column 1.
2. Tax-exempt status may be challenged by for-profit providers, distracting attention from the business and increasing its costs.	2. No challenge to tax-exempt status of the parent is likely so long as the parent does not spend disproportionate resources on the subsidiary.	2. Tax-exempt status may be difficult to obtain if issue of unrelated income arises and, if obtained, it may be susceptible to challenge.
3. There is the possibility of legal and financial liability if the division's activity is ruled unrelated, and liability can be retroactive.	3. Generally, no legal or financial liability inures to the nonprofit parent.	3. No legal or financial liability inures to the nonprofit parent in setting up the separate NPO.
B. Financial Considerations		
1. The division can share overhead expenses.	1. All costs are borne directly by the business.	1. Costs are borne by the new nonprofit.
2. Capitalization (funding) can come from the parent, reducing time and cost to the division.	2. Capitalization can come from a mix of sources—i.e., from the nonprofit parent and outside financing—and may take time to arrange.	2. Capitalization can be enhanced by ties with the nonprofit.
3. Sources of capital are limited to charitable organizations, the board, and individuals, through grants or program-related investments. Equity capital is unobtainable.	3. Sources of capital are likely to come from venture capitalists, banks, or individual investors, as well as from the nonprofit parent. Capital can be equity or debt. Grants are unavailable.	3. Same as column 1.
4. Earnings are not taxable. They can go directly to the parent for program use.	4. Earnings are taxable. Money is returned to the parent through dividends or royalties.	4. Earnings are not taxable and go directly for program use.

[2]*Nonprofit World,* September/October, 1986. Used with permission. See also Norman A. Sugarman, "Planning Techniques for Operating an Unrelated Business, in *N.Y.U. 14th Biennial Conference on Tax Planning for the Charitable Sector,* (Matthew Bender, N.Y.: 1985), pp. 15–18 ff; Brad Caftel, "Forming a For-Profit Subsidiary," in *Economic Development & Law Center Report,* Spring 1986.

FIGURE 9–3. ORGANIZATIONAL OPTIONS FOR NONPROFIT ENTERPRISE (continued)

Retain as a Program Division	Create a For-Profit Subsidiary (Wholly or Partially Owned)	Create a Separate NPO
5. There is no equity. The program, if it does well, cannot be sold later for a profit. It can, however, be spun off later, as a for-profit.	5. If the business grows and succeeds, it can be sold, with the proceeds going to the nonprofit parent in proportion to the parent's contribution. The relation between the parent and the subsidiary must be at arm's length at all times.	5. There is no equity.
6. Financial risk is likely to be less than as a for-profit.	6. Financial risk is likely to be greater than as a program division.	6. Same as column 1.
C. Operational Administration Considerations		
1. Control over the division is retained by the nonprofit parent, which can direct its growth and operations.	1. Total control may be given up, as may majority ownership.	1. Control over the operation by the separate NPO may be retained.
2. Executive leadership may take fewer business risks and expand the business more slowly than a for-profit.	2. Executive leadership may take more risks to expand the business more quickly than as a nonprofit.	2. Executive leadership may take more risks to expand the NPO than if a program division.
3. Board and staff committees can slow decision-making on issues needing fast resolution.	3. Operations can be streamlined and decisions made quickly.	3. Operations can be streamlined and decisions made relatively quickly.
4. Tension may arise at the staff level if salary and expense disparities exist.	4. Tension over salary and expense differentials is reduced, but "raiding" the parent for staff may introduce such tension.	4. Tensions are reduced, but "raiding" the parent may introduce tensions.
5. New career paths may be created to promote talented staff. Internal communication may increase.	5. Career movement into the for-profit, after start-up, will be unlikely. Communication between parent and subsidiary may decrease.	5. New career paths from within will probably not develop.
6. Cost sharing may become increasingly complex and hard to administer.	6. Budgets are distinct and must be funded directly. "Arm's length" relationships will apply.	6. Budgets are distinct and must be funded directly.
7. Increased prominence of the division may cause internal rivalries and raise questions about the mission of the nonprofit.	7. Mission conflicts are minimized.	7. Mission conflicts are minimized.

FIGURE 9–3. ORGANIZATIONAL OPTIONS FOR NONPROFIT ENTERPRISE (continued)

Retain as a Program Division	Create a For-Profit Subsidiary (Wholly or Partially Owned)	Create a Separate NPO
D. Marketing Considerations		
1. The division may be enhanced, locally, by its close connection with, and use of, the parent's name.	1. The business may be enhanced, nationally, by its separation from a locally familiar organization.	1. The business may be enhanced locally and nationally, by both trading off on the parent name and looking distinct from a local agency.
2. Marketing may call attention to the division's activities, increasing the chances of IRS or private legal action.	2. Marketing is limited only by financial resources.	2. Marketing may have to be limited to reduce the chance of IRS or private legal action.
3. Great success may cause confusion as to the real mission of the organization, with unknown effects on future fundraising activities.	3. No confusion over mission will occur.	3. No confusion over mission will occur, although there may be overlap in people's minds about fundraising goals and strategies.
4. The "image" of a nonprofit organization engaged in enterprise is sometimes suspect in the business world. On the other hand, successful new programs reflect well on the whole organization.	4. The "image" of for-profits is consonant with the business world.	4. Same as column 1.
E. Board Considerations		
1. Board reaction to growth of the division is not predictable, especially regarding its fundraising obligations.	1. Growth would be supported and looked on positively. No conflicts over mission can occur.	1. Growth would be supported and looked on positively. No conflicts over organizational goals can occur.
2. The board may not have the time or expertise to support the division.	2. The board may only partially overlap with that of the parent. Additional expertise can be made available through the appointment of new members.	2. The board may only partially overlap with that of the parent. Additional expertise can be made available through the appointment of new members.

one entity to the other. It applies to the rental or other shared use of space, personnel, services, equipment, or supplies. Again, competent professional help is needed in such arrangements.

USING A SISTER CORPORATION

There may be situations in which it is advantageous to use a sister corporation, although it is usually preferable to use a subsidiary. A sister corporation's shares might be owned by individuals, rather than by the nonprofit, but unless those people are directly involved with the nonprofit as officers, directors, or staff, the relationship would be tenuous and impermanent. Since there could be no income received as dividends from a sister corporation by the nonprofit, any profits could only be made available to the nonprofit as payment of rent, interest, staff services, royalties, and the like. The only way that any of this income would become taxable to the nonprofit would be if there were control through its board of directors. (See the earlier section, "Creating a Separate Affiliate.")

LIMITED PARTNERSHIPS AND JOINT VENTURES

The advantage of either a limited partnership or a joint venture is that the entity is not itself taxed, but passes through any profits (or losses) to the participating organizations and individuals. It is more flexible than a corporation and makes it easier to attract outside capital. There are several variations, all of which are governed by state law:

• A limited partnership must normally have at least one general partner who manages the enterprise and has unlimited liability for debts and claims. The limited partners usually have legal liability only to the extent of their investment, sometimes plus a stated amount or percentage, and they commonly have a limited voice in decision-making. The nonprofit would often be a limited partner in such an arrangement, a business firm or investor the general partner, although the reverse can be the case. Such a firm would normally have a continued existence. A syndicate is one type of limited partnership. The IRS now accepts these arrangements, but will scrutinize them to make certain that there is a genuine tax-exempt purpose involved.

• A joint venture is a form of partnership between two organizations for the accomplishment of a particular task, after which it is dissolved. A tax-exempt community development corporation may, for example, form a joint venture with a business firm to build low-rent housing. The co-venturers are usually fully liable for debts and claims. Day-to-day management is in some cases assigned to one of the two parties.

As with a business corporation set up by a nonprofit, expert legal help is a must to ensure that the interests of the nonprofit are fully protected. The IRS has set aside any tax exemption related to such arrangements where it can be demonstrated that profits will inure primarily to the benefit of a business firm or private investor.[3]

---

[3]See IRS General Counsel Memoranda 39005 (6/28/83) and 37259 (9/17/77).

THE FEASIBILITY STUDY

For any nonprofit, setting up an income producing venture is a high-risk proposition. The nonprofit is flirting with business failure and loss of tax-exempt status. Worse yet, the new venture could drag your existing nonprofit down with it, unless you have protected yourself against that possibility. Before embarking on any such venture, it is essential to conduct a feasibility study. There are two major parts of such a study, the marketing aspect and the financial aspect, which are the same as the components of a business plan. The financial study is developed after a decision to go ahead is made. In examining feasibility, it is wise to keep in mind the most common reasons for new business failures:

- Inadequate business experience in general, and in the specific line of business in particular. Each line has its own quirks and special problems that can become pitfalls to the unwary. This applies not only to marketing and operations management but also to financial management. You must therefore have a knowledgeable manager in charge.

- Inadequate funds to start up and to ride out any rough weather. Most enterprises can expect to lose money in the first year at least, before they get up to speed and develop the know-how and customer base.

- Inadequate planning and reliance on "flying by the seat of the pants." This is especially true where you do have an experienced manager! No amount of experience can substitute for good planning.

If you find these considerations scary, this might be a good time to consider dropping the whole idea. Otherwise, proceed with your feasibility study and reconsider this, depending on its outcome.

The Market Potential

Whether you plan to sell services or products, the first question that needs to be answered is: Can we generate enough sales to earn an adequate profit? That means not only enough sales volume, but enough profit margin on these sales to cover administrative, advertising, and selling costs, plus enough profit to make the venture worthwhile. To answer this fundamental question, the following points must be considered:

What products or services would be the most desirable, meaning that they are not only potentially the most profitable, but also that they fit in best with the knowledge and experience of your organization, or at least of someone you can get to manage the venture. This is the "product-first" approach. A few tips regarding the criterion follow (we use the word "product" to refer to services as well, to save space).

Despite the myth that businesses want only to compete, the fact is that most successful businesses try to avoid head-to-head competition by (1) coming up with products that no one else in their market has and seeking geographic areas that are not well served; (2) trying to differentiate their products from the competition by features, names, the advertising appeals and slogans used, auxiliary services and facilities offered; and (3) seeking a "market niche" that is going unfilled because it is either too small to be of interest to larger competitors, or merely has unrecognized potential. Examples are the Ford Mustang, which first recognized the potential post-World War II mass market for a sports-type car, and the personal computer, which IBM did not invent, but for which it discovered the market only after Apple and others developed it.

Note: The one who invents a product or discovers a new market is not always the one who owns it for long. Often as not they "come a cropper" as a result of the kind of problems involved in a new business, described above. A good example that comes to mind is the first computer spreadsheet program called Visicalc, a brilliantly original product, and a major factor in the creation of the microcomputer market. It no longer exists, however, having lost out to Lotus 1-2-3, which came later.

You'd do well to take the above to heart and not assume that being a business means trying to do better what everyone else is doing right next door. That's usually a losing proposition, romantic as it may seem, although it may work better in the nonprofit than in the business field.

The product-first approach.   If you are starting with the product-first approach, you will have to do market research that takes the product as a given, as part of your feasibility study. It should include the following:

1. Determining who the potential customers or clients are for your product, and making preliminary estimates of their number, locations, per capita income, and growth trends.

2. Identifying any cultural, social, or economic issues affecting customers, including pricing. Is yours a convenience product, a luxury, or a necessity to your target customers? That will affect your location as well as your pricing scheme.

3. Identifying the market area for your product in geographic terms, considering convenience, accessibility and transportation issues, public and private (i.e., parking facilities). If other than a retail operation, accessibility and transportation issues must be considered regarding suppliers as well as customers. (Shipping costs can price you out of a market.)

4. If your products are to be marketed to business firms, other nonprofits, or government agencies, identifying potential customers, their geographic distribution, size level, quantities purchased, and growth trends.

5. If you plan to sell merchandise, unless it is a retail store, a study must be made of the best distribution channels for reaching your customers. There are many ways to do so, including direct sales (door-to-door, direct mail, or media solicitation), wholesalers, sales or manufacturers' agents, jobbers, and drop-shippers, among others. Each method has its advantages and disadvantages, which relate to the amount of sales push you can expect and the various costs and risks involved. These include such things as selling costs (commissions, shipping, advertising, and travel), plus the bearing or shifting of the risks and carrying costs of customer credit and inventory. A chart summarizing these methods and their pros and cons appears as Fig. 9–4.

6. Determining who the likely competitors are in the same market, their size and market share, and their sales volume, if possible, plus their pricing structure.

7. Establishing a pricing plan, based on the above considerations and your costs. (This is discussed later, under Financial Considerations.)

8. Making a conservative estimate of your potential sales, in units as well as dollars for the next three to five years. (You can't really estimate dollar sales unless you first know what prices you'll charge. If they are set by the market, it will be feasible at this point. If not, see Financial Considerations.)

The customer-first approach.   The opposite approach is to start with an intended target group of customers and ascertain what they are willing and able to buy. It is much like a needs assessment,

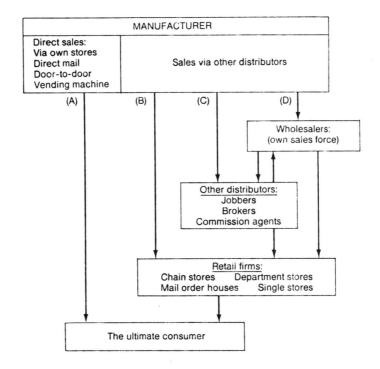

FIGURE 9-4. STANDARD CHANNELS OF DISTRIBUTION.

such as was described in Chapter 8, and requires a different kind of market research that proceeds from their interests and needs, coupled with their ability to pay.

You must first determine what is wanted, then proceed to the steps described in the product-first approach. This involves sifting through alternative products or services that might meet the same need, to pick the most promising one. It requires more work than deciding in advance what is needed, but it has the advantage of gearing your whole orientation to customer wants, which can pay off not only in greater sales but also in repeat business and strong word-of-mouth advertising—often the best kind.

Marketing pros speak of "The Marketing Concept," which in essence means running the whole organization in a way that maximizes consumer interest and satisfaction. It tends to put greater emphasis on product quality, quality control, and customer service, and it is the secret of Japan's success in foreign markets, especially our own. A chart that attempts to illustrate the interrelationships involved in the marketing concept is shown as Fig. 9–5.

Financial Considerations

The basic elements to be considered in evaluating the feasibility of the business being considered are: start-up capital needs for fixed assets and working capital, where you can get it, basic overhead costs, profit margins on products, cash flow issues, and projected profits. This will be only a preliminary estimate, to be sharpened up in the actual business plan itself.

1. Start-up capital.   Start-up will have to cover any needed real estate, vehicles, furniture and equipment, installation (including wiring, plumbing, or flooring), remodeling or decorating, plus a beginning inventory of merchandise or raw materials, if merchandise is to be sold or manufactured, legal fees, licenses and permits, utility and rent deposits, plus any needed advertising, printing or promotional costs announcing your opening, where appropriate.

In addition to these one-time outlays, some of which you can obtain on credit and pay over time, you must obtain enough working capital to pay for at least the first three or four months' operations, or until your sales are enough to cover them. That includes salaries, payroll taxes, and employee benefits; rent (or mortgage and tax payments, if any); utilities including telephone; insurance; delivery or shipping; professional fees; supplies; repairs and maintenance; advertising and promotion; and commissions, if any.

2. The costs to make, buy, and sell your products, preferably on a per unit basis. Applying these to your projected sales levels in units will give you a starting point in setting prices, since you want to generate a profit margin large enough to cover all expenses plus provide an adequate profit. (See discussion of Break-Even Analysis in Chapter 6.)

3. Estimate your prices, taking into account the factors already discussed under Market Potential and the prices charged by any likely competitors in your market. From that information, estimate your sales in dollars and your gross margin (sales minus cost of goods or services sold).

4. Now you are in a position to prepare projected operating statements for the first three to five years, and to see whether they show an adequate rate of return on invested capital—for any outside investors, as well as for your own agency. This must include the effect of projected interest paid on borrowed funds, as well as income taxes—federal and state—on your net income. If the net income is little more than you can get on bank certificates of deposit or other alternative investments, forget the whole thing.

5. If the ROI (return on investment) looks promising, the last step is to project the monthly cash flow for at least a year, taking into account the timing issues affected by credit given customers and received from vendors of materials, equipment and services, seasonal borrowing and repayment of loans, and dividends to outside investors, if any. (The coverage of cash and capital budgeting in Chapter 7 is fully applicable here.)

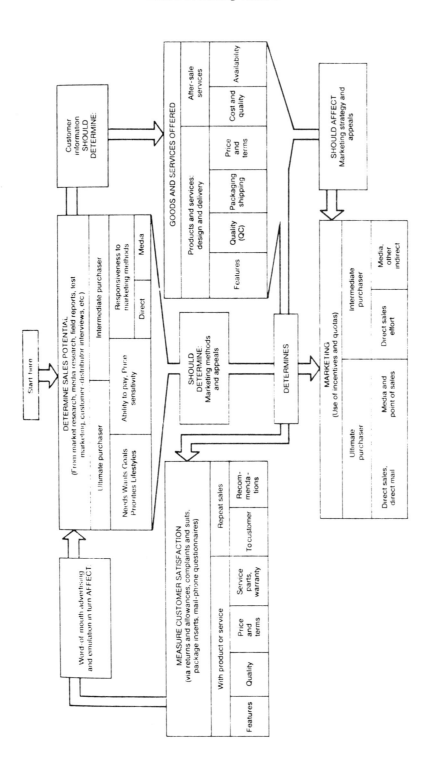

FIGURE 9–5. A MODEL OF THE MARKETING CONCEPT.

BASIC DECISIONS INVOLVED IN PLANNING

Organizational Form

Based on the discussion at the beginning of this chapter, decide on whether your enterprise will be (1) tax-exempt or taxable; (2) whether it will be part of your present agency, an affiliate, or a subsidiary; (3) if a taxable enterprise, whether it should be a corporation, limited partnership, or joint venture.

Decide also the acceptable degree or limit of ownership or control you want to keep, and how much to relinquish to outsiders. That may involve consideration of who will serve on the board or who will act as the managing partners. Other issues that may have to be considered, with legal advice, follow:

- The powers of the board and its fiduciary duties, which should be contained in the articles of incorporation. These are similar to, but may differ from, the ones described in Chapter 2.

- Provision for disposition of assets on dissolution, also in the articles.

- Buy–sell agreements between owners, which govern the transferability of shares of stock or partnership interests in the event that someone wants out, dies, or becomes incapacitated. Often the entity is given the right of first refusal (i.e., the right to make the first bid) to buy out any individual.

- Covenants, such as one not to compete, between partners, co-venturers, or stockholders.

- By-law provisions regarding voting rights and procedures, assigning the power to sign checks and contracts, dealing with conflicts of interest, and the like.

    Reminder: All of the above matters may have legal, tax, or financial implications that must be fully considered with the help of expert advice.

Types of Funding Sought

Investment of its own funds by the nonprofit forming the affiliate is usually a starting point. A word here on terminology: financial types differentiate equity—meaning permanent ownership investments—from long-term debt, which must be paid interest and eventually repaid. (The latter is sometimes lumped together with equity interests as capital investment, a debatable practice.)

A stockholder seeks a return on investment in the form of either dividends or a saleable increase in value; a partner's return may be a guaranteed payment or a share of profits; lenders usually expect current interest and repayment at a future date, or a series of installment payments. The difference is that dividends do not necessarily have to be paid, especially if funds are low, whereas there is usually little or no discretion with payments of profit shares, interest, or maturing loans.

On the other hand, interest is tax-deductible, dividends are not. (As noted, partnerships pay no separate federal income tax, though some states levy an unincorporated business tax.) Clearly, the pros and cons of the three types of long-term funding need to be weighed.

The proportions of equity and debt you desire for long-term funding must also be decided, which may come down to what you can get. New ventures do not find it easy to raise cash either way, because of the risks involved to investors. Banks rarely are interested. Insurance companies may be a source of long-term loans. Small Business Investment Corporations (SBICs) are a possible source of equity capital. You may find private investors and local business firms your best bet, especially if they know you and have some connection with your agency, such as board membership.

ELEMENTS OF A BUSINESS PLAN

You don't just walk in the door and ask investors or lenders for money: a sound business plan is the key instrument in attracting the outside funding you have decided to seek in the form of equity capital (ownership investments) and long-term loans. This document is based on the kind of strategic planning approach described in Chapter 3. Differences from a strategic plan will be observed in the outline that follows; they will suggest the differences required in the planning process. The outline resembles a funding proposal in many respects. The sequence is appropriate for a plan to be used in—or as—a prospectus for potential investors or co-venturers. The issues dealing with the choice of organizational form should already have been decided, and are therefore unnecessary.

THE OUTLINE

1. Overview or summary. A brief statement covering the most important aspects of your plan. This is your "grabber." Unless it makes a good first impression, you may get no further with the reader. Whatever you have to say that makes yours an exciting venture should be said here, in concise form.

2. Description of the business.
   a. What you plan to sell and what genuine or perceived need it fills; whether you will make it, have it made, or buy it, and from whom.
   b. Why the features or benefits of your product or service are better than its existing competition; how and where it will be obtained, made, or delivered.
   c. Why you think yours will be a profitable enterprise: what it has going for it, in the way of uniqueness and management know-how, and what return on investment you anticipate.
   d. The form of organization and planned methods of long-term funding, including any already committed or anticipated from others.

3. The market for your product. This section is essentially a brief statement of the results of your analysis of the potential market for your products already done in your feasibility study (see above). It should cover who and where your customers are, how many of them and how big the market is; what the motivating factors are to buy: price, prestige, convenience or saving time. What you expect your market share to be and by when; whether and how fast the market is growing.
   a. Your marketing plan. How your prices will be determined; your terms of sale (cash, credit, etc.); quality control and customer service policies, and most important, how you plan to win customers: via which distribution channels or methods and what advertising and sales promotion efforts. (This section and the next could be headings separate from the Market for Your Product.)

    b. The competition. This section should identify your closest competitors, their similarities and contrasts with your own planned operations; their pricing policies, competitive strengths and weaknesses; whether their sales curve is rising, falling, or flat; and what competitive edge or advantages you expect to have. (Competitor's sales may not be easily determined.)

4. Physical plant. This should be a brief statement of your space needs and where you plan to locate your premises and any branches; whether you plan to rent or buy. It should describe your needs in the way of capital equipment: vehicles, machinery, computers, office furniture and equipment.

5. Your management team. The point stressed in the section on proposal writing, that funding sources invest in people as much as in programs, applies here with equal force. The best plan in the world will fail if it lacks a management able to carry it out. Here is the place to convince your "angels" that their money will be in good hands.

    To do this convincingly you must indicate your organizational design (an organization chart is necessary): identify your key managers, including your CEO, line managers and staff members in the areas of marketing, finance and accounting, human resource administration. Their authority, responsibilities, and accountability need to be spelled out. The basis of their compensation and of any incentives offered should be explained.

    Their backgrounds and qualifications for the job are particularly important: resumes should be included as an appendix. If any are yet to be engaged, indicate what efforts you are making to recruit and, if necessary, train them. If any consultants or other professionals will play an important role, they too should be described.

    a. Personnel issues. A projection of your immediate and future needs, and potential sources, of other personnel, together with the types needed; whether they will be full-time or part-time, permanent, seasonal, or temporary; also whether fixed salaries or hourly wages will be paid. Develop personnel policies, including employee benefits and incentives, as well as recruiting and training methods, if appropriate.

6. Financial requirements and prospects. This is the payoff section of your business plan, where you get to the point. It consists of two major parts:

    a. Why you need money and how it will be used: for start-up, research and development (familiarly referred to as "R & D" in the business world), expansion, etc. How much you need, when, and in what form (debt or equity), including the expected ROI by investors (in dividends or growth) or lenders (in interest or possible growth). Where the funds will come from to pay dividends, interest, and loan principal. Also make clear the nature and terms of your own organization's contributions to the venture, in the form of any cash or cash equivalents, rented or owned premises and utilities, machinery, vehicles, computers, furniture or other equipment, as well as any operating or support personnel. Depending on whether it is to be a partnership, joint venture, or corporation, the form in which these resources are to be provided will vary: i.e., as an equity investment or long-term loan, and the return you expect on each, whether in money or other assets or values.

    b. Recent financial statements, if you are already operating, and financial projections (called "pro formas" in business) for three to five years down the road: operating statements, balance sheets, and cash flow projections. This is the basis for your statement about ROI and repayment of loans. The statements should be accompanied by an explanation of the assumptions on which they are based: changes in market size and market share, in population and demographics, economic conditions, including inflation, etc., related developing technologies, or any other relevant factors that may affect your prospects.

7. Appendix. This is the place for any exhibits that will help or further explain your proposition. It should include any of the following that are appropriate to your situation:

- Product or service descriptions, specifications, and especially any pictures (=1,000 words)

- Statistical data, questionnaires, or other bases for your projections of market potential

- Data regarding competitors and their market share

- Relevant patents or copyrights

- Possible advertising copy or appeals

- Relevant laws or regulations, including those that are tax-related (e.g., the Low Income Housing Tax Credit)

- Any favorable publicity or reviews of your products, services, officers, or company.

SUMMARY

Even though for-profit ventures require a different mind set than is common in the nonprofit world, we hope that this chapter and Chapter 8 have made clear the similarities between the two. Just as the best nonprofits put service to their clients and to society in the forefront of their thinking, the same to a great extent has been true of the most successful business firms.

Japan has taught us a lot in that regard: you see more Hondas and Toyotas on the road these days than Fords and Chevrolets because Americans found that they could rely on these Japanese products, and because the government of Japan was able to invest in promoting consumer industries freed of the burdens of a military-industrial complex. There is no necessary contradiction, it would appear, between profits and service to society.

Chapter 10

Accounting Literacy for Non-Accountants

Accounting is just a means to an end. Its products are for use in planning, analysis, and decision-making. Sometimes the fact that its language was developed, not by its users, but by its producers may tend to get in the way.

We have no desire to make accountants of our readers. But to make effective use of budgets and financial reports in winning the battle for survival, you need a degree of literacy in Accounting as a Second Language. Certain important basic concepts need explaining: they are known collectively as "GAAP," short for "Generally Accepted Accounting Principles." They have been evolved to provide a degree of uniformity—a common language and framework—for the communication of financial data between those who prepare and use it.

GAAP seeks to provide accounting information that possesses the characteristics of understandability, relevance, timeliness, and reliability. In addition, it aims for a degree of uniformity that can make it consistent between periods and comparable between different organizations. Its aim is for fairness of presentation, rather than perfect precision, a goal often too expensive to obtain, if not downright illusory. GAAP is best approached with the understanding that accounting is not a true science, but an evolving art. It is, nonetheless, a powerful tool, once both its potentials and limitations are understood.

GAAP FOR NONPROFITS: THE STATE OF THE ART

Until recent years, the nonprofit world has enjoyed—or suffered from—the benign neglect of accountancy's rule-makers. It is undoubtedly the great expansion of both the public and private nonprofit sector as major factors in the economy that has brought a new focus by the FASB and AICPA[1] on the need for codifying the piecemeal or inadequate accounting guidelines for nonprofits. Only a trickle of rule-making has been forthcoming in the nonprofit area, as contrasted with a veritable Niagara in the business sector.

Until 1978, AICPA's only guidelines were embodied in separate documents known as audit guides, which necessarily contained accounting and reporting standards deemed appropriate for the type of nonprofit covered. These documents were as follows:

[1]Financial Accounting Standards Board and American Institute of CPAs.

Hospital Audit Guide
Audits of Colleges and Universities
Audits of Voluntary Health and Welfare Organizations
Audits of Certain Nonprofit Organizations
Audits of State and Local Governmental Units
Statement of Position 78-10, Accounting Principles and Reporting Practices for Certain Nonprofit Organizations

The *Statements of Position* (SOPs) issued beginning in 1974 were a new type of unofficial guideline undertaken by the Institute to provide some guidance to public accountants in areas of accounting and reporting rules not yet covered by official *Statements of Financial Accounting Standards* (SFAS), which are the exclusive province of FASB. SOP No. 78-10 was an effort to codify "Accounting Principles and Reporting Practices for Certain Nonprofit Organizations"—namely those not already covered by the audit guidelines. The FASB lent some force to these SOPs and the audit guides by issuing SFAS No. 32, which conferred upon these guidelines a newly created favored status of "Preferable Accounting Principles." This does not make them fully binding on independent public accountants, except in a limited situation,[2] but has the practical effect of approving the SOPs as stop-gap rules that most public accountants will follow. The SOPs are expected to be superseded eventually by official rules issued by the FASB. To date only a conceptual framework for such rules has been released, "Objectives of Financial Reporting by Nonbusiness Organizations" *(Statement of Financial Concepts No. 4).*

In our discussion of GAAP below, we have attempted a broadly generalized treatement because we recognize the current state of flux in this area. The publications just described are guidelines for public accountants in connection with external financial reporting, and only three of them are likely to be directly relevant to your organization: SOP No. 78-10, *Audits of Certain Nonprofit Organizations*, or perhaps *Audits of Voluntary Health and Welfare Organizations* (which are defined as those involved with health, welfare, or community services). We cover specific provisions of SOP No. 78-10 later in this chapter. The comparable provisions of the last-named audit guide are essentially the same, but that publication should be referred to by readers involved with organizations it covers, where they require specific guidance.

Accounting principles and practices prescribed by AICPA or FASB are binding only on licensed public accountants, not on the enterprises whose books or statements are involved. They are thus mandatory only for external financial reports, if a public accountant's opinion ("certified statement," in the colloquial term) is required. On the other hand, consideration both of usefulness and practicality generally leads to adoption of the same rules for most internal as well external financial reporting, as we try to demonstrate throughout this book—with exceptions or reservations noted where appropriate.

Complexity of Accounting Resulting from Real-World Problems

Here are some examples of problems accounting must confront to solve:

● Different kinds of users differ in their level of expertise, knowledge, and understanding, and in their specific information needs.

---

[2]They are the legitimate basis for a change in accounting principle or practice: i.e., the way a given item is treated in reporting.

- Accounting is used for different purposes at different levels of an organization and outside of it.

- The same economic events—exchanges and uses of resources—can be portrayed in different ways: the most reliable and useful way is not always the simplest. Again in the quest for objectivity, accounting differs from economics in generally using the cost rather than the value of assets in financial reports (with certain exceptions). "Value" is still viewed with suspicion as a term prone to subjective bias.

- As its central focus, accounting seeks to measure as reliably as possible the revenues *earned* and expenses *incurred* in a given period of time, which are not always the same as revenues collected and expenses paid in the same period. This is done for greater objectivity, since the real question is not what was *paid* for, but what goods or services were given or received. Payment dates can be arbitrarily manipulated. The main goal is to record and report events in a rational, systematic, and objective manner, for which cash basis accounting is ineffective.

The Rationale for Cash Basis Accounting

Most people intuitively keep their personal financial records and prepare their income tax returns on a basis of money received or paid, the obvious and simplest way. Even at that they can make serious errors on their returns, such as not deducting for a casualty loss because they did not pay the repair bill until the following year.

The only good argument for recording and reporting economic events only when cash is immediately involved (the cash basis) is its familiarity and simplicity. It is also true that for a given nonprofit, use of the cash basis may sometimes not make a difference in results. The AICPA expressly recognized this in SOP No. 78-10 and states that, "If financial statements prepared on the cash basis are not materially different from those prepared on the accrual basis, the independent auditor may still be able to conclude that the statements are presented in conformity with generally accepted Accounting principles (Par. .013)."

This provision, it should be noted, is no blank check to use cash basis at will: the burden of proof will be on the auditor, if challenged. The reasons why should soon become apparent.

Cash Basis Accounting: The Pitfalls

Accrual accounting is not as simple as cash basis, nor as obvious. But it tells the whole truth where cash basis is often dangerously deceptive. A business has a different motive for using this method than does a nonprofit: it matches expenses incurred to revenues earned in the same period in order to measure profits correctly, not manipulated by payments; but a nonprofit's reasons are quite as important. Consider these situations if you're in doubt:

- A youth center reports its operations on a cash basis. At the end of its fiscal year it shows a nifty excess of revenues and support over expenses of $10,000. The board is delighted with the Executive Director's performance and votes her a raise. What it doesn't know is that she failed to submit $15,000 in unpaid expense bills, already past due. Simple system—bad decision!

- XYZ Community Concerts, also on the cash basis, collects $5,000 near the end of its fiscal year for tickets to performances early next period, and thereby shows a $3,000 excess of revenues over expenses for the year. Its board reduced ticket prices for next year before discovering that the new year's first quarter shows a loss because admissions revenue for the period fell off by the $5,000 already reported, while all performance costs were charged to the new quarter. What price simplicity?

Other situations in which the cash basis misled an organization's leaders would involve cases in which things looked worse than they really were, due to unreported revenues that would have been reflected on an accrual basis. Similarly, a payment in the current period of expense incurred in the previous period can make things suddenly look bad (whereas they had look surprisingly good at the end of the previous period).

In short, while to simplify is desirable, to oversimplify complex processes is potentially disastrous. It is for these reasons that the rules of GAAP require that such a statement prepared on a cash basis be labeled, not an operating or income statement, but that it bear a title such as Statement of Income Collected and Expenses Paid; and no auditor's opinion may be expressed as to whether or not it fairly presents the results of the organization's operations for the period. These rules apply only to external financial reports, and have the escape hatch noted above, if the resulting figures are substantially the same as if prepared on the accrual basis.

Instead of the operating statement, consider the balance sheet of an organization. It is intended to be a statement of financial condition, showing what the organization owns (its assets) and what it owes (its liabilities). The trouble is, if a balance sheet were prepared on a cash basis it would omit major amounts owed to or by the organization. As a result it would present as distorted a picture of the nonprofit's financial condition as the operating statement would of its revenues and expenses. A board that relied on it to make financial decisions could get a falsely favorable or unfavorable impression, leading to potentially harmful actions.

The excess of assets over liabilities, the fund balance, represents the "cushion" or net worth of the nonprofit. Should it be a negative quantity (i.e., a deficit), the organization would be at least technically insolvent. Using the cash basis, this figure or comparison becomes almost meaningless, for major assets or liabilities are omitted, or they may be over- or understated, if only partially included. Thus a false "cushion" would be common, since liabilities are more likely to be omitted than assets .

Would a supplier extend credit or would foundations approve grants to a nonprofit, knowing that its liabilities exceeded its assets? A cash basis "balance sheet" does not rule out such a possibility, which is why it is unacceptable.

How Cash Basis Can Distort Balance Sheets

Suppose Nonprofit X had assets consisting of $1,000 cash and $5,000 in equipment. Even though it had unpaid expense bills totaling $8,000, which it expected to pay out of a forthcoming grant or revenues to be earned, it would show no liabilities on a balance sheet prepared on a cash basis, therefore a fund balance of $6,000. In fact, it has a *deficit* of $2,000—the excess of what it owes ($8,000) over its total assets ($6,000). A balance sheet prepared on the accrual basis would "tell it like it is," by showing the liability and deficit, whereas a similar statement prepared on cash basis would be grossly misleading.

Again, GAAP requires that if a statement is thus prepared, it be labeled, not a balance sheet, but a Statement of Assets & Liabilities Resulting from Cash Transactions, with no auditor's opinion as to whether it fairly presents the organization's financial condition at the date indicated.

Aside from the requirements of GAAP, some states require that forms reporting annual operations be prepared on an accrual basis. The fact that operating budgets are almost intuitively prepared on an accrual basis, as explained in Chapter 6, is still another reason for preparing internal as well as external financial reports on the same basis, for purposes of comparing actual operating statements vs. operating budgets for both control and performance evaluation.

In view of all the many cited reasons that make use of the accrual basis desirable and often necessary, the argument that the cash basis is so much easier to understand and use becomes less convincing. It would seem appropriate only for small organizations that have little or no unpaid expenses or uncollected revenue at the end of any reporting period.

Note: The point should be stressed here that we refer to the use of accrual basis for reports, and not necessarily for day-to-day bookkeeping. This distinction is explained in Chapter 12.

ACCRUAL BASIS: HANDLING SPECIFIC ITEMS

The accrual basis classifies revenues and expenses by taking into account not only the accounting period in which the bill is paid, but more importantly, the period in which the activity involved occurred. It shows the *earning* of the revenue or support or the *incurring* of the expense. There are three possible periods in any situation: past, present, or future, and both the payment and the related activity could occur in any of those three time frames. The term "earned" has a somewhat different meaning for a nonprofit than for a business, since it may indicate that funds received have been used in the manner specified by their donor.

In each case, it is the relationship between "when it happens" and "when it is paid" that determines whether the particular item of revenue or expense should be classified ("recognized") as:

1. Current revenue or expense, if all of it was earned or incurred as well as used during the current period and the amount was all paid for in the current period.

2. Accrued revenue or expense, if earned or incurred in the current period which benefited, to the extent *not* paid by the end of the period.

3. Deferred revenue or prepaid expense, to the extent paid in advance during the current period, where all or part of it will benefit a future period. Note that deferred revenue represents an obligation to render a service or do something in the future and is treated therefore as a liability, not revenue. Similarly, a prepaid expense represents the right to receive a service or use something in the future that already has been paid for, and is thus treated as an asset, not an expense.

A "Real-World" Example Using Accrual Accounting

To illustrate these concepts in a graphic way, let us suppose that you are taking a three-day cross-country trip by train, departing from the East Coast the night of December 30. Your organization closes its books on December 31. It keeps them (with incredible precision) on the accrual basis, for it wants to know how much of the expense of the trip applied to this year, how much to next. Suppose the sleeper fare for the trip was $1,100, and that you are due to arrive in Chicago at midnight of December 31, which is $300 of the total fare, we'll assume.

Ride now, pay later.   If you charged the fare to your credit card, you could look at it this way: when you arrived in Chicago, $300 of the expense would have been incurred, and would apply to this year. You also should really owe only that amount at that point on your credit card, assuming you could get a credit for the balance, say if you decided to go by air the rest of the way. Your score is $300 in expense incurred, and $300 owed as a liability.

Note also that the $300 was building up—accruing, we call it—as the miles clicked off and that the actual expense incurred and liability accrued was less than that, before you reached Chicago. The fact that you didn't pay for the trip until your credit card bill came in January of next year is irrelevant here. The $300 of expense applied to this year, not next. The payment was not an expense, the trip was: that's what was paid for (the $800 balance is next year's expense).

Paying cash "up front."   Now let's turn it around a bit: suppose instead of charging the fare to your credit card, you paid cash for it. At that point, before you leave, have you incurred an expense? You may think so, but the answer is no. Proof is the fact that you should be able to get a refund, if something prevents your going at the last minute. Why? Because you have not received the services you paid for. What you have here is a prepaid expense, which is not an expense at all, but an asset until you get what you paid for.

As the miles click away, you are getting service you paid for and thus incurring the expense. When you arrive in Chicago, you'll have incurred $300 of expense, will have gotten that much service, and therefore will have used up $300 of the asset, which will still be worth the balance of $800. This is the cost of the rest of the trip, which will be an expense of next year (January 1 and 2). When you reach San Francisco, you'll have incurred the remaining $800. No more asset—all "expensed."

The important point is that the time of payment was irrelevant to the period in which the expense was incurred. In both cases—one unpaid, one prepaid—the $300 expense was for December, the $800 balance for January.

From the railroad's viewpoint.   Let us now look at the same question as it applies not to expense, but to revenue. If we look at the same $1,100 fare from Amtrak's point of view, the railroad earned no revenue until it took you for a ride. Though you charged the $1,100 on your credit card, Amtrak had earned revenue of only $300 when you reached Chicago, even though it would not collect for a month or more. The amount due from you was an asset.

It would have earned only the same $300 of revenue at that point, even if you had paid cash in advance. The rest would be unearned revenue—a liability—until you reached San Francisco, for at Chicago it still owed you the rest of the trip, or a refund, if you cancelled.

To tie up the relationships: Amtrak had revenue to the extent you had an expense, based on services rendered and received. On your arrival in San Francisco, if you had used credit, Amtrak had an $1,100 asset (an account receivable) and you an $1,100 liability (account payable or accrued expense payable), until you paid your bill. If you paid the fare in advance, they had an $1,100 liability (Unearned Income); you had an $1,100 asset (Prepaid Expense) until they delivered what they had promised: delivering you to San Francisco. In between the two coasts, services were being rendered, which finally accumulated to $1,100.

Of course, no organization would ever break down a single trip between periods in this way, but the example does illustrate the whole theory of accrual basis accounting, in a way that may facilitate both understanding and remembering the concept.

What Happen to Accruals and Prepayments Later

What happens to accrued and deferred items left over from the previous period in the following period? When accrued revenue is recorded on the books, its subsequent collection represents, not revenue, but settlement of the prior claim. It cannot therefore be recognized as revenue a second time in the following period, when collected. The same applies to accrued expense: payment of the amount owed, already recorded as an expense when accrued, must be recorded, when subsequently paid, as settlement of a debt, not as an expense a second time.

Thus the collection of revenue previously recorded as an accrual represents the reduction of an asset—a "receivable"; the payment of an expense previously recorded as an accrual represents the reduction of a liability—a "payable."

Similarly, where collection or payment precedes the actual performance of the service paid for, or use of the goods purchased, it is not the date of payment that governs its treatment ("recognition") as revenue or expense, but which period benefited from the related activity. Thus, collection in advance (e.g., for tickets to a future performance) is not revenue, because not yet earned: it becomes revenue, and is transferred to a revenue account, once the obligation to perform the service is satisfied.

Expenses paid for in advance, or supplies purchased, become expenses when the related benefits have been received: when the services paid for have been performed, or the supplies used. At that point, the portion of the previously deferred amount that now relates to the past, rather than future periods, is transferred to the appropriate revenue or expense account ("amortized"), by way of recognition that the activity in question has taken place.

So much for general concepts and rules. Now let us apply them to specific items that might be found in typical nonprofit situations.

Traditionally, small nonprofits have not accrued uncollected revenues, but have treated them as revenue of the period in which received. Revenues of such organizations are more frequently received before they are earned (program grants, dues, subscriptions, and admissions) or are not earned by any specific acts (contributions and general-purpose grants).

Revenues Earned Though Not Yet Received

Unrestricted grants. Any uncollected portions of grants that have been approved and are unrestricted as to purpose, or of program grants whose purposes have already been satisfied, can be treated as accrued revenue and entered both as a grant receivable (on the balance sheet at the end of the current period) and as grant revenue (on the operations statement of the current period).

Program service fees. Any that have already been earned, but not yet paid for by clients or members, can be treated similarly to uncollected grants, as accounts receivable and program revenue.

Pledges. Although the existing guidelines of the AICPA deal with pledges differently for different kinds of nonprofits, the Financial Accounting Standards Board (FASB) has tentatively concluded[3] that as long as they are unconditional, they should be recognized as revenue or support when received, just as though they were accounts receivable.[4] (If conditional, they should be accrued when any conditions have been substantially met.)

If the donor has indicated the period for which the pledge is being made, and it is to be collected during that period, it should be set up as a pledge receivable at the full amount likely to be collected (which may be less than the amount pledged). The pledge should be recognized as revenue in the

---

[3]Status report No. 203, July 14, 1989, p. 6.

[4]An allowance for potentially uncollectible pledges should be set up at statement dates, by an adjusting entry similar to that used to set up the allowance for depreciation. The amount of the "Allowance for Uncollectible Pledges" should be an estimate based upon recent experience: an educated guess is to be preferred over crystal-gazing.

period specified. This is a bit complicated, where the pledge spans two or more accounting periods, either because so specified, or because it will be paid in two installments.

If pledges are numerous, or the total amount is substantial, they should be analyzed on a worksheet, and the totals sorted between deferred, current, and accrued revenues. Record-keeping for pledges is covered in Chapter 12.

Other accrued revenues.   These would consist of any other categories of revenue (dues, subscriptions, etc.) where amounts remain uncollected after related services have been performed; usually these would be delinquent amounts. If substantial in total, they should be treated similarly to uncollected grants, at the estimated collectible amount.

EXAMPLES OF DEFERRED REVENUES

These are amounts received in the current period but not yet earned, as explained above. In succeeding periods, the portions earned must be recognized as revenue, by transferring them to current revenue accounts from the deferred revenue category, which represents only an obligation to render the service (a liability), and not revenue.

Restricted program or contract grants.   Ordinarily funds are approved and received on such grants before any directly related expenses are incurred. There are two ways to deal with the situation: (1) The grant can be recognized as revenue in either the period approved or the period collected. If uncollected, it would be accrued, as we have explained, under uncollected grants. (2) The grant can be recognized as revenue as the program expenses are incurred.

The effect of (1) is to show the entire revenue immediately, without any related expenses. If this occurs near the end of an accounting period, the revenues for that period may show a substantial injection, whereas the expenses of the following period will exceed the related program revenue. This practice may distort the financial picture for the board or the treasurer.

Only method (2) conforms with GAAP, since its purpose is to match expenses against related revenues. This is the method prescribed for external financial reporting by AICPA's SOP 78-10. The procedure is to treat the original approval or collection of the program grant not as current revenue, but as deferred program revenue, before the funds are actually used. As program expenses are incurred, equivalent revenues should then be transferred out of the deferred category and treated ("recognized") as current program revenue. The unexpended portion of the grant will continue to be reported as deferred revenue, until it is used up.

Pledges.   Where a donor has specified the period to which a pledge applies, it should be similarly recognized as revenue in that period. Thus a pledge accrued in one period, designated as intended for the next, should be treated in a manner similar to a restricted grant: the amount to be recognized in the next period should be treated as deferred revenue or support, and transferred to current revenue (amortized) or support in the periods designated.

Dues and subscriptions.   Where received in advance and covering a specified period, these should be treated in the same manner as the previous items: deferred and amortized over the periods to which they apply. In addition, they may present a particular problem, if dues also cover a subscription to a publication of the organization, in which case the publication's value should be allocated to subscription revenue.

If dues are in substance contributions, and no services are to be provided the member, they should be recognized when collected, or when accrued, if the practice is to accrue uncollected dues.

Advance ticket sales and reservations.   Where a nonprofit sells tickets and collects money in advance for a performance or an event to take place in the future, the amounts received are deferred revenue until the event is held, and are only then recognized as current revenue. If the event is to take place in the same accounting period as the advance payment, the item can be treated as current revenue immediately. Note, however, that it may still represent a liability rather than revenue (if the amount is refundable) because of cancellation of the event, nonattendance, or other reasons.

ACCRUED EXPENSES: WHAT THEY ARE AND HOW TO DEAL WITH THEM

Accrued expenses are expenses incurred but not previously recorded and still unpaid. Generally speaking the typical small nonprofit is much more involved with this type of accrual than with revenue items, and failure to consider them is likely to cause problems. Although the number of accrued expense items may be substantial, they offer fewer technical problems than do accrued revenues.

Strictly speaking, all liabilities that arise out of services received by an organization may be thought of as accrued expenses. The term itself is ordinarily applied, however, only to those that do not originate with invoices entered on the books during the period through a journal, but are recorded only at the time statements are being prepared. The other types are generally referred to as accounts payable (or vouchers payable). Bookkeeping aspects are covered in Chapters 11 and 12.

Examples of Typical Accrued Expenses

Salaries and wages.   If part or all of a payroll has been earned but remains unpaid at the end of an accounting period, its full amount before withholding taxes is called accrued salaries or wages—alternately salaries or wages payable. If less than a full pay period is involved—e.g., three days of a five-day week—that proportion has been earned in, and is considered an expense of the current period, as well as a liability (owed to employees).

Payroll or other taxes.   Whether payroll taxes or other taxable items, they are additional expenses accrued or payable to the extent that they apply to the current period. This is illustrated in Fig. 12–5 (entry 5), which takes this problem into account.

Estimated unpaid utilities.   These are other examples of additional expenses and liabilities that need to be recorded at the end of a period, or when statements are being prepared.

Unpaid travel vouchers.   These and other out-of-pocket expenses to be reimbursed are also accruals of expenses and liabilities, if unpaid at the statement date.

Interest.   Interest owed to date on a loan or mortgage is still another example.

The list could be expanded to include many other examples of expenses or taxes incurred during a period but remaining unpaid at its end. They must be reflected on financial statements of the period as expenses (on the operating statement) and liabilities (on the balance sheet); otherwise there will be an incomplete, perhaps distorted picture of the cost of operations, and of the financial condition.

As with accrued revenue items, when these expenses are actually paid in the following period, the payment entry is not treated again as expense, but as eliminating a liability, which therefore has no effect on the operating statement, even though it affects cash flow. This is one way that GAAP matches expenses that apply to a given period against the revenue earned in that period.

Prepaid Expense Items Are Assets

Prepaid expenses are the reverse of accrued expenses. Instead of being unpaid at the period's end, they are prepaid: i.e., expenses of the next period paid in advance in this period. Like accrued expenses, this could be true of almost any type of expense. Any time all or part of an expense that has already been paid for really benefits a future period rather than the current period, the future benefit is treated as prepaid. This sometimes requires an entry reclassifying (amortizing) the future portion from expense to prepaid expense. Since that is a future benefit, it is then treated as an asset, no longer as expense, and therefore included in the balance sheet, not the operating statement. Examples of Prepaid Expense Items (illustrated in the expense budget worksheet, Table 5–5) follow.

Supplies (program supplies, printed materials).   When purchased, these are sometimes treated as expenses, although properly assets, since they are of future benefit. If so treated, and all used up by a statement date, no harm is done, for no entry is required: they have become expenses. If, however, any material quantity of supplies remains unused, that quantity will have to be reclassified as prepaid ('material" means significant). A preferred method, where the cost of supplies is substantial, is to treat them as assets (prepaid expense) when purchased, and transfer the part used to expense instead. This helps avoid losing track of prepaid items.

Insurance.   Here is another common example, where the policy runs past the statement date. The same options as above are available for recording the unexpired portion at the statement date. Treating the original payment as prepaid insurance rather than as insurance expense has the same advantage as noted for supplies. The prepaid portion should be amortized (transferred to expense) over the remaining life of the policy.

Interest.   If paid in advance on a loan or installment purchase, interest presents the same problems and can be treated the same ways. If total loan payments are greater than the value of what was received in cash or equipment, the difference represents prepaid interest (it may be called a discount or finance charge) and should be so treated. The prepayment is then amortized over the time period to which it applies.

Matters of Terminology

On a semantic note, the words *deferred* and *prepaid* mean the same thing; however they are generally used in somewhat different contexts. If an item is initially entered in an expense or revenue account, and a portion is later treated as a prepaid item because it relates to the activities of a subsequent period, the act of postponing its recognition as expense or revenue is called *deferral*. Where this treatment is used from the outset, it is designated *prepaid expense* or *deferred revenue*. (The latter is sometimes called *unearned* or *prepaid* revenue. Of these the first seems proper, the second confusing, for revenues are received by the entity, not paid.)

ACCRUALS AND DEFERRALS: ALL A MATTER OF TIMING

The purpose of accruing unpaid/uncollected expense/revenue items is to pull them back in time into the current period—the one in which they were incurred/earned. Otherwise the cash payment for the transaction, when entered, will record it in the wrong period.

The purpose of deferring such items is the reverse: the cash has already been paid or received and entered. Deferral serves to postpone the expense or revenue, i.e., to push it forward in time into future periods.

In either case, the treatment must be reversed in subsequent periods. The expense or revenue that had been accrued must then be treated not as expense or revenue when the cash transaction occurs and is entered, but as the reduction of the asset or liability set up in the accrual. This shields subsequent periods from duplicating the expense or revenue.

Similarly for a prepaid or deferred item: In subsequent periods, the expense or revenue that had been deferred and treated as an asset (expenses) or a liability (revenues) must receive the reverse treatment. The process, called amortization, undoes the deferral to the extent appropriate, and restores or transfers the next period's share of the expense or revenue to the related expense or revenue account.

In the case of deferrals, the process of going in the oppposite direction in the following period is sometimes referred to as a "reversal" of a previous deferral or accrual. (The bookkeeping entries embodying the processes described are covered in the Appendix to Chapter 12). Note that with respect to prepaid or deferred items (not accruals), the subsequent treatment can be variously described as reversal or amortization—and also as a "write-off" or a "write-down."

With respect to accruals as well as deferrals, in the subsequent period, regardless of the choice of words, there is usually a transfer from a balance sheet account to an operating statement account. The reverse occurs in the period in which the item is accrued or deferred. Thus the balance sheet may be viewed as the temporary file cabinet for expense and revenue items being shifted between periods, in whole or in part. It may also be seen as a time window through which an expense or revenue item must pass in order to shift its effect from one period to the next.

Compromise or Hybrid Methods

Some nonprofits go halfway to accrual basis accounting by applying the method to expenses, but not to revenues. The result may be to understate current revenues while reflecting expenses properly. It will thus generally result in a more conservative picture of both operations and financial condition than full accrual basis. Where this is consistently the situation, it is probably an unobjectionable compromise.

If, however, substantial program or support revenues are received in advance and treated as current revenue rather than being deferred as described above, the revenues and financial picture are overstated. This applies to many different items, ranging from program grants to advance ticket sales, subscriptions, and membership dues, all of which represent deferrals when received. If substantial amounts of revenue remain unearned by the end of the period, they should be deferred, and not treated on a cash basis. If the pattern and amount of such unearned revenues do not vary materially from year to year, cash basis accounting is acceptable, since one year's overstatement will be offset by the understatement resulting from failure to defer revenues at the end of the previous year. (Nonetheless the balance sheet will distort the financial conditions.)

HOW TO DEAL WITH EQUIPMENT AND OTHER LONG-LIVED ASSETS

This is a major area in which nonprofits traditionally resisted GAAP, a subject on which there were conflicting views among accountants in that field. Again the issue of simplicity versus usefulness arises. Consider the problem in broad outline. If a nonprofit buys a major item of equipment, say the station wagon we dealt with in the last chapter, when does its cost become an expense? When it is bought? When it is paid for, say, on installments? When it is junked or traded in? Does the cost of owning it, aside from upkeep, have anything to do with these dates?

If it were rented instead, the problem would take care of itself: the cost of having the use of it would be the monthly rental over the period of use. GAAP has traditionally applied the same concept to ownership: i.e., spread the net cost to own the item over the period of use. The name of this cost is *depreciation*, a term and concept much misunderstood, yet easy to demystify. Depreciation is not the loss in value of an asset with time. It is used for buildings which often increase in value. It is merely a way of saying that the cost of "fixed assets," as they are often called (or "plant assets") is an expense relevant to the periods during which they are used. In other words, the periods which benefit from that use should bear their share of the asset's cost. In Chapter 12 under "Adjusting Entries," we illustrate a depreciation calculation, using 20% of asset values (meaning their costs); in other words, we assumed a five-year useful life and a depreciation rate of one-fifth per year.

This seems logical when viewed in the light of accounting theory. Many nonprofits have chosen to use a cash basis approach, which charged the cost of fixed assets to the period in which they were paid for. Aside from distorting total operating costs for that period and periods of use, it also made the assets disappear, as far as the books and the balance sheet were concerned. While unlikely for a station wagon, this loss of accountability in the records makes it easier to forget that an asset exists, and may help lead to its actual disappearance.

Accounting for Fixed Assets

The technical side of the subject is not complicated, and need not be of particular concern to anyone but accountants and bookkeepers. Actually the net cost of the asset (after subtracting what it is expected to be worth when disposed of) is treated in effect as a prepaid expense, which is amortized over its expected useful life. The asset cost is "capitalized"—treated as an asset—not an expense. Instead of reducing the cost of the asset by this amount each period, it is accumulated in a separate account, which is subtracted from the cost of fixed assets on the balance sheet as "accumulated depreciation" or "allowance for depreciation."

The remaining balance is usually referred to as the "book value" of the assets, which generally bears little if any relationship to their actual value on a sale or trade-in. When a fixed asset is disposed of, the difference between anything received for it and its book value is either a gain or a loss on disposition. (Trade-ins are more complicated and will be handled in dealing with bookkeeping.)

The above treatment of fixed assets, which corresponds with GAAP, is no longer optional for nonprofits. FASB Statement No. 93 requires that they be set up as assets, not charged off in the period paid for, and that their cost be amortized via depreciation accounting. Where fixed assets are received as donations, they should be capitalized at an appraised or estimated value and depreciated thereafter as though purchased. Assets owned but not previously capitalized should be similarly appraised, and capitalized, and depreciation accounting should be used.[5]

---

[5] The increase in total assets must be offset by an increase in fund balance.

Depreciation Accounting

While SOP 78-10 covers only external financial reports, there are several different compelling reasons why nonprofits should find this method of accounting for fixed assets a desirable one:

- Reasons previously noted:

    1. the fluctuations and distortions of expenditures in periods when fixed assets are purchased or paid for and those in which used without any apparent cost, other than upkeep.

    2. loss of accountability in the books and records.

- On the balance sheet both total assets and fund balance will be understated by this amount if this method is not used, giving a distorted picture of the nonprofit's resources and financial condition.

- The nonprofit's board may be misled if fixed assets are charged off as purchased. In later periods operating costs will be artificially reduced, giving a false sense of well-being, until the time comes to replace the asset. That is when "the roof will fall in." (Perhaps literally, if the asset in question is the nonprofit's own building!) While depreciation does not provide replacement funds (unless funded separately, discussed in Chapter 7 under "Capital Budgeting"), it does serve as a reminder of concealed replacement costs.

- Unless depreciation accounting is used, buying fixed assets instead of renting them conceals such operating costs. This is potentially a way of manipulating operating statements and misleading the board.

- Nonprofits that charge for their services, and whose intention is to charge for all costs (including cost to replace assets used), will undercharge if depreciation cost is ignored.

- Nonprofits with program grants from government or foundations may be underfunded if relevant depreciation is not recognized as part of program cost.

- Nonprofits may be subject to a tax on "unrelated business income" (See Chapter 1). Depreciation is a tax-deductible expense for that purpose.

There are so many excellent reasons to capitalize and depreciate fixed assets, we believe it should be right up there with accrual accounting as a "must" for nonprofits that own any fixed assets. That is why we have included it as part of internal financial reporting and for both operating and proposal budgets, even though entirely discretionary for all three.

Note: One way to avoid the whole problem is to buy nothing and rent everything. It is simpler if you don't mind raising the extra funds rentals usually require.

IN-KIND CONTRIBUTIONS (DONATED GOODS AND SERVICES)

This topic was introduced in Chapter 6, in terms of the rationale for recording and reporting such resources. Not all such items are required to be recorded or reported for external purposes by accounting or tax rules, even though they may be for internal purposes where desirable. Summaries of the current externally imposed rules are as follows:

THE AICPA GUIDELINES

Donated Goods

If significant in value, fixed assets, supplies, or other goods should be entered at their estimated value and the same accounting methods used as though purchased. They represent revenue or support in the period received, as well as assets. Any estimated value used should have some objective basis, such as an outside appraisal.

Donated Facilities

If office space or other space or equipment is supplied rent-free, the facilities should be recorded as both an in-kind contribution and as rent expense of the period in which used, as illustrated in the operating budgets in Chapter 5. Again, the fair value of the space should be used as the amount. If reduced rent rather than free rent is provided, the rent expense should be reported at its fair value and the reduction as an in-kind contribution. Free use of telephone is still another example.

Donated Services

This is a more complex area, for the guidelines limit the reporting of such volunteer services to a rather narrow category and require that others be excluded. Reportable services are those in which *all* of the following circumstances exist:

- Significant administrative or professional services, integral to the nonprofit's functions, that would be performed by paid staff in the absence of volunteers.

- Services of volunteers whose activities are as subject to control as if they were employees.

- Services whose monetary value can be clearly measured.

- Services rendered for the benefit of outsiders, and not principally for members. (This would exclude membership organizations like unions, religious, social, and fraternal organizations.)[6]

These rules would seem to leave few other types of in-kind services subject to external financial reporting. A survey of 5,000 preparers of financial statements for nonprofits by the FASB found that 68% received contributed services, but only 8% reported their value in their financial statements.

That is not to say that other types may not be appropriately reported for internal reporting or budgeting, or for proposal budgets. Whether or not recorded on the books, or reported on external financial statements, the reasons for disclosing the value of such services for internal purposes or grant proposals, as explained in Chapter 6, should not be overlooked. Their fair value may be shown as a footnote or in some other informal manner, if not as part of the operating revenues and expenses.

Examples of donated services that may lend themselves to such treatment include consulting or other professional services, or volunteers delivering a material portion of the nonprofit's program or support services. Staff members paid token salaries, or substantially underpaid, may be considered as contributing the difference for the purposes indicated above.

---

[6]At this writing, the FASB has tentatively concluded that "donated services need not be recognized unless they create or enhance a continuing asset." *Op. cit.,* p. 7

Donated Securities

Where a nonprofit is given marketable stocks or bonds rather than money, goods, or services, the security should be treated (1) as an investment asset, at its quoted market value on the date of the gift, and (2) as revenue or support at the same value. If later sold, any difference between its original value and net proceeds is reported as a gain or loss on investments.

Note: SOP 78-10 gives nonprofits different optional methods for reporting the value of any marketable securities owned, methods that reflect changes in market value. This would result in a "paper" gain or loss being reported for each such change in valuation. These methods, after adoption, are required to be followed consistently. Those most generally appropriate to small nonprofits are market value and the lower of cost or market value. ("Cost" would be the original value, in the case of donated securities.) Fig. 10-1 presents an overview of accounting methods applicable for specific uses.

INTERNAL REVENUE SERVICE RULES

The U.S. Annual Return of Organization Exempt From Income Tax (IRS Form 990) has its own separate reporting requirements, covering "noncash contributions" and "donated services or facilities," which differ from those described above. (See Chapter 16.)

BASIC CONCEPTS OF FUND ACCOUNTING

Fund accounting is a subject primarily applicable to governmental and nonprofit accounting, although it has certain business parallels, such as escrow accounts and sinking fund accounting. It is a technique developed to facilitate accountability for resources of an organization that have been earmarked for a specified purpose. It applies particularly to funds whose use has been legally restricted to a specified purpose by the terms of the grant, appropriation, or loan that provided the funds.

The purpose of fund accounting is to segregate, in the accounts and reports, details of all resources and obligations of the separate fund and of all transactions that affect these accounts. It does not necessarily require the opening of separate bank accounts, unless so specified by its terms; separate accounts in the ledger generally suffice. However, these must constitute a self-balancing group of accounts—assets, liabilities, and fund balance—as though for a separate entity. On financial statements, these accounts are then reported, usually in a separate column for each such fund in a manner similar to the way separate programs are shown on a program budget or operating statement in a columnar format.[7]

The same technique may be used optionally for unrestricted funds earmarked by the board for a specified use, such as a plant or fixed asset fund. Funds may actually be classified as between: restricted and unrestricted (the latter may include those restricted by board decision rather than by the donor); current (or general) fund and special purpose funds (plant or investment); expendable

---

[7]While columnar form is preferred, it is not mandatory: restricted fund assets, liabilities, and fund balances may be listed in the appropriate section of the financial statement, as in layered format budget. Statements in standard fund accounting form are illustrated in Chapter 16.

Type of item	*Use for:*			
	External reports	*Internal reports & operating budgets*	*Accounting for grants**	*IRS forms*
Accrual of revenues	Required only for certain specified types.	Desirable for appropriate types and situations.	Optional	(Whatever method used on books)
Accrual of expenses	Required if material	Desirable if material	Optional (desirable)	(Book method)
Depreciation accounting	Generally required	Desirable and preferred	Optional (desirable)**	(Same) Use for unrelated business income
Deferral & amortization of prepaid expenses	Required if material.	Desirable if material.	Optional (desirable)**	(Whatever method used on books)
Deferred recognition of revenues	Required only for specified types and situations.	Desirable for appropriate types and situations, if material	Optional (see note)	(Same as above)
*Recording in-kind contributions** Equipment or material, securities (supplies, etc.)	Required if material and value determinable	Desirable	Desirable	Required
Facilities (space, use of equipment)	Required (same)	Desirable	Desirable**	Excluded except as supp. information
Personal services: necessary administrative services performed by volunteer employee substitutes (but see text above)	Required if equivalent to employee status	Desirable	Desirable**	(Same as above)
Other personal services	Not reported	Desirable	Desirable	(same as above)
Allocation of expense: Share of any direct fixed expense paid jointly (e.g. office space used)	Required	Optional: Classify between controllable and noncontrollable. (Use with care!)	Desirable**	Partial allocation required
Share of indirect expenses (e.g. support services)	Not required	Optional: All are noncontrollable. (Use with care!)	Desirable**	Optional

*In accounting for grants, follow specific instructions of funding agency.
**Includes excess of value received over an amount paid.

**FIGURE 10–1. NONPROFIT ACCOUNTING METHODS—
APPLICABILITY TO DIFFERENT USES**

and unexpendable funds. The former are funds for current expenses, the latter are funds invested in fixed assets or received as endowments.

The small nonprofit may not be involved with many such accounting problems: however, restricted program grants are *not* uncommon. Such a grant should properly be handled as a separate restricted fund on the records, and certainly in reports to the funding agency. Such reports are dealt with in Chapter 15. Needless to say, they should be derived from the accounts set up for the restricted fund to which all appropriate program and overhead expenses have been charged. On the other hand, SOP 78-10 does not mandate external financial reporting on a fund accounting basis, even where restricted funds exist. It does indicate that such reports "should disclose all material restrictions," and should identify restricted items as such, wherever reported.

Accounting for Grants and Contracts

Fund accounting theory divides the accountability for resources received by a nonprofit into three categories:

- General or unrestricted funds, which the agency is free to use as it sees fit.

- Restricted funds, which represent resources received by the agency with strings attached: i.e., conditions imposed mandating their use only for specified purposes. These may consist of restricted grants from foundations, corporations, government agencies, or other donors. They may also take the form of contracts, which are usually from government agencies. Endowments, bequests, and charitable trusts are the other major sources of restricted funds available only for prescribed uses.

- A third category includes funds whose use is restricted not legally, but voluntarily, by a decision of the governing body, e.g., the board of directors. These are set aside or earmarked in the accounts as "Board-Restricted Funds," and so reported on financial statements. Examples are plant funds, reserves for various purposes. The board can, of course, remove any restrictions it has imposed.

Note: Be careful not to assume that the words "funds" or "Fund Balance" mean that there is cash available in the same amount. You could even have hundreds of thousands of dollars in a fund balance and zero in actual money. The figure, as explained later, only represents the difference between the total assets and total liabilities: if your assets are buildings or amounts due to you, and exceed your debts, you could have a large fund balance and no money! Or this might be true of a particular fund.

Grants Received in Advance—Deferred Revenues

When funds are received in advance under a restricted grant or contract, they are not properly treated as income, since the restriction is an obligation to perform certain services, as described in the governing document. They should be set up on the books and financial reports as Deferred Revenue, in effect a liability offsetting the value of the resources received.

As expenses are paid out of the funds received, an equivalent amount should periodically be transferred out of Deferred Revenue into Revenue from Grants (or Contracts). Eventually, both the restricted cash account and the Deferred Revenue account will be reduced to zero, and the revenue account will equal the total of the grant expenses paid out. A moment's thought will indicate, therefore, that there will never *be* a fund balance for this grant or contract, unless there are funds left over—which the funding agency may or may not let you keep.

Reimbursement Grants—Accrued Revenues

In the more common situation, grant or contract expenditures are not received until they have been made. There is no deferred revenue in such cases; none was received so it cannot be deferred. Although the amounts paid out could be charged directly to an account for grants or contracts receivable, that would lose track of the nature of the expenditures.

The right way is to charge expenditures to the appropriate expense accounts, earmarked as to the specific program, grant, or contract, and taken out of general fund cash. A second entry accrues the amount due from the funding agency (usually on a monthly basis) and the revenue earned. When the expenditures are reimbursed, it is used to reduce the receivable and becomes general fund cash again. Note that here too there is no resulting fund balance, unless the funding agency were to somehow pay out more or less than was expended.

How Can Restricted Grants or Contracts Improve Your Fund Balance?

If you are only paid for expenses attributed to the grant or contract, clearly you must include in the expenses charged to it not only direct expenses you would not have incurred otherwise, but some part of your other operating expenses, such as rent, utilities, and administrative expenses, which may be indirect, but unavoidable if the program involved is to go on functioning. How to do this is discussed in the section "The Proposal Budget" in Chapter 8.

Another way your agency's over-all fund balance could be affected by a grant or contract would be if you had the kind that provided for installment payments of a fixed or predetermined amount, regardless of the related expenditures. In that situation, current expenditures might be more or less than the amounts received. In that case the fund balance relating to the program could be either positive or negative, at least until a final settlement is made at the end of the related period.

HOW TO HANDLE TRANSACTIONS BETWEEN FUNDS

One of the main record-keeping problems of fund accounting is that of transfers between funds, such as temporary borrowing of restricted fund cash by the general fund, or expenditures affecting both funds. In effect, two sets of books are involved:

Handling Borrowing Between Funds

Amounts borrowed (or spent) by the general fund from restricted fund cash should be set up in the general fund accounts as a loan payable to the restricted fund and in the restricted fund accounts as a loan receivable from the general fund, and the cash account of the latter reduced. If a loan, the amount should be shown as an increase in the general fund cash. If spent directly out of general fund cash, solely for general fund purposes, it should be charged to the appropriate expense or asset account in the general fund and loan receivable and payable accounts set up in the two funds, to disclose the accountability. On repayment of the loan, these entries would be made in the opposite direction.[8]

Handling Joint Expenditures

Amounts paid out of one fund's cash for the benefit of two funds should be split between them on the books, as appropriate. Thus a bill for supplies totaling $100 (of which $60 is for unrestricted and $40 for restricted purposes) if paid out of general fund cash, would be treated as follows:

General Fund Accounts	**Restricted Fund Accounts**
Charge $60 to Supplies	Charge $40 to Supplies
Charge $40 as a Loan Receivable or Advance to Restricted Fund	Credit General Fund with a loan payable or advance of $40
Reduce Cash balance by $100	

If and when this loan payable or advance is later reimbursed by the restricted fund, that account will be closed or reduced and the fund's cash balance reduced. In the general fund, cash will be increased and the interfund loan account closed or reduced.

HANDLING PERMANENT TRANSFERS BETWEEN FUNDS

Where one fund may have accumulated an unneeded excess of liquid assets and a fund balance (total assets minus total liabilities) in excess of any anticipated needs, the board may decide to transfer the excess permanently to another fund, or to general fund, so that it may be put to other required uses. The board may do so by a resolution, unless the fund in question is a restricted fund under the terms of a grant, contract or other legally binding document. If this is done, an entry on the books is required, reducing the fund balance account of the fund being tapped and its cash account (or account for the noncash asset being transferred). A second entry would be made increasing both the cash or other asset account and the fund balance account of the fund to which the excess funds are being transferred. (No loan or advance account would be involved in this case.)

ARE SEPARATE CHECKING ACCOUNTS NEEDED?

Although the point was made above that separate bank accounts are not necessary for fund accounting, unless required by the terms of the grant or contract, it may be a good idea to consider using them anyway, unless the organization's books are being kept by a knowledgeable person. One of the problems of fund accounting and monitoring of restricted funds is that it is easy to overlook any interfund charges and transfers where all the money "is in the same pot." Using separate bank accounts brings about a clear and conscious segregation of the money in the

---

[8]You may encounter rules or objections about such loans from some funding agencies.

respective funds, which serves to protect their integrity in record-keeping as well as making it harder to tap them for some other use without authorization or control.[9]

It requires a conscious act to violate the restrictions on a fund by spending it for an improper purpose, or even to "lend" funds to another fund. Drawing a check on a common bank account and charging it to the wrong account on the books is prone to both abuse and honest error.

If your bookkeeping is done manually by a skilled bookkeeper or accountant, fund accounts can be set up using a Chart of Accounts like the one illustrated in Table 12–2. A separate cash account can be set up for each fund, as well as any other asset and liability accounts needed, plus a fund balance account for each. Individual revenue and expense accounts are best set up using a uniform coding system such as the one shown in the illustration. If you do your bookkeeping using a computer, either in-house or via a service center (see Chapter 11), you may well have to use a prescribed coding scheme different than the one illustrated. In either case, your financial reports will be no more accurate than the way transactions are coded—a serious responsibility.

Organizations use different coding patterns, which may use additional digits for separate funds and/or programs and may then use a four-digit or five-digit account code such as that shown in Table 12–2. As noted in Chapter 11, designing an effective accounting system, especially for a multifund or multi-program agency, should be entrusted to a professional accountant, particularly if you need to track both separate funds and different programs.

---

[9]The legal rule against "commingling of funds" generally does not apply to depositing accountable funds in the same bank account as other funds. It has to do with losing track of this accountability by inadequate record-keeping.

Chapter 11

How to Design (or Choose) Your Management Information System

If you have been struggling along with just a checkbook and informal, homemade financial records, this chapter is "must" reading. It is an overview of ways to solve your record-keeping problems, to handle them more effectively. It is intended not for bookkeepers but for the leadership itself.

The first point is that, although keeping books is hardly the mystery it may seem, *designing* or even selecting the bookkeeping *system* calls for a "pro." There are many alternatives available; bookkeepers are often unaware of this, since they have often learned only a particular way of doing things, which may not be the best or the most appropriate for your organization. There are shortcuts, needs for special information, special problems to be solved, and internal control aspects. All of these require the expert advice of a trained accountant, one familiar with the special needs of nonprofit organizations.

It is also foolhardy to leave responsibility for incorporating the safeguards of internal controls in the hands of anyone they are supposed to control!

THE GOAL OF SYSTEM DESIGN

Before describing available systems, it should be helpful to outline what your system should be able to provide. We begin by asking what information the organization's leadership needs to run it properly? Fig. 11–1 attempts to do this.

Everything You Need to Know About Systems

If you are not charged with doing the record-keeping yourself, you need not know how to *do* it, but you do need to know different ways it *could* be done. "We always did it that way!" is neither a convincing nor a meaningful reason for using a given system, especially if it does not give you capabilities shown below. Here then is a brief survey of available methods for solving these problems, in nontechnical terms intended to demystify matters. The alternatives range from the simplest (and possibly least adequate) to the most comprehensive. Details on how to follow these methods in actual use are supplied in the next chapter.

System Capability	Purpose of Feature
I. BASIC INFORMATION NEEDED BY NONPROFITS	
• Internal controls, including capability of being audited (below)	Protection and accountability for resources • Possible audit by CPA or funding agency
• Supply details of revenues and expenses, by type	• Internal reports, for budget control • External reports for government, funding agencies and others
• Funds received/paid: From whom and to whom	• Accountability and proof of payment
• Funds owed to/by the organization: totals and details	• Follow-up on collection and payment (to maintain credit standing)
• Details of employee earnings & withholdings	• Payroll tax reports and payments
• Nonmonetary activity measures: hours, type and amount of services performed	• Required where lobbying is engaged in (see Chapter 16, also below)
• Cost details, by program, function, or client	• Required for pricing and billing by nonprofits charging for services (see below)
II. INFORMATION NEEDED FOR EFFECTIVE MANAGEMENT AND PERFORMANCE EVALUATION	
• Details of employee earnings, by program	• Program planning and evaluation; control of administrative costs; comparison with budget
• Nonmonetary activity measures: hours, type and amount of services performed by staff and volunteers	• (same)
• Other cost details, by program or function	• (same)
• Records of other organization resources and obligations: assets and liabilities	• Accountability and control

FIGURE 11-1. GOALS OF MANAGEMENT INFORMATION SYSTEMS

SAFEGUARDING YOUR RESOURCES

Before describing the various ways you can meet your accounting and bookkeeping needs, it is well to understand that your books can only be as reliable as they reflect what really happened. After all, what good is it for your accounts to tell you that you received $1,000 if $1,200 came in but $200 of it stuck to someone's fingers en route?

A True Story

A community center owed much of its success to the enthusiasm of its members, many of whom served as volunteers, working on committees and assisting the paid staff by handling all sorts of odd jobs. One young man regularly volunteered to collect at the door for tickets purchased for the film series and other events. To save money, the center ran off its own informal tickets which the patrons handed to another volunteer, who collected them at the door, as in a theater.

The program director became concerned over the fact that, in spite of good attendance, the cash turned in each time seemed far below the attendance. She also began to notice that selling tickets was the one task for which Mr. X was willing to volunteer.

At the accountant's suggestion, two steps were taken; a second person was asked to help him at the box office, counting cash. In addition, a tally was made of tickets turned in at the door.

You may not be too surprised to learn that there was a sudden improvement in the total cash turned in for deposit after subsequent events, nor to learn that Mr. X lost his interest in volunteering to help the center. (With such friends, who needs enemies?)

Moral: Encourage people to be honest by making dishonesty difficult. That way you can keep your faith in human nature.

On a more ambitious scale of operations is the story that broke in the press not long ago about the Spingold Foundation in New York, whose president was accused of looting it of nearly $7 million between 1982 and 1988—more than half its 1982 assets! He paid himself, among other things, a total of over $5 million in excessive fees during the period, as its operating deficits rose from $126,000 in 1983 to nearly $2 million for the first half of 1988! The board itself was charged with responsibility for allowing all this to happen. (*Tax Exempt News*, Vol. 10, No. 12, December, 1988, p. 1)

This kind of experience is familiar to auditors, who have heard over and over the shock and dismay expressed in the cry, "But he was one of our most trusted people!" And then comes the auditor's sad but cynical reply, "Naturally!—Who else is in a position to steal?"

The corollary, which we see not as cynicism, but as merely good sense, is *not* that people can't be trusted but rather that it is the most trusted people who need protection against the temptation of unguarded treasure. Or, to put it in other words, "Don't make a thief of an honest man." (And carry fidelity insurance, just in case! See below.) Knowledgeable people actually appreciate the existence of adequate internal controls, because they are better protected against possible suspicion or accusation when effective controls exist.

Let us consider safeguards before we look at the books.

THEFT AND EMBEZZLEMENT: IT CAN HAPPEN IN YOUR ORGANIZATION

One of society's myths that has been long in dying is that there are only "good guys and bad guys," that people are either honest or crooked. Yet the files of law enforcement agencies reveal a different picture. One recalls a dear old lady who was the bookkeeper of a union local for many years and straight as a die. Yet she was discovered to be embezzling from the local, not because she was greedy or evil but to help her ne'er-do-well son, who had been losing money gambling. And she is only one example of many that could be cited. Ask any detective or criminal defense attorney.

They will also tell you what we have found: when confronted with having taken money, every culprit has the same story: "I only borrowed it and would have paid it back!"

So much for philosophy, which is essential to break down the attitude "It can't happen here!" Funds and other resources entrusted to a nonprofit by funding sources and supporters need to be safeguarded, which is another aspect of accountability. That means a number of different things which this chapter is designed to explore:

- Physical and financial safeguards over resources
- Assignment of personnel to duties
- Systems of authorization and approval of expenditures
- Methods for verifying that these safeguards are actually operating and effective
- Insurance to cover any losses you are unable to prevent

Fraud and Other Problems

Accountability for resources actually covers a much wider spectrum of problems than people stealing money. Nonprofits also have more frequent problems in the area of petty theft of other items, as well as errors, waste, and incidents of being cheated by suppliers of goods and services. A brief list of examples follows:

- Overpayments or duplicate payments of bills, through error or because a supplier of goods or services was unscrupulous.
- Staff or volunteers helping themselves to supplies, postage stamps, excessive use of equipment, or facilities for personal purposes.
- Padding of expense vouchers or overtime claims, or doing personal work during paid working hours.
- Not collecting for dues, subscriptions, or tickets, etc.
- Wasteful use of supplies, vehicles, equipment, and utilities, including telephone and electricity.

The reader's negative reactions can already be anticipated. No, we are not out to promote a threatening or pinchpenny atmosphere! But in an environment where no one (and everyone) owns things, it is just too tempting to be careless, to forget about accountability, and, worse, to take the contradictory attitudes of bewailing the usual shortage of funds while squandering or wasting the limited resources on hand.

Red Tape vs. Red Ink

Internal controls ("red tape") exist to protect the organization against losses, essentially by acting both as preventive medicine and as a deterrent to waste, error, and fraud.

It was pointed out above that the books of account *prove* nothing, reflecting merely what the bookkeeper recorded. The "paper trail" making up the system of internal controls is in place to make sure that "things are done right" and that what the books and financial reports show is what really happened and exists: facts, not fancies. To indicate how important the concept is, the rules of the accounting profession discourage the independent auditor's "certifying" a financial report in the absence of adequate internal controls.

INTERNAL CONTROL

Six Principles to Follow

Accountants have developed, the hard way, a clear set of principles for designing or evaluating an internal control system. They make good common sense, are based on sound behavioral concepts, and are easy to grasp:

1. Personnel handling assets and records should be screened for both competence and integrity.

2. A system should be established requiring a proper signature or initials authorizing the purchase of goods and services and then of approving the related payment.

3. Only individuals with proper authority should be able to authorize such transactions, and the terms of the transaction should be checked for compliance with those authorized.

4. Access to assets should be limited to those who are *authorized.*

5. Periodic independent comparisons should be made between actual assets on hand and recorded accountability for such assets.

6. Assigned and actual duties should not be incompatible from a security viewpoint: different individuals should perform each of the following functions:

- Authorization of a transaction
- Recording the transaction
- Custody of assets involved
- Comparison of actual assets on hand with amounts indicated by accounting records

Just in case the reasons for principle No. 6 are not self-evident, no one should be in a position to make off with or waste the organization's assets, and then to conceal the fact of having done so.

You may believe that that's a tall order for a small nonprofit, and we agree. It may even be a hardship in many cases. It may mean reorganizing certain functions, reassigning duties, even pressing volunteers into unaccustomed services. On the other hand, we urge you to consider the potential consequences of *not* establishing the controls—the kinds of accountability—that this chapter prescribes. Our aim here is consciousness raising. You should be aware that this issue is a serious one.

A Procedures Checklist

Translating these general principles into more concrete terms, before developing specific procedures, we have devised the following checklist:

☐ All money paid to the organization should follow the rule, "Do not stop: go directly to the bank account." More on this later.

☐ Never should two of the steps of authorization, payment and the related bookkeeping, be performed by the same individual.

☐ Commitments for goods or services should be only those authorized, either by the budget or by other properly constituted authority.

☐ Valuable assets should be protected by physical safeguards and only authorized personnel given access. Incoming cash needs extra protection to make sure it gets recorded and deposited.

☐ Cross-checking and verifying quantities, prices, and arithmetic on bills should become "SOP" (standard operating procedure), along with checking that a transaction has been properly authorized or approved.

☐ Verification of balances of cash and other assets (and liabilities) should also become SOP.

☐ Adequate insurance coverage should be maintained to protect the nonprofit against various kinds of insurable losses.

☐ Internal control procedures and requirements should be detailed in writing, in outline form at the very least. Turnover of personnel can otherwise lead to uncertainty of responsibilities and "buck passing" if there are no clearly specified procedures.

☐ If possible, an independent public accountant should be engaged to help design and evaluate the internal controls and to conduct an annual audit, a standard part of which is an appraisal of their effectiveness. First and foremost, you should understand that deterrence is far more effective and reliable than detection, which may come "after the horse is stolen" anyway. You may be surprised to learn that detection of fraud is *not* considered to be a basic purpose of a routine independent audit and cannot be relied upon to discover any but the clumsiest efforts to embezzle.

Thus we return to our earlier thesis: "Keep 'em honest," by an ounce of prevention.

A Checklist for Control of Cash Received

If you normally receive small cash payments for services, dues, contributions, subscriptions, etc., it should come as no surprise that this is your most vulnerable area for losses. Nonprofits use a wide variety of methods that involve collecting small amounts in bills and coins, ranging from coin boxes and raffles to special events such as dinners and theater parties. Control over such collections is an accountant's nightmare, but there are a variety of methods, mostly familiar.

● Duplicate prenumbered receipts should be used wherever feasible. The signed originals are issued, the duplicates are retained, and all are accounted for by serial number, including any cancelled as void. This applies also to raffle books and other coupon books for tickets to special events. The total of each batch of receipts should be compared with the amount of the related bank deposit. The checking of numbers and amounts should not be done by anyone who handles the cash.

● When such receipts are not feasible—for example, when a tray, hat, or canister is used to collect money—substitute measures may be devised. Canisters should be serially numbered and numbers accounted for when the canisters are picked up. They should be sealed or so designed that they cannot be opened without breaking either the seal or the canister itself. A basic principle is that two people independently count all cash collected and each signs or initials a cash report. This principle also applies when cash or many checks are received by mail. (The practical organizational problems in this area are discussed below.)

● Cash collected should be deposited as quickly as possible after the two-person count is completed and the cash report signed. When necessary delays are common—for example, collections received and counted too late in the day, or when an immediate trip to the bank is impractical—a safe should be provided for the purpose, with the combination given only to an authorized cash custodian. Alternatively, a lockbox or night depository at the bank may be used, if feasible.

● Currency collected should not be used for petty cash payments, but deposited intact, to maintain the "audit trail"; otherwise tying in collections with deposits requires complicated bookkeeping, and effective control is easily lost.

● Checks received in the mail should, as noted, be tallied by two people and an endorsement stamped on them immediately. A stamp which records the name of the bank and the account number is additional protection against the check being deposited by someone in a fraudulent account. Yes, someone else can deposit checks made out to your organization, a fact that is (perhaps fortunately) not well known.

● Incoming funds should always be deposited in a checking account, which should never be bypassed by a deposit directly in a savings account. Otherwise, there may be no record of the deposit in the books, and the savings account balance may be incorrect or unrecorded.

● Bank deposit slips should be prepared in duplicate and one copy date-stamped by the bank and kept on file by the nonprofit to permit tracing checks received by the bank. Listing the name of each payor also helps.

Buying Goods and Services

Earlier in this chapter we emphasized the necessity of a system of authorization to incur expenses or acquire assets. That step must come before the approval of a bill or a payroll; once an order has been placed or someone put on payroll or retainer, there is usually a contractual commitment and no way to avoid payment, if the other party carries out its end of the transaction.

The operating budget is the underlying authority to make commitments, and if commitments arise of a type not budgeted—hiring by the Center of a consultant for Program A would be an example—approval is needed, either from the board or from an official to whom authority for such decisions has been delegated by the board.

Step 1. With respect to commitments that are within budgeted categories and amounts, an officer or administrator with duly constituted authority should sign or initial the authorizing document, which represents a contract for the goods or services. This could be a purchase order, lease, other written contract, or letter or memorandum covering the hiring of staff or professionals. Two things should be apparent here:

● that there be clearly designated areas of authority

● that the individual with that authority abide by the budget in exercising it (staying within budgeted amounts is covered in Chapter 13).

Step 2.   The approval of the actual bill or payroll covering goods or services received should not receive an automatic OK based on Step 1. Verification should be made that the nonprofit was charged for what was authorized. That means checking bills and payrolls against purchase orders or other authorizing documents for description, quantities, and prices (arithmetic should also be checked, especially when substantial dollar amounts are involved). One way nonprofits are bilked is by being charged for more than was requested and/or at a higher price. (Arithmetical errors also occur, usually in the other party's favor.) As with authorization, approval should also be recorded by signature or initials.

Step 3.   Another important procedure when supplies or equipment are purchased is to have someone compare what was actually received with what the invoice says was delivered and to initial this fact (or to report any discrepancy). Similarly, payrolls should be checked for validity of names and hours worked. Only when all of these procedures are followed can you really say that. To summarize:

Step 1: We had a right to incur this expense.
Step 2: We received what we asked for.
Step 3: We were charged only for what we got, and for the right amount.

Recording Verification and Payment

Nonprofits would do well to borrow from business the rubber-stamp approval form shown below, which provides spaces for the whole authorization, verification, and approval process, plus a record of payment. This stamp can be made up commercially and applied to each invoice as received. Each blank, except "Material Rec'd on" is for entry of the initials of the person who carried out the particular step, up to approval for payment. The remaining blanks provide space to identify the check issued and to indicate the account to which the invoice and payment are to be charged.

RUBBER STAMP VERIFICATION AND PAYMENT RECORD

Material Rec'd on _____ by _____

Description & Quantities OK _____

Invoice Checked to Order:

    Prices: _____ Quantity: _____

Checked Extensions & Total: _____

Approved for Payment: _____

Paid by Check No. _____

    Date: _____   Net Amt.: _____

Charge Invoice to a/c # _____

Charge Payment to a/c # _____

Comments: _____

If the cash basis is used, only the account charged for the payment would be shown. The accounts referred to are, of course, those in the organization's bookkeeping system, not a charge account with a supplier. The account number will be determined from the chart of accounts, as described in Chapter 12.

A Checklist for Handling Payments

Cash paid out can cause almost as many problems as incoming cash if not properly handled.

● Any payments in actual currency should be traceable to amounts withdrawn from the checking account. No payments should be made by diverting incoming cash, and no payments should be made directly out of a savings or money market account, because adequate control records are unavailable in either case. If all collections are deposited in the checking account intact, the funds cannot be withdrawn without a duly signed check.

● The savings or money market account should be used only as a reserve to which funds are transferred by check and from which they are transferred *by teller's check* (not cash) to the checking account, as needed (some accounts permit telephone transfers).

● A petty cash fund should be maintained if it is frequently necessary to pay in currency for small routine items such as incoming delivery charges, minor retail purchases of office supplies, etc. Such a system is described below. A signed receipt, bill, or cash register printout should be obtained as proof of all such payments.

● Payments by check should, when possible, be approved (Step 2) by an authorized individual, preferably not the one who signs the check. The resolutions or signature cards on file with banks (including savings banks) should provide for two signatures, certainly so if the bookkeeper is authorized to sign checks and, in any event, for checks larger than a specified amount. Without this safeguard, the bookkeeper could well conceal an embezzlement by burying it in the accounts. *Preparing* checks is a somewhat safer function for a bookkeeper, but only if signers really know what they are signing!

● Before a payment is approved, the invoice or other document should be inspected to make certain that Steps 1, 2, and 3 above have been fulfilled and recorded. Of course, the check should not be signed by anyone other than the person charged with approval, unless approval (Step 2) has been noted.

● Payment by check for expenses of staff or volunteers, such as travel advances or reimbursement, not paid directly to the provider of the service, should be requested on an expense voucher, approved by an authorized person. The voucher form, which can be designed and reproduced inexpensively, should also provide spaces for the date, details, and purpose of the trip or other expenditure, name of payee, date and number of check, and account charged. (Such forms are also called "check requests" or the like.)

● It was explained previously that the number and date of the check issued (and amount, if different from the invoice total), should be recorded on the invoice or voucher. Better yet, a big "PAID" stamp may be even more effective in preventing paying the same item twice, unfortunately a common mistake and one not too commonly reported by the recipient of the check. Monthly statements from vendors should be inspected as a verification of the status of vendor accounts.

● Checks should be made payable to a named person or organization, not to "Cash," except for checks reimbursing petty cash, and never should be issued in blank. Cash checks are about as safe as currency—meaning not at all—since they may be lost or stolen.

• A check protector should be used to emboss the amount and prevent it from being raised.

• Spoiled checks should be saved, not discarded, to account for all check numbers, and the signature section should be torn off. The checkbook should be kept locked up, along with spare fillers.

Warning: None of the above safeguards will help if the people involved just go through the motions of initialing or signing, without actually verifying whatever was supposed to be verified. As a matter of fact, that is worse than no system of approval at all, because it creates a false sense of adequate internal control. Zipping through a pile of checks and signing them automatically, on the strength of one's confidence or trust in an associate, is creating just the kind of temptation warned against earlier. You might as well leave all your cash lying around loose. Yes, it gets the irksome job done faster and cuts the red tape, but it invites red ink.

Two other dangerous variants should be noted. Where two signatures are required on a check, signing it *because* the other person has signed it and found it valid is almost as bad as going away on a trip and signing a bunch of blank checks in advance because you won't be around. What a temptation that presents, especially if the other signer happens to be the bookkeeper!

Bank Reconciliation: A Key Security Device

One of the advantages of paying by check, and running all incoming funds through a checking account, is that you have an outside, independent cross-check on the flow of cash. At the end of each month,[1] you should regularly receive a bank statement reporting all activity for the period, accompanied by your cancelled checks, plus any "debit" or "credit" memoranda that have been issued. You are then in a position to perform a bank reconciliation, which accomplishes several things if it is done properly and *not by your bookkeeper*.

• It determines the accuracy of your checkbook balance.

• It helps locate any errors in your balance due to errors in math or to unentered deposits, checks, bank charges or credits.

• It reveals differences between amounts entered in your checkbook, including deposits, and those actually received by the bank.

• It sometimes uncovers errors made by the bank in balances or amounts—even items charged to your account in error. (Banks *do* make mistakes.)

• It may uncover cash received and recorded but never deposited (possible "sticky fingers" issue).

• It may uncover forged checks, or checks signed by unauthorized individuals, when cancelled checks are compared with check stubs or other records of checks known to have been issued.

• It may uncover checks made out to and/or cashed or deposited by recipients other than those indicated on payment records.

---

[1]Some banks may wait 2 or 3 months, or end the statement at a date during the month. Most will shift to a regular end-of-month statement on request.

● The mere fact that a proper monthly bank reconciliation is being done generally acts as a deterrent to all but the most inexperienced embezzler.

If your organization has not been in the habit of doing a regular monthly bank reconciliation, or if you have been doing it in a mechanical way—merely to verify the "accuracy" of your checkbook balance—the above list of benefits that can be gained by tapping all of its potential should help convince you to do it right. Even if you are not interested in the detailed procedures, which are explained in Appendix 11A, the question of who does the bank reconciliation is of great significance to the organization. Done by the wrong person, it loses much of its value.

Who should do the bank reconciliation?   As already stated, it should *never* be the bookkeeper—a statement that surprises only people inexperienced in financial control. A bookkeeper is just in too good a position to forge checks, or to prepare unauthorized checks, get them signed by an official who signs mechanically, cover the theft in the books, and then to remove and destroy the checks in doing the reconciliation. Beyond that, it is also undesirable to have *anyone* who signs checks, including the treasurer, do the reconciliation, to prevent the possibility that they might make out a check to themselves, for example, which would not be revealed by the reconciling process and could be disposed of.

In smaller nonprofits, nonetheless, the reconciliation is often done by the treasurer. The bank should have standing instructions to mail the monthly statement and cancelled checks directly to that officer's home address, so no one else can get to it first, for reasons that should be apparent. If the treasurer must delay doing the reconciliation for any reason, or does not do it, he or she should at least examine the cancelled checks and any bank memoranda without delay. That way, at least any improper items charged to the bank account can usually be spotted early enough to do something about them.

A situation that should not be permitted is one in which the treasurer, who signs checks, is also the bookkeeper *and* does the bank reconciliation. No one should be placed in that untenable situation, for the sake of the individual and that of the organization. While the situation is not at all an unusual one, it results from the board either not realizing its danger or not taking seriously the need to do something about changing it.

Savings Accounts

There are a few problems specific to savings accounts. For one, passbooks should be physically safeguarded, being somewhat more dangerous than blank checks. Second, interest should be entered by the bank monthly if material in amount, but at least quarterly, and the amount entered in the ledger account.

A worksheet record should be maintained of the balance, deposits, interest, and withdrawals, with the date, source, or use of each transaction fully identified, since there is usually no formal journal involved. The balance on the worksheet should of course be compared with the passbook balance.

Two Key Reminders: (1) All funds should pass through the checking account on their way into or out of the savings account, so that the only savings account deposits or withdrawals will be transfers between these accounts. (2) Two authorized signatures normally should be required on withdrawals from savings. Note that the above comments also apply to money market accounts.

OTHER SPECIFIC AREAS OF CONTROL

Payrolls: Payments and Record-Keeping

This is an area of basic importance for several reasons:

- Payroll usually represents the largest part of the budget of service-type nonprofits, unless little or no paid staff is employed.

- Payroll padding—payment for services not received or excessive pay—is a favorite form of embezzlement.

- Since a nonprofit's personnel are rarely paid adequately, and since its funds apparently belong to no one in particular, it somehow does not feel like stealing to some people when they find an opportunity to get paid more than they are supposed to be paid.

- Some nonprofits have grants or other arrangements providing that certain personnel be paid *directly* by another agency, out of a grant, even though employed by the nonprofit. This can lead to a loss of accountability for such activity, unless it is recorded and reported.[2]

Internal control principles require the following procedures:

1. A record of some sort should be maintained of people added to and taken off the payroll. Responsibility for such decisions should be assigned to specific, authorized individuals. The record of hiring should contain the person's name, signature, Social Security number, starting date, rate and basis of pay, hours and days per week, plus any fringe benefits to be received, including vacation and sick pay. Whoever approves payrolls should receive notices of termination, which should disclose the date effective, name, Social Security number, any severance pay, and a brief indication of the reason for the termination.

2. Raises in pay or increases in fringe benefits should also be approved in writing by an authorized official and recorded in the personnel file.

3. Employees should turn in signed time sheets or cards, which should be used to determine earnings and overtime pay, as well as for allocating their salaries to activities.

4. Before it is paid, each payroll should be reviewed and approved by an authorized person for the validity of the names, rates, hours, and amounts listed. This is the time to spot payroll padding, especially by excessive rates or hours. Fictitious overtime, people paid while on unpaid leave or vacation, before their starting date or after termination—or fictitious employees—all are potential areas to watch. Items that seem questionable should always be questioned. If nothing else, this keeps people on their toes and acts as a deterrent to payroll padding.

5. When the payroll is paid, which preferably is by individual check, the cancelled checks should be compared, at least periodically, with the payroll sheet. If payment is by cash, signed receipts should be obtained. A way that payments to fictitious or terminated employees may be detected is to compare endorsements on checks or signed receipts with the original signature on file at hiring. This too could well be done periodically, or on a test basis regularly.

---

[2]Both the grant and payroll expense should be reflected.

Guarding Receivables: Amounts Due from Others

One of the advantages of using the accrual method for revenues is that it creates accountability for their subsequent collection, by recording the amounts receivable as assets when due, to be later reduced when the funds are received. When such receivables involve numerous items, such as dues, subscriptions, and pledges, a card index or other auxiliary record may be kept of the amounts due and collected, even if the revenue is recorded on a cash basis.

Once the receivable is set up, there should be control over any subsequent "write-offs" cancelling or reducing uncollectible amounts. The advantage of the accountability created by the receivable is lost if anyone is in a position to intercept incoming collections and cover this up by writing off the amounts due. Such write-offs should require authorization by an appropriate official, such as the treasurer, provided the treasurer is not the bookkeeper. Such items should not be written off as uncollectible until adequate efforts have been made to collect them.

The card file is a control over collections in that the uncollected receivables act as a reminder to follow up by mail or phone. The file should be kept current by adding new members, subscribers, or pledgors and deleting any terminations.

How to Safeguard Marketable Securities

If the organization owns shares of stock, bonds, certificates of deposit, or other investments, they should be protected against loss or theft, since they are negotiable—fraudulently, if not legitimately. They should be kept in a bank vault or safe, with access permitted only to a specified custodian.

A record should be kept on file with a full description of each certificate, including any donated, with indication of its serial number, dates issued and acquired, plus interest-due dates, if any. The record should also show where the securities are physically located and name the custodian or persons who have access to them in order to fix responsibility in case of loss.

The certificates should be inspected and accounted for periodically and collection of interest due or dividends declared followed up. A signed receipt should be obtained whenever possession of certificates is transferred, even on a temporary basis.

One way negotiable securities are improperly used, aside from outright theft and sale, is "borrowing" them clandestinely to use as collateral for a personal loan. The proceeds of such a loan can also be used by an embezzler to cover up a cash shortage, if necessary.

Protecting Fixed Assets

Office and program furniture and equipment, vehicles, and other lasting assets also require controls over accountability. As with the other assets mentioned, the basis of accountability is a written record of all assets on hand, with a full description, including date acquired, cost, location, custodian, and serial number if any. Assets received as donations should be included. A card file, notebook, or commercially printed forms can be used for this purpose.

Physical safeguards are also necessary, especially for vulnerable items such as typewriters and calculators, which should be bolted or chained to desks if feasible. They should also be protected against the elements, accidental damage, and physical abuse. Metal identification tags, which can be attached with epoxy, are helpful safeguards. A receipt should be obtained when such items are loaned or transferred to a new custodian or user.

A periodic inventory should be taken of fixed assets, comparing the record of what should be there to what in fact is, and any shortages should be followed up with the custodian for explanation. The inventory takers should be alert to signs of damage or other impairment to the usefulness of the asset.

Controlling Other Valuable Materials

Many nonprofits have valuable items such as art materials, props, costumes, or other office or program materials, which should be controlled and accounted for in much the same manner as fixed assets. Staff and volunteers should be deterred from helping themselves to such supplies and impressed with the notion that they are valued resources that must be safeguarded and accounted for.

Checklist of the Various Types of Insurance

There are several areas in which proper insurance is essential to the protection of a nonprofit's resources. In our Expense Budget Worksheet for the Center (Table 5–5) we included three of the principal types, intended to protect against certain hazards: liability, workmen's compensation, and fire insurance. Health insurance is actually a fringe benefit protecting employees from loss, not the organization.

- Auto insurance often combines insurance for damage to the vehicle or to others, plus loss by theft, fire, and medical costs of an accident. Liability coverage is normally required by law.

- Owner/landlord/tenant liability insurance covers different situations and types of liability, depending on whether the premises are rented or owned. It generally insures against claims by any nonemployee on the premises, whether volunteer, client, patron, or tradesperson, resulting from accidental injuries incurred. Employee claims may also be covered if they are not covered by a workmen's compensation policy.

- Workmen's compensation insurance, as its name indicates, pays employees for injuries sustained in the course of employment and is a coverage usually required by law.

- Fire insurance covers loss to property and the contents of that property owned by the insured, whether the premises are owned or rented. Comprehensive insurance covers other casualty losses as well, such as losses from the elements.

- Robbery, burglary, and theft insurance covers various types of losses of money or property. It should be carried, especially when large amounts of cash or other valuables are frequently on hand or transported by personnel of the nonprofit in a risky manner. It covers against money stolen by individuals outside the organization.

- Fidelity insurance ("bonding" employees) is an additional and inexpensive protection against embezzlement, one that all nonprofits should carry. It reimburses the organization for any embezzlement losses, provided its records are adequate to demonstrate that such an act took place, meaning internal controls.

Fidelity insurance also has a preventive value: insurance companies do not enjoy paying claims;

therefore, they screen "trusted employees" for any past record of misdeeds and are not loath to press charges against embezzlers, when a nonprofit might be. Awareness of this is in itself a deterrent to the sophisticated, who are the very people from whom protection is most needed.

There should be no more hesitancy about fidelity insurance than about auto or fire insurance. No one accuses a nonprofit's personnel of being reckless drivers or arsonists just because such insurance is carried. The organization has a right to "bond" all people in a position to embezzle money or securities in safeguarding its resources, as a part of the accountability expected of it.[3]

Financial Management Includes People Management

Until you obtain fidelity insurance, follow the earlier recommendation that employees expected to handle valuables and/or financial records be carefully screened, and that all references be checked. (The insurance carrier will also do so, routinely, as noted.) A clue to a possible security problem is the consistent failure of a bookkeeper or other person in charge of financial records to take a vacation. Experienced auditors view this suspiciously, for the individuals may be afraid to let anyone else handle their records, possibly because they have been "doctored" and/or might reveal an embezzlement.

Why Two Are Better than One When Counting Money

Finally, you may have thrown up your hands at the strong recommendation that two people open mail, count cash, sign checks, etc. with the common laments that "It would only slow things down," "Two people can conspire to steal as well as one!," and/or "We just haven't enough people." Long professional experience leads to rejection of these arguments. First, haste makes waste; better safe than sorry. Second, in order to conspire, one person must propose it to another, which is a very risky proposition and also a good reason why close friends or relatives should not be the two involved. The individuals doing it should be rotated, to break up or lessen the opportunity for collusion.

As for the problems of the very small office, nonprofit *or* business, with limited staff the danger of loss from error or embezzlement is too serious to permit acceptance of the third excuse. If necessary, officers, program staff, including part timers, and/or volunteers should be pressed into service to be the second person required. The tasks involved, except check-signing, are usually mechanical ones, requiring no training or experience, and usually a limited amount of time. It is a case of "where there's a will, there's a way."

A Final Word About Internal Controls

Although the subject of fraud and theft is a delicate one, its overall importance can be underestimated only at grave risk to the organization. We have pointed out that independent public accountants often cannot "certify" (express an auditor's opinion regarding) your financial report in the absence of adequate internal controls. The concept behind this rule is that the figures generated from the books of account may be unreliable or meaningless without such controls.

Therefore, whether or not you have any need for a certified statement, you need reliable informa-

[3]Another type of insurance to consider is liability insurance for officers and/or board members, covering them personally for claims of creditors or others against the organization. (See Chapter 2.)

tion in managing your organization and its resources and in having the accountability required by all those interested parties outside your goldfish bowl. Those are reasons enough to make sure that your organization does not spring a leak somewhere that drains it as fast as you can fill it with other people's money.

THE TEN COMMANDMENTS OF ACCOUNTABILITY

Thou shalt . . .

● divide the handling of resources and related record-keeping between different people.

● provide that expenditures be authorized (or at least reviewed and approved) by an official other than the one initiating them.

● assign different people to the counting, recording, and depositing of funds received or due to be received.

● provide for a continuous or periodic inventory of physical properties and securities, identifying location and custody.

● monitor your activities to protect your tax exemption, funding, and solvency.

Thou shalt not . . .

● let the same individual be in *sole* charge of handling certain resources as well as the related records.

● let the same individual be in *sole* charge of both authorizing (or approving) expenditures and signing the checks.

● let the same person do bank reconciliations and sign checks, unless a second signature is required.

● pay expenses out of undeposited funds received.

● use a savings account for deposits or withdrawals that bypass your checking account.

BOOKKEEPING METHODS: FROM RUDIMENTARY TO PROFESSIONAL

Once your data have been sanitized, many ways to record them are available.

Checkbook Plus Columnar Worksheet Approach

This method is used by many very small nonprofit groups, and is normally used as a cash-only system. It usually involves entering: (1) details of cash received on one worksheet, sorting them into categories by using a separate column for each type, adding up the columns to obtain totals for reports, and (b) doing the same for each check issued, on a second worksheet, deriving total expenditures by type in the same fashion.

Limitations of the Approach

1. Failure to keep track of resources or obligations, such as equipment or balances owed by or to the organization. (Although a full "one-write" system can do so for each separate outside

amount due, it does not maintain a current balance of the *total* of amounts due. Lack of such control totals also makes the system prone to errors that a self-balancing double-entry system would disclose and help locate.)

2. Inherent limitation in the number of categories into which activities can be classified, due to the practical limits in the number of columns available and the need for analysis where different accounts must be combined in the same column; thus these methods are practical only when an extremely limited number of accounts is required (see Chapter 12 under "Chart of Accounts"). What it offers in simplicity it loses in the reduced amount of information provided for control and evaluation of operations and financial status.

3. Clumsiness in operating and proneness to errors of many types; nonetheless it is widely used and can be worked with by resourceful individuals as an acceptable substitute in very small nonprofits. It should be viewed as a stopgap system, however, to be upgraded as soon as resources (funds and people) permit.

Description of the Approach   (**Note:** Worksheets are illustrated in Chapter 12.)

● *Checkbook* (plus memo records of sources of any cash received and spent without being deposited and of payments made by cash, not check)

● *A worksheet for cash received and deposited* (with provision for six to twelve columns, plus item space, depending on the number of different types or sources of funds collected)

● *A worksheet for cash disbursed* (with provision for at least twelve or thirteen columns, plus item space)

Essential checkbook details: Required in nearly *all* systems:

● Explanation of each amount received, identifying its source and nature

● Explanation of purpose and classification of each check issued, in addition to name of payee

● All bank debit and credit memos and service charges, entered as though they were payments or deposits, with explanation

● Transfers to or from savings or money market accounts, properly entered

● Checkbook balance reconciled with bank statement monthly (Outstanding checks over 3 months old should be canceled and added back to the balance of the cash account through a worksheet entry, not merely by corrections to the checkbook balance.)

Column headings—cash receipts worksheet (see Fig. 12-1)

1. "Date received" (in date column at far left)

2. "Received from" (in item space) (name of source or of category, if group totals are small, amounts are entered for a day, week, etc.)

3. "Date deposited" (can use narrow column)

4. Separate memo column for "Total deposited" recommended to permit tracing items to deposits and to facilitate bank reconciliations

5. (First actual money column): "Total received" (if there are two or more checking accounts, a column worksheet is needed for each)

6. Detail columns as required, for recurring items; common examples are:

a. "Membership" (or dues)

b. "Contributions" (individual)

c. "Admissions," "Fees," "Tuition," "Subscriptions," etc.; any or all, as applicable: a separate column for each

d. "Grants received" (plus program or other identification, if not obvious from name shown in "Received from" column

e. "Special events" or a specific column and name for each, if more than one occurs; e.g., "Annual dinner," "Mail fund drive," "Theater party"

7. *Plus* an overflow column, headed "Other" (or "Miscellaneous") for occasional items not warranting a special column, with one or two description columns used for identifying the type of item, such as "Loan received," "Interest," or "Dividends," etc.

Column headings—cash disbursements worksheet (see Fig. 12–2). This worksheet uses basically the same scheme as that of the cash receipts worksheet described above.

1. "Date paid" (date column at far left)

2. "Paid to" (in item space) (for name of payee)

3. "Check number" (use a narrow column) (if not a check, enter "DM" or "SC" for bank debit memo or service charge)

4. (First money column) "Amount of check" (total or net amount paid) (if there are two or more checking accounts, a column or worksheet will be needed for each account, to separate the entries)

5. Detail columns, with headings, as required, for recurring items; common examples are "Salaries," "Transportation," "Office supplies and/or expense," "Program supplies," "Taxes," etc. Separate columns are desirable for expenses of different activities or programs, including "Special events."

a. "Salaries" or "Payroll": checks may be entered here in their net amount, if a payroll worksheet or register is used to accumulate the gross amounts earned and the amounts withheld; otherwise separate columns will be needed to record:

1) "Gross earnings" for the actual expense; tax withheld columns for:

2) "Federal income tax" or "FWT"

3) "FICA" or "Soc. Sec." (Social Security tax)

4) "State income tax" or "SWT"

5) In some states, columns for disability and/or unemployment tax, if withheld

6) In some cities, a city income tax; it can be seen that these complicate the worksheet, explaining why a separate payroll register may make more sense; one is also necessary when a single payroll check is cashed to make payments in cash; a "one-write" system can handle either method, and more conveniently.

b. Other detail column headings will vary in category and number, depending on which expenses occur frequently; certain items paid once a month or less often can be entered in the "Other" column: rentals, telephone, utilities, and installment payments.

6. Again, an overflow column headed "Other," "Miscellaneous," or "Sundry" is needed and is used in the same way as described above for the cash receipts worksheet.

Note also that it may sometimes be important to identify items more specifically within a column that is used for somewhat different items of the same general type, such as different kinds of office expense or office supplies. The basic test is what specific information may be useful or needed later. *Remember:* it is easier to record it currently than try to reconstruct it later!

Drawbacks to using worksheets.   Whereas both worksheets should be totaled and balanced monthly, *cumulative* totals are needed for various reports, giving rise to certain problems:

- If totals are accumulated from month to month, certain *monthly* totals are not provided, except at the end of the first month of the fiscal year. However, the totals of cash received and paid each month may be needed for the bank reconciliation, and totals for each quarter are required for payroll tax reports.

- The "overflow" column should be analyzed each month. It is clumsy to carry forward and analyze these summaries cumulatively.

- If the recurring types of revenue or expense change during the year, column headings cannot be easily changed to accommodate the fact without creating problems. Furthermore, as new recurring categories are added, it is clumsy to use worksheets with more than 12 or 13 columns, even though they are commercially available.

- The systems do not themselves provide for keeping track of asset or liability balances other than cash.

The development of formal double-entry bookkeeping undoubtedly arose partly to solve these problems. There are other solutions, however, to some of them:

- To get monthly or quarterly totals for revenues received or expenses paid, it is necessary only to subtract the cumulative totals at the beginning of a period in question from those at the end.

- If column headings are changed (not merely added), the cumulative total of each detail column eliminated must be transferred to become part of the overflow column and must be included in its summaries thereafter.

- One solution for expanding categories is to use the columns for *groups* of similar or related items and then to analyze and summarize each column periodically, as is done for the overflow column.

The test is always how much detail is actually meaningful to administrators or board. For example, the total costs of a program or activity (e.g., fundraising, special events) *may* be adequate information. In such cases a column accumulating such costs may not have to be analyzed.

Note: It is well to enter the nature of each item in any event, in case an outside agency later requests more detail: e.g., for IRS forms.

The cumulative column totals, with details analyzed as needed, are of course used to prepare the revenue and expenditures section of the financial reports and tax forms.

As with the worksheet approach, a one-write system requires little training or know-how, and is relatively inexpensive to operate in terms of personnel or materials. These systems are commercially available (see "Resources" below).

Features Provided in One-Write Systems

1. They can simultaneously provide the equivalent of the above worksheet data plus (by use of carbons, etc.) help in maintaining other records required for keeping track (in detail) of amounts owed by the nonprofit and in preparing payroll records required, and can do this on the payment end, as a byproduct of the writing of the checks themselves. These systems are widely used in business for just such labor-saving purposes and for eliminating the inevitable transcribing errors.

2. They can be used as the basis for a full double-entry bookkeeping system, if desired (currently or eventually) with the addition of a general ledger.

3. "One-write" systems can be used, by adding suitable forms, to record transactions on a full accrual basis. Thus pledges and other amounts due can be recorded as they are committed; expenses can be recorded as incurred, before payment; balances due from or to others kept track of, by name of debtor or creditor.

4. Some systems offer other features, such as the simultaneous preparation of signed receipts to donors or others while entering the cash received worksheet and/or preparing deposit slips. When statements or other reminders are sent to members or donors, they can also be prepared as a byproduct of recording the related charge or pledge in the individual's account, and recording the total of such entries in a journal when accrual accounting is used—or for memorandum purposes, when not so used.

Limitations of the system.   The same limited-classification problem exists here as in the worksheet method. (1) If used without a general ledger, it has all the limits of the system described using worksheets, plus the same clumsiness in operation and susceptibility to errors.[4] (2) When the system is used to prepare checks as well as cash records, the problem of separation of functions for internal control purposes arises (see above). In that case, the authority to approve and sign checks should be fully divorced from the check-writing function and underlying documents always carefully reviewed first.

As was noted above, these systems have many of the other limitations and problems of the worksheet approach, yet offer certain useful features. The column headings for the cash receipts and cash disbursements journal forms (See Figs. 11–2 and 11–3) are nearly the same as those used with the worksheet approach. All of the information regarding the use of worksheets is fully applicable here and should be studied when a "one-write" system is used for these journals. When used in conjunction with a general ledger, however, many of the problems and limitations noted will not be present.

The added features and capabilities available, described above, are usually explained and/or demonstrated by representatives of the supplier. Illustrations of forms for cash receipts and cash disbursements are shown below in Figs. 11–2 and 11–3. Application to payroll record-keeping is shown in Fig. 11–4.

---

[4]Another serious problem, mentioned above, is the problem of keeping track of asset and liability balances.

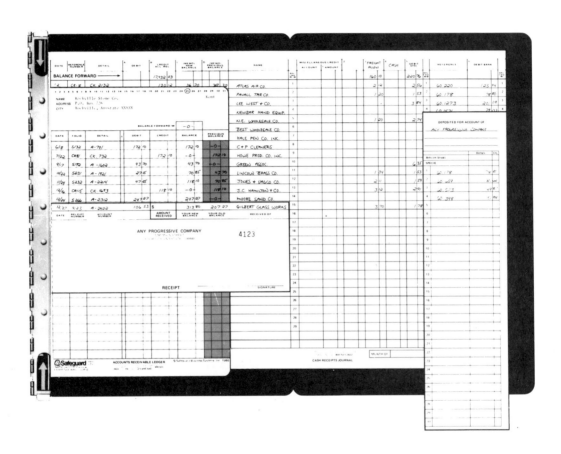

FIGURE 11–2. ONE-WRITE SYSTEM: CASH RECEIPTS JOURNAL.

Note: This system also provides for simultaneous preparation of both a receipt for the payer and an entry on the deposit slip (on the right).

Source: Safeguard Business Systems, Inc., Ft. Washington, PA 19034. Used with permission.

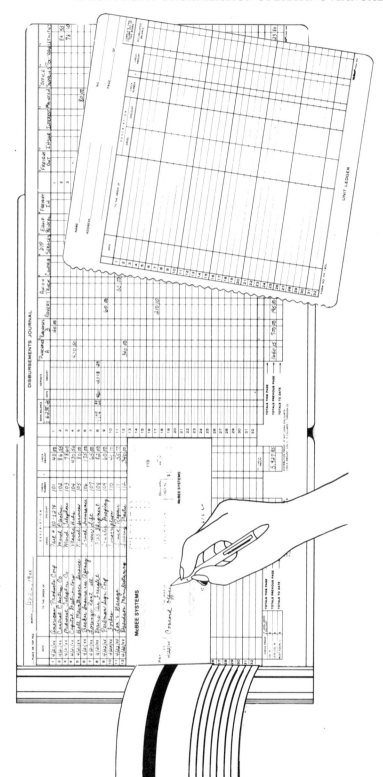

FIGURE 11–3. ONE-WRITE SYSTEM: CASH DISBURSEMENTS JOURNAL.

Note: This system permits simultaneous preparation of checks and the Cash Disbursements Journal. Note that checks are "shingled"—i.e., overlapped and attached at left-hand edge, for ease in handling and automatic positioning on consecutive lines of the journal sheet. Note optional "Unit Ledger Card" at right. This can be used for charges to programs or accumulating payments for preparing Forms 1099. (See Chapter 17.)

Source: McBee Systems, a division of Litton Industries, Belleville, NJ 07109. Used with permission.

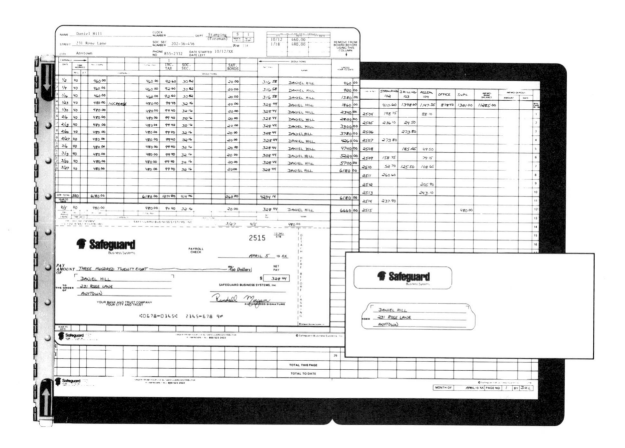

FIGURE 11-4. ONE-WRITE PAYROLL SYSTEM

Note: 1. Shingled checks with stub at top showing details of withholdings (lower left part of illustration). 2. Employee earnings record to accumulate details of salary and withholdings for payroll tax reporting (under paycheck and in register with stub). 3. Payroll journal (bottom layer), with provisions for distribution or allocation of salary expense to programs or functions (the right half of the journal that is fully visible).

Source: Safeguard Business Systems, Inc., Ft. Washington, PA 19034. Used with permission.

Using an All-Worksheet Approach

Some small nonprofits manage to "have their cake and eat it" by using a summary worksheet to convert cash basis journals to double-entry records. This is possible with both cash worksheets and "one-write" journals, though it usually works effectively only in the hands of a skilled accountant or bookkeeper trained in its use.

The summary worksheet solves one major problem of worksheets already noted: carrying forward balances of asset and liability accounts. It does not solve the other problems of a cash worksheet, such as its limitations in classifying expenses. Basically, the technique involves use of an additional worksheet, which lists previous balances of asset, liability, and fund balance accounts in a pair of columns. To this worksheet is transferred the column totals of the cash receipts and cash disbursements worksheets, which are entered in additional columns. Figures on each line are then added horizontally, to provide a trial balance, as in a true double-entry system, which then forms the basis of financial statements, including a balance sheet. (The summary worksheet is shown in Fig. 11–5.)

If financial statements are to be prepared in conformity with proper accounting principles, particularly when depreciation or accrual accounting is to be used, adjusting entries will be required. The entries can be added to the worksheet, which may result in too many columns for convenience, or the ending trial balance figures can be transferred to and used on a standard accountant's worksheet (see Fig. 12A-7) to prepare the statements.

Other Substitutes or Short-Cuts

Organizations can sometimes gain some of the capabilities of a true double-entry or accrual system by common-sense improvisations such as the following:

Control of "receivables": When a full-fledged accrual system is not used, and there is no ledger for pledges, dues, grants, or other amounts uncollected, such items can be controlled and followed up by using either index cards or worksheets listing names, amounts, due dates, date bill, notice or statement sent, date and amount collected, and balance due. As noted in Chapters 5 and 7, this information is of great value in preparing budget forecasts and assessing current financial status. When statements of account are mailed, copies of statements, filed alphabetically, can serve as the "ledger."

Control of "payables": The same approach—using index cards or worksheets—can be used for control and follow-up of unpaid bills and balances due various creditors for supplies, fees, utilities, etc. An unpaid bills file should be used as a supplement, but not as a substitute, since bills may be misplaced or lost. (They should always be stamped "PAID," with the check number, when paid in full.) Like the suggested record of receivables, this type of record is quite valuable for ongoing budgeting and assessing current financial status.

Accounts (some optional	Previous Trial Balance* at ____ 199__		Cash Receipts Transactions		Cash Disbursement Transactions		Ending Trial Balance at ____ 199__	
	(Dr)	(Cr)	(Dr)	(Cr)	(Dr)	(Cr)	(Dr)	(Cr)
Cash			(Total recd.)			(Total paid)		
Accounts receivable								
Property and equipment								
Accumulated depreciation (if used)								
Accounts payable								
Equipment installments due								
Payroll taxes payable								
Fund balance								
Revenues								
(examples only)								
Foundation grants								
Program revenues								
Other (list accounts)								
Expenses								
(examples only)								
Salaries (or detail accounts)								
Rent								
Utilities								
Telephone								
Supplies expense								
Consulting fees								
Travel								
Payroll taxes								
Depreciation expense (if used)								
Totals								

*This would show only asset, liability, and fund balance accounts if used with cumulative year-to-date totals from cash worksheets or "one-write" journals. It could also be used with monthly or quarterly totals, in which case it would be prepared each month or quarter and the ending trial balance used as the previous trial balance for the next period's summary worksheet.

**FIGURE 11–5. SUMMARY WORKSHEET
TO CONVERT SINGLE-ENTRY FIGURES TO DOUBLE-ENTRY**

Who Needs Full-Fledged Double-Entry Books?

First a note on terminology. Double-entry accounting merely means keeping track of the dual aspects of each transaction. As explained in Chapter 12, each transaction is an exchange, meaning that goods or services are being received or supplied, and funds are paid or promised in exchange. Even a checkbook usually provides both aspects of the exchange, but it is clumsy for keeping track of them independently. The worksheet and one-write system are improvements, with the limitations noted previously. They are a crude form of double entry, nonetheless. Combined with the summary worksheet described, in the hands of an accountant they can provide some of the benefits of a true double-entry system.

A full-fledged set of double-entry books can, however, provide unlimited kinds of information, tailored to the user's needs. The reason it has swept the world since its origins in the fifteenth century in Italy is simply that it is the most all-encompassing and flexible record-keeping method yet devised. Even computerized accounting is firmly grounded in it. And for many good reasons.

Purposes and advantages of the full double-entry system

1. The system is, as noted, self-balancing; i.e., entries must be made symmetrically, their dual nature reflecting the two sides of any exchange: e.g., what we gave and what we got for it, or what we got and how we got it. Thus most errors that upset this balance are soon apparent, and can be tracked down, usually without great difficulty. (Unnoticed errors in your books can be costly. Examples are paying the same bill twice or failing to collect an amount due.)

2. The system is far more comprehensive; it keeps track of all resources and obligations, if the accrual basis is used, because of the duality referred to above. It thus affords a picture of your current financial condition as well as an analysis of the revenues, expenses, and other transactions that produced it. Double entry thus satisfies the first four of the capabilties listed in Fig. 11–1.

3. Because it is an integrated system, it permits the preparation of an integrated set of financial statements required for external reporting to government and funding agencies. Attempting to construct such reports is well-nigh impossible by any other means, and certainly unreliable.

4. When the requirement or possibility of an external audit—by public accountants or by government agency—exists, double entry can provide "auditable" records, if properly used, whereas makeshift systems cannot. It provides what is called an "audit trail."

5. The system is capable of unlimited expansion of the information it provides. It can give you more detailed and useful analyses, without clumsy, time-consuming procedures. This flexibility is a major advantage of the method.

6. Its further flexibility is seen in the fact that it can be used not only with full accrual basis accounting but also with a simplified accrual basis described below, or even with cash basis accounting. (The basis used is independent of the use of the double-entry method itself.)

7. Even a worksheet approach or a "one-write" system can become a basic element of a double-entry bookkeeping system (its "input") with addition of the missing elements (described below): a general ledger plus provision for noncash entries. As a matter of fact, some small nonprofits use this approach as a practical compromise, instead of a full set of journals, by using regular staff who lack bookkeeping training to enter the day-to-day transactions and using an outside accountant, bookkeeper, or computer service center to handle the nonroutine entries, ledger, and financial statement preparation on a quarterly or monthly basis.

8. Another approach to a double-entry system, using a summary worksheet in place of a general ledger, is used by some very small nonprofits. It can be used with either cash worksheets or a "one-write" system, but generally works well only when handled or supervised by an accountant. This system was described above.

Elements of a complete double-entry system. Without getting too technical, here is a general overview of what is meant by a full double-entry set of books. (The "how-to" description is covered in Chapter 12 for self-study or review by whoever is responsible for actually keeping the books. Fig. 12–12 illustrates the full flow of information from transaction documents to financial reports.)

Types of journals. The word "journal" comes from the Italian word for "day" (giorno) and is also used in the names of daily newspapers to indicate a daily record of events, which is what a journal is. Also called a "register" (cf. cash register), a journal is thus a diary for recording events of a financial or operational nature as they occur, classifying and grouping them for transfer (usually by a group total) periodically to a ledger (see below). Most commonly, there are separate journals for cash received and cash disbursed and a general journal for noncash transactions and adjustments.

In a *full* accrual system, journals are added for: (1) bills received, but not paid, called an "accounts payable journal" or "register," and (2) revenues frequently recorded as billed out, called an "accounts receivable journal" or "register"—sometimes given a name more descriptive of the type of revenues earned, such as service fees, pledges, dues, etc. Other journals or registers may be added, though they are not necessarily unique to a double-entry system. A payroll register is the most common and is described below.

The general ledger. This is in essence a filing system, to which the totals of like items, classified in the journal, are transferred ("posted" is the term used) and accumulated for eventual use in preparing financial reports. It will contain a page or "account" for each category, to which totals are posted monthly, and the cumulative balances updated.

Types of Accounts Found in the General Ledger

Revenue accounts:	Grants, service fees, dues, etc.
Expense accounts:	Salaries, rent, utilities, payroll taxes, etc.
Resources ("assets"):	Accounts receivable—total due from others for revenues, etc.; equipment and other fixed assets, supplies, etc.
Obligations ("liabilities"):	Accounts payable—totals due to others for expenses, installment contracts or loans; also, obligations of the organization for services paid for in advance and not yet rendered
Fund balances:	The difference between assets and liabilities, representing the "net worth" of an organization or fund

The chart of accounts. This is not actually a separate element, but rather in effect the operating manual of the system, listing all of the accounts to be used, what goes into each, and for what purpose. Note that the classification of the accounts must correspond to that used in budgets, to ensure uniformity and comparability of actual with budgeted amounts.

Principal types of subsidiary ledgers (where applicable).   These may be maintained either as part of a full accrual system or as memorandum records in a cash basis or simplified accrual system. They include the following.

Accounts receivable ledger is a generic term for ledgers used for related groups of accounts with members, donors, funding agencies, clients, subscribers, etc., to keep track of amounts due from them. Specific ledgers might be used for pledges receivable, dues receivable, or any other group of like accounts too numerous to be carried individually in the general ledger.

Accounts payable ledger is a type of subsidiary ledger common to nearly every type of organization; it is used to keep track of amounts due to creditors sending bills for good or services.[5]

The great importance of maintaining records of both receivables and payables, not only for follow-up, but for budgeting and assessing financial status, has already been noted (see "Other Substitutes or Short-Cuts" above).

Fixed asset ledger is of particular value to nonprofits owning numerous items of equipment used for the office, transportation, school, or programs. This ledger facilitates control over and accountability for such property, which helps to protect it against loss and to establish insurance claims when stolen, damaged, or destroyed. The ledger should show physical location, detailed description (including serial number), date acquired, and cost and accumulated depreciation of each asset, plus the name of its custodian.

Payroll records   Tax and labor laws are quite specific in requiring complex record-keeping in this area, perhaps the most cumbersome and time-consuming area of all. Whether staff is paid by check or cash, and regardless of the type of bookkeeping system used, three separate records are required for *each* salary payment:

1. An employee pay slip (or check attachment) indicating amount earned, taxes and other amounts withheld, and net amount paid.

2. An employee's earnings record, which accumulates the above amounts for each employee, by quarter and annually, for use in preparing payroll tax reports and withholding statements.

3. A payroll journal or register, listing all paychecks or cash payments for each pay period and showing the details described above in 1. Column totals for each period are then entered in the cash disbursements journal and/or posted directly to the general ledger. (The payroll details may be entered instead in the cash disbursements journal, but see Chapter 12 on this.)

Some idea of the potential record-keeping burden involved in payrolls can be gained by realizing that a weekly payroll covering ten employees will usually involve recording a combined total of over 9,000 *individual amounts per year* on the pay slips (or check stubs), employee earnings records, and payroll registers!

Methods for preparing payroll records

"One-Write" system: Permits preparing all three records with one writing (see above), which cuts the work by two-thirds.

Computer service center: Widely available for payroll, inexpensive and practicable even for fairly small organizations. Not only does it provide all three records, it can also, for one price, prepare the paychecks, payroll tax reports, and annual withholding slips. Moreover, in many cases payroll information can be updated by phone once the basic payroll data are submitted.

---

[5]When bills are paid regularly each month, this ledger may be eliminated by use of a voucher register, which provides for keeping track of unpaid bills within the journal itself. (This is explained in Chapter 12.)

Keeping payroll records the hard way: Very small nonprofits can also prepare these records manually; in this case, a commercially available payroll book should be used: one with features designed to overcome a little of the drudgery involved. They have little but their price to recommend them and can accommodate only a payroll with a very limited number of employees.

Important Supplementary Records

Additional records of value can and should be used whenever appropriate, regardless of the general bookkeeping system employed.

Receipt books.   Reference was made earlier to the importance of using duplicate, prenumbered receipts as a means of controlling collection of numerous small amounts of money, by cash or check. The most practical way is use of a receipt book designed for the purpose. The best type is one printed to order, with the name of the organization and provisions for identifying the type of payment (dues, donation, subscription, tickets, etc.).The carbon copies remaining in the book, after signing and detaching the receipts, can be totaled periodically by category, if desired, and only the totals entered in the cash receipts journal to save numerous individual entries. (The individual receipts can be posted to the appropriate receivables ledger, if one is maintained, to keep track of individual balances.)

Petty cash records.   Most organizations find frequent occasion to pay out small amounts in cash rather than check, for such items as postage or delivery charges due, small items of office supplies, local fares, and the like. The best way to maintain control and accountability is by using a so-called imprest fund, which is entrusted to a single custodian, responsible for both the funds and accounting for their expenditures. This is the only situation in which the principles of internal control permit both functions to be handled by the same individual. However, it is designed to make the custodian fully accountable for funds put in his or her care.

The basic idea is to maintain a fund of a specified amount—usually determined from experience as being the amount of cash that is paid out in a month or so—for costs that cannot be conveniently paid by check. The funds are usually kept in a cash box that is kept under lock and key by the sole custodian. (No one else should be permitted access, if the system is to work properly, for accountability must be pinpointed to a single person.)

A signed receipt, which should be prenumbered and preferably bear the custodian's initials, should be obtained for each payment and a cash register or delivery slip or other document stapled to it as a proof of authenticity. All receipt numbers should be accounted for and the box checked periodically to ensure that the total cash remaining, plus receipts obtained, equals the correct amount of the imprest fund.

When the cash runs low, a check should be issued and cashed, reimbursing the fund for the total amount of petty cash slips on hand. This serves the dual purpose of (1) restoring the original balance of cash and (2) recording the amounts expended on the books of account, by breaking down the amount of the check into the categories represented by the petty cash slips, which have been summarized for that purpose. This provides a self-balancing system, easily audited as often as necessary, and providing adequate control over a slippery area. It works well as long as no one but the custodian has uncontrolled access to the petty cash fund, and that includes officers and administrators!

Savings account records.   As was noted earlier, no funds should be deposited into or withdrawn from an organization's savings account without passing through its checking account on the way in or out, or serious holes may appear in cash accountability. Should violations of this rule occur, a running record in worksheet or notebook form should be kept of where funds came from and/or to whom they were paid and for what purpose. (This applies as well to money market accounts.)

The need for nonmonetary records.   A well-run nonprofit often needs a number of nonfinancial records, which may include any or all of the following:

Employee (and sometimes volunteers') time reports and weekly summaries thereof, indicating activities to which their time applied. If your organization is a tax-deductible charitable organization that tries to influence legislation, such records are necessary to establish the amount of such activity to the IRS's satisfaction.

Records of services performed: Clients served: number, types of service, hours of staff or volunteer time, or other units of service output (especially important when cost per client or per unit of service—per hour, per day, etc.—is to be calculated for program or other performance evaluation purposes, or pricing services).

In-kind contributions received in goods, facilities, or services; their value or some basis for calculating value should be recorded (e.g., hours of service rendered).

Records for controlling accountability over custody, and for current and advance sale of tickets, raffle books, coin canisters, reservations, subscriptions, etc.

Miscellaneous organizational documents affecting financial records and management, such as bylaws, board resolutions and minutes, leases, contracts, and the like; these are often the basic authority for substantial payments.

How Computer Service Centers Can Ease the Task

Representatives of larger firms, such as Accounting Corporation of America and Automatic Data Processing, Inc., will explain the use of their input forms and procedures. The key to a good system is a well-designed chart of accounts, as explained in Chapter 12. (You may have to conform with a coding system prescribed by the service center.)

In addition,the use of well-designed "one-write" computer input forms, prepared in duplicate (so the copy may be retained), may combine some of the best features of both systems and can also minimize the cost of the data processing as well, when monthly journal *totals* are submitted rather than numerous individual transactions. The latter alternative requires only that your staff *code* all transactions to indicate the accounts affected, and shifts *all* bookkeeping functions to the computer. Some service centers even accept coded check stubs, or coded adding machine tapes of transactions, as input. To avoid headaches and delays in resubmission, all input details should be double-checked and proven before submitting as input. For example, cash receipts and disbursement totals should be submitted preferably after being used in the bank reconciliation.

Note, however, that the more *details* submitted, the higher the charges, so the cost/benefit aspect should also be considered. The desirability of risking the loss of original records, such as check stubs, is another consideration. (One solution is to prepare your checks in duplicate, with the "dummy" (unsigned) copy coded and submitted instead of check stubs.)

Problem area: Unlike a manually posted general ledger, the version printed out by a computer will probably show only the beginning and ending balances of each account, plus postings to the accounts for the current period. For example, if transactions are submitted monthly, it is necessary to review all 12 months' printouts to see the details of activities in any account for the year. If desired, the service center often can supply a full year's activity, by account, for an extra charge.

Features of computerized accounting

1. Subsidiary ledgers for accounts receivable and payable can also be maintained by computer. However, this may well be expensive for most small nonprofits, as well as impractical, due to the delay in receiving printouts needed for day-to-day follow-up of collections and payments.

2. Where a voucher register is used in lieu of an accounts payable ledger, a computerized approach is less practicable, except for posting to general ledger (see Chapter 12).

3. The worksheet used for preparing financial reports (see below) is eliminated. All adjusting entries are submitted to the service center and posted to the general ledger. Financials are printed out directly from the adjusted ledger balances. (Adjusting entries made during the fiscal year for interim reports must be reversed when the next period's transactions are submitted.) The printouts can include journals as well as ledger accounts and financials, if desired, for reference to transactions in chronological order, bank reconciliations, etc.

4. The computer can print out many variations of report formats, including percentage relationships between items, figures for the current period *and* the year-to-date. These figures can be displayed, if desired, with the same periods for the previous period, or with budgeted figures. They can show either unexpended balances or variances between budgeted and actual items of revenue and expense. These are, of course, "add-on extras."

The rapid development of computer applications and services has led to three different approaches for bookkeeping and accounting purposes; at least one of them is within the means of many small nonprofits, and another is affordable by many others without any substantial investment in equipment.

Computer service centers are now located in cities of modest size, and are always accessible by mail in any event. Many of them offer a complete bookkeeping/accounting service for small organizations that requires little or no training of personnel. Transaction data can be submitted in any of several different forms—including coded check stubs (at some centers); on input forms supplied (in all centers); or even using the "one-write" system forms as inputs (in many cases). Their use costs much less than hiring a full-charge bookkeeper, and the best such firms can provide professionally designed accounting records and financial reports whose level of sophistication is limited only by the amount the organization is willing to spend for them. The one drawback is the delay in receiving your "books"[6] and records after sending the data.

Time-sharing terminals, which are computer input units that can "talk" to a remote computer in machine code, over your telephone line, are a more sophisticated (and faster) way of utilizing electronic data processing. They generally require more training of personnel, plus funds for renting or buying the equipment. The printouts available may or not be as complete or adequate as those provided by the service center that delivers its output by mail or similar nonelectronic means. This system should nonetheless become more common in the near future.

Your Own In-House Computer

If you are already using a computer system for purposes other than accounting, and are comfortable with it, you may want to explore using it to keep your books and generate reports. We do not

---

[6]"Books" will of course come in the form of computer printouts, for which special binders are available.

recommend using a computer for that purpose first. Learning to do your own accounting is enough of a challenge without learning to use a computer as well: despite what you may have heard, you still need some knowledge of accounting. Even if you have a skilled bookkeeper or accountant on staff, unless that person or someone else in the office is comfortable with a computer, you are likely to be buying trouble during the transition.

Quite aside from learning the accounting program, a knowledge of basic computer operations and problems is essential. We provide a primer on the subject, and how to go about getting into the world of computers, as Appendix 11C of this chapter.

WHO SHOULD DO YOUR BOOKKEEPING?

Who should *not* do it was explained in detail under Internal Control above: first, anyone who handles cash; second, anyone who has sole authority to sign checks; or even if the authority is joint, unless the cosigner does a thorough job of scrutinizing checks and the supporting bills or vouchers, and verifies not only that the expenditures were authorized but that the proper goods and services were actually received. This having been said, there are a number of alternative approaches to this serious problem, depending on the financial and human resources available.

A "Full-Charge" Bookkeeper

If resources permit, hire a full-time bookkeeper, one experienced in double-entry bookkeeping, including operation of a general ledger. Otherwise, use an experienced part-time bookkeeper until then. Knowledge of double entry is essential if a manual general ledger is used, especially if full accrual basis is employed. This knowledge is valuable even if other bookkeeping methods are used; it will provide better results. A professionally trained accountant should be available for consultation by the bookkeeper regarding unusual entries or problems and to review the work periodically.

Nonprofit accounting and bookkeeping have their own particular goals and problems; consequently bookkeepers, and accountants as well, whose experience is limited to the world of business ordinarily need a certain amount of reorientation to the nonprofit world. A "strictly business" approach can otherwise cause certain problems, as well as helping to solve the basic ones. This book can be used for such a reorientation by bookkeepers and accountants—one of its intended purposes.

Other Staff

Administrative or other support staff can learn to operate major portions of the bookkeeping system, with a little instruction and help from someone already knowledgeable. Actually, there is no great mystery about learning to be a full-charge bookkeeper, given the motivation and an average ability with figures. Chapter 12 plus the material in Chapter 10 are intended as a self-study approach to basic bookkeeping and accounting theory.[7] There are of course many books and courses available for more in-depth study of the subject.

Until the necessary know-how has been acquired, such staffers should handle only the "input" phase of the bookkeeping. This is the worksheet, "one-write" forms or journals, or computer input forms plus subsidiary ledgers for receivables and/or payables. An outside accountant or book-

---

[7]See also the fully worked out Accounting Cycle of Center for Community Services in Appendix 12A.

keeper can be used to post the general ledger and prepare financial statements on a monthly or quarterly basis.

Officer or volunteer: An unpaid treasurer or other volunteer can sometimes be used, when there is no other feasible solution, if he or she has some bookkeeping background. An individual member, currently unemployed or employed only part-time, can sometimes be found for this job. This is rarely a good arrangement, for its continuance may be undependable; it also may result in tension, when other staff is paid. It is better to pay a stipend of some sort to avoid this problem.

Note: It is worse to have unpaid personnel handling funds, as well as books, than to have paid staff do so!

A practical mix

1. Have the best available level of personnel do the "inputs" mentioned above.

2. Use an outside accountant or computer service center to prepare the general ledger and the financial statements, on a monthly—or at least quarterly—basis.

3. If the above approach is not economically or financially feasible, which should apply only to very small nonprofits, use the "one-write" or worksheet approach, and have an outside accountant prepare your annual reports. Note that this is a minimal use of accounting, of little value for control or performance evaluation.

4. In any event, a professional accountant should prepare, or at least review, annual reports to the IRS and state agencies, and compile, or at least review, annual financial reports. If you can interest a local professional in donating his or her services to your organization for the purpose, you will have found a solution to a very important problem. An effort to do so is strongly recommended to all underfunded nonprofits: it can help avoid many headaches, ranging from inability to obtain or retain funding to difficulty with the IRS or state regulatory agencies.

It may be apparent by this point that systems design is not a do-it-yourself project. A brief outline of where to go for professional assistance or advice follows.

General Professional Assistance

This includes independent public accounting firms or practitioners, or accounting professionals employed in business or government; depending on your financial situation, you may be able to obtain their help on a one-shot or occasional basis as a contribution or at a low fee.

A nonprofit organization in your area may offer technical accounting assistance; examples are VISTA, public interest accounting groups,[8] umbrella organizations for nonprofits in certain fields (arts, human services, etc.). (You may have to do some investigating to locate such aid, but it is well worth the effort.)

"One-write" systems. Suppliers help in the design of the forms and records without charge. Leading suppliers are McBee Systems, Shaw Walker Co., and Safeguard Business Systems, Inc. (see "Business Forms & Systems" in the Yellow Pages.)

Computer service centers. These can be found in the Yellow Pages under "Data Processing Services." Two leading national firms are Accounting Corporation of America and Automatic Data Processing, Inc. They offer systems advice and provide a wide variety of services, some designed especially for nonprofit organizations. There are in addition many regional and local

---

[8]Accountants for the Public Interest, 1625 I Street, N.W., Suite 517, Washington, DC 20006 may be able to direct you to one nearby.

firms providing payroll service and sometimes other services described above.

Other bookkeeping record forms.   More traditional manual forms such as those described above for payroll, receipt books, time sheets, etc., can be obtained from large commercial stationers and from a number of mail order houses catering to such needs, such as Accountants' Supply House of New York.[9]

---

[9]A chart of a fully developed accrual system and its flow of data are shown in Figure 12-12.

APPENDIX 11A

Bank Reconciliation

The word "reconciliation" means, among other definitions, "to adjust differences." The process has two general goals: (1) to "tie in" the checkbook balance at the end of a period with the balance according to the bank's records, and adjust it, if incorrect; and (2) to detect any errors, irregularities, or embezzlement (accountants use the term "defalcation"). The process of reconciling the two balances is based on the fact that certain information is included in each of them that may not be taken into account in the other.

The logic behind the process is this.

Balance per Your Records	Balance per Bank Statement
May need adjustment for data originating with the bank:	Often needs adjustment for deposits or checks in transit:
Examples:	*Examples:*
Subtract: bank service charges, bad checks, promissory notes paid to or through the bank	*Add:* late deposits not yet credited by bank
Add: credit memos for loan from bank, promissory notes collected, interest credited, etc.	*Subtract:* checks issued that have not yet cleared the bank

Once each balance has been adjusted for items it had not reflected, the two balances should agree, be "reconciled." If not, then you have made a mechanical error either somewhere in the reconciliation (in math, an incorrect figure, or an omission) or in your records, or the bank has made an error. The procedure is straightforward.

How to Adjust the Bank Statement Balance

1. Sort the returned checks in numerical order.

2. Assuming this is not the first bank reconciliation for the account, obtain the one for the previous month, or the last one done. Check off all old outstanding checks listed on it that have cleared on this month's statement.[10] As you handle each check, it should be inspected for authenticity—proper signature, payee, and endorsement—to ensure that it is a legitimate payment. This is a primary control over forgeries and embezzlement and so should not be done mechanically.

3. Any old outstanding checks that have still not cleared represent a difference between your

---

[10]If no reconciliation was done last month, checks for all months since the last one was done will have to be checked this way.

balance and the bank's and need to be carried over to the current month's reconciliation, as a deduction from the bank's balance.

4. Next, check off on your check stubs, or other payment record, the current month's checks that have cleared, inspecting them for validity as in step 2. Any not checked off and still outstanding must be used as deductions from the bank's balance.

5. Check any deposits in transit on the previous bank reconciliation to see that they have cleared the bank.

6. Compare your deposits for the current month with those credited by the bank. Any which have not been so credited should be *added* to the bank's balance. After this step you normally have the "adjusted balance" according to the bank.

Adjusting the Balance per Your Books

7. Look for any debit memos from the bank not already deducted from your checkbook balance. Such memos (e.g., for service charges, bad checks) should be subtracted from your balance. (Banks sometimes show service charges on their statement without including a debit memo, so don't overlook such items.) Certified checks issued but not yet cleared will also show up as debit memos, so don't list such checks in step 4 above, since these amounts have already been taken out of your account.

8. Look for any credit memos from the bank not already added to your balance and add them. (These are less common.) After this step you will normally have the adjusted balance per your checkbook, which should agree with the balance in step 6.

An illustration of a typical bank reconciliation format is shown in Figure 11A–1.

BANK RECONCILIATION
January 31, 19x1

Per Books			Per Bank Statement		
Balance, Jan. 31		$2,005[a]	Balance, Jan. 31		$2,790
Add: Bank loan not entered		2,000[b]	Add: Jan. 31 deposit in transit		1,500[c]
		4,005			4,290
Less:					
Service charge	5.[b]		Less: Outstanding checks:[d]		
Bad check	100.[b]		#	Amount	
		105	(Dec.) 222	50.	
			(Jan.) 262	100.	
			(Jan.) 264	150	
			(Jan.) 265	90.	390
Adjusted balance		$3,900	Adjusted balance		$3,900

[a] Balance from general ledger (cash account) or checkbook.

[b] From bank statement: not yet entered on books.

[c] From cash receipts journal (or checkbook); not shown on bank statement, since items have not cleared the bank yet.

[d] From cash disbursements journal or checkbook, not yet cleared.

FIGURE 11A–1. BANK RECONCILIATION

Note: The $2,000 bank loan had not been entered on the center's cash records, nor had the $5 service charge or the bad check (usually coded "NSF"). These items must be entered as adjustments through the journals and added to or subtracted from the checkbook balance. Items on the bank statement side should either clear automatically the following month or else must be carried forward and used again until they do. (Example above is the December outstanding check, No. 222, which did not clear in December *or* January.) If a check continues outstanding for several months it should be stopped, added back to the balance, and generally a new check issued, to replace the original check.

How to Locate Differences

If the two adjusted balances—per books and per bank statement—do not agree, retrace your steps, looking for the following errors.

- Outstanding checks (i.e., not cleared) you failed to list and subtract from the bank's balance.

- Late deposits in transit (not cleared) you did not add to bank's balance.

- Debit or credit memos, or service charges for which no debit memo was received, not taken into account.

- Errors in the bank reconciliation in addition, subtraction, listing of amounts, or the direction used (e.g., subtracted instead of added).

- Differences between actual amounts of individual checks or deposits and amounts shown in your checkbook or cashbook.

- Error in the balance shown in your own records: adjustments listed in 5 and 6 above will not produce a correct adjusted balance if you have made errors in arithmetic in your checkbook or cashbook or if the balance at the beginning of the period has not been reconciled; in that case, you may have to reconcile one or more prior months as well.

- Occasional bank failure to return a canceled check charged to your account, which you will assume is still outstanding; the only way to detect this is to check the canceled checks against the checks listed on the statement (a preliminary test is to add up the canceled checks and compare the total with the total of those charged on the statement); any such charge should be challenged.

- Bank omission of a copy of a debit or credit memo applied to your account; these charges or credits are usually shown with letters such as "DM," "CM," etc., next to them, which aid in distinguishing them from checks.

9. After "tying in" the two balances, one final step is required before the process is complete. All adjustments needed to *your* balance must be used to adjust the checkbook balance *and* the balance in your ledger account. The latter is done by making entries in the proper journals, either your general journal or your cashbook. The bank reconciliation should be filed for use the following month.

10. Should you find that the bank has made an error, it should be called to their attention and corrected, not merely to tie in the balances. The error, once corrected, will eliminate itself in the following period. The most common bank errors are charging an account for someone else's check, charging or crediting the wrong amount of a check or deposit, and crediting a deposit to the wrong account. All these types of errors should show up if steps 2–6 are done carefully. Ways to find other bank errors were explained when the errors were mentioned.

APPENDIX 11B

Available One-Write Systems Designs and Computer Service Centers

One-Write Systems

The major suppliers of these systems offer a wide variety of labor-saving features. These include the simultaneous posting of nearly all related records, journal forms designed for computer input, and window envelopes that save addressing of checks (or even save imprinting of return address). One-write systems combine different functions in one set of forms, for example, cash disbursements, plus payroll, plus accounts payable bookkeeping. Samples of such combination forms and features are supplied in Figs. 11B-1-11B-4. Additional systems available can be ascertained from the suppliers themselves, who also offer free assistance in selecting the appropriate system design (from their own catalog, of course).

Computerized Accounting

The leading service center firms in this field offer a wide variety of output formats, including all standard financial reports described in Chapter 13,[11] plus numerous types of comparative and analytical report formats, including those described in Chapter 15. Examples are comparisons of actual vs. budget, with variances shown, for the current month or quarter vs. the same period last year; for the year to date this year vs. that period last year; for the entire year vs. last year. Percentages can be shown instead of or in addition to variances. Unexpended budget to date can be shown.

Breakdowns of activity by program and support function are possible, with totals for each of these categories. Fund accounting balance sheets or other statements can be printed out, and even calculation of cost per unit of each activity if desired. Of course, these special features entail an extra charge, which must be weighed against the benefit of having specialized reports printed by computer rather than prepared manually from basic reports.

One-Write Plus Computer

It is possible and often advantageous to combine the use of computer service centers with the use of one-write systems, once the system is properly set up. Although the computer centers can accept input directly from coded check stubs, without the use of journals, in practice this is often a clumsy arrangement, since there are no records to refer to until the printouts are received. There are ways around this, such as using a duplicating checkbook and retaining carbon duplicates of checks and stubs issued and photocopying stubs before mailing, but these methods are also clumsy for refer-

[11]Balance Sheet, operating statement, etc.

ence purposes. The processing costs are greater when all details are submitted rather than journal totals. All details then appear in the general ledger accounts, too, which is often an unnecessarily clumsy way to work, rather than submitting monthly totals. But it is in just these areas that the objective advice of a professional accountant can be of most value. Although the representatives of the computer firms can give advice as well, they cannot be expected to be as objective about your needs.

Other Available Formats

One-write system suppliers and data-processing companies offer users a wide variety of special applications and designs. Although these may cost somewhat more than the standard package, there is often a great saving in time, labor, and payroll costs over more traditional ways of doing the same thing or the hidden cost of not doing it as well.

One-Write System Designs   (See Figs. 11B-1–11B-4.)

- Combined cash disbursements, payroll, and accounts payable system.
- Cash disbursement system with provision for fund accounting records.
- Cash receipts journal with provision for simultaneous preparation of donor receipt and/or deposit slip.
- Computer input format with combined cash disbursements and payroll (one format provides a "sub-account" column for functional account codes).
- Many other specialized applications and designs are available.

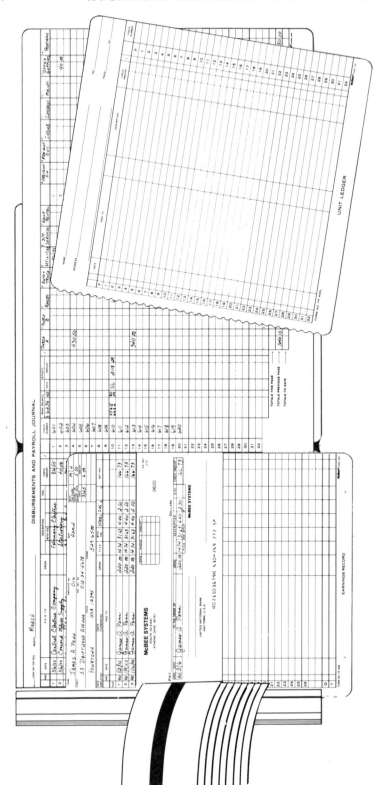

FIGURE 11B–1. COMBINED PAYROLL AND CASH DISBURSEMENT SYSTEM. PAYROLL APPLICATION.

Source: McBee Systems, a division of Litton Industries, Belleville, NJ 07109. Used with permission.

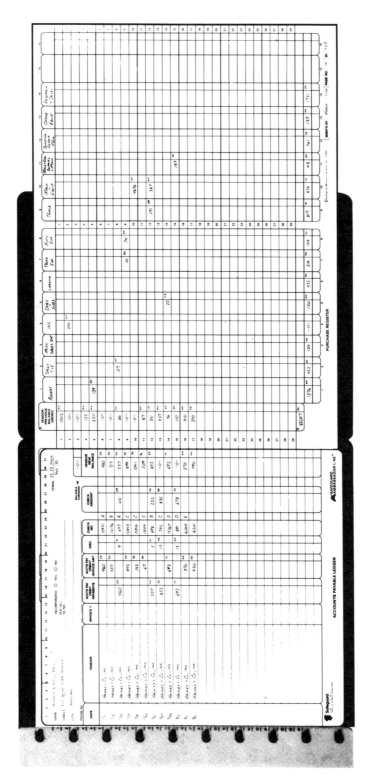

ACCOUNTS PAYABLE JOURNAL AND LEDGER PLUS CASH DISBURSEMENTS JOURNAL AND CHECKS.

FIGURE 11B–2. STEP 1: ENTERING INVOICE IN ACCOUNTS PAYABLE JOURNAL AND LEDGER.

Note: Top layer is the creditor's ledger account ("Haines & Co., Inc."); underneath it is the Accounts Payable Journal (here called a "Purchase Register").

Source: Safeguard Business Systems, Inc., Fort Washington, PA 19034

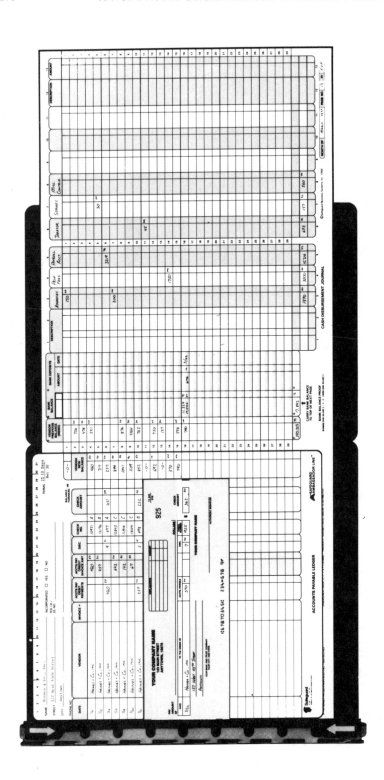

FIGURE 11B–3. STEP 2. PREPARING CHECK TO VENDOR AND ENTERING IN VENDOR'S ACOUNT AND CASH DISBURSEMENTS JOURNAL

Note: Check on top, with provision for vendor's name and address (used with window envelope), details of bills being paid (upper box), gross amount, discount and net amount. Creditor's ledger account underneath check, Cash Disbursements Journal as bottom layer.

Source: Safeguard Business Systems, Inc., Fort Washington, PA 19034

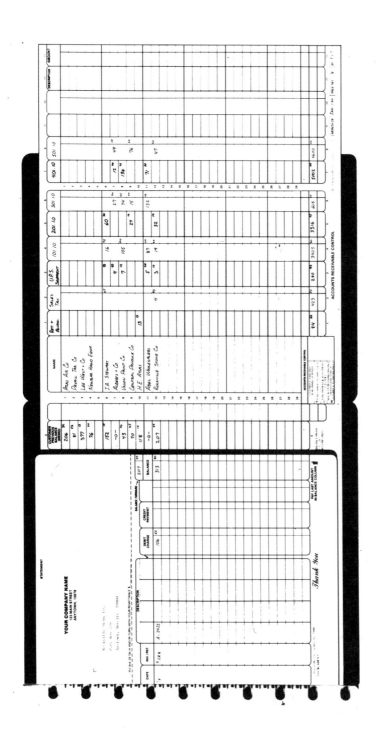

FIGURE 11B–4. MULTI-PURPOSE ONE-WRITE SYSTEM. ACCOUNTS RECEIVABLE JOURNAL AND LEDGER PLUS CASH RECEIPTS JOURNAL. ACCOUNTS RECEIVABLE APPLICATION. ENTERING AND POSTING OF OWN INVOICE ILLUSTRATED.

Note: Top layer is a monthly statement, prepared cumulatively as bills or collections are entered and posted to the individual's Accounts Receivable ledger account, and in the Accounts Receivable Journal (bottom layer)—or Cash Receipts Journal (not shown). Note provision for recording credits to accounts ("Return and Allowances"), sales tax or other charges, and analysis of the charges by category (under "Sales Distribution" columns).

Source: Safeguard Business Systems, Inc., Fort Washington, PA 19034

APPENDIX 11C

Getting Started with Computers

In the past few years, the trend to using microcomputers on the part of even the smaller non-profit has been unmistakable. (As pointed out in Chapter 8, some computer and software companies have encouraged this trend by donating or sharply discounting their products for nonprofits.) Look at it this way: those ever-present and very handy digital calculators are now sold for the price of a good pen, though they seemed a miracle when they first appeared. The microchip that made them possible gave birth to the microcomputer as well. Get ready for a sales pitch on why you need one. One good reason is that most of the calculations and graphs set forth in this book can be done almost instantaneously, without even the key strokes needed for your calculator. (And just try drawing graphs and charts with that!)

There are computer programs worth much more than their cost that can take the number-crunching out of your planning and decision-making as if by magic. You can do "what if?" projections in which you can instantly predict the effect of a given change in price, activity level, fixed or variable costs, on your bottom line—or calculate the revenue you need to produce a given target profit. You can even do this using break-even analysis, and can print out all these projections if you want to. And that's just the beginning—although it's possibly the very best use for a microcomputer.

Those Magical Spreadsheet Programs

The computer programs (or "software") that let you work this magic are called spreadsheet programs, since they look like a multicolumn worksheet such as you have seen many times. (Did you ever see one that has 256 columns, though?) Spreadsheets are what *made* the microcomputer industry in the first place; not many machines were sold before the first spreadsheet (Visicalc) came along. It was the realization that a manager could, in effect, become his or her own controller, by using the power of this electronic brain, that made the industry take off.

Naturally, spreadsheet software became *the* hot item, and the competition for this market has become fierce. Some of the more popular spreadsheet software programs (which have made the pioneer, Visicalc, obsolete) are the following: Lotus 1-2-3, PlanPerfect (from WordPerfect Corp.), MultiPlan (from Microsoft), SuperCalc, Quattro, and Excel (also from Microsoft), which works only with the fastest new personal computers (PCs). Lotus has been the most widely used of all, although you can get a lot of arguments by favoring any one of them (so I won't, much as I'm tempted). Below are some of the planning and decision-making tools they all make painless.

- Developing budgets and other forecasts and projections, such as projected cash flow and cash requirements.

- Doing allocations of overhead between departments, products, and other segments for budgeting or reporting purposes.

- Doing "what if?" projections, as mentioned above, with alternative assumptions and variables, to see their effects on the bottom line or to see required sales.

- Recasting financial reports to use alternative formats, i.e., isolating controllable and noncontrollable contribution margin, generating financial ratios and trends, and converting some of these to graphs and charts, such as pie or bar charts.

- Deciding the best alternative in such decisions as buy or make, buy or lease, add or drop a program, equipment replacement, alternative pricing methods, bids and special orders, and most profitable use of space and facilities.

Where You Come In

Will a microcomputer do everything for you? Frankly, we aren't at 2001 yet and you can't just ask "Hal" for the answers by talking to him. Someone has to feed the numbers in, even when there are canned calculations. In some cases, someone has to know how to set up the spreadsheet so that feeding in the numbers is all you have to do. There is a certain amount of skill involved here, but the important thing is that you don't have to be a computer programmer to do any of it. Anyone with average intelligence and some patience can learn to use a spreadsheet for all it's worth—which is plenty! And if you haven't the time to learn how, there are always other ways to get that job done, including buying "off-the-shelf" software that sets it all up for you (called "templates" in the industry).

A number of firms have been supplying these templates for some time now. Finally, in the spring of 1988, Lotus Development Corporation decided to cash in on this market itself. It announced that it would sell a 1-2-3 Small Business Kit, consisting of a copy of Lotus 1-2-3, a selection of add-on applications for financial analysis and planning, plus six months of toll-free unlimited telephone support for the small business owner or manager.

Templates

Here are some examples of typical template software already on the market.

- Break-even analysis
- "What if?" analysis (also called sensitivity analysis)
- Cash flow projection statement
- Cash requirements analysis
- Analysis of sales variances
- Depreciation and amortization
- Pro forma (projected) income statement
- Pro forma balance sheet
- Product or program profitability analysis

Other Good Reasons to Own a Computer

This is a clear instance where "the race is to the swift." The use of microcomputers by executives is becoming old stuff: if *you* don't do it, you could easily lose out to competitors who do. It helps make the right decisions, fast, because all the information needed is at your fingertips. But there are other uses of these little electronic powerhouses that can make a big difference in your staff's productivity as well as your own. Here we can only review them briefly.

The productivity that computers make possible.   To put it in general terms first, a computer is an extremely fast and reliable robot that can store, organize, find, retrieve, and print (if desired) masses of the information with which you have to deal constantly, and one that never tires or gets sick (well, not often). Think of it as a combination of typist, private secretary, file clerk, copy machine, and calculator rolled into one, and you'll get a rough idea of its capabilities.

Some more specific ways to use your personal computer are:

- To send or receive "flash" reports up or down the line, either by direct link or with a diskette or a printout. You can even communicate with other computers.

- To act something like a telex machine, for communicating written messages and data to others inside or outside the unit or firm. (As with a telex, you can transmit at any time of the day or night and leave the message to be read later. This is what electronic mail and "bulletin boards" are all about.)

- To act as a private secretary who never forgets to remind you about appointments, finds phone numbers quickly (even dials them), helps you manage your time, and handles your executive files efficiently. (I have a program that beeps at me while I'm writing this and flashes a reminder about a phone call I have to make!)

- To use with software that provides training programs for mastering specific management skills, some of which simulate real-world situations.

Improving office and sales productivity.   Quite aside from using the micro yourself, there are numerous ways to improve productivity and accuracy in many areas of your organization by using a microcomputer.

- Keeping your books and printing financial reports. This can include anything from your journals and general ledger to your receivables, payables, payrolls, and inventory. This can mean, if you wish, preparation of computerized billing, posting, and statement preparation; purchase order, receiving report, invoice entry, voucher, and check preparation; automatic inventory updates (even reorders) for sales, purchases, and completed production; job cost tracking; budgetary control and variance reporting. In fact, you name it. If there is a regular business record-keeping activity, somebody smart has already designed computer software to automate it.

- Handling correspondence and direct mail fundraising. Many nonprofits start using computers when they discover how powerful they are for writing (not just typing) letters, direct mail pieces, proposals, contracts, or other kinds of documents. (You're already flooded with computerized sales and charitable appeals. These use the computer's ability to merge a form letter with a mailing list, inserting into the text the date, name, address, and salutation—even inserting your name or other personal information, such as how much was given last time.) Lawyers often use computers in writing standard contracts (they call them "boilerplate"), by assembling paragraphs from computer files and inserting the client's or other party's name automatically wherever it is to appear.

● Doing marketing and analysis. Analysis by program, type of service rendered, territory, or client/patient is "a piece of cake" for a micro. Spreadsheet software is often used this way. There are some accounting programs that facilitate this job without the need for separate software.

● Managing information. Computers automate information management of all kinds, not just for accounting: tracking of employee activity for productivity analysis, for example, third-party billing, or client or patient tracking.

Specialized Software Available

You can find PC software for all kinds of applications listed in computer magazines and catalogues (see the lists later in this appendix). Here is a list of examples that have been advertised:

- Fund accounting
- Project management
- Fundraising and pledge tracking
- Mailing list management
- Desk-top publishing (newsletters, catalogues, etc.)
- Personnel management and pension management
- Real estate: rental property management
- Construction management
- Investment management

There is undoubtedly software available for still other industries and uses; you just have to look for it. Computer user groups exist as well as computer societies and clubs in many cities, not to mention computer "bulletin boards" you can access with a modem. These resources can all be gold mines of information.

How *Not* to Go About Getting Your First Computer

After all those glowing words about the marvel that is the microcomputer, it's time for a serious note of caution about buying one. Most people don't rush into a marriage or a partnership, or, if they do, they're often sorry. Though buying a computer isn't quite so serious a step, you may well spend as much of your life with a PC as you do with a spouse or partner, so the parts of the system you buy must be as compatible with *you* as they are with each other.

Many personal computers have ended up ignobly as very expensive doorstops. Aside from the investment involved, computers do take some time to learn. (Don't believe those alluring ads that speak of how "user-friendly" they are; that is true only in a relative sense.) Before you decide to buy one, be prepared to invest some time and feel frustration in your rite of passage to that magical new world. If you can handle that, you'll be very happy you did.

A Hard Look at Hardware

Don't approach buying the hardware as you would buying a typewriter or other office appliance, where what you see is what you get ("WYSIWYG," in today's jargon). Most of today's PCs work quite well, and a salesperson can easily persuade you that any one of them is the greatest thing since sliced bread! The problem is that what you see is a piece of hardware that is only *potentially* wonderful. (We use the shorthand "PC" throughout, although it usually refers to IBM-compatible computers. Their leading competitor for serious use is the Macintosh made by Apple.)

Think of the choice as though you were deciding whether to buy a VCR with a VHS or Beta format. Even if you preferred the picture on the Beta machine, you'd have to consider whether you could find blank or prerecorded cassettes for it. (On the East Coast, at least, my family has started to have trouble finding them for our Beta VCR.) "What has that to do with a computer?" I can hear you ask. It's the same problem exactly: Remember that a computer is basically a dumb machine. The programs you load into it tell it what to do. And when you find that "absolutely marvelous program," like the ones just described, it has to work on the machine you own—or forget it!

That's just another way of saying that first you find the right software and then you get the hardware. The problem is that computer stores are really in business to sell hardware, where the big markup is. The software is a sideline (like tape for a VCR) that few sales clerks know enough about to help you very much. The point is to know what you want before you go shopping, not just to go see what's on the shelf.

Don't be a Soft Touch for Software

Point number two: The hype in the highly competitive computer field is like that in any other. If you go by the ads or brochures that describe software programs, each one is miraculous and better than the next. Promotional pitches tell the truth in nearly all cases, but what they don't say may be more important than what they do. Even if a program does all the things the ad says it does, the way it does them may be clumsy. Furthermore, it may not do something you assume it will. (The ads never tell you what the products can't do!) The only way to be safe, therefore, is to go by what they call an "A/B" comparison test in the hi-fi stores: Compare the features of competing software side by side, after making a list of which are the most important to you.

If all these warnings have you a bit nervous about the whole thing, don't despair. Just watch your step! If you're asking yourself who has time for all this, you're on the right track. After all, you go to doctors or lawyers for their expertise rather than going to medical or law school yourself. What you need here, too, is a genuinely knowledgeable specialist (sometimes two different ones) who does have the time and can avoid your wasting time chasing down blind alleys.

The reason it sometimes takes two is that, unless you're lucky, computer experts rarely understand your own needs in more than a generic or superficial way. (That includes sales clerks.) They may be able to help you with the more generalized types of software, such as spreadsheet or word processing programs, but when it comes to the more specialized applications, especially various accounting functions or software designed for a particular kind of program, you need someone to interpret for you. Now that you see both the potentials and the pitfalls, we can look at a sensible way to go about computerizing that takes both into consideration.

A Common-Sense Plan

Here is a step-by-step approach that puts first things first and can save you some of the time and headaches many people have experienced.

Step one: Learning the buzz words.   This is not a detailed glossary of computer terms, but merely a list of those that come up repeatedly in conversations with the experts:

● CPU (central processing unit). This is the computer itself. The other components (keyboard, monitor, printer) are called the peripherals.

● Keyboard. This means just what you think it means. (For general business use, forget about a joystick or light pen, two other "input" devices.) Most keyboards are basically the same as that of a typewriter, except that they usually have a few special keys added with labels like "Enter," "Cntrl," "Alt," and the like, the uses of which you may have to learn from the user's manual, just as you would for a new car. The "mouse" is an input device gaining favor.

● Monitor. (Also called the VDT, for video display terminal, or CRT, for cathode ray tube.) They come in two types, color and monochrome (which may be black and white, black and yellow, etc.). You pay for color, as you would in a TV set, which is almost the same thing electronically. Mine can pinch-hit as a boob tube.

● Modem. This is an optional device that lets you plug your computer into a telephone line so that you can communicate with other computers. It also makes possible access to services that can put incredible amounts of information at your fingertips, as though your monitor is located in the New York Public Library. This aspect of using a PC is one you should explore for its own sake: To some people, it is the most important reason to own one.

● Operating system. Watch out for this one. Older IBM computers and compatibles use one called MS.DOS or PC.DOS; the hot new IBM PC, the PS/2, uses one called OS/2; and both use a different one from the Apple and Macintosh lines—not to mention other hardware that uses still others. This subject is the meat of experts. The operating system may itself be a specialized type of software of which part or all resides in the hardware itself, in dedicated (specialized) types of computers. (Program software is usually called application software, to distinguish it from operating system software.)

● Printer. This looks like a typewriter without a keyboard (and some typewriters double as printers), but the choice of which to buy can sometimes be a key one. Printers differ in speed, the kind of typefaces they can generate, and other features that can be important to you. And they too must be fully compatible with your CPU and program software. You can do without a printer for some personal uses, but not for business use.

● RAM (random access memory). This is the working memory of the computer. Think of it as the room you have on your desk for the papers you're shuffling today. The bigger your desk is, the more room you have to work with. (But you can pile papers in layers on your desk, if you're like me. You can't in RAM.) Size has generally been stated in "Ks," or kilobytes. (One K equals 1,000 characters. 2 Ks equal about one double-spaced page of typing.) (You will also run across the term ROM, meaning read-only memory, the kind you can read but not change.) The RAM size is important, especially if you use programs that are so-called "space hogs" or want to use two or more programs at the same time, which you can do with some types.

● Storage (or mass storage). This generally means the permanent memory, as distinct from the working memory (RAM). Think of it as the filing cabinets where you *should* keep all that stuff on your desk when you're not using it. Most PCs for business use have a hard disk inside, which may store as much as 40 to 80 times the data that the RAM can hold. This is an important feature to look for, since you can run out of room for data such as accounting records, correspondence files, etc. You need room for your programs as well, some of which use up a lot of room.

• Diskettes. Better known as floppies, these come in two sizes now: 5¼", the traditional size, and the newer 3½" size. You will handle a lot of these, since the software you buy usually comes in this form. They're also the most common way to "back up" your hard disk files, just in case anything goes wrong with your computer. File backup should become almost a religious observance! There are other more efficient methods available, if you're willing to spend money to save time. They involve buying additional hardware.

You will hear other terms, but most of us "nontechies" have little occasion to use them. You'll rarely need to deal with the names or different types of program languages, or with compilers or interpreters.

Step two: Deciding how to use your PC.   You don't have to buy all the headaches yourself in order to get the benefit of computers, although not many people will tell you that. There are three ways to approach computer use, and you may want to adopt two or even all three for different purposes:

1. You can operate on a 100 percent do-it-yourself basis, which means you have to find the right software, learn how to use it right, and deal with any bugs in it or in your hardware (not that bugs happen so often).

2. You can send some of your "laundry" to a service center to process. Many firms with PCs don't use them for payroll work, which is the biggest nuisance in accounting; they leave this to service centers, many of which can take the payroll data by phone. Others have a center do everything in the bookkeeping area and use the PC only for such things as spreadsheets and word processing. The finished laundry is picked up, mailed, or delivered in printed form, ready to read and use. Usually a copy is kept of whatever is sent for use in the interim.

3. There is still a third option that some firms find a good compromise. They use a modem to connect their PC with a service center that provides what is called time-sharing. That means you use the center's mainframe computer, and its frequently superior software, and speed, to process your own data, delivering your laundry *via your own computer's printer.* You thereby save the time it takes to get data to and from the service center, usually at least a few days. You also save the cost of their entering your data manually, so it's much cheaper. (Or you can get a better printout delivered by mail or courier.)

Don't jump off the dock. If you are going to learn how to use a computer for the first time, it's not a good idea to use a program that will take a lot of learning itself. Until you're comfortable with a PC, you'll do well to use it for something that comes fairly naturally, like word processing. Unless you're a stranger to a typewriter, you'll find that a word-processing program not only is understood easily but makes typing itself much less frustrating. The more sophisticated electronic typewriters that have been on the market awhile can do some of the same things, only not as well.

If you're not interested in doing your own typing, your secretary can learn to use the PC for that, when you're not using it. In that case the first software you use should be a spreadsheet program, which takes a bit more getting used to. Don't plunge in and try playing it by ear. Just as a typewriter or word processor confronts you with a blank sheet of paper to type on, a spreadsheet is like a blank worksheet: You have to create the worksheet data itself. If you want it to make use of the terrific features of most spreadsheet programs, you have to learn how to use them.

You can learn the basic moves without much trouble. It's when you want to do the fancy functions and find the many short-cuts that you need the manual. Take time to study the manual, and do use the tutorial program that comes with the best software. It will save you lots more time in the long run. We'll look at this subject in more depth later.

The last software anyone should start with is an accounting program, however tempting it may look. It's best for a new user to get comfortable in front of that monitor first. After you know your way around the basic features, it will then be time to tackle the complexities of accounting programs, if accounting is to be a major use of your microcomputer.

Your first computer, like the new kid on the block, may have to face resistance from your staff, based on the fear that the computer may cost them their jobs, either because they can't figure it out or because you may need fewer people. (Saving on payroll may in fact be one of the reasons you bought it.) Someone will have to be taught how to use the PC (unless it's only for your own use), and you'll have to decide who is the best choice in terms of availability and talent.

Step three: Calculating what it will cost. How much to budget for the system will of course have to be considered carefully. There is not only the obvious cost of the hardware and software; there are often other costs to be aware of. Accessories, a service contract, training and future support, possible installation or delivery costs not borne by the hardware vendor, furniture, computer supplies, all these need to be budgeted. And you can save yourself time and trouble by engaging a consultant, who rarely works for free. More on that later.

Special system issues to consider. The physical security and accessibility of your computer must be considered. Computers are targets for thieves and people who might want to use them for their own purposes, business or personal (playing games, for example). That suggests that they should be kept locked and anchored. Will more than one person need to use a PC? Will there be arguing over who gets priority? If you can't solve this problem by scheduling who uses it when, you may need more than one machine. Then you may have another problem: What if more than one user has to have access to the same data files? Unless you want to make duplicate copies of your files on floppy diskettes, there are two main approaches to these kinds of problems, and you need a consultant to help you choose between them. They are called local area networks (LANs) and multiuser systems and may take different hardware and investments of funds. For example, LANs usually involve using separate computers, whereas multiuser systems may permit using only a single computer plus two or more terminals, which may cost less altogether. This is a complex and rapidly changing field, so be careful.

How much is it worthwhile to spend? You can apply the approaches shown in Appendix 7A. A computer consultant may be able to help you in this area. The issue of how long the investment will take to pay back its cost is more complicated. Your return on investment should be measured in less tangible ways: you will need to consider the increased bottom line resulting from making the whole agency operate more efficiently and effectively.

Step four: Choosing the system. You can't expect to find out here which hardware or software is best for you, because situations and needs vary. But a checklist of things to cover should be of some help.[12]

A checklist for computerization:

1. Consider using a consultant, as discussed above. (Don't just go to a store.)

2. Evaluate and choose (1) software, (2) hardware (see above). Don't forget that they must be *compatible*, or they're a useless combination.

3. Rank features: essential versus desirable (establish priorities).
   a. What can it do? Is it *really* "user-friendly"? (How long will it take to get used to?)

   b. Are the different functions (modules, etc.) integrated? Will they interact with each other automatically?

   c. What are the procedures for saving data to the hard disk? For making backups? Any special features for these?

   d. What about security? (Can you limit access to certain files or functions with a password?)

   e. Will the hardware and software meet your foreseeable needs regarding capacity? Can the system expand with you, without having to be replaced?

   f. How fast is the printer? Can it print letter quality or near letter quality (NLQ) that is satisfactory for your needs? Is it fully compatible with the software you expect to use? How does it handle any graphics you plan to use?

4. Check quality of "documentation" (a readable and usable instruction manual, etc.) and user support by vendors, including warranties, service contracts, updates for improvements.

5. Ask for a list of present users of the software, and ask them their experience with it. (The vendor should be proud to give you some names in your immediate area.)

6. Shop among vendors: manufacturers, stores, discount houses, and mail order houses. How long has a vendor been in business? How long has the particular product been on the market? Brand new ones may sound exciting but are untested and may have undiscovered bugs.

7. Follow these steps in the installation.
   a. Arrange for expert installation and training (by vendor or consultant). (It's not as easy as it may sound to install software yourself, and this can take a lot of time until you get it right.)

   b. Continue manual parallel processing of records until you're sure everything is working fine, for several months at least.

   c. Order supplies (paper, diskettes, etc.).

The following section has some additional resources you should find useful in your exploration of this brave new world.

Some Computer Resources

Keeping abreast of developments.   If you are new to the PC world, you'll soon discover what a fast-changing field it is, especially in the software area. This is one product that takes very little

---

[12]There are publications that go more deeply into this than space permits here. One is a free pamphlet published by the U.S. Small Business Administration, called "How to Get Started with a Small Business Computer," by M. M. Stewart and A. C. Shulman (Management Aid No. 2.027). It offers more detailed checklists in all areas that must be considered.

capital to develop and produce. It comes out of the teeming brains of thousands of "hackers," who made the industry one of the greatest Cinderella stories in history. Therefore it's essential to keep up with the latest developments, which books can't do. Computer magazines are your main source of news, leads on resources, and even a certain amount of know-how. Several of them contain listings of available hardware and software; all write reviews of the leading makes, and needless to say, all have numerous ads for new products that you can explore further.

Because of the dynamics of the software field, one thing to be aware of is that software companies keep updating and improving their products and label each new update or revision with a "version" or "release" number. It's important to know which version you're getting, therefore, and whether it is the latest. Some versions may not be compatible with your hardware.

Computer resources.   There have been dozens of books and periodicals in this field, some of which are no longer around. A few are listed here to get you started, but this is not to say that they are necessarily the best or most up to date. Libraries, book stores, and magazine racks are a good place to start, but you'll find that some material is intended for programmers or advanced users, so you can't go just by the title. If you want to find what's best for your needs, ask someone knowledgeable. (Reference librarians are, incidentally, one of the most valuable and least known resources for just about anything in print.)

Software testing and rating service.   Some commercial PC periodicals also review software. One publication that resembles *Consumer's Report* in that it accepts no advertising and *only* does comparative reviews and ratings is *The Software Digest Ratings Report*, One Winding Drive, Philadelphia, PA 19131.

Books on personal computers.   There are so many books on computers that choosing any of them is probably unfair. Most of them are general books on using a PC for various purposes. Instead of a list of such books, therefore, here is a list of publishers offering "how-to" books on one or more of the following subjects: (1) learning to use a PC; (2) learning to use spreadsheet software; (3) setting up specific types of Lotus 1-2-3 spreadsheets. Many of these books not only teach you how to set up specific worksheets but offer templates on diskettes to do it *for* you, which you can order from them. (These most commonly relate to Lotus 1-2-3 or other Lotus products, such as Symphony or Jazz. If you choose spreadsheet software other than Lotus 1-2-3, the specific keystrokes may be somewhat different; but your own software may be able to convert the templates from Lotus 1-2-3 to its own format.) The best idea is to write or phone for a catalogue. (Note that Lotus and 1-2-3, as well as Symphony and Jazz, are trademarks of Lotus Development Corp.)

Some publishers specializing in books on computers and software.
Curtin & London, Inc., P.O. Box 363, Marblehead, MA 01945
Osborne McGraw-Hill, 2600 Tenth St., Berkeley, CA 94710
Prentice-Hall (Bracy Computer Books), Englewood Cliffs, NJ 07632.
Que Corp., 11711 North College Ave., Carmel, IN 46032
Central Computer Products/4-5-6 World, P.O. Box 803, Fillmore, CA 93015 (a catalogue house of Lotus-compatible software)
Computronix, Inc., 46C Route 303, Valley Cottage, NY 10989 (also a catalogue house with Lotus plus other interesting software packages for business)

Computer-based self-study.   Self-training programs are the most up to date and effective way to learn how to use computers or software. The following are companies that supply such training programs specifically for Lotus products; some use videotape as well as computer diskettes:

American Management Assn., 9 Galen Street, Watertown, MA 02172
American Training International, 12638 Beatrice St., Los Angeles, CA 90066
Edutrends, 25 Clifton Rd., Oak Ridge, NJ 07438
Intellisance Corp., 1885 Lundy Ave., San Jose, CA 95131-1899
McGraw-Hill Training Systems, 1221 Ave. of the Americas, New York, NY 10020
Microworx, 12983 Ridgedale Dr., Minnetonka, MN 55434

Where to find a consultant.   Some of the computer chains have genuine experts of various kinds, who are usually based in certain of their stores. In the Boston Yellow Pages directory, consultants are listed under "Computers—System Designers & Consultants" and "Computers—Software & Services." You can also locate a consultant by asking around, preferably among people in agencies that are similar to yours in size and services offered. Or you can contact the Independent Computer Consultants Association, Box 27412, St. Louis, MO 63141, for the name of someone in your area. (Their WATS line number is 800-GET-ICCA.) A few words of caution are necessary first, however.

How to Choose the Consultant.

1. Perhaps it's not necessary to persuade you not to choose someone who can make money from the sale of a product he or she recommends, unless you've already decided which product you want.

2. Get recommendations from a consultant's present or former clients, not only in writing but also by follow-up direct contact.

3. Ask about the consultant's background and credentials regarding training and experience, not only as a technical expert but also as a consultant. These don't necessarily require the same skills. If you can do some sort of credit check, it might help avoid hiring a deadbeat.

4. Get everything you can in writing: what specific services will be provided, how long they should take to finish, what they should accomplish for you, and some estimate of what the total cost will be, even if an hourly or daily rate is quoted. You might be able to agree on a schedule of stages, to be paid for as each is completed.

5. A good consultant should not present you with canned solutions, but should first become thoroughly familiar with just what you need and take it from there. You should usually be offered options and alternatives that look at the most cost-effective solutions, not just the quickest and cheapest ones.

6. Finally, your consultant should deal with the questions of installation, training, and future support, whether he or she is to provide any of them or not. As a matter of fact, all of the issues raised above under "Step four: Choosing the system," should be considered whether you're dealing with a consultant or handling the job yourself.

Note: Appendix 11C is adapted from Arnold J. Olenick, *Managing to Have Profits*, McGraw-Hill, New York: 1989, and is used with permission.

Chapter 12

Keeping the Books:
A Step-by-Step Guide to
Do-it-Yourself Accounting

This chapter is designed for practical use by anyone entrusted with the responsibility for "keeping the books," whether or not books, in the conventional sense, are actually used. It adopts a cookbook approach, a step-by-step how-to-do-it kit for putting into practice the "why we do it this way" represented by Chapters 10 and 11. Use it as an owner's manual or instructions for assembly, when and as needed.

Here we will describe in detail how to operate the alternative systems, from simple to complex, that were more generally described in Chapter 11, and will additionally develop in greater detail the accounting model itself. We will show you how to use full double-entry books, using debits and credits in a self-balancing system. This chapter is a primer (or refresher) on the subject.

HOW TO USE THE CASH RECEIPTS WORKSHEET (Fig. 12-1)

1. Larger amounts received should be entered individually, once in the "Total" column, and then classified by an entry in the appropriate distribution column, on the same line.

2. Any other items may be either entered in detail or grouped and entered as a daily or weekly total, if numerous, e.g., many small contributions, dues, or admissions payments. An entry should in each case be made in both the "Total" and the appropriate detail columns. An amount can be split between columns if it combines different types of items, e.g., one check received covering dues plus a contribution.

3. When a deposit is made, it should be for the total of all items in the "Total" column since the last deposit date shown, and the date entered with the amount of the deposit shown, if a separate column is used for the purpose, as recommended. (This permits tracing items deposited, if necessary, and also helps in reconciling the bank statement.)

4. At the end of the month, all columns should be totaled. The combined totals of the detail columns should agree with that of the "Total received" column. The latter's total will agree with that of the "Total deposit" column only if deposits made during the period are only of items

entered in the same period. Otherwise, other items will create a difference between "Total received" and "Total deposited."

5. The columns of this worksheet will then yield the figures for the "Cash receipts" section of your financial report. Only the "Other" (overflow) column will have to be summarized and totaled by category ordinarily, since it will contain items of different kinds. (Accountants call this an "analysis and summary" or "recap.")

Note: Fig. 12–1 illustrates the above.

HOW TO USE THE CASH DISBURSEMENTS WORKSHEETS   (Fig. 12–2)

1. Every check ordinarily is entered individually. However, when a separate payroll worksheet or register is used, the totals of each payroll may be entered on a single line, with the string of payroll check numbers indicated (e.g., "P/R check Nos. 125–135").

2. In the manner described for cash receipts, the amount of the check is entered in both the "Amount of check" column and the appropriate detail columns, splitting the amount between two or more columns whenever more than one account is being charged.

3. If columns for withholdings are carried in the cash disbursements worksheet, payroll checks must be entered in the appropriate gross earnings and deductions columns. (The latter are *negative* columns, of course, indicating subtractions from gross, and must be so used in balancing the worksheet later. Payments to governments of taxes withheld will cancel the withheld amounts.)

4. The employer's payroll taxes (the balance of social security, disability, and unemployment taxes) are expenses.

5. Payments representing loans or installment contracts are balance sheet transactions, not expenses, except for any interest included.

6. The worksheet should be totaled monthly (or whenever carried over to a new page) and the column totals balanced; i.e., the detail columns should add across to the total column. (Any deduction columns should of course be subtracted from the combined totals of the other detail columns in verifying the balance.)

Note: Fig. 12–2 illustrates the above.

BREAKING DOWN REVENUES AND EXPENSES BY PROGRAM

When a dual coding or classification scheme is used to break down revenues and expenses by program and function, manual journals become somewhat clumsy to use. In addition to the columnar distribution by type of revenue or expense, each entry in a column must be further broken down by program or other function (function here means nonprogram expenses, such as administration or fundraising, as noted previously.) This can be done by entering next to each distribution entry a code number or letter identifying the program or function to which it applies. At the end of the month—or whenever the journal is closed and posted—these codes are summarized at the bottom of each column, so that a single amount can be posted to each account. Alternatively, the columns could be used for programs, and the type of expense indicated by an account code.

Date Received 19xx	Received From	Date Deposited	Total Deposit (Memo)	Total Received (Dr)	Member-ship Dues (Cr)	Contri-butions (Cr)	Admis-sions (Cr)	Tuition (Cr)	Grants Received (Cr)	Special Events (Cr)	OTHER Account	OTHER Amount (Cr)
Jan. 3	QRS Foundation	Jan. 3	5,000	5,000					5,000			
4	I. Gottbucks			1,000		1,000						
5	Patrons—Advanced Ticket Sales	5	1,300	250			250					
5	Sundry Small Cash Donations			50		50						
10	Dues—19xx (10 members)	10	300	300	300							
15	Sales of Theater Party Tickets			200							200		
20	MNO Foundation	20	3,200	3,000					3,000			
25	Ticket Sales (at Door)	26	200	200			200					
30	Sales—Theater Party Tickets	30	150	150							150		
31	Last National Bank	31	2,000	2,000								Loan from Bank	2,000
	Total Received for Period		12,150	12,150	300	1,050	450		8,000	350		2,000

FIGURE 12-1. CASH RECEIPTS WORKSHEET (OR JOURNAL).
For the Period January 19xx

Note: Where "(Dr)" or "(Cr)" are shown in column headings, they apply only to the use of these forms as journals in a full double-entry system, and mean "debit" or "credit," as explained later.

Note: This procedure applies to all manual bookkeeping systems, whether worksheets, standard journals, or one-write journals.

DOUBLE-ENTRY BOOKKEEPING

It may seem a bit intimidating to the uninitiated, but a set of double-entry books is nothing more than a well-designed system for sorting and filing information about the finances and operations of an organization for retrieval when needed. Bookkeeping operates under a clearly defined set of rules no more complicated than those of any parlor game, and it is easy to master. Once learned, the bookkeeping rules open wide the bookkeeping process itself and aid in the understanding of the financial reports based on it and for which it exists.

The reports are designed to depict, in summary fashion, the actual events in the life of the organization that are measurable in dollars. They show where it stands financially. These economic exchanges in which the enterprise engages with other entities or individuals may include buying and selling[1] goods or services for cash or on credit, and paying or receiving the related funds. It is the duality of these exchanges—what was given, what was received—that creates the need for double-entry, so that both aspects of each exchange are accounted for.

Keeping Double-Entry Books on a Cash Basis

As discussed in Chapter 10, cash basis accounting, the simplest method, does not fully record economic events. The period in which it records an event is the one in which payment occurs. The fact that the other part of the exchange may have occurred in a different period is ignored, which may distort its significance.

Nonetheless, from a purely mechanical standpoint, double-entry books can be kept on a cash basis. What was given or received for the money is also recorded, even though it may be in the wrong period, i.e., the one in which the cash settlement occurs, not when the goods or services were supplied.

Five categories of accounts used in cash basis bookkeeping follow:

1. Assets (cash, equipment, etc.)

2. Liabilities (loans or withholding taxes owed)

3. Expenses (services paid for: salaries, utilities, etc.)

4. Revenues (payments for services rendered: dues, subscriptions, etc.)

5. Fund balance (the difference between total assets and total liabilities on the balance sheet at the end of a period).

A separate page ("account") in the general ledger is reserved for each specific account in each of these categories. As an exchange occurs, an entry is made in a journal, recording both sides of the transaction: what was paid (or received) and what it was paid for. The journal is used to list these

---

[1]The word "selling" will often have a meaning somewhat different from its meaning in a business context, particularly when free services are provided.

Date Paid 19xx	Paid to	Check No.	Net Amount Cash (Cr)	Payroll Exp. (Dr)	Office Exp. (Dr)	Office Supp. (Dr)	Program Supplies (Dr)	Prof. & Consltg. Fees (Dr)	Stationery & Printing (Dr)	Travel Exp. (Dr)	Utilities Exp. (Dr)	OTHER Account	OTHER Amount (Dr)
Jan. 2	Speedyprint Corp. (Xeroxing)	101	20		20								
4	Best Variety Stores, Inc.	102	10			10							
7	Payroll (Week ended 1/6/xx)	103	700	700									
10	Edison Electric Corp.	104	65								65		
14	Payroll (Week ended 1/13/xx)	105	700	700									
15	Western Airlines, Inc. (for ED)	106	150							150			
15	Budget Motels Corp.	107	60							60			
20	I. Knowall, PC	108	200					200					
21	ABX School Outfitter, Inc.	109	120				120						
21	Payroll (Week ended 1/20/xx)	110	700	700									
24	Tops Office Supply	111	50			15			35				
25	Tops Office Supply–Typewriter	112	300									Office Equipment	300
28	Payroll (Week ended 1/27/xx)	113	750	750									
30	Best Variety Stores, Inc.	114	15			15							
30	Internal Revenue Service	115	900									Pay. Taxes Withheld	600
												Pay. Tax Expense	300
Total Paid for Period			4,740	2,850	20	40	120	200	35	210	65		1,200

FIGURE 12–2. CASH DISBURSEMENTS WORKSHEET (OR JOURNAL).
For the Period January 19xx

Note: Where "(Dr)" or "(Cr)" are shown in column headings, they apply only to the use of these forms as journals in a full double-entry system, and mean "debit" or "credit," as explained later.

exchanges in chronological order and to assign each to two accounts (sometimes more), in which its twofold aspects are to be recorded later. Since the system is designed to be self-balancing, it is based on a simple algebraic equation, which must be kept in balance:

Debits ——————→ Equal ——————→ Credits

What is received = What is given in exchange

(funds, goods, or services) (funds, goods, or services)

(Asset) Cash (received)	Cash (paid: Asset reduced)
(Asset) Equipment, etc. (received)	Equipment, etc. (reduction of asset: disposed of)
(Liability paid) (reduced)	(Liability) Promise to pay giver
(Expense) Services received (called "expenses," which represent the price of such services)	(Revenues) Services rendered (the *price* of services rendered, not necessarily rendered to those paying for them, in a nonprofit)
	Fund balance. (Total assets minus total liabilities)

Each account in the ledger is usually shaped like a "T," although a third (balance) column is sometimes added. The vertical line of the "T" represents the equals (=) sign in the equation. Entries on the left of this line are called "debits," those on the right "credits." (The terms do *not* by themselves mean increase or decrease, for that depends on the normal balance of a particular account.)[2] Typical ledger account formats look like this:

T-account format

CASH

(Debit side)	(Credit side)

Account with balance column

CASH

Debit	Credit	Balance

Derived from the above model, the rules are as follows.

Type of account	Normal or positive balance	Therefore, entries for	
		Increases are:	Decreases are:
Assets	Debit	Debits	Credits
Expenses	Debit	Debits	Credits
Liabilities (debts)	Credit	Credits	Debits
Revenues	Credit	Credits	Debits
Fund balance	Credit	Credits	Debits

(A deficit is a negative balance in a Fund Balance account, and therefore appears as a Debit balance.)

[2]The word "charge" is also used as a substitute for "debit."

Some typical transactions would be classified thus in a journal, applying these rules as follows:

			Entry for accounts affected	
Accounts affected	Type	Direction	Debit	Credit
1. Cash paid for employee services received: $300				
a. Salary expense	Expense	Increase	$ 300	
b. Cash	Asset	Decrease		$ 300
2. Cash received on a grant: $100,000 (for program services to be performed)				
a. Cash	Asset	Increase	10,000	
b. Grant received	Revenue	Increase		10,000
3. Money borrowed: $2,000 (for promise given to repay)				
a. Cash	Asset	Increase	2,000	
b. Loan from X	Liability	Increase		2,000
4. Loan payment: $1,000 (promise partially redeemed)				
a. Loan from X	Liability	Decrease	1,000	
b. Cash	Asset	Decrease		1,000

Note: The headings in the above format may be used as a guide to determine the entries required for any given transaction, using the rules stated above.

Hint: *Think Cash.* Once you begin to recognize increases and decreases in Cash as debits and credits, respectively, the other side of each entry (source or use of cash) must be the opposite (credit or debit, respectively).

Actually, separate columnar journals are used for cash receipts and cash disbursements, and the columns are headed with the names of the accounts most frequently affected, with "debit" or "credit" also shown in the heading (or their abbreviations, "Dr" or "Cr"). This makes the above process nearly a mechanical one for most entries. What is more, since entries in the cash receipts journal represent increases to Cash, the cash column will always be a "debit" column, the others therefore "credit" columns. Similarly, in the cash disbursements journal, the cash entry is a "credit" (decrease), the others are therefore normally "debits."[3]

Typical journals are illustrated above. Note that these forms are essentially identical, whether used in a worksheet system, or as journals in a double-entry bookkeeping system. In the latter case, one of three forms of books may be used to hold the journal pages, all of which are available from commercial stationers. Twelve- or 13-column forms are recommended.

- A bound journal, with an adequate number of blank columns, plus item space at left.

- A "post-binder," which uses loose journal page fillers and thus usually costs less in the long run.

- A standard loose-leaf binder, which uses journal fillers punched for a three-ring binder.

The arrangement of column headings depends only on what is most convenient, since labeling a column "Dr" or "Cr" means it can be on the left *or* right. It is not related to whether a manual or "one-write" system is used.

[3]Payroll deductions, if shown in this journal, would also be "credit" columns since they would represent increases in liability accounts.

General Ledger Entries

After all entries for the period (usually a month) have been made in each journal, all of the columns are totaled and balanced across,[4] and the "Overflow" ("Other" or "Sundry") column is analyzed and summarized. In these respects, the journal operates the same way as the worksheet described above, which in fact it closely resembles.

However, instead of using these records as the direct source of financial reports, with all the problems that entails (see Chapter 11), the monthly figures from each journal are transferred and entered ("posted") to the general ledger accounts, following the directions in the column headings as to the account name and whether to enter as a "debit" or "credit" (i.e., on the left side or right side).

To illustrate, using the four transactions worked out above, the eight amounts from the four transactions would be posted (entered) as shown below. (The items are cross-referenced by number to the transactions above.)

Cash				Salary expense	
(increases)		(decreases)			
(2a)	10,000	(1b)	300	(1a)	300
(3a)	2,000	(4b)	1,000	(services received)	
	12,000		1,300		
(Balance = 10,700)					

Grants received

	(2b)	10,000
(services to be performed)		

Loan from X

(decrease)		(increase)	
(4a)	1,000	(3b)	2,000
(promise partially redeemed)		(promise given to repay)	
		(Balance = 1,000)	

One arrangement popular with accountants is to group related accounts on a single page, creating what they call a "railroad account," with one column for total and the others for details, such as the part of a given expense charged to each program and function. It not only saves turning pages; it speeds statement preparation.

To provide a cross-reference for tracing entries when necessary, each page in the journal should be numbered, and each posting to the ledger should include this posting reference (e.g., "CD 7" = page 7 of the Cash Disbursements journal). Similarly, the number of the general ledger account to which each total or individual amount is posted should be shown next to the item in the journal; e.g., "101" might be the account number for Cash.

---

[4]To make sure the total of the debits equals the total of the credits.

Note that an entry to decrease the balance of an account is *never* made by inserting and subtracting an amount on the side of its balance; all entries on each side *may only be added.* You subtract by making an entry on the opposite side from the balance. (Think of algebra, where moving a variable to the other side of the equal sign changes its sign from positive to negative, etc.) The subtraction is done as a separate calculation and the balance entered in the item space, or balance column if one is provided.

Note the following results from the above postings: If we add the two accounts with "debit" balances (Cash $10,700 plus Salary expense $300), they total $11,000, which equals the sum of the two "credit" balance accounts: (Grants received, $10,000 plus Loan from X, $1,000).

If these were the only accounts and had no previous balances (for example, when the organization began), the balances would represent the following:

1. The balance of Cash available (the Assets)

2. The amount still owed to X (Liability)

3. The revenues collected during the period (Grants received)

4. The expenses paid for the period (Salary expense)

Preparing Simple Financial Reports on the Cash Basis

Cash basis financial statements could then be prepared as follows:

Balance Sheet (cash basis)[5]

Assets—Cash	$10,700	
Equities (see Chapter 10)		
Liabilities—Loan from X	1,000	
Fund Balance (excess of Assets over Liabilities)	9,700	
Total equities	$10,700	(which equals total Assets)

Operating Statement (cash basis)[5]

Revenues received—grants	$10,000	
– Expenses paid—Salaries	300	
= Increase in Fund balance	$ 9,700	(see above)
(Equals Fund Balance above, since it started at zero)		

Note: These are minimal statements, of course, shown only to illustrate how the amounts are used. See Chapter 13 for illustrations and discussion of actual statement formats.

ACCRUAL BASIS ACCOUNTING

As explained in Chapter 10, accrual basis refines the accounting process further, by measuring the timing aspect of *both* sides of an exchange or other event. Its goal is to record not only the

[5]As noted in Chapter 10, statements prepared on a cash basis should be called by names other than those shown above.

period in which a given payment occurred but also the period which *benefited* from funds paid out, or was the one in which the *activity* occurred, for which funds were received.[6] Put another way, revenues are recognized as such (recorded as revenues) in the period "earned." Expenses are matched against the related revenues or period; i.e., a cost associated with earning specific revenue, or with the general operations of a period, is recognized (recorded as expense) during the period that benefited.

But—and this is where the distinction becomes sharper—when the payment occurs in a period different from that of the *recognition* of revenue or expense, the payment is not recorded as revenue or expense but as an asset or liability account set up for that purpose. The process, though not the bookkeeping entries, is fully explained in Chapter 10, and should be studied carefully in conjunction with the following explanation of the bookkeeping entries.

The new types of entries and accounts required to accomplish the above results are as follows.

Type of transaction or exchange	Additional accounts required[7]
1. Expense incurred and recognized currently, prior to payment (expense accrual)	Accrued Expense or Accounts Payable (Liability Accounts)
2. Funds paid in advance for *future* services or benefits (deferral or prepayment of expense, not yet *recognized* as expense)	Prepaid Expense (or Fixed Asset account, for which Depreciation accounting is used) (Asset Accounts)
3. Revenue recognized currently prior to collection (revenue accrual)	Pledges, Grants, or other Accounts Receivable (Asset Accounts)
4. Funds collected in advance for goods or services to be delivered in the future (e.g., tickets, reservations, grants) (deferral of revenue not yet recognized)	Unearned or Deferred Revenue or Advances (Liability Account)

The explanation of how these transactions are handled is explained fully in Chapter 10. The actual bookkeeping entries involved are as follows:

Transaction (numbered as above)	Current entry and types of account used[7]	Subsequent entry and types of account used
1. Expense accrual (and later payment)	Dr. Expense account Cr. Liability account	Dr. Liability account Cr. Cash
2. Expense prepayment (and later recognition of portion actually used)	Dr. Prepaid expense Cr. Cash	Dr. Expense account Cr. Prepaid Expense (see also entries for Depreciation of fixed assets)
3. Revenue accrual (and later collection)	Dr. Receivable account Cr. Revenue account	Dr. Cash Cr. Receivable account
4. Revenue deferral (and later recognition of portion earned)	Dr. Cash Cr. Unearned or Deferred revenue	Dr. Unearned Revenue Cr. Revenue account

---

[6] The business analogy for the activity would be the period in which the funds were *earned* by the delivery of goods or services.

[7] Actual specific accounts would be used instead of the generic account names shown (see "Chart of Accounts").

Note that current transactions 2 and 4 are cash disbursements and cash receipts, respectively, and are entered in the journals provided for the purpose, which should provide the appropriate column headings (in addition to "Cash") if such items are common. They should otherwise be entered in the "Overflow" column.

Transactions 1 and 3 may, if frequent, require special journals (illustrated in Figs. 12–3A and 12–3B for accruing expenses (Accounts Payable Journal or Register) or accruing revenues (Accounts Receivable Journal or Register, or more relevant title). If such items are infrequent, they may be entered instead through the General Journal, which has only "debit" and "credit" columns and can handle any type of entry (Fig. 12–4).

Periodic adjusting entries are also required, and will be described in the next section.

Date	VENDOR	Accounts Payable (Cr)	Program Supplies (Dr)	Professional & Consulting (Dr)	Office Expense (Dr)	Stationery & Printing (Dr)	Travel Expense (Dr)	Utilities Expense (Dr)	Office Supplies (Dr)	OTHER		
										Account	PR	Amount (Dr)

FIGURE 12–3A. ACCOUNTS PAYABLE JOURNAL/REGISTER
Month of _____, 19xx

Date	Source	Accounts (Pledges) Receivable (Dr)	Pledge Revenue (Cr)	Dues Earned (Cr)	Program Revenues (Cr)	OTHER		
						Account	PR	Amount (CR)

FIGURE 12–3B. ACCOUNTS RECEIVABLE JOURNAL/REGISTER
Month of _____, 19xx

Date	Accounts	PR	DR	CR

FIGURE 12–4. GENERAL JOURNAL

Note: "PR" column is for inserting the "posting reference," i.e., the account number to which posted.

SIMPLIFIED ACCRUAL BASIS

This is a hybrid system, widely used, and is a compromise between the Cash Basis and full accrual.

Advantages of Simplified Accrual Basis

- It simplifies daily use of the bookkeeping system, which is maintained on a Cash Basis during the year.

- It permits preparing Accrual Basis statements at the end of any period, by adjusting the accounts for incomplete exchanges, i.e., those in which only one side has been completed by the date of the financial statement (e.g., unpaid bills).

Disadvantages of Simplified Accrual Basis

- It does not integrate uncollected revenues due or unpaid expenses incurred into the bookkeeping system for follow-up *during* the period.

- It is more prone to error and omissions, due to this lack of integration, especially omission of uncollected or unpaid items at statement date.

- For a nonprofit of any size or complexity, it tends to provide inadequate managerial information on a current basis.

Nonetheless, by using the "Substitutes or Short-Cuts" described in Chapter 11, many small nonprofits get by with it fairly well, especially if they have the periodic services (quarterly or at least annually) of a professional accountant.

Procedures for Simplified Accrual Basis

- Same journals are used as in Cash Basis. Thus only cash received and disbursed are routinely recorded.

- At the end of your fiscal year, or whenever a financial statement is required, usually on a monthly or quarterly basis, so-called "adjusting entries" are made in the General Journal and are posted to the General Ledger to adjust the accounts to an accrual basis, for financial statement purposes (see the heading "Adjusting Entries" in the following text).

● Certain entries so posted must then be "reversed" (entered again in the reverse direction) at the beginning of the next month. Alternatively an accountant's worksheet, described below, can be used for interim adjustments, which eliminates the need for reversal entries, since the books themselves are not affected by the adjustments until accounts are "closed" at year-end, as described later.

ADJUSTING ENTRIES

Adjusting entries are those designed to accomplish the following adjustments required by accrual basis accounting, as explained in Chapter 10.

1. *To accrue expenses:* unpaid bills or unbilled expenses or taxes at the end of the period. The entries will be made as shown above under "Current entry" (transaction 1). Typical accrued expenses will be for unpaid salaries, payroll taxes (employer's share), professional and consultants' fees, or any other current expenses that were unpaid as of the date in question.

Note: Some small organizations simulate expense accruals by writing checks to pay all their expenses at the end of a month in which an operating statement is to be prepared. They do not mail the checks until there is enough cash to cover them. (This may create an overdraft in your cash balance, which can be viewed as accrued expense or as accounts payable at that date.)

2. *To defer prepaid expenses*, if they were originally charged to a current expense account when paid. Unlike the entry shown in transaction 2, since the payment was not debited to a prepaid expense account, it must now be deferred—i.e., reclassified as prepaid, by an entry like this:

> Dr. Prepaid expense (or a specific account in this category)
>   Cr. Expense (the account previously charged).

The amount entered should represent only the still unused portion of the expense item; i.e., for services not yet received or materials still unused. Any part representing current expense should remain in the current expense account. (Does not apply to expenses deferred when entered.)

3. *To accrue revenues* (where these are recognized for statement purposes), representing uncollected receivables earned as of the date in question. The entries will be made as shown in transaction 3, "Current entry.")

4. *To defer unearned revenues* that were credited to current revenue accounts when collected. Unlike transaction 4, which treats them correctly, since the collection was not in fact credited to a deferred or unearned revenue account, it must now be deferred—i.e., reclassified as deferred as follows:

> Dr. Revenue (the account previously credited)
>   Cr. Deferred (or Unearned) Revenue (or a specific account in that category).

The amount entered should represent only the still unearned portion of the revenue item, and any earned portion left in the revenue account.

5. *To charge off ("amortize") prepaid expense.* Any prepaid expense accounts that already have balances—usually at the beginning of the fiscal year—can either be adjusted to the correct prepaid (unused) balance, by transfer of the used portion to the related expense account (see transaction 2, "Later entry" column), or all such accounts can be closed out entirely to the related expense accounts (see "When to Reverse Entries" below). In the latter case, entry 2 above will again be necessary; in the former, entry 2 is taken care of by this adjustment.

6. *To charge off ("amortize") unearned (deferred) revenues.* Any such accounts that have balances are handled in the same manner as in entry 4: either adjust as shown in transaction 4, "Later entry" column, or close such accounts out to their related revenue accounts by reversal entries (see below). In the latter case, entry 4 above will again be necessary; in the former case, entry 4 above is taken care of by the adjustment.

7. *To recognize depreciation of fixed assets.* This entry is similar in intent to entry 5 above. The portion of each class of fixed asset (e.g., building, vehicles, equipment) used up during the period is calculated as shown below, and an entry made debiting Depreciation expense. The credit is not, however, to the asset account itself, but to an account called "Accumulated Depreciation," which is also identified by the class of asset; for example, Vehicles. Such accounts, which have credit balances, are in effect the credit (decrease) side of the related asset accounts, and are subtracted from such accounts on the balance sheet, rather than on the books themselves. They are called "contra-asset" or "valuation" accounts. In this way the original cost of each fixed asset is still carried and presented to statement users. The entry is shown below.

Depreciation calculations are simple enough: since an asset will eventually be sold or traded in at the end of its useful life, in most cases, its estimated value at that time (called "salvage" or "residual" value) is first subtracted from its cost. The balance is the portion of cost that will be used up during the period owned. The calculation is thus:

$$\text{Annual depreciation} \quad = \quad \frac{\text{Cost} - \text{Salvage value}}{\text{Estimated no. of years of useful life}}$$

If depreciation is calculated for less than a full year—for interim reports, or for an asset bought during the year—the appropriate fraction of the year is multiplied by the annual depreciation.

Illustration: A station wagon was purchased July 1, for $8,400. You expect to use it for four years and then trade it in or sell it for $2,000. For a statement prepared as of September 30 (after the wagon has been owned 3 months), the depreciation expense would be:

$$\text{Annual depreciation} \quad = \quad \frac{8,400 - 2,000}{4} \quad = \quad \$1,600$$

$$\text{Three months' depreciation} \quad = \quad \frac{3}{12} \quad \times \quad \$1,600 \quad = \quad \$400$$

At September 30, Dr. Depreciation—Vehicles $400
              Cr. Accumulated Depr. Vehicles $400

Note: The above is a description of simple "straight-line" depreciation, generally used on books and for financial statements. More complex or specialized calculations for accelerated methods may be used on tax returns to defer any tax or Unrelated Business Income.

8. *To provide for uncollectible receivables or pledges* and for the write-off of losses on uncollectibles.

a. Setting up the allowance. This adjustment is made, like others, at closing or statement dates. It resembles the allowance for depreciation in appearance, since it involves a debit to an expense account, to recognize the estimated loss in value of the asset in the current period, and a credit to an allowance account (contra-asset), which reduces the balance sheet value at which the asset is carried. The amount of the provision is based on one or more of the following analyses: (1) past experience regarding such losses, as a percentage of the annual total of such items (pledges received or program service revenues earned) or of the receivables outstanding; (2) credit standing of those owing the money; or (3) evidence of apparent uncollectibility, based on unsuccessful collection efforts or refusal to pay. For example, if it has been estimated by such analyses that $1,500 of Pledges receivable will be uncollectible, the adjusting entry establishing the allowance would be:

> Dr. Provision for Uncollectible Pledges $1,500   (expense account)
> Cr. Allowance for Uncollectible Pledges $1,500.

The allowance account would be a subtraction from Pledges Receivable on the balance sheet.

b. Handling the write-offs. When information is received that specific receivables have become definitely uncollectible, at any time during the year, a write-off entry may be made. This is not a true adjusting entry, though made through the general journal. If the previous entry setting up the allowance had been made at year end on December 31, 19x1, and actual losses during 19x2 were $1,350, an entry recording the losses would appear as follows:

> Dr. Allowance for Uncollectible Pledges $1,350
> Cr. Pledges Receivable $1,350.

Note: If there is a balance (debit or credit) in the allowance account at the time the adjustment to set up the new allowance is made, the amount in the first entry will generally have to take this into account. Thus, if the first entry setting up the allowance at December 31, 19x1 was being made for the first time, there would be no balance in the allowance account. But at the end of 19x2, before the new adjustment, the account would have a balance of $150: $1,500 minus the write-off of $1,350. If the estimated amount uncollectible at the end of 19x2 was again $1,500 (by coincidence), the amount in the entry setting up the new provision for uncollectibles during 19x3 would have to be not $1,500 but only $1,350, since the account would already have a credit balance of $150, which would bring the new balance to $1,500 after posting the new adjusting entry.

When the provision is based on a percentage of total pledges (or service revenue) received, rather than on the balance outstanding, the amount already in the account need not be considered, however.

Note: Entries writing off receivables as uncollectible are dangerous and should be made only on written authorization from the board or duly authorized officer, since they can be used to cover up misappropriations of collections on the accounts written off.

9. *Allocation entries.* When accounts are maintained and expenses reported on a functional and program basis, any expenses directly chargeable to a function or program are debited to the appropriate program expense account (see Table 12–2). (Handling split invoices and payments is discussed below.) Indirect or overhead expenses are usually allocated periodically by journal entry, either individually or as the total of the group, such as by use of an intermediary account called Administrative and General Expense.

WHAT ACCOUNTS SHOULD WE USE?—THE CHART OF ACCOUNTS

The accounts provided in the general ledger should be chosen with the information required for your financial statements uppermost in mind, as well as what is needed for other purposes, such as budgetary control, analysis of operating and financial performance, and compliance with reporting requirements of funding and regulatory agencies. Each chart must be tailored to the activities of the specific organization. (Two examples of such charts are shown in Tables 12–1 and 12–2). Several important factors to consider in creating a workable chart of accounts follow. You must take into account future needs as well as present ones. Allow for potential expansion in the number and type of accounts, to avoid having to insert account numbers with letters added. (Notice how blocks of account numbers are provided for each category in Tables 12–1 and 12–2.)

Accounts used should lend themselves to the classifications required by reports to funding agencies or regulatory agencies, such as the IRS, your state's charities registration agency, or your parent body, if any, in the case of a local affiliate.

You should decide which specific details are worth measuring separately and which similar ones can be combined into a single account. (Again, this could change over time, when a particular item of revenue or expense grows large enough to keep track of separately.) Otherwise time will be wasted analyzing accounts to obtain needed detail. (The rule is "don't scramble the eggs if you want to separate the whites and yolks later." It is easier to combine accounts than to analyze them.)

If expenses and/or revenues are likely to be reported or analyzed by particular fund, program, activity, or function, the accounts used should make this possible without your having to "unscramble the eggs." It is also important that uniform or similar account names be used for each such fund, program, activity, or function to permit their being added together in operating statements, using the program (or functional) columnar format illustrated in Chapter 13 (Table 13–5).

The most effective uniform account codes consist of a "prefix" of one or two digits identifying the function, followed by a "suffix" of two digits identifying the type of expense—the so-called "natural expense" classification. This is illustrated in Table 12–2.[8]

Related account groupings (assets, expenses, etc.) should be assigned blocks of sequential account numbers, which facilitates statement preparation. For the same reason, groupings should follow the order in which they will appear on financial statements, such as assets, liabilities, and fund balance accounts; revenue accounts, program expenses, fundraising expenses, and administrative expenses.

---

[8]Additional sophistication (and complexity) can be added by using activity prefixes before asset, liability, and fund balance account codes, where the former are assigned to specific activities. This coding is particularly appropriate when fund accounting is used.

TABLE 12-1. ILLUSTRATIVE CHART OF ACCOUNTS (ACCRUAL BASIS)—NO. 1: VOLUNTEER SERVICE ORGANIZATION WITH A SINGLE PROGRAM OR FUND

Balance Sheet Accounts		Operating Statement Accounts	
Acct. No.	Title	Acct. No.	Title
Assets		**Revenues**	
101–104	Cash accounts	400	Membership Dues
105–109	Accounts Receivable	410–419	Contribution accounts (by type, including in-kind)
110–114	Supplies Inventories		
115–119	Prepaid Expense accounts	420–429	Grants Received (specific grants)
120–124	Property and equipment accounts and related accumulated depreciation accounts	430–439	Investment income accounts (interest, dividends)
		440–449	Fundraising and special events
125–199	Other asset accounts (as needed)	450–459	Advertising and other revenues (as needed)
Liabilities and fund balance			
200–204	Accounts Payable	**Expenses**	
205–209	Short-term liability accounts	500–503	Salary accounts
210–214	Payroll Taxes Payable	504	Office Temporaries
215–219	Accrued Expense or Tax accounts	505–509	Payroll tax and fringe benefit accounts
220–224	Unearned (deferred) revenue accounts	510–519	Occupancy expense accounts (rent, utilities, janitorial, insurance expense, repairs, maintenance)
225–229	Long-term debt accounts		
300	Fund Balance account	520–529	Office expense accounts (printing, stationery, postage, supplies used, telephone, equipment rentals, dues and subscriptions, etc.)
		530–539	Transportation (auto, fares, other travel costs)
		540–549	Professional and consulting fees
		550–559	Program expenses
		560–569	Fundraising expenses (mailing, printing, special events)
		570–574	Depreciation expense accounts

**TABLE 12–2. ILLUSTRATIVE CHART OF ACCOUNTS (ACCRUAL BASIS)—NO. 2:
ART CENTER WITH MULTIPLE PROGRAM FUNCTIONS**

Balance Sheet Accounts (account groups)		Suffixes (natural account codes)	
Acct. No.	Title	Acct. No.	Title

Assets

101–109	Cash accounts (general and restricted funds; savings, etc.)		
110–119	Accounts receivable (various)		
120–129	Inventories (supplies, merchandise)		
130–139	Property and equipment accounts and related accumulated depreciation accounts		
150–199	Other asset accounts (as needed)		

Revenues

10–19	Admissions earned accounts (by event or type)
20–24	Tuition earned accounts (by type or course)
25–29	Dues earned (by class of membership)
30–33	Contributions (by type: individual, business)
34	In-kind contributions: goods or services
35–39	Grants (restricted, unrestricted, etc.)
40–44	Special events (by event)
45	Publication sales
46	Advertising revenue
47–49	Investment revenues (interest, dividends, gains)

Liabilities and Fund Balances

200–209	Accounts payable (various)
210–219	Short-term liabilities
220–229	Payroll taxes payable
230–239	Accrued expense and tax accounts
240–249	Advance ticket sales, etc. (subscriptions or single events)
250–259	Other unearned (deferred) revenue accounts (tuition, etc.)
260–269	Long-term debt accounts
300–309	Fund Balance accounts

Expenses

50	Salaries—Administrative
51	Salaries—Other staff
52	Office Temporaries
53	In-kind Services
54–59	Payroll tax and fringe benefit accounts
60–69	Occupancy expense accounts
70–79	Office expense accounts
80–82	Professional and consulting fees
83–89	Other direct activity supplies and expense accounts
90–94	Special events expense accounts
95–99	Depreciation Expense accounts

Operating Statement Accounts

Prefixes (activity codes)

400	Program Activities
500	School Activities
600	Gallery Activities
700	Fund-raising Activities
800	Administration (general)
900	Unallocated Expenses

Note: An account code is formed by adding a two-digit suffix code to the first digit of the above activity codes. Example: School administrative salaries would be account 550 or 500-50.

Account names should be consistent from period to period, to facilitate comparisons. The same revenue and expense categories (accounts) should be used for budgeting as for bookkeeping, if actual performance is to be compared with budget.

Next to each account in the chart of accounts, instructions should be supplied for what type of entries should be entered as debits and as credits. The chart then becomes a bookkeeping manual for entering transactions in journals or coding them for computer input.

The Advantages of Dual Coding

Since similar accounts for each function will have the same two-digit suffix, and all expenses of a function will share the same prefix, the coding scheme is organized and systematic. Also, it expedites preparation of reports and speeds analysis of current expenses, either by function or by type of expense. Computerized bookkeeping virtually requires this approach, but all types benefit from it.

In internal program (functional) statements, or budgets prepared in columnar form, the statement columns may be headed with the appropriate prefix codes ("400," "500," etc.) shown directly under the program and support function headings, with the suffix codes shown next to the related revenue and expense accounts, listed vertically. The resulting matrix format permits reading totals vertically by function and/or horizontally by type of expense, as shown in Table 13–5.

How to Enter a Split Invoice or Payment

A single bill or check may sometimes apply to more than one program. When it is coded for entry, the person responsible has two alternatives, depending on the situation.

1. If the portion that applies to each program is readily apparent, the debit side of the entry is merely split between the two accounts in the amounts indicated; for example, an invoice received for supplies, half for Program "A," half for Program "B." (Alternatively, policy may call for using a certain standard breakdown.)

2. If the item will have to be reallocated later, it may be debited to either account and an adjusting entry made transferring the allocated portion to the other. A general fund account can be used temporarily and split later or a Suspense Account set up and used for all transactions for which the coding is not yet clear, and cleared out later by journal entries.

RECURRING JOURNAL ENTRIES

When interim financials are prepared *during* the year—quarterly or monthly—most adjusting entries required are predictable and can be made most conveniently through a "Recurring Journal" (i.e., one for recurring adjusting entries). This is a form of General Journal with dr. and cr. columns for each quarter (Fig. 12–5) (or month). The standard adjusting entry accounts are entered in the item space provided to the left, as in a worksheet. The specific entries required will depend on whether the full or simplified accrual basis is used (Fig. 12–6).

Entries for full accrual basis: As indicated in Chapter 10, under the heading "What Happens to Accruals and Prepayments Later?" these follow-up adjustments are required.

	First quarter			Second quarter		
	PR	Dr	Cr	PR	Dr	Cr
1. Dr. Expense Accounts Cr. Prepaid Expense Accounts To write off expired insurance, supplies used, etc.[9]						
2. Dr. Unearned Revenue Accounts Cr. Revenue Accounts To recognize earning of revenues received and originally deferred.						
3. Dr. Depreciation Expense Accounts To record allowance for current depreciation, per schedule Cr. Accumulated Depreciation Accounts						
4. Dr. Expense Accounts Cr. Accrued Expenses (Liability Accounts) Estimated expenses not entered in the Accounts Payable Journal.						
5. Dr. Payroll Tax Expense Accounts Cr. Payroll Taxes Payable To record employer's share of social security, unemployment, and other payroll taxes borne by employer						
6. Dr. Accounts Receivable Accounts Cr. Revenue Accounts To record revenues earned but uncollected (this could apply to all or most accrued revenues where no special journal is used to accrue them.)						

FIGURE 12–5.

Another type of recurring entry may be the regular requirement to allocate portions of joint expenses of programs or functions.[10]

Entries for simplified accrual basis: The same recurring entries may be used with the simplified accrual basis. In addition, it may be necessary to add the following entries, as appropriate.

---

[9]Traditionally, explanations for entries are written after the entries as shown, since their purposes are not always self-evident.
[10]See above.

	First quarter			Second quarter		
	PR	Dr	Cr	PR	Dr	Cr
7. Dr. Prepaid Expenses						
Cr. Expense Accounts						
To defer prepaid expenses charged to expense accounts prematurely						
8. Dr. Revenue Accounts						
Cr. Unearned Revenues						
To defer unearned revenues credited prematurely to revenue accounts						

FIGURE 12–6.

Note: A way to simplify further the problem of accruing unpaid expenses and/or taxes (as in entries 4 and 5) is to write checks for all such unpaid items by the end of the period for which financial statements are to be prepared, but to *hold* some of the checks until the bank balance is adequate. This can result in a negative checkbook balance, temporarily. The next step is to make an adjusting entry for the checks being held, as follows.

> Dr. Cash (checking account)
> Cr. Accrued Expenses (& Taxes, if appropriate)
> (or Accounts Payable)

Since the entries for these checks were charged to the appropriate expense accounts in the Cash Disbursements Journal, the net effect of these entries is the same as if the accruals had been made, since there will be debits in the expense accounts and credits to a liability account. (The effect on the cash account is canceled by the entry above.)

THE TRIAL BALANCE KEEPS YOUR BOOKS IN ORDER

It is important to make sure that your books are in balance at the end of each posting cycle, whether monthly or less often. (The less often you balance your books, the harder it will be to locate errors; the longer you wait, the more detail you will have to review.) The proving device is known as a trial balance (not to be confused with a balance sheet). A trial balance is simply a list of all accounts, with debit balances listed in one column and credit balances in another. The total of the two columns should be equal; if not, start hunting down the error (or errors). The steps, depending on the type of error, usually follow this order.

Four Steps in Locating a Trial Balance Error

1. Check the totals of the trial balance itself for errors.

2. Compare the trial balance amounts with corresponding ledger balances, for errors in listing.

3. Check arithmetic in all accounts (balances and totals).

4. Check all postings back to the journals. You should find your error along the way; the totals of debits and credits in the journals themselves should have been proven equal *before* you posted to the ledger.

Common Types of Errors and Ways to Locate Them

1. Differences of 1, 10, 100, etc. often result from errors in adding or subtracting. (Check the items in steps 1 and 3 above.)

2. Differences evenly divisible by 9 often result from transposing adjacent digits (e.g. 795 for 975) or from a "slide" (e.g. 7.52 for 75.20). These are usually errors in transferring figures from journal to ledger or ledger to trial balance or in entering them on your calculator. If you have made a slide, dividing the difference by 9 will automatically disclose the amount itself: e.g. 75.20 − 7.52 = 67.68; 67.68 ÷ 9 = 7.52! A transposition is harder to locate. (Check the items in steps 2 and 4 above, including your adding machine tapes, if you have any.)

3. It is always possible that your error combines two or more errors, which will not respond to these tests until all but one is found. In that case, follow the steps in order.

Note: The trial balance does not prove that all transactions have been entered or properly classified but proves only mathematical balance.

CLOSING ENTRIES

At the end of each fiscal year, after all adjusting entries have been made and posted to the ledger, all revenue and expense account balances are transferred ("closed") to the Fund Balance account, so that they will have zero balances for the start of the next fiscal year. This is illustrated below.

Expense accounts:

Dr.   Fund Balance (for *total* of expenses)
   Cr.   Salary Expense (for its adjusted balance)
   Cr.   Rent Expense (for its adjusted balance, etc.)

Revenue accounts:

Dr.   Grants Received (adjusted balance)
Dr.   Membership Dues (adjusted balance)
   Cr.   Fund Balance

These entries update the Fund Balance account, which now incorporates the effect of all revenues and expenses for the year.

At this point, all revenue and expense accounts should have zero balances. Only Asset, Contra-asset,[11] Liability, and Fund Balance accounts should still have balances remaining. The total of the Liability, Contra-asset, and Fund Balance account balances should equal the total of the Asset account balances. This type of proof is known as a "post-closing trial balance."[12]

The next fiscal year will thus begin with the balances carried forward in these accounts and with zero balances in all revenue and expense accounts. The revenue and expense accounts are then ready to accumulate and measure the activities of the new year, as though you had to reset a tape recorder index to zero. An organization's fiscal year need not end December 31, but can come at the end of any month. (See Chapter 2 for a discussion of which month to choose.)

Ruling Off Accounts

If a manual ledger is used, lines are usually ruled in ink above and below the final totals of debits and credits in each account, as shown below, to indicate that they have been closed. Any remaining balances in Asset, Contra-asset, Liability, and Fund Balance accounts are entered in ink on the side of the account with the *lower* total and added to it, so that total debits and credits in the account are equal. These accounts are ruled off as well; however, the balance is then "brought down" (re-entered) on the opposite side—i.e., the one with the higher total (normal balance), marked "balance" and dated the first day of the new fiscal year. (Or start a new ledger page.)

Closings of two types of accounts are illustrated in Fig. 12–7.

Accounts are not ruled off—or even formally "closed" in some cases—when computerized or other machine bookkeeping is used, since new ledger sheets or cards are created for the next fiscal year.

When to Reverse Entries

Where the practice is to reverse adjustments entered on the books, at the beginning of the next period, the adjusting entries 1 through 4 above are the ones to be reversed. (See above under "Adjusting Entries.") The entries are merely the same as the related adjusting entries, with debit and credit accounts reversed, to undo or cancel their effects on the accounts. They are usually *required* at interim dates when books and statements are prepared via computerized methods, unless interim adjustments are entered on a worksheet in lieu of the books.

Depreciation entries are not usually reversed, nor are the amortization entries of the type described above. It is essentially accrual entries that must be reversed as well as deferral of revenues.

Payment of an accrued expense, or collection of accrued revenue, can be applied directly to the related payable or receivable, thus eliminating the need for reversing entries. Any difference between the amount paid and amount previously accrued is transferred to the related expense or revenue account.

---

[11]Such as "Accumulated depreciation."

[12]If the totals are unequal, there is an error somewhere, if you have posted your closing entries. See "Four Steps in Locating a Trial Balance Error."

Temporary Accounts

(Revenue and Expense)

(Any) Expense Account

19x1		19x1	
Jan. 31 (increase)	1,000	Feb. 28 (refund)	200
Nov. 30 (increase)	1,500	Dec. 31 (closing entry)	2,300
	2,500		2,500

Same Expense Account

19x2
(Note zero balance on following Jan. 1)

Real (Permanent) Accounts

(Asset, Liability, and Fund Balances)

(Any) Asset Account

19x1		19x1	
Jan. 31 balance	10,000	Feb. 28 (reduction)	500
Nov. 30 (increase)	1,000	Dec. 31 balance	10,500
	11,500		11,500

Same Asset Account

19x2	
Jan. 1 balance	10,500

FIGURE 12–7. CLOSING THE ACCOUNTS

FUNCTIONS OF THE ACCOUNTANT'S WORKSHEET

At the end of the fiscal year, or whenever financial statements are to be prepared, a convenient (though not essential) tool is the accountant's worksheet.[13] Its function is to expedite preparation of the statements, by adjusting the accounts "off the books," sorting their balances into those used on the operating or activity statement and those used on the balance sheet, and disclosing the excess of revenues over expenses (or vice versa) in the process.

The "financials" can then be expeditiously prepared, since the accounts used on each statement need merely be transferred mechanically. A worksheet consists of five pairs of debit/credit columns, as follows. (See also Fig. 12A–7 in Appendix 12A).

1. Trial balance (dr/cr)
2. Adjusting entries (dr/cr)
3. Adjusted trial balance (dr/cr)
4. Operating Statement (dr/cr)
   (Expenses and Revenues)
5. Balance Sheet (dr/cr)
   (Assets and Liabilities)

Steps in Preparing the Worksheet

The trial balance itself is the first step in the preparation process. It is entered in the first pair of columns on a ten-column worksheet.[14] The adjusting entries may then be entered in the pair of columns provided for them, though they should be prepared first in journal form, either on a separate worksheet or in the General Journal itself.[15]

Next, each trial balance figure is adjusted by adding and/or subtracting horizontally the amounts in the adjustment columns, the adjusted figures then being entered in the Adjusted Trial Balance columns. In effect, each line on the trial balance simulates the corresponding ledger account, with an adjustment on the same side as the balance added (e.g., when both are debits) and one on the opposite side subtracted.[16]

When the first three pairs of columns are completed (and the totals of all three pairs are in balance), the next step is that of distributing each of the adjusted balances to one of the four blank columns. Expense and Revenue account balances will be entered in the debit and credit columns, respectively, of the Operating Statement section. Asset accounts will be entered in the debit column of the Balance Sheet section, and contra-assets (e.g., Accumulated Depreciation), Liability, and Fund Balance accounts in the credit column.[17]

Finally, the four statement columns are totaled and the difference between each pair calculated: the difference between total revenues and expenses (which will be closed out to Fund Balance at year end) should equal the difference between the debit and credit column totals in the Balance

---

[13]Not to be confused with the type of worksheet described earlier, used as a substitute for a formal journal.

[14]Available in blank ruled pads from most commercial stationers, usually with 12 or 13 columns provided, plus item space.

[15]At year end, all adjustments must finally be entered on the ledger through the journal.

[16]If a *negative* figure results, the balance should be entered on the opposite side.

[17]Of course, if an account has a negative balance—one opposite from its normal balance—it is so entered. Thus a deficit balance in the Fund Balance account would be a *debit.*

Sheet section. In preparing the actual Balance Sheet, this amount is added to and included in the Fund Balance figure.

THE ACCOUNTS PAYABLE LEDGER: KEEPING TRACK OF WHAT YOU OWE

In a full accrual system (unless a Voucher Register is used), a separate book or set of ledger cards is maintained, one account for each vendor or supplier from whom purchases are made on credit. In addition to posting monthly totals from the Accounts Payable Journal or Register, each line (representing an invoice) is posted to the credit side of the particular vendor's account in the Accounts Payable Ledger and the balance updated.

When a payment is made to such a vendor, the decrease in liability is posted to the debit side of the account, and its reduced balance is shown. The account will thus indicate the unpaid balance, if any, which may represent one or more invoices. Each payment is "keyed off" (coded) with a letter indicating the bills being paid, which are in turn coded the same way; thus any unpaid items will not be coded and will be readily spotted (referred to as "open items").

Entering Reference Data

As each bill or payment is posted from a journal, a similar cross-referencing system is used: next to the item in the journal, a subsidiary ledger posting reference is entered, which may be an account number (if used), the first letter of the vendor's name, or merely a checkmark to indicate that it has been posted. In the vendor's account, the journal page number is entered to the left of the amount posted. The above steps are illustrated in Fig. 12–8. (Only a portion of each journal or account is shown. Transactions are not based on Center for Community Service data but are chosen to illustrate particular situations.)

Balancing Details Against the Total Due

At the end of each month a schedule, or adding machine tape, should be prepared listing unpaid balances. The total should agree with the balance of the Accounts Payable account in the General Ledger (account 201 in the above illustration). If the amounts disagree, the difference should be tracked down. Most commonly it will result from one or more of the following errors:

1. A bill received and entered in the Accounts Payable Journal but not posted to a vendor's account.

2. A bill entered directly in a vendor's account without first being entered in the Accounts Payable Journal.

3. A *payment* of a bill charged in error to an expense account rather than to Accounts Payable, but entered as a debit in the vendor's account. (Once a bill has been entered in the Accounts Payable Journal and charged to expense, its subsequent payment is not an expense but a reduction of the Account Payable.)

4. An arithmetical error in the schedule or in an account balance.

1. Accounts Payable Journal or Register

AP 23
(Journal page reference)

Month of January, 19xx

Invoice Date	Vendor	PR	Accts. Payable (Cr)	Printing & Staty. (Dr)	Supp. (Dr)	Equip. Rentals (Dr)	Other (overflow) Acct.	PR	Amount (Dr)
Jan. 3	ABC Staty	A	115.00	115.00					
10	Rent-All Co.	R	250.00			250.00			
12	Central Supply Co.	C	96.00		96.00				
30	Ma Bell Tel.	M	350.00				Tel.	570	350.00
	Totals (Jan.)		2,872.00	421.00	233.00	450.00			1,768.00
(General Ledger posting references)			201	572	571	575			

Note: Posting references for items in "Other" column appear next to the related amount.

2. Cash Disbursements Journal

CD 35

Month of January, 19xx

Date Paid	Paid to	PR	Check No.	Net Cash (Cr)	Accts. Payable (Dr)	Payroll (Dr)	Off. Exp. (Dr)	Other Acct.	PR	Amount (Dr)
Jan. 10	Payroll check		205-210	820.		820.				
15	ABC Staty.	A	211	85	85					
	Rent-All Co.	R	212	500	500					
29	Ma Bell Tel.	M	249	400	400					
				7,541	3,105	3,280.	510			646
(G/L Posting references)				101	201	900	572			

FIGURE 12–8.
POSTING FROM SPECIAL JOURNALS TO ACCOUNTS PAYABLE LEDGER ACCOUNTS.

3. Selected Vendor Accounts in Accounts Payable Ledger

ABC Stationers

Date (of bill or check)	Invoice or Check Number	PR	Dr	Cr	Balance Cr or (Dr)
Dec. 15	#A423	AP22		(A) 85.00	85.00
Jan. 3	#A521	AP23		115.00	200.00
15	#211	CD35	(A) 85.00		115.00

(Payment of previous month's bill keyed off as "(A)" leaving current Jan. 3 bill unpaid at Jan. 31.)

Central Supply Co.

Date	Number	PR	Dr	Cr	Balance
Jan. 12	26-233	AP23		96.00	96.00

(No payment yet: new vendor.)

Ma Bell Telephone Co.

Date	Number	PR	Dr	Cr	Balance
Dec. 20	23-1000- 15	AP22		(A) 400.00	400.00
Jan. 29	249	CD35	(A) 400.		-0-
30	24-1011- 16	AP23		350.00	350.00

(Old bill paid before new bill entered: keyed off.)

Rent-All Company

Date	Number	PR	Dr	Cr	Balance
Nov. 15	2653B	AP21		(A) 250.00	250.00
Dec. 29	3721B	AP22		(A) 250.00	500.00
Jan. 10	4823C	AP23		250.00	750.00
15	212	CD35	(A) 500.00		250.00

(Old bills for two previous months paid at once and keyed off, leaving current bill unpaid.)

PDQ Supply, Inc.

Date	Number	PR	Dr	Cr	Balance
Dec. 28	763	AP22		125.00	125.00

(No payment on bill previously entered.)

FIGURE 12-8.

POSTING FROM SPECIAL JOURNALS TO ACCOUNTS PAYABLE LEDGER ACCOUNTS.

(continued)

Needless to say, all errors located should be promptly corrected. Error 1 is obviously corrected by making the missing posting; error 2 by making the missing entry in the journal, through the General Journal if the others are closed; error 3 by a correcting entry through the General Journal; error 4 by correcting the erroneous figure.

USING THE VOUCHER REGISTER: A SHORT-CUT SUBSTITUTE FOR THE ACCOUNTS PAYABLE LEDGER

This is not an additional book of account, but one used to eliminate the *need* for an Accounts Payable Ledger, by keeping track of unpaid bills in an alternate form of journal, which provides for a record of payments as well as bills received (see Fig. 12–9). The entries illustrated are to record the December bills shown in Vendor Accounts in Fig. 12–8. (Such accounts would not be used in a Voucher Register system.)

Month of December, 19xx

Invoice Date	Vendor	Voucher No.	Paid		Vouchers Pay. (Cr)	Printing & Staty. (Dr)	Sup-plies (Dr)	Equipt. Rental (Cr)	Other		
			Date	Check No.					Account	PR	Amount (Dr)
Dec. 15	ABC Stat.	101	Jan. 15	211	85.	85.					
20	Ma Bell	102	29	249	400				Tel.	570	400.
28	PDQ										
	Supp.	103			125.		125.				
29	Rent-All	104	15	212	250			250			
	Totals										
	(Dec.)				3,220	560.	440	450			1,770
(G/L posting references)					201	572	571	575			

FIGURE 12–9. VOUCHER REGISTER

Note that the only unpaid December invoice shown is that of PDQ Supply Co., as indicated by the lack of an entry in the "Paid" section. The date and number of the checks issued in payment of the other three invoices correspond with those shown in Figure 12–8 in the respective vendor accounts. They are entered from the check stubs as payment is made, providing indication of payment plus the same date and check number record that would be provided by a vendor's ledger account.

After the totals (and items in the "Other" column) are posted, a schedule or adding machine tape is prepared of items remaining open (unpaid) in the Voucher Register. The total of such items should correspond with the balance of the Vouchers Payable account in the General Ledger.[18]

[18]Usually used instead of "Accounts Payable."

(The schedule should also agree with the bills in the unpaid bills file as of the date the last check issued was recorded in the "paid" section of the Voucher Register.)

Voucher numbers are assigned in sequence as a bill is entered and are recorded on the bill itself. This helps avoid entering and paying a bill twice. (All paid bills should of course be stamped "PAID" and the date and check number shown, as explained in Chapter 11.)

Problems in Using a Voucher Register

1. Unless all bills are paid regularly—on a monthly basis—the system becomes clumsy to operate, since one must look back two or more months to locate open (unpaid) items.

2. Unless each bill is paid in full, it is clumsy to keep track of balances due, since a partially paid bill might appear paid if the check is recorded. The solution is, in effect, to cancel the entry of the original voucher and reenter it on the next two vacant lines as two vouchers, one for the amount paid, the other for the unpaid balance.

Thus Voucher 123 for $500, on which $300 has been paid, would be reentered as Voucher 123A for $300 (with payment noted) and Voucher 123B for $200, which would appear as unpaid. An entry would be made next to the original voucher (123) in the "Paid" section, reading "see 123A and B."

In larger organizations especially, a Voucher Register system works best when the following procedures are followed.

- Numbered voucher slips are prepared in duplicate, and one copy is filed in numerical order, the other filed in an unpaid voucher tray, by due date, behind date index guides.

- When the due date is reached, and the related invoice is paid, the voucher is removed, stamped "PAID," with date and check number; the payment entry is made in the Voucher Register, and the vouchers filed alphabetically in the vendor's file folder. This affords a cross-reference, since entries can be traced either by vendor's name, or by voucher number in the numerical file of voucher slips.

- Voucher numbers are assigned and entries made for *all* cash disbursements, whether they represent invoices or other payments, such as payrolls, staff expenses, or other cash expenditures for which there is no vendor account. So used, the voucher becomes an approval document for all expenditures and should therefore provide space for authorizing signatures or initials, as described in Chapter 11 and illustrated by Fig. 11–1.

WHEN AN ACCOUNTS (OR PLEDGES) RECEIVABLE LEDGER IS USED

This is used in a full accrual system, if revenues are accrued frequently enough to warrant a special journal and subsidiary ledger. The forms and procedures parallel those used for Accounts Payable, except that we are dealing now not with our debts and our payments but with amounts due us and our collections. We will therefore be posting from the Accounts Receivable Journal *debits* to the individual accounts receivable from clients, donors, or members, representing increases in amounts owed to us; and *credits* (from the Cash Receipts Journal), representing decreases in amounts owed to us, when we collect (Fig. 12–10).

The same procedures are used for posting references and keying off items as were described previously and also for reconciling the total of uncollected balances with the balance of the Accounts (or Pledges) Receivable account in the General Ledger. Balances will normally be debit rather than credit balances, of course.

If a receipt book is used for collections, and entries in the Cash Receipts Journal represent page or group totals, rather than individual payments, the postings to the Accounts Receivable ledger are made from the carbon copies of the individual receipts, and so numbered, rather than from the journal. (The monthly totals are of course posted to the General Ledger.)

An Accounts Receivable ledger can be used as a memorandum follow-up record, even when the books are kept on a cash or simplified accrual basis. In this case, the debit entries for bills or pledges receivable are made from bills or statements mailed, since there is no journal from which they can be posted. There will also be no Accounts/Pledges Receivable account in the General Ledger, except at year-end.

Collections are posted the same way, from the Cash Receipts Journal or receipt book, and the ledger account balances are updated for follow-up. There is in this case no tie-in between these balances and the General Ledger, which will show all collections as revenue rather than as reductions of Accounts/Pledges Receivable.

(Name of Client, Patient or Other Debtor)

Date (of invoice)	Invoice number	PR	Dr	Cr	Balance Dr or (Cr)

FIGURE 12–10. TYPICAL ACCOUNT IN AN ACCOUNTS RECEIVABLE LEDGER.

KEEPING PAYROLL RECORDS

A Payroll Journal or Register is illustrated in Appendix 12A (Fig. 12A-4), with entries for an entire quarter for the Center for Community Services, Inc. As explained in the footnote, this journal is normally totaled and balanced for each pay period. If salaries are paid monthly, these totals are posted to the General Ledger; if weekly, biweekly, or semimonthly, the totals for the month are summarized ("recapped," in accounting jargon) and the month's total for each column posted.

Only the net total of each period's payroll is entered in the Cash Disbursements Journal and entered (debited) to Net Payroll (or "Payroll Control"). This account should have a zero balance after postings are made from both the payroll and cash disbursements journal. (This keeps the details out of the latter journal.)

Pay Slips or Check Aprons

The details on each line of the Payroll Journal (Fig. 12A-4) are entered from the employee's pay statement. If a one-write system is used, the same information is simultaneously entered on both as a byproduct.

Employee Earnings Record

The information on each line of the Payroll Journal is also entered on what amounts to a ledger card for each employee, which contains a cumulative record of earnings and deductions for each quarter and year. The quarterly and annual totals are used in connection with reports to government agencies explained in Chapter 17, including unemployment compensation, FICA, and income taxes. Again, if a one-write system is used, this record is also prepared as a byproduct of the other two, as illustrated in Fig. 12-11. Note that the right half of the Payroll Journal provides columns for charging payroll to specific functions or activities.

Time Records

Although some payroll record forms provide for keeping track of hours per week worked by each employee, required by minimum wage and/or wage/hour laws, the well-run nonprofit may need to go beyond that in cases when an employee works on more than one function or program, as mentioned in Chapter 11. In such cases, it is quite desirable to have each such employee submit a weekly time sheet, which should be reviewed and signed by his or supervisor, with a breakdown of the number of hours or percent of time spent on each activity. This information has many uses, including control of personnel effort and allocation of expenses for internal and external financial reporting, compliance with IRS requirements regarding lobbying, etc. (As a short-cut, time sheets can be submitted one [different] week per month to find percentages.)

This is a more complex problem in practice than it is in theory. If a staff member splits his or her time between two or more programs, a problem arises in charging the appropriate amount of payroll expense to each.

If actual hours are charged based on the time sheets, which is clearly the correct thing to do, there will often be a variance between the amount charged and the amount allowed according to a grant or contract, one that may cause a problem with the funding agency.

If, in order to avoid this problem, the agency makes a practice of charging exactly what the contract or grant provides, regardless of the actual amount of time spent, a different issue arises: the funding agency is perhaps being misled regarding what it is getting for its money.

There is no perfect solution to this dilemma, except one, which has been argued for many years: contracts and grants should not be based on too tight a control over line items: what should be important is the program results, what it does for the clients or patients and how many of them were served. As long as the agency delivers the goods within the allotted funds, the amounts spent for each line item should be unimportant. Until that happy day arrives, each nonprofit must decide what is best for itself in handling this question.

In our opinion, you should always use your mission, purposes, and goals as a starting point in any tough decision, and that would seem to counsel a viewpoint that says, "The patient or client could care less about line items; just do a good job satisfying his or her needs." (Now all you have to do is sell that to your funding agency.)

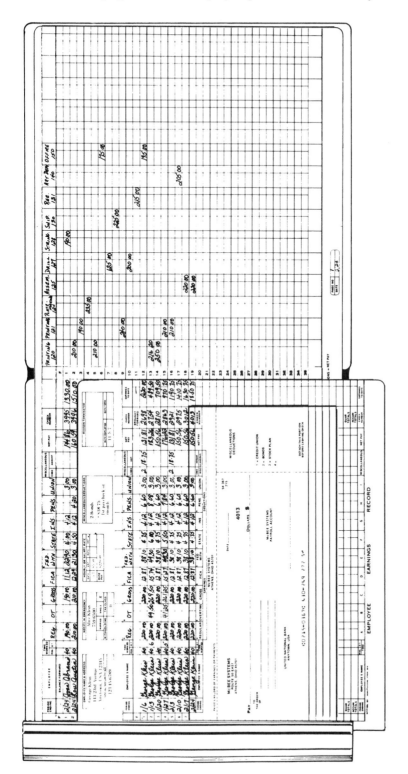

FIGURE 12-11. ONE-WRITE PAYROLL SYSTEM.

Notes:

1. Shingled checks with stub at top showing details of withholdings (lower left part of illustration).

2. Employee earnings record to accumulate details of salary and withholdings for payroll tax reporting (under pay check and in register with stub).

3. Payroll Journal (bottom layer), with provison for distribution or allocation of salary expense to programs or functions: the right-hand half of the journal that is fully visible.

Source: McBee Systems, a division of Litton Industries, Belleville, NJ 07109. Used with permission.

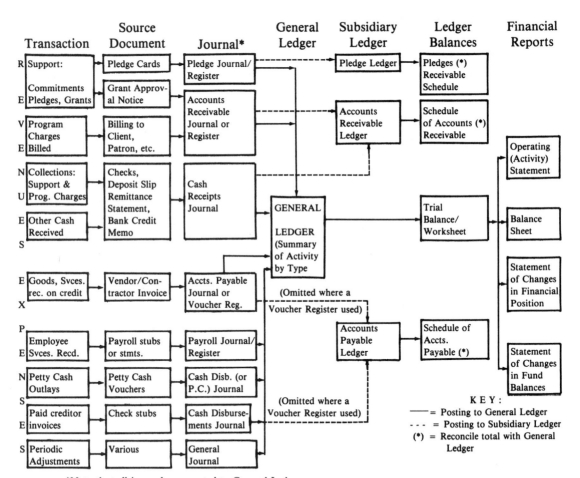

*Note that all journals are posted to General Ledger.

FIGURE 12–12. FLOW CHART OF FULL ACCRUAL ACCOUNTING CYCLE.

APPENDIX 12A

Illustration of the Full Accounting Cycle

So that we do not leave the bookkeeping process somewhat abstract, let us return to our imaginary nonprofit, Center for Community Service, Inc., and work through a summary of its actual transactions for the first quarter ended March 31, not those we budgeted in Chapter 5, but the actual transactions used in Table 14-1 (the cash worksheet and budget) and also on the financial statements in Chapter 13. We will ignore functional classifications here to simplify the illustration. We first list below (Table 12A–1) summaries of the *actual* data for revenues and expense as well as actual cash received and disbursed, which will of course differ somewhat from *budgeted* amounts listed in Chapter 5. We will then illustrate the following.

- The chart of accounts (Fig. 12A-1)
- The required entries in four journals
- How the journals are posted to the general ledger
- Adjusting entries
- The trial balance and worksheet, with adjustments

TABLE 12A–1. SUMMARY OF FIRST QUARTER TRANSACTIONS* (Accrual basis used)

Item No.	Revenues Earned	Amount	Item No.	Revenues Received	Amount
	Grants:				
1	ABC Foundation	$ 5,000	1	ABC Foundation	—
2	XYZ Foundation	15,000	2	XYZ Foundation	$15,000
3	State Agency	2,200	3	State Agency	2,200
4	Program "A" services	3,800	4	Program services	3,800
5	In-kind contribution (rent)	1,500	6	In-kind rent (non-cash item)	—
6	Membership dues	1,000	6	Dues	1,000
7	Interest	90	7	Interest	90
	Expenses Incurred			**Expenses Paid**	
8	Gross salaries[1]	17,750	8	Net salaries[1]	12,425
9	Less: taxes withheld	(5,325)	9	(See Item 31 below)	—
10	Payroll taxes accrued	1,567	10	Payroll taxes paid	674
	Employee benefits	625		Employee benefits	375
11	Rent expense (in-kind)	1,500	11	Rent paid (non-cash item)	—
12	Electricity and heat	750	12	Electricity and heat	750
13	Water	75	13	Water	75
14	Janitorial service	450	14	Janitorial service	450
15	Telephone	345	15	Telephone	345
16	Printing and stationery (bought and consumed)	388	16	Printing and stationery	388
17	Postage	260	17	Postage	260
18	Travel and conferences	685	18	Travel and conferences	685
19	Supplies bought (and used)	725	19	Supplies bought (and used)	725
20	Equipment rentals	600	20	Equipment rentals	600
21	Consulting fees	1,200	21	Consulting fees	1,200
22	Legal fees	275	22	Legal fees	275
23	Accounting fees	650	23	Accounting fees	650
24	Office expense	188	24	Office expense	188
25	Insurance–liability (1 year of 4 prepaid)	50	25	Insurance–liability (4-year policy: prepaid)	200
26	Insurance–workmen's compensation	75	26	Insurance–workmen's compensation	75
27	Insurance–fire	25	27	Insurance–fire (prepaid previous December)	—
28	Depreciation on equipment	645	28	(Depreciation is a non-cash item)	
	Non-Revenue Items Received			**Non-Expense Items Paid**	
29	Loans received–January	2,000			
30	Loans received–April	1,500			
			31	Paid withheld taxes to government agencies	4,650
			32	Paid equipment installments	600

* See the General Journal (Figure 12A-3) for accrued revenues and expenses, the Cash Receipts and Cash Disbursements Journals for amounts received or paid (Figures 12A-2 and 12A-3—refer to corresponding item numbers).

[1] See Payroll Journal (Figure 12A-4) for details of amounts withheld.

101 Cash	550 Salaries—Administration			
110 Grants Receivable	551 Salaries—Program A			
130 Prepaid Insurance	522 Salaries—Program B			
140 Equipment	560 Rent Expense			
141 Accumulated Depreciation	561 Electricity and Heat			
210 Equipment Installments Due	562 Water			
211 Loans Payable—Bank	563 Janitorial Service			
220 Payroll Taxes Payable—Federal Income	570 Telephone			
221 P/R Taxes Payable—FICA	571 Supplies Expense			
222 Accrued P/R Taxes—Unemployment	572 Office Expense			
230 Accrued Expenses	573 Printing & Stationery			
300 Fund Balance	574 Postage			
900 Payroll Control	575 Equipment Rentals			
500 Foundation Grants	576 Insurance Expense			
510 Government Grants	580 Professional Fees			
515 Program Revenues	581 Consulting Fees			
520 Dues (Revenue)	585 Travel & Conferences			
525 Interest Revenue	590 Payroll Tax Expense			
530 In-Kind Contributions	591 Employee Benefits			
	599 Depreciation Expense			

FIGURE 12A–1. CHART OF ACCOUNTS.

Item No.	Received From	Cash Rec'd (dr)	Program Revenues (cr)	Dues (cr)	Interest Revenue (cr)	Loans Payable (cr)	Other Account	PR	Amount (cr)
2	XYZ Foundation	15,000					Grants Rec'ble	110	15,000
3	State Govt.	2,200					Grants Rec'ble	110	2,200
4	Sundry Patrons	3,800	3,800						
6	Various Members	1,000		1,000					
7	Last National Bank	90			90				
29	Last National Bank	2,000				2,000			
30	Last National Bank	1,500				1,500			
	Total Cash Receipts 1st Quarter	25,590	3,800	1,000	90	3,500			17,200
	(Posting References) (1)	101	515	520	525	211			

FIGURE 12A-2. CASH RECEIPTS JOURNAL
QUARTER ENDED MARCH 31.

Notes:

1. Note that column totals have been posted to the accounts identified above by posting references, except for the "Other" column, from which entries must be posted individually, and appropriate posting references entered for each. Item numbers refer to those listed in Table 12A-1.

2. To save space, only a single figure has been entered to represent the total of each item of revenue. In practice, there would be a number of items each month for such accounts as program service fees and dues, and the journal would be totaled and posted each month.

Item No.	Paid To	Check No.	Cash (Net Amount) (Cr)	Net Payroll (Dr)	Travel etc. (Dr)	Supplies Expense (Dr)	Office Expense (Dr)	Consulting Fees (Dr)	Other Account	PR	Other Amount (Dr)
8 & 9	Net Payroll (see Note 2)	(Var.)	12,425	12,425							
10	IRS/Inc. Tax & FICA	102	1,100						Inc. tax	220	1,000
									FICA Pay.	221	100
10	State Unemp. Ins.	103	674						P/R Tax Accrued	222	674
10	Assoc. Health Svce.	104	375						Accrued Health	230	375
12	Local Utility Co.	105	750						Elec./Ht.	561	750
13	District Water Co.	111	75						Water	562	75
14	Reliable Maint. Corp.	112	450						Jan. Svce.	563	450
15	Bell Telephone Co.	113	345						Tel. Exp.	570	345
16	Best Stationers Inc.	119	388						Printg. & Staty.	573	388
17	U.S. Postmaster	120	260						Postage	574	260
18	(Staff members)	121-4	685		685						
19	General Supply Co.	125	725			725					
20	Universal Rentals Inc.	126	600						Rental Equipt.	575	600
21	Ann Expert PhD	127	1,200					1,200			
22	Lee Galeagle, Esq.	128	275						Prof. Fees	580	275
23	T. Account, CPA	129	650						Prof. Fees	580	650
24	Bottled Water Inc.	130	188				188				
25	Premium Casualty Co.	131	200						Prepaid Ins.	130	200
26	State Insurance Fund	132	75						Ins. Exp.	576	75
31	IRS/Inc. Tax & FICA	133	3,550						Inc. Tax	220	2,825
									FICA Pay.	221	725
32	Office Equipt. Corp.	134	600						Installment Pay.	210	600
	Total Cash Disbursements		25,590	12,425	685	725	188	1,200			10,367
	Posting References		101	900	585	571	572	581			

FIGURE 12A-3. CASH DISBURSEMENTS JOURNAL
QUARTER ENDED MARCH 31

Notes:

1. See footnote (1) for Cash Receipts Journal.

2. Only single figures have been entered, to represent the total of each type of disbursement. In practice there would be a number of checks each month for salaries and the other expenses shown in column headings. Note that check numbers missing above appear in the Payroll Journal, Fig. 12A-4. (A "Net Payroll" column as shown above is used here; details of salaries and withholdings are posted from separate Payroll Register or Journal as shown in Fig. 12A-4.)

3. Item numbers refer to transactions listed in Table 12A-1.

Pay Period	Employee	Salaries Earned (Dr)				Taxes Withheld (Cr)			Net PR (Cr)	Check No.
		Admin.	Prog. A	Prog. B	Total	Inc. T	FICA	Total		
Jan.	E. Director	1,667			1,667	454	102	556	1,111	106
	A. Assistant	667			667	118	41	159	508	107
	A. Leader		1,333		1,333	324	82	406	927	108
	B. Service			1,500	1,500	382	92	474	1,026	109
	B. Versatile			750	750	134	46	180	570	110
Feb.	E. Director	1,667			1,667	454	102	556	1,111	114
	A. Assistant	667			667	118	41	159	508	115
	A. Leader		1,333		1,333	324	82	406	927	116
	B. Service			1,500	1,500	382	92	474	1,026	117
	B. Versatile			750	750	134	46	180	570	118
Mar.	E. Director	1,666			1,666	454	102	556	1,110	134
	A. Assistant	666			666	118	41	159	507	135
	A. Leader		1,334		1,334	324	82	406	928	136
	B. Service			1,500	1,500	382	92	474	1,026	137
	B. Versatile			750	750	135	46	180	570	138
Total for Quarter		7,000	4,000	6,750	17,750	4,237	1,088	5,325	12,425	
Posting Reference		550	551	552		220	221		900	

FIGURE 12A-4. PAYROLL JOURNAL OR REGISTER
QUARTER ENDED MARCH 31

Notes:

1. See footnote (1) for Cash Receipts Journal. (There is, however, normally no "other" column in a payroll journal.)

2. Monthly pay period assumed, totaled, and posted here for the quarter as for the other journals, to save space. This journal would actually be totaled and posted at the end of each pay period (weekly, semimonthly, or monthly). Only the net total of the checks for each period would be entered in the Cash Disbursements Journal.

Item × No.[4]		PR	DR	CR
1, 2, & 3	Grants Receivable	110	22,200	
1 & 2	Foundation Grants (ABC & XYZ)	500		20,000
3	Government Grants (State)	510		2,200
	To accrue revenues at 1/2/x			
	ADJUSTING ENTRIES (for Worksheet) (See Note 3 below.)			
	A			
11	Rent Expense	560	1,500	
5	In-kind Contributions	530		1,500
	Office space for quarter donated			
	B			
10	Payroll Tax Expense	590	1,567	
	Employee Benefits—Health Ins.	591	625	
	Payroll Taxes Payable—FICA (Employer share)	221		1,088
	Accrued Payroll Taxes—Unemp. Ins.	222		479
	Accrued Expenses—Health Ins.	230		625
	To accrue expenses for quarter			
	(See Expense Budget Worksheet for details.)			
	C			
25	Insurance Expense—Liability Insurance	576	50	
	Prepaid Insurance	130		50
	To write off expired portion for quarter (Note 5)			
	D			
27	Insurance Expense—Fire Insurance	576	25	
	Prepaid Insurance	130		25
	To amortize for quarter (Note 5)			
	E			
28	Depreciation Expense	599	645	
	Accumulated Depreciation	141		645
	Estimated depreciation for quarter			

FIGURE 12A-5. GENERAL JOURNAL

Notes:

1. It is assumed here that no special journals are used to accrue revenues or expenses; i.e. that the Simplified Accrual Method is being used.

2. The numbers in the "PR" (Posting Reference) column are those of the General Ledger accounts to which the amounts have been posted.

3. Adjusting entries A through E above were entered on Worksheet, but not posted to General Ledger accounts until after the Trial Balance was prepared. (See Worksheet).

4. Item numbers refer to those listed in Table 12A-1.

5. "Write off" and "amortize" are alternate terms.

Cash			(101)
Jan. 1 Bal.	2,000	Mar. 31 CD	25,590
Mar. 31 CR	25,590		
	27,590		
(Bal. = 2,000)			

Grants Receivable			(110)
Jan. 2 GJ	22,200	Mar. 31 CR	15,000
(Bal. = 5,000)			2,200
			17,200

Prepaid Insurance			(130)
Jan. 1 Bal.	150	Mar. 31 GJ (C)	50
Mar. 31 CD	200	31 GJ (D)	25
	350		75
(Bal. = 275)			

Equipment		(140)
Jan. 1 Bal.	12,885	

Accumulated Depreciation		(141)
	Jan. 1 Bal.	5,154
	Mar. 31 GJ (E)	645
		5,799

Equipment Installments Due		(210)
Mar. 31 CD	600	Jan. 1 Bal	1,200
		(Bal. = 600)	

Loans Payable—Bank		(211)
	Jan. 31 CR	2,000
	Mar. 31 CR	1,500
		3,500

P/R Tax Payable—Fed. Inc. Tax		(220)
Jan. 31 CD	1,000	Jan. 1 Bal.	1,000
Mar. 31 CD	2,825	Mar. 31 PR	4,237
	3,825		5,237
		(Bal. = 1,412)	

P/R Tax Payable—FICA		(221)
Jan. 31 CD	100	Jan. 1 Bal.	100
Mar. 31 CD	725	Mar. 31 PR	1,088
	825	31 GJ (B)	1,088
			2,276
		(Bal. = 1,451)	

Accrued P/R Tax—Unemp. Ins.		(222)
Jan. 31 CD	674	Jan. 1 Bal.	674
		Mar. 31 GJ (B)	479
			1,153
		(Bal. = 479)	

Accrued Expenses		(230)
Mar. 31 CD	375	Jan. 1 Bal.	375
		Mar. 31 GJ (B)	625
			1,000
		(Bal. = 625)	

Fund Balance		(300)
	Jan. 1 Bal.	6,532

Payroll Control Account		(900)
Mar. 31 CD	12,425	Mar. 31 PR	12,425
		(Bal. = 0)	

Foundation Grants		(500)
	Jan. 2 GJ	20,000

Government Grants		(510)
	Jan. 2 GJ	2,200

FIGURE 12A-6. GENERAL LEDGER ACCOUNTS

Notes:

Most entries are dated March 31, the end of quarter, which may not correspond with dates per Cash Flow Worksheet (Chapter 14, Table 14-1).

1. Posting reference page numbers omitted, due to space limitation.

2. Balances shown are after posting adjusting entries, A–E. (Trial Balance shown on Worksheet is of balances before these entries were posted.)

Program Revenues	(515)
Mar. 31 CR	3,800

Dues	(520)
Mar. 31 CR	1,000

Interest Revenue	(525)
Mar. 31 CR	90

In-Kind Contributions	(530)
Mar. 31 GJ (A)	1,500

Salaries—Administration	(550)
Mar. 31 PR	7,000

Salaries—Program A	(551)
Mar. 31 PR	4,000

Salaries—Program B	(552)
Mar. 31 PR	6,750

Rent Expense	(560)
Mar. 31 GJ (A)	1,500

Electricity & Heat	(561)
Mar. 31 CD	750

Water	(562)
Mar. 31 CD	75

Janitorial Service	(563)
Mar. 31 CD	450

Telephone	(570)
Mar. 31 CD	345

Supplies Expense	(571)
Mar. 31 CD	725

Office Expense	(572)
Mar. 31	188

Printing & Stationery	(573)
Mar. 31 CD	388

Postage	(574)
Mar. 31 CD	260

Equipment Rentals	(575)
Mar. 31 CD	600

Insurance Expense	(576)
Mar. 31 CD	75
31 GJ(C)	50
Mar. 31 GJ(D)	25
	150

Professional Fees	(580)
Mar. 31 CD	275
31 CD	650
	925

Consulting Fees	(581)
Mar. 31 CD	1,200

Travel & Conferences	(585)
Mar. 31 CD	685

Payroll Tax Expense	(590)
Mar. 31 GJ (B)	1,567

Employee Benefits	(591)
Mar. 31 GJ (B)	625

Depreciation Expense	(599)
Mar. 31 GJ (E)	645

FIGURE 12A-6. GENERAL LEDGER ACCOUNTS (continued)

Account Name	Trial Balance (Before Adjustments)		Adjusting Entries		Adjusted Trial Balance*		Operating Statement		Balance Sheet	
	Dr	Cr	Dr	Cr	Dr	Cr	Dr	Cr	Dr	Cr
Cash	2,000				2,000				2,000	
Grants Rec. (ABC Fdnt)	5,000				5,000				5,000	
Prepaid Insurance	350			(C) 50	275				275	
Equipment	12,885			(D) 25	12,885				12,885	
Accumulated Deprec.		5,154		(E) 645		5,799				5,799
Equipment Install. Due		600				600				600
Loans Payable—Bank		3,500				3,500				3,500
Payroll Taxes Pay.—Fed.WT		1,412				1,412				1,412
Payroll Taxes Pay.—FICA		363		(B) 1,088		1,451				1,451
Accr. Pay. Tax—Unemp.		-		(B) 479		479				479
Accrued Expense		-		(B) 625		625				625
Fund Balance		6,532				6,532				6,532
Payroll Control		-								
Foundation Grants		20,000				20,000		20,000		
Government Grants		2,200				2,200		2,200		
Program Revenues		3,800				3,800		3,800		
Dues		1,000				1,000		1,000		
Interest Revenue		90				90		90		
In-Kind Contributions (Rent)		-		(A) 1,500		1,500		1,500		
Salaries—Administration	7,000				7,000		7,000			
Salaries—Program A	4,000				4,000		4,000			
Salaries—Program B	6,750				6,750		6,750			
Rent Expense (Donated)			(A) 1,500		1,500		1,500			
Electricity & Heat	750				750		750			
Water	75				75		75			
Janitorial Service	450				450		450			
Telephone	345				345		345			
Supplies Expense	725				725		725			
Office Expense	188				188		188			
Printing & Stationery	388				388		388			
Postage	260				260		260			
Equipment Rental	600				600		600			
Insurance Expense	75		(C) 50		150		150			
Professional Fees	925		(D) 25		925		925			
Consulting Fees	1,200				1,200		1,200			
Travel & Conferences	685				685		685			
Payroll Tax Expense	-		(B) 1,567		1,567		1,567			
Employee Benefits	-		(B) 625		625		625			
Depreciation Expense			(E) 645		645		645			
Decrease in Fund Balance**								238	238	
	44,651	44,651	4,412	4,412	48,988	48,988	28,828	28,828	20,398	20,398

Note:
Fund Balance after
Closing Entries:

Balance Jan. 1   6,532
less decrease   (238)**
Balance Dec.31   6,294

**FIGURE 12A-7. WORKSHEET
FOR THE QUARTER ENDED MARCH 31**

Notes:

*Trial Balance was prepared before posting adjusting entries shown to General Ledger accounts. Entries were posted to General Ledger afterwards, thus balances shown in Ledger correspond to Adjusted Trial Balance above.

**Decrease in Fund Balance represents excess of expenses over revenues.

Part Three

Operational Management

Chapter 13

Financial Reports: Making Your Figures Talk to You

SOME IMPORTANT REASONS WHY YOU NEED FINANCIAL REPORTS

Accounting was invented to serve the internal needs of organizations. It was not imposed from without by the government or other agencies. Its primary use has always been to answer the questions

- How are we doing?
- Where are we at?
- How did we get there?

In addition to providing an overall picture of the organization, internal reports serve another important purpose: evaluation and review by officers and board members of the performance of program and support personnel in carrying out the organization's plans and achieving its goals. Reports to outsiders—government agencies, creditors, stockholders, etc.—were a later development, and are covered in Chapters 15 and 16. The basic functions described above are performed by different financial reports; each is described below, with an explanation of its purpose and use.

THE OPERATING STATEMENT: COUNTERPART TO THE OPERATING BUDGET

The Operating Statement of the Center for Community Service, Inc., for the quarter ended March 31, 19xx is shown in Table 13–1. It has been prepared from the worksheet (Fig. 12A–7) in Appendix A to Chapter 12.[1] Note how its form corresponds to that of the budget for the period shown in Table 5–6. Both use the line-item format, which is the simplest one, used by most small nonprofits, especially those with only a single program.

As suggested by the alternate names, the Operating Statement is a summary of the current period's activities as reflected by revenues and expenses; as such it is the counterpart of the operating

---

[1] It might be useful to trace the figures.

TABLE 13-1. CENTER FOR COMMUNITY SERVICE, INC.
OPERATING STATEMENT, QUARTER ENDED MARCH 31 (Line-Item Format)

Revenues

Grants	$22,200	
In-kind (free rent)	1,500	
Program revenues	3,800	
Dues	1,000	
Interest	90	
Total Revenues		$28,590

Expenses

Salaries	$17,750	
Payroll fringe costs	2,192	
Occupancy	2,775	
Telephone	345	
Printing & Stationery	388	
Postage	260	
Travel & Conferences	685	
Supplies	725	
Equipment rentals	600	
Professional & Consulting fees	2,125	
Office expenses	188	
Insurance	150	
Depreciation	645	
Total Expenses		28,828
Decrease in Fund Balance (Note b)		(238)
Fund Balance—January 31, 19xx		6,532
Fund Balance—March 31, 19xx		$ 6,294

---

[a]This is a very simple form of statement which does not group support (grants, contributions, and dues) separately from program revenues, nor group overhead items separately from program expenses. Some accounts are combined above in the same way as on the budget (Table 5–6): e.g., Salaries and Occupancy costs.

[b]This item could be alternatively entitled "operating deficit" or "excess of expenses over revenues."

budget described in Chapter 5, the latter setting forth the plan of operations, the former showing the actual results of the operations. The so-called "bottom line," representing any excess of revenue over expenses (or vice versa) is usually labeled as such, or called "increase (or decrease) in fund balance," and is not interpreted as a profit or loss, as it would be on a comparable business statement.[2] (It should be obvious.that a nonprofit should seek to break even at least, or be prepared for financial difficulties.)

The format of an operating statement is identical to that of an operating budget; as a matter of fact, for the two to be of much use, they must be set up in a manner that permits an item-by-item comparison of planned and actual amounts for each category of revenue and expense to calculate variances.

BUDGET VARIANCE REPORTS

Now take the process one step further by combining the budgeted and actual figures on a single report, where they are compared line by line, and you have what is called a budget variance report. By adding a third column for the amount under or over budget, usually headed "Variance," you can see whether the organization is under or over par for the period, or if the report is only for a part of the fiscal year, you can determine how much is left in the budget in uncommitted funds.[3] A budget variance report for the center's quarter ended March 31 is shown in Table 13-2, which combines Table 5-6 and Fig. 12A-7.

Comments on Table 13-2:   Review of the variances shown in Table 13-2 raises the following issues.

- A minor drop (5%) in anticipated program revenues is seen.

- Although small in amount, the variance of 28% in interest received may need investigation.

- The 25% increases in utilities costs should be checked to see whether it is due to increases in rates or in usage, or to errors in budgeting.

- The other variances, all unfavorable, should be similarly investigated, particularly travel and office expenses, which were 90% and 109% over budget, respectively.

- The center may well be in need of better controls over expenditures, certainly with respect to any items showing unfavorable variances not due to circumstances beyond its control, such as price changes or unanticipated expenses such as the extra $150 in legal fees. Note that the contingency reserve of $250 was grossly inadequate to cover the unfavorable variances, which totaled $1,020 more than the reserve, as indicated by the net unfavorable variance of that amount in the change in fund balance. (Instead of the operating surplus of $782 budgeted, there was an operating deficit of $238.)

USING VARIANCE ANALYSIS

When variances appear on a budget variance report, they may indicate various conditions and require investigation, especially if substantial. They may result from changes in price or activity

[2]The terms "operating surplus (or deficit)" or "operating margin" are sometimes used.

[3]Note that this is possible only with statements prepared on the accrual basis; otherwise, unpaid bills will not be considered. A different format is required (see Table 13-4).

**TABLE 13–2. CENTER FOR COMMUNITY SERVICE, INC.
BUDGET VARIANCE REPORT, QUARTER ENDED MARCH 31 (Line-Item Format)**

	Budget	Actual	Variance (Note a)	Percent Variance (Note c)
REVENUES				
Foundation Grants:				
ABC (Program A)	$ 5,000	$ 5,000	$ -	
XYZ (Program B)	15,000	15,000	-	
State Grant	2,200	2,200	-	
In-kind contribution (free rent)	1,500	1,500	-	
Program A Service revenues	4,000	3,800	200 U	5
Dues	1,000	1,000	-	
Interest	125	90	35 U	28
Total Revenues	28,825	28,590	235 U	1
EXPENSES				
Salaries (Note b)				
Administration	7,000	7,000	-	
Program A	4,000	4,000	-	
Program B	6,750	6,750	-	
Payroll fringe costs	2,192	2,192	-	
Occupancy (Note b)				
Rent (donated)	1,500	1,500	-	
Electricity and heat	600	750	150 U	25
Water	60	75	15 U	25
Janitorial service	450	450	-	
Telephone	300	345	45 U	15
Printing & stationery	306	388	82 U	27
Postage	245	260	15 U	6
Travel & conferences	360	685	325 U	90
Supplies	570	725	155 U	27
Equipment rentals	600	600	-	
Professional fees	775	925	150 U	19
Consulting fees	1,200	1,200	-	
Office expenses	90	188	98 U	109
Insurance	150	150	-	
Depreciation	645	645	-	
Contingency reserve (budgeted)	250	-	250 F	100
Total Expenses	$28,043	$28,828	$ 785 U	3
Increase or (Decrease) in Fund Balance	782	(238)	(1,020) U	

[a]"F" = favorable variance; "U" = unfavorable variance.

[b]Note optional addition of "% Variance" column.

[c]Accounts are shown in detail for control. (Budget details for Occupancy derived from Budget Worksheet, Table 5–5.

levels affecting quantities used, as well as from unanticipated new items or from errors in budget estimates (see Chapter 5). If variances are to be analyzed in a useful way, figures must be shown in a comparable manner. Thus, if the analysis is made during the fiscal year, rather than at year end, the comparable interim budget allowances must be the measuring rod. For example, actual expenses at midyear can only be compared with amounts budgeted for the same period, unless uncommitted funds rather than variances are being measured. (Table 13-4 is for this purpose.)

If the variance is small, the usual conclusion is that revenues are coming in as budgeted or that expenses are being properly controlled. On the other hand, if several different items are included in a single expense category, there is always the possibility that one is too high and another too low, so that they mask each other. Good budgetary control requires that the items be broken down in full detail to avoid this trap.

If a variance is quite large (in proportion to the item itself), you have a clear signal that something needs looking into. Showing variances as percentages flags such items. While it is obvious when revenue is lower or expense higher than budgeted, it may even be the case when the variance is a "favorable" rather than an "unfavorable" one, the terms accountants use. A large favorable revenue variance (more than budgeted) may result from successful activity that should be identified so that the reasons for it may be repeated, if possible, and the individuals reponsible supplied the motivation to continue their good work, in the form of reward or praise. If an expense variance is large and favorable, the same might apply, but it might also signal the possibility that someone is cutting corners by skimping on necessary expenses that might hurt in the long run. One common example is saving money by not having needed repairs done, or by short-changing program activities in a harmful way.

Variance Analysis Pinpoints Responsibility for Departures from the Budget

You can see this when costs are broken down on operating statements between different programs, or between program and support services costs. This is called responsibility accounting, and was touched on in Chapter 6. Its proper use requires that personnel be held responsible (accountable) only for costs over which they have either direct or at least partial control. Here the question is not only "who decides?" but also "who is in a position to influence the decision?" Thus it is a matter not only of who signs the checks but also of who has the authority to hire or to order materials or services and how much genuine authority is delegated over the particular expense. In managerial accounting theory, the rule is to evaluate performance of personnel—usually administrators of programs or support activities—on the basis of controllable expense variances. These are variances in expenses (or revenues) over which personnel have direct or indirect control.

When Variance Analysis Should Be Done

Variance analysis should be done as often as feasible, at least quarterly, and corrective measures taken when indicated. The possibility should never be overlooked that a variance has resulted from an error in the budget estimate rather than in the actual amount of the item in question. When appropriate, the budgeted amount should be revised. This is especially indicated when the activity level has changed substantially, resulting in a corresponding change in program expenses or revenues. Budgeted expenses should be restated to reflect the effect of actual volume on variable costs (see Chapter 6).

NONPROFITS WITH MORE THAN ONE PROGRAM

In Chapters 5 and 6 we explored alternate budget formats for nonprofits with two or more programs (see Tables 5–7, 5–8, 6–2, and 6–4), together with certain other issues, such as allocating overhead and joint expenses between activities. Since operating statements will be compared with their related budgets, when these formats are used for budgets they will obviously be used for the statements as well. The bookkeeping required to produce this breakdown in the accounts is explained in Chapter 12.

When Supporting or Segmental Schedules Are Needed

There are situations in which it is desirable to show some of the figures of an operating statement on a separate "schedule," which is an accounting term for a "list." For example, in a multiprogram operation, it might be desirable to supply each program director with only the budgeted and actual figures for his or her own program, rather than the overall performance report, for political reasons.*

It may also be desirable to reduce the amount of detail on an operating statement by showing only revenues and total expenses by program or activity, providing the details of expenses on separate schedules. This is referred to as a condensed presentation of expenses on the operating statement. An example is shown in Figs. 15–1 and 15–2.

When the columnar format is used rather than the layered format in presenting multiprogram operating data, it is more convenient to compare actual vs. budgeted figures on separate schedules, to avoid a format that would otherwise have nine or more columns, covering budgeted, actual and variances, for two or more programs plus support services.

Handling of Restricted Grants and Funds Is Facilitated by Variance Reports

A brief explanation of fund accounting was set forth in Chapter 10. Control over expenditures budgeted for a particular restricted grant or fund, whether restricted legally or by voluntary board action, is also facilitated by variance reports, which state such items separately. Although it may be acceptable for one program or fund to borrow from another temporarily when short of money, such transfers should be clearly treated as loans. They should not merely be charged to another fund as an expense, on the theory that "it's all our money anyway." Clearly, the "borrowed" money should be repaid as soon as practicable. (Some funding agencies even require that interest be charged.)

Illustrations of alternate budget variance report and operating statement formats for nonprofits maintaining separate funds or operating multiple programs are shown in Tables 13–3 and 13–5. A variation illustrated is the division of revenue between "support" and operating revenues. "Support" is defined as revenues from grants and contributions, as differentiated from operating revenues, money earned in operating the organization (dues, fees, ticket sales, etc.).

A DETAILED ANALYSIS OF THE BUDGET VARIANCE IN FUNCTIONAL FORMAT

Breaking down the comparison of actual and budgeted figures for programs and support services is like switching a microscope to a higher-powered lens. It brings the finer details into view

---

*This does not promote teamwork or good morale, however.

**TABLE 13–3. CENTER FOR COMMUNITY SERVICE, INC.
PERFORMANCE REPORT, QUARTER ENDED MARCH 31**
(Program or Functional Layered Format)

	Budget	Actual	Variance
Support and Revenues			
Support			
Foundation grants (combined)	$20,000	$20,000	—
Government grants	2,200	2,200	—
In-kind contributions—rent	1,500	1,500	—
Fundraising events	—	—	—
Total support	$23,700	$23,700	—
Revenues			
Program A service revenue	$ 4,000	$ 3,800	200 U
Dues	1,000	1,000	—
Interest	125	90	35 U
Total revenue	$ 5,125	$ 4,890	235 U
Total support and revenue	$28,825	$28,590	235 U
Expenses[a]			
Program services			
Program A:			
Salary—Program Director	$ 4,000	$ 4,000	—
Payroll fringe costs	478	478	—
Travel	150	200	50 U
Telephone	75	80	5 U
Supplies	570	725	155 U
Total Program A	$ 5,273	$ 5,483	210 U
Program B:			
Salaries—Program Dir. & asst.	$ 6,750	$ 6,750	—
Payroll fringe costs	846	846	—
Consultant	600	600	—
Telephone	75	125	50 U
Travel	30	300	270 U
Equipment rental	600	600	—
Printing—brochures	150	150	—
Postage	75	25	50 F
Total program B	$ 9,126	$ 9,396	270 U
Total program services (carried forward)	$14,399	$14,879	480 U

**TABLE 13-3. CENTER FOR COMMUNITY SERVICE, INC.
PERFORMANCE REPORT, QUARTER ENDED MARCH 31
(Program or Functional Layered Format) (continued)**

	Budget	Actual	Variance
Total program services (brought forward)	$14,399	$14,879	480 U
Expenses (continued)			
Support services			
Administration			
Administrative salaries	7,000	7,000	—
Payroll fringe costs	868	868	—
Travel and conferences	180	185	5 U
Legal and accounting	775	925	150 U
Occupancy:			
Rent (donated)	1,500	1,500	—
Electricity and heat	600	750	150 U
Water	60	75	15 U
Janitorial services	450	450	—
Telephone	150	140	10 F
Stationery and postage	51	53	2 U
Other[b]	490	338	152 F
Total administration	$12,124	$12,284	160 U
Fundraising			
Consultant	$ 600	$ 600	—
Printing	125	205	80 U
Postage	150	215	65 U
Total fundraising	875	1,020	145 U
Total support services	12,999	13,304	305 U
Depreciation	645	645	—
Total expenses	28,043	28,828	785 U
Operating surplus or (deficit)[c]	$ 782	$ (238)	(1,020) U

[a]Breakdown of expenses between programs and support services not provided for in chart of accounts in Appendix 12A. Actual expense totals were allocated above in order to permit comparison with functional budget. (Table 5-7, first quarter. Note: Joint costs not allocated.)

[b]May be desirable to show an item this large in detail. It includes office expense, insurance, and the contingency reserve of $250 (budget only).

[c]Alternate caption.

and permits pinpointing responsibility for variances. That is really "making your figures talk to you."

Example 1. It turns out that the whole unfavorable variance in telephone expense is traceable to Program B, which was budgeted for only a fourth of the total. The natural question would be "What's going on there?"

Example 2. Similarly, of the $325 overall unfavorable variance in travel and conferences per Table 13–2, it turns out that $270 was also caused by Program B. There may of course be good, defensible reasons for this, which the program director should be asked to supply. Is she traveling and running up phone charges in connection with setting up the new program, or could some of this expense be improper?

Here is another interesting question. Why, if Program B incurred the budgeted expense of printing brochures, is its postage expense only a third of budget? Is this an indication that the brochures were not mailed out as planned? If so, why weren't they?

It seems that the whole variance in supplies was in Program A. That makes it even more significant, although it was also inevitable, since all supplies were charged to that program.

Example 3. The other new bit of information that surfaced from analyzing the programs is the fact that nearly the entire budget overage in printing can be traced to fundraising activity, and it went 43% over budget on postage, although there was only a small ($15) unfavorable postage variance for the whole budget. (This illustrates how a favorable variance—for postage in Program B—can mask an unfavorable one, unless expenses are broken down this way.) Do the variances in printing and postage used for fundraising reflect unexpected, unplanned activity, or waste of some kind?

Isolating the Effect of Volume Changes

Variances can be misleading, since they may result from causes you may not be able to do much about; for example, if your funding is sharply reduced below what was budgeted, you have little choice but to cut expenses accordingly. Thus if a program proposal that was budgeted for is turned down, you obviously must eliminate the budgeted expenses of that program as well as the anticipated revenue. These are not really true variances. If you receive fees or other reimbursement for program services, either from clients, patients, patrons, etc., and the volume of such services increases or decreases sharply, any related *variable* expenses will change proportionately.

To avoid reading misleading signals into such variances from budgeted amounts, the effect of changes in revenue and activity must somehow be isolated or neutralized. In the first situation cited—a cutback or cancelling of a planned program and its associated revenue—the solution is to revise the budget by eliminating both the revenue and expenses involved. In the second, there are two available alternatives:

Flexible budgeting. Instead of staying with the originally budgeted expenses, all variable expenses (and the variable part of mixed expenses) are recalculated based on the actual new volume of activity. This involves using the equations for such expenses explained in Chapter 6 and multiplying the cost per unit by the actual number of units of service (or goods) provided. Any variances from these revised budgeted figures will result from causes other than changes in activity level.

Analyzing components of variances. Analyzing variances into the components resulting from volume changes and those resulting from other causes, such as those discussed previously. This has essentially the same effect as flexible budgeting, except that it provides information that may be useful to management as to the effect of the volume change itself.

Aside from analyzing variances from budgeted figures, another profitable study is to compare changes in figures against those of the previous period, usually for a year. When the number of service units each period are known, it is not too difficult to determine the following pieces of useful information.

1. What part of a revenue increase or decrease resulted from the change in number of units and what part, if any, from changes in average price charged. This is best done separately for each fee-for-service program activity.

2. The same information can be determined for program costs: the separate effects of volume changes and changes in the cost per unit. This can be separated into payroll costs and other costs, again preferably by program activity.

The calculations involved in all of these analyses are probably best left to an expert accountant, using managerial accounting techniques.

Report Formats that Stress Expenditure Control

While the distinction between variance analysis and expenditure control is somewhat subtle, the latter is more commonly used as a current, pragmatic tool, particularly on the part of functional managers, such as program directors, executive directors and fund-raisers. A variance report seeks to answer the question "How well did this activity do, compared with its budget (plan) for the period?" as measured by variances. A budget expenditure control report, on the other hand, asks "How much do we have left in the budget for the year?"

A variance report compares actual versus budgeted figures for the same period, while an expenditure control report compares actual expenses for the year to date (or period to date, if a project budget spans two or more years) against the budgeted figures for the entire year (or project). Table 13–4 illustrates an expenditure control report for the Center as it might appear for January through September.

Restricted Funds. The expenditure control format can serve the additional purpose of insuring that revenue or support received under restrictions for their use are not overspent or misspent. This may apply to grants, donations, endowments, or to investment income from assets in restricted funds, including any gains or losses from their sale or other disposition.

ANALYSIS OF BUDGET EXPENDITURE CONTROL REPORT (Table 13–4)

1. In the Revenue section the Balance column represents revenue still to be earned in the fourth quarter. (Comparing this with the fourth quarter budget items in Table 5–6 indicates in effect a $225 decrease required in budgeted revenues,[4] most particularly for fundraising events ($400) to allow for the overage through Sept. 30.) (The figures in the Annual Budget 19xx column are from Table 5–6.)

2. Only printing and stationery appear to have already gone over budget for the year (by $19). However, note that because of heavy travel and conference expense to date, only $220 is left for the fourth quarter, although $360 was originally budgeted. Board policy governs the question of

---

[4]$25,600 balance vs. $25,825 budgeted; i.e., actual revenues to Sept. 30 were $81,400, or $225 more than the $81,175 budgeted.

TABLE 13–4. CENTER FOR COMMUNITY SERVICE, INC.
BUDGET EXPENDITURE CONTROL REPORT, NINE MONTHS ENDED SEPTEMBER 30

	Annual Budget 19xx	Actual through Sept. 30	Budget balance or (shortage)
Revenues			
Foundation grants	$61,000	$51,000	$10,000
Government grants	8,800	6,600	2,200
In-kind rent	6,000	4,500	1,500
Fundraising events	11,000	4,600	6,400
Program revenues	17,000	12,500	4,500
Dues	2,700	1,800	900
Interest	500	400	100
Total revenues	$107,000	$81,400	$25,600
Expenses			
Salaries	$ 71,000	53,250	17,750
Payroll fringe costs	7,662	5,949	1,713
Occupancy	10,440	7,830	2,610
Telephone	1,120	845	275
Printing & stationery	581	600	(19)
Postage	525	490	35
Travel and conferences	1,320	1,100	220
Supplies	1,140	1,100	40
Equipment rentals	2,305	1,705	600
Professional fees	6,400	4,925	1,475
Office expense	330	255	75
Insurance	600	450	150
Contingency reserve	1,000	750	250
Depreciation	2,577	1,933	644
Total expenses	$107,000	$81,182	$25,818
Operating surplus or (deficit)	$ —	$ 218	$ (218)

Notes: 1. The report could be presented in layered functional format as in Table 13–3 permitting control of expenditures by program and function.

2. Separate reports can be prepared and supplied to each functional administrator (program and fundraising) showing only the relevant revenues and expenses.

3. A separate section could be added showing funds received and used for nonrevenue/expense purposes. Or, you could have a supplementary report in the format of a statement of sources and uses of funds prepared, showing budgeted and actual figures and balance.

TABLE 13–5. CENTER FOR COMMUNITY SERVICE, INC.
OPERATING STATEMENT, QUARTER ENDED MARCH 31 (Program or Functional Columnar Format).

	Total	Program services: A	B	Administration	Fund raising[a]
Support and revenue					
Grants	$22,200	$5,000	$15,000		$2,200
In-kind contributions	1,500				1,500
Program service revenue	3,800	3,800			
Dues	1,000				1,000
Interest	90				90
Total support and revenue	$28,590	$8,800	$15,000	—	$4,790[a]
Expenses					
Salaries					
Program personnel	10,750	4,000	6,750		
Support personnel	7,000[b]	1,000	2,000	$2,500	1,500
Payroll fringe costs	2,192	478	846	868	
Occupancy	2,775[b]	1,110	1,388	166	111
Telephone	345	80	125	140	
Printing and stationery	388		150	33	205
Postage	260		25	20	215
Travel & conferences	685	200	300	185	
Supplies	725	725			
Equipment rentals	600		600		
Professional & consulting	2,125		600	925	600
Office expenses	188[b]	75	94	11	8
Insurance	150[b]	37	76	36	1
Depreciation	645[b]	405		155	85
Total expenses	$28,828	$8,110	$12,954	$ 5,039	$2,725
Excess (deficiency) of revenue over expenses	$ (238)	$ 690	$ 2,046	$(5,039)	$2,065

[a]These items are arbitrarily allocated here to fundraising, although they could have been allocated to administration. The latter is here viewed as being a cost center that generates no revenues.

[b]Actual amounts for period, allocated on bases used in Overhead Allocation Worksheet shown in Chapter 6 (Table 6–1): joint expenses were allocated here.

whether the small overage in printing and stationery means that no more may be ordered this year. This policy governs how strictly line items are controlled and to what extent it is permissible to go over on some items as long as offset by reductions in other items or by increased revenues.

3. Overall results for the year to date indicate good budgeting and control, since the balance of the contingency reserve is more than the operating deficit by $32.

Operating Statement in Columnar Format

A valuable form of operating statement is shown in Table 13–5. It contains only the actual figures for the first quarter of the year: the budgeted figures for the year were shown in the same format in Table 5–8.

This form of statement (also called the matrix form) has one obvious disadvantage compared with the budget variance format shown as Table 13–3: it does not lend itself to showing variances when there are two or more programs, since the number of columns would be tripled. On the other hand, it provides information the other format does not, without difficulty:

- The total expenses of each program or function can be compared directly with its revenue and support, and a bottom line derived.

- Revenues and expenses can be viewed in two diffrent ways: either by how much of each item related to each program or function ("where did we spend our payroll money?") or what the detailed revenues and expenses of each program or function were for the period. Although these could be compared against the separate budgeted figures, and variances derived, this would be clumsy, as noted above.

Our view is that the budget variance report in layered format shown in Table 13–3 is best for managerial control and evaluation during the year, and the columnar statement format is a useful adjunct for analysis on an annual basis. Software for microcomputers, to our knowledge, is thus far unable to generate the columnar format, although mainframes can, and the forms can be supplied by some computer service centers, such as Accounting Corporation of America. If your agency has an annual audit by a public accountant, you may receive a "statement of functional expenses" as part of the audit report, which presents the expense portion of the columnar operating statement in the same matrix form as shown here. That will provide the same two-dimensional view at least of the expenses, by line item and by program or function. This format is shown in Fig. 15–2.

Comments on Table 13–5: Note how this columnar arrangement permits matching directly the revenues and expenses for each program and support function.[5] The excess of revenues over expenses for the two programs can be interpreted either (1) as an "operating surplus" or "savings" in the program, if all expenses incurred for the period have been recognized; or (2) as partly reflecting the costs of any activities postponed to a later period. Examples of the latter would be unused (or unordered) supplies, or delays in obtaining planned services. It does not necessarily reflect unexpended cash on hand, where revenues have been accrued. Note that the nonprogram revenues of $4,790 fell $2,974 short of the combined costs of support services ($5,039 + $2,725 = $7,764), which

---

[5]It is also possible on either statement format to match certain specific expenses even more directly with related revenues by directly subtracting them in the revenue section and showing the revenue net of the associated expense. Common examples are revenues from fundraising activities minus fundraising expense, and membership dues minus the share paid to parent bodies, showing the organization's share net.

is also reflected in the difference between the "bottom line" in these columns ($5,039) and $2,065. These costs were apparently covered by the $3,500 in bank loans obtained in January and March, per Table 14–1.

Operating Statement with General Expenses Reallocated

Where essentially all revenues are earned, as with human service agencies funded by state contracts, it is common to take the further step of reallocating administrative and fundraising expenses in total to programs or contracts. This is usually done on a separate line, after the subtotals of all columns, as subtraction from the totals in the columns for administrative expense and fundraising and addition of the allocated amounts in the program columns. The allocation is usually made on some logical basis, such as the percentage of total revenue earned by each program, although other bases, such as the percentage of total program expense or of payroll costs may be used.

USING THE BOTTOM LINE IN PERFORMANCE EVALUATION

What may not be so apparent is that there are two ways of using financial data in evaluating performance: (1) deciding whether a program is at least breaking even, and whether "the price is right," and (2) evaluating a program director's performance, where he or she has considerable autonomy in running it. Responsibility accounting was discussed above and more fully in Chapter 6. It relates not only to a middle manager's responsibility for line-item variances but also to his or her responsibility for the bottom line, in a decentralized organization. Where all costs, direct and indirect, including administration and fundraising, are allocated to programs, the bottom line can be misleading in evaluating the program director as a middle manager. To use it for both purposes overlooks the fact that it is the net income or loss after *all* expenses, which means after some which are uncontrollable by that individual.

This problem has long been recognized and dealt with in the business world by arriving at an intermediary level of net income, usually labeled "controllable profit" in business. A similar line on the operating statement of the agency—or budget variance report prepared for a single program— could be called "controllable net income" or the like; other, uncontrollable expenses could then be subtracted from this figure to arrive at the bottom line. In that way, the performance of the program director could be evaluated separately from that of the program itself.

OTHER USES OF THE BOTTOM LINE IN DECISION-MAKING

In a multiprogram agency, where all expenses have been allocated to programs, the bottom line can be misleading when one or more programs shows a loss. The temptation is to solve the problem in one of the following ways, any of which might do more harm than good (it is assumed that your program director was not the problem).

1. Raise the price. If you do, the result may be losing so much "business" that the loss is increased; if the price is one set by or negotiated with a third party funder, you may not be able to raise it at will. Policy considerations and what your target population can afford are other constraints, as is competition.

2. Cut costs. This is fine if it means genuine economy or efficiency but dangerous if it reduces the quality of service. That also can lose you more than the savings in lost "business," especially if you have competition.

3. Change the nature of the program so that it will attract more users. This puts you in collision with your mission: it may be a program important to your clients or patients.

4. Drop the program entirely, to eliminate the "loss."

As for the first three alternatives, only the second has any potential at all to help, and that only if you don't damage the quality of your service by your economies. It is the fourth that may therefore seem quite tempting and logical. Often, however, that can result from a superficial use of the bottom line.

Consider this: when you have allocated all expenses to your programs, inevitably some of them will be expenses that would continue to exist, with or without that program. If its bottom line showed a loss of, say, $2,000, what if the allocated expenses included part of your rent and of your administrative payroll, which would go on even if you dropped the "losing program"? What if these totalled $5,000?—If you did eliminate this program, the $5,000 would merely be shifted to the remaining ones. What that really means is that the program was absorbing $3,000 of common expense, and that in dropping the revenue it generated, matters would get worse, not better. If you don't believe it, look at the arithmetic:

Program revenues (assumed)	$100,000
Less: Direct program expenses	97,000
Contribution to overhead (common or general expense)	3,000
Less: Allocated overhead	5,000
Net loss	($2,000)

Thus the option of dropping the program would be self-defeating, since the agency's overall bottom line would be worse off by the $3,000, which the program was generating to pay part of the overhead! (This is a good example of the way figures can cause the wrong decision, if you jump to conclusions.)

Three other options might be mentioned that were not suggested previously: (1) Consider changing the allocation percentage, to shift some of the expenses to other programs, if a negative bottom line is offensive to some of your board members. (2) Try to get the board to recognize and accept its own responsibility for fundraising, as we pointed out in Chapters 4 and 6. (3) Perhaps best of all, prepare your statements in the form shown above, which will always keep your eye on the ball and prevent making costly mistakes.

USING TREND AND RATIO ANALYSIS

Value and Limitations of Trend Analysis

Variance analysis is only one measure of how good performance is. It compares actual revenues and expenses with what was planned. It is a measurement of accountability by personnel charged with carrying out the plan, and seeks to answer the question, "Are we getting and spending what we expected to?" There are, however, other ways of evaluating performance that do not make use of budgeted figures at all. The most common and obvious one, called *trend analysis*, asks, "How are we doing compared with last year?" The comparison, which can be made between quarters or months as well, is another way of viewing and deciding results, i.e., whether they are better or worse than last time. Even in the absence of a budget, comparative data are useful for evaluating results. However, since the activity level or direction may have changed, they are not usually adequate by themselves.[6]

Several Useful Applications of Ratio Analysis

Another measuring device is *ratio analysis,* which may be used in more than one way. It involves calculating the percentage of each item of expense to total revenues, including contributions and grants, or it may show the percentage of each item of program expense to program revenues or total program costs. Comparison of these percentages between periods, aside from changes in dollar amounts, is particularly useful where the level of activity changes, since comparison of expenses in dollars is not very useful when activity levels change. The discussion of cost behavior in Chapter 6 (in the discussion of break-even analysis) is relevant here as well. Some expenses vary directly with activity level, others may not; consequently not all expense ratios will behave in the same way. For example, program supplies may in some cases vary in direct proportion to the level of activity, but office supplies may vary but little. In studying ratios, therefore, figures should be looked at critically, in relation to their true significance, and not mechanically or abstractly.

The importance of ratios is in the clues they may provide to what is going on, not as absolute measures of good or bad performance. Just as in variance analysis, an increasing ratio for a given expense is sometimes fully justified, a decrease in another not necessarily desirable. For example, an increase in the ratio of program supplies expense to total program expense or revenue could indicate inflationary price increases, or it could reveal use of higher quality supplies. On the other hand, it could disclose excessive quantities purchased or consumed. A decrease in this item might reveal an unwarranted skimping on either quantity or quality that could be bad for the program's effectiveness.

Another use of ratio analysis is to compare the organization's expense ratios with those of other comparable nonprofit (or profit-making) organizations or with averages of ratios for organizations in the same field of activity. This use is not too common in the nonprofit field. It is generally possible for only a limited number of organizations where such data are published, such as colleges and universities, hospitals, and others that bridge the profit and nonprofit fields.*

Ratio Analysis and Control of Overhead Costs

Ratio analysis may also be used in a more limited way comparable to the budgetary control approach. Nonprofits exist not to perpetuate themselves but to provide certain program services that funding agencies, members, or clients are willing to pay for. The general administrative and fund-raising costs of the organization are frequently looked at suspiciously by these constituents, and, as noted in Chapter 8, by state regulatory agencies, who commonly see them as targets of criticism

---

[6]Published corporate reports routinely furnish comparative data for the last five years for use by investors and others in evaluating performance.

*Few nonprofits are really comparable, and averages are treacherous.

and prime candidates for budget cuts. It is useful to establish a justifiable percentage relationship between such "overhead" costs and total funds received or spent. Any substantial increase in the ratio of administrative or fundraising expenditures should be avoided and/or investigated by officers and board. Although they may increase in dollar amount with an increase in the level of activity, they should generally *decrease* as a percentage rather than increase or even remain stable. These are known as the "economies of scale." What this means is that overhead costs generally grow much more slowly than program costs, which usually vary more directly with volume of activity. Therefore, overhead decreases as a percentage of the total.

Important Questions on Pricing

Where the organization is paid for its goods or services by those served or by third parties, the *cost per unit* becomes a still more important piece of information. When services are free, this figure is one that the nonprofit will try to keep at a minimum (or at least optimum) level, but need only define consistently and not necessarily with any precision. Once it is decided to charge a price for goods or services, a whole series of questions eventually surfaces. Here is where the "bottom line" point of view often comes into headlong conflict with the goals of the nonprofit organization. The two major issues that arise are (1) should we set our price to break even, should we try to make money, or should our goal be to recover only part of our cost per unit? (2) What do we mean by cost per unit?

Price vs. Cost per Unit

The answer to the first question is one that will have to be thoughtfully considered and debated by the board itself as a major policy question, unless the board has already established an ongoing policy on this question. The answer cannot be found in a book on accounting or financial management, for it goes to the very essence of what the organization is. Obviously any organization that is constantly "in the red" on an overall basis cannot long survive. That is not the question. The questions that must be answered are the following:

- Should program activities collectively bring in total revenues adequate to defray their costs; i.e., to break even overall?

- Is a particular program popular enough to permit a price that brings in an excess over cost, which can be used to help pay for other, less popular programs?

- Is a particular program of sufficient importance to the goals of the organization that it should be subsidized, if necessary, by charging a price less than cost, or should certain clients be served at a lower price or without charge?

- Can economies of scale result in a given program's revenues equaling or exceeding cost when a certain break-even point is reached in the number of clients served?

Problems in Defining Cost per Unit

We explored the question of allocating overhead costs in some depth in Chapters 5 and 6. We pointed out the distinctions between direct program costs and joint or indirect costs of a program. We also addressed the more knotty problem of whether support costs of general administration and fundraising also should be allocated to programs. In determining the cost per unit of output (goods or service), a choice must be made among these alternatives. The following considerations usually govern this choice:

• Direct program costs are invariably used at least as the *minimum* cost, for a starting point. (Managerial accountants call these separable or incremental costs, which presumably would not be incurred if the program did not exist. There is little that could be argued about here.)

• Joint or indirect costs are sometimes included, such as a percentage of the cost of rented space that applies to the program or a percentage of the salary of an administrator whose time is spent supervising more than one program. A good case can be made for allocating a portion of any costs that are clearly of direct benefit to the program, despite the nuisance involved in making such allocations.

• A more controversial issue is whether to allocate the cost of support services which are only of indirect benefit to the program, such as general administration and fundraising. This issue was explored in Chapter 6, at some length. A major question is whether such overhead costs, loosely defined as costs that would be incurred whether or not the program existed, should be related to program revenues at all, or whether they should be covered by grants and fundraising activities. Again, this is a policy decision for the board, one based on the overall philosophy and goals of the organization itself.

Note: The fact that any such allocation must be made on an inherently arbitrary basis and that selecting some other basis changes the resulting "cost" should give one pause before using the method. A related issue is whether there are other sources of support for a program, such as foundation or government grants. Such income would help cover program costs and allow a lower price to be set.

Special Circumstances

Usually, there are sources of funds other than program revenues, but, if not, then the organization will have little choice but to assure that all costs are covered by program revenues. That should not prevent pricing one program below or another above cost, so long as total revenues cover total costs.

If depreciation accounting is used, as recommended, and program equipment is to be replaced when necessary out of program revenues, rather than through special fundraising drives or grants, the depreciation cost should be considered part of the cost per unit, regardless of which of the above methods of determining cost is used.

WHAT SHAPE ARE WE IN?—THE BALANCE SHEET AS THE ANSWER

The cash-flow worksheet tells us what funds we expect to have on hand to pay bills and other obligations as they come due. It also helps us to plan how much we'll need and where it should come from. The organization's balance sheet[7]—and it may properly only be so designated if prepared on an accrual basis—is a report of its current financial situation and discloses the following information at a minimum.

---

[7]Sometimes called a "statement of financial position," or simply "position statement." (Where prepared on a cash basis, the comparable statement would be called "Statement of Assets, Liabilities and Fund Balances Prepared on a Cash Basis.")

Assets Checklist

- The cash balance at the balance sheet date

- Receivables: amounts due to us from funding agencies, members and donors (if dues or pledges are accrued), from employees for any loans or advances, or other amounts coming to us

- Temporary investments: savings or money market accounts, certificates of deposit (time deposits), stocks or bonds held, or other investments

- Inventories of merchandise, if any is being sold, or of supplies

- Prepaid expenses: expenses paid in advance for services to be received in the future

- Fixed assets: land, building, vehicles, furniture, equipment, etc.

- Sundry other assets that may be held, such as security deposits with utilities, landlords, etc.

Liabilities Checklist

- Accounts payable: amounts due suppliers and other nonemployees for goods or services

- Installments payable: on equipment purchased

- Accrued expenses: amounts owed for other services rendered, including unpaid payrolls, interest on loans

- Taxes payable: generally for payroll taxes withheld or employer taxes due but unpaid (may include Unrelated Business Income sales or property taxes where applicable)

- Unearned (deferred) revenue or advances: for services paid for in advance by patrons or members

- Loans payable: short- or long-term loans from others

- Mortgages payable: on property owned by the organization.

Fund Balance

The fund balance is the difference between total assets and total liabilities: the "net worth" of the organization. An illustration of a balance sheet, showing how that of Center for Community Service, Inc. might appear at March 31, is shown in Table 13–6.

USEFUL INFORMATION IN A BALANCE SHEET

Are We Solvent?   This generally means that our current assets are greater in total than our current liabilities. These are defined respectively as assets expected to be turned into cash within a year and liabilities (or portions of them) that are due for payment within that same period. The ratio of the former to the latter is known as the "current ratio" and is a rough indicator of current financial well-being. A common rule of thumb is that a 2:1 ratio is a comfortable one in a good many cases, although this may vary by type of business or organization. (It means that there are twice as many dollars expected to come in during the year, from current assets held, as debts that will come due. It reflects the financial picture at a given moment of time, however, and is not the same as a cash budget for the year.)[8]

It should be fairly obvious that if current liabilities are greater than current assets, we have real problems. Such is the case in Table 13–6, the balance sheet of the center at March 31. The cash budgets shown cover only the first quarter of the year, but note that the $3,500 in bank loans was obtained in January and March and will have to be paid eventually ($2,000 in April). The delayed check of $5,000 from the ABC Foundation should straighten this out. The second quarter operating budget (Table 5–6) projected an excess of revenues over expenses of $3,327, whereas the

TABLE 13–6. CENTER FOR COMMUNITY SERVICE, INC. BALANCE SHEET, MARCH 31

ASSETS	
Current Assets	
Cash	$ 2,000
Grants Receivable	5,000[a]
Prepaid Insurance	275
Total Current Assets	$ 7,275
Fixed Assets	
Equipment	12,885
Less: Accumulated Depreciation	5,799
Total Fixed Assets	7,806
Total Assets	$14,361
LIABILITIES AND FUND BALANCE	
Current Liabilities	
Loan Payable—Bank	$ 3,500
Equipment Installments Payable	600
Payroll Taxes Payable	3,342[b]
Accrued Expenses	625
Total Current Liabilities	8,067
Fund Balance	6,294
Total Liabilities and Fund Balance	$14,361

[a] From ABC Foundation
[b] Withheld and accrued taxes.

third quarter shows an operating deficit of $3,972. The $1,500 left after paying the $3,500 in loans should cover the difference.

The balance sheet in this case discloses a less comforting short-term picture than the operating budget, which projected a $782 operating surplus for the first quarter. Remember that the center was actually $1,020 worse off than the projection according to its budget variance report (Table 13–2). It would thus appear that either new sources of support or revenue must be found or expenses pared somewhere, possibly some of each. Increasing loans would stave off the problem but not solve it, since they must eventually be repaid.

What Resources Do We Own?   In addition to our checking accounts what do we own that could be tapped if necessary to pay maturing debts? These are, of course, any other current assets, with the probable exception of prepaid expenses and supplies, which rarely yield much cash.

[8]If you get involved in a business venture, other balance sheet ratios may become important, such as debt/equity, asset turnover, etc. Ask your accountant.

What Do We Owe, and When Is It Due? This information is needed in conjunction with the preparation of a cash budget. Current installments of long-term debts, such as mortgages and installment contracts, must be recognized as current liabilities that will come due shortly. Unearned revenue and advances do not represent cash obligations. They represent obligations to perform a service, unless the related service cannot be rendered, in which case a refund may be required. (An example is advance sale of tickets to a concert or other event, paid for before it takes place.) But rendering the service will mean additional expenses.

FUND ACCOUNTING BALANCE SHEETS

When a nonprofit uses formal fund accounting, generally when it has received or voluntarily created one or more retricted funds, such as a plant or endowment fund, the balance sheet should reflect this situation. For internal purposes, this serves to keep the board and officers aware of borrowing between funds, if this is properly recorded (see discussion of Fund Accounting in Chapter 10). It also reminds officers and staff of the need to repay any funds borrowed by a fund or laid out for one fund by another. Balance sheets segregating items by fund or program can, like operating statements, be prepared in either the layered or columnar format. The latter generally afford a better overview of the organization and of the interrelationships between funds (see Table 13–8).

TABLE 13–7. CENTER FOR COMMUNITY SERVICE, INC. BALANCE SHEET, MARCH 31
(prepared on a fund accounting basis, layered format[a])

ASSETS		LIABILITIES & FUND BALANCE	
	Current Funds—Unrestricted (General Fund)		
Cash	$ 1,500	Loans payable—bank	$ 3,500
Due from Programs	978[b]	Payroll taxes withheld	1,775 [c]
Prepaid insurance	275	Accrued expenses and taxes	868
			6,143
		Fund balance (deficit)	(3,390)[d]
Total	$ 2,753	Total	$ 2,753
	Current Funds—Restricted (Program Funds)		
Cash	500[b]	Due general fund	978 [b]
Grants receivable	5,000[e]	Accrued expenses and taxes	1,324 [c]
		Fund balance	3,198 [d]
Total	$ 5,500	Total	$ 5,500
	Plant Fund (Equipment)[f]		
Equipment	12,885	Equipment installments	600
Less: accum. depreciation	5,799	Fund balance	6,486 [d]
Total	7,086	Total	7,806
Total—all funds	$15,339	Total—all funds	$15,339

[a]Based on the assumption that both program funds are restricted to program use and that a separate Plant Fund has been mandated.
[b]Represents cash advanced by the General Fund for program expense. (No entry had been made on the books for this.)
[c]No allocation made of withheld taxes, only of accrued payroll taxes and expenses.
[d]Note that the sum of the three separate fund balances equals $6,294, the combined Fund Balance shown in Table 13–6.
[e] Delayed receipt of approved grant for Program A.
[f]Plant Fund assumed to be a restricted fund.

Illustrations of balance sheets for the Center prepared in both formats are shown in Tables 13–7 and 13–8. Other variations of each type exist, there being no standard format.

THE STATEMENT OF CHANGES IN FUND BALANCES

When a nonprofit has more than one fund, showing a single figure for fund balance on the balance sheet doesn't explain where it came from. Ordinarily, you should be able to add the net income, or subtract the net loss, from the fund balance at the end of the previous period as discussed above. Yet, even when there is only a single fund, that may not be adequate, if any adjusting entries have been made to the account itself, such as to correct errors of the previous period.

TABLE 13–8. CENTER FOR COMMUNITY SERVICE, INC.
BALANCE SHEET, MARCH 31
(prepared on a fund accounting basis, columnar format[a])

		Current Funds		
	Total	**Unrestricted (general fund)**	**Restricted (program funds)**	**Plant[b] fund (equipment)**
Current Assets				
Cash	$ 2,000	$ 1,500		
Grants receivable	5,000		$ 5,000	
Inter-fund balances	—	978	(978)[c]	
Prepaid insurance	275	275		
Total current assets	$ 7,275	$ 2,753	$ 4,522	
Fixed Assets				
Equipment	$12,885			$12,885
Less: accumulated depreciation	5,799			5,799
Total fixed assets	7,086			7,086
Total assets	$14,361	$ 2,753	$ 4,522	$ 7,086
LIABILITIES AND FUND BALANCES				
Current Liabilities				
Loans payable—bank	$ 3,500	$ 3,500		
Equipment installments	600			600
Payroll taxes withheld	1,775	1,775		
Accrued expenses and taxes	2,192	868	1,324	
Total current liabilities	8,067	6,143	1,324	600
Fund Balance or (deficit)	$ 6,294	$(3,390)	$ 3,198	$ 6,486

[a]See notes to Table 13–7.
[b]Plant Fund assumed to be a restricted fund.
[c]Actually a current liability: shown on this line to offset (cancel) the receivable in the general fund.

Enter the statement of changes in fund balance. If there is only one fund, i.e., the general fund, it is a simple statement that starts with the fund balance at the end of the preceding period, adds or deducts any adjustments to the closing balance made this year, and finally adds or deducts the net income or loss for the current period to arrive at the new ending balance.

If there are two or more funds, the statement shows all of them in columns, plus a total column. It presents the same information for each fund, but also provides for any permanent transfers between funds. This did not apply in the case of the Community Service Center, so Table 13–9 uses zeroes to show a transfer that might have been made from the current fund to the plant fund. (The zero in parentheses represents a minus figure.)

TABLE 13–9. CENTER FOR COMMUNITY SERVICE, INC.
STATEMENT OF CHANGES IN FUND BALANCES, QUARTER ENDED MARCH 31, 19xx

	Total	General Fund	Restricted Funds	Plant Fund
Balance, Jan. 1	$6,532	($416)	$462	$6,486
Transfers		(0)		0
Net Income or (Loss)[a]	(238)	(2,974)	2,736	
Balance, March 31	($6,294)	(3,390)	$3,198	$6,486

[a]This is an alternative caption for the one used in Table 13–5, "Excess (Deficiency) of Revenue Over Expenses." It is preferred by many people for its brevity.

OVERALL GUIDELINES FOR DIAGNOSING FINANCIAL PROBLEMS

Awareness that a financial problem exists usually hits you when there's not enough money in the bank to pay what you owe. With proper use, financial data should allow anticipation of such a problem. Mounting expenses or shrinking income may be one cause but are by no means the only cause, as indicated in the discussion of the statement of cash flows.

Analyzing such a statement is in fact an excellent starting point; unfortunately, the statement cannot be prepared until the operating statement and balance sheet are finished. If your problem is in the operations area, a big loss will show up quickly, and further analysis of what caused it will be necessary. That usually means doing a budget variance report and perhaps also comparing the line items with the operating statement for the previous period.

A more detailed analysis may be worthwhile, analyzing variances in earned revenues between those caused by changes in activity level and those caused by changes in prices charged (or reimbursed). The same kind of analysis may be of value for expenses: using a flexible budget or comparative analysis that further pinpoints the problem. If there is no loss for the period, these analyses may not answer the question of "what happened?"

Analysis of comparative balance sheets and the statement of cash flows can reveal whether the shortage in cash resulted from such things as using cash for nonexpense purposes, such as buying equipment, paying off loans or old liabilities, etc., or whether there has been a build-up of receivables, investments or inventory, if you have one. The point here is that "you can't have your cake and eat it too." Put another way, you can't pay bills or payrolls out of profits if the cash hasn't been collected or has been spent. This point was made earlier, of course, but cannot be stressed too often.

WHY YOU SHOULD INCLUDE NARRATIVE COMMENTS IN YOUR FINANCIAL STATEMENTS

Although the financial reports of a nonprofit described in this chapter may resemble those of a business enterprise in most respects, they are by themselves far less adequate for management or for external use. First, operating and financial performance of a business can be more readily expressed in purely monetary terms. The "bottom line" of profit or loss is what the enterprise is all about, after all. What is more, the statement users, both insiders and outsiders, understand the language. Accounting is called "the language of business."

With the typical small nonprofit, neither of these advantages exists. Its performance cannot be judged solely in monetary terms; its financial statements do not themselves gauge either the efficiency or effectiveness of its performance, and users of the reports often either "do not speak accounting" or, even if they do, cannot obtain an adequate picture of results from them. It is for this reason that narrative or other explanatory comments become a most valuable, if not essential, part of financial reports. Such analytical observations, cogently and concisely written, can give meaning to the numerical abstractions of the financial statements, which may otherwise be of little value to the board member or officer for whom accounting is not even a second language.

Examples of Interpretive Comments That Can Bring Bare Numbers to Life

- Comments regarding substantial variances, including explanations of why they occurred

- Comments on the measured efficiency and/or effectiveness of the organization's operations in attaining its goals and its objectives for the period, including output measures of services provided and/or number of volunteer hours enlisted

- Comments on the organization's financial condition and its financial performance during the period, including new funding prospects, renewal or nonrenewal of major grants and the like

- Possible comments on improvements needed or accomplished in the system of internal controls; changes in the number, scope, or nature of programs and/or key personnel; other important developments or facts that help shed light on the meaning of the financial data

THE USE OF GRAPHICS IN REPORTING

Most people, even accountants, find it easier to grasp the significance of arrays of figures when presented in the form of charts or graphs, especially when studying trends or making comparisons of related figures. A good illustration of this is the two presentations of the same data in Figs. 8–1.A and 8–1.B. Although it may require a bit of skill, which may mean finding someone else who can do the artwork, the effort is worthwhile, especially if the data are to be presented to your board, funding agency or large donors. If you use a computer, spreadsheet programs can generate the most common types of charts and graphs, such as the pie chart in Figs. 8–1 and 13–1.

Pie charts lend themselves best to ratio analysis, showing the percentage of income or total expense for each major expense category or the percentage of total revenue and support by category. Changes in these percentages between years are more clearly grasped than are columns of numbers. Line and bar graphs are better for showing trends and comparisons in actual amounts of income and expense. Stacked or segmented bar graphs can also show relationships between income and expense for a period and then compare them with the same relationships vs. other periods.

Examples of these types of graphic presentation are shown in Fig. 13–1. The illustrations are for business applications but can be readily adapted to nonprofit use, with a bit of imagination. There are still other types of bar charts and graphs, some of which can be generated by microcomputers from spreadsheets of data, as can these, depending on the features of the particular software.

Fiscal Year 1988

The Government Dollar

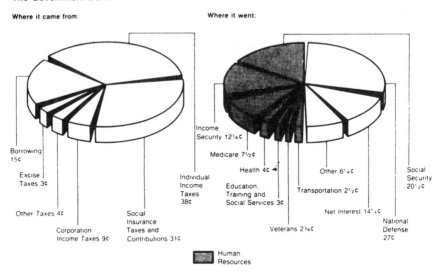

Where it came from:

Borrowing 15¢
Excise Taxes 3¢
Other Taxes 4¢
Corporation Income Taxes 9¢
Social Insurance Taxes and Contributions 31¢
Individual Income Taxes 38¢

Where it went:

Income Security 12¼¢
Medicare 7½¢
Health 4¢
Education, Training and Social Services 3¢
Veterans 2¾¢
Net Interest 14¼¢
Transportation 2½¢
Other 6¼¢
Social Security 20½¢
National Defense 27¢

Human Resources

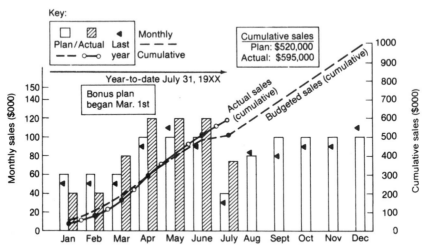

Cumulative and monthly sales, planned and actual, Jan.–July 19XX, combining bar chart and line graphs.

FIGURE 13-1. EXAMPLES OF GRAPHIC REPRESENTATION

Note: From Arnold J. Olenick, *Managing to Have Profits,* New York: McGraw-Hill, 1989, pp. 132-133.

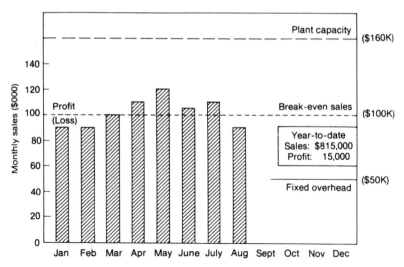

Sales versus profits, showing capacity and break-even, Jan.–Aug. 19XX, using bar chart.

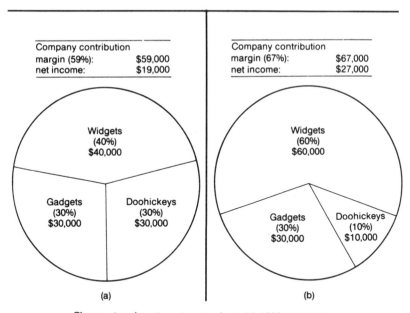

Changes in sales mix, using pie chart: (a) 1988, (b) 1989.

FIGURE 13–1. EXAMPLES OF GRAPHIC REPRESENTATION (continued)

Chapter 14

Cash Management

As we suggested in Chapter 7, although directing its programs is the main function of a non-profit, it can neglect husbanding its cash only at its peril. Preparing a cash budget is only a good first step: monitoring the cash actually available and forthcoming is a life-and-death matter. If yours is the rare nonprofit that is always "loaded," you might think this chapter is not for you: even then there are unexpected turns of events that might change that.

One mistake any organization can make is to assume that, as long as it monitors its operating budget carefully, nothing bad can happen. Not so! The problem is that of timing and of cash flow that has nothing to do with revenue or expenses, directly at least. This point, covered in Chapter 7, bears repeating here.

Timing. Since, as noted in Chapter 7, operating budgets are inevitably prepared on an accrual basis—whether you realize it or not, whether you keep your books that way or not—they indicate when revenues are to be earned and when expenses are to be incurred, and not when cash is to be collected or paid. Confusing the two can be a near-disaster in minding the store.

Transactions not affecting the operating budget. You do not receive cash only from revenues. Cash is also borrowed, received from the sale of investments or other assets, etc. You pay out cash not only for expenses but also to repay funds borrowed, to pay installments of mortgage principal, withheld taxes, purchases of equipment, etc.

The monitoring of your cash situation therefore requires its own tracking device, independent of the budget variance report. Cash management is a purely financial specialty, although one not hard to learn.

WHY YOU NEED A CASH FLOW WORKSHEET AND BUDGET

As a practical matter, the cash budget described in Chapter 7 cannot accurately predict what funds will actually be received or paid, only a forecast. Consequently the figures projected must be constantly monitored and modified as necessary. The working version of a cash budget is a "shirt-sleeves" document rather than a formal one. The worksheets illustrated in Tables 7–2 and 7–3 merely project anticipated amounts for the periods indicated, but do not provide columns to enter the *actual* cash in and out, the actual cash balances resulting, or any temporary loans needed to cover unanticipated shortages. (Sources of additional cash other than loans, including transfers from a savings account, can of course be substituted if available, as discussed below.)

A working version useful for cash management is illustrated in Table 14–1. We call it a cash flow worksheet and budget, although the name is discretionary, as are other internal accounting forms. Although it has been completed here for all 3 months, in real use the actual amounts for each month would be entered at the end of that month. The actual amounts of cash received and paid are recorded monthly for comparison with budgeted figures and for monitoring their impact on projected cash balances.

Table 7–2 projected what was expected to happen in the first quarter. Let us assume that the board has a standing policy of requiring that a minimum balance of $2,000 be maintained, and that things fail to work out just as planned. The ABC Foundation's installment of $5,000 due in February is not received even by March 31; therefore, the cash flow picture will change. Table 14-1 reflects the new situation and the way it can best be projected in the revised and updated cash budget. (To avoid irrelevent repetition, we have condensed the budgeted and actual expense payments. The actual total paid for expenses can be derived from the books of account and need not be shown in detail.)

The following differences between budgeted and actual amounts will be seen upon inspection: (1) the delay in the payout of the ABC Foundation grant of $5,000 budgeted for February, and (2) the difference between actual and estimated balances, reflecting other differences between budgeted and actual expenses as well as revenues.

REQUIREMENTS FOR CASH MANAGEMENT

For routine cash management, what is required is a weekly list of amounts due staff, suppliers, and others, for use by the treasurer or whomever authorizes or makes payments. If you are able to schedule payments (including payroll) on a monthly basis, the list of "payables," as accountants refer to them, can be prepared that way, but important new bills that may be due during the month must still be scheduled for interim payment.

The cash budget has to be monitored constantly, of course, and modified as required by actual developments. That is where the cash flow budget and worksheet come in—and pay off. You can't overlook the interrelationship of the following figures, when authorizing and making payments:

1. The budgeted payments for the period.

2. The actual bills, payrolls, and other obligations on hand and due.

3. Known *additional* priority payments coming up soon.

4. The checkbook balance, which reflects actual rather than budgeted cash transactions; this balance should be reconciled monthly to both the bank statement and the cash balance according to your books.[1]

5. Money definitely coming in soon.

---

[1]Since the cash budget projects the *estimated* balance at the end of each payment period (a month, or sometimes a week), this figure must always be adjusted to the *actual* balance when that date arrives; in addition, all subsequent monthly balances projected must be corrected by the same amount, in a chain reaction.

If your cash is as tight as that of most nonprofits, you'll need a budget worksheet each month like the sample budget shown below in Fig. 14–1. As was pointed out in Chapter 7, this is for detailed planning within the month: *who* do we pay *when*, based on how much we'll have in the bank each week. On the other hand, if you have maintained an adequate cash balance, it may not be necessary, since you'll always have enough to meet your regular payroll as well as paying your bills, which is usually done monthly.

Depending on how often you pay your staff—weekly, biweekly, semimonthly or monthly—this worksheet helps you schedule the issuing of checks. Use it to answer the questions "What do we have to pay this month and when? How much do we have in the bank? How much more is

TABLE 14–1. CASH FLOW WORKSHEET AND BUDGET, FIRST QUARTER
(based on Table 7–2 data and actual cash flow)

	January		February		March	
	Budget	**Actual**	**Budget**	**Actual**	**Budget**	**Actual**
Balance—beginning of month	$ 2,000	$ 2,000	$ 3,285	$ 3,900	$ 7,919	$ 3,193
Cash Receipts—Revenues						
Grants—ABC	—	—	5,000	(not received; expect in April)		
—XYZ	5,000	5,000	5,000	5,000	5,000	5,000
—State	800	800	700	700	700	700
Program A services	1,000	1,400	2,000	1,800	1,000	600
Dues	500	600	400	300	100	100
Interest	20	10	20	10	85	70
Total cash revenues	$7,320[a]	$ 7,810	$13,120	$ 7,810	$ 6,885	$ 6,470
Nonrevenue Receipts						
Temporary loans						
Budgeted (due April)	2,000	2,000	—	—	—	—
New—unbudgeted	—	—	—	—	—	1,500[b]
Total cash receipts	9,320	9,810	13,120	7,810	6,885	7,970[-]
Total cash available	$11,320	$11,810	$16,405	$11,710	$14,804	$11,163
Cash Disbursements						
Expenses						
Salaries	5,917	5,917	5,917	5,917	5,916	5,916
Less: taxes withheld	1,775	1,775	1,775	1,775	1,775	1,775
Net salaries	4,142	4,142	4,142	4,142	4,141	4,141
Other cash expenses[c]	2,593	2,468	2,369	2,400	2,168	3,047
Total expenses paid	6,735	6,610	6,511	6,542	6,309	7,188
Nonexpense payments						
Withholding taxes paid	1,100	1,100	1,775	1,775	1,775	1,775
Equipt. installments	200	200	200	200	200	200
Loans repaid (Apr.)	—	—	—	—	—	—
Total cash disbursed	8,035	7,910	8,486	8,517	8,284	9,163
Balance—End of Month	$ 3,285	$ 3,900	$ 7,919	$ 3,193	$ 6,520	$ 2,000[d]

[a] In-kind contribution (donated rent) omitted.

[b] Temporary loan (or other source) of $1,500 required to increase ending balance to minimum of $2,000 in accordance with Board policy. Repayment must be budgeted.

[c] Other Expenses budgeted per Table 7–2. Excludes donated rent and depreciation.

[d] Assumed a policy of the Board to maintain a minimum balance of $2,000 at all times.

coming in and will it be soon enough?" Proper planning can help prevent these questions from driving you up a wall. This is one big area where you can't afford *not* to plan, or the day may come when all the chickens come home to roost and the wolf is at your door—looking for those chickens, no doubt.

Cash Budget Worksheet for Current Month

		Week ending			
	Budget for month	**Scheduled payment:**			
Item		**(Date)**	**(Date)**	**(Date)**	**(Date)**
Rent					
Payroll					
Payroll tax deposits (Federal and state)					
Consultants					
Utilities					
Telephone					
Suppliers					
Co. A					
Co. B					
(etc.)					
Totals					

FIGURE 14-1. SAMPLE BUDGET FOR CURRENT MONTH.

CASH PROSPECTS AND PROSPECTING

Remember, in cash budgeting, timing is everything. Monthly budgets are essential; even weekly budgets may be necessary; $1,000 coming in tomorrow may be more crucial than $5,000 six months from now. Cash budgeting is more than projecting how much money is expected and when. It implies or involves planning ways to *make sure* cash comes in when expected.

Following up on Funding Proposals

Foundations and other funding agencies generally operate on established schedules in their handling and processing of grant requests. Part of the nonprofit's planning/budgeting process involves ascertaining from each agency its grant application deadlines and its schedule of steps in processing, including dates of preliminary and final approval. Contact must be maintained to keep abreast of the progress of each application through its final disposition, amount of approved grant, and schedule for payment obtained. (Needless to say, this schedule becomes an item in the cash budget for follow-up.) (The "Cautionary Tale" that began the Overview of Part Two is relevant here.)

Developing Fundraising Projects

Annual or special fundraising events, such as dinners and benefits, require lead time for planning and arrangements. They often represent a substantial part of projected revenues, and their reliable scheduling can be important not only from a revenue viewpoint but also for the associated expenses. Fund drives aimed at members, major donors, and/or the general public also need to be carefully scheduled and the timing pattern of resulting contributions projected. Records and follow-up of pledges are part of the planning process.

Keeping After Dues, Pledges, and Contributions

In Chapter 11 we described record-keeping procedures that include systems to keep on top of membership dues status and contribution potentials. These are basic tools in cash-flow management and are your basis for follow-up on collections and for routine solicitation to help bring in the cash promptly, by billing or other follow-up, on a planned cycle.*

Stop-Gap Loans

These may be needed at certain dates, as revealed by cash-flow projections. They need to be scheduled, and arrangements should be made in advance to obtain them when needed. These often take time and effort and can't be relied upon for a last-minute bailout.

Timing and Planning in Scheduling Payments

If you do this on a hit-or-miss basis, the odds are you'll miss and then have to go scurrying around in a panic. Here is another job where timing and planning are everything.

First, and above all, someone in authority, commonly the treasurer, has to decide priorities, in terms of both ongoing, routine situations and in a cash crunch. This is basically a policy matter, with the board as final arbiter; unfortunately you cannot call a board meeting every time you are in a bind, so you need a routine order of priorities for the treasurer's guidance.

As an example, there ought to be a policy for who gets paid first, staff or outside suppliers of goods or services. And when that isn't enough help, when things get really tight, *which* suppliers and *which* staff members get paid, and in what order? Real-world constraints will of course operate here, such as the axiom that the squeaky wheel gets the grease. On the other hand, that can sometimes result in danger: wheels that may not squeak much can suddenly stop turning if ignored too long in favor of those that do.

Fig. 14–1 above provides a systematic way to handle this important task. The Appendix to this chapter shows an original, fairly simple yet reliable method of accomplishing the following important tasks:

- Monthly cash budgeting for expenses and payroll taxes, to prevent running out of cash

- Authorizing and scheduling or prioritizing payment of expenses

- Accruing unpaid expenses, without converting your books from the cash basis or calling in an accountant.

*Specialized computer software is available for this purpose.

How to Handle a Low Cash Balance

If your nonprofit is lucky enough to have a savings account with enough in it, that is an obvious source of extra cash. If this is not a possibility, one or more of the following may help.

- Speed up collections of revenues and other amounts due the organization, as much as possible.
- Find new sources of revenues that can be collected quickly, including special pledges, assessments, and donations.
- Borrow money as discussed below.
- Sell (or cash in) assets that are not needed, preferably when no loss results.
- Get agreement of certain friendly creditors to wait.
- Reduce expenses to the extent possible, without adversely affecting activities, if possible.

Temporary Investments Can Be a Good Source of Funds

If you are holding any temporary investments, and they are readily convertible to cash, without a loss, they are a prime source of funds. When substantial grant or other funds are received in a lump sum, and will not be expended very soon, unneeded balances should be transferred temporarily to secure, liquid investments, such as short-term certificates of deposit or well-managed money market funds. The interest generated is an added source of revenue, unless the grant contract provides that it be rebated.[2]

If another investment is held (e.g., stock or bond certificates), which can only be turned into cash at a loss compared to cost, one possibility is to use it as collateral for a temporary loan. You may not be able to borrow 100% of its current market value, but it's better than taking a permanent loss if you sell it. You can make sure of the loan and also cut the rate of interest that way, and still collect interest or dividends on the investment while it is held as collateral.

Another financial device that acts as a spur to improving your financial picture is leaving a savings account intact and using it as 100% collateral for a loan at a low interest rate. Instead of using up the account and thereby lulling yourself to sleep about your cash flow, the existence of the loan and the unavailability of the funds in the savings account will act to spur your efforts to pay off the obligation and free up the funds.

If you do not have such resources to draw upon, you may be able to obtain a short-term bank loan, or to borrow from one or more members, patrons, or perhaps trustees. If you have a payment due to come in soon on an approved grant, showing the related correspondence should facilitate the loan. What it often comes down to in the end is "beg, borrow, or stall."

Ways to Improve Cash Flow

As was pointed out above, cash flow management is a responsibility quite separate from operating management and involves a different set of tools. Below are listed some of the techniques that can be used to improve your cash picture:

---

[2]For example, Office of Management and Budget (OMB) Circular A-110 requires that nonprofits return interest earned on federal grants to the federal government.

Ways to maximize a bank balance

● Use an interest-bearing account, one tied in with a money-market component. Keep minimum in noninterest-bearing component or accounts, and transfer into them as needed.

● Use a bank lockbox or other device to get cash collections into your account faster. (Usually this involves a post office box address handled by bank personnel. This also should reduce any risk elements in your office.)

● Use out-of-state banks for paying bills, so that cash stays in your account longer, a favorite device of business firms known as "working the float."

Collecting cash faster or paying it more slowly

● Receivables.   If you are owed money, whether by clients, patients, third-party payers, or funding agencies, the importance of keeping on top of these amounts cannot be stressed too greatly. You need a schedule of amounts owed, when they were billed or approved, and when they are due, as a control mechanism, one to be monitored as carefully as your cash balance, to which it is intimately related. Slow payers must be contacted via monthly statements and by phone if necessary. Even though it may be uncomfortable for a nonprofit, the use of collection agencies and/or attorneys should not be ruled out as a last resort. Look at it this way: it may come down to your credit rating vs. theirs. (Some state agencies have instituted accelerated payment systems. Yours may be one of them. Find out.)

● Pledges.   The same tracking should be done on pledges, though clearly a somewhat different approach needs to be used for collection. Few nonprofits will want to follow the example of a New Jersey charity, which began to sue people who had reneged on pledges. This was described by one observer as cutting off your nose to spite your face.

● Notes receivable from people who owe you money can be obtained, since they can be cashed at your bank, at a discount based on its interest charges.

● Buying on credit.   This is hardly a new idea; nevertheless, there may be things for which you customarily pay cash at local retail stores, or travel expenses, that could be charged on credit cards or billed to you on credit.

● Cash discounts.   If you do have the cash to get discounts on supplies and such, they are worth much more than may be realized. The common terms of "2/10 net 30" (2% off if paid in ten days, full amount due in 30) are equivalent to 36.7% interest a year (we'll spare you the proof, but believe it). That makes it even worth borrowing to pay your bills early, if you can.

● Consignment purchases.   If you buy merchandise for resale, such as books, or if you are engaged in a business venture involving merchandise sales, buying on consignment is a common business practice, when acceptable to vendors. It means you don't owe anything until you sell the goods: meanwhile it belongs to the vendor—although you must bear any risks of loss, theft, fire, etc.

● Other terms of sale.   Watch for the FOB terms. FOB shipping point means the buyer pays all freight and insurance costs; FOB destination means these are borne by the seller. Quantity discounts on purchases are other terms of sale that can save you substantial money where they apply.

● Lease vs. buy.   Cash outflow may be slower on a lease, depending on how you pay for new assets.

Inventory levels and purchases: The other side of the coin in quantity purchases is tying up too much money in inventory. There is obviously a trade-off here. Only if you sell or use what you buy pretty quickly does it make sense to buy much more than you need to satisfy customer demand or your own needs. It is best to calculate about how much you need per day and multiply this by the number of days it takes to send in and receive a reorder. That will give you what's called the amount of "safety stock" you need at a minimum, to keep from running out of an item.

For excess inventory, take a leaf from the retailer's book and sell off at a discount when you're overstocked. Their saying is "cut the price until it moves."

Other saleable assets.   If you get into a real cash bind, consider selling off anything you don't really need, including any investments.

Note: As a general principle, keep in mind that you can't pay payroll or bills with receivables, inventory, or anything else except cash.

BANKING RELATIONS AND BORROWING

Your bank can be one of your most valuable resources, if you choose and use it in a sophisticated way. Don't just choose the nearest bank, thinking only of convenience: It can affect your operations in a number of ways.

- *Choosing your bank.*   Aside from location, there are other considerations, such as how big your bank is in relation to your own agency; too big and you may not get adequate service, too small and they may not offer adequate facilities or services, such as phone transfers, for example, or lockbox arrangements. You might consider using a bank close by to make deposits and cash checks, then transfer the funds to one that can meet all your banking (and borrowing) needs, including waiving any service charges.[3]

- *Developing a relationship.*   Don't wait until you desperately need to borrow money to meet your banker. Do it when your balance is high: you'll get a better reception. Let your banker know you or whoever would go to him or her for a loan as a person, not a voice on the phone. Think of the bank as a potential funding agency, and deal with it accordingly. Introduce your board chairperson or president (your CEO). Find out who is in charge of approving loans and get to know that person. If it will help and not hurt your image, send a copy of your audit report and copies of press releases. If you apply for a loan, offer the bank a seat on your board, to keep an eye on things.

- *Understand what the bank looks for.*   Banks are not in business to take real risks, since they are lending other people's money. They want to see a strong leadership, good financial management, adequate insurance coverage, and a decent financial condition. If you owe too much to others, they'll be less likely to become just another creditor on line.

Making a Loan Proposal

The conventional wisdom about banks is that they are always ready to lend money to people who don't need it. As a general principle, most of the points raised in Chapters 8 and 9 about grant proposals and business plans apply to making a proposal for a bank loan. You should approach a

---

[3]Many banks do this for nonprofit customers.

bank the way you would an investor in a business venture. The basic considerations are the same from the banker's viewpoint, the primary ones being an adequate return on investment—here meaning the rate of interest—and the financial strength to repay the loan when due. The banker may request a cash flow projection covering the period of the loan, as a way of evaluating the prospects of being paid back.

Bankers are usually skilled in financial statement analysis. If your current ratio (see Chapter 13) is poor, or your accounts receivable or inventory turn over too slowly, bankers see this as a risk factor. If you have been delinquent in meeting payments on a mortgage or other installment loans, they anticipate being in the same boat if they lend you money. They will look for assets you could pledge as collateral—investments, receivables, etc.

The best idea is to adapt your best grant proposal—or business plan, if you have one—as the basis of your loan proposal. Most of the information needed is already there. Calculate exactly how much you need, and for what specific purposes. Don't just ask how much they'll lend you! Also state when and how you can pay it back.

If you have been operating for some years and can show a satisfactory financial condition and management, the best plan is to request a line of credit. That means you can borrow up to a certain maximum amount at any time you need it, without making a new application or proposal. Many banks expect you to "clean up" such loans periodically, not let them run on forever.

Just as in fundraising and starting or funding a business venture, you can't expect to succeed unless you have done all your homework, are able to present all the necessary documents and projections, and are able to answer all likely questions. You will succeed to the extent that you are able to inspire the loan officer's confidence that you are a "pro" who knows exactly what you're doing and what is expected of you and your agency.

Keep in mind, however, that most banks have had very little experience lending money to nonprofits and may view them as a far greater risk than a business of the same size. Part of your job is to overcome that viewpoint by showing your professionalism. Many small business firms are not such great risks either.

Other Sources of Loans

If you are turned down by your own bank, don't despair: assuming you've done a professional job presenting your case, it may just be that they are overextended at the moment. Try shopping around for another bank that has more loan money available. Ask around among knowledgeable people about which banks might be approached. Members of your board from the business community might know, or perhaps your public accountant.

If you own property, even with a mortgage, it may be worth far more than the balance on the mortgage: you may well be able to refinance the mortgage to generate more money. (You also might consider doing so if the current mortgage interest rates are lower than you are paying, a good way to save money.)

The U.S. Small Business Administration can lend money to nonprofits as well as small business firms, if they have been turned down by banks. (That doesn't mean you can depend on getting a loan from them.) There are in some areas of the country revolving loan funds run by nonprofit organizations that will make emergency short-term loans to smaller nonprofits at below-market interest rates. These are certainly worth looking into, although they do not generally lend large sums.

Repaying Loans

It probably goes without saying here that if you want to be able to borrow again in the future, or even if you just want to continue buying on credit, it is essential to pay amounts due on loans.

WHAT IS HAPPENING TO OUR FINANCIAL CONDITION? USING THE STATEMENT OF CASH FLOWS

It is useful to study the nonprofit's financial situation, not only at a moment in time, as shown by its balance sheet, but also to learn what is happening to it. Not only "Where are we?" but also "How did we get there?" is important. The operating statement provides one part of the answer. Did revenues exceed expenses? Did we at least break even? It does not take into account nonrevenue sources of funds nor nonexpense uses of them.

What a Statement of Cash Flows Contains

The Statement of Cash Flows is also called a Statement of Sources and Uses (or Applications) of Funds or, more simply, a Funds Statement. It is illustrated in Table 14–2 and presents: (1) the net effect of operations (revenues minus expenses), i.e., the operating surplus, to use one of its shorter titles; (2) nonrevenue funds received, such as loans or advances; (3) nonexpense items paid, such as payments on loans or installments, or for inventory, prepaid expenses, equipment, or security deposits; (4) changes in accounts receivable and accounts payable balances. The difference between sources and uses of funds will equal the change in the cash balance during the period. Since a cash flow worksheet is usually a month-by-month document, it would be clumsy to use in lieu of a Funds Statement, since a statement showing totals for a year or a quarter is more useful for financial analysis.

The Statement Shows How the Nonprofit Has Managed Its Finances

This is distinct from its operating performance, which is depicted in the Operating Statement. It is called a "where-got, where-went" statement colloquially in some financial quarters, which is fairly descriptive. For example, the Operating Statement might indicate a substantial operating surplus for the period, yet cash might be very low because a lot of money was paid out for equipment or to retire a large loan. Since this reflects financial policy decisions, it is important. The Funds Statement would make this clear.

If accounts payable are increasing, it may mean either that bills are not being paid or that you are incurring expenses faster than you should. If receivables are increasing, efforts to collect may be lagging. If you carry inventories that are increasing, you may be headed for trouble by overbuying merchandise that may not be too easily sold. These are examples of important signals that can be provided by the funds statement. Not only is it required as a standard part of external reports by GAAP, it can provide valuable insights to leadership as part of internal reporting as well.

TABLE 14-2. CENTER FOR COMMUNITY SERVICE, INC. STATEMENT OF CASH FLOWS, FOR THE YEAR ENDED DEC. 31

Cash flows from operations		
Net income per Income Statement[a]		$(1,155)
Adjustments to convert to cash basis:		
Add back depreciation	2,580	
Add back amortization of Prepaid Insurance	100	
Changes in current asset/liability balances:[b]		
Net (Increase)/Decrease in accts. receivable	0	
Net (Increase)/Decrease in accounts payable	0	
(Increase)/Decrease in accrued expenses	225	
(Increase)/Decrease in accrued taxes	(574)	
(Increase)/Decrease in taxes payable	$1,024	
Total adjustments		3,355
Net cash from operations		$2,200
("Net cash used for operations" if negative)		
Cash flows from investment		
Proceeds of sale of fixed assets[c, d]	0	
Payments for purchase of fixed assets	0	
Money market account investment/transfer	0	
Net cash from (used for) investments		0
Balance		$2,200
Cash flows from financing		
Funds borrowed	1,000	
Payments on loans or installments	(1,200)	
Net cash from (used for) financing		$ (200)
Net increase (decrease) in cash		2,000
Add: Cash balance—beginning of year		2,000
Cash balance—end of year		$4,000

[a]It is possible, but far more time-consuming, to work with the details of income and expenses instead. This is a short-cut. Variances between budgeted and actual income and expense are better measured using budget variance report as shown in Tables 13-2 and 13-3.

[b]Changes in balances are required to adjust operating transactions from the accrual basis to the cash basis.

[c]Actual cash proceeds of sale are substituted for gains or losses on the sale of assets.

[d]Items with zero amounts are included to show some other possible inflows and outflows.

Statement of Cash Flows Explained

The information in this statement can be prepared from a worksheet containing the balance sheets at the beginning and end of the period, in this case January 1 and December 31, aligned in parallel columns. By subtracting the beginning from the ending balance for each item, the changes in balances are derived. These represent changes in assets and liabilities, which can be converted to changes in the cash inflows and outflows by using a worksheet such as the one illustrated in Fig. 14-2.

CENTER FOR COMMUNITY SERVICE, INC.
WORKSHEET FOR STATEMENT OF CASH FLOWS,
YEAR ENDED DEC. 31

Balance Sheet Account Balances
Jan. 1, 19xx to   Dec. 31, 19xx

Name of account	Debit	Credit	Debit	Credit	Cash Inflows	Cash Outflows
Cash	2,000		4,000		(See Below)	
Prepaid insurance	150		50		100	
Equipment	12,885		12,885			
Accum. deprec.—Equipment		5,154		7,734	2,580	
Loan payable—bank		0		1,000	1,000	
Equipt. installments due		1,200		0		1,200
Fed. Inc. tax withheld		1,000		1,420	420	
FICA tax withheld		100		704	604	
Accrued unemp. insurance		674		100		574
Accrued expenses		375		600	225	
Fund balance		6,532		5,377	(Note)	1,155
	15,035	15,035	16,935	16,935	4,929	2,929

Less: total outflows   2,929

Net cash inflow   2,000

Note: The reduction of the Fund Balance account during the year by $1,155 was the result of the net loss.

FIGURE 14–2. WORKSHEET FOR STATEMENT OF CASH FLOWS

WHAT TO DO IF YOUR REPORTS TELL YOU THAT YOU HAVE A FINANCIAL CRISIS

Nonprofits can on occasion face a financial crisis. For people lacking experience with managing the financial problems of an organization, the human tendency is to panic and to thrash about for the "quick fix." The danger here is to fall into bureaucratic opportunism in the process and to lose sight of values and goals. The businessman who complains that only he "knows what it means to have to meet a payroll" is actually hinting at this point in part.

Staff Salaries are at the Top of the List

Most organizations, whether nonprofit or profit-seeking, have learned the hard way that morality and self-interest join forces to put the payment of current salaries at the top of any list of priorities. (The bankruptcy statutes do the same, incidentally.) Employees are the last group of creditors that should be made to wait, in spite of the fact that they are least able to resist—or rather *because* of that fact. Cutting salaries—or worse, asking people to go off payroll temporarily and work as volunteers—is another way of handling matters, which may be defensible but only as a last resort in a real crisis, never as a temporary expedient.

We discussed morale factors involved in the process of budgeting. People usually work in the nonprofit field, where the pay is generally lower, out of idealism and a love for what they are trying to accomplish for others. It would be unconscionable that they of all people should be deliberately exploited in a crunch by their own organization.

Not too different from this situation, in our opinion, is the not unknown practice in new and/or unfunded nonprofits of hiring a key employee with the understanding that an important part of the job will be to raise funds for his or her own salary. This, too, is taking advantage of both idealism and the desire for the position, to have a staff person assume what is primarily a board responsibility. Is it really fair to hire people if you lack money to pay them? Even if it works, the relationship it creates between the board and the staff member is an inauthentic one: if a person is, in effect, paying his or her own salary, by that person's own efforts, in what sense is the board or the organization the employer?

Use Caution When Asking for Loans from Organization Supporters

Although there is nothing inherently wrong with borrowing temporarily from a member or other supporter of the nonprofit, there is harm in making the individual wait much longer than expected for repayment. It is a good way to lose such supporters, who may also be influential in the organization and the community; people do talk when they feel abused, and no nonprofit needs to make enemies.

Stalling Creditors Can Hurt Your Credit Rating

In a genuine crisis there may be no alternative, but to stall paying creditors, without their agreement for delay, is a guaranteed method to weaken an organization's credit standing. This is another lesson from the private sector, for a good credit standing is a combination of ability and trustworthiness about meeting obligations when due. The same applies of course to loans, whether from banks or supporters.

A particularly dangerous practice, which is covered more fully in Chapter 17, is that of delaying payment of one potent class of creditors: federal, state, and local government tax agencies. The issue here is not the nonprofit's credit but the effect on its *existence*, direct or indirect. Worst of all is the once-common practice of not paying withholding taxes. This is employees' money, and heavy penalties can be imposed not only on the organization but on its responsible officers personally.

FACING THE HARD QUESTION: "TO BE OR NOT TO BE?"

Although gradual attrition can bring a nonprofit to the same situation, it is more commonly the onslaught of a continuing financial crisis that forces an agonizing reappraisal of the organization's continued viability and survival prospects. It is at this point that the board, in consultation with key staff members, must ask and seek clear answers to the following basic questions governing the organization's continued existence.

Questions for a Needs Reassessment

- Do we have the right programs? Enough services? Too many to fund adequately?

- Are there other programs—nonprofit, governmental or business—that are (or may be) capable of meeting the same needs of the same people? Can they perhaps do it better or for less money?

- If there are, why should people come to us, not them? Do potential supporters know we are here?

- To what extent are competing programs siphoning off support from us in the way of clients, members, patrons, donors and/or funding agencies?

- Are economic conditions, shifting population-mix or other developments operating to undermine our viability?

- How reliable are our present sources of funding? Why should they continue, in view of the above answers?

- How committed and effective is our leadership: key staff, officers, committee chairs, the board itself?

Possible Alternative Solutions

Depending on the answers to these questions, consideration of one or more of the following alternative courses of action might be essential.

- Develop new grant proposals for present or new funding agencies, either for present programs, if you can demonstrate a continuing need not filled by others or for valid *new* programs suggested in the course of the reassessment.

- Reconsider and change programs offered, to attract greater support of users and funds. Change the program "mix." Seek auxiliary income sources, such as thrift or gift shops, sale of ads in publications. (See Chapter 9.)

- Maximize public relations and/or advertising efforts and publicity via publications and other organizations, to enhance the image and public awareness of the organization (if that is a major problem and funds permit). It may be possible to obtain the donated services of PR or marketing professionals.

- Reorganize or reconstitute any weak elements of the leadership referred to above, if that is found to be a source of problems.

● If success in going it alone appears unlikely, consider cooperating and pooling certain resources (facilities, personnel) with competing programs for mutual advantage, instead of weakening each other. A division of labor involving the offering of complementary services that each can do best would be better than continued competition.

● In the absence of other possibilities, consider a merger with (or into) another compatible nonprofit, or liquidation if that is not a possibility.

Avoiding a Serious Financial Outcome

We have stressed from the beginning of this book the accountability of the nonprofit. What its leadership needs to address when a crisis of survival develops is not only the organization's legal and moral obligations, but also the likelihood that there are potential personal obligations in such a situation, even legal responsibility for certain debts. You need legal advice at that point, and the following considerations need to be weighed carefully.

● Since no one personally owns the assets of a nonprofit, on its dissolution, any assets remaining after all of its debts have been paid can be transferred to another nonprofit; otherwise they revert to the ownership of the state in which the organization was incorporated. If any assets are thus transferred, an attempt should be made to have the successor nonprofit assume any unpaid debts.

● If, after converting all assets to cash, there are insufficient funds to pay all debts, legal procedures must be followed in determining who gets how much, and legal advice is therefore needed.

● Any creditors who go substantially unpaid can harm the personal reputation, and therefore possibly the credit, of officers and board members. This may prompt special fundraising efforts, or personal donations, by them to prevent this outcome.

● As previously noted, should withholding taxes go unpaid, responsible officers, such as the treasurer, may be subject to personal liability for them, plus penalties of up to 100% of the amount of the tax, at least in the case of federal taxes withheld. Clearly this is one obligation that will have to be given high priority to avoid such a consequence.

We want to conclude this discussion on a somewhat more positive note. Planning such as we have been describing can accomplish one of two positive outcomes. It can help prevent the kinds of difficulties described, or, if they occur, it can make resolving them easier.

APPENDIX 14A

Using Checks for Cash Budgeting and Expense Accruals

Here is a way to do both of these things well, if you do it carefully. It involves writing checks as soon as bills and payrolls are approved, even if your bank account lacks the funds to cover them. The idea is to accomplish the following:

●Get all of your expenses on your books, paid or not (i.e., accruing them, in effect) as well as other upcoming payments due;

●Disclose your true cash position, including how much you need to cover all upcoming payments;

●Prevent spending money you have no business spending—such as money to cover withholding taxes that belongs to the government;

●Provide a systematic way to pay bills according to their proper priorities and due dates.

STEP-BY-STEP PROCEDURE

1. Periodically, perhaps once a week, all approved bills and payrolls should be sent to whomever writes checks (see "Requirements for Cash Management" in Chapter 14). Checks should also be written covering taxes withheld plus employer taxes due, even though not due until the following month or later. It will be helpful if all checks are then arranged in the approximate order in which they will be paid, as well as is known at this point, with a "PAY DATE" slip attached showing approximate due dates.

2. Checks should be prepared (but not yet signed) for all payments due, regardless of when. This may well result in a negative cash balance: it will equal the total amount that will be currently due, if you actually send out checks only up to the amount of the balance you had before you started writing them.

3. The checks should next be grouped by due date and priority, as finally decided by the Treasurer, Financial Manager, or whomever makes such decisions, and any corrections necessary made on the attached "PAY DATE" slips. It is useful to have a file folder or slot for each group, with labels such as "DUE THIS WEEK," "DUE NEXT WEEK," "DUE NEXT MONTH," "DUE MONTH AFTER NEXT," and perhaps "DUE IN OVER TWO MONTHS."

4. Show a cumulative total of the amount in each folder, and increase or decrease it as bills are added or paid. That way, you can always get a quick picture of your cash situation at any time. (See #5 below.)

5. Finally, whoever is keeping on top of making actual payments looks through the first folder (at both the checks and the supporting documentation) and either signs the checks or sends them to whomever will do so. Keeping the total in each folder up-to-date as explained in #4 makes it possible to make sure you have enough money to cover them, as follows:

Balance (or overdraft) per check book or One-Write Journal	$ XXXX
Add back the totals of all categories of payments *not yet due*	<u>XXXX</u>

The total (or difference) is your actual cash balance after paying the bills you are about to mail. If it is too low, hold back enough to avoid an overdraft, taking into account also any checks you are certain to receive and deposit in the next day or two. For bills due later, you can take into account sums you expect to receive during the same time slot.

6. Note that you are now in a position to prepare an operating statement that includes accrued expenses, although not accrued or deferred revenue. This will make it possible to calculate your variances in a way that is far more meaningful than those derived from cash basis statements.

Part Four

Outside Accountability

Chapter 15

Financial Reporting to Others

EVERYBODY ELSE'S BUSINESS: REPORTS REQUIRED

In the Overview to Part Two, we put heavy stress on the idea of accountability as living in a goldfish bowl. To this point we have concentrated on how to stay afloat and have dealt with accountability as an internal matter. This chapter is about people outside the goldfish bowl itself: the reports required for financial accountability to those from whom we receive our funds.

Any person or organization supplying funds, or free goods or services to a nonprofit does so for a mixture of selfish and unselfish motives, although in most cases the latter predominate. The giver of funds expects them to be used for worthy purposes, which the gift is intended to promote. It should come as no surprise that those supplying substantial donations or grants will in some cases request an accounting for the way these resources have been used. In addition, those who supply another important necessity—credit—in the form of loans or for goods or services received on credit, may request financial statements that demonstrate financial health before risking a credit loss.

Individuals or Organizations Who May Ask for Financial Reports

- Foundations or corporate donors
- Other private or governmental funding agencies, e.g., United Way
- Large donors
- Banks and individual lenders of funds
- Large creditors, landlord, mortgage holder, equipment supplier (on installments), contractors,or major suppliers
- Parent or umbrella organizations.

What To Include in the General Purpose Financial Reports

The most commonly used reports are those that present an overall picture of the operations and financial condition of the organization, described in Chapter 13: the operating statement, under one or another of its various names,[1] balance sheet,[2] and statement of cash flows.[3] We have already presented illustrations of these statement forms in Chapters 13 and 14, including variations that set forth more detailed information on a fund accounting or programmatic basis. The forms of statements used for external reporting are generally no different from the various forms shown in the last chapter, except that performance reports comparing actual with budgeted figures are not generally released to outsiders other than parent bodies. In some cases only the basic, condensed form of statements referred to above are so released, even though the more detailed formats are used internally for purposes of evaluation and control of operations and finances.

Who Decides Report Form and Content?

Although no one can dictate the kind of reports a nonprofit prepares for internal use, for external reporting it may often be a different story. Not only can the form of report be mandated, in certain cases, but also the accounting methods by which it is prepared, e.g., whether accrual basis is required, whether depreciation accounting must be used, how to handle in-kind contributions, etc. Thus funding agencies, such as foundations making large grants to the organization, United Way (which required affiliates to use GAAP—generally accepted accounting principles: see Chapter 10), or other major interested parties may specify such requirements. Or any of the various users of the organization's reports listed above may require that they bear the "opinion" (sometimes incorrectly referred to as the "certification") of a CPA. This requirement often produces the same result indirectly, for independent public accountants are required to adhere to GAAP in examining financial statements. This is merely another way of saying that they must require their clients to prepare such statements on the basis of GAAP. Appendix 15A "Audits by a Public Accountant" will give you a better idea of what goes on when you ask a professional to examine and attest to your financial statements.

AICPA Guidelines for CPAs Auditing Nonprofits

Chapter 10 cited the AICPA publications, which contain the guidelines used by public accountants in their audits and reports for nonprofits of different types. Until the Financial Accounting Standards Board (FASB), which makes the basic rules of accounting, issues governing documents on the subject, AICPA guidelines will usually be followed by public accountants (known familiarly as GAAP and GAAS), which cover accounting, auditing, and reporting standards.

The IRS issues its own rules covering annual reports by nonprofits (Form 990, etc.), which are covered in Chapter 16. The rules differ in some areas, most particularly regarding the treatment of in-kind contributions of services and facilities.

These guidelines do not in fact require that *all* nonprofits use accrual basis accounting, or specify the particular form of financial statements to be used. However they do indicate that most nonprofits should in fact allocate any joint costs among organizational functions they benefit; that they use accrual basis accounting, with specified exceptions, as explained in Chapter 10; and that all use depreciation accounting. The reasons for this were spelled out in Chapter 10 and will not be repeated

---

[1]E.g., statement of activity; statement of support, revenue and expenses; income statement; statement of cash receipts and disbursements (for nonprofits on a cash basis, or as a supplementary statement, when on an accrual basis).

[2]Also called a statement of financial condition, statement of financial position, or position statement.

[3]Also called a statement of source and applications of funds, statement of sources and uses of funds, or simply funds statement.

here. That chapter sought to explain what it is that GAAP seeks to accomplish, not for accountants but for users of financial statements and the characteristics that financial statements should have to meet the needs of such users.

General-purpose financial reports are usually released to outside users annually only, showing the results for the fiscal year, and not on an interim (quarterly or monthly) basis, except when a parent or umbrella organization or a major funding source or lender is in a position to insist on an interim report.

How Each Type of Report Is Used

Operating statements, which are sometimes issued in one of the formats illustrated in Chapter 13 (without the inclusion of budget and variance figures), are used by people outside the organization primarily as an indication that it is not operating badly "in the red," since an operating deficit inevitably results in a poor financial condition eventually, if not immediately.[4] It also gives the reader some idea of the scale of operations of the nonprofit, since the larger the revenue and expense figures are in absolute size, the larger the organization. This can, however, be misleading, when any substantial portion of program or support services is rendered by volunteers or by altruistic individuals serving at salaries that are nominal or far below the going rate. As was suggested in Chapter 10, to the extent permitted by SOP 78-10, such services should be stated at their value, and the unpaid portion shown as an in-kind contribution. Any services that cannot be so treated can be handled by a footnote to the report, or by comment in accompanying narrative remarks, in a communication from the president or chairperson of the board accompanying the financial report.

Note: As you may recall, the name *operating statement* was cited as a generic one, preferred by many accountants. The standardized title recommended by the AICPA publications cited above is statement of support, revenue, and expenses and changes in fund balances (see Fig. 15-1). This is actually two statements combined, since it does not end with the "bottom line" figure showing an agency's net income or loss. The recommended, if clumsy, terminology for that line is "excess (deficiency) of public support and revenue over expenses," (the figure $407,000 in the left-hand column of Fig. 15-1). This line is then followed by any "other changes in fund balances"; it is added to these and to the "fund balances, beginning of year" to arrive at "fund balances, end of year." Anything in parentheses is a minus figure, representing a transfer to another fund, in this section of the statement.

Balance sheets, which may be issued in any of the formats illustrated in Tables 13-6, 13-7, and 13-8, are used by outsiders to gauge the solvency and liquidity of the organization—i.e., its ability to pay its debts. Sources of restricted funds may also want to see whether the restrictions are being observed, as would be disclosed on a balance sheet in the form shown in Tables 13-7 and 13-8.

Statement of cash flows has become a standard part of the general-purpose financial report, and is now required to be issued. It is used to evaluate the financial performance of the nonprofit, whereas its operational performance is portrayed by its operating statement. Sources of funds and their uses, other than in operations, can be readily ascertained from this statement. For example, if the organization is operating at a large deficit and covering its financial needs through substantial borrowing, this could well be a warning signal to a prospective lender or large donor. If funds

[4]Since Table 13-5 clearly discloses any excess or deficiency of specific program revenues over expenses, it is more common to show the functional breakdown of expenses on a separate schedule of functional expenses, presenting the basic operating statement in the form shown in Table 13-1.

VOLUNTARY HEALTH AND WELFARE SERVICE
Statement of Support, Revenue, and Expenses and Changes in Fund Balances
Year Ended December 31, 19X2 with Comparative Totals for 19X1

| | 19X2 | | | | Total all funds | |
| | Current funds | | Land, building and equipment fund | Endowment fund | | |
	Unrestricted	Restricted			19X2	19X1
Public support and revenue:						
Public support:						
Contributions (net of estimated uncollectible pledges of $195,000 in 19X2 and $150,000 in 19X1)	$3,764,000	$162,000	—	$2,000	$3,928,000	$3,976,000
Contributions to building fund	—	—	72,000	—	72,000	150,000
Special events (net of direct costs of $181,000 in 19X2 and $163,000 in 19X1)	104,000	—	—	—	104,000	92,000
Legacies and bequests	92,000	—	—	4,000	96,000	129,000
Received from federated and nonfederated campaigns (which incurred related fundraising expenses of $38,000 in 19X2 and $29,000 in 19X1)	275,000	—	—	—	275,000	308,000
Total public support	4,235,000	162,000	72,000	6,000	4,475,000	4,655,000
Revenue:						
Membership dues	17,000	—	—	—	17,000	12,000
Investment income	98,000	10,000	—	—	108,000	94,000
Realized gain on investment transactions	200,000	—	—	25,000	225,000	275,000
Miscellaneous	42,000	—	—	—	42,000	47,000
Total Revenue	357,000	10,000	—	25,000	392,000	428,000
Total support and revenue	4,592,000	172,000	72,000	31,000	$4,867,000	$5,083,000
Expenses:						
Program services:						
Research	1,257,000	155,000	2,000	—	$1,414,000	$1,365,000
Public health education	539,000	—	5,000	—	544,000	485,000
Professional education and training	612,000	—	6,000	—	618,000	516,000
Community services	568,000	—	10,000	—	578,000	486,000
Total program services	2,976,000	155,000	23,000	—	3,154,000	2,852,000
Supporting services:						
Management and general	567,000	—	7,000	—	574,000	638,000
Fundraising	642,000	—	12,000	—	654,000	546,000
Total supporting services	1,209,000	—	19,000	—	1,228,000	1,184,000
Total expenses	4,185,000	155,000	42,000	—	$4,382,000	$4,036,000
Excess (deficiency) of public support and revenue over expenses	407,000	17,000	30,000	31,000		
Other changes in fund balances:						
Property and equipment acquisitions from unrestricted funds	(17,000)	—	17,000	—		
Transfer of realized endowment fund appreciation	100,000	—	—	(100,000)		
Returned to donor	—	(8,000)	—	—		
Fund balances, beginning of year	5,361,000	123,000	649,000	2,017,000		
Fund balances, end of year	$5,851,000	$132,000	$696,000	$1,948,000		

FIGURE 15–1

VOLUNTARY HEALTH AND WELFARE SERVICE
Statement of Functional Expenses
Year Ended December 31, 19X2
with Comparative Totals for 19X1

	Program services					Supporting services			Total expenses	
	Research	Public health education	Professional education & training	Community services	Total	Management & general	Fundraising	Total	19X2	19X1
Salaries	$ 45,000	$291,000	$251,000	$269,000	$ 856,000	$331,000	$368,000	$ 699,000	$1,555,000	$1,433,000
Employee health and retirement benefits	4,000	14,000	14,000	14,000	46,000	22,000	15,000	37,000	83,000	75,000
Payroll taxes etc.	2,000	16,000	13,000	14,000	45,000	18,000	18,000	36,000	81,000	75,000
Total salaries and related expenses	51,000	321,000	278,000	297,000	947,000	371,000	401,000	772,000	1,719,000	1,583,000
Professional fees and contract service payments	1,000	10,000	3,000	8,000	22,000	26,000	8,000	34,000	56,000	53,000
Supplies	2,000	13,000	13,000	13,000	41,000	18,000	17,000	35,000	76,000	71,000
Telephone and telegraph	2,000	13,000	10,000	11,000	36,000	15,000	23,000	38,000	74,000	68,000
Postage and shipping	2,000	17,000	13,000	9,000	41,000	13,000	30,000	43,000	84,000	80,000
Occupancy	5,000	26,000	22,000	25,000	78,000	30,000	27,000	57,000	135,000	126,000
Rental of equipment	1,000	24,000	14,000	4,000	43,000	3,000	16,000	19,000	62,000	58,000
Local transportation	3,000	22,000	20,000	22,000	67,000	23,000	30,000	53,000	120,000	113,000
Conferences, conventions, meetings	8,000	19,000	71,000	20,000	118,000	38,000	13,000	51,000	169,000	156,000
Printing & publications	4,000	56,000	43,000	11,000	114,000	14,000	64,000	78,000	192,000	184,000
Awards & grants	1,332,000	14,000	119,000	144,000	1,609,000				1,609,000	1,448,000
Miscellaneous	1,000	4,000	6,000	4,000	15,000	16,000	21,000	37,000	52,000	64,000
Total expenses before depreciation	1,412,000	539,000	612,000	568,000	3,131,000	567,000	650,000	1,217,000	4,348,000	4,004,000
Depreciation of buildings and equipment	2,000	5,000	6,000	10,000	23,000	7,000	4,000	11,000	34,000	32,000
Total expenses	$1,414,000	$544,000	$618,000	$578,000	$3,154,000	$574,000	$654,000	$1,228,000	$4,382,000	$4,036,000

FIGURE 15-2.

generated in operations are being too rapidly tied up in equipment purchases, leaving inadequate cash and/or working capital, that might also be viewed negatively by funding sources or other users.

Statements of functional expenses are essentially the same as the operating statement in program or functional columnar format shown in Table 13–5, except that the support and revenue section is omitted. This statement is discussed in Appendix 15A in connection with the problem of auditing the propriety of the methods of allocating indirect or shared expenses to programs and support services.[5]

Note that the reason this statement is needed is that the statement of support, revenue and expenses (etc.) shows no line-item detail of expenses, only the total by program or support function. This statement or schedule is thus a supporting schedule for that statement, permitting the further breakdown by types of expense shown in the operating statement formats in Chapter 13.

SPECIAL-PURPOSE REPORTS TO FUNDING AGENCIES

Foundations, government agencies, and other institutional sources of grants and loans commonly have their own reporting formats, which may differ somewhat from those presented in Chapter 13. Generally speaking, these will correspond with the budget formats they incorporate in their grant application forms or "RFP" (request for proposal). The principal differences may be a greater amount of detail, a somewhat different expense classification scheme (chart of accounts), or a specific requirement that program revenues and expenses be separately presented, which is not mandatory under SOP 78–10. Aside from reporting formats, they may require that books be kept on a fund accounting basis[6] or even that a separate bank account be maintained for their grant funds. Since he who pays the piper calls the tune, it is clear that, if you want their money, you will do as they say. (Although they may not be able to take it back sometimes, they will find the relationship one that is somewhat less than habit-forming for the future.)

Why Some Funding Agencies Require Detailed Reports

There is a serious accountability issue on the part of the funding agency, since it too may be a tax-exempt organization whose status may be endangered by acts of its grantees. In fact, in some cases, the Internal Revenue Code requires a specific level of supervision by such organizations over nonprofits to which it makes grants, in order to help it administer these provisions of the law.[7] Understanding a foundation's own problems in this respect may help lessen resentment of the added paperwork and record-keeping sometimes involved in a grant. It is not necessarily just "bureaucratic make-work."

Specific Requirements of Grantors

Any or all of the following may be prescribed by the terms and conditions of a grant from a public or private funding agency.

---

[5]This statement is illustrated in Fig. 15–2.

[6]One foundation even requires that a full set of separate books be kept for all transactions relating to a grant it makes.

[7]See for example Section 4945(d) and (h) of the Internal Revenue Code.

- That a specified account classification be used (The same classifications should be used on both the proposal budget and reports.)
- That fund accounting be used on the books for the grant
- That grant funds be kept in a separate bank account (not too common, but sometimes required)
- That accrual accounting (or possibly cash accounting) be used with respect to the grant accounts
- That depreciation accounting be used (or not used) in relation to the grant
- That interim progress reports be submitted on the use of grant funds, usually on a quarterly basis (This may be the basis for receiving grant installments.)
- That only specific items of overhead (administrative and joint expenses) are allowable or that such costs are allowable on the basis of a specified percentage limit, based on the total amount of the grant, total payroll for the program, or a combination of these.

It should be clear that complete guidelines or other instructions should be obtained from the funding source, read carefully, and followed closely in submitting grant proposal budgets and reports of grant expenditures to the agency. Since, unfortunately, there are wide variations in terminology used in accounting, it is particularly important to understand and speak the same language as that spoken and understood by the funding agency. Otherwise you may have trouble explaining and/or defending items in your proposal budget or financial reports indicating "where the money went." It is also important to establish credibility as a responsible, accountable grantee, for "repeat business." Aside from following the rules of the game, meeting report deadlines is important, as is making sure that your figures are internally consistent, i.e., that related figures in different places "tie in" with each other. When they do not, an impression is given of sloppiness in accounting, which hardly encourages confidence.

HOW TO MANAGE YOUR GRANT

When you get your grant approval, you will naturally contact the grant officer or foundation manager to find out when you can expect your check, whether it will be in installments, and what if anything you are required to do in order to get it, such as obtaining required matching funds or other commitments. Most of the other aspects of grant management are dealt with in the main body of this chapter. Needless to say, if you want to stay in the good graces of your funding source, you will make sure to stay within your budget, deliver what you have promised within the time frame you indicated, avoid playing games with the budget, and submit interim and/or annual reports as required, in the format and by the dates prescribed. Aside from ensuring that you get all the funds you expect, living up to your obligations may result in your being able to come around again in the future.

Note: Foundation managers and grant officers also network and exchange experiences. Even if you never plan to seek another grant from the same agency, you want to keep your credibility and good name in the foundation and nonprofit world, because they are what will keep you afloat in long-range terms. (Consider the alternative.) Even rejection of a grant proposal should be accepted in good grace.

It is well to keep in mind that a program grant is not a gift but a contract to deliver services in exchange for money. Although not as widely used for foundation grants, the term "contract" is commonly used as part of the standard jargon in government agency grants, and with good cause.

Padding Allocated Expenses (A Word of Warning)

A related issue, one fraught with danger, is that some nonprofits see an opportunity for "profit" in the allocation area. If unreasonable allocations are made to a program, or, worse, if the total of an expense allocated to all programs equals more than the actual total of the line item, the nonprofit is playing a potentially dangerous game, one that is specifically discussed and barred by the OMB circular mentioned previously. To illustrate, the circular states the following regarding allocated payrolls.

> (2) Reports reflecting the distribution of activity of each employee must be maintained for all staff members ... whose compensation is charged, in whole or in part, directly to awards. ...
>> (a) The reports must reflect an *after-the-fact* determination of the actual activity of each employee. Budget estimates ... do not qualify as support for charges to awards.
>> (b) Each report must account for the total activity for which employees are compensated. ...
>> (c) The reports must be signed by the individual employee. ...

That would seem to take care of things quite nicely, since (1) more than 100% of an employee's time could not be allocated to his or her activities; (2) actual time spent on the grant program, not a before-the-fact estimate, must be used; and (3) the *employee* is the one making the determination. This is just another way of pointing out that you are up against "pros" on the other side.[8]

The overall conclusion would seem to be that a nonprofit should seek a reasonable and fair allocation of its indirect costs to program budgets but should resist the temptation to make a profit out of such allocations, if it values its future credibility.

Playing Games May Cost You Money

The temptation may exist to pad or load proposal budgets and/or the charging of actual expenditures against grant funds; in fact, a cynical attitude often expresses itself in this area on the part of people who are idealistic in other respects. It is not intended here to moralize, only to point to the difference between short- and long-range self-interest. Grant officers of funding agencies are often skilled at detecting unreasonable charges. Sometimes they tend to become cynical on the subject and may look with suspicion even on wholly valid items. Another potential that should not be overlooked is that the agency with which you may consider playing games sometimes has an audit capability, which exists in the case of government agencies and large foundations (see Appendix 15A). In the event of an audit, improper charges are not difficult to detect from your own records, and clear evidence of this can be most embarrassing, not to mention the likely reaction next time you come knocking at their door for funds.

Again, a reminder is in order about accountability. Not only are you spending someone else's money for purposes other than what they intended, you may also overlook the fact that the funding

---

[8]In July, 1981, the media carried an expose of hospitals that padded their budgets in requesting funds from a state funding agency, allegedly at the recommendation of a major accounting firm.

agencies, too, are allocating other people's money to you. These are contributions or taxes given to them to promote particular socially desirable purposes and for which they in turn are accountable. The moral is that if you want to stay afloat in the nonprofit environment, remember the goldfish bowl you're in. And remember that, unlike a business, the money received by the organization as restricted grants, endowments, and contracts is not its own to do with as it sees fit, except within the restrictions and limitations imposed by its funding sources.

OTHER MEASURES OF OPERATING PERFORMANCE

Productivity and Efficiency: Ratio of Output to Input

Although these terms are hardly in widespread use in the nonprofit field—certainly among small organizations—all political signs point to their assuming increasing importance to funding agencies, especially governmental agencies. The terms are unfortunately subject to misuse and misunderstanding and will be discussed here only in terms of their technical meaning to economists and managerial accountants, not in any ideological context.

Efficiency or productivity is the ratio of output (goods or services) to input (costs). An example would be a day-care center's cost per day to care for a child. Note that whether reducing this cost advances or interferes with the center's program goals is quite a different matter, one requiring independent analysis. Cutting out lunch, or cutting down its size or quality would be an easy but stupid way to increase efficiency; yet reducing the cost per child while maintaining the quality of the care is a constructive effort that requires a critical review of possible savings by eliminating waste in the use of resources. For example, it might be possible to use more qualified volunteers to save payroll, or to buy food or supplies at more favorable prices.

Benefit/Cost Analysis

Program benefits, also called results or outputs, are hard to measure directly in a meaningful way. How do you measure client satisfaction or the "success" of a program? What is usually measured instead is some *quantity* of service, but some way of judging quality or value should also be used. While comparison of alternate methods of delivering a particular service by bare "efficiency" calculations (cost per unit of output) may be unsatisfactory, a feasible approach is to ask:

- Since they cost about the same amount, which one appears to produce a better result, in terms of both quantity and the value to the client? or
- Since the results appear about equal, which approach costs less?

When funds are supplied to a nonprofit by agencies, clients, or members, the funding parties are entitled to expect the maximum of service efforts and accomplishments for their money, within the constraints imposed by quality considerations. In this sense, efficiency and productivity are in no way alien to the purposes of the nonprofit. They mean merely getting the most out of the resources you have.

Another use of benefit/cost analysis was described in the Appendix to Chapter 7, under "Capital Budgeting Where Benefits as Well as Costs Are Involved." This is a more scientific application of the concept, since the benefits involved are measurable in monetary terms.

Despite the difficulty in measurement, especially in the human-services field, the evaluation of program results or so-called outputs is absolutely essential if a nonprofit is serious about carrying out its mission. A business can use its bottom line as a measure of success; not so a nonprofit.

HOW TO MEASURE PROGRAM RESULTS OR EFFECTIVENESS

This is an area different from measuring productivity or efficiency, one perhaps more important in evaluating programs, yet at the same time more difficult. It seeks to measure what our organization is actually accomplishing rather than what it costs. Measurement is usually in units rather than in dollars: how many clients served, how many children placed in foster care? Whereas variance, trend, and ratio analysis measure inputs—i.e., the cost of rendering service—these are output measures; costs themselves are not the issue. (Productivity and efficiency measures are thus the link that relates input and output or costs and benefits.)

Difficulties in Measuring Output

This is as yet a frontier in performance measurement, with little in the way of agreed-upon terminology or methodology. Only partial, tentative procedures have been developed, for what is being measured in each case has meaning only in relation to the goals and objectives of the organization.[9] As one author put it, it is hard to know when you're there until you have determined where "there" is. For example, what are the criteria that represent effective or "good" performance? What do you measure? Is quantity of output alone a meaningful measure, without regard for the quality of the service? How about the extent to which program services meet the total need for such services in the community?

To be more specific and graphic, let us suppose that the Center we have been referring to has a program for training and placing the hard-core unemployed in meaningful jobs, and that it is able to report that 150 people were so assisted this year, compared with 100 last year. That looks like good performance: a 50% increase in output. But what if there are 5,000 such individuals in the community? How much of an impact does such an effort have? Or, to take another tack, what if there were only 300 such unemployed, but that, of the 150 placed, only 20 were still gainfully employed at the end of a year? These are more meaningful measures of the effectiveness of the program in dealing with the problems it was intended to address. The problem of defining criteria and performance indicators for measuring results can thus be seen as one that is as complex and elusive as it is crucial.

Performance measurement in the nonprofit world, especially that of human services, is still a fairly young field. It involves the selection of meaningful performance indicators—measures of desirable performance—a choice in which sincere people can have sharply different opinions, which will tend to reflect their own value systems. Since what is often being measured is a question not of fact but of judgment or opinion, it is frequently best to use more than one indicator and to check indicators against each other for validity.

A common problem is that the indicators chosen are often not the most meaningful ones, which may be too difficult to obtain or are the most open to challenge on reliability or validity. The easy

---

[9]See *Developing Client-Outcome Monitoring Systems,* The Urban Institute, 1981; also *Evaluating Your Agency's Programs,* by M. J. Austin and Associates (Sage Publications, 1982, Beverly Hills, CA); *Program Evaluation Kit* (2nd ed.), Joan L. Herman, Ed. (Sage Publications, 1990: Newbury Park, CA); and *Reporting of Service Efforts & Accomplishments,* (Financial Accounting Standards Board, 1980.)

way out is therefore sometimes taken: to choose the ones that are the easiest and/or most acceptable. That may mean measuring the wrong thing.

The relationship between performance measurement and achievement of the organization's goals and objectives was explored in Chapter 3, under "Management by Objectives."

Why You Should Present Nonmonetary Data in Reports

Chapter 12 points out the need to keep the necessary records of number of clients or members served, hours of staff and volunteer time, etc. Although these data are not a formal part of the operating statement or performance report itself, which expresses results only in dollars, it is often useful to provide it in an accompanying narrative report to the board, along with other comments and performance measures such as those described above. Such explanations are of major importance in evaluating performance of a nonprofit, whose progress towards its goals cannot be measured in monetary units, because its true "bottom line" is service, not profits.

Both Chapters 6 and 10 pointed out another area in which a nonprofit should seriously consider presenting data not involving monetary transactions. This is donated goods or services, when substantial. When rent-free space is used, or when volunteers perform a substantial part of the nonprofit's work, these facts should be disclosed in internal reports, whether or not they are required for external reporting. If it would be necessary to pay for such services otherwise in order to function, serious consideration should be given to estimating their dollar value and presenting it on internal reports, as a reminder of what it would cost to continue such services or facilities, should such "in-kind contributions" no longer be received.

Behavioral Problems in Performance Evaluation

Everyone wants to look good, and, even though the rewards for good performance by nonprofit personnel are primarily nonmonetary, human nature requires us to act in ways that will earn us "Brownie points" in one form or another. In Chapter 6 we described some of the games people play with budgets when they are being drawn up. There are still others that are even more common in carrying out the plans that the budget embodies, and in shaping activities in a way that will result in good performance evaluations. Although such things do not happen too often when a genuine atmosphere of teamwork and mutual trust exists, it may be useful to identify some of the more common games played in nonprofits, just in case.

Games Nonprofit People Play

Spend it all: A favorite pastime, well-known in government agencies especially, is to make sure that whatever is in the budget gets spent by the end of the period, whether the expenditures are necessary or not. The underlying assumption, learned the hard way, is that coming in *under* budget, instead of benefiting the administrator responsible, will likely result in a reduction in the budget allowance next time. There is no incentive to save money in such an atmosphere, unless staff are rewarded in some manner for savings, and their own estimates of how much is needed are given enough weight in the budget process. (This issue was discussed in Chapter 6.)

Shell game: Hide excessive or unauthorized expenditures by calling them something else that will pass muster, a game often played when a program is over budget on one line item and under on another. At top levels in an organization, this may take the form of charging costs of one program or support activity to another that is either under budget, or in the early stages of a grant. A good system of internal controls, one that reviews expenditures for proper authorization and classification, is the best defense against this popular indoor sport (see Chapter 12).

Freeloading: The story is told of the man caught stealing money whose defense attorney counseled him, "Why be a jerk and steal money when you could just as well borrow it and not pay it back, like a gentleman?" In nonprofits, no one ever thinks of it quite this way, but the practice of "borrowing" people and supplies charged to one program or activity and using them on another, without any cost to the user, is a dandy budget-stretcher. This is especially true since the user may end up looking better than the "lender" on performance reports. A far worse practice is, of course, what the law calls "theft of services," in which personal needs are met at the expense of the organization. Helping oneself to stamps or abusive use of the phone, or using personnel for personal errands or work—the list could go on and on. Sadly, this is rarely seen as stealing; you may even find the point uncomfortably annoying; yet funds are provided to a nonprofit by others for the purpose of carrying out certain activities, none of which are personal activities of the staff. Here, again, the internal controls described in Chapter 11 should be devised to minimize such misappropriation of resources. This is an area of accountability that needs attention, or the practice can grow like a cancer, since cynicism tends to be contagious, as does its slogan, "Why not? Everyone does it!"

Playing with numbers: Manipulation of monetary and nonmonetary figures takes other subtle forms. One involves pushing expenses into the following period to avoid going over budget. With a cash basis system that can be done merely by not submitting bills for payment. In an accrual system, it is accomplished by not submitting bills to be entered, or having them postdated by the supplier. Another technique is to make output performance look better than it is by finding unproductive gimmicks. The cynical slogan here is, "The only thing that counts is what gets counted."

That human nature is the same the world over is illustrated in a *New York Times* story (1-1-89) about a socialist economy (which also operates as a nonprofit). It seems that there was a severe soap shortage in 1988. Here is why:

> Reporters who looked into the soap crisis ... discovered explanations that would mystify a western consumer. The Svododa soap factory in Moscow had tons of cheap soap sitting in warehouses, but truckers had already delivered enough soap to earn their bonuses for 1988, and were coasting until the new year.

In other words, any more deliveries would have no benefit, but could be added to their 1989 reports to make the next year's quota easier to meet.

USING PERFORMANCE MEASUREMENT TO MOTIVATE DESIRABLE PERFORMANCE

Modern management theory holds that people in even the most idealistic of environments cannot be expected to work against their own self-interest. The methods used for evaluating and rewarding staff must therefore be based on criteria and "performance indicators" (measures) that harmonize their own personal goals with those of the organization. The problem often is that true organization goals (long-term) or objectives (short-term) are unstated, unclear (to management as well as staff), unagreed upon among management (or with staff), conflicting (mutually inconsistent), or even based on a hidden agenda. As a result, personnel may get no clear sense of direction, a confused sense based on mixed signals, or even a false sense. They need to know what is considered good performance, how it will be measured, and preferably how it will be rewarded.

To be more specific, if the day-care center referred to above has a stated policy of offering quality care, but measures performance—perhaps for PR reasons—by the number of children cared for, the program director may try to win "Brownie points" by admitting more children than staff can handle effectively. Although this will appear as productivity (lower cost per child), as well as greater output in terms of services, what will disappear is the claimed quality. Clearly, some indicator other than the number served should be used in evaluating the program director, since quality of care probably increases in inverse ratio to the ratio of children to staff.

A Case in Point

Consider a college department in a university making a similar claim of quality education. How is this measured, and how in fact will its faculty and administrators be evaluated? From the viewpoint of administrators, charged with staying within their budgets, the temptation may be to schedule large classes and/or use part-time or lower-paid teachers to achieve "productivity." Or, if they are persuaded that quality is really the goal, they may hire only academic "stars," people with advanced degrees and prestigious publications, who will attract talented students and faculty.

From the faculty member's viewpoint, depending on which signals are believed, emphasis will be placed on improving teaching quality and resisting increases in class size or on winning academic credentials via publications and research. From the student-client's viewpoint, if teaching is done in huge lecture classes and/or by teaching assistants, while the "stars" pursue research, the claim of quality becomes a violation of truth in advertising. Here is a clear and typical case illustrating unagreed upon or conflicting goals. The true goal may be a publicly unannounced one, such as building the prestige of the university, college, or department, or attaining or maintaining accreditation, if faculty academic credentials are in fact being emphasized. The true goal may be overcoming budgetary problems, if productivity is the name of the game, or if admissions standards are lowered, to attract more tuition-paying students. It may even be a genuine concern for real education, where faculty knowlege and teaching ability are prime criteria rather than formal credentials and scholarly work.

The point here is not to argue which is the correct goal. That is up to a governing board. What is essential is that all personnel, from top to bottom, understand what the goal really is, so that they know whether they can accept it and work toward it comfortably. They need to be secure in the knowledge that they will be evaluated and rewarded on the basis of their efforts in advancing that goal, and not run afoul of some administrator's hidden agenda. There is nothing that increases staff turnover and destroys morale as much as such a breach of trust.[10]

[10]Two leading concepts in prevailing management theory are known as MBO (management by objectives) and goal congruence, meaning that organizational goals and objectives must be shared ones, founded in self-interest.

APPENDIX 15A

Audits by a Public Accountant
(A Checklist)

REASONS FOR AUDITS

- Request for an audited statement by a funding agency, parent body, lender or major donor.
- Opinion of an independent public accountant required as part of annual report to state regulatory agency.
- Desire to enhance the credibility of financial reports to users.
- To help improve financial controls and safeguards, or accounting and reporting systems, as preventive medicine against embezzlement, though not primarily designed to detect it.
- The audit may not be one you requested, but one contracted for by one of your funding agencies, governmental or private (that will often be a more limited audit, focused on your compliance with the terms of a grant or contract).

WHAT AN AUDIT INVOLVES

An "audit of the books" is a serious misnomer. The accounting ledgers and journals are only the starting point. The audit aims at determining whether the figures entered are valid ones, based on the underlying documents, such as bills, checks, etc. An audit includes:

- A review of the system of internal controls covering authorization and approval of expenditures and safeguarding of assets.
- Tests of entries and verification of their authenticity by inspection of vouchers, bills, checks, and other documents, on a test basis.
- Verification of asset and liability balances by direct correspondence; review of asset valuations for reasonableness.
- Review of proper tax compliance and of maintenance of tax-exempt status in organizational activities and annual reporting.
- Review for compliance with GAAP in financial reports, including adequate disclosure of contingent (potential) liabilities and anticipated losses affecting the financial condition.

Note: Only an "independent public accountant"—one not directly involved with your nonprofit financially or organizationally—may "attest" to your financial reports, i.e., lend any assurance of their reliability to other parties. What is more, a clean bill of health may not be given if there are any substantial departures from GAAP, inadequate internal controls, inadequate disclosures, or limitations imposed by the client on the scope of the audit. The licensed professional is bound by GAAS (generally accepted auditing standards) as well as GAAP, which represent a public trust, and also by potential legal liability to those who rely on the statements. (The auditor may also be liable to the client for negligent work.[11])

For reasons indicated above, a "quick and cheap" audit is often a bad bargain in the long term; one done on a truly professional basis is usually a productive investment.

A word of caution: If a public accountant's audit turns up any shortcomings in your system or statements that are sufficient to prevent an "unqualified opinion" (meaning a clean bill of health), and these cannot be corrected, three alternatives are available: (1) a "qualified opinion," disclosing the inadequacies, or, if they are too serious for that, (2) refusal to issue an opinion at all, or (3) an "adverse opinion," which is worse than none. The latter is a course not taken often.

Documentation

One of the more troublesome issues for public accountants and their nonprofit clients is the lack of underlying documentation to support the allocation of indirect or shared expenses. A schedule (or statement) of functional expenses included in an audit report sets forth the way payroll and other expenses have been allocated to programs. The public accountant normally tests or otherwise verifies that these have been done correctly, which means factually. If there are no time sheets submitted by the staff to back up such allocations, a qualified opinion or disclaimer of opinion may result, which may cause trouble.

Reference is made here to the section, "Padding Allocated Expenses (A Word of Warning)," where federal guidelines for allocating payroll are quoted. Nonpayroll expenses are easier to document persuasively, since they are usually evidenced by bills, on which the allocations can be shown. If they are not so shown, the auditor has the same problem in accepting them as valid. The importance of keeping good files of all documents supporting expenses and other payments should be clear.

The Management Letter

An invaluable by-product of a good audit is the so-called "management letter." You should ask for one, since they are not submitted automatically. Such a letter is usually a detailed report on the auditor's findings regarding the strengths and weaknesses of your accounting and management information system, covering your internal controls, including documentation, safeguards over cash and other assets, cash flow problems, and the like. It is ordinarily a confidential report for use only by the agency itself.

---

[11]One nonprofit successfuly recovered payment from a large CPA firm whose substandard audit failed to uncover several hundred thousand dollars stolen by its bookkeeper over a number of years.

Chapter 16

Working to Keep Your Exemption Alive

Once your group has become tax-exempt, it still has to file annual returns with the IRS and other government agencies. Even if your group owes no taxes, you have to file information returns to prove that you're playing by the rules. (This chapter deals only with the returns peculiar to exempt organizations. Chapter 17 covers employment taxes and other returns that exempt organizations, like business firms, are often required to file.)

ANNUAL IRS REPORT FORMS FOR EXEMPT ORGANIZATIONS

If your organization's annual gross receipts are normally under $25,000 and the IRS knows your current address but has not sent you a Form 990 or 990EZ package with a preaddressed label, you are not required to file Form 990 or 990EZ. ("Gross receipts" is a different figure from "Total revenues." It is the total of all revenue and support, before deducting any costs, such as those deducted on several lines of page 1 of the form.)

If your gross receipts are normally under $25,000 but you did receive a preaddressed Form 990 or 990EZ, the IRS asks that you attach the peel-off label, check the box near the top indicating that your gross receipts are normally under $25,000, and sign and mail the form to the address given in the instructions. "Normally below $25,000" is explained below under "Forms 990 and 990EZ Deciphered." If your agency is filing for its first or second fiscal year, the minimum is higher, as explained below.

Even if your gross receipts *are* normally $25,000 or more, you may not have to complete the full, multi-page Form 990. A much shorter Form 990EZ has been introduced for use by organizations which would otherwise have to file a Form 990 but which had gross receipts of less than $100,000 for the year in question, and which had total assets at the end of that year of less than $250,000.

The 990EZ is much simpler than the 990. It does away with the Statement of Functional Expenses, the detailed breakdown of expenses, allocations of those line items between programs, management, and fundraising that the 990 requires of all 501(c)(3) and 501(c)(4) groups (except that the total expenses for each program must still be reported by those groups). The 990EZ also boils the balance sheet down to two or three lines, omits the Analysis of Income-Producing

Expenses (and its accompanying Relationship of Activities to the Accomplishment of Exempt Purposes), and omits the Information Relating to Taxable Subsidiaries. In addition, the Other Information section is much shorter, inquiring into fewer subjects.

It appears that as Form 990 has been beefed up recently to police the activities of the larger organizations, the IRS, whether out of compassion for the smaller groups, or simply because it realized that it couldn't deal with that level of detail on all the small groups (which constitute the majority of groups), introduced the 990EZ. It was a smart move, as otherwise there could well have been a massive political backlash against the 990's new requirements.

Use of Form 990EZ has no effect on the other forms you use. If you have to file Schedule A (Form 990), you still use that form. (As of this writing, there is no special version of Schedule A for the 990EZ.) You might still use a full 990 if your state or funding agency requires it, or if you are set up to use the 990 already, expect not to qualify to use the 990EZ every year, and want to maintain consistency of format from year to year.

All nonprofits classified by the IRS as "private foundations" (including private operating foundations) must file Form 990-PF instead of Form 990, regardless of gross receipts. As pointed out in Chapter 1, you may not think of yourself as a foundation at all, but the IRS may have determined that you are one, either in the Determination Letter granting your tax exemption, or in a later year.

CASES WHERE YOU MAY BE EXEMPT FROM FILING

There are exemptions from having to file Form 990 for churches and church-affiliated organizations and below-college-level religious schools, federal instrumentalities, and some state institutions. Some exempt organizations file other forms instead of the 990, such as private foundations (Form 990-PF), black lung benefit trusts (990-BL), employee benefit plans (Form 5500), and section 501(d) religious or apostolic organizations (Form 1065-Partnership Return). (See "Instructions for Filing Form 990.")

All 501(c)(3) groups that claim they are not private foundations (see Chapter 1), and that have to file Form 990, must also file Schedule A for Form 990, to show that they are still eligible for 501(c)(3) status and for "non-private-foundation" status.

If your group has gross income of $1,000 or more from an "unrelated trade or business" in any particular year, you'll also have to file Form 990-T, which is not an information return, but a tax return. (As pointed out in Chapter 9, this applies to activities you may not realize fit the IRS definition.)

Finally, if your group has net investment income and expenses to influence elections you may also have to file Form 1120-POL. (But remember that Section 501(c)(3) organizations may not spend *any* money on influencing elections.)

You Must Also Report to State Agencies

In addition to the federal forms, you'll probably also have to make annual filings with your state's Corporations, Tax, Public Charities and/or Secretary of State's offices. Because state requirements vary, this chapter focuses on the federal forms. Check with the state offices just listed, to find out what they require.

UNDERSTANDING THE FEDERAL FORMS

The main body of this chapter consists of discussions of the most commonly used federal forms. However, before we plunge into the forms in detail, we will take a quick look at the function of each of the forms in maintaining a group's accountability. After this overview, in a section called "Going for Help," we have included some suggestions about how and when professional advice should be sought to help in completing the forms. Mistakes can have major consequences.

IRS Form 990: Return of Organization Exempt from Income Tax (and Short Form 990EZ)

Forms 990 and 990EZ are the key elements in maintaining your tax-exempt and tax-deductible status via your accountability to the federal government. Taken together with the accompanying Schedule A (required only of 501(c)(3) organizations), they combine an annual financial report of your activities and affairs with an updating of your eligibility and specific tax status, based on a series of questions about what you have been doing and where you get your funds.

Note and read carefully the statement in very small print that appears just above the space for the signature of the appropriate officer of your organization. It also applies to your accountant or attorney who prepares the return for you, if any. This declaration covers all information contained in the Form and its supporting schedules and statements, and the penalties of perjury it refers to are stated in the Internal Revenue Code. (Section 7206 provides fines and/or imprisonment for anyone who willfully makes and signs a statement or return, under penalty of perjury, that he does not believe to be materially true and correct, and this includes the preparer of the return. This penalty applies to all tax and information returns, not merely to Form 990.)

Filing the Return: Form 990 or 990EZ is due by the fifteenth day of the fifth month after the end of the organization's fiscal year. There is a penalty of $10 a day for late filing, or for filing an incomplete return, up to a maximum of $5,000. After due notice of failure to file by the IRS, *the person or persons responsible for filing can, in addition, be assessed a penalty of the same amount **personally.*** The same applies to incomplete returns. The moral: file complete information and on time. Do not leave questions that are not applicable to your organization with blanks in the space for answers. Enter "N/A" or zero instead.

Schedule A (Form 990)—Organization Exempt Under 501(c)(3)

This form is required only of 501(c)(3) organizations, as its title indicates, and private foundations are also excused from filing it, since its principal purpose is to determine whether the organization filing has become a private foundation, based on its sources of revenue. It is what the IRS looks at in deciding whether your group is "publicly supported" and therefore should not be treated as a private foundation. In evaluating whether your group qualifies, the basic test is largely mathematical. For example, the receipt of a large contribution from a board member can actually hurt you in this area, as it might inflate your "total support" without increasing your "public support," thus effectively reducing your public support as a percentage of the total. Many other variables need to be watched as well. Chapter 1 discusses, in some detail, the tests involved as well as the kinds of funding that may help and the kinds that may hurt.

IRS Form 990-T—Exempt Organization Business Income Tax Return

This is a special return unlike Form 990, since it is an income tax return, not an information return. Any organization otherwise exempt from income tax is required to file it for any fiscal year in which its total income from an unrelated trade or business is $1,000 or more. So the main question is: what do they mean by an "unrelated trade or business"? There are two types:

1. One that is regularly carried on and is not substantially related to the tax-exempt purpose of the organization. This is a factual issue, and the question of whether a business is or is not "substantially related" is sometimes a bit difficult to answer with any assurance. There are, however, exceptions even within this category:

a. Where the work is carried on by volunteers: i.e., without compensation;

b. Where the activity consists of selling merchandise, all of which has been received by the organization as donations;

c. An activity carried on by a 501(c)(3) organization primarily for the convenience of its members, employees, patients, etc.

2. While rental income is generally not treated as unrelated business income, it is so classified for 501(c)(7) and (9) organizations, for rentals of "personal property," property that is mortgaged—i.e., what is called "debt-financed property"—and rents received from an 80% or more "controlled corporation." (See Chapter 9, "Setting Up a Subsidiary Business Corporation— General Considerations.")

Still another area is one related to the first one, termed "exploited exempt activity income," which refers to income from an activity associated with an exempt activity but which does not in fact advance the exempt purposes of the nonprofit. If this sounds like a hair-splitting issue, it often is. IRS Publication 598, "Tax on Unrelated Business Income of Exempt Organizations," gives as an example of taxable income the sale of endorsements of lab equipment by an exempt scientific organization. This is considered to be a commercial exploitation of its reputation by an exempt organization. A nontaxable activity cited is the sponsorship by a university of dramatic and symphonic performances to which the general public is invited through advertisements, with tickets being sold by the university. Here the key is the IRS view that such performances contribute to the exempt (educational and cultural) functions of the institution, whereas the sale of endorsements by the laboratory do not.

Advertising revenue from a nonprofit's periodicals is a special case of this, and is handled separately on the Form 990-T.

The following typical cases illustrate how these provisions are usually interpreted by the IRS:

Examples of Unrelated Business Income: Operation of a boutique with paid staff (but not if the staff is all volunteers, nor if all merchandise is donated to the organization); advertising income from a newsletter; regular (but not occasional) bingo games or the like; and parking lot fees (unless all services are by volunteers or the lot is operated primarily for the benefit of members, employees, or clients).

Examples of "Substantially Related Activities":   Thrift shops selling donated merchandise (even with paid staff); a luncheonette or gift shop operated by a hospital for the sale of candy, flowers, or newspapers (assumed to be of benefit to employees, patients, or visitors); any business whose services are substantially all performed by volunteers without compensation.

Activities Not Regularly Carried On: Occasional fundraising events, craft fairs, and other activities engaged in on an irregular basis that don't rise to the level of an ongoing business, even if they don't "contribute importantly to advancing" your group's exempt purpose.

(Form 4562, *Depreciation*, may also be required of groups that have to file a 990-T, as a supporting schedule to the 990-T.)

See Chapter 9, under "Possibly Taxable Types of Income," for an in-depth discussion of Unrelated Business Income.

Form 1120-POL—Return re: Electoral Activity

Any 501(c) organization that spends more than $100 on influencing the selection of individuals for public or political party office, including nomination, election, or appointment, whether at the federal, state, or local level, must file form 1120-POL. This form is *not* filed by a 501(c)(3) organization, for it is prohibited from any such activity.

GOING FOR HELP

The consequences of errors, omissions, or even missed opportunities in completing these returns can be serious, whether in terms of additional taxes, penalties or, worse yet, possibly jeopardizing your tax-exempt or tax-deductible status. Therefore, if you undertake preparing the above forms on a do-it-yourself basis, first of all because you can save badly needed dollars, second because you get a much better handle on what is being submitted (and what you are signing!) you will still need professional advice. For one thing, the Internal Revenue Code does not stand still, nor do the IRS Regulations that interpret it, not to mention their rulings or new court decisions, which can affect its application to particular situations.

While the number of public accountants and attorneys who are expert in this area is not very large, you would be well advised to find one who can at least review your returns before they are filed. He or she can make sure there are no problems of which you may be unaware, or tax-saving opportunities you may have missed. Not to do this would be a case of "penny-wise, pound-foolish." Such a professional can also be a valuable resource by telephone while you are working on your returns, since it should be clear by now that a number of tricky questions are likely to arise. If you follow professional advice, the subsequent review will consist of checking for things that did not occur to you, and will minimize the likelihood of having to make changes (and dig up additional needed data) too close to the due date of the return.

This last point should also suggest the obvious about preparing tax and information returns in general. If you put them off to the last minute, a common human failing, the result may be a hurry-up job in order to meet the deadline. We hope that the dangers of sloppy work have become so apparent by this time that you will allow yourself enough time and space to do careful and thorough tax returns. (If you need further convincing, Appendix 16A will explain briefly how the IRS audits such reports. The best thing to do about an IRS audit is to avoid one, and the best way to do that is to prepare returns that do not invite scrutiny.)

Note: The remainder of this chapter is intended as reference material. It is not intended to be read for enjoyment, but for use as you work on the returns. However, it does contain information that supplements the information in Chapter 1, and may be useful in answering questions you may have come up with on your own.

GETTING STARTED ON YOUR IRS FORMS

The federal forms can be obtained, with accompanying instructions, from your nearest IRS office. (The instructions also indicate when the returns are due and where to file.) We have illustrated and explained the use of forms for 1989, and all references in this chapter to line, column, and part numbers relate to those forms. Yet IRS forms do change sometimes, and these references may have to be adapted accordingly. It works best, incidentally, if you do your Form 990 (or 990EZ) first, then the others, as required, in the following order: 990-T, Schedule A (Form 990), and lastly, 1120-POL.

Before you start, make sure you have all the information you'll need, as explained below, so that you can concentrate on return prepartion, without having to interrupt the process to chase down bits and pieces of information. You'll need your adjusted trial balance at fiscal year-end, your general ledger, very likely your cash receipts and cash disbursements journals (unless your ledger provides all the necessary detail, which is unlikely), payroll records, allocation worksheets, etc. [Where expenses must be allocated, on Forms 990-T, Schedule A (Form 990) Part VI, Lobbying Expenditures and 1120-POL, use the same approach explained below in instructions for Form 990, Statement of Functional Expenses.]

Preparing IRS Form 990

As mentioned, IRS Form 990 is the key element in maintaining your tax-exempt and tax-deductible status via your accountability to the federal government. How to assemble the figures and enter them on the forms, and what significance the lines and questions have, is explained below in detail.

Forms 990 and 990EZ Deciphered

We include as Appendix B a section of IRS Package 990-2, which is normally received by Sec. 501(c)(3) organizations each year with its forms, if they have filed Form 990 previously. This material contains completely filled-in forms 990 and Schedule A, plus required supporting schedules, plus explanations and supporting materials that show where the entries come from and why.

Note: The forms may change from time to time, so there may be different line numbers, etc. on the 1990 or later forms. Use with care therefore.

Heading Information: Mostly self-explanatory. Note the provision for partial reports by very small nonprofits (see boxes for organizations with gross receipts of normally not over $25,000 or between $10,000 and $25,000.) Note also that the instructions define "gross receipts" as being, not the total revenue shown, but the sum of all revenues *before* deducting directly related costs, such as the expenses of rental income, cost of assets sold, expenses of special events and cost of goods sold.*

The IRS defines "normally not more than $25,000" on an averaged basis, over a three-year period, up to and including the year just ended. Groups that have not been around for three years can qualify as having "normally not more than $25,000" as follows:

(a) groups that have been in existence a year or less can have received or have pledged to them up to $37,500 their first year and still qualify; and

---

*That means Total Revenue *plus* all amounts subtracted from those amounts on the form.

(b) groups in existence between one and three years qualify if their gross receipts and pledges for the first two years average $30,000 or less.

Even if your gross receipts are normally more than $25,000, note that if the total revenue for the fiscal year is $25,000 or less, some parts of Form 990 need not be completed.

Support and Revenue: Items that seem self-explanatory have been omitted.

"Direct public support" is defined in the instructions to include dues from members paid for support of the organization, rather than for services or benefits received in a direct sense. The value of any merchandise or other direct benefits given to members should be deducted from the total dues and that value entered as membership dues. (Dues of nonprofits exempt under sections 501(c) other than 501(c)(3) are often of this nature. Your record-keeping should keep track of this allocation, either for each transaction or by a formula.)

Indirect public support refers to funds from the United Way or similar fundraising organizations that raise funds for several organizations. It also includes funds from parent or subordinate groups, or groups that share the same parent organization as the reporting group. It does not include funds from sales promotions where the purchaser is told that a part of the price will go to the reporting group, which is "direct support" and is reported on the previous line.

Government grants. Include amounts paid to your group for the benefit of the public or to help you further your exempt purpose. Do not include amounts paid to you under contract to provide a service or other benefit only to the government agency itself, such as help with its internal problems. Those amounts are reported as other revenue, or as program service revenue. Form 990 has you enter each of these 3 categories separately, on different lines. 990EZ combines them all into one number. Each form asks you to attach a schedule listing all the items.

Program service revenue. This is the total of funds collected in the course of conducting activities that further your exempt purpose (except to the extent that other, more specific lines apply).

Membership dues. Include here only the part covering purchase of goods or services (see "Direct Public Support" above). If the dues you receive include a portion collected for your parent body (such as the "per capita" dues a union local collects for its international), that portion is not revenue, but a liability, and should be excluded. IRS considers only the part of the dues received for your own unit's use to be "gross receipts" for this purpose. This rule may qualify you to file only a partial report, if it brings your "gross receipts" down below $25,000.

Rents. Some nonprofits have rental income, either from a subtenant, or from renting out part of a building they own. The rental expenses deducted are a percentage of overall costs of occupancy, based on space. (See "Occupancy" on the Overhead Allocation Worksheet, Table 6–1.) (Not a separate item on the EZ, so include it under "Other revenue.")

Sale of assets. This would apply to a sale of equipment, investments, or any other asset except merchandise (reported under Gross Sales). The cost would be the amount shown on the books, reduced by any accumulated depreciation, in the case of fixed assets like equipment or buildings.

Special fundraising events and activities. The form calls for entering total receipts and directly connected expenses of each event. To meet this requirement, a record of these items will have to be kept, or the amounts entered separately on the general ledger, which is preferable.

Gross sales. These three lines (a), (b), and (c) are used to report any sales of merchandise in a related fundraising activity such as a gift or thrift shop. (It may also represent unrelated business income.)

Fund balance at beginning of year is usually from the adjusted trial balance, unless there have been other changes in the fund balance account during the year, in which case the balance at the end of the previous year is used; the net amount of other changes during the year is shown on the next line, with explanation attached showing the amounts involved.

Fund balance at end of year is derived arithmetically as shown, and must also agree with the amount shown as the fund balance at the end of the year, as shown on the balance sheet (see below). **Note:** Supporting Schedules, which include a list of contributors of over $5,000, are required by the instructions in support of the line for contributions. They require the amounts and dates of grants, as well as the name and address of the contributor, which includes organizations as well as individuals.

Statement of Functional Expenses.   On the 990EZ, total figures are used, but the full 990 requires that a line-by-line breakdown between "Program Services," "Management and General," and "Fundraising" be shown by all 501(c)(3) and 501(c)(4) organizations and 4947(a)(1) trusts. (Other users of the full 990 may use the "total" column and ignore the rest, unless their state or funding agencies require otherwise.) Making the three-way split requires an allocation of each expense category between the three functions, such as discussed in Chapters 5 and 13, though the IRS instructions permit you to use "a reasonable method of allocation" if your accounting system itself does not do so. (However, these figures "should be accurate," so a wild guess is clearly not acceptable.) Whatever method you use, make sure to keep a worksheet or other record of how you arrived at your allocation for each expense: e.g., salaries, by estimate of percentage of time spent by personnel on each function; rent, by percentage of space used, etc. The calculations should of course be kept with your copy of the Form 990, as well as the explanations.

Now, as for the figures entered in columns (B), (C), and (D): you can use the Overhead Allocation Worksheet in Chapter 6 (Table 6–1) and the resulting Annual Operating Budget with Joint Fixed Costs Allocated to Function (Table 6–2), but use actual rather than budgeted figures in the total column. That requires some adjustment of figures, such as eliminating any donated rent included in "Occupancy," and using the same percentages of actual expenses as those used in the budget worksheet, or derived from the figures in Table 6–2, where necessary. The resulting breakdowns would first be made on a worksheet like Table 6–1, unless already prepared for internal or external financial reports. The final allocations would be those we entered on the form itself. Note that Table 6–1 provides a column headed "Basis of Allocation"; this should satisfy the IRS as explaining the method used, which should be acceptable. Note that percentage breakdown of the executive director's actual time may differ from the budgeted percentage.

Statement of Program Services Accomplishments.   The expense allocation referred to above will have to break total expenses down by program as well as showing total program expense. In other words, the worksheet mentioned will require a column for each program, as in the budget worksheet mentioned (Table 6–1). This section's dollar figures can be omitted unless you are a 501(c)(3) or a 501(c)(4). In any case, you'll have to write the essay they ask for, even if dollar figures are not required.

Balance Sheets.   Note simpler requirements if Form 990EZ is used. The amounts in column (A), "Beginning of Year," would be taken from the previous year-end balance sheet. The year-end balances are of course taken from the worksheet in Appendix 12A (Fig. 12A–7). Note that supporting schedules are required for Other Assets and Other Liabilities. This is the case where there are a number of different accounts on the trial balance that must be combined on the form. Actually, where there is only one item, it is sufficient to enter the identity of the item directly on the form itself. The other asset lines are self-explanatory. (A few require attached schedules.)

Most of the lines under Liabilities apply to nonprofits using the accrual method in their reports (which we urge elsewhere in the book). The captions are mostly self-explanatory. The caption "Support and revenue designated for future periods" is used for items of deferred or unearned revenue, which appear as liabilities on your balance sheet. Where grant funds have been received and not yet fully expended in situations where the fully correct method of handling unexpended funds described in Chapter 10 is used, in accordance with AICPA's SOP 78-10.[1] (This type of item was referred to as Deferred Revenue.)

The end-of-year Fund Balance is *calculated* from the worksheet (Fig. 12A–7) and must agree with the same figure at the bottom of Part I of Forms 990 and 990EZ.

If all figures are correct, the total assets on the balance sheet should equal the total of liabilities and fund balances. (It is important to check that they do; otherwise the credibility of the Form 990 may be questioned by IRS.)

List of Officers, Etc.   Paying expense accounts for travel or other outlays on behalf of the organization [column (E)] is not unusual.[2] The main problem here is an estimate of time spent on the position, called for in column (B). Where there is no compensation, IRS should accept "part" as a sufficient time estimate.

Other Information.   This one looks easy and innocent enough, but it is probably the most dangerous part of the entire report, since in many cases a careless answer can precipitate an IRS audit and possible loss of your exempt or tax-deductible status.

The main purpose of "Other Information" is to disclose to the IRS any changes or additions to information previously submitted in the following important areas, especially in your original application for exemption:

- Newly added or discontinued program activities.

- Any changes or additions to your organizing documents (articles of incorporation, etc.) or bylaws (see Chapter 2).

- Any Unrelated Business Income received during the year.
Note: Starting in 1989, Form 990 has included a schedule containing questions designed to determine whether a Form 990-T should have been filed for the year. (See "Analysis of Income-Producing Activities" above.)

- Political activities. This is the way IRS checks up on whether you may be violating the prohibitions or limitations of the Revenue Code that apply to your organization. The instructions require you to enter the amount spent, loaned, or even promised in connection with the nomination, appointment, or election of anyone to a public office, and points out the requirement to file a Form 1120-POL if your political expenses and net investment income exceed $100 for the year. Watch out for this one: it is too easy to answer carelessly, which could invite serious trouble if, on audit, the facts prove different from your answer. And if your answer is that you spent over $100 to influence an election and received over $100 in interest, dividends, etc., you had better file the Form 1120-POL, or face trouble. *But note this:* The word "spent" includes allocated salary of any staff who were involved and allocated phone or mailing expenses.

- In-kind contributions. Since this information is optional, why enter it? The point is that since this form is open to public inspection, any such items tend to make you look good, and can also

---

[1] See Chapter 10, under heading "Accrual Basis: Handling Specific Items."

[2] The instructions call for entering only amounts that exceeded actual expenses, or were not accounted for: these are taxable income to the individual.

explain why there is no rent expense in Occupancy expense (Part II). You might also want to include the value of donated services of volunteers or professionals, for the same PR reasons. (A funding source may ask to see your 990.)

Analysis of Income-Producing Activities. This appears only on the full 990. As to each program or category of income, a classification must be made between unrelated business income, income excluded from being treated as unrelated business uncome under sections 512 through 514, and income related to the organization's exempt purpose. (As to the last category, an explanation is also required.) On the 990EZ, you are simply told to attach a statement showing why any income from business activities does not have to be reported on a Form 990-T tax return as Unrelated Business Income.

Schedule A (Form 990)—Organization Exempt Under 501(c)(3)

This form is required only of 501(c)(3) organizations, as its title indicates. Private foundations are also excused from filing it, since its principal purpose is to determine whether the organization filing has become a private foundation, based on its sources of revenue.

Part I—Compensation of Five Highest Paid Employees. This is required only for employees —other than officers, directors, and trustees—who are paid more than $30,000 each. Unfortunately, it probably will too rarely apply to readers of this book.

Part II—Compensation of Five Highest Paid Persons for Professional Services. This applies to consultants, attorneys, CPAs, and other individuals who are not employees or directors of the nonprofit, and only those paid more than $30,000. Only the type of service and amount of compensation is required here, plus the name and address of each person.

Part III—Statements About Activities. This is a further extension of the type of questions asked in Form 990, "Other Information," and covers activities of 501(c)(3) organizations that are subject to particular constraints or controls. The same cautionary comments apply here.

Lobbying activities: Note that in addition to the "yes" or "no" answer, the total amount paid or incurred must be entered, plus a detailed statement detailing the activities and classifying the expenses. Where an election has been made to use the specific dollar limits prescribed in Section 501(h), a Form 5768 must be filed to qualify, and Part VI of Schedule A must be completed.*

Transactions with related parties: These are transactions that might be prohibited and taxable—if you lose your exclusion from private foundation status. (See Chapter 1 about this.) To minimize your risk you should keep these kinds of transactions to a minimum, or better yet, try to avoid them. The transactions listed are among those that pose a danger of "private inurement"— someone making an excessive "insider" profit at the organization's expense.

Part IV—Reason for Non Private Foundation Status: This Support Schedule is very important. It is what the IRS looks at in deciding whether your group is "publicly supported" and thus should not be treated as a private foundation (see also Chapter 1 and discussion above of Schedule A, "Understanding the Federal Forms").

Some types of groups have automatic exclusions from private foundation status, as discussed in Chapter 1. If you qualify to check one of their boxes you don't have to rely on the mathematical tests and can skip the rest of this Part.

If you are relying on Section 509(a)(1) and Section 170(b)(1)(A)(iv) or (vi) [we'll call this the "170(b)(1)(A)" test] or on the Section 509(a)(2) test, you'll have to complete this Part. It's enough to

---

*The rules cited above re: allocated expenses apply here as well.

pass either test, but in either case, you'll fill in almost all the lines, even some that are mainly relevant to one or the other of the tests. Many groups that meet one test may also meet another. You should try working through both tests to see which gives your group a greater margin of safety, before you decide which test to choose on your Form 990, Schedule A.

The first thing you may notice is that the Support Schedule does not include the year just ended but covers the four prior years. In fact, if your group has had a "material change" in its sources of support in the year just ended, you will have to make up a *five-year* version of the Support Schedule, adding the year before the first year printed on the form. A "material change" means a *major change* that could result in your group's failing to pass the public support test. It does not mean merely the receipt of an unusual grant that you can simply exclude from the computation by moving it onto the last line of the Support Schedule (as explained below), but it relates more to the beginning or ending of a major ongoing source of support, like a major ongoing grant, a major change in membership dues receipts, or a related or unrelated business.

Proceeding through the Support Schedule (note that "support" is used here differently from elsewhere: unlike the term "total revenues" on the 990, the Support Schedule excludes capital gains; unlike the way "support" is used on financial reports discussed in Chapter 15, the Support Schedule does include money earned by the group):

Gifts, grants, and contributions received. Include here the same amounts that are included in this category on the Form 990 for each year, except that you may exclude any unusual grants that would cause you to fail the "public support" tests. These are large or unexpected grants that are from "disinterested persons" (i.e., people who become "substantial contributors"—and thus "disqualified persons"—solely because of the size of their gift, not because of any other ties to your group). You can exclude them from the computation by moving them onto the last line of the Support Schedule and providing details about them as described below.

Membership fees received. See our earlier instructions for the Form 990 on how to categorize membership dues as being contributions or fees.

Gross receipts from admissions, merchandise sold or services performed, or furnishing of facilities in any activity that is not a business unrelated to the organization's charitable, etc. purpose. Include here your gross receipts from activities that advance your exempt purposes. (See Chapter 1 and also the discussion of the Form 990-T in this chapter on how to distinguish between related and unrelated business activities.) For convenience, we refer to these as "related gross receipts."

Gross income from interest, dividends, amounts received from payments on securities, loans, rents, royalties and unrelated business taxable income (less section 511 taxes) from businesses acquired after June 30, 1975. This is where you report most of your taxable income. Notice that you deduct your Form 990-T taxes (section 511) before including your unrelated business taxable income. Don't forget to make this deduction, which makes it easier for you to qualify if you rely on the 509(a)(2) test.

Net income from unrelated business activities not included on the line above. This is where you report unrelated activities that are not in the line above, either because you've had them since before June 30, 1975, or because they don't rise to the level of a business. (See Chapter 1 and also the discussion of the Form 990-T in this chapter on how to distinguish between unrelated activities that are and are not businesses.) Note that this income is reported on a net basis. While such contributions are not taxed on the Form 990-T, they still work against you in computing your public support percentage. (However, they don't affect the "not more than one-third from gross investment income plus unrelated business taxable income after taxes" since they're not "taxable income.")

Tax revenues levied for your benefit and either paid to you or expended on your behalf and *The value of services or facilities furnished to you by a governmental unit without charge.* These are self-explanatory. They only apply where government gets into the act. As to the second, if you got something that is not normally provided to the public, and it is clearly of significant value, you may have to have someone (like an accountant or appraiser) put a value on what you got.

Other income, except capital gains. This is your "Total other revenue" from Part IV of your Form 990 for the year involved, minus anything you've included on any of the other lines of the Support Schedule.

After that, you total the lines up to this point and enter them on the next line. For groups that rely on the 509(a)(2) test, this is "Total support."

Then you subtract the related gross receipts (the third line of the Support Schedule) and enter that figure on the line below. For groups that rely on the 170(b)(1)(A) tests, this is "Total support."

Then you take 1% of the first Total support (the one that includes related gross receipts). If larger than $5,000, this is the maximum related gross receipts from any one individual in any one year that will count toward public support for a group that relies on 509(a)(2). (If this line is less than $5,000, $5,000 is the limit.)

On the next pair of lines, if you rely on the 170(b)(1)(A) tests, you enter, on line **a**, 2% of the second Total support (the one that excludes related gross receipts), attach a list of contributors whose total gifts for the time period covered by the Support Schedule exceed this figure and how much they contributed, and enter, on line **b**, the total of all the excess amounts. In making up your list of contributors, remember that a husband and wife count as one contributor, as do all members of a disqualified entity (see Chapter 1 about those). Contributions from governments or other publicly supported organizations that use the 170(b)(1)(A)(iv) test don't have to be listed here unless they were simply passing along a contribution that was earmarked for your group. Such earmarked contributions *would* be listed. (Lists of contributors are not open to public inspection.)

If you rely on the 509(a)(2) test, you skip that pair of lines and go instead to the next pair of lines. These are each broken down by year. On the first line you include, in full, all contributions from disqualified persons, as described in Chapter 1. On the second line you include the excess of any related receipts in one year from one individual (other than "disqualified persons") that exceed the greater of 1% of Total support (see the explanation a few lines back) or $5,000. For each line, you have to attach lists of individuals included on those lines. The lists show the total amounts from each individual each year, not just the excess amounts. If you got amounts from these individuals that were not related receipts, you should show those amounts separately on your list, labeled as not being related receipts, and not include them in the calculation of how much to report as excess related receipts.

Finally, the unusual grants we discussed above get totaled here, and you attach a list that describes each of them, including its amount and nature, who you got it from and when and why it should be treated as unusual (see the reasons outlined above).

Now do the arithmetic to see if your group meets its tests, as described in Chapter 1. If you are relying on 170(b)(1)(A) and don't meet the one-third level of public support, but do meet a 10% level, you should attach a statement on how you meet the "facts and circumstances" test described in Chapter 1.

Part V—Private School Questionnaire. This part of Schedule A only applies to private schools that are relying for exclusion from private foundation status on the basis of being a school.

(This is one of the automatic exclusions that avoid the Support Schedule's one-third of support tests.) Its purpose is to make sure that private schools comply with the civil rights laws. See IRS Publication 557 for details in this area.

Part VI—Lobbying Expenditures by Public Charities (Cross Reference: Chapter 1, "Political and Legislative Activity"). This part of Schedule A only applies to groups that have filed an election to be allowed to lobby, under Section 501(h). This election is filed on Form 5768 (see Chapter 1, "To Elect the Lobbying Provision or Not?").[3]

Boxes (a) and (b) ask about whether your group is part of an "affiliated group" and, if so, whether the law's "limited control" provisions apply. (See Chapter 1, and the form's instructions, for an explanation of these.) If you are part of an affiliated group, you have to complete column (a) with the whole group's numbers, and column (b) with your own group's. If your group is considered affiliated only because its or the other group's governing instrument provides that one group's decisions on national issues control the other's, the controlled group need only complete column (b) and use its own expenses, while the controlling group completes column (b) including the controlled group's expenses on national issues along with its own.

Total (grass roots) lobbying expenses to influence public opinion is explained in Chapter 1.

Total lobbying expenses to influence a legislative body is lobbying directed at the government, rather than at the public, as described in Chapter 1.

Total lobbying expenses. This is the sum of the first two. Don't forget about allocated expenses (see above). Skip the next line for now, and go on to:

Total exempt purpose expenditures. This is "Total functional expenses" from Part II of Form 990 for the year involved, plus any expenses from other lines that are associated with "related revenues," such as the expenses of a special fundraising event that furthers the group's exempt purposes in itself (aside from the money raised) or the cost of goods sold in a shop that is operated to further the group's exempt purposes, uses all volunteers, sells only donated merchandise, etc.

Other exempt purposes expenditures. Now go back up a line and subtract total lobbying expenses from total exempt purposes expenditures, to get "Other."

Lobbying nontaxable amount and *Grass roots nontaxable amount* come from a table printed on the form, and are based on your total exempt purpose expenditures. The grass roots nontaxable amount is simply 25% of the lobbying nontaxable amount.

Then comes a four-year computation. There are several exemptions from having to complete this in full:

1. Groups that are filing Schedule A for their first year of IRS recognition of 501(c)(3) status can skip it entirely.

2. Tax years prior to IRS recognition of 501(c)(3) status can be omitted.

3. If this is the first through third year of your 501(h) election, you need only fill in the columns for each of your 501(h) years and the total column, unless you have exceeded one of the ceiling amounts (the ceilings are 150% of the nontaxable amounts). If you exceed a ceiling, you have to include all of your IRS-recognized 501(c)(3) years.

Unless you fill in all the years, you have to attach an explanation of why you did not have to, in terms of these rules, which are based on the instructions to the form. Your explanation should also include the ending date of your first 501(h) year and whether the election was revoked before the

---

[3]Form 5768 is called Election/Revocation of Election by an Eligible Section 501(c)(3) Organization to Make Expenditures to Influence Legislation.

beginning of the year for which this Schedule A is filed.

Part VII—Information Regarding Transfers, Transactions, and Relationships with Other Organizations. This portion of Schedule A is designed to ferret out relationships with other tax-exempt organizations (including political action committees exempt under section 527) that are not section 501(c)(3) charities. It calls for reporting of many kinds of transactions and relationships. It is looking for conduit transactions.

There are exceptions from this reporting, which are spelled out in the form's instructions. Grants and contributions are not included, nor are "arms-length" transactions (meaning a fair exchange of value on both sides) with unrelated organizations where less than $500 is involved.

Even if more than $500 is involved, fees for subscriptions, conferences, or seminars paid to the unrelated organization need not be reported if you paid the going rate charged to the general public, or if you provided the goods, assets, or services to the other organization as part of carrying out your exempt purposes and you gave the other organization no better a deal than you were also giving to the general public.

If you gave or got less than fair market value in a transaction, you have to report it, even if it was for less than $500.

If a non-501(c)(3) exempt organization is related to or affiliated with you, you have to report all transactions with it, regardless of the above, and also describe its relationship to your organization in the following section of this Part.

Groups are considered related to or affiliated if more than 25% of the officers, directors, or trustees of one group are also officers, directors, or trustees of the other, or if one or more of the officers, directors, or trustees of either group is chosen by the officers, directors, or trustees of the other. (This form of relationship is called "common control.") You are also considered related or affiliated if the two groups work together on a continuous or recurring basis (not just once or twice), or share facilities, equipment, or paid personnel.

There are lines for answering yes or no to numerous kinds of transactions. If an answer is yes, and the exceptions above don't apply, then you have to identify the transaction by: where on Schedule A the transaction's result is included; what the values of the goods or services involved were (on both sides of the transaction); the name of the other group, and a short note about the transaction and the relationship between the groups.

After that, you are asked to name the organizations to which you are related, what section of the Internal Revenue Code they're exempt under, and what the relationship is.

Form 990-T: The Way You Report Unrelated Business Income

(See definition above under "Understanding the Federal Forms.")

While form 990 is used primarily to monitor your continuing right to your tax exemption, with no tax involved, Form 990-T is an income tax return, which can cost you unbudgeted money. Our advice is therefore to have it prepared by a tax professional. (All page and Part references are to the 1989 form.)

Page 1. Heading data: In Box "B," a code must be entered (from the list provided in the instruction booklet). You may find that more than one code is needed for your unrelated business activities, either because you have more than one, or perhaps because your single activity can be classified more than one way. Use the closest codes you can find.

Lines 1 to 5. These lines are used by nonprofits with low unrelated business gross income—

$10,000 or less. It is a condensed version of page 2, though the resulting tax is the same, since it is calculated for either one on the following lines. The source of the figures on lines 1 and 2 would be your adjusted trial balance or operating statement at the end of your fiscal year, and the comments below for page 2 should be read for ideas, even though you show only the totals on page 1.

Page 2: Taxable Income Computation (Gross Income Over $10,000)

Part I—Unrelated Trade or Business Income.   *Gross receipts or sales, etc.*: similar to that on Form 990; however it only includes sales that represent an unrelated business activity. For example, if you run a thrift shop that sells only donated merchandise, its sales would not be included on this line (even if you had other sales that had to be included).

Cost of goods sold is just what the name indicates, and is calculated in Schedule A at the bottom of the page. How you arrive at the inventory figures can be a complex subject, one on which you can use professional accounting advice. Basically, you count the number of each item on hand, multiply the quantity of each by its original cost, according to invoices, and total the products of these calculations to get the grand total.[4]

Gross profit is the difference between the first two lines. The other lines in Part I are figures transferred from the supporting schedules shown, where the amounts are computed:

Capital gain net income: This is a complex issue, where it exists. It is another case where an accountant or other tax expert may need to be consulted, if the item is large. The instructions offer detailed explanations in this area, but a nonprofit selling an asset for a substantial amount of money (or for other property) could pay a substantial, unnecessary tax on it without adequate professional help in the accounting area.

Partnership income is one few nonprofits would be likely to have, unless two or more joined together in a joint venture of some kind and shared the proceeds or profits. In that case a statement of the details would be required as an attachment.

Rent income: the explanation of the equivalent line on Form 990 applies here as well, though rental income is only reported here in the situations described in the beginning of this section of the chapter: i.e., those in which rents are considered to be unrelated business income. The details would be reported in Schedule C of the return. (Example: rent from a "Controlled Corporation.")

Unrelated debt-financed income is a narrowly defined type of taxable income previously mentioned, generally from renting mortgaged property. (See instructions if applicable.) Again, details are shown in a separate Schedule E.

If you are a Social or Recreational Club covered by 501(c)(7) or Voluntary Employees' Beneficiary Association covered by 501(c)(9), any *net income from investments*, minus any set aside for purposes approved of in the instructions, is taxable, and shown in Schedule F, and on this line.

If you control another nonprofit or business organization, certain of its income is taxable to your organization. The calculation is made in Schedule G, per instructions.

Exploited exempt activity income was explained in the overview for this form at the beginning of this chapter. Any income not derived from advertising is reported here, after being calculated in Schedule H, in accordance with instructions.

Advertising income derived from your nonprofit's publications is reported here, after being calculated in Schedule I, in accordance with instructions.

Other income is any kind of unrelated business income not mentioned on previous lines, but not any other kind of income. You do not want to pay tax on nontaxable types. The instructions give examples.

---

[4]Since we are into business tax accounting here, as we are for other items, such as depreciation, expert advice can save money. There are several ways to value inventory, and to compute depreciation, which can cut taxes.

Part II—Deductions Not Taken Elsewhere. This lists expenses and any deductible losses, other than those already deducted either on line 2 or in one of the attached schedules supporting other lines. Most of these items are self-explanatory; some require that you attach a supporting schedule, or refer you to instructions that explain them further. These would be reported on either a cash or accrual basis, whichever you use on your books. Clearly, since it is more common to have accrued expense than accrued revenue, unless you provide goods or services on credit, it is to your advantage to use the accrual method for activities representing unrelated business income, because it saves you paying tax to the extent that accrued expenses exceed accrued revenues. Where you sell merchandise, the Revenue Code requires that you use the accrual method for merchandise transactions—sales and purchases both. The instructions—even Publication 598—are not explicit in this regard. However, Publication 598 states that accounting methods that apply to tax returns apply to those filed on Form 990-T, and all taxpayers are required to use the accrual method for merchandise transactions, even if they use the cash basis otherwise.

Another general guideline to watch is that if you have allocated any expenses in calculating any of the income reported in Part I, you can only use the unallocated remainder in Part II. The deductions on these lines are only those properly allocable to your unrelated business income: you must therefore eliminate any portion that applies to other program or support activities. Only a few bear explanation:

Salaries represent the business share of related salaries.

Bad debts (uncollectible receivables) should be reported by whatever method you use on your books, if any, as explained in Chapter 10. If you use the allowance (also called the "reserve") method, you must attach a schedule similar to Schedule F on a Corporation Income Tax Return (Form 1120). (Applies mainly to sales on credit.)

Taxes: this deduction generally includes payroll, property, and any sales tax expense incurred by the organization (which may be on its own sales for tax not collected but due). If you have to pay a state or local income tax, *that* is deductible, but not the federal tax on unrelated business income paid, nor most federal excise taxes, etc. (See instructions.)

If your nonprofit makes *contributions to other tax-deductible organizations,* there are specific limitations as to the amount deductible and other rules, set forth in the instructions.

Depreciation is calculated on an attached Form 4562 or similar schedule. This is one area in which more sophisticated accounting methods can save taxes, particularly since the tax law permits you to use a different (faster) method of depreciation on the return than you do on your books. The so-called accelerated depreciation methods used by business firms to reduce income taxes can save you money here as well, and the Revenue Code permits even faster write-offs than before, even a 100% write-off of new equipment (up to certain ceilings). If this tax is of any size, you should obtain expert advice in this area, particularly if you have any depreciable assets. (The methods described on the back of Form 4562 are not a full description of available options).

Depletion and fringe benefits are specialized deductions which also require professional advice, if applicable to you.

Other deductions: like Other income, only deductions not previously used that are applicable to your unrelated business income can be taken here, and a schedule attached. (Don't overlook allocating rent, salaries, etc.)

Advertising loss is a deduction that requires expert advice. It is only deductible if the direct cost of your advertising exceeds your advertising income, which would be unlikely, and not true in our Schedule I; however, if part of that cost represents allocated overhead expense that you would have anyway, it would make sense. But note that you cannot include in advertising costs any of the costs of producing or circulating your publication, as Schedule I indicates: these are called "readership" costs. If these exceed subscription income, they can reduce your net income from advertising but cannot be used to create a deductible advertising loss. To make matters worse, you are required to allocate a portion of your membership dues, if they cover a free subscription, to Subscription income (or Circulation income, as it is called in Schedule I). The result is to reduce further any net loss on circulation that could be used to reduce your taxable advertising income entered on page 2. (See Schedule I.)

Net operating loss is, as indicated, another tricky area. However, if your total deductions and losses are larger than your income for this or any other prior or subsequent year, it is a net operating loss that can be used to obtain a refund of earlier year taxes or to reduce your taxable income in future years. If this applies, you probably need help with the calculation.

After all the above lines are completed, you reach "the bottom line" of *"Unrelated Business Taxable Income"*—or profit, after deducting the same up-to-$1,000 Specific Deduction described previously. (This figure is the equivalent of the one on line 5, page 1, when the short-form calculation for under-$10,000 situations is used.)

Schedule A:

Completing Page 1: The next step is to go back to page 1 and calculate the tax, if any. If your nonprofit is part of an affiliated group—meaning that one of the group's units owns shares in another, item 6 might apply, and it would be wise to consult both the instructions and a tax professional. (This could apply if a nonprofit owned the controlling shares in a taxable business corporation.)

Using the taxable income from page 2, the tax is calculated and entered on page 1 if this is a corporation, using the corporate tax rates shown in the instructions. (As we have noted in earlier chapters, the various tax rates used in this book are only for illustration: instructions accompanying current year's income, payroll, and other tax returns should always be consulted.) Taxpayers on a fiscal year must therefore apportion their taxable income between calendar years when tax rates change (based on the number of days in their fiscal year that fell in each calendar year), and use the applicable rates.

If your group is a trust, rather than a corporation, tax rates for trusts would be used instead of corporate rates, as shown in the instruction booklet. (If you are neither a trust nor a corporation— e.g., an unincorporated association—you are required to use corporate tax rates.)

The various tax credits shown in the tax calculations again are special situations requiring professional help.

The next line is the total of tax due, before any payments or other credits.

Tax due is the line to worry about, since it is what you will owe IRS, if you have an unpaid tax.

Make sure to check the answers to questions about foreign bank accounts and trusts, and to get help if either one should be "yes." Also make sure your return is signed and dated by an officer. If it was prepared for you by a professional (not by anyone in your own organization), the preparer should also of course sign and supply the information required. Note once more the declarations in small print that your signature is being appended to, and remember the earlier admonitions about penalties.

New Schedule for Form 990: As a stopgap for the moves in Congress to tax, eliminate, or limit nonprofit efforts to earn income from unrelated business-type ventures, the IRS added a new schedule to 1989 Forms 990 and 990-PF, to require disclosure of revenues from such ventures. An itemized list of all such activities is required, setting forth the following information for each:

- A description of the activity
- The gross receipts derived
- Whether the income is related or unrelated to the agency's exempt purpoes (i.e., per its corporate charter, etc.)
- If unrelated but exempt for some other reason, the Revenue Code section which exempts it (e.g., interest).

(See the discussion of Congressional developments in this area in Chapter 9, under "How Much Taxable Income Is Too Much?" So, if you fail to report UBI on a Form 990-T, the IRS can spot it on Form 990.)

FORM 990-PF: WHEN IRS DECIDES YOU ARE A "PRIVATE OPERATING FOUNDATION"

We discussed "Avoiding Private Foundation Status" and "The 'Private Operating Foundation' Option" under those sections in Chapter 1.

We won't go into detail about the Form 990-PF, which is the return filed by private foundations. Much of it is very similar to the Form 990, although the level of detail each asks for varies, so our explanation of the Form 990 should be helpful in getting a basic understanding of what the 990-PF is looking for. There are parts of the 990-PF that relate to investment income, which is primarily relevant to foundations that have a nest egg and make grants to other organizations. They're not relying on this book, however, since they have their own lawyers and accountants. (You should too, but we'll try and help you as much as we can. They can take care of themselves, so we'll skip those parts of the form.)

The most important section of the Form 990-PF for readers of this book is Part XV—Private Operating Foundations, which is the test that must be met by 501(c)(3) groups that are not grant-making foundations and which carry out their own exempt activities, but can't meet the "public support" tests or avoid foundation status any other way. Their only choice is to qualify as an operating foundation. This requires that they directly spend in pursuit of their exempt purposes at least 85% of the lesser of their adjusted net income (from Part I of the Form 990-PF) or their minimum investment return (from Part IX of the Form 990-PF), and also meet one of the following: an "assets test," and "endowment test," or a "support test." These are computed in one of two ways. You get your choice whether to simply add up the last four years or whether to meet the test for each of three of the four years (you'd only do this if one of the years is so bad that it would kill a four-year total, so you want to leave it out altogether). You have to be consistent. Whichever method you use for the 85% expenditure test, you have to use the same method for the other test you select (assets, endowment, or support).

First off, about the mysterious question about whether you are a 4942(j)(3) or (5) organization: (j)(5) organizations are elderly care facilities. They get to skip much of this section, but they have to use the endowment test outlined below. The instructions indicate which lines they can skip.

If you don't have investments, your bank account will be the basis for the minimum investment return, which is a hair under 5% of your assets. This figure will probably be smaller than your adjusted net income. Showing that you've spent 85% of the lesser of these directly on your exempt purposes will probably not be difficult.

Similarly, the assets test requires that 65% of your assets be devoted directly to your exempt activities or related businesses. Again, this should not be difficult for most of our readers.

The endowment test requires that you directly spent or made grants in pursuit of your exempt purposes amounting to two-thirds of your minimum investment return. Unless you've got lots of investments, and relied on adjusted net income for the 85% test because it was less than 5% of your investments, you'll have little problem with this test.

If, for some reason, you can't meet either of these tests, you'll meet a new version of the public support test, which is very different from the ones for public charities. Instead of one-third, you're looking to show (1) that 85% of your non-investment support comes from the general public and from at least five exempt organizations that are not private foundations controlled by the same people that control your group or funded by the same "disqualified persons" that fund you (and who keep you from qualifying as a public charity); (2) that not more than 25% of your non-investment support comes from any one of the exempt organizations; and (3) that not more than half of your total support comes from investment income.

If you can work your way through that, the rest of the Form 990-PF should be a breeze.

APPENDIX 16A

Avoiding Audits by the IRS

The best thing to do about this kind of audit is to do your best to avoid it, and the best way to avoid it is to file your annual report (Form 990) and other IRS reports—payroll tax and information returns—properly, as pointed out elsewhere. The reason this is so important is that there are three ultimate weapons government agencies have against nonprofits: (1) denial of tax exemption; (2) ending your right to raise funds publicly; and (3) cancelling your charter, if you operate as a corporation. The IRS has only the first of these weapons; your state government has all three.

WHY IRS AUDITS NONPROFITS

Usually what the revenue agents may have some reason to suspect is evidence of one or more of the following failures:

- Ineligibility for tax-exempt status. This could result from misrepresentations of your actual purposes and activities in your original Application for Recognition of Tax-Exempt Status, or from engaging in activities not permitted of tax-exempt organizations after obtaining exemption, or while awaiting it, such as electoral activity.

- Failure to comply with the requirements relating to Unrelated Business Income, lobbying, or self-dealing.

- Failure to file payroll or information returns required by the Internal Revenue Code.

WHAT THE IRS AGENT WILL BE EXAMINING IN THE AUDIT

In this and all other types of audits, it is important to understand that the phrase "audit the books" is misleading, since anyone can put anything on the books, without the entry having any relation to reality. The books are merely the starting point, since they are the source of your reports—or certainly should be. What is being audited is the actual legal and supporting documentary evidence of exactly what activities took place during the period under audit. It may also involve interviews with people who know what went on: there will certainly be inquiries regarding questionable items and activities, and how they are answered can affect the outcome of the audit.

In addition to examining underlying documents of bookkeeping transactions, such as bills, checks, receipts, and vouchers, the Revenue Agent will ordinarily examine contracts, leases, minutes of board meetings, your IRS exemption letter, copies of any previous IRS audit reports, your corporate charter and bylaws (or equivalent association documents). In addition, he or she may examine things that might surprise you, yet provide even better evidence than formal records of your actual activities: your own press releases and clippings, newsletters, program publications, and correspondence. These often reveal what may not be otherwise apparent, and it is embarrassing to have your own words used against you.

How deep the examiner may go depends on what information he or she may have to begin with, or may turn up in the early stages of the audit. Good records tend to be reassuring; sloppy ones, to invite a closer look. The "auditor's instinct" is operating, and new avenues can be opened by an answer to a question that seems innocent to the person asked, yet may have deeper significance to the agent. It is common for more than one year to be examined at a time.

How you deal with the agent is quite important, since revenue agents generally have considerable latitude in arriving at their findings. In theory at least, they are not your adversaries, and therefore should be treated with full cooperation and respect, however annoying or disruptive the intrusion may seem. If your organization is in good shape regarding its record-keeping and reporting, you should be less apprehensive and therefore more relaxed. Remember the old saying, "A guilty conscience is its own accuser." Usually the first time around, even administrators who have done their record-keeping conscientiously tend to be unnecessarily nervous.

SEVERAL KEY REASONS TO HAVE PROFESSIONAL REPRESENTATION IN AN IRS AUDIT

In view of the potentials for trouble, it is usually the better part of valor to have a tax professional represent you in dealing with the revenue agent. Public accountants are experienced in this role, act as a buffer in handling questions and requesting documents, which can save you much time personally, expedite the audit, and perhaps most important, protect you against yourself, where verbal statements are concerned. He or she should relay the questions and the answers and advise you regarding the significance and ramifications of particular inquiries.

Because they have a sophisticated awareness of the revenue agent's discretionary latitude—or should have if they are experienced in handling audits—tax pros usually extend themselves to satisfy the agent, even where a seemingly unreasonable position is being taken. Experience has proved it more sensible to work things out cooperatively at the agent level than to rely on having the tough position reversed by appealing it above. Another word to the wise: there may be a temptation, especially in answer to a revenue agent's question in a vulnerable area, to give a deceptive or nonresponsive answer. Most people unfamiliar with the Revenue Code are unaware of Section 7207 which imposes criminal penalties for furnishing false information to the IRS—of up to $10,000 ($50,000 for corporate defendants) and/or a year's imprisonment. (The penalties for signing a false statement or a document that indicates that it is made under the penalties of perjury, or for assisting or counseling in its preparation, meaning a public accountant or attorney, are up to $100,000 ($500,000 for corporate defendants) and/or three years' imprisonment. Need we say more?)

If (or when) the focus of the audit indicates possible problems regarding the organization's continued tax exemption, or if there is reason to believe beforehand that it is vulnerable in this regard, competent legal counsel should be called upon, either for direct representation with the agent, or for advice and guidance in the handling of the audit. This is an area in which fewer public accountants are expert, and a knowledgeable attorney can contribute more, since the issue often turns around the interpretation of the law and documents describing activity, rather than financial records, even though the latter may also be relevant. Appeals from a revenue agent's findings can be made via various channels but should not be undertaken without appropriate professional aid.

There appears to be an increase in enforcement activities by the IRS in challenging tax exemptions in recent years.

A Few Tips in Handling an IRS Audit

There was enacted not long ago a Taxpayer's Bill of Rights. It requires that IRS auditors inform you of your rights before an initial audit; that you may be represented by a qualified person, including a CPA or attorney to whom you have given a properly executed Power of Attorney (IRS Forms 2848 or 2848-D); that you have a right to record conferences with IRS personnel.

While the IRS has the right to see all relevant documents, it does not have the right to go fishing through your files freely, nor to examine any correspondence with your attorney, which is privileged. Any such correspondence, memos, etc., should therefore be removed from any documents requested.

APPENDIX 16B

Sample IRS Form 990 and Form 990, Schedule A

Supplemental Instructions and a Completed Sample of Form 990 and Schedule A (Form 990)

This part of the instructions provides a set of facts and a filled-in example to assist you in preparing a complete and accurate Form 990 and Schedule A (Form 990) for 1990.

To avoid having to respond to requests for missing information, please complete all applicable line items; answer "Yes," "No," or "N/A" (not applicable) to each question on the return; make an entry (including a "-0-" when appropriate) on all total lines; and enter "None" or "N/A" if an entire part of Form 990 does not apply. If one or more applicable line items are not completed, we will consider the return incomplete and contact you for the missing information. The penalty of $10 a day for failure to file a return under section 6652(c) also applies if a return is submitted with required information missing.

The illustrated example of a completed Form 990 and Schedule A (Form 990) for 1990 was prepared using the following facts.

The Family Service Agency of Utopia, Inc., a not-for-profit organization, is exempt from income tax under section 501(c)(3) of the Internal Revenue Code. The agency is a member of the National Association of Family Service Agencies. Its principal programs include: (1) adoption of infants and children; (2) foster home care; and (3) counseling individuals and families.

The agency was incorporated September 16, 1968. It received a letter dated January 25, 1971, notifying it that it had been determined not to be a private foundation within the meaning of section 509(a).

The agency uses the fund method of accounting and is on the accrual and calendar-year basis. The books are in the custody of the bookkeeper, Ms. Nancy Ward at 1414 West Ash Drive, Utopia, PA 11111.

All contributions are considered available for unrestricted use, unless specifically restricted by the donor. Pledges are recorded in the books of account when the agency is notified of the pledge, and allowances are provided for amounts estimated as uncollectible. Bequests are recorded as income at the time the agency has established a right to the bequest and the proceeds are measurable.

A substantial number of volunteers have donated significant amounts of their time to the organization's adoption program. No amounts have been reflected in the financial statements, however, for donated services.

In accordance with the affiliation agreement with the national organization, a portion of the unrestricted support from the public is remitted to the national organization for its use as determined by its board of directors. Additional grants are made to individuals and organizations as determined by the agency's board of directors.

For its annual dinner/dance, the agency paid $800 (fair rental value) to rent a hall, kitchen, tables, dishes, etc., from the Fraternal Society of Utopia, an unrelated section 501(c)(10) fraternal lodge. This was the agency's only transaction with exempt organizations not described in section 501(c)(3). The agency is not affiliated with or related to any such organization.

Depreciation of $5,200 was computed for buildings and equipment on a straight-line basis.

The expenses for the year are allocable as follows:

Statement of Functional Expenses

	Program Services			Supporting Services		
	Adoption	Foster Home Care	Counseling	Mgmt. & General	Fund Raising	TOTAL
Salaries	$ 25,600	$ 25,100	$126,900	$33,100	$36,800	$247,500
Pension plan cont. .	100	....	100	100	....	300
Other emp. benefits	1,700	1,400	6,300	2,100	1,500	13,000
Payroll taxes, etc. .	3,000	2,300	12,400	3,000	3,100	23,800
Professional fees .	63,000	300	61,200	2,600	800	127,900
Supplies	3,900	21,300	1,300	1,800	1,700	30,000
Telephone . . .	9,500	1,000	1,100	1,500	2,300	15,400
Postage & shipping .	2,900	1,300	8,900	1,000	9,000	23,100
Occupancy . . .	2,550	21,100	11,250	1,500	1,350	37,750
Interest	....	....	100	800	....	900
Rental & maintenance of equipment .	3,550	1,100	1,250	1,500	1,350	8,750
Prtg. & publications .	5,400	400	6,400	300	1,600	14,100
Travel & trans. . .	12,500	2,000	2,200	2,300	3,000	22,000
Conferences, etc. .	3,700	7,100	2,000	4,500	400	17,700
Specific assistance to individuals .	16,500	24,300	5,000	....	....	45,800
Membership dues .	500	....	....	....	....	500
Awards & grants— To national org. .	10,000	....	3,000	....	....	13,000
To indvs./other organizations .	11,000	11,900	....	....	....	22,900
Insurance . . .	10,450	10,100	5,100	600	50	26,300
Other expenses . .	1,250	500	400	100	2,050	4,300
Depr.-bldgs./equip. .	700	600	2,900	600	400	5,200
Total functional expense: .	$187,800	$131,800	$257,800	$57,400	$65,400	$700,200
Payments to national org.						12,400
Total expenses						$712,600

We made the following entries in Form 990 and Schedule A (Form 990) and have attached explanatory schedules.

Form 990, Part I

Line 1a.—We have entered the $473,700 of direct contributions received from the public and the $9,600 received from legacies and bequests.

Line 1b.—We have entered the amount of $223,500 received through the United Way organization and the $4,000 collected through the local auxiliary.

The financial statements for the Family Service Agency of Utopia, Inc., are given below:

Statement of Revenue, Expenses, and Changes in Fund Balances

For the Year Ended December 31, 1990

	Current Funds		Land, Bldg., & Equip. Fund	Endow- ment Fund	TOTAL
	Unrestricted	Restricted			
Revenue:					
Public support—					
Received directly—					
Contributions (net of estimated uncollectible pledges of $19,500)	$460,100	$ 6,200	$ 7,200	$ 200	$473,700
Special events (net of costs of direct benefit to participants of $18,000)	10,400				10,400
Legacies & bequests	9,200			400	9,600
Received indirectly—					
Collected through local auxiliary	4,000				4,000
Allocated by federated fundraising organizations (net of their related fundraising expenses estimated at $12,300)	223,500				223,500
Total public support	707,200	6,200	7,200	600	721,200
Revenue and grants from governmental agencies		300			300
Other revenue:					
Membership dues—individuals	1,600				1,600
Program service fees	2,300				2,300
Sales of materials and services (net of direct expenses of $1,000)	400				400
Endowment and other investment income	30,500	700			31,200
Miscellaneous revenue	2,800				2,800
Gains (losses) on investments	(2,000)			2,500	500
Total other revenue	35,600	700		2,500	38,800
Total revenue	742,800	7,200	7,200	3,100	760,300
Expenses:					
Program services—					
Adoption	187,100		700		187,800
Foster home care	131,200		600		131,800
Counseling	244,100	10,800	2,900		257,800
Total program services	562,400	10,800	4,200		577,400
Supporting services—					
Management & general	56,800		600		57,400
Fundraising	65,000		400		65,400
Total supporting services	121,800		1,000		122,800
Payments to national organization	12,400				12,400
Total expenses	696,600	10,800	5,200		712,600
Excess (deficiency) of revenue over expenses	46,200	(3,600)	2,000	3,100	47,700
Fund balances, beginning of year	446,300	10,000	156,800	191,700	804,800
Other changes in fund balances:					
Acquisition of fixed assets	(7,000)		7,000		
Mortgage payment	(400)		400		
Fund balances, end of year	$485,100	$ 6,400	$166,200	$194,800	$852,500

BALANCE SHEET
December 31, 1990

ASSETS	Current Funds Unrestricted	Current Funds Restricted	Land, Bldg., & Equip. Fund	Endowment Fund	TOTAL
Current assets:					
Cash, including $115,000 in interest-bearing accounts	$121,100	$ 300			$121,400
Short-term investments, at cost (approximates market)	100,000	7,100			107,100
Receivables:					
Program service fees, less allowance of $200	600				600
Pledges, less allowance of $11,200	58,900				58,900
Grants		1,000	$ 4,800		5,800
From affiliated organizations	1,000				1,000
Interfund receivable (payable)	2,000	(2,000)			
Inventory, at lower of cost or market	7,000				7,000
Prepaid expenses and deferred charges	13,800				13,800
Total current assets	304,400	6,400	4,800		315,600
Noncurrent investments	279,600			$194,800	474,400
Land, buildings, and equipment, at cost, less accumulated depreciation			174,800		174,800
Total assets	$584,000	$6,400	$179,600	$194,800	$964,800

LIABILITIES AND FUND BALANCES

	Unrestricted	Restricted	Land, Bldg., & Equip. Fund	Endowment Fund	TOTAL
Current liabilities:					
Accounts payable and accrued expenses	$ 39,300				$ 39,300
Support & revenue designated for subsequent period	59,600				59,600
Total current liabilities	98,900				98,900
Mortgage payable, 6%, due 1992			$ 3,200		3,200
Amounts payable under capital lease			10,200		10,200
Total liabilities	98,900		13,400		112,300
Fund balances:					
Current unrestricted:					
Designated by the governing board for—					
Long-term investment	279,600				279,600
Purchase of new equipment	10,400				10,400
Undesignated—available for general activities	195,100				195,100
Current restricted for:					
Professional education		$4,000			4,000
Expansion of services		2,400			2,400
Land, building, and equipment:					
Unexpended restricted			4,800		4,800
Equity in fixed assets			161,400		161,400
Endowment				$194,800	194,800
Total fund balances	485,100	6,400	166,200	194,800	852,500
Total liabilities and fund balances	$584,000	$6,400	$179,600	$194,800	$964,800

Line 2.—We have entered the total of program service revenue from Part VII, lines 93(a) and (g). This included $2,300 in consultation fees and $300 in fees from government agencies.

Line 3.—We have entered $1,600 of membership dues and assessments. These dues are not equivalent to contributions because members receive benefits and privileges (educational publications and counseling services) which have a monetary value in excess of their dues payment. Therefore, they are reported on line 3. (See the discussion of this principle in the specific instructions for line 3 of Form 990.)

Lines 4 and 5.—We have entered the $14,800 received in interest income and $16,400 received in dividends for the year.

Line 8.—We have entered $24,200, the selling price of securities sold, and subtracted their cost basis and the sales expense. We entered the $500 gain on line 8d.

Line 9.—We have reported the revenue of $28,400 less direct expenses of $18,000 from special fundraising events and activities. As there were no contributions included in gross revenue from these events, we entered "-0-" on line 9a. All of the $18,000 of expenses attributable to this function are reportable here and none in Part II.

Line 10.—We have reported, on line 10a, $2,000 in gross sales of educational publications, less $600 of returns and allowances. On line 10b, we entered $1,000, the cost of goods sold, and entered the $400 gross profit on line 10c.

Line 11.—We have entered the gross amount of other revenue received from the sale of an easement. This amount was also reported in Part VII on line 103(a).

Line 13.—We have entered the program services expenses from line 44, column (B) of Part II.

Line 14.—We have entered the management and general expenses from line 44, column (C) of Part II.

Line 15.—We have entered the fundraising expenses from line 44, column (D) of Part II.

Line 16.—We have entered the portion of the unrestricted support from the public that was remitted to the national organization.

Lines 17 and 18 are self-explanatory.

Line 19.—We have entered the net asset balance at the beginning of the year from line 74, column (A) of Part IV.

Line 21.—We have entered the total of lines 18, 19, and 20. This computed net asset figure agrees with the end-of-year net asset balance from line 74, column (B) of Part IV.

Form 990, Part II

From the breakdown of the expenses provided, we have listed the organization's expenses attributable to program services; management and general; and fundraising functions. In column (A), we reported the total expenses for each line of columns (B), (C), and (D). The total of column (A) was entered on line 17, "Total expenses," of Part I. The expenses in Part II include only those that are not reported on lines 8b, 9b, or 10b of Part I. The expenses of the special fundraising events and activities are reported on line 9b of Part I and, therefore, are not also reported in Part II. In this example, the expenses listed in the program service column include those attributable to adoption services, foster home care, and family counseling.

Form 990, Part III

We have listed and described the organization's three program services and indicated the expenses attributable to each. Statistical information regarding the number of individuals, families, and organizations served is also provided. We have entered the amount attributable to donated services in the narrative section for "Adoption Services."

Form 990, Part IV

We have completed beginning and end-of-year balance sheets. **Note:** For the sake of brevity, the beginning-of-year balance sheet was not given in the statement of facts.

Form 990, Part V

We have entered the name, address, and other required information for each officer and director even though some of them serve without compensation. We entered "-0-" when there were no amounts to enter. (**Note:** For the sake of brevity, specific names, addresses, titles, and hours worked were not given in the statement of facts.)

Form 990, Part VI

Lines 76 through 81.—From the facts given, the appropriate answer to each of these questions was either "No," "N/A," or "-0-."

Line 82.—We have entered the amount of $8,000 in donated program services that was also reported in the narrative section of Part III.

Line 92.—We have entered "N/A" because the organization is not a section 4947(a)(1) charitable trust.

Form 990, Part VII

We have listed both consultation fees and fees from government agencies as the organization's only source of program service revenue for the year. None of the organization's other receipts constitute program service revenue as defined in the instructions for line 2 of Part I and column (B) of Part II.

In column (d), we have entered the amounts received from income-producing activities that do not further the charitable purposes of the agency (other than by providing funds for such purposes) and the income from which would be taxable as unrelated business income but for specific provisions in the Code that render such income non-taxable. We have also entered the appropriate exclusion codes (from the Instructions for Form 990) to indicate the Code provision that excludes each amount from classification as unrelated business income.

In column (e), we have entered the amounts received from activities that contributed to the agency's related or exempt purposes.

Form 990, Part VIII

We indicated the line number for the related or exempt function amounts we entered in column (e) and explained how each reported activity contributed importantly to the accomplishment of the agency's exempt purposes.

Form 990, Part IX

We have answered "N/A" because we answered "No" to question 78c of Part VI.

Schedule A (Form 990)

Part I.—We have entered the compensation and contribution to employee benefit plans for each employee listed.

Part IV.—We have checked block 11a, based on our sample facts, and entered the appropriate information on lines 15 through 28. The amounts shown on these lines are from returns for previous years that are not part of this example.

Part VII.—We have entered the required information regarding the agency's rental of facilities and equipment from a fraternal organization for the annual dinner/dance. Note that this does not constitute a "sharing of facilities or equipment" (line 51c) which connotes a continuing arrangement and joint or alternating use of the same assets (sharing of office space and equipment, for example). Because there was no such sharing and because the agency was not otherwise affiliated with or related to the fraternal organization, we answered "No" to question 52a.

Form **990**	**Return of Organization Exempt From Income Tax**	OMB No. 1545-0047
	Under section 501(c) of the Internal Revenue Code (except black lung benefit trust or private foundation) or section 4947(a)(1) charitable trust	19**90**
Department of the Treasury Internal Revenue Service	**Note**: You may have to use a copy of this return to satisfy state reporting requirements. See instruction E.	

For the calendar year 1990, or fiscal year beginning _____ , 1990, and ending _____ , 19 ___

		A Employer identification number (see instruction S2)
Use IRS label.	Name of organization · Family Service Agency of Utopia, Inc.	12 ⋮ 3456789
Other-wise, please print or type.	Number, street, and room (or P.O. box number) (see instruction S1.) 1414 West Ash Drive	**B** State registration number (see instruction E) 567890
	City or town, state, and ZIP code Utopia, PA 11111	**C** If application for exemption is pending, check here ▶ . . . . ☐

D Check type of organization—Exempt under section ▶ ☒ 501(c)(3) (insert number), OR ▶ ☐ section 4947(a)(1) charitable trust (see instruction C7 and question 92.)

E Accounting method: ☐ Cash ☒ Accrual ☐ Other (specify) ▶ _____

F Is this a group return (see instruction Q) filed for affiliates? . . . . ☐ Yes ☒ No
If "Yes," enter the number of affiliates for which this return is filed _____
Is this a separate return filed by a group affiliate? . . . . ☐ Yes ☒ No

G If either answer in F is "Yes," enter four-digit group exemption number (GEN) ▶

H Check box if address changed ▶ ☐

I Check here ☐ if your gross receipts are normally not more than $25,000 (see instruction B1). You do not have to file a completed return with IRS; but if you received a Form 990 Package in the mail, you should file a return without financial data (see instruction A5). Some states require a completed return.

Note: *Form 990EZ may be used by organizations with gross receipts less than $100,000 and total assets less than $250,000 at end of year.*

Section 501(c)(3) organizations and 4947(a)(1) trusts must also complete and attach Schedule A (Form 990). (See instruction C1.)

Part I Statement of Revenue, Expenses, and Changes in Net Assets or Fund Balances

1	Contributions, gifts, grants, and similar amounts received:			
a	Direct public support	**1a**	$483,300	
b	Indirect public support	**1b**	227,500	
c	Government grants	**1c**		
d	**Total** (add lines 1a through 1c) (attach schedule—see instructions)	**1d**		$710,800
2	Program service revenue (from Part VII, line 93)	**2**		2,600
3	Membership dues and assessments (see instructions)	**3**		1,600
4	Interest on savings and temporary cash investments	**4**		14,800
5	Dividends and interest from securities.	**5**		16,400
6a	Gross rents	**6a**		
b	Less: rental expenses	**6b**		
c	Net rental income or (loss) (line 6a less line 6b)	**6c**		
7	Other investment income (describe ▶ _____)	**7**		
8a	Gross amount from sale of assets other than inventory	(A) Securities 24,200	**8a**	(B) Other
b	Less: cost or other basis and sales expenses	23,700	**8b**	
c	Gain or (loss) (attach schedule) . . .	500	**8c**	
d	Net gain or (loss) (combine line 8c, column (A) and line 8c, column (B))	**8d**		500
9	Special fundraising events and activities (attach schedule—see instructions):			
a	Gross revenue (not including $ ____–0–____ of contributions reported on line 1a)	**9a**	28,400	
b	Less: direct expenses	**9b**	18,000	
c	Net income (line 9a less line 9b)	**9c**		10,400
10a	Gross sales less returns and allowances	**10a**	1,400	
b	Less: cost of goods sold	**10b**	1,000	
c	Gross profit or (loss) (line 10a less line 10b) (attach schedule)	**10c**		400
11	Other revenue (from Part VII, line 103)	**11**		2,800
12	**Total revenue** (add lines 1d, 2, 3, 4, 5, 6c, 7, 8d, 9c, 10c, and 11)	**12**		$760,300
13	Program services (from line 44, column (B)) (see instructions)	**13**		577,400
14	Management and general (from line 44, column (C)) (see instructions)	**14**		57,400
15	Fundraising (from line 44, column (D)) (see instructions)	**15**		65,400
16	Payments to affiliates (attach schedule—see instructions)	**16**		12,400
17	**Total expenses** (add lines 16 and 44, column (A)).	**17**		$712,600
18	Excess or (deficit) for the year (subtract line 17 from line 12)	**18**		47,700
19	Net assets or fund balances at beginning of year (from line 74, column (A)) . . .	**19**		804,800
20	Other changes in net assets or fund balances (attach explanation)	**20**		–0–
21	Net assets or fund balances at end of year (combine lines 18, 19, and 20) . . .	**21**		$852,500

For Paperwork Reduction Act Notice, see page 1 of the separate instructions.

Form **990** (1990)

Form 990 (1990)   Page **2**

Part II — Statement of Functional Expenses

All organizations must complete column (A). Columns (B), (C), and (D) are required for section 501(c)(3) and (c)(4) organizations and 4947(a)(1) charitable trusts but optional for others. (See instructions.)

Do not include amounts reported on line 6b, 8b, 9b, 10b, or 16 of Part I.		(A) Total	(B) Program services	(C) Management and general	(D) Fundraising
22	Grants and allocations (attach schedule)	$ 35,900	$ 35,900		
23	Specific assistance to individuals	45,800	45,800		
24	Benefits paid to or for members				
25	Compensation of officers, directors, etc.	42,800	26,600	$ 8,800	$ 7,400
26	Other salaries and wages	204,700	151,000	24,300	29,400
27	Pension plan contributions	300	200	100	
28	Other employee benefits	13,000	9,400	2,100	1,500
29	Payroll taxes	23,800	17,700	3,000	3,100
30	Professional fundraising fees				
31	Accounting fees				
32	Legal fees				
33	Supplies	30,000	26,500	1,800	1,700
34	Telephone	15,400	11,600	1,500	2,300
35	Postage and shipping	23,100	13,100	1,000	9,000
36	Occupancy	37,750	34,900	1,500	1,350
37	Equipment rental and maintenance	8,700	5,900	1,500	1,350
38	Printing and publications	14,100	12,200	300	1,600
39	Travel	22,000	16,700	2,300	3,000
40	Conferences, conventions, and meetings	17,700	12,800	4,500	400
41	Interest	900	100	800	
42	Depreciation, depletion, etc. (attach schedule)	5,200	4,200	600	400
43	Other expenses (itemize): a Dues	500	500		
b	Professional Fees	127,900	124,500	2,600	800
c	Insurance	26,300	25,650	600	50
d	Miscellaneous	4,300	2,150	100	2,050
e					
f					
44	**Total functional expenses** (add lines 22 through 43) Organizations completing columns B-D, carry these totals to lines 13-15.	$700,200	$577,400	$57,400	$65,400

Part III — Statement of Program Service Accomplishments (See instructions.)

Describe what was achieved in carrying out your exempt purposes. Fully describe the services provided; the number of persons benefited; or other relevant information for each program title. Section 501(c)(3) and (4) organizations must also enter the amount of grants to others.

Expenses (optional for some organizations—see instructions)

a Counseling – The organization provided 5,954 hours of counseling to individuals and families. A total of 635 cases were assisted involving 2,426 individuals. The agency also made a grant to its national affiliate for a research project.

(Grants and allocations $ 3,000) $257,800

b Adoption Services – The agency placed 50 children in adoptive families. This included counseling for 189 birth parents. Five adoptions involved children from foreign countries. There were 65 home studies completed during this year. (This program was assisted by $8,000 of donated services in 1990.) Under the Adoption

(Grants and allocations $)

c Services program, the agency made grants to three organizations for related services.

(Grants and allocations $ 21,000)   187,800

d Foster Care – The agency placed 28 children in 16 foster homes. Agency also made grants to two other organizations providing foster home care for hard-to-place children.

(Grants and allocations $ 11,900)   131,800

e Other program services (attach schedule)   (Grants and allocations $)

f Total (add lines **a** through **e**) (should equal line 44, column (B)). ▶ $577,400

Part IV **Balance Sheets**

Note: *Where required, attached schedules and amounts in the description column should be for end-of-year amounts only.*

					(A) Beginning of year		**(B)** End of year
	Assets						
45	Cash—noninterest-bearing				$ 4,000	45	$ 6,400
46	Savings and temporary cash investments				244,700	46	222,100
47a	Accounts receivable	47a	$ 1,800				
b	Less: allowance for doubtful accounts	47b	200		1,800	47c	1,600
48a	Pledges receivable	48a	70,100				
b	Less: allowance for doubtful accounts	48b	11,200		46,000	48c	58,900
49	Grants receivable				4,600	49	5,800
50	Receivables due from officers, directors, trustees, and key employees (attach schedule)					50	
51a	Other notes and loans receivable (attach schedule)	51a					
b	Less: allowance for doubtful accounts	51b				51c	
52	Inventories for sale or use				6,100	52	7,000
53	Prepaid expenses and deferred charges				9,600	53	13,800
54	Investments—securities (attach schedule)				430,700	54	474,400
55a	Investments—land, buildings, and equipment: basis	55a					
b	Less: accumulated depreciation (attach schedule)	55b				55c	
56	Investments—other (attach schedule)					56	
57a	Land, buildings, and equipment: basis	57a	188,000				
b	Less: accumulated depreciation (attach schedule)	57b	13,200		168,500	57c	174,800
58	Other assets (describe ▶ _____)					58	
59	**Total assets** (add lines 45 through 58)				$916,000	59	$964,800
	Liabilities						
60	Accounts payable and accrued expenses				$ 46,000	60	$ 39,300
61	Grants payable					61	
62	Support and revenue designated for future periods (attach schedule)				61,600	62	59,600
63	Loans from officers, directors, trustees, and key employees (attach schedule)					63	
64	Mortgages and other notes payable (attach schedule)				3,600	64	3,200
65	Other liabilities (describe ▶ Payable under capital lease)					65	10,200
66	**Total liabilities** (add lines 60 through 65)				$111,200	66	$112,300
	Fund Balances or Net Assets						
	Organizations that use fund accounting, check here ▶ ☒ and complete lines 67 through 70 and lines 74 and 75.						
67a	Current unrestricted fund				$446,300	67a	$485,100
b	Current restricted fund				10,000	67b	6,400
68	Land, buildings, and equipment fund				156,800	68	166,200
69	Endowment fund				191,700	69	194,800
70	Other funds (describe ▶ _____)				-0-	70	-0-
	Organizations that do not use fund accounting, check here ▶ ☐ and complete lines 71 through 75.						
71	Capital stock or trust principal					71	
72	Paid-in or capital surplus					72	
73	Retained earnings or accumulated income					73	
74	Total fund balances or net assets (see instructions)				$804,800	74	$852,500
75	**Total liabilities and fund balances/net assets** (see instructions)				$916,000	75	$964,800

Form 990 (1990)   Page **4**

Part V   **List of Officers, Directors, and Trustees** (List each one even if not compensated. See instructions.)

(A) Name and address	(B) Title and average hours per week devoted to position	(C) Compensation (if not paid, enter zero)	(D) Contributions to employee benefit plans	(E) Expense account and other allowances
Anita Hurlimann 10 Paradise Drive, Utopia, PA	President 10 hrs./wk.	-0-	-0-	-0-
John S. Brown, Ph.D. 15 Heavenly Place, Utopia, PA	Executive Director 50 hrs./wk.	$42,800	$1,810	-0-
Janet Newhouse 20 Musical Drive, Utopia, PA	Vice President 10 hrs./wk.	-0-	-0-	-0-
Jim Jones 5 Scenic Rd., Utopia, PA	Treasurer 2 hrs./wk.	-0-	-0-	-0-
Zenobia Boyce 23 Wonderful Way, Utopia, PA	Secretary 3 hrs./wk.	-0-	-0-	-0-

Part VI   **Other Information**

		Yes	No
76	Did you engage in any activity not previously reported to the Internal Revenue Service? **76**		X
	If "Yes," attach a detailed description of each activity.		
77	Were any changes made in the organizing or governing documents, but not reported to IRS? **77**		X
	If "Yes," attach a conformed copy of the changes.		
78a	Did your organization have unrelated business gross income of $1,000 or more during the year covered by this return? **78a**		X
b	If "Yes," have you filed a tax return on **Form 990-T**, Exempt Organization Business Income Tax Return, for this year? **78b**	N/A	
c	At any time during the year, did you own a 50% or greater interest in a taxable corporation or partnership? **78c**		X
	If "Yes," complete Part IX.		
79	Was there a liquidation, dissolution, termination, or substantial contraction during the year? (See instructions.) . **79**		X
	If "Yes," attach a statement as described in the instructions.		
80a	Are you related (other than by association with a statewide or nationwide organization) through common membership, governing bodies, trustees, officers, etc., to any other exempt or nonexempt organization? (See instructions.) **80a**		X
b	If "Yes," enter the name of the organization ▶ _____ _____ and check whether it is ☐ exempt **OR** ☐ nonexempt.		
81a	Enter amount of political expenditures, direct or indirect, as described in the instructions . **81a** -0-		
b	Did you file **Form 1120-POL**, U.S. Income Tax Return for Certain Political Organizations, for this year? **81b**		X
82a	Did you receive donated services or the use of materials, equipment, or facilities at no charge or at substantially less than fair rental value? . **82a**	X	
b	If "Yes," you may indicate the value of these items here. Do not include this amount as revenue in Part I or as an expense in Part II. See instructions for reporting in Part III . . . **82b** $8,000		
83a	Did anyone request to see either your annual return or exemption application (or both)? **83a**		X
b	If "Yes," did you comply as described in the instructions? (See General Instruction L.) **83b**	N/A	
84a	Did you solicit any contributions or gifts that were not tax deductible? **84a**		X
b	If "Yes," did you include with every solicitation an express statement that such contributions or gifts were not tax deductible? (See General Instruction M.) **84b**	N/A	
85a	*Section 501(c)(5) or (6) organizations.*—Did you spend any amounts in attempts to influence public opinion about legislative matters or referendums? (See instructions and Regulations section 1.162-20(c)) **85a**	N/A	
b	If "Yes," enter the total amount spent for this purpose . . . . **85b** N/A		
86	*Section 501(c)(7) organizations.*—Enter:		
a	Initiation fees and capital contributions included on line 12. **86a** N/A		
b	Gross receipts, included on line 12, for public use of club facilities (See instructions.) . . **86b** N/A		
c	Does the club's governing instrument or any written policy statement provide for discrimination against any person because of race, color, or religion? (See instructions.) **86c**	N/A	
87	*Section 501(c)(12) organizations.*—Enter amount of:		
a	Gross income received from members or shareholders . . . . **87a** N/A		
b	Gross income received from other sources (Do not net amounts due or paid to other sources against amounts due or received from them.) . . . . **87b** N/A		
88	*Public interest law firms.*—Attach information described in the instructions.		
89	List the states with which a copy of this return is filed ▶ _____ Pennsylvania _____		
90	During this tax year did you maintain any part of your accounting/tax records on a computerized system? **90**	X	
91	The books are in care of ▶ Nancy Ward _____ Telephone no. ▶ (123) 456-7899		
	Located at ▶ 1414 West Ash Drive, Utopia, PA 11111		
92	*Section 4947(a)(1) charitable trusts filing Form 990 in lieu of **Form 1041**,* U.S. Fiduciary Income Tax Return.— . Check here ▶ ☐ and enter the amount of tax-exempt interest received or accrued during the tax year . . ▶ **92** N/A		

Form 990 (1990)   Page **5**

Part VII Analysis of Income-Producing Activities

Enter gross amounts unless otherwise indicated.	Unrelated business income		Excluded by section 512, 513, or 514		(e) Related or exempt function income (See instructions)
	(a) Business code	**(b)** Amount	**(c)** Exclusion code	**(d)** Amount	
93 Program service revenue:					
(a) Consultation fees					$2,300
(b)					
(c)					
(d)					
(e)					
(f)					
(g) Fees from government agencies					300
94 Membership dues and assessments					1,600
95 Interest on savings and temporary cash investments			14	$14,800	
96 Dividends and interest from securities			14	16,400	
97 Net rental income or (loss) from real estate:					
(a) debt-financed property					
(b) not debt-financed property					
98 Net rental income or (loss) from personal property					
99 Other investment income					
100 Gain or (loss) from sales of assets other than inventory			18	500	
101 Net income from special fundraising events			1	10,400	
102 Gross profit or (loss) from sales of inventory					400
103 Other revenue: (a) Sale of easement			18	2,800	
(b)					
(c)					
(d)					
(e)					
104 Subtotal (add columns (b), (d), and (e))		-0-		$44,900	$4,600

105 TOTAL (add line 104, columns (b), (d), and (e)) ▶ $49,500
(Line 105 plus line 1d, Part I, should equal the amount on line 12, Part I.)

Part VIII Relationship of Activities to the Accomplishment of Exempt Purposes

Line No. ▼	Explain below how each activity for which income is reported in column (e) of Part VII contributed importantly to the accomplishment of your exempt purposes (other than by providing funds for such purposes). (See instructions.)
93a	Fees for marriage counseling--one of our exempt purposes.
93g	Fee from county for finding foster homes for 2 children--this furthers our exempt purpose of ensuring quality care for foster children.
94	Members are social service workers who receive information and advice on problem cases from our staff as part of our counseling, adoption, and foster care programs.
102	Sale of educational materials to members and persons receiving counseling--part of our overall counseling program.

Part IX Information Regarding Taxable Subsidiaries (Complete this Part if you answered "Yes" to question 78c.)

Name, address, and employer identification number of corporation or partnership	Percentage of ownership interest	Nature of business activities	Total income	End-of-year assets
N/A				

Under penalties of perjury, I declare that I have examined this return, including accompanying schedules and statements, and to the best of my knowledge and belief, it is true, correct, and complete. Declaration of preparer (other than officer) is based on all information of which preparer has any knowledge.

Please Sign Here

▶ *John S. Brown* | 3/23/91 ▶ Executive Director
Signature of officer | Date | Title

Paid Preparer's Use Only

| Preparer's signature ▶ | | Date | Check if self-employed ▶ ☐ |
| Firm's name (or yours if self-employed) and address ▶ | | ZIP code | |

SCHEDULE A (Form 990) <small>Department of the Treasury Internal Revenue Service</small>	**Organization Exempt Under 501(c)(3)** (Except Private Foundation), 501(e), 501(f), 501(k), or Section 4947(a)(1) Charitable Trust Supplementary Information ▶ Attach to Form 990 (or Form 990EZ).	OMB No. 1545-0047 19**90**

Name	Employer identification number
Family Service Agency of Utopia, Inc.	12 ⋮3456789

Part I   **Compensation of the Five Highest Paid Employees Other Than Officers, Directors, and Trustees**
       (See specific instructions.) (List each one. If there are none, enter "None.")

(a) Name and address of employees paid more than $30,000	**(b)** Title and average hours per week devoted to position	**(c)** Compensation	**(d)** Contributions to employee benefit plans	**(e)** Expense account and other allowances
Roshan Contractor, M.S.W. 41 Allegro Way, Utopia, PA	Dep. to the Director 45 hrs./wk.	$36,000	$1,634	-0-
Mehroo Aziz 50 Mountain View, Utopia, PA	Ch. Counseling Services 45 hrs./wk.	$52,000	$1,490	-0-

Total number of other employees paid over $30,000 . . . . ▶	-0-	

Part II   **Compensation of the Five Highest Paid Persons for Professional Services**
       (See specific instructions.) (List each one. If there are none, enter "None.")

(a) Name and address of persons paid more than $30,000	**(b)** Type of service	**(c)** Compensation
None		

SAMPLE

Total number of others receiving over $30,000 for professional services . . . . ▶		

Part III   **Statements About Activities**

		Yes (1)	No (2)
1	During the year, have you attempted to influence national, state, or local legislation, including any attempt to influence public opinion on a legislative matter or referendum?	1		X
	If "Yes," enter the total expenses paid or incurred in connection with the legislative activities. $ _____			
	Complete Part VI of this form for organizations that made an election under section 501(h) on Form 5768 or other statement. For other organizations checking "Yes," attach a statement giving a detailed description of the legislative activities and a classified schedule of the expenses paid or incurred.			
2	During the year, have you, either directly or indirectly, engaged in any of the following acts with a trustee, director, principal officer, or creator of your organization, or any taxable organization or corporation with which such person is affiliated as an officer, director, trustee, majority owner, or principal beneficiary:			
a	Sale, exchange, or leasing of property?	2a		X
b	Lending of money or other extension of credit?	2b		X
c	Furnishing of goods, services, or facilities?	2c		X
d	Payment of compensation (or payment or reimbursement of expenses if more than $1,000)?. See Part V,	2d	X	
e	Transfer of any part of your income or assets? . . . . Form 990	2e		X
	If the answer to any question is "Yes," attach a detailed statement explaining the transactions.			
3	Do you make grants for scholarships, fellowships, student loans, etc.?	3		X
4	Attach a statement explaining how you determine that individuals or organizations receiving disbursements from you in furtherance of your charitable programs qualify to receive payments. (See specific instructions.)			

For Paperwork Reduction Act Notice, see page 1 of the instructions to Form 990 (or Form 990EZ).   Schedule A (Form 990) 1990

Schedule A (Form 990) 1990   Page **2**

Part IV   Reason for Non-Private Foundation Status (See instructions for definitions.)

The organization is not a private foundation because it is (please check only **ONE** applicable box):

5 ☐   A church, convention of churches, or association of churches. Section 170(b)(1)(A)(i).

6 ☐   A school. Section 170(b)(1)(A)(ii). (Also complete Part V, page 3.)

7 ☐   A hospital or a cooperative hospital service organization. Section 170(b)(1)(A)(iii).

8 ☐   A Federal, state, or local government or governmental unit. Section 170(b)(1)(A)(v).

9 ☐   A medical research organization operated in conjunction with a hospital. Section 170(b)(1)(A)(iii). **Enter name, city, and state of hospital** ▶ ....

10 ☐   An organization operated for the benefit of a college or university owned or operated by a governmental unit. Section 170(b)(1)(A)(iv). (Also complete Support Schedule.)

11a ☒   An organization that normally receives a substantial part of its support from a governmental unit or from the general public. Section 170(b)(1)(A)(vi). (Also complete Support Schedule.)

11b ☐   A community trust. Section 170(b)(1)(A)(vi). (Also complete Support Schedule.)

12 ☐   An organization that normally receives: (a) no more than ⅓ of its support from gross investment income and unrelated business taxable income (less section 511 tax) from businesses acquired by the organization after June 30, 1975, and (b) more than ⅓ of its support from contributions, membership fees, and gross receipts from activities related to its charitable, etc., functions—subject to certain exceptions. See section 509(a)(2). (Also complete Support Schedule.)

13 ☐   An organization that is not controlled by any disqualified persons (other than foundation managers) and supports organizations described in: (1) boxes 5 through 12 above; or (2) section 501(c)(4), (5), or (6), if they meet the test of section 509(a)(2). See section 509(a)(3).

Provide the following information about the supported organizations. (See instructions for Part IV, box 13.)

(a) Name(s) of supported organization(s)	(b) Box number from above

~~SAMPLE~~

14 ☐   An organization organized and operated to test for public safety. Section 509(a)(4). (See specific instructions.)

Support Schedule (Complete only if you checked box 10, 11, or 12 above.) Use cash method of accounting.

Calendar year (or fiscal year beginning in) ▶	(a) 1989	(b) 1988	(c) 1987	(d) 1986	(e) Total
15 Gifts, grants, and contributions received. (Do not include unusual grants. See line 28.)	$742,300	$696,800	$640,600	$594,300	$2,674,000
16 Membership fees received	1,100	1,500	1,500	1,400	5,500
17 Gross receipts from admissions, merchandise sold or services performed, or furnishing of facilities in any activity that is not a business unrelated to the organization's charitable, etc., purpose	31,200	26,400	30,600	24,900	113,100
18 Gross income from interest, dividends, amounts received from payments on securities loans (section 512(a)(5)), rents, royalties, and unrelated business taxable income (less section 511 taxes) from businesses acquired by the organization after June 30, 1975	26,000	27,700	22,100	20,400	96,200
19 Net income from unrelated business activities not included in line 18					
20 Tax revenues levied for your benefit and either paid to you or expended on your behalf					
21 The value of services or facilities furnished to you by a governmental unit without charge. Do not include the value of services or facilities generally furnished to the public without charge.					
22 Other income. Attach schedule. Do not include gain (or loss) from sale of capital assets					
23 Total of lines 15 through 22	$800,600	$752,400	$694,800	$641,000	$2,888,800
24 Line 23 minus line 17	769,400	726,000	664,200	616,100	2,775,700
25 Enter 1% of line 23	8,006	7,524	6,948	6,410	

26 Organizations described in box 10 or 11:
   a   Enter 2% of amount in column (e), line 24   . . . . $ 55,514
   b   Attach a list (not open to public inspection) showing the name of and amount contributed by each person (other than a governmental unit or publicly supported organization) whose total gifts for 1986 through 1989 exceeded the amount shown in line 26a. Enter the sum of all excess amounts here   . . . . ▶   -0-

(Continued on page 3)

Part IV   Support Schedule (continued) **(Complete only if you checked box 10, 11, or 12 on page 2.)**

27   Organizations described in box 12, page 2:   N/A

   a   Attach a list for amounts shown on lines 15, 16, and 17, showing the name of, and total amounts received in each year from, each "disqualified person," and enter the sum of such amounts for each year:

     (1989) .... (1988) .... (1987) .... (1986) ....

   b   Attach a list showing, for 1986 through 1989, the name and amount included in line 17 for each person (other than "disqualified persons") from whom the organization received more during that year than the larger of: (1) the amount on line 25 for the year; or (2) $5,000. Include organizations described in boxes 5 through 11 as well as individuals. Enter the sum of these excess amounts for each year:

     (1989) .... (1988) .... (1987) .... (1986) ....

28   For an organization described in box 10, 11, or 12, page 2, that received any unusual grants during 1986 through 1989, attach a list (not open to public inspection) for each year showing the name of the contributor, the date and amount of the grant, and a brief description of the nature of the grant. Do not include these grants in line 15 above. (See specific instructions.)   N/A

Part V   **Private School Questionnaire**
         (To be completed ONLY by schools that checked box 6 in Part IV)   N/A

		Yes (1)	No (2)
29	Do you have a racially nondiscriminatory policy toward students by statement in your charter, bylaws, other governing instrument, or in a resolution of your governing body?	**29**	
30	Do you include a statement of your racially nondiscriminatory policy toward students in all your brochures, catalogues, and other written communications with the public dealing with student admissions, programs, and scholarships?	**30**	
31	Have you publicized your racially nondiscriminatory policy through newspaper or broadcast media during the period of solicitation for students, or during the registration period if you have no solicitation program, in a way that makes the policy known to all parts of the general community you serve?	**31**	

     If "Yes," please describe; if "No," please explain. (If you need more space, attach a separate statement.)

32	Do you maintain the following:		
a	Records indicating the racial composition of the student body, faculty, and administrative staff?	**32a**	
b	Records documenting that scholarships and other financial assistance are awarded on a racially nondiscriminatory basis?	**32b**	
c	Copies of all catalogues, brochures, announcements, and other written communications to the public dealing with student admissions, programs, and scholarships?	**32c**	
d	Copies of all material used by you or on your behalf to solicit contributions?	**32d**	

     If you answered "No" to any of the above, please explain. (If you need more space, attach a separate statement.) ------------------

     ----

33	Do you discriminate by race in any way with respect to:		
a	Students' rights or privileges?	**33a**	
b	Admissions policies?	**33b**	
c	Employment of faculty or administrative staff?	**33c**	
d	Scholarships or other financial assistance? (See instructions.)	**33d**	
e	Educational policies?	**33e**	
f	Use of facilities?	**33f**	
g	Athletic programs?	**33g**	
h	Other extracurricular activities?	**33h**	

     If you answered "Yes" to any of the above, please explain. (If you need more space, attach a separate statement.) ------------------

     ----

34a	Do you receive any financial aid or assistance from a governmental agency?	**34a**	
b	Has your right to such aid ever been revoked or suspended?	**34b**	

     If you answered "Yes" to either 34a or b, please explain using an attached separate statement.

35	Do you certify that you have complied with the applicable requirements of sections 4.01 through 4.05 of Rev. Proc. 75-50, 1975-2 C.B. 587, covering racial nondiscrimination? If "No," attach an explanation. (See instructions for Part V.)	**35**	

Part VI   **Lobbying Expenditures by Public Charities** (see instructions)
                  (To be completed ONLY by an eligible organization that filed Form 5768)

Check here ▶ **a** ☐   If the organization belongs to an affiliated group (see instructions).

Check here ▶ **b** ☐   If you checked **a** and ''limited control'' provisions apply (see instructions).   N/A

Limits on Lobbying Expenses		**(a)** Affiliated group totals	**(b)** To be completed for ALL electing organizations
36 Total (grassroots) lobbying expenses to influence public opinion	36		
37 Total lobbying expenses to influence a legislative body	37		
38 Total lobbying expenses (add lines 36 and 37)	38		
39 Other exempt purpose expenses (see Part VI instructions)	39		
40 Total exempt purpose expenses (add lines 38 and 39) (see instructions)	40		
41 Lobbying nontaxable amount. Enter the smaller of $1,000,000 or the amount determined under the following table—	41		

If the amount on line 40 is—	**The lobbying nontaxable amount is—**
Not over $500,000	20% of the amount on line 40.
Over $500,000 but not over $1,000,000	$100,000 plus 15% of the excess over $500,000
Over $1,000,000 but not over $1,500,000	$175,000 plus 10% of the excess over $1,000,000
Over $1,500,000	$225,000 plus 5% of the excess over $1,500,000

42 Grassroots nontaxable amount (enter 25% of line 41)	42	
(Complete lines 43 and 44. File Form 4720 if either line 36 exceeds line 42 or line 38 exceeds line 41.)		
43 Excess of line 36 over line 42	43	
44 Excess of line 38 over line 41	44	

4-Year Averaging Period Under Section 501(h)

(Some organizations that made a section 501(h) election do not have to complete all of the five columns below. See the instructions for lines 45–50 for details.)

Calendar year (or fiscal year beginning in) ▶	**Lobbying Expenses During 4-Year Averaging Period**				
	(a) 1990	**(b)** 1989	**(c)** 1988	**(d)** 1987	**(e)** Total
45 Lobbying nontaxable amount (see instructions)					
46 Lobbying ceiling amount (150% of line 45(e))					
47 Total lobbying expenses (see instructions)					
48 Grassroots nontaxable amount (see instructions)					
49 Grassroots ceiling amount (150% of line 48(e))					
50 Grassroots lobbying expenses (see instructions)					

Schedule A (Form 990) 1990   Page **5**

Part VII   Information Regarding Transfers To and Transactions and Relationships With Noncharitable Exempt Organizations

51 Did the reporting organization directly or indirectly engage in any of the following with any other organization described in section 501(c) of the Code (other than section 501(c)(3) organizations) or in section 527, relating to political organizations?

		Yes	No
a Transfers from the reporting organization to a noncharitable exempt organization of:			
(i) Cash	**51a(i)**		X
(ii) Other assets	**a(ii)**		X
b Other Transactions:			
(i) Sales of assets to a noncharitable exempt organization	**b(i)**		X
(ii) Purchases of assets from a noncharitable exempt organization	**b(ii)**		X
(iii) Rental of facilities or equipment	**b(iii)**	X	
(iv) Reimbursement arrangements	**b(iv)**		X
(v) Loans or loan guarantees	**b(v)**		X
(vi) Performance of services or membership or fundraising solicitations	**b(vi)**		X
c Sharing of facilities, equipment, mailing lists or other assets, or paid employees	**c**		X

d If the answer to any of the above is "Yes," complete the following schedule. The "Amount involved" column below should always indicate the fair market value of the goods, other assets, or services given by the reporting organization. If the organization received less than fair market value in any transaction or sharing arrangement, the column should also indicate the value of the goods, other assets, or services received.

(a) Line no.	(b) Amount involved	(c) Name of noncharitable exempt organization	(d) Description of transfers, transactions, and sharing arrangements
b(iii)	$800	Fraternal Society of Utopia	Rental of hall, kitchen, dining room equipment and supplies for the agency's annual dinner/dance.

SAMPLE

52a Is the organization directly or indirectly affiliated with, or related to, one or more tax-exempt organizations described in section 501(c) of the Code (other than section 501(c)(3)) or in section 527?   ☐ **Yes**   ☒ **No**

   b If "Yes," complete the following schedule.

(a) Name of organization	(b) Type of organization	(c) Description of relationship
None		

FAMILY SERVICE AGENCY OF UTOPIA, INC.
EIN: 12-3456789
Form 990 (1990) Schedule Attachment

Part I, line 1d: Contributions, gifts, grants, etc.

> No single contributor gave $5,000 or more during the year.

Part I, line 8c: Sale of assets other than inventory

Proceeds from sales of
Publicly traded securities	$24,200
Cost and sales expenses	23,700
Gain	$ 500

Part I, line 9: Special fundraising events and activities

	Dinner/ dance	Celebrity auction	Raffle	Total
Gross revenue	$14,500	$9,200	$4,700	$28,400
Less: Direct expenses	11,200	3,700	3,100	18,000
Net income	$ 3,300	$5,500	$1,600	$10,400

Part I, line 10: Sales

Proceeds from sale of educational publications	$1,400
Cost of publications sold	1,000
Gross profit	$ 400

Part I, line 16:

Payments to affiliates	$12,400

> Two percent of unrestricted contributions collected
> were paid to the National Association of Family Service
> Agencies for its general operations, as required by our
> affiliation agreement with that organization.

Part II, line 22: Grants and allocations

Family Counseling:
National Association of
Family Service Agencies
Milwaukee, Wisconsin	$ 3,000

Adoption Services:
National Association of
Family Service Agencies	$10,000

Utopia Adolescent Center
Utopia, Pennsylvania	5,000

Utopia Children's Services
Utopia, Pennsylvania	6,000
	$21,000

Foster Home Care:
Utopia Children's Services	$ 5,000
Utopia Adolescent Center	6,900
	$11,900

FAMILY SERVICE AGENCY OF UTOPIA, INC.
EIN: 12-3456789
Form 990 (1990) Schedule Attachment

Part II, line 42: Depreciation AND Part IV, line 57 -- Land, buildings, equipment

Asset	Date acquired	Cost	Prior years' depreciation	Method	Useful life	Current depreciation
Land	1988	$ 45,500	--	--	--	--
Office equip.	1983	3,000	$2,450	S.L.	8 years	$ 350
Office equip.	1990	11,500	--	S.L.	8 years	1,150
Building	1988	128,000	5,550	S.L.	30 years	3,700
Total		$188,000	$8,000			$5,200

Part IV, line 54: Investments securities (end of year)

Common Stock	Number of Shares	Book Value (cost)
A Corporation	4,000	$ 98,000
B Corporation	1,600	17,400
C Corporation	1,000	22,100
D Corporation	1,200	58,200
E Corporation	800	43,700
F Corporation	2,000	109,200
G Corporation	1,000	62,400
H Corporation	600	16,500
I Corporation	900	46,900
Total		$474,400

Part IV, line 62: Support and revenue designated for future periods

		Designated for Year		
	1990	1991	1992	Total
Received prior to 1990	$20,000	$20,800	$20,800	$61,600
Received in 1990		9,000	9,000	18,000
Expended (earned) in 1990	(20,000)			(20,000)
Balance at end of 1990	$ -0-	$29,800	$29,800	$59,600

All of the above represent grants designated by contributors to support adoption
services in future periods.

FAMILY SERVICE AGENCY OF UTOPIA, INC.
EIN: 12-3456789
Form 990 (1990) Schedule Attachment

Part IV, line 64: Mortgages and other notes payable

    Mortgage Payable to State Bank of Utopia $3,200
        @ 6% per annum

Form 990 (1990), Schedule A
    Part III, Item 4

    Organizations receiving grants are required to furnish:

    1. A copy of their section 501(c)(3) determination letter from the IRS.

    2. Audited financial statements for the two preceding years.

    3. Evidence of service quality and effectiveness in reaching poverty
       level population.

    4. Quarterly report of services delivered.

Chapter 17

Other Tax-Reporting Obligations

Don't let the title of this chapter suggest that it is a grab-bag of relatively unimportant odds and ends, since we just spent the last chapter on a single type of report. The annual report is required for maintaining a tax exemption that applies primarily to income taxes. It does not automatically exempt you from all other types of returns. Some of these other returns are required to be filed quarterly or even monthly, and must therefore be dealt with much more often.

Among the other returns that must be filed are these:

- Payroll taxes: federal, state (and some cities)
- State and local sales and use taxes (you only *think* you're exempt!)
- Property taxes on realty and personal property
- Excise taxes
- Federal and state information returns on payments to nonemployees.

ASPECTS COMMON TO MOST RETURNS

The Figures on Books and Returns Must "Tie In"

For the sake of accuracy—and credibility in case of an audit—the figures used on all returns, with the possible exception of certain property taxes, should be derived from and tie in with your books of account, using worksheets to assemble them, to permit tracing back down the "audit trail." For example, since you must file Form 990 in most cases, which shows your total payroll for the year, it is courting trouble to submit quarterly or annual payroll tax returns to the IRS that do not add up to the same total.

Tax Dollars Are Saved Mainly by Planning

Aside from the tax on Unrelated Business Income or taxes imposed on political activities (lobbying or electoral), and penalties for nonfiling, the last chapter was not about tax costs—unless you lost your exemption. It was about information returns. This chapter is in a different ball park, one played in by tax-exempt and business organizations alike for the most part. The know-how needed here has a direct payoff in dollars, and most of it must be applied long before you fill out the tax form itself. Most taxes are saved through planning ahead, before a transaction occurs, and not by the way it is reported on a tax return. For this reason, you would do well to get professional advice from the outset, or as soon as you can, regarding the basic tax-planning issues that may affect your organization. A professional accountant is a valuable resource in such matters. If you cannot afford to engage one for a fee, try to obtain volunteer assistance from a knowledgeable member of your organization, a sympathetic practitioner or a public interest accounting group.

How to Use Professional Help

It is not necessary to have a professional prepare your returns, which are pretty routine in nature, once you understand the forms. The main thing is to get advice in regard to who or what is taxable or nontaxable, and to have the accountant show the ropes to the person who will be responsible for filing the returns. Beyond that, it is helpful to have an annual review of the way the returns are being prepared, how they tie in with the books, and what kind of worksheets are being used and retained. This sort of help can save you a lot of time, embarrassment, and often badly needed money in taxes and penalties avoided.

Anyone with average intelligence, plus some perseverance, can fill out the kinds of tax forms described in this chapter. The information needed is usually contained in an instruction sheet accompanying the form, and these instructions should be followed, quite literally, to avoid problems with the agency involved. The material presented for each type of tax will therefore focus, not on how to fill out the form (except for federal forms which are uniform), but on the underlying concepts you need to understand in doing your tax planning and record-keeping. These concepts should control what you will have to enter on the tax forms themselves.

SOME FACTORS THAT MAY MAKE TRANSACTIONS TAXABLE

The biggest problem in tax planning is that there is no single, simple rule governing what is taxable or nontaxable, except the phrase "it all depends." Thus a given payment or collection may or not be subject to a specific tax, depending on the following factors:

- Whether the organization filing the return is subject to the tax, based on exempt status or location.

- Whether the organization is required to collect the tax from someone else who is subject, and pay it over.

- Whether the other party to the transaction is in fact an employee, customer, or vendor, or something else.

- Whether the type of payment is one that is subject to the tax, and whether part or all of it is nontaxable.

To make matters more complicated, where taxes imposed by states are concerned, each state makes its own rules covering these issues, making generalizations about them difficult. It therefore goes without saying that you need to know the specific rules of any state in which you operate, which may mean that you need to file returns in more than one state, even if you have only one office, if any of your people or activities are across state lines. With these words of caution, we can proceed to examine each of the major tax compliance obligations that may apply to your own nonprofit.

THE PAYROLL TAX JUNGLE

The complicated requirements of payroll record-keeping were explained in Chapters 11 and 12. The complexities of the payroll tax laws are what create these requirements. Since most of the operating expense of a typical nonprofit consists of payroll and related taxes and fringe benefits, this area becomes one of central importance—and a major headache. It is important to realize that the amount of *withheld* income and Social Security taxes you must handle for government agencies is much larger than the amount of the payroll taxes borne by your own organization. These are funds that do not belong to the nonprofit, but that it is collecting from its employees in trust for the federal or other government. They must be paid over as quickly as the rules require, or penalties and interest can be expected—expenses that are unbudgeted and unnecessary in a well-run organization.

Exemptions from Payroll or Withholding Taxes[1]

The basic rules regarding "covered employers" and "covered employment" are these:

- Federal and state income tax withholding: no exemption available for any type of nonprofit; all employees covered.
- Social Security (FICA) tax and withholding: starting in 1984, all nonprofits became taxable.
- Federal Unemployment Tax: 501(c)(3) organizations are exempt; other nonprofits generally taxable.
- State Unemployment Taxes: nonprofits are taxable in many states. (For guidance, refer to agency collecting this tax of any state in which your employees operate.)
- State Disability Benefits Tax: governed by state law.

Who Is an Employee?

This is the next definitional hurdle and an important one, since *only* employees are covered by payroll taxes, not everyone who may perform services for the organization. The answer is not a simple one, and may be different if you are dealing with state or federal agencies, in some cases. One common-law definition of an employer–employee relationship, used by the IRS and many states: "An employer–employee relationship exists where (1) the employer has the right to control and direct the detailed means of performing the services and their result, even if the right is not exercised; (2) the employer has the right to discharge; and (3) in some cases, the employer furnishes the

---

[1]See IRS Circular E for special rules covering students, nonresident aliens, clergy, and members of religious orders.

tools and workplace."[2] Any of these or other factors, such as working for only a single employer, may be held to prove employee status.

Most other states use a general statutory definition that provides that "Service for pay is employment, *unless* (1) The "written and actual agreements provide that the individual is free from control and direction in doing his job; and (2) his work is done away from the business premises or outside the usual course of business; and (3) he is customarily engaged in an individually established occupation."[3] This is a far more inclusive definition, leaving a far smaller gray area than does the common-law approach.

One gray area clarified by the Revenue Code covers the situation where the same person may render services to the organization both as an employee and as a so-called "independent contractor"—the term covering all nonemployees rendering services. Here the rule is that "if half or more of the services performed during a pay period constitute 'employment,' all of the services are deemed to be employment"[4] (and vice versa).

IRS has begun a crack-down on the abuse of the category of "independent contractor," which has become widespread in recent years, since it saves both the employer and employee payroll taxes. (We consider it short-sighted on the part of employees, since it also denies them unemployment compensation and Social Security coverage for the salary involved.) If you are uncertain whether an individual genuinely fits this category, you can obtain a ruling from IRS by completing and submitting Form SS-8, which is a questionnaire covering the facts of the relationship.

Should you arbitrarily treat employees as independent contractors, and be found wrong, your organization will have to pay IRS all the withholding and payroll taxes it should have paid in, plus penalties and interest. That could really hurt. (Your state tax agency will also demand the same payments.) Worse yet, the responsible officer might be held personally liable.

What Are "Taxable Wages"?

This term has two meanings: (1) wages subject to employment taxes and withholdings, meaning all payments to individuals considered to be employees, with a few specified exceptions; and (2) the net amount of such wages on which a given tax is calculated, which may be less than the total paid, since there may be an upper limit to the portion taxable.

1. Gross wages (the first meaning): here again, federal and state rules may differ. For the IRS, include all remuneration, whether in cash, goods or services, and whether called salary, bonus, vacation or sick pay, commission, or severance pay. If the organization furnishes meals or lodging to an employee, they are considered taxable (gross) wages for all purposes, unless furnished for the employer's convenience and on the employer's premises. In the case of lodging, it must be a condition of employment: e.g., the apartment furnished a building superintendent. The phrase "convenience of employer" generally means that the employee's presence must be continuously available, or that there is a short lunch hour (45 minutes or less) and no place nearby to eat.

If meals or lodging are not for the employer's convenience, they are considered wages subject to all federal employment taxes, and at their fair market value. If it is for the employer's conven-

---

[2]Arnold J. Olenick, *Managing the Company Tax Function* (Englewood Cliffs, NJ: Prentice-Hall, Inc., 1976), p. 92.

[3]*Ibid.*, p. 93

[4]*Ibid.*, p. 93

ience, the same value is subject only to Social Security and Federal Unemployment Taxes. Some states exempt these from State Unemployment Tax.

2. Net Taxable Wages (the other meaning): both the federal and state taxes on employers (and the Social Security Tax withheld on employees) are imposed on total wages up to a specified limit per employee. (This limit does not affect income tax withholdings, of course.) The tax rate, multiplied by this limited amount, computed on an annual, cumulative basis for each employee, yields the tax on each employee. The sum of these equals the total tax due for the period, usually a calendar quarter. Since this would be a needlessly time-consuming way to calculate the tax, a worksheet is used instead, which accumulates the portion of employee salaries that is currently taxable, totals these amounts, and multiplies the rate times this total.[5]

How to Report and Reconcile Wages Earned

Regardless of whether the organization keeps its books on a cash or accrual basis, wages are reported for payroll taxes on a *cash* basis, i.e., the period *paid* governs, not the period in which the wages were earned. This results in the need to reconcile wages reported with wages earned, if there has been a delay in paying salaries and the amounts have been accrued on the books, or where the practice is to accrue the unpaid part of salaries for a pay period that ends, or is paid for, after a statement date. Quarterly and annual worksheets for calculating net taxable wages and taxes due, and for reconciling all figures with general ledger accounts, are shown at Figs. 17–2 and 17–3.

A NOTE ON TAX TERMINOLOGY

The advice commonly given to "watch that language," in order to spot both the pitfalls and the opportunities in the tax laws, must be taken literally. This is as good a time as any to define the most commonly used terms, in addition to the explanations already given, so that they can be used as a shorthand in the remainder of the chapter, and can be part of your vocabulary when handling tax responsibilities.

- *Gross Wages* (or *Gross Sales*): The total amount of the item, before any deductions, exemptions, etc., for nontaxable portions (sometimes called "Total Wages," etc. on forms).

- *Net Taxable Wages* (or *Sales*): The so-called "tax base," i.e., the amount by which the tax rate is multiplied to arrive at the total tax (called Taxable Payroll or Taxable Sales also).

- *Adjustments, Deductions, or Exemptions*: Nontaxable items subtracted from the gross figure to arrive at the net. The term "adjustments" is also used at times to refer to a direct addition or subtraction from the amount of tax itself, as on IRS Form 941.

- *Credit*: An allowance that may be subtracted directly from the amount of the total tax previously calculated.

- *Tax Base*: A shorthand term used by professionals, meaning the net taxable wages or sales figure (or assessed value of property) by which the tax rate is multiplied to get the total tax

---

[5]The tax rate and the limit on the amount subject to tax may change annually. For example, in 1990, the Social Security (FICA) tax rate was 7.65% on employee plus 7.65% on employer, times a limit of $50,400 per employee, the maximum being indexed for inflation thereafter.

(before any credits). The term is usually used on tax forms.

• *Tax Deposits*:   Prepayments of taxes against the final amount due for the quarter or year, usually made through a commercial bank, in the case of federal taxes. The total of deposits for the period is then shown on the tax form and subtracted from the net tax for the period, to arrive at the balance due, if any, or overpayment. This system is also used by some states for collecting sales and use taxes as well as payroll taxes, except that payments are usually made directly to a state tax agency, not through a bank.

• *Tax vs. Withheld Tax*:   The issue here is whose money is it? Federal and state income taxes and half of the amount paid the IRS for Social Security taxes are taken out of the employee's pay, as is often part of any tax on disability benefits, and even on unemployment compensation in some states. The only actual "taxes" paid on payroll by the employer, therefore, are (1) the other half of Social Security, (2) federal and state unemployment taxes (except any part of the state tax that is withheld), and (3) disability benefits tax, with the same exception. Sales taxes are usually added to the bill paid by the customer, unless included in the price already, so the *customer* is paying it; the same often applies to excise taxes, such as the gasoline tax. Use taxes are supposed to be paid also by the buyer direct to the state. Property taxes are of course paid by the owner, directly or via installment payments on a mortgage through a bank.

The following checklist shows the types for which your nonprofit may be responsible, depending upon whether it pays wages, fees or other payments, owns property, sells merchandise or services, and also on the state in which it is located.

REPORTING EMPLOYMENT/PAYROLL TAXES

Of the eleven types of reporting forms listed in Fig. 17–1, seven relate to payrolls or other compensation. These constitute the major tax problem areas faced during the year by both nonprofit and business organizations, and they involve both the federal and state governments, and some cities.

Payroll Tax Returns Required by the IRS

Through the toils of the Internal Revenue Service, the federal government collects three different kinds of taxes on employees and employers: (1) Income tax withheld from salaries, (2) Social Security taxes, half withheld from employee, half imposed as a tax on employer; and (3) Federal Unemployment Tax, all borne by the employer. Since the taxes are reported uniformly by all U.S. employers, it has been possible to provide a worksheet that is tied in with filled-in forms, plus detailed instructions for preparing both the Form 941—on which both income and Social Security taxes are reported—and the Form 940, covering Federal Unemployment Tax. This material is in Appendix 17A, for use when you need it. [Note that annual federal and state information returns reporting *individual* withholdings of income and FICA taxes, and other payments not subject to withholding (Form 1099), are explained later in this Chapter. Note also that only nonprofits exempt under IRS Sec. 501(c)(3) are exempt from filing Form 940.]

Type of tax	Imposed by	IRS form no. (if any)	Frequency of returns*
Employment/Payroll			
☐ Income Tax Withheld	U.S., state (& a few cities)	941	U.S.: quarterly; State: various
☐ Social Security (FICA)	U.S. (combined return)	941	Quarterly
☐ Federal Unemployment	U.S. (501(c)(3)s exempt)**	940	Annually
☐ State Unemployment	State	—	Quarterly
☐ State Disability Benefits	State	—	Quarterly or annually
Sales and use taxes	State and/or local	—	Quarterly
Property taxes:			
☐ Real Property	State or local	—	Commonly semiannually (issued by tax agency)
☐ Personal Property (equipment, etc.)	State or local	—	Commonly annually
Excise taxes information returns	Federal and/or state	(var.)	Commonly annually
☐ Individual Taxes Withheld for year	Federal, state	W-2, W-3	Annually
☐ Other payments (fees, interest, etc.)	Federal and state	1099, 1096	Annually

FIGURE 17-1. CHECKLIST OF COMMON TAX AND INFORMATION RETURNS.

*Tax deposits or interim payments on account may be due more frequently than tax returns (see explanation for specific taxes).

**See IRS Circular E re: other exempt organizations.

WORKSHEETS FOR STATE/LOCAL PAYROLL TAXES

Worksheets for federal returns have, as noted, been provided in Appendix 17A. Worksheets for use in preparing state returns (and returns for cities imposing an income tax) are shown in Figs. 17-2 and 17-3. For purpose of comparison and integrating the illustrations, we have invented five employees whose earnings illustrate the five most common situations regarding taxability of amounts earned during the quarter prescribed by the U.S. and a typical state government. The same people and earnings are used throughout all worksheets.

All data on earnings, withholdings, as well as names and Social Security numbers are entered from the Employee Earnings Records described in Chapters 11 and 12—usually a card for each employee, unless a payroll book is used. Columns and significant amounts on the worksheets are identified by numbers or letters and are cross-referenced to the text. Wherever used, the phrase "Taxable Wages" means the Tax Base—i.e., the amount to be multiplied by the tax rate on the return—since all earnings entered are assumed to be "taxable" in the sense of being covered by the tax law involved.

State (and City) Income Tax Withheld

Columns (4) and (5) of Quarterly Worksheet #1 (Fig. 17–2) provide for income taxes withheld for state or city tax agencies. The totals (items K and L) are entered on the form for reporting such withholdings, if reported quarterly. If they are recorded monthly, these amounts are obtained from the credits to the State or City Withholding Tax Payable account on the general ledger or from the Payroll Journal, Cash Disbursements Journal, or worksheet, depending on which is used to record taxes withheld.

State Quarterly Unemployment Tax Returns

Also referred to as state unemployment insurance, these returns are required of most employers, including nonprofit organizations (check your state's requirements on this). This tax is integrated with the Federal Unemployment Tax, which allows credit on its reporting form for the tax paid the state against the gross federal tax, as will be explained below. The federal unemployment tax law requires that the unemployment tax of all states covers nonprofits employing four or more people for twenty weeks or more, as well as all employees of elementary and secondary schools, even if church-related.

The state unemployment tax rate is generally different for each employer, and tries to take account of how stable each employer's record of employment (and unemployment) is. The less turnover, the lower the tax rate. In addition, some states permit an employer to reduce the tax rate by

Quarter Ended: 12-31

(1) Employee's name	(2) Soc. Sec. number	(3) Current quarter earnings	(4) (5) Income tax withheld Current quarter		(6) (7) Income tax withheld Year-to-date	
			State (A)	City (A)	State	City
A. Jones	xxx-xx-xxxx	2,500	125.	—	250.	—
B. Reilly	xxx-xx-xxxx	3,500	175.	—	350.	—
C. Levy		4,500	225.	—	900.	—
	xxx-xx-xxxx					
D. Lee	xxx-xx-xxxx	7,500	375.	—	1,500.	—
E. Diaz	xxx-xx-xxxx	10,000	500.	—	2,000.	—
Total payroll		28,000	1,400.*	—	5,000.**	—
		(F & G)	(K)	(L)		

FIGURE 17–2. QUARTERLY PAYROLL TAX WORKSHEET #1
(For State and/or City Income Tax Withheld)

*Totals withheld per earning records should agree with total credited to state and city withholding tax payable accounts in the general ledger during quarter: (K) above.

**At the end of the fourth quarter of the calendar year, the year-to-date total of income tax withheld for each employee (as shown on his or her earnings record and entered above) is used for the withholding statement.

making voluntary payments into the state's unemployment insurance fund. Another special arrangement is one such as provided in Massachusetts, which permits nonprofit organizations to elect to reimburse the state for any unemployment benefits paid its former employees, rather than pay a tax in advance. All such possible tax savings should be looked at.

Quarter Ended: 12-31

(1)	(2)	(3)	(4)	(5)	(6)	(7)
Employee's name	Social Security number	Earnings through previous quarter	Current quarter earnings	Earnings this year (cumulative) (3) + (4)	Excess S.U.T. wages (over $7,000)	Taxable S.U.T. wages current quarter
A. Jones	xxx-xx-xxxx	2,500	2,500	5,000	—	2,500
B. Reilly	xxx-xx-xxxx	4,000	3,500	7,500	500	3,000
C. Levy	xxx-xx-xxxx	13,500	4,500	18,000	4,500*	— *
D. Lee	xxx-xx-xxxx	40,800	7,500	48,300	7,500*	— *
E. Diaz	xxx-xx-xxxx	48,000	10,000	58,000	10,000*	— *
Total payroll			28,000	136,800	22,500*	5,500(G)

Multiply by employer S.U.T. rate 2.7% (Assumed rate)

Employer contribution = 148.50

FIGURE 17–3. QUARTERLY PAYROLL TAX WORKSHEET #2
(For State Unemployment Tax Returns)

*Exceed $7,000 limit previously.

As previously indicated, the unemployment tax is generally a tax imposed entirely on the employer,[6] and each is advised at the beginning of the calendar year what rate is to be used for that year's returns. The worksheet shown in Fig. 17–3 makes provision for accumulating the data for this tax and for calculating it. Columns 3, 4, and 5 are used to enter each employee's earning record and to calculate the taxable portion. The limitation (maximum taxable wage) is much lower than it is for FICA Tax: it is $7,000 per employee in many states, but others have higher limits. To illustrate the calculation, we can use the data for B. Reilly, who went over the limit in the current (fourth) quarter:

			Col No.
Earnings year-to-date through 3rd quarter	=	$4,000	(3)
Current quarter earnings		3,500	(4)
Total earned through end of 4th quarter	=	7,500	(5)
Less: Limitation (maximum taxable)		7,000	
Balance is the excess over $6,000		500	(6)
Taxable portion of wages for current quarter: ($3,500 minus $500)	=	$3,000	(7)

[6]A few states have permitted the employer to deduct part of the tax from employee salaries.

The total taxable wages for all employees ($5,500: see G) is then multiplied by the employer's contribution (tax) rate, assumed in this case to be 2.7%, to yield the tax due ("Employer's Contribution") for the period, here $148.50. (See last line, column 7 of worksheet.) All the basic arithmetic is first done on the worksheet, proven with the related ledger accounts, and then merely copied onto the tax forms in the proper spaces. The worksheet then becomes a supporting document for the tax form, justifying the figures reported. (No illustration of a state form is presented, since no two states are alike.)

State Disability Benefits Tax

This is a tax to cover sick pay, and the method of assessing and paying it varies widely. In some states it is not a true tax, but a compulsory form of insurance, carried with an insurance company; others permit a choice between paying the state or carrying the insurance. The tax (or premium) may be levied entirely on the employer, or deducted in part from the employee, in a few states.[7] It may be a flat amount per employee or a percent of total (gross) payroll. The tax sometimes is deducted from salaries, up to the $7,000 limit per employee. In that situation, a column can be added to the same worksheet (#2), though it is not necessary, since the tax is computed on the total. In practice, the specific instructions of the state or insurance company must be followed.

HOW A COMPUTER PAYROLL SERVICE CAN ALMOST PAY FOR ITSELF

The point has been made and stressed previously that payrolls and payroll taxes are perhaps the greatest single headache in the whole area of financial management and control. The numerous bits and pieces of information involved and the related record-keeping were explained in Chapters 11 and 12. The idea proposed in those chapters of having the whole job done by a computer service center may look even more attractive, since a widely available type of service can not only do all your payroll record-keeping, as well as prepare paychecks or slips, it can also prepare your quarterly worksheets and returns as a by-product, as well as your annual W-2 (withholding tax) slips. The cost is not great, and the saving in time and error-correcting and headaches is.

WHY YOU MUST RETAIN YOUR PAYROLL RECORDS

You are not finished just because you have filed all your payroll tax returns. Both the IRS and state agencies have the right to audit your payroll records, as do other agencies, in connection with wage-and-hour laws and insurance policies. The IRS requires that you retain payroll records for audit four years after the due date of the tax or date paid, whichever is later. Some agencies keep the returns permanently, as evidence they were filed. State rules vary, and may even require longer periods. "Payroll records" mean not only your payroll journals and employees' earnings records, but also your payroll tax worksheets and retained copies of your payroll tax forms as well. And don't forget that making sure they all tie in with your general ledger and annual information returns (Form 990 and state form) is important in case you are ever audited in these areas.

---

[7]Not many states require such coverage at all.

Be Aware of Penalties and Interest Imposed

There are penalties for not complying with these tax obligations, particularly heavy at the federal level. They are imposed for late filing, failure to pay tax and, the worst one of all, failure to withhold taxes. The following civil penalties are imposed by the IRS (*plus* interest from the date payment was due):[8]

- Failure to make tax deposits when due

- Failure to file return, including information returns like W-2

- Failure to pay tax due per return, understating tax due, or overstating tax deposited in advance

- Payment with a bad check

- Willful failure to withhold, account for, or pay tax as required. This penalty can be imposed on the responsible officer or employee *personally*, and is a heavy one: it can be as much as 100% of the amount of the tax.

In addition to the above civil penalties, the Internal Revenue Code has additional muscle to enforce tax compliance obligations in the form of criminal fraud penalties. The chief distinction between civil and criminal fraud is that in the latter case, intent to defraud must be proven, but the penalties range from heavy fines (for willful attempt to evade tax) to prison terms (up to five years for the same offense). These penalties are not, incidentally, limited to payroll taxes, but apply to all tax and information returns required by the IRS.

The one area in which nonprofits are most likely to run into serious trouble with IRS is in taking a carefree attitude about payroll taxes, usually due to ignorance of the potential consequences. The writers have encountered small organizations that assumed they could pay salaries in full, without any withholding to one or all employees, merely by taking the position that what they were paying was not a salary, or that the individual was something other than an employee. If you try to do this, you had better have a good case, based on the definitions of employee at the beginning of this chapter, because you risk the 100% penalty that can be imposed personally on the officer or employee responsible for such matters. If you just are not sure about a person's status, IRS provides form SS-8 which you can use to get a ruling.

In 1981 Congress increased the penalties imposed on employees who falsify their W-4 forms by exaggerating the number of withholding exemptions to which they are entitled, to evade tax. The new penalties are $500 (civil) or $1,000 (criminal).

YOU MUST COMPLY WITH SALES TAX REGULATIONS

There seems to be a misconception in this area of taxation to the effect that a tax-exempt organization is exempt from sales taxes entirely. Although many states do in fact exempt you from sales tax on what you buy, once you get the appropriate exemption form and number, they do not exempt you from sales tax *collection* and *payment* on any merchandise or taxable services you sell to non-exempt customers, unless for resale. Since some nonprofits raise funds by operating a shop

---

[8]The interest rate is the average "prime rate" charged by banks; penalties range from 5% to 100% of tax due. (Interest will be compounded daily.)

of one kind or another, or by other sales of goods or services, this is another area fraught with danger. The danger is that if you go blithely on your way selling taxable items without collecting the necessary sales tax, you can find, when it's too late to collect the tax, that you should have done so, and must now pay it out of your own limited funds!

Just to make the pill more bitter, if you have never filed a sales tax return, there is no statute of limitations on how long the government agency can wait to audit you and for how many years back you can be required to pay the uncollected tax—plus interest and probable penalty. (If you are engaged in this type of activity, and believe yourself not subject to tax, you are better off filing a sales tax return showing a zero liability, and reporting sales as nontaxable: at least you are putting the agency on notice that you're "in business," can't be accused of tax evasion, and the normal statute of limitation of several years for audit or assessment will start running from the date you file.)

If you are subject to the tax on Unrelated Business Income described in Chapters 1, 9, and 16, there is a good possibility you may also be subject to sales tax on the sales of that "business." Your best bet is to get a copy of the instructions that accompany the sales tax return, and better yet, check out the way the activity in question is viewed as to taxability by the agency involved. For example, sales tax applies not only to sales of merchandise in some states, but also to certain kinds of service; also tax is imposed on rentals of equipment in some states. Another thing to watch is for sales that are not taxable, whether because of what is sold (food, for example) or who buys it; e.g., an out-of-state buyer to whom the merchandise is being shipped, another tax-exempt organization, or a buyer for resale. It is important to obtain the exemption or resale number for your files in the last two cases, to substantiate the facts.

Another thing to watch is for part of a sale of taxable merchandise that may not be taxable, such as shipping charges: these should be added in separately, after the tax on the merchandise is calculated and added. Since the rules vary widely between taxing jurisdictions (states and cities), the best thing to do is read the instructions carefully. What is important to remember is this: once you get your exemption certificate, you will be exempt from paying sales or use tax on what you buy; but remember that you may be required to collect and pay over sales taxes on goods or services that you sell. This is an area where professional advice may be required, because failure to collect and pay in the tax can result in your later having to pay it out of your own funds, as already noted, plus penalty and interest.

RECORD-KEEPING FOR SALES TAXES

As with other kinds of taxes, it is important to keep back-up records, both for tax return preparation and for support of the returns filed, in case of audit. If a cash register is used, the tapes should be kept on file for the length of time specified by the taxing authority (usually the statute of limitations for audit of the return). The same applies to any worksheets or other lists used in preparing the tax returns. These should show exempt or other nontaxable transactions, supported by files of exemption or resale certificates, or other documents supporting nontaxability. Remember that all sales are deemed taxable (to you) unless you can document their nontaxability.

Sales are generally recorded on a cash basis as well as sales taxes collected. If they are recorded on an accrual basis, sales tax returns are generally required to be filed on the same basis as is used on the books of account. Sales tax refunded or credited on credit sales are often deductible from the tax return of the period in which this occurred. That could mean amending prior returns.

Bookkeeping Entries

If you are required to collect and pay to the government sales taxes on any of your revenues, you will need an extra column in your cash receipts journal (or worksheet) and a separate account to record such items, entitled "Sales Tax Payable." This is a liability account, not revenue, because the amounts you collect are on behalf of the sales tax agency, and are owed to it, just as the withholding taxes on payroll are owed. The difference is that here you are collecting something extra, whereas withholding taxes are subtracted from salaries. When you pay over the sales tax to the government, the entry is the same as you would make for the payment of any other debt: a debit to the sales tax payable account and a credit to cash. (If there is any difference in the amounts collected and due, usually because you failed to collect the right amount of tax, any adjustment should be made through sales tax expense; e.g., if too little was collected, debit the account, credit sales tax payable for the difference, or vice versa, if too much was collected.)

If you should be in the position of selling on credit, and sales tax is involved, the entry would be as follows:

> Dr. Accounts receivable
> Cr. Appropriate revenue account
> Cr. Sales tax payable

It is important that sales tax return copies be kept on file permanently, as proof of filing, otherwise the statute of limitations on audit remains open permanently. Supporting worksheets and documents should of course be retained as well. The latter should include records of any sales returns, allowances, or refunds. The period for which these records should be retained is the one specified in the instructions accompanying the tax form, or the underlying statute: i.e., the statute of limitations for audit. (It is important to remember that if no return is filed, the statute remains open indefinitely.)

PROPERTY TAXES YOU MAY HAVE TO PAY

If your exempt organization is fortunate enough to be classified as one that is educational, religious, or charitable, its realty and personal property (equipment, vehicles, etc.) will probably be considered exempt from property taxes imposed by your state or other local taxing jurisdiction. If you are classified as a Section 501(c)(3) organization for federal purposes, this exemption may well apply. If you are not so exempt under state or local law, however, a knowledge of how such property is taxed (or exempted) is important.

Factors That Affect Real Property Taxation

The exemption of property is based, not on who owns or benefits from it, but on how it is used. Property is generally tax-exempt if used for educational, religious, or charitable purposes. If your organization is engaged in this type of activity, it may be able to obtain an exemption from real estate tax altogether on its own property, though it will likely have to pay the tax indirectly as part of rent if the property is leased from someone else who is taxable.

There are few controllable factors in the area of the tax on realty, other than where you choose to locate. Even nearby towns or cities may have much higher or lower tax rates or assessment practices, so this is a question that lends itself to investigation and planning. The tax assessors of neighboring taxing districts often set widely different assessed valuations on similar property, and the rates themselves may be quite different. For example, an area that is almost entirely residential and lower middle class may have a higher tax rate than one which has a large amount of business property in its tax base. If you expect to own your own building, this issue is worth considering in advance. Realtors or the tax assessors' offices in the area under consideration can supply an estimate of what to expect in the way of real estate tax, if you are not eligible for exemption.[9] Another tax-saving possibility is that of appealing or protesting the assessed valuation on your property. You will do much better with professional assistance here.

Some exempt organizations pay realty tax voluntarily as a political policy or civic obligation.

How to Minimize Personal Property Tax

The same exemptions from tax apply to personal property, which most states or localities impose, and should of course be your first line of defense, if available. When imposed, it usually applies to equipment, vehicles, and merchandise inventory, any of which could be owned by a nonprofit organization. About half of the states also tax intangibles, such as investments, although U.S. Treasury bonds and notes are exempt from such tax.

These taxes are assessed as of a given date, in most states, which results in a loophole for taxpayers willing to play such games as sharply reducing merchandise inventory by that date, or moving vehicles out of the state. Other states have sought to close this loophole by using averages, mileage of vehicles, or merely taxing the property whether or not it is in the state on assessment day, as long as it has been for part of the year. Reference to state or local law is necessary to determine which rule applies. Unlike the tax on realty, you may be able to avoid or reduce the effect of the tax on vehicles by renting them from a lessor in another state that does not tax them, which may reduce the effective rental. But the issue of renting versus owning should of course take into account all of the factors covered in the discussion of Capital Budgeting in Chapter 7. Renting them in your own state saves only the direct tax on ownership; your rental will usually include this tax, passed along by the lessor.

Other Ways to Minimize Tax on Personal Property

- Buy merchandise on consignment, not outright. Consigned merchandise does not belong to you. (This is a good idea for nontax reasons, since you need not pay for it if you cannot sell it.)

- Vehicles or equipment: reduce value due to damage, obsolescence, or abandonment, including useless equipment still owned. Use accelerated depreciation, where book value used.

- Tax on intangible personal property: may apply not only to investments, but also to bank accounts and receivables, based on balances at the assessment date. Values can be reduced by lowering the balances: collecting receivables, writing off uncollectible accounts or worthless investments, setting up a reserve for uncollectibles, selling for cash; paying bills to reduce cash at

---

[9]If you have a mortgage on your property, you may be better off paying this tax as part of your monthly or quarterly installments, whether or not required to, as a cash budgeting device.

assessment date; using funds, including from other investments, to buy U.S. bonds or notes; valuing investments at current market value, if below cost, etc.

As with other taxes, it is important to keep good records to support the valuation of property as of the assessment date, especially if you take advantage of the kinds of tax-saving devices described above, and also to keep track of where it is located on that date and who else owns it, if held on consignment or rented. Files documenting losses in value of intangibles, with independent evidence, such as market quotations, news items or correspondence received regarding worthlessness, loss in value or uncollectibility, are important back-up for claims of reduced value for tax purposes, especially in the hands of tax professionals called in where valuation is being disputed by the tax assessor.

FEDERAL AND STATE EXCISE TAXES

This is a type of tax that comes and goes, as the needs for revenue or regulatory agencies change. Federal excise tax has been levied on automobiles, gasoline, gas-guzzling autos, telephone calls, airline tickets, alcoholic beverages, and tobacco. Exemption from certain of these taxes may be available to tax-exempt organizations in certain categories. Section 501(c)(3) organizations may be exempt from the tax on telephone calls; schools and hospitals are exempt from federal excise taxes in general. If your organization is exempt and has been paying a tax which it need not have paid, such as the telephone excise tax, a tax refund may be available. Again, professional advice is always desirable, though not always essential if you want to explore the tax labyrinth on your own. Check your phone bill for the amounts involved, to see whether it is worthwhile.[10]

Some states also levy excise taxes, some of which are, in effect, property taxes, where they are paid annually and based on the value of the asset. If a state levies a tax on admissions, you may have to collect it if you stage performances or special events. The question of exemption from these types of taxes should of course also be explored. If you have taxable transactions, you should find out what sort of records you must keep, such as ticket stubs or other attendance records for performances or special events. State excise taxes may also be imposed on such items as vehicles, gasoline, alcoholic beverages, and wagering, which covers lotteries (but commonly exempts lotteries, bingo, etc. run by nonprofits exempt from other taxes.)

FEDERAL AND STATE INFORMATION RETURNS YOU MUST FILE

Forms W-2 and W-3

This category of return deals not with a tax obligation, but with the requirement to report certain types of payments to the federal and state tax agencies, for their use in enforcing the tax law with regard to reporting income from salaries subject to withholding.

The forms you are most likely to be responsible for are IRS Forms W-2 and 1099, as well as their state equivalents. Form W-2 was commented on briefly in connection with employers' quarterly federal tax returns. It is a multipurpose form, which reports to both the IRS and Social Security Administration the following types of information:

---

[10]This tax was due to expire after 1990, but may have been extended.

- Federal income tax withheld
- Taxable wges
- FICA wages (up to maximum taxable)
- FICA tax withheld
- Other compensation (most commonly travel or expense allowances)
- Pension data.

It also contains, of course, the name, address, and I.D. numbers of both the employee and the employer. The state income tax withheld is shown on the same form, with extra copies used for state returns.

There is a separate transmittal form used in each case, indicating the number of withholding forms being sent to the tax agency. (The IRS form is Form W-3. It also requires that total wages and withholdings for the entire year's payroll be reported, as well as total FICA wages and taxes.) **Note:** The W-3 and W-2 forms are now sent, not to the IRS, but to the Social Security Administration, as the instructions state.

Forms 1099 and 1096

These forms, and their state equivalents, are often loose ends in the sphere of reporting obligations. They are intended to prevent taxable income going unreported, where no tax is withheld from a payment, since not required by law. Since payments in the economic system which fit this description cover numerous kinds of transactions, the tax laws focus on only certain types, primarily those made to individuals, few of whom keep books, rather than to businesses, which do.

The types of payments and the number of the form on which they are required to be reported, *for any payee who received the amounts indicated during the calendar year,* are as follows:

Type of payment	Form used
• Fees, commissions, or other form of compensation not subject to withholding, of $600 or more	1099-MISC[11]
• Rents or other payments, including prizes and awards to nonemployees, totaling $600 or more,[12] or royalties of over $10	1099-MISC[11]
• Interest paid to any person (except a corporation) totaling $10 or more	1099-INT
• Coops must file Form 1099-PATR on patronage dividends.	

There are other forms covering other types of payments, but these are the ones a nonprofit is most likely to find applicable. As noted, states have equivalent forms, and it is possible to obtain carbonized sets of these forms, as well as of W-2 Forms, to facilitate preparing both the federal and state returns simultaneously. The transmittal form for submitting your 1099 forms is Form 1096, which reports the number sent, by type.

---

[11] Excludes payments to a corporation.

[12] The most common types for nonprofits would be fees paid to consultants, lawyers, accountants, or other professionals, considered to be independent contractors. A for-profit subsidiary must also file Form 1099-DIV for dividend payments.

It is important that you obtain the Social Security number (or employer's identification number) of anyone for whom you file either a W-2 or 1099 form, since the IRS cannot make much use of them without these numbers, and can impose a $50 penalty for each omission.

The main problem with the 1099 forms is in deciding who they must cover. You will recall that in our discussion of who is an employee, near the beginning of this chapter, we distinguished so-called independent contractors. Basically, the question of who must be reported on a Form 1099 revolves around that distinction, in the case of payments for services. If you have paid for services a total exceeding $600 during the year that do not require withholding, a 1099-MISC is required. To go back over a whole year's payments in order to do this would be a waste of time and effort. The practical approach is to set up a worksheet covering such payments at the beginning of the calendar year. Its headings would be as follows:

- Name of payee
- Address
- Identification number
- Total paid to payee (derived by totaling the monthly or quarterly columns horizontally)
- Columns for the months (or quarters of the year).

As you make payments of the type described, they can be entered on the worksheet. At the end of the calendar year, you need only add the monthly or quarterly columns across on each line to get the amount for Form 1099. (If a total is under $600, no form need be filed.)

Note: The IRS (and state agencies) impose penalties on organizations which fail to file these forms. Although they are not likely to be very costly for most nonprofits, they do represent a waste of money that could be better used on program activities. The IRS imposes a $50 penalty for each form not filed and each form for which a copy is not supplied to the individual covered.

Other required information returns are listed in Circular E.

TAX RETURN CONTROL AND TAX BUDGETING

A note of caution was sounded near the beginning of this chapter to the effect that failure to be religious about your tax obligations can result in needless penalties and interest charges which most small nonprofits can ill afford. Just the payroll tax payments alone generally represent a major cash-flow issue for most organizations. To illustrate, if you add up the total taxes, including withholdings, that Nonprofit X was obligated to pay in for the quarter ending March 31, 19x1 per Fig. 17–5, they come to about $13,266, which is nearly one-half of the payroll for the quarter of $28,500. Since payroll usually is the bulk of a nonprofit's budget, managing the payment of payroll taxes plus possible others mentioned is a major cash-flow problem in some cases, and failure to take it seriously flirts with the substantial penalties and interest described earlier in the chapter.

Tax Calendars Will Keep You Up-to-Date

Nearly every office has some kind of a desk calendar or diary, which the user relies on as a reminder of appointments, phone calls to make, etc. This gadget can also serve as insurance that all tax and information returns are filed by their due dates. What is needed is a list of regular due dates,

Type of tax	Tax form number	Monthly deposit or return (15th of next mo.)	Quarterly (end of next mo.)	Annual return	Example
Federal tax deposit					
(Covering WT & FICA)	(Coupon)	X or	X		Jan. due 2/15
USWT & FICA	941		X		Q/E 3/31 due on 4/30
State WT	State form	X or	X		(Varies)
State unemployment tax	State form		X		(See 941)
State disability benefit	State form (or Ins. Co.)		X		(See 941)
Federal unemployment tax	940	Quarterly deposit may be required		X	1990 due 1/31/91
State sales tax	State form	X or	X		(Varies)
Annual USWT returns:					
Employee copies	W-2			1/31	(see 940)
Soc. Sec. Admin. returns	W-2 & W-3			2/28	1990 due 2/28/91
Annual information returns	1099 & 1096			2/28	(Same)
Annual U.S. return of organization exempt from tax	990	For fiscal year ending 12/31: 5/15; 1990 due 5/15/91 (Due 4½ mos after end of fiscal year)			
Exempt organization business tax return	990-T				(Same)
State & local property taxes	State form	(Due dates vary: usually semiannual or annual returns)			

FIGURE 17–4. DUE DATES OF TAX RETURNS AND DEPOSITS*

Dates are for illustration only. They may vary with amounts withheld and taxes due, as well as with particular state. (See IRS Circular E for payroll tax deposit requirements, depending on amount of taxes due. See also the notes below Fig. 17–5.) Only IRS form numbers listed. You may be able to pay quarterly or may have to pay during a month.

which can be compiled from the instructions accompanying the forms you are required to file. Federal due dates are the same for everyone (although the Form 990 due date depends on when your fiscal year ends), but those for state and local returns may vary, though most payroll taxes are due on much the same basis in most states. To illustrate the frequency with which such returns are due, and to provide a model you may wish to follow—though with adaptations to your own state rules and your fiscal year, a chart of due dates is shown in Figure 17–4. (No state is identified, although the dates are common ones.)

Type of tax	Due date	Amount and month of payment/collection			Total for quarter (opt.)
Estimated payments due		Jan.	Feb.	March	
Federal Tax Deposit (WT + FICA)	15th	2,730	3,172	3,172	9,074
State Withholding Tax	15th	550	700	700	1,950
State Dis. Ben. Tax (1%) (4th quarter of prior year)	31st	55			55
State Unemployment Tax (2.7%)	31st	149			149
Federal Unemp. Tax Deposit (.7%)	15th	38			38
State Sales Tax	20th			500	500
Real Estate Tax (½ year)	1st		1,500		1,500
Total Tax Due		3,522	5,372	4,372	13,266

Estimated Taxes Collected or Withheld	Rate	Monthly Tax Base	Jan.	Feb.	March	
Fed. income tax (WT)	(Var)	$9,300	1,775	1,775	1,775	5,325
FICA	7.5%*	9,300	698	699	698	2,095
State withholding tax	5.0%	9,300	465	465	465	1,395
State dis. ben. tax	0.5%	9,300	47	47	47	141
State sales tax	5.0%	3,300	165	165	165	495
Total taxes collected withheld			3,150	3,150	3,150	9,451
Net budgeted tax outlays			372	2,221	1,222	3,815

FIGURE 17–5. NONPROFIT X, TAX BUDGET WORKSHEET
Quarter ending March 31, 1989

*1989 rate

What to Do About Late Filings

Where a difficult situation makes it impossible to file a return on time, it is possible in certain cases to obtain an extension of time to file, if application is made before the due date. This is not available for certain returns, such as Form 941, and where it is possible the effect is to avoid assessment of any penalty for late filing, although interest is usually mandatory for any late payments.* Even where IRS or a state agency will not grant an extension, it is often possible to obtain a waiver or abatement (cancellation) of such a penalty, where you are able to state in writing, under penalty of perjury, a convincing "reasonable cause," one indicating that it was impossible to file on time despite good faith efforts at compliance. But ignorance of the filing requirement is not an acceptable reason, nor are oversight, lack of funds, or usually unavailability of information needed to prepare the return.

*A Form 941 may be filed up to 10 days later, if all taxes due have been deposited.

Interest is mandatory on late payments, and will not be waived for cause by most agencies. It is thus desirable to pay at least an estimated amount on time, where circumstances prevent the return itself being prepared and filed, since interest generally runs on any unpaid balance up to the date of payment. Since there are separate penalties for late filing, in the reverse situation in which you are merely short of funds, it is safer to file the return without payment, since waiting until you can pay might trigger a penalty for late filing as well as late payment.

Getting Payments Credited

Since you are dealing with computerized record-keeping at the other end, be careful to comply with prescribed procedures for filing and paying as regards addresses, identification numbers, and documentation. Always show your Employer Identification Number on each check, to make certain you get credit: numbers are more reliable than names, which may be similar. Keep a supply of Tax Deposit forms on hand (for payments connected with Forms 941 and 940), and use the one for the correct period. If you don't have a federal tax deposit form, write a letter with your payment, stating the amount, type of tax, period for which due, and your employer I.D. number. (IRS normally sends you a coupon book containing a supply of Forms 8109, on which your Employer I.D. number is preprinted.)

CASH-FLOW BUDGETING FOR TAXES CAN AVOID NEEDLESS PENALTIES

The Cash Budget Worksheets in Chapter 7 (Tables 7–2 and 7–3) took into account the timing difference between collection and payment of payroll taxes. For example, the withheld taxes due in January were less than those due in February and March, because they had been withheld in December of the previous year, when some highly-paid employees were over the maximum on Social Security (FICA) taxes. It may be desirable to set up a Tax Budget Worksheet on a monthly basis, especially where sales or property taxes are due in addition to payroll taxes, in order to project the estimated tax payments for the overall cash budget. The key to these projections is the operating budget for the related periods, which should contain the following information used in the projections:

- Estimated payrolls, by quarter and month
- Estimated employer taxes (not withholdings) and property taxes (plus any others customarily incurred)
- Estimated sales or other taxable revenues.

Depending upon how substantial a given tax is and how much it fluctuates during the year, either a rough percentage estimate of the related tax base may be used (e.g., total payroll or sales for the month), or a careful calculation made that considers such questions as when each employee will exceed the cut-off for unemployment and FICA taxes. The latter will, of course, be more precise, unless there are unbudgeted changes in payrolls or tax rates.

The Tax Budget Worksheet can be set up as shown on Fig. 17-5, with the figures derived for each tax each month. The excess of taxes due over taxes collected or withheld can then be entered on the Cash Budget Worksheets as a single figure for net taxes. Or, the collections and payments due can be shown separately to flag the actual amount of payments to be anticipated.

If all taxes are carefully budgeted, payment crises and the needless costs of penalties and interest can be successfully avoided.

Note that in Fig. 17–5 January payments budgeted relate to payroll for December or the previous quarter ended December 31. Sales tax payments relate to estimated collections for months of December, January, and February. Federal tax deposits indicated are based on the current requirement that cumulative taxes due of $500 to $3,000 at the end of any month be deposited by the 15th of the following month for income and FICA taxes, and quarterly for federal unemployment tax, when tax since last payment exceeds $100. (Should undeposited taxes total $3,000 or more at the end at any time, you must deposit them within three banking days of the related payroll.)

Note: All tax rates used in Fig. 17-5 are assumed, and should not be relied on for your own use.)

A method of "tax budgeting" that also serves the purpose of accruing employer payroll taxes, without making adjusting entries, is used by many nonprofit and business organizations. It is done primarily to avoid penalties and interest resulting from not having enough money in the bank to pay payroll taxes (including withholdings) when due. It works this way: when payroll checks are made out, a single check is made out for each monthly or quarterly tax payment that will be due, based on the salaries for that payroll period. This has the effect of setting aside the coming payroll tax obligations as well as accruing them on the books when the checks are entered and posted. The checks themselves are held until they are actually due.

You may note the similarity to the use of this practice described in the Appendix to Chapter 14 for accruing expenses, to avoid having to make adjusting entries. Their use for payroll taxes can be a far more important one, since it does not avoid merely making adjusting entries, but also risking penalties and interest on payroll taxes. It is also justifiable as to the withheld taxes since the amounts deducted from salaries do not belong to the organization at all: it is merely acting as a withholding agent for the federal and state governments. Also, if you enter salaries net when paid, and add the payment of taxes withheld to get gross salaries, this does so in the same month, rather than the next.

APPENDIX 17A

Preparing Federal Employment Tax Reports

This Appendix provides the following practical aids in assembling the required information and preparing Employer's Quarterly Federal Tax Return (IRS Form 941) and Employer's Annual Federal Unemployment Tax Return (IRS Form 940):

- Comprehensive worksheet form for assembling data, containing sample payroll information.

- Detailed instructions for using the worksheets and forms, explaining the sample data and how it was obtained.

- Illustrations of filled-in Forms 941 and 940, showing how the sample data are entered and the forms completed.

EMPLOYER'S QUARTERLY FEDERAL TAX RETURN (FORM 941)

This form is used to report both taxes—income taxes withheld and the Social Security (FICA) taxes—imposed on employer and employee. It formerly required a listing of the amount of taxable FICA wages (i.e., up to the maximum covered) for each employee during the quarter, but has been simplified to require that only the total of such taxable wages be reported. A worksheet calculating and listing the underlying details must therefore be prepared anyway, and kept on file with your copy of the return. The information regarding the amount earned to date by each employee, and therefore the amount that still falls within the taxable limit, is obtained from the Employee Earning Record described in Chapter 12. The worksheet used for the U.S. quarterly return (Form 941) is shown at Figure 17A–1. (This form is somewhat complicated because it covers FICA and income tax withholdings on one worksheet.)

The worksheet shows five employees, who typify the five common situations regarding taxability of salaries paid during the quarter. The information in the "Earnings through previous quarter" and "Current quarter earnings" columns is obtained from the employee earnings records—usually a card for each employee. (Total earnings for the current quarter are added to those of the previous quarters.) We have keyed the figures on the worksheet to those on the Form 941, so you can trace them and see where they come from (or go). You will also find a list of these key letters (shown in parentheses) below the worksheet, with a brief comment on each. (Note that "taxable wages" is used throughout to mean the tax base, up to the amount of the limitation.)

Quarter ended 12-31-89

(1)	(2)	(3)	(4)	(5)	(6)	(7)	(8)	(9)
					Excess	Taxable	Taxes withheld	
Em-	Social	Prior		Cumulative	FICA	wages (for	Current	Quarter
ployee's	Security	earnings	Current	earnings	wages	FICA)		federal
name	number	to date	quarter	this year	(over	current	FICA	income
(A)	(A)	(A)	earnings	(3) + (4)	$48,000)**	quarter	(A)	(A)
A. Jones	xxx-xx-xxxx	2,500	2,500	5,000	—	2,500	187.75	373.80
B. Reilly	xxx-xx-xxxx	4,000	3,500	7,500	—	3,500	262.85	608.40
C. Levy	xxx-xx-xxxx	13,500	4,500	18,000	—	4,500	337.95	653.90
D. Lee	xxx-xx-xxxx	40,800	7,500	48,300	300	7,200	540.72	1,310.40
E. Diaz	xxx-xx-xxxx	48,000	10,000	58,000	10,000	—		2,379.00
		108,800	28,000	136,800	10,300	17,700	1,329.27	5,325.50 (J)
			(G)		(I)	(F)		

Add: employer tax @ 7.51%   1,329.27

Taxes withheld per books*   Total FICA Tax   2,658.54 (M)

Total Form 941 Taxes   7,984.04 (N)

	FICA	Federal income
October	445.05	1,800.00
November	433.15	1,725.50
December	451.07	1,800.00
Total 4th Q	1,329.27	5,325.50

Less: federal tax deposits:
- Nov. 15th 2,670.00
- Dec. 15th 2,631.00
- Jan. 15th 2,682.00

Total federal tax deposits   7,983.00 (O)

Balance due with Form 941   1.04 (P)

FIGURE 17A–1. QUARTERLY PAYROLL TAX WORKSHEET #3 (for Form 941 taxes).

*All totals per employee earnings records should be reconciled with totals per entries in general ledger accounts for wages and withheld taxes.

**1989 FICA tax rate = 7.51% on maximum earnings of $48,000. Maximum was increased in 1990 to $51,300; the rate became 7.65%.

Note: At the end of the fourth quarter of the calendar year, columns can be added to the right side of the worksheet to show total FICA and federal income taxes withheld for the year for each employee, as shown on their earnings records. This can be used in preparing their withholding slips (W-2s). (See Figure 17-2, Worksheet #1, columns (6) and (7) for an illustration of this in connection with state and city income taxes withheld.

Explanation of Key (Form 941 Items Only)[13]

(A) Data obtained from employee earnings record for each employee (Cols. 1 to 4, 8, and 9).

(F) FICA taxable wages (Col. 7): Amount is derived as in following example, from cumulative earnings:

[13] See Figures 17A-1 and 17A-2.

		Col.
D. Lee earned through previous quarter = $40,800		(3)
Add: Current quarter earnings	7,500	(4)
Total earned to date	48,300	(5)
Less: Limitation (maximum taxable)	48,000	
Balance = excess (nontaxable)	300	(6)
Taxable portion of current quarter earnings: ($7,500 - 300 excess)	7,200	(7)

(G,F, and J) Tie in the totals (cols. 4, 8, and 9) with total payroll expense for the quarter, on a cash basis, and total of amounts withheld, as shown by general ledger accounts. Here is an example of adjustment of earnings to cash basis:

Salary expense per general ledger account: Oct. =	$ 9,000
Nov. =	9,500
Dec. =	10,300
Total salaries earned 4th quarter	28,800
Less: accrued salaries as 12/31 =	800
Equals salaries paid, 4th quarter	28,000

(F) (Col. 7) This figure is entered on Form 941 on the line "Taxable FICA wages paid."

(J) (Col. 9) Entered on Form 941 on the line "Total income tax withheld from wages," etc.

(M) (Col. 9) This figure represents the full 15.02% FICA tax (1989) rate.

(N) (Col. 9) This figure is the total of income taxes withheld and total FICA taxes (15.02%) and is entered as "Total taxes" on Form 941.

(O) (Col. 9) This figure represents total of payroll taxes paid in during the quarter against the eventual liability. (See definition of tax deposits.) This employer's total U.S. withholdings and taxes falls between the $500 and $3,000 per month bracket, therefore deposits of total taxes due must be made monthly, by the 15th of the next month, in accordance with instructions accompanying Form 941. (It has been assumed that monthly payments are also required by the state in this case.) The IRS automatically sends employers Form 8109, the Federal Tax Deposit form used for remitting these taxes via your bank, not directly to the IRS itself. (See Instructions.)

(P) (Col. 9) The figure of $1.04 represents the difference between amounts deposited on account and the final amount determined to be due when preparing the Form 941. Errors in calculating Social Security tax withholdings on individual employees during the quarter often result in such minor discrepancies. Since the 15.02% tax due is calculated on the total taxable earnings, any discrepancy in either direction is automatically accounted for on this line, and becomes an amount due or a refund. To be realistic, we have thus assumed a $0.52 error in FICA tax withheld, resulting in a balance due of twice that amount.

Form **941**	**Employer's Quarterly Federal Tax Return**
(Rev. January 1989) Department of the Treasury Internal Revenue Service	4141 ▶ **For Paperwork Reduction Act Notice, see page 2.** **Please type or print.**

Your name, address, employer identification number, and calendar quarter of return. (If not correct, please change.)

Name (as distinguished from trade name) Nonprofit X	Date quarter ended 12-31-89	OMB No. 1545-0029 Expires: 5-31-91
Trade name, if any	Employer identification number 00-0000000	T FF FD FP I T
Address and ZIP code Anywhere, U.S.A. 00000		

If address is different from prior return, check here ▶ ☐

IRS Use

1 1 1 1 1 1 1 1 1 1   2   3 3 3 3 3 3   4 4 4

5 5 5   6   7   8 8 8 8 8   9 9   10 10 10 10 10 10 10 10 10 10

If you do not have to file returns in the future, check here . . ▶ ☐   Date final wages paid . . . . ▶

If you are a seasonal employer, see **Seasonal employer** on page 2 and check here . . . ▶ ☐

1a	Number of employees (except household) employed in the pay period that includes March 12th . ▶	**1a**	
b	If you are a subsidiary corporation AND your parent corporation files a consolidated Form 1120, enter parent corporation employer identification number (EIN) . . ▶ **1b** —		
2	Total wages and tips subject to withholding, plus other compensation . . . . ▶	**2**	(G) 28,000 00
3	Total income tax withheld from wages, tips, pensions, annuities, sick pay, gambling, etc. . ▶	**3**	(J) 5,325 50
4	Adjustment of withheld income tax for preceding quarters of calendar year (see instructions) . ▶	**4**	
5	Adjusted total of income tax withheld (see instructions)	**5**	5,325 50
6	Taxable social security wages paid . . . . . $ ___17,700__00__ × 15.02% (.1502) .	**6**	(M) 2,658 54
7a	Taxable tips reported . . . . $ _____ × 15.02% (.1502) .	**7a**	
b	Taxable hospital insurance wages paid . . . . $ _____ × 2.9% (.029) . .	**7b**	
8	Total social security taxes (add lines 6, 7a, and 7b)	**8**	2,658 54
9	Adjustment of social security taxes (see instructions for required explanation)	**9**	
10	Adjusted total of social security taxes (see instructions) . . . . ▶	**10**	2,658 54
11	Backup withholding (see instructions)	**11**	
12	Adjustment of backup withholding tax for preceding quarters of calendar year . . . . . ▶	**12**	
13	Adjusted total of backup withholding	**13**	
14	Total taxes (add lines 5, 10, and 13)	**14**	7,984 04
15	Advance earned income credit (EIC) payments, if any . . . . ▶	**15**	
16	Net taxes (subtract line 15 from line 14). **This must equal line IV below** (plus line IV of Schedule A (Form 941) if you have treated backup withholding as a separate liability)	**16**	7,984 04
17	Total deposits for quarter, including overpayment applied from a prior quarter, from your records . ▶	**17**	7,983 00
18	Balance due (subtract line 17 from line 16). This should be less than $500. Pay to IRS . . . ▶	**18**	1 04
19	If line 17 is more than line 16, enter overpayment here ▶ $ _____ and check if to be: ☐ Applied to next return **OR** ☐ Refunded.		

Record of Federal Tax Liability (Complete if line 16 is $500 or more.) See the instructions on page 4 for details before checking these boxes.

Check only if you made eighth-monthly deposits using the 95% rule ▶ ☐   Check only if you are a first time 3-banking-day depositor ▶ ☐

Do NOT Show Federal Tax Deposits Here

Date wages paid		Show tax liability here, **not deposits.** IRS gets deposit data from FTD coupons.		
		First month of quarter	Second month of quarter	Third month of quarter
1st through 3rd	A		I		Q
4th through 7th	B		J		R
8th through 11th	C		K		S
12th through 15th	D		L		T
16th through 19th	E		M		U
20th through 22nd	F		N		V
23rd through 25th	G		O		W
26th through the last	H		P		X
Total liability for month	**I**	2,670.00	**II** 2,631.00	**III** 2,683.04
IV Total for quarter (add lines **I, II,** and **III**). **This must equal line 16 above** . . . . ▶				7,984.04

Sign Here

Under penalties of perjury, I declare that I have examined this return, including accompanying schedules and statements, and to the best of my knowledge and belief, it is true, correct, and complete.

Signature ▶ *Lotta Figgers*   Title ▶ Treasurer   Date ▶ Jan. 30, 1990

FIGURE 17A–2. FORM 941.

Other Questions About Filing Form 941

The above comments contained in explanation of the figures on the form and supporting worksheet cover most aspects of its preparation. Other procedural steps are explained fully on the instruction sheet on the back of the form, which should be read and followed carefully. The current Circular E, Employer's Tax Guide, published by the IRS, contains all the other necessary information, including withholding tax tables for both income tax and FICA taxes. A Form W-4, Employee's Withholding Allowance Certificate, must be obtained from each employee, stating number of exemptions and marital status, in order to be able to use the withholding tax tables.[14]

Note that in addition to the quarterly Form 941, employers are also required to file two other types of forms, which are submitted annually to the Social Security Administration, not the IRS. These are a Form W-2, annual Wage and Tax Statement, for each employee, accompanied by a Form W-3, Transmittal of Income and Tax Statements. (The Social Security Administration processes them for its records and forwards the data to the IRS afterwards.) You can obtain all necessary tax forms, and your employer identification number, from IRS.

EMPLOYER'S ANNUAL FEDERAL UNEMPLOYMENT TAX RETURN (FORM 940)

A Section 501(c)(3) organization is exempt from this tax. As previously noted, the federal and state unemployment taxes form an integrated system. The tax base is the same, and a stated allowance is taken on the federal return against the gross tax rate for taxes paid the state. Since the return is for a whole year, rather than a quarter, the worksheets for quarterly returns cannot be conveniently used to prepare it, but are the source of data for the Annual Unemployment Tax Worksheet shown in Fig. 17A–3, which sets up the information for Form 940, and also provides a full-year worksheet for tying in and supporting the payroll and tax expense accounts between the books, financials, and tax returns for audit purposes.

As was done with the Form 941 and state unemployment tax returns, we have keyed the worksheet to its sources and to the tax return, Form 940, which is illustrated in Fig. 17A–4. Note that the figures for the fourth quarter, ended December 31, are from the fourth quarter worksheet for state unemployment tax returns. Gross Earnings (Col. 1) are the total of Current Quarter Earnings from the four quarter worksheets.

A check on any errors in calculating the tax on quarterly returns can also be made from this worksheet, based on the old axiom, "The whole is equal to the sum of its parts." The total tax for the year should be calculated by multiplying the rate by the total taxable wages for the year. The total tax in cols. 4 and 5 (marked with the letters D and E) should be the same, whether the four quarterly taxes are added or the tax on the taxable wages for the year "C" in col. 3 is computed.

Another tie-in should be made between the totals A, D, and E, and the total salary expense and tax expense, by type, on the trial balance or general ledger at year-end, taking into account any accruals, as explained earlier in this Appendix.

---

[14]Same form is used to obtain employee's Social Security number.

	(1)	(2)	(3)	(4)	(5)
Company: Nonprofit X			State: Mass.	Year 19xx	
			State Unemployment Tax		
Quarter ended	Gross earnings	S.U.T. excess earnings	Taxable wages	Tax (2.7%)	Fed. unemp. tax (0.8%)
March 31	38,800	12,500	26,300	710.10	210.40
June 30	35,500	28,500	7,000	189.00	56.00
Sept. 30	34,500	29,000	5,500	148.50	44.00
Dec. 31	28,000	22,500	5,500	148.50	44.00
Annual totals[5]	136,800	71,500	44,300	1,196.10	354.40
	(A)	(B)	(C)	(D)	(E)

FIGURE 17A–3. ANNUAL UNEMPLOYMENT TAX WORKSHEET (for Form 940)

Notes:

[1] Reconcile totals with general ledger balances: gross earnings, taxes paid and/or accrued.

[2] Sources of quarterly entries are totals of the columns indicated below on Fig. 17-3, Quarterly Payroll Tax Worksheet #2 (State Unemployment Tax Returns):

No. of Column Above	*Comparable Column on Fig. 17–3*
(1) Gross Earnings	(4) Current Quarter Earnings
(2) S.U.T. Excess Earnings	(6) Excess S.U.T. Wages
(3) S.U.T. Taxable Wages	(7) Taxable S.U.T. Wages

[3] Letters on bottom line refer to text and Form 940 entries.

[4] Section 501(c)(3) nonprofits are exempt from Federal Unemployment Tax and need not file Form 940.

[5] Includes $12,000 paid an unlisted employee in earlier periods.

A Final Point About Form 940

Although it is filed once a year, by January 31 of the next calendar year, tax deposits are required quarterly at any point at which the cumulative tax due for the year to date exceeds $100.00. In our illustration, the first-quarter tax was over $100 ($210.40) and therefore a deposit had to be made by April 30, the last day of the month after the end of that quarter. The next time the $100.00 figure was reached was in the fourth quarter, so the tax for the second, third, and fourth quarters, totaling $144.00, was paid at the end of January. As a result, there was no tax due with the return, since all of it had already been paid in. If, however, the total tax for the last three quarters had totaled under the $100.00 minimum, the balance due would be paid with the tax return—or it could also be deposited and credit taken on the Form 940.

Tax deposits are made to your bank, as for those on Form 941, and the same transmittal form (Federal Tax Deposit Form 8109) is used, which IRS supplies automatically with your tax forms.

Form **940**
Department of the Treasury
Internal Revenue Service

**Employer's Annual Federal
Unemployment (FUTA) Tax Return**
▶ For Paperwork Reduction Act Notice, see page 2.

OMB No. 1545-0028

1989

		T	
		FF	
		FD	
		FP	
		I	
		T	

If incorrect, make any necessary change. ▶

⌐Name (as distinguished from trade name)
Nonprofit X
Trade name, if any

Calendar year
1989

Address and ZIP code
⌐ Anywhere, U.S.A. 00000

Employer identification number
⌐00‑ 0000000⌐

A Did you pay all required contributions to state unemployment funds by the due date of Form 940? (See instructions if none required.) . . . ☒ **Yes** ☐ **No**

If you checked the "Yes" box, enter the amount of contributions paid to state unemployment funds . . . . ▶ $ 1,107.00

B Are you required to pay contributions to only one state? . . . . ☒ **Yes** ☐ **No**

If you checked the "Yes" box: (1) Enter the name of the state where you are required to pay contributions . . . ▶ Massachusetts

(2) Enter your state reporting number(s) as shown on state unemployment tax return. ▶ 00000

C If any part of wages taxable for FUTA tax is exempt from state unemployment tax, check the box. (See the Specific Instructions on page 2.). . . . . ☐

Note: *If you checked the "Yes" boxes in both questions A and B and did not check the box in C above, you may be able to use Form 940-EZ.*

Part I Computation of Taxable Wages (to be completed by all taxpayers)

1	Total payments (including exempt payments) during the calendar year for services of employees	1	115,800	00
2	Exempt payments. (Explain each exemption shown, attaching additional sheets if necessary.) ▶ _____	Amount paid		
		2		
3	Payments for services of more than $7,000. Enter only the excess over the first $7,000 paid to individual employees not including exempt amounts shown on line 2. Do not use the state wage limitation.	3	71,500	00
4	Total exempt payments (add lines 2 and 3)	4	71,500	00
5	Total taxable wages (subtract line 4 from line 1). (If any part is exempt from state contributions, see instructions.) ▶	5	44,300	00

Part II Tax Due or Refund (Complete if you checked the "Yes" boxes in both questions A and B and did not check the box in C above.)

1	**Total FUTA tax.** Multiply the wages in Part I, line 5, by .008 and enter here	1	354	40
2	Total FUTA tax deposited for the year, including any overpayment applied from a prior year (from your records) .	2	354	40
3	**Balance due** (subtract line 2 from line 1). This should be $100 or less. Pay to IRS . . . . . ▶	3	−0−	
4	**Overpayment** (subtract line 1 from line 2). Check if it is to be: ☐ **Applied to next return,** or ☐ **Refunded** . ▶	4		

Part III Tax Due or Refund (Complete if you checked the "No" box in either question A or B or you checked the box in C above. Also complete Part V.)

1	Gross FUTA tax. Multiply the wages in Part I, line 5, by .062 . . .	1		
2	Maximum credit. Multiply the wages in Part I, line 5, by .054	2		
3	Credit allowable: Enter the smaller of the amount in Part V, line 11, or Part III, line 2 .	3		
4	Total FUTA tax (subtract line 3 from line 1)	4		
5	Total FUTA tax deposited for the year, including any overpayment applied from a prior year (from your records)	5		
6	**Balance due** (subtract line 5 from line 4). This should be $100 or less. Pay to IRS . . . . . ▶	6		
7	**Overpayment** (subtract line 4 from line 5). Check if it is to be: ☐ **Applied to next return,** or ☐ **Refunded** . ▶	7		

Part IV Record of Quarterly Federal Tax Liability for Unemployment Tax (Do not include state liability.)

Quarter	First	Second	Third	Fourth	Total for Year
Liability for quarter	210.40	56.00	44.00	44.00	354.40

Part V Computation of Tentative Credit (Complete if you checked the "No" box in either question A or B or you checked the box in C above—see instructions.)

Name of state 1	State reporting number(s) as shown on employer's state contribution returns 2	Taxable payroll (as defined in state act) 3	State experience rate period 4 From— To—	State experience rate 5	Contributions if rate had been 5.4% (col. 3 x .054) 6	Contributions payable at experience rate (col. 3 x col. 5) 7	Additional credit (col. 6 minus col.7) If 0 or less, enter 0. 8	Contributions actually paid to the state 9

10 Totals . . . . ▶						

11 Total tentative credit (add line 10, columns 8 and 9 only—see instructions for limitations) . . . . ▶

If you will not have to file returns in the future, write "Final" here (see general instruction "Who Must File") and sign the return. ▶

Under penalties of perjury, I declare that I have examined this return, including accompanying schedules and statements, and to the best of my knowledge and belief, it is true, correct, and complete, and that no part of any payment made to a state unemployment fund claimed as a credit was or is to be deducted from the payments to employees.

Signature ▶ *Lotta Figgers*   Title (Owner, etc.) ▶ Treasurer   Date ▶ Jan. 30, 1990

Form **940** (1989)

FIGURE 17A-4. FORM 940.

APPENDIX 17B

Adjusting Entries to Accrue Payroll Taxes

This seems a more helpful place to discuss the bookkeeping aspects of payroll taxes than placing them in the earlier discussion of adjusting entries, where they would have little meaning without an understanding of the way the taxes work.

Although payroll tax returns are based on salaries actually paid during the period covered, not those earned, if the books or financial statements are kept on the accrual basis, it is necessary to accrue payroll taxes on the payroll for the period, covering payroll accrued as well as paid. There is nothing difficult about the entries themselves, since they are like any other expense accrual. The amount of tax due is derived from quarterly worksheets like Figs. 17–3, 17A–1, and 17A–3, and the entry is a debit to each appropriate tax expense account and a credit to a taxes payable or accrued taxes account.

What makes these entries a bit different is the fact that while part of certain taxes is withheld, the other part is an expense of the employer. It is the latter that need to be accrued, to the extent not already paid in by tax deposits; and it is these deposits that complicate matters. In order to visualize the process, let us use the data already available on the worksheets to see how it would appear on the general ledger and what adjusting entries would be required for accrued taxes. The accounts as they would appear before these entries are shown in Fig. 17B–1.* All credits have been made from the payroll journal (or cash disbursements). It is assumed here that adjusting entries are made only quarterly, not monthly. Figures relating to prior months are omitted for the sake of simplicity; only accounts for taxes withheld and tax deposits made are shown, since the tax expense accounts will have zero balances (except for past quarter payments) until the taxes for the fourth quarter are accrued.

FIGURE 17B-1. TAX WITHHOLDING AND DEPOSIT ACCOUNTS—UNADJUSTED

U.S. W.T. payable		FICA taxes payable		State W.T. payable			
	Oct. 1,800.00		Oct. 445.05	Nov. 450.00	Oct. 450.00		
	Nov. 1,725.50		Nov. 433.15	Dec. 400.00	Nov. 400.00		
	Dec. 1,800.00		Dec. 451.07		Dec. 550.00		
	Bal. 5,325.50		Bal. 1,329.27		1,400.00		
				850.00	Bal. 550.00		

*Showing only 4th Quarter entries

Disability benefits tax payable		U.S. tax deposits	
Oct.	9.20	Nov.	2,670.00
Nov.	9.00	Dec.	2,631.00
Dec.	9.30		
	——	Bal.	5,301.00
Bal.	27.50		

The amounts to be accrued are derived by comparing total taxes due for the quarter according to the quarterly worksheet with any taxes already paid in. The latter covers the U.S. tax deposits and payments to the state on withheld taxes. There were no payments on account of disability benefits or federal unemployment tax. The calculations, keyed to the worksheet figures on Fig. 17A–1, are as shown in Fig. 17B–2.

Total income tax withheld for quarter	(J, col. 9)	$5,325.50
Total FICA tax due at 15.02% (1989 rate only)	(M, col. 9)	2,658.54
Total taxes reported on Form 941, 4th Q.	(N, col. 9)	7,984.04
Tax liability already on general ledger at Dec. 31:		6,654.77
(U.S. W.T. payable: 5,325.50 + FICA tax pay: 1,329.27)		
Balance—accrued FICA tax		1,329.27

FIGURE 17B–2. FICA TAX ACCRUAL (FORM 941)

The adjusting entry for FICA tax accrued (also called "FOAB Tax" by many accountants, for Federal Old Age Benefits, and Social Security tax by others) would then be made as follows:

Dr.	FICA tax expense	$1,329.27	
	Cr. FICA taxes payable		$1,329.27

The adjusting entries for federal unemployment and state unemployment tax are in this case quite simple, since nothing has been paid in on account during the quarter. In order to be consistent with data previously given, however, we will need to take into account the fact that since adjustments are made quarterly, and no payments of federal unemployment tax were made for the two previous quarters (since the accumulated amount due was under $100), there would be a balance in the Accrued Tax account representing second and third quarter tax: $56.00 + $44.00, or $100.00, before the new adjusting entry. The federal unemployment tax due for the fourth quarter was $44.00. The state unemployment tax is $148.50. The two accruals can be combined into a single entry, as follows:

Dr.	Federal unemployment tax expense	$44.00	
	State unemployment tax expense	148.50	
	Cr. Accrued taxes		$192.50

This leaves only the disability benefits tax accrual of $27.50. The adjusting entry is straight-forward (it assumes employer and employee each pay 0.5% of tax base):

Dr.	Disability benefits tax expense	$27.50	
	Cr. Disability benefits tax payable		$27.50

Notice how the liability is added to the withholding account, where one exists, as in the case of FICA and disability benefits taxes, or to Accrued Taxes in other cases, such as unemployment taxes.

After these adjustments have been posted to the general ledger, entries in the payroll tax accounts for the quarter will look like this:

PAYROLL TAX ACCOUNTS AFTER FOURTH QUARTER ADJUSTING ENTRIES

U.S. W.T. payable

Oct.	1,800.00
Nov.	1,725.50
Dec.	1,800.00
Bal.	5,325.50

FICA taxes payable

Oct.	445.05
Nov.	433.15
Dec.	451.07
J.E.	1,329.27
Bal.	2,658.54

State W.T. payable

Nov.	450.00	Oct.	450.00
Dec.	400.00	Nov.	400.00
		Dec.	550.00
	850.00		1,400.00
		Bal.	550.00

Disability benefits tax payable

Oct.	9.20
Nov.	9.00
Dec.	9.30
J.E.	27.50
Bal.	55.00

U.S. tax deposits

Nov. 15	2,670.00
Dec. 15	2,631.00
Bal.	5,301.00

Accrued taxes

June	49.00
Sept.	38.50
J.E.	44.00
Bal.	131.50
J.E.	148.50
Bal.	280.00

FICA (FOAB) tax expense

J.E.	1,329.27

(State unemp. tax)
(Fed. unemp. tax)

State unemployment tax expense	Federal unemployment tax expense	Disability benefits tax expense
J.E. 148.50	J.E. 44.00	J.E. 27.50

Note: On the Balance sheet at December 31, 19xx, this agency would show the tax liabilities contained in the accounts as follows: the U.S. tax deposits shown in that account which were made on account of the liabilities shown in the U.S. W.T. and FICA tax payable accounts, would be subtracted from the sum of the tax liability acounts, and the balance shown as a current liability, as payroll taxes payable. The amount would be the sum of all the above liability accounts, net of the deposits, derived as follows:

U.S. W.T. payable	$5,325.50	U.S. W.T. and FICA taxes	$2,683.04
FICA tax payable	2,658.54	State unemployment tax	148.50
Total reported	7,984.04	Federal unemployment tax	131.50
Tax deposits made in Nov. & Dec.	5,301.00	Disability benefits tax	55.00
Bal. due at Dec. 31	2,683.04	Payroll taxes payable	3,018.04
(carried forward to next column)			

To complete the cycle, when the U.S. tax deposit is made January 15, 19x1 ($2,682.00) and the $1.04 balance due is paid with Form 941 (see last line on quarterly worksheet, Figure 17A–1, col 9, letter P), the $2,682.00 will be charged to the U.S. tax deposit account, and the balance of the account, now $7,983.00, distributed to the tax liability accounts as follows:

Dr.	U.S. W.T. payable	$5,325.50	
	FICA taxes payable	2,658.54	
Cr.	U.S. tax deposits		$7,983.00
	Cash		1.04

This entry cleans out the balances of all three accounts as they appear before posting any January withholdings. (It actually combines the $1.04 payment and the transfer of the tax deposit account.)

The December 31 balances of the other accounts will be cleaned out by the payments of the other taxes with the respective returns, or the January tax deposit, in the case of the federal unemployment tax.

Bibliography

BOOKS AND PAMPHLETS

Chapter 1

Independent Sector, *Tax Exempt Organization's Lobbying & Political Activities Accountability Act of 1987—A Guide for Volunteers and Staff of Nonprofit Organizations* (Independent Sector, Washington, DC: 1988)

Internal Revenue Service Publication No. 557, *Tax Exempt Status for Your Organization*

Internal Revenue Service Publication No. 598, *Tax on Unrelated Business Income of Exempt Organizations*

New York University *Conference on Tax Planning for the Charitable Sector* (Matthew Bender, New York: 1985)

Marylin E. Phelan, *Nonprofit Enterprises: Law and Taxation* (Callaghan & Co., Wilmette, IL: 1989) Updated annually.

Chapter 2

Bruce R. Hopkins, *The Law of Tax-Exempt Organizations*, 5th ed. (Ronald Press, John Wiley & Sons, New York: 1987)

Howard L. Oleck, *Non-Profit Corporations, Organizations & Associations*, 5th Ed. (Prentice-Hall, Englewood Cliffs, NJ: 1988)

See also Chapter 1 listings.

Chapter 3

John M. Bryson, *Strategic Planning for Public and Nonprofit Organizations* (Jossey-Bass, San Francisco: 1988)

Chapter 4

John Carver, *Boards That Make a Difference* (Jossey-Bass, San Francisco: 1990)

W.R. Conrad and W.E. Glenn, *The Effective Voluntary Board of Directors* (Swallow Press, Chicago: 1976)

E.W. Anthes & J. Cronin, *Personnel Matters in Nonprofit Organizations* (Independent Community Consultants, P.O. Box 1673, West Memphis, AR 72301: 1987)

Joan Flanagan, *The Successful Volunteer Organization* (Contemporary Books, Chicago: 1981)

Giving USA (American Association of Fund-Raising Counsel, New York: an annual)

Sandra Trice Gray, *An Independent Sector Resource Directory of Education & Training Opportunities* (Independent Sector, Washington, DC: 1987)

Cyril O. Houle, *Governing Boards* (Jossey-Bass, San Francisco: 1989)

Daniel L. Kurtz, *Board Liability Guide for Nonprofit Directors* (Moyer-Bell, Ltd., Mt. Kisco, NY: 1988)

Brian O'Connell, *The Board Member's Book* (Foundation Center, New York: 1985)

Chapters 5–7

R. Braswell, K. Fortin & J.S. Osteryoung, *Financial Management for Not-for-Profit Organizations* (John Wiley & Sons, New York: 1984)

Anthony J. Gambino, *Financial Planning & Evaluation for the Nonprofit Organization* (National Association of Accountants, Montvale, NJ: 1981)

Chapter 8

Thomase E. Broce, *Fund Raising: The Guide to Raising Money from Private Sources* (University of Oklahoma Press: Norman, 1979)

Kent E. Dove, *Conducting a Successful Capital Campaign* (Jossey-Bass, San Francisco: 1988)

Joan Flanagan, *The Grassroots Fundraising Book* (Contemporary Books, Chicago: 1982)

Michael Seltzer, *Securing Your Organization's Future* (Foundation Center, New York: 1987)

Harold J. Seymour, *Designs for Fund-Raising* (The Fund-Raising Institute, Ambler, PA: 1988)

Robert F. Sharpe, *Planned Giving Idea Book* (Thomas Nelson, Nashville, TN)

Carole C. Upshur, *How to Set Up and Operate a Non-Profit Organization* (Prentice-Hall, Englewood Cliffs, NJ: 1982)

(See also Chapter 8, under "Zeroing in on Grants," and "Government Grants and Contracts," for directories and other publications listing grants. Foundation Center, New York, NY, also publishes other directories and research materials on foundation and corporate grants.)

Chapter 9

Marylin Brentlinger & Judith Weiss, *The Ultimate Benefit Book* (on fundraising events) (Octavia Press: 1987; Obtainable from American Council on the Arts, New York, NY, which publishes a number of arts-related books.)

J.C. Crimmins & Mary Keil, *Enterprise in the Nonprofit Sector* (Partners for Livable Places, Washington, DC: 1983)

Paul B. Firstenberg, *Managing for Profit in the Nonprofit World* (Foundation Center, New York: 1986)

IRS Publication 1391, *Deductibility of Payments Made to Charities Conducting Fund-Raising Events*

Philip Kotler, *Marketing for Nonprofit Organizations* (Prentice-Hall, Englewood Cliffs, NJ: 1975)

C.H. Lovelock & C.B. Weinberg, *Marketing for Public and Nonprofit Managers* (John Wiley, New York: 1984)

Arnold J. Olenick, *Managing to Have Profits* (McGraw-Hill, New York: 1989)

Edward Skloot, Ed., *The Nonprofit Entrepreneur* (Foundation Center, New York: 1988)

Public Relations and Publicity

Public Interest Public Relations, Inc., *Promoting Issues & Ideas: A Guide to Public Relations for Nonprofit Organizations* (Foundation Center, New York: 1987)

Robert H. Ruffner, *Handbook of Publicity and Public Relations for the Nonprofit Organization* (Prentice-Hall, Englewood Cliffs, NJ: 1984)

Chapters 10–14

Malvern J. Gross, Jr. & William Warshauer, *Financial & Accounting Guide for Nonprofit Organizations* (Ronald Press, New York: 1979)

Emerson O. Henke, *Introduction to Nonprofit Organization Accounting* (Kent Publishing Co., Boston: 1980)

National Health Council, National Assembly of National Voluntary Health & Social Welfare Organizations and United Way, *Standards of Accounting & Financial Reporting for Voluntary Health & Welfare Organizations* (National Health Council, New York: 1989)

Byron Stone and Carol North, *Risk Management and Insurance for Nonprofit Managers* (Society for Nonprofit Organizations, Madison, WI: 1989)

Chapter 15

Financial Reporting to Others

Robert Lefferts, *The Basic Handbook of Grants Management* (Basic Books, New York: 1983)

United Way of America, *Accounting & Financial Reporting: A Guide for United Ways and Not-for-Profit Human Service Organizations* (United Way, Alexandria, VA: 1974)

U.S. Office of Management and Budget, *OMB Circular A-110: Grants & Agreements with Institutions of Higher Education, Hospitals, & Other Nonprofit Organizations; OMB Circular A-122: Cost Principles for Nonprofit Organizations*

Performance Evaluation

Robert N. Anthony & David W. Young, *Management Control in Nonprofit Organizations* (Richard D. Irwin, Homewood, IL: 1984) (Chapters 11 to 13)

Michael J. Austin, *Evaluating Your Agency's Programs* (Sage Publications, Beverly Hills, CA: 1982)

Brace, Elkin, Robinson & Steinberg, *Reporting of Service Efforts and Accomplishments* (Financial Accounting Standards Board, Stamford, CT: 1990)

Reginald K. Carter, *The Accountable Agency* (Sage Publications, Beverly Hills, CA: 1983)

Anthony J. Gambino, *Financial Planning & Evaluation for the Nonprofit Organization* (National Association of Accountants, Montvale, NJ: 1981) (Chapter 6)

Henry M. Levin, *Cost-Effectiveness—A Primer* (Sage Publications, Beverly Hills: CA: 1983)

The Urban Institute, *Developing Client-Outcome Monitoring Systems* (Urban Institute, Washington, DC: 1981)

Chapter 16

See references for Chapter 1.

Chapter 17

Internal Revenue Service, Circular E, *Employer's Tax Guide*

IRS Publication 539, *Employment Taxes*

IRS Publication 510, *Excise Taxes*

IRS Publication 916, *Information Returns*

COMPREHENSIVE WORKS

Robert N. Anthony & David W. Young, *Management Control in Nonprofit Organizations* (Richard D. Irwin, Homewood, IL: 1984)

Tracy D. Connors, *The Nonprofit Organization Handbook* (McGraw-Hill, New York: 1980)

Patricia V. & Daniel M. Gaby, *Nonprofit Organization Handbook* (Prentice-Hall, Englewood Cliffs, NJ: 1979)

Arnold J. & Philip R. Olenick, *Making the Nonprofit Organization Work* (Prentice-Hall, Englewood Cliffs, NJ: 1983) (Out-of-print predecessor to this book.)

Thomas Wolf, *The Nonprofit Organization* (Prentice-Hall, Englewood Cliffs, NJ: 1984)

Frederick J. Turk & Robert P. Gallo, *Financial Management Strategies for Arts Organizations* (ACA Books, New York: 1984)

PERIODICALS

The Chronicle of Philanthropy, P.O. Box 1989, Marion OH 43305

Foundation News, Council on Foundations, 1828 L St. NW, Washington, DC 20036

Fund Raising Management, Hoke Communications, Garden City, L.I., NY 11530-5771

Grassroots Fundraising Journal, P.O. Box 14754, San Francisco, CA 94114

NonProfit Times, c/o The Support Center, 1410 Q St. NW, Washington, DC 20009

Nonprofit World, Society for Nonprofit Organizations, 6314 Odana Rd., Suite 1, Madison, WI 53719

The Philanthropy Monthly, by the Non-Profit report, P.O. Box 989, New Milford, CT 06776

Tax Exempt News, Whitaker Newsletters, Inc., P.O. Box 340, Fanwood, NJ 07023

Tax Monthly for Exempt Organizations, c/o Harmon & Weiss, 2001 S Street NW, Suite 430, Washington, DC 20009

Technical Assistance Resources

ACTION—The National Volunteer Agency, 806 Connecticut Ave. NW, Washington, DC

Accountants for the Public Interest, 1625 I St. NW, Suite 717, Washington, DC 20006 (Publish *National Directory of Volunteer Accounting Programs*)

Association for Volunteer Administration, P.O. Box 4584, Boulder, CO 80306

Directory of Consultants & Management Training Programs, MLP Enterprises, 236 East Durham St., Philadelphia, PA 19119

Executive Service Corps, 622 Third Ave., New York, NY 10022

The Foundation Center, 79 Fifth Ave., New York, NY 10003–3050
(Contact for cooperating library nonprofit collections in your area; also for its catalog of publications and research aids.)

Grantsmanship Center, 1031 South Grand Ave., Los Angeles, CA 90015

Independent Sector, 1828 L St. NW, Washington, DC 20036

National Congress for Community Economic Development, 1612 K St. NW, Suite 510, Washington, DC 20006

National Society of Fund Raising Executives, 1990 Main St. NW, Washington, DC

SCORE (Service Corps of Retired Executives), 1129 20th St. NW, Washington, DC

The Society for Nonprofit Organizations, 6314 Odana Road, Suite 1, Madison, WI 53719.
Publishes *Nonprofit World, Resource Center Catalogue* and the *National Directory of Service and Product Providers to Nonprofit Organizations*

The Support Centers, 1410 Q St. NW, Washington, DC 20009

U.S. Small Business Administration, 1441 L St. NW, Washington, DC (Offices in many cities.)

Volunteer: The National Center for Citizen Involvement, Arlington, VA

Volunteer Lawyers for the Arts, 1285 Ave. of the Americas, New York, NY

Volunteers of America, 3813 North Causeway Blvd., Metairie, LA 70002

Index